Translating the Literature of Scripture

A Literary-Rhetorical Approach to Bible Translation

SIL International
Publications in Translation and Textlinguistics 1

Publications in Translation and Textlinguistics is a peer-reviewed series published by SIL International. The series is a venue for works concerned with all aspects of translation and textlinguistics, including translation theory, exegesis, pragmatics, and discourse analysis. While most volumes are authored by members of SIL, suitable works by others will also form part of the series.

Series Editors

Freddy Boswell
Mary Ruth Wise

Volume Editors

Betty Eastman
Ågot Bergli

Production Staff

Bonnie Brown, Managing Editor
Margaret González, Compositor
Kirby O'Brien, Cover Design

Translating the Literature of Scripture

A Literary-Rhetorical Approach to Bible Translation

Ernst R. Wendland

SIL International
Dallas, Texas

© 2004 by SIL International
Library of Congress Catalog Card Number: 2004108320
ISBN: 1-55671-152-2
ISSN: 1550-588X

Printed in the United States of America

The Scripture quotations used in this publication, when not my own literal or concordant translation of the Hebrew or Greek text, are in the main taken from the following English versions: the *New International Version* (NIV) © 1984 by the New York International Bible Society; the *Revised Standard Version* (RSV) © 1973 by the Division of Christian Education of the National Council of Churches of Christ in the U.S.A.; the *New Revised Standard Version* (NRSV) © 1989 by the Division of Christian Education of the National Council of Churches of Christ in the U.S.A.; the *Today's English Version* (TEV) © 1976 by the American Bible Society; the *Contemporary English Version* (CEV) © 1995 by the American Bible Society; and *God's Word* (GW) © 1995 by God's Word to the Nations Bible Society. All these are used by permission, for which I am grateful.

Distributed by Eisenbrauns, Inc., in conjunction with SIL International. Copies may be purchased from:

Eisenbrauns, Inc.
P. O. Box 275
Winona Lake, IN 46590-0275, U.S.A
and
International Academic Bookstore
SIL International
7500 West Camp Wisdom Road
Dallas, TX 75236,-5699
Voice: 972-708-7404
Fax: 972-708-7363
Email: academic_books@sil.org
Internet: http://www.ethnologue.com

Contents

To

All my SIL and UBS colleagues

From whom I have learned so much—
perhaps taking longer than I should have, but as they say in Chichewa,
mau a akulu akoma akagonera
"the words of the elders sound sweeter once they've slept the night."

And with whom I have had such an exciting and enriching experience
over the years, discussing the various problems and possibilities of
translating the Word of God in the literary form of a "new song," and
in as many as possible of the languages resulting from Babel.

מִזְמוֹר שִׁירוּ לַיהֹוָה שִׁיר חָדָשׁ
כִּי־נִפְלָאוֹת עָשָׂה ...
הוֹדִיעַ יְהוָה יְשׁוּעָתוֹ
לְעֵינֵי הַגּוֹיִם גִּלָּה צִדְקָתוֹ: (Ps. 98:1a–2)

καὶ ᾄδουσιν ᾠδὴν καινὴν λέγοντες,
Ἄξιος εἶ λαβεῖν τὸ βιβλίον
καὶ ἀνοῖξαι τὰς σφραγῖδας αὐτοῦ,
ὅτι ἐσφάγης καὶ ἠγόρασας τῷ θεῷ ἐν τῷ αἵματί σου
ἐκ πάσης φυλῆς καὶ γλώσσης καὶ λαοῦ καὶ ἔθνους. (Rev. 5:9)

Foreword

If an author uses a particular literary device in writing, what are the translator's constraints? This question often crosses the desk of a translator, and the answer will reflect one's theory of translation. Failure to heed the function and impact of literary devices can, on the one hand, leave one feeling that the meaning-intention of the author has not been accurately reflected. On the other hand, slavish adherence to reproducing a particular literary or rhetorical device can produce a stilted translation that obscures the author's intended purpose and meaning. This is a dilemma! How do we proceed?

Ernst Wendland has done a favor for the practitioners of Bible translation in laying an excellent groundwork for further study of this topic and, in doing so, has addressed a neglected topic. For if we dismiss the issues surrounding the translation of literary devices, saying out of hand that it cannot be done successfully, I believe that we do a great disservice to our field, and that we are forced to admit that our theory of translation, which we have deemed to be completely adequate, is instead porous.

In his preface, Wendland states, "It needs to be stressed at the outset that there is not just one possibility here—a single 'right' or 'wrong' way of doing it. Rather, a number of *options* in terms of application are available to a translation team depending on their capabilities and many other circumstances." I believe this is a statement made with an eye towards that difficult intersection of translation as art and translation as science. Some say translation is like the science of mathematics, where one plus one always equals two, and that if we adhere to certain rules, restrictions, and guidelines, we will come out with the "right answer." Others, though, insist that translation is more like an art form. If you asked three translators to translate the same passage, you would probably come up with three different translations, just as if you asked three artists to paint your portrait, it is highly doubtful if the three portraits would end up exactly the same.

Translation is probably best thought of as a mixture of art and science, not an either/or proposition. Such is the nature of Wendland's task. In addressing the issue of literary translation, he helps us to proceed with more expertise in this art cum science, equipped with an increasing number of proper tools for improving our finished product.

Freddy Boswell
Translation Coordinator
SIL International

Preface

A verbally competent individual can start reading the Bible either at its beginning or at its ending and will not fail to come to the conclusion that this text is not ordinary religious or ideological discourse, for it is indeed *literature*. This is clearly manifested in the lyric-liturgical description of the primeval Creation event in Genesis 1 and in Christ's epistles to the seven churches in Revelation 2–3, with their repeated, purposefully arranged panels:

(a) "And God said..."   [introduction]
(b) "Let there be..."   [pronouncement]
(c) "And it was so."   [result]
(d) Action Report   [fulfillment of b]
(e) "God saw it good."   [evaluation]
(f) "And God called/blessed"   [naming/blessing]
(g) "And there was evening/morning"   [conclusion]

(a) "Unto the angel of the church of X write" [addressees]
(b) "These things says the one"   [author]
(c) "I know your works that"   [evaluation]
(d) "But I have this against you, that"   [condemnation]
(e) A call to repentance/fidelity   [appeal]
(f) "He who overcomes..."   [promise]
(g) "He that has an ear, let him hear..."   [exhortation]

Many diverse stylistic features distinguish these structurally prominent portions of the Scriptures—parallel patterning, rhythmic utterance units, figurative language, dramatic direct speech, a climactic manner of composition, and many more. Literary qualities are not restricted to the extremities of the sacred corpus—they are seen throughout in varied combinations and concentrations. One must therefore "read" (apprehend, analyze, assess) the Bible as literature in order to avoid the most elementary error of interpretation, namely, failing to correctly discern the essential nature of the verbal forms whereby the intended manifold meaning of the message has been expressed. In this book, then, I present certain key aspects of a literary-rhetorical approach to the analysis and translation of the Scriptures. (At times I will abbreviate the designation *literary-rhetorical* to *literary* or just *L-R* to save space; however, the two aspects should always be understood as operating together.)

I am grateful to various translation colleagues for their encouragement as well as critical response to this material, which has been circulating in various forms for a number of years now. In particular, I would like to single out the reviewers for their helpful corrective and constructive criticism of my first draft. Their comments along with the excellent editorial work of Betty Eastman made a significant contribution to the ultimate quality of this production. They cannot, of course, be held responsible for any deficiencies that surely remain.

My primary aim is to contribute to recent initiatives undertaken by the major organizations in the field to prepare a comprehensive evaluation and restatement of their recommended philosophy and practice of Bible translation. In this effort, several longstanding principles and procedures may have to be discarded, some new ones added to take their place, and certain guidelines that were recommended in the past will have to be revised or modified to a greater or lesser extent in view of recent scholarship. As in the case of some crucial related areas of focus, namely, cultural anthropology, communication, biblical text analysis, linguistics, research in mass media, and indeed the greatly expanding field of translation studies itself,[1] so also this examination of biblical literature seeks to maintain an appropriate *balance* among three fundamental points of concern: theoretical principles, application in the field, and pedagogical training.[2]

While I do wish to be current in terms of the latest translation theories, I want to limit this input to those concepts, terms, models, and methods

---

[1] For a discussion of the term *translation studies* with reference to "a recognized academic discipline (or 'interdiscipline'…),'" see Chesterman and Wagner 2002:35–36; for a recent exemplified survey of the field, see Munday 2001; for definitions and longer explanations of its terminology, see Shuttleworth and Cowie 1997 and Baker 1998.

[2] The present text is an expansion and further illustration of Wendland 2002b.

that are actually necessary and helpful when applied to the work of Bible translation, which is different from secular translation in a number of respects. For one, the text to be translated is regarded as the sacred, authoritative Word of God; hence its essential content and/or intent cannot be "revised" or otherwise modified in an effort to improve, update, or render it more relevant to a contemporary audience and sociocultural setting (i.e., "transculturation"). For another, the Bible consists of a selected anthology of diverse, but pervasively intertwined literary works (i.e., manifesting extensive "intertextuality"), composed by some forty authors living over a span of roughly 1,600 years; as a result, a comprehensive "interpretive framework" is required to govern the understanding of any given biblical text, especially in the prophetic and epistolary books. Another difference is that the Scriptures are meant to be read and heard aloud, many portions having been circulated first in oral form. Contemporary translators must take this preferred mode of transmission into serious consideration as they carry out their work.

My proposals, which arise from these considerations, will also have to be teachable, either using the present arrangement or some modified format. This concern applies both in formal courses of translator training and also informally as when a translation consultant is guiding the "above average" sort of translator that a literary-rhetorical approach requires. (There will probably be some significant regional differences in this last respect.)

The central issues to be dealt with in this presentation may be summed up in the following questions: What does it mean to translate the *literature* of *Scripture*—or its corollary, to translate the *Scriptures* as *literature*? Why introduce the subject of "literature" into the practice of translation at all? Is there a possible conflict of interests here since the Bible is a distinctly "theological" as well as a highly sacred book? Is not the task of the translator difficult enough without complicating the procedure by literary technicalities? To be sure, these queries must be addressed and answered in a satisfactory manner before we can proceed very far in our study.

Assuming, then, that an adequate response can be given, we are able to go into more detail: How can past and present methods of studying literature (*literary* criticism) and the formal discourse of persuasion (*rhetorical* criticism) help us to better understand, analyze, transmit, and teach translators about the diverse artistic texts of the Scriptures? (For a good survey of L-R studies see House 1992.) I begin in chapter 1 with the subject of literature in general as it is related to Bible translation, considering some of the key issues with respect to definition, the medium of communication, quality, scope, methodology, prominent precursors, motivation, and characteristic features. An important issue to be considered in this connection is that of degree—the relative amount of "literariness" and rhetoric that is actually manifested, either in an original text or in its translation into another language.

It needs to be stressed at the outset that there is not just one possibility here—a single "right" or "wrong" way of doing it. Rather, a number of *options* in terms of application are available to a translation team depending on their capabilities and many other circumstances. I hope that my presentation comes across as being flexible enough to fit just about any translation program, from the less to the more literal and/or content-based in its fundamental ethos and outlook. My treatment of this wide-ranging subject must necessarily remain more suggestive than substantive due to space restrictions. Nevertheless, I trust that it will prove adequate to stimulate some creative thinking along "literary" lines and also to provide readers with at least some idea of its breadth and diversity as well as importance for Bible translators. I must also emphasize the fact that the literary approach that I will be focusing upon in this book in no way diminishes the need for considering translation from a more *linguistic* perspective as well (e.g., Dooley and Levinsohn 2001); to a large extent these methods complement and reinforce one another, in addition to overlapping in a number of key areas.

Chapter 2 presents an overview of past and current studies that relate to a specifically "literary" type of version, both in the practice of Scripture translation itself and also in the field of contemporary secular approaches to the subject. In subsequent chapters I discuss various aspects of four prominent qualities of literature that contribute to the overall unity and communicative dynamics of the biblical text, namely, *tectonicity* (chap. 3), *artistry* (chap. 4), *iconicity* (chap. 5), and *rhetoricity* (chap. 6). I survey such important topics as genres, archetypes, the structural features of discourse, various formal or stylistic constituents of the elusive quality known as "artistry," and five distinct methods of rhetorical study, namely, those which stem from the rabbinic tradition, classical Greco-Roman oratory, Greek epistolary conventions, speech-act theory, and argument-structure analysis. This last topic is especially emphasized since it is not always given the attention it deserves in current Bible translation theory and practice.

In the second half of the book, beginning with chapter 7, attention is shifted from the more technical aspects of analyzing the source-language (SL) text to applying the results within the framework of an actual Bible translation program. First, I offer some practical guidelines for conducting a literary-rhetorical study of biblical literature, whether narrative or nonnarrative discourse. This leads to the consideration, in chapter 8, of a preliminary requirement, namely, the need for carrying out a systematic examination of oral and written verbal art in a given target language (TL): What are some things to keep in mind when conducting such an essential, complementary exercise, and how does a literary, or "oratorical," version compare with other translation types? In chapter 9 I survey translation and teaching methodology with special reference to how current techniques may be augmented through the adoption of a literary perspective and set of procedures. In chapter 10 the application of a literary approach is illustrated by a specific research project in the Chichewa language (a Bantu language of south-central Africa) with respect to the analysis and translation of a familiar poetic passage (Psalm 23), as well as the procedures for and results of testing this translation. Chapter 11, the final chapter, is an overview of steps for organizing a literary-rhetorical translation project. Three appendixes follow: appendix A with various test samples relating to chapter 10, appendix B with another literary-rhetorical analysis (Psalm 1) and several sample translations, and appendix C with an inductive teaching lesson that highlights a general literary-rhetorical perspective on the Book of Malachi. A variety of shorter, illustrative studies of different biblical passages are offered along the way to further demonstrate the relevance of a literary-rhetorical approach and how it might be performed.

A major goal of recent UBS and SIL theoretical initiatives is to produce some updated teaching resource manuals for translation consultants and translation team exegetes. The latter are, ideally, persons who have received the minimum of a bachelor's degree from a recognized theological college or seminary and at least a year's training in the theory and practice of communicative Bible translation, and who are either mother-tongue speakers of the TL or are very fluent in its use. The present volume is intended to make an initial and introductory contribution to this global training effort with particular reference to the field of literary and rhetorical studies.

This subject obviously surpasses the abilities and resources of one individual. I have learned a lot from others while doing the research for this book and certainly have not covered the field. Therefore, input from readers in the form of corrections, suggestions for improvement, additional topics, relevant works not listed in the Bibliography, and clearer illustrations is warmly encouraged. All comments and criticisms may be directed to me at wendland@zamnet.zm or erwendland@hotmail.com. I would also appreciate contributions of some annotated examples of a more-or-less literary rendition (along with a literal English back translation) that I can include in a translation workbook and practical guide that is being prepared for translators.

During our deliberate movement in the direction of some new perspectives and approaches, two critical questions continually confront us: First, in *which* specific areas of this broad field of study do we need some theoretical or procedural revision and expansion? Second, *how* can we best develop and communicate this material pedagogically as well as encourage its effective use when translating the Word of God *as literature* in the many diverse languages and Scripture-use settings of the world today? Your comments are most welcome!

Ernst R. Wendland
Bible Society of Zambia and
Centre for Bible Interpretation and Translation in Africa
University of Stellenbosch

Abbreviations

AV	Authorized Version
BL	*Buku Lopatulika*
BY	*Buku Loyera*
CEV	*Contemporary English Version*
CL	common language
DTS	descriptive translation studies
FE	functional equivalence
GNB	*Good News Bible*
GW	God's Word
HV	hymn version
J-E-P-D	Jahwist-Elohist-Priestly-Deuteronomist textual "sources" (alleged)
KQ	key question
LET	literary equivalent translation
LiFE	literary functional-equivalence
L-R	literary-rhetorical
LXX	Septuagint
M	message
MT	Masoretic Text
NASB	*New American Standard Bible*
NBV	*Nieuwe Bijbel Vertaling*
NEB	*New English Bible*
NIV	*New International Version*
NJB	*New Jerusalem Bible*
NLT	*New Living Translation*
NP	noun phrase
NRSV	*New Revised Standard Version*
NT	New Testament
OT	Old Testament
PL	popular language
PR	poetic rendering

R	receptor
REB	*Revised English Bible*
RQ	rhetorical question
S	source
SL	source language
TEV	*Today's English Version*
TL	target language
TT	target text
UBS	United Bible Societies
YL	your language

1

The Study of Literature in Relation to the Bible and Its Translation

The main subject of this book is an approach to Bible translation that is based on a literary and rhetorical (i.e., form-functional) study of the Hebrew and Greek Scriptures. The following quotations emphasize the importance of this approach:

> If I were to start again, I would study **literary criticism** in depth. There is probably no field which has made a more important contribution to my own understanding of the Bible and which has more relevance to Bible translation....Couple a literary approach to the study of the biblical text with a **discourse analysis** and you get an understanding of the text that is directly relevant to translation. (Philip Stine 1999:1, 3, boldface added)
> Literary translations are published as part of the cycle of economic activities within a multimillion-dollar industry....The tendency within these external forces is to downgrade the artistry to want the translator to be a compliant cog helping turn the wheels of a vast machine more virtual by the day. If we value what we read in translation, then **the artistic quality of literary translation has to be safeguarded**. (Peter Bush,[3] boldface added)

---

[3]From the abstract for a lecture entitled "Recent Developments in the Publishing Industry and the Impact on Literary Translation," given on March 23, 2000, at the UMIST Centre for Translation Studies. Peter Bush is Director of the British Centre for Literary Translation. His warning has great relevance for Bible translation, especially with regard to the focal feature of "artistic quality."

> We have here indeed what may very probably be the most complex type of event yet produced in the evolution of the cosmos. (Ivor Richards, cited by Fawcett 1997:1)[4]

> And [Paul] reasoned in the synagogue every Sabbath, and **persuaded** both Jews and Greeks….[M]any came to [Paul] at his lodging, to whom he explained and solemnly testified of the kingdom of God, **persuading** them concerning Jesus from both the Law of Moses and the Prophets, from morning till evening. (Acts 18:4 and 28:23, NKJV, boldface added)[5]

Here at the outset it should be recognized that our *focus of attention* is literature, written verbal art; our *corpus under investigation* is the Holy Scriptures, composed of the sacred canonical Hebrew and Greek Testaments; and our *principal goal* is a stylistically sensitive, literary-rhetorical rendering of the dynamic Word of God into the languages of the world.

1.1 Definition: What "literature" is

The adoption of a literary approach during text analysis and translation presupposes that the Bible is in fact literature—that the various books which it includes, whether as wholes or in part, are generally regarded as being literary in character and consequence. It will help us if we understand what, precisely, these commonly used terms mean to most Bible interpreters and translators. Many people assume that they know what is being referred to simply because they have heard the words so often. But if you ask them to define *literature*, for example, it quickly becomes obvious that familiarity does not necessarily mean understanding. This is really not surprising since even the experts do not always agree.[6]

The issue of definition is of considerable importance. It will affect both what one looks for in the original texts of the Scriptures and also how one

---

[4]An idiomatic translation does not simply "evolve," and neither did the cosmos, as the patent complexity of either creative operation clearly suggests. My point in quoting Richards concerns the magnitude of this task and the overwhelming challenge that we place before most Bible translators, many of whom have not been adequately prepared to carry out a basic exegesis of the original text, let alone confront its literary-rhetorical dimension.

[5]Such authorial testimony coupled with the implicit witness of the expertly composed text itself, at least in most passages, would suggest that both the oral and the written proclamation of the chosen spokesmen of God are quite "literary" in character. The Scriptures do evince, by and large, an artistically embellished style of writing and a rhetorically shaped discourse. The twofold purpose of the sacred writings, as in all contemporary preaching, teaching, and Bible translation, is to enable (through the operation of the Holy Spirit) a given audience to clearly understand the text and to motivate them to respond positively to the gospel of Jesus Christ and the kingdom of God.

[6]With reference to the terms *literature* and *translation*, José Lambert observes: "Neither concept is simple or well defined in most cultures" (1998:130).

decides to deal with this in any version where the literary qualities of the target language are seriously considered as translational options.

Various definitions of *literature* have been proposed. *Webster's New World Dictionary* (1988) includes as part of its definition this pertinent entry: "all writings in prose or verse, esp. those of an imaginative or critical character...considered as having permanent value, excellence of form, great emotional effect, etc." This definition encompasses form ("prose or verse"), content ("value"), and function ("effect"), the three interrelated features that are the essential diagnostic components of any oral or written verbal message, whether artfully or poorly composed. It is important to note here, however, that not just any sort of text is included within the scope of literature. Evaluation is inevitably involved: a document that can be characterized as literary is one that is generally regarded as being "permanent," "excellent," even "great" with regard to beauty, imagination, and presumably also subject matter, impact, appeal, and relevance.

Clearly a considerable degree of subjectivity is involved in any such characterization and evaluation: Who is to say what constitutes value, excellence, or, indeed, greatness with reference to emotional effect? Furthermore, there appears to be an implicit bias against specifically *religious* writing, which in the main is neither imaginative (i.e., fictive) in nature nor "critical" in a literary sense. In any case, the notion of imagination needs to be extended to include what Thiselton (1999:169) refers to as "the multilayered coding of 'open' or 'literary' texts (as against flat, one-point, 'closed' or 'handbook' texts of, for example, engineering and building construction)." Such manifold "coding" would encompass both thematic/semantic meaning as well as functional/pragmatic implications stimulated by literary "resonances, intertextual allusions, new perspectives, [and] transformed horizons" (ibid.:171).

This brings us to a more technical definition of what constitutes literature. According to Robert de Beaugrande (1978:101), it is a text that is distinguished by a "poetic use of language": polyvalence (in terms of its semantic character), polyfunctionality (in the pragmatic dimension), dense structuration, expanded grammar and vocabulary (including novel usages), and a regular "non-fulfillment of reader expectations" (i.e., through textual surprises and aesthetic delights). Alonso Schökel (1963:380) adds, "Literary language shows a preference for multiplicity and complexity, it exploits the double personal factor, makes use of connotation, allusion, suggestive ambiguities, it seeks out the unexpected novelty, the surprise, it transposes language to the realm of metaphor, imagination, symbol."

In addition, it would seem necessary to add as another distinctive characteristic of literature the stamp of widespread scholarly or public recognition and approval. Gideon Toury draws our attention to the fact that "literature is first and foremost a cultural institution," manifesting verbal models, norms, strategies, features, and techniques that are regarded as being literary by one or more social groups within a given linguistic community (1995:170–171). Although an extratextual, qualitative assessment may be made simply by popular acclaim, this activity is usually carried out and substantiated by recognized literary experts, scholars, critics, and actual artists.[7] In this respect then, numerous critical studies,[8] coupled with a massive popular appeal, have conclusively demonstrated—on the basis of both stylistic *form* and communicative *purpose* or *effect*, let alone inspirational *content*—that the biblical corpus does indeed contain literature, a great deal of *good* literature, in fact. It would therefore stand to reason that many of the principles, perspectives, and procedures (but not necessarily the same presuppositions) used in the analysis of secular literature may be helpful when studying various Scripture texts. This book is intended to provide a selective overview of some of these literary viewpoints and techniques to show how they might be profitably utilized for this purpose by ordinary Bible translators in their effort to prepare a rendering of the original message in their language that is *functionally equivalent* in certain *situationally relevant* respects.[9]

1.2 Medium: Literature versus orature

The focus of our attention is termed "literature" because the Bible happens to be a collection of written documents. It is important to recognize, however, that reading in ancient times was only rarely a completely

---

[7]The formal systematic, theoretical, or "scientific" study of literature is technically referred to as "poetics," or for those who have a special linguistic interest, "stylistics" (Preminger and Brogan 1993:697, 930, 1227).

[8]A representative selection of such critical works may be found in the Bibliography of this book.

[9]The term *functional equivalence* was popularized with reference to Bible translation by de Waard and Nida (e.g., 1986:36–37). However, similar functionally based approaches were being practiced by secular translators prior to this, most notably by proponents of the German *Skopostheorie* school (see Nord 1997, J. House 1977, and the helpful survey in Gutt 1991, chap. 1). The present study, along with Wendland 2002b, combines insights from both sources in an effort to further develop and nuance the concept of functional equivalence so that it becomes a more useful tool for Bible translators as they analyze the original text and reconstruct it in their mother tongue. My particular aim is to promote this method (as one possible option) by means of a translation style that would be regarded as "literary," or its equivalent in one or more significant formal respects, based on standard or recognized criteria in the target language.

individual, private, and silent affair. Rather, texts—the sacred Scriptures in particular—were normally meant to be read aloud and in public[10] (see Ezek. 33:30–31; Acts 8:30, 15:21; Col. 4:16; 1 Thess. 5:27). Documents were also frequently composed orally, that is, by verbal dictation either to oneself or to a scribe, with aural reception on the part of the intended audience in mind. This means that there is a perceptible *oral overlay* that characterizes much biblical literature, including, most notably, a relatively high incidence of lexical recursion, colloquial speech "extenders," composition with a preference for structural parallels, rhythmic utterance sequences, and other appeals to the phonological dimension of discourse (alliteration, punning, etc.), as well as audible transitional and boundary-marking devices. It may also mean, though this point is more debatable, that certain techniques commonly practiced in the production of ancient Jewish and Greco-Roman rhetorical discourse (see sec. 6.2.2) were employed in the writing of New Testament hortatory literature.

Orally composed and communicated discourse differs in a number of important respects from written literature, depending on the genre concerned. The more important features that are normally (not always) present in oral art include the following: a greater amount of exact repetition, for emphasis as well as compositional marking; the use of many formulaic expressions, aural structural signals, and direct speech orienters; more hyperbolic, exclamatory, even bombastic language; less descriptive or expository detail; more freedom in word order; a significant semantic dependency upon prosody (e.g., stress, pitch, pause, tempo) and nonverbal communication devices such as gestures, resulting in more ellipsis and anacolutha; and the tendency to use relatively less complex, more paratactic syntactic construction and a less diverse, more predictable (speaker-specific) vocabulary. Some scholars propose the terms *orature* for spoken discourse and *verbal art* to include both oral and written texts.

The *medium* of transmission is of vital concern in the case of the Scriptures because most people of the world receive the text in some oral-aural form rather than in writing. This is especially true in non-Western countries or where there is a relatively low literacy rate. In such regions, as well as in areas where not much written literature is available to the masses, translators must give special attention to the acoustic nature of their text. This requires a great deal of preliminary research into the oral genres, or orature, of a given speech community before undertaking a translation intended for their use. There are important questions to consider: What are the features that distinguish, whether explicitly or intuitively, natural oral and written discourse in

---

[10]A classic study of this subject is Achtemeier 1990, an important qualification to which was given by Frank Gilliard 1993. Another salient essay on this issue is Parunak 1981. See also Wendland 1994a.

language-culture X, and how do such differences affect the basic perception and understanding of most people? To what extent do factors pertaining to speech register (sociolinguistic style) and sociocultural setting modify the standards of public acceptability? What influence do diverse communication and media-related settings have upon the basic procedures for producing a meaning-oriented Bible translation?

One fact seems certain, as Linton (1986:32) says: "The beauty of any translation is best sensed in oral rendition." He adds this important peda-gogical note: "What the stylist of a modern translation of the Bible needs is not alone a mastery of the technicalities of prosody but a sensitive ear, kept in tune by habitually reading aloud both poetic and prose passages, giving full value to accented syllables."

1.3 Quality: "Good" versus "poor" style in verbal art

The notion of literary style is an elusive one, for it may be defined with varied degrees of generality and from different perspectives, such as authorial intention, compositional qualities, and audience effect. The *American Heritage Dictionary of the English Language* (1992:1785) points us in the direction of a workable definition: The term *style* refers to "[t]he way in which something is said, done, expressed, or performed" (italics added). More specifically, it is "[t]he combination of *distinctive features* of literary or artistic expression, execution, or performance *characterizing* a particular person, group, school, or era" (ibid., italics added). We might add here "language."

Basic to the concept of style is a quantitative or qualitative differentiation according to such variables as selection, frequency, distribution, and ar-rangement. To accurately describe and evaluate such characteristics one must carry out an explicit or implicit *comparison*. Thus one written narrative or letter, for example, is either *similar* to or *different from* another with respect to a specifiable set of linguistic and/or literary features.[11] Furthermore, where the verbal objects under consideration belong to the broad category of "art," then the factor of *evaluation* usually becomes relevant. Text A is better or worse than text B—more or less attractive, moving, compelling, evoca-tive, novel, etc.—with respect to qualities x, y, and/or z. In place of "text B,"

---

[11]Many stylists refer to such textual differences as a deviation from the norms of ordinary oral or written discourse. However, the term *deviation* has a rather negative connotation. Thus, as far as good literature is concerned, a more positive perspective on the nature of style may be sought. For example, it may be viewed as a creative "realization" of the expres-sive potential inherent in a particular language, whether its sound structure, vocabulary, syntax, or text arrangement. Stylistic creativity is manifested particularly in multifaceted, multifunctional communication, where there is a special emphasis upon the emotive-affective and aesthetic dimensions of language.

some sort of generally accepted *standard* may be employed as the basis for the comparative estimation that is made.

The problem is that criteria such as "good" or "poor" are very subjective. Like "beauty," these criteria frequently lie very much in the eye of the beholder or the ear of the hearer. Any type of literary appraisal is further complicated when it comes to a translation; in this case, standards such as relative intelligibility and accuracy or fidelity with respect to a source text come into play. The goal of assessment is not completely irrelevant or unattainable, however, because there are specific procedures that can be followed in order to achieve a certain measure of objectivity. The most reliable of these are based upon some form of textual comparison, as previously suggested, because such an exercise gives us something more concrete to evaluate and to debate with reference to when a judgment is being made. For example, we can ask which of the three following renderings of Song of Songs 8:6–7 sounds more poetic (i.e., artistic, expressive, evocative, or memorable) in English and why. (Can you then match each text to the version that it comes from—NRSV, TEV, or REB?)

A

Set me as a seal upon your heart,
as a seal upon your arm;
for love is strong as death,
passion fierce as the grave.
Its flashes are flashes of fire,
a raging flame.
Many waters cannot quench love,
neither can floods drown it.
If one offered for love
all the wealth of his house,
it would be utterly scorned.

B

Close your heart to every love but mine;
hold no one in your arms but me.
Love is as powerful as death;
passion is as strong as death itself.
It bursts into flame
and burns like a raging fire.
Water cannot put it out;
no flood can drown it.
But if anyone tried to buy love
with wealth,
contempt is all they would get.

                    C

        Wear me as a seal over your heart,
        as a seal upon your arm;
        for love is as strong as death,
        passion cruel as the grave;
        it blazes up like a blazing fire,
        fiercer than any flame.
        Many waters cannot quench love,
        no flood can sweep it away;
        if someone were to offer for love
        all the wealth in his house,
        it would be laughed to scorn.

On the basis of their manifest styles of translation, it may be apparent that these texts—A, B, and C—are, respectively, from the REB, TEV, and NRSV. With that in mind, the next step would be to specify the main textual features that lead you, as the analyst, to this conclusion, for your decision in this respect is not an arbitrary matter.

Some additional questions would be: What improvement(s) could you suggest in the way of translating any given line more "poetically," and what are your reasons for making such a proposal? How possible or feasible is it then to compose a version that incorporates the most artistic and expressive words, phrases, and lines selected from all three texts, including your own suggestions? What do you think of the following attempt? Identify the salient poetic features to be found in any of these versions.

        Wear me as a seal right over your heart,
        Or like a gold bracelet upon your wrist.
        Surely love is as strong as death itself,
        Such passion fierce as the fickle grave.
        It flashes forth—a searing, blazing fire,
        More furious far than any wooden flame.

        Pouring water cannot quench such love,
        Neither rain nor flood can drown it out.
        Truly, should someone try to buy a love
        As this with all the goods he did possess,
        Harsh scorn he'd get—a laughing stock!

Whatever you decided and however you arrived at this decision, you see that a reasoned stylistic assessment is clearly possible. In many instances it is also necessary. During their everyday working procedures, for example, a Bible translation team is continually called upon to rate one particular rendering in relation to another with regard to compositional felicity, fluency, clarity—in a word, *naturalness* in the TL. This comparative process must always be textually based, systematic, and more or less feature specific so that any difference of opinion may be examined individually on its own merits. (See Wendland 2000a for an example of such a practical procedure.)

A less precise procedure may be carried out by comparing, with respect to its literary value, a given text of Scripture ("A") to a similarly worded, parallel Scripture text ("B") instead of to an alternative translation of A. Another option is for text A to be compared stylistically to several similar Scripture passages, or even to generically similar secular texts in the same language or in related languages. Similarly, translations and original compositions of a particular genre in the target language may be compared on the basis of their key formal features (see Chesterman and Wagner 2002:73). A given translation can also be evaluated in relation to some of the recognized universal literary norms for that genre (e.g., lyric or praise poetry). One specific goal of such training exercises is to instill within translators the *literary competence* to carry out such an analytical, comparative exercise more or less intuitively. (See chap. 8 for some proposals in this regard.)

1.4 Scope: The extent to which the Scriptures contain literature

A problem of judgment confronts us where the Bible is concerned. On what basis can any sort of an authoritative evaluation of style be made, especially of the Old Testament, since there is not a large corpus of extant ancient literature with which a comparison may be carried out? How much genuine literature do the Holy Scriptures really contain? Can degrees of "literariness" or "rhetoricity" be confidently established when a specifically *religious* corpus is being appraised largely in terms of itself?[12] This difficulty is not as great in the case of the New Testament, but here it is the lack of comparative texts of a closely similar nature or genre that is the problem. Then too, how can a collection so "theological" in nature be viewed as "literary" at the same time?

A related concern is the matter of *credibility*: Who may serve as a reliable judge in evaluating ancient religious texts written in dead

---

[12]Christiane Nord points out that "if we look at the fundamental importance that the sender's intention and the receiver's expectations have for the function and effect of texts, we must admit...that literariness is first and foremost a pragmatic quality assigned to a particular text in the communicative situation by its users.... Receivers...interpret [specific textual signals and stylistic] features as literary in connection with their own culture-specific expectations, which are activated by certain extra-textual signals" (1997:82). I might add that the interpretive activity of the "receivers" of a translation is also influenced by their relative degree of literary sophistication and expertise (i.e., competence + experience), both in terms of their own language as well as in relation to the language and culture of the original text.

languages? Obviously, a conclusion is much less credible if one is forced to make an aesthetically motivated or oratorically oriented choice merely on the basis of some translation into another language. Only proven masters of the original languages and modern techniques of literary-linguistic analysis will be in a position to make authoritative and credible decisions in such matters.

While I do recognize the importance of issues such as these, I will not be able to resolve or fully pursue them within the confines of the present study. I can simply state that my own opinio rests on both the studies of recognized scholars in the field and also my own detailed comparative analyses, which are guided by generally accepted literary methods and standards (see Ryken and Longman, eds. 1993:15–37; Ryken 1992:14–32).[13] I therefore assume the biblical writings' relative coherence (with regard to *unity*), excellence (with regard to *artistry*), and forcefulness (with regard to *rhetoric*), whether in general or with respect to specific texts. My evaluation is based upon the identification and analysis of such important literary features as extensive compositional patterning (design-balance-symmetry); the appropriateness of verbal style with respect to semantic content and pragmatic intent; the heavy presence of allusion and various other types of conceptually enriching intertextuality; a dynamic, often dramatic, manner of expressing the point of a text; a great amount of graphic imagery, symbolism, and evocative figurative language; a high incidence of special phonological devices, including rhythmic expression and sonic recursion, utilized to embellish the message or accent its theme(s); a variety of literary genres, usually occurring in rhetorically mixed and combined forms; and the harmonious interweaving or juxtaposition of all these features and conventions within a given pericope to create cohesion, interest, impact, and appeal.

Furthermore, there are several important formal characteristics that appear, in their combination, to be distinctive of (though individually not unique to) the corpus of biblical literature. These characteristics are: the great diversity of subgenres that occur, often in combination within the same text; a preference for discourse units that are relatively short, whether in prose or poetry; a spare, unembellished, often episodic narrative style in which much (obviously background material) is left unsaid; a corresponding affinity for a concise, aphoristic manner of expression (e.g., the wisdom literature of the Old Testament and the discourses of Christ); the ubiquitous presence of dramatic direct speech or a "spoken mode" of presentation (e.g., the legislative discourse of the Pentateuch or prophetic and epistolary literature); elaborately constructed architectonic patterns, both linear and

---

[13]Even such unlikely candidates as Leviticus in the Old Testament and Jude in the New have recently been shown (by Douglas 1999 and Charles 1993, respectively) to manifest an excellent literary structure and a persuasive style of composition.

concentric, based on repetition; and, above all, a profoundly realistic point of view that focuses upon common, life-related human experiences, whether good or bad, but all "pervaded by a consciousness of God" (Ryken and Longman 1992:34) and the thematic perspective that his divine purposes are always being carried out in relation to a world that he created, redeemed, and will one day submit to eternal judgment.

When considering such formal and thematic features, however, it needs to be emphasized that the literature of the Bible is not "pure" literature.[14] Rather, as primarily *religious* discourse, these writings should be generally classified as "applied" literature, that is, composed in order to serve a larger utilitarian or functional purpose, one that is essentially theological, spiritual, and moral in nature.

Since terms such as *literary, artistic,* and *rhetorical* are generally regarded as having a positive connotation, and since they tend to be viewed as referring to relatively subjective qualities, differences of opinion will inevitably arise in cases where they (or related criteria) are used in the discussion that follows. Nevertheless, the important task before us is not primarily evaluative and certainly not prescriptive in nature. It is rather to describe, apply, and assess some of the commonly used tools of literary and rhetorical criticism in order to better ascertain their validity and utility in the process of Scripture translation. To what extent do these analytical techniques and procedures help us to *understand* a particular biblical text more accurately and completely in terms of form, content, and function? How do they then enable us to *communicate* the Bible's essential message more effectively in another language—perhaps even as acknowledged "literature" in that language?[15]

In anticipation of a fuller discussion in the next chapter, we might stress the fact that there are *degrees of literariness* in any text designated as a literary one, including Holy Scripture. Important differences may therefore be displayed in terms of both quality, or excellence (with regard to artistry, persuasiveness, impact, appeal, etc.), and quantity (how concentrated, where distributed, etc.). Similarly, there is a basic continuum of possible translational options, in other words, *degrees of mediation* manifested by translators as they work to re-express the source language (SL)

---

[14]The distinction between "pure" and "applied" literature, derived originally from David Robinson, is pointed out by V. P. Long (1994:152). It applies even to biblical texts that are obviously fictional in character, such as the parables of Christ.

[15]The term *literary translation* is ambiguous: Does it refer to the translation of a document that is regarded as being literary in the source language, to a translation that is itself appraised as literary in nature according to TL norms, or to both (see Toury 1995:168)? I have adopted the third sense as my default reference point—namely, the literary rendering of a literary source text (the Scriptures). This issue will be considered further in the next chapter.

text in the target language (TL), their mother tongue. A little actually can go quite a long way, even in a relatively literal version, through the consistent usage of just a few recognized vernacular literary techniques, for example, felicitous word choice, pleasing lexical collocations, utterance rhythm (equilibrium + variation), alliteration or assonance (euphony), and balanced syntactic parallelism. There are also degrees of application evident in a more overtly literary translation since various strategies of stylistic use are available on all levels of linguistic-literary structure from phonology to discourse texture. This will be determined by the overall guiding principles as stated in the translation manifesto (or *Brief*) of the project as a whole.

1.5 Methodology: A literary-rhetorical (L-R) approach

The eclectic, structure- and function-oriented L-R translation method that I am proposing and will be illustrating in this book can be summarized[16] by its features of theoretical orientation and practical text-processing procedure as follows:[17]

- This *discourse-centered* (top-down and bottom-up),[18] *genre-based* approach highlights the salient compositional features (or distinctive "markers") of organization, cohesion, progression, and projection within a biblical document. The parts of a text are thus analyzed and translated in terms of the linguistic and literary whole, and the whole correspondingly in terms of its constituent compositional parts, with respect to the creative genius of both the SL and also the TL in general comparative relief.
- A prominent *pragmatic-functional* component assumes that the producer of a text, whether the original author or a present-day translator, arranges its form and content to carry out particular communicative goals. This may be done at selected linguistic levels, with varying degrees of specificity, and within possibly diverse

---

[16]The summary given in this section, as well as the various L-R procedures suggested in this book, may be compared with current secular approaches to literary translation, several of which will be surveyed in the next chapter.

[17]This rather concentrated program statement summarizes the main principles to be discussed and illustrated in the following chapters. The proposed methodology will therefore have to be considerably "unpacked" by instructors before it can be made intelligible to average mother-tongue translators and then applied by them in the field. However, I have tried to simplify certain concepts where possible. The notion of "function," for example, is not used in the strict semiotic sense of Toury (1995:12), but rather is based upon an elementary communication model (e.g., de Waard and Nida 1986, chap. 5).

[18]For a concise definition and illustration of the difference between "top-down" and "bottom-up" text processing, see Dooley and Levinsohn 2001:28.

frames of sociocultural and situational reference. The target audience then "processes" and further interprets this same text by means of a context- and setting-sensitive intuitive-inferential process based on personal as well as group learning and experience.

- The representation of the author's intended *meaning* (denotation + connotation; ideational + interpersonal + textual significance) is viewed as being manifested either *explicitly*—that is, stated overtly in the discourse—or *implicitly* through his motivated selection of specific literary forms (from macrogenres to microstylistic features) and also by their ordered arrangement. These signs serve to compose the original SL text according to a comprehensive strategy of communication that incorporates certain important *presuppositions* as well as pragmatic *implications*.[19]

- Careful investigation is made with regard to the influence of the overall *contextual framework* upon the interpretation of a given passage or pericope, whether by the original or contemporary audience. This includes both its *co-textual* environment, immediate as well as removed in space or time (i.e., intra- and interdocumentary resonance), and also the *extratextual* setting. The latter involves a gradient of mutually interactive, situational "frames" and "filters" of cognitive, emotive, and volitional relevance (e.g., sociocultural, ecclesiastical, and literary standards, values, and norms).[20]

- Special attention is devoted to the previously overlooked *artistic* (formal) and *rhetorical* (interpersonal) dimensions of biblical discourse. Together these determine the relative appeal (aesthetic attraction) and impact (persuasive power) of the original message as it was produced (conceived, composed, and conveyed) and processed (heard, read) during the primary act of verbal creation. There is a prominent manifestation of the "expressive," "directive," and "poetic" functions of communication.

- There is a major interest in the key *oral-aural* dimension of the text of Scripture, with reference to the process of initial text transmission

---

[19]"In order to give the receiver a clue as to the intended function of a particular text, senders provide their texts with markers of function or intention on various levels or ranks" (Nord 1997:69). To what extent do Bible translators need to provide analogous functional signals (structural, stylistic, extratextual) in their TL texts to preserve a basic level of meaning equivalence on the pragmatic level of discourse?

[20]Among these frames of relevance would be conventional cognitive-based constructs, such as *scenarios* (visual settings), *scripts* (verbal exchanges), and *schemata* (event sequences) (see also Wilt 2002a). Frames normally act as filters to limit in certain respects what may be said in any given sociocultural situation—and how. This leads to compensatory language strategies, such as "generalization," category "alteration," and "deletion" (see Katan 1999:85ff.).

(including its composition and reception) and also its subsequent translation (including re-composition and possibly re-formatting). This manifold transformation must be investigated with due regard for differences in the respective communication frameworks, involving language, literary tradition, current convention, sociocultural (including religious) setting, media network, and the interpersonal situation.

- This heuristic model considers the principal *stylistic qualities* of a literary version in terms of three integrated sets of features: unity, diversity, and rhetoricity; structure, patterning, and foregrounding; imagery, sonority, and dramatics (see Wendland 2002b, chap. 6). The first set includes general foundational factors, presumed to be operational in all literary texts; the second set pertains largely to the macrostructure of discourse; the third is associated more with the microstructure of literary composition. These characteristics are complementary and closely interconnected, often overlapping, with respect to their manifestation in the diverse texts of Scripture; they must therefore be analyzed and applied accordingly during the derivative, synthetic act of translation.

- The process of analysis and interpretation is governed by a *holistic* conception of the individual books of the Bible as distinct religious documents. This is true also of the entire received corpus—the Holy Scriptures. The whole is seen to consist of a complete, variously integrated (both topically and textually), mutually illuminating and interpreting collective canon of sacred literature. This primary *synchronic* perspective does not discount the need to also investigate the dynamic *diachronic* process of textual and canonical development and interrelationship (intertextuality).

What is the aim of this type of form-functionally focused analysis? To what need does it respond? What benefit does it contribute to translation studies? In general it can be said that, like all meaning-centered methods, an L-R approach, whether applied fully or only in part, aims to achieve effective audience-sensitive, interlingual communication. To this end, it offers certain analytical techniques intended to help translators understand the literary and rhetorical nature of the Scriptures more correctly and completely. Finally, it suggests various ways in which the biblical text may be *re*composed using an appropriate L-R style within the diverse and disparate context of another language-culture, verbal tradition, and situational setting.[21] More specifically, these analytical procedures are designed both to uncover and also to convey the special significance of the principal literary and rhetorical devices that the biblical author employed when communicating his intended message in the initial event of message composition, transmission, and reception. Translators are often tempted to ignore such features in their work, either because they do not recognize and understand them or because they feel that they are merely meaning-*less* embellishments that can be ignored in their primary struggle to convey the basic semantic content ("information") of the original text.

Obviously, the preceding list of concerns is a great deal to keep in mind and distinguish during any text analysis. It may also be complemented by other theoretical and practical perspectives.[22] Nevertheless, it represents at least one area of engagement for initiating a study of the magnificent complexity of biblical discourse in a manner that gives due consideration to its oft-neglected aesthetic dimension as part of a larger, situationally framed perspective on literary communication via translation.

Such a discourse-framed, stylistically oriented approach to analysis is essential if one wishes to effectively come to grips with any biblical composition as an instance of literary—as well as theological—communication. While the theology of the text is paramount, the didactic divine message is always encased in human artistic and rhetorical forms, writ both large (e.g., a poetic genre such as the "woe" oracle) and small (e.g., a Pauline metaphor), and these forms are often specific to the language and literature concerned, whether Classical Hebrew or Koine Greek. They constitute the inventory from which the inspired writer made a specific selection and arrangement in order to best represent his message to the intended receptors. Thus a systematic, holistic, and context-conscious investigation of his stylistic technique and compositional strategy will usually pay dividends as far as helping the translator organize and interpret the principal ideas conveyed by the original work.

A thorough analysis of a given instance of literature must always precede and form the basis for its ultimate re-creation in another language.

---

[21]It should be noted that the task of the translator is to formally *recompose*, or re-express, the biblical message in the TL, *not* to create a new or different message, whether with respect to meaning or function. This point may need to be emphasized in the event that mother-tongue translators become motivated to adopt an L-R approach too enthusiastically in their work. In my experience, however, I have only rarely found this to be the case. All too often just the opposite occurs and a team either makes no effort to deal with stylistic concerns or is unable to do so.

[22]For example, with respect to the literary structure and patterning of biblical discourse, see Dorsey 1999; for an emphasis upon biblical rhetoric and the sociological context, see Robbins 1996.

Such an examination is carried out by means of two distinct, but related operations, which may be diagrammed as follows:

```
                                                    MACROstructure
     stylistic (compositional) /                    > focus on FORM
                            /      \ microSTRUCTURE
LITERATURE ➔ LITERARY
                       \
     rhetorical (argumentational)  >   focus on FUNCTION
                                       (text in context)
```

Assuming then that we are beginning with an acknowledged instance of literature in the SL, a text may be analyzed with special attention to either its form or its function. In the case of *form*, a "stylistic" analysis is undertaken: The compositional organization and aesthetic features of the text are investigated on the macro- and/or microstructure of the discourse as a whole, usually in relation to its intended (SL) or perceived (TL) meaning. In the case of *function*, a "rhetorical" analysis is undertaken: It is the argumentational dynamics and affective dimension of the discourse that are in focus—how the author shaped his text in order to move or persuade the intended audience to adopt a certain conclusion, opinion, perspective, conviction, or motivation (purpose) in relation to the message, whether as a whole or in relation to selected portions. Both types of literary analysis are required, first to permit fuller *understanding* of the original, and second to prepare one for adequately *communicating* its significance and relevance to others. Where translation is involved, this same twofold analytical process must be conducted also with respect to literature in the TL—first in general, to determine the genre-based inventory and artistic resources that are available, and then with specific reference to the text at hand.

1.6 Motivation: Why study and translate the Bible as literature

In section 1.4 I stated why I believe the Bible should be studied as literature. To lend greater credence to the case, I can do no better than to cite Robert Alter's (1987:21–22) rationale at length. What this expert practitioner of the art of biblical criticism artfully says about the "Hebrew Bible" with special reference to Judges 11 applies just as fully to the Greek Testament (note that the italics have been added by me):

> What can be inferred from all this about the workings of *the literary impulse* in the Hebrew Bible? Perhaps the most essential point is that

literary art is neither intermittent in its exercise nor merely ancillary to the writers' purposes—in this central regard, our passage from the beginning of the Jephthah story is thoroughly characteristic of the whole corpus. To be sure, the writer here is deeply concerned with questions of political leadership, community and individual, the binding nature of vows and pledges, the relationship of father and daughter, man's real and imagined obligations before God; but as a shaper of narrative he engages these complex issues by making constant artful determinations, whether consciously or intuitively, about such matters as the disposition of character, the deployment of dialogue, the attribution or withholding of motives, the use of motifs and thematic key words, the subtle modification of near-verbatim repetition of phrases. *For a reader to attend to these elements of literary art is not merely an exercise in "appreciation" but a discipline of understanding: the Hebrew vehicle is so much the necessary medium through which the Hebrew writers realized their meanings that we will grasp the meanings at best imperfectly if we ignore their fine articulations as literature.*

This general principle applies as much to biblical poetry as to prose. A line of Hebrew verse, whether it occurs in a grim denunciation in the Prophets, in an anguished question of divine justice in Job, or in the exultation of a psalm of praise, is likely to evince a certain characteristic structure dictated by the formal system of biblical poetry, of which the poets, whatever their spiritual aims, were exquisitely aware. The predominant patterns within the line are in turn associated with a number of characteristic movements for developing the poem as a whole; and some poetic compositions exhibit truly intricate structural features, involving refrainlike devices, strophic divisions, rondo movements, concentric designs, and much else. This is hardly surprising to find in any poetic corpus, but *these are not qualities that our usual preconceptions of Scripture have encouraged us to look for in biblical poetry; and as with the prose, an inattention to the literary medium runs the danger of becoming an inattention to the close weave of meanings.*

Since we are here talking about the manifold *meaning, or "sign*ificance," of the biblical message (implicit as well as explicit, semantic and pragmatic), the imperative implication of comments such as these affects translators as well as exegetes and interpreters. The artistry of biblical form inevitably impinges upon its content, for in far more cases than most of us are probably aware, this literary form constitutes an essential and inseparable part of the total meaning that it conveys. This is true whether we are talking about an individual figure of speech (e.g., "the shepherd and his sheep") or an entire genre (e.g., a parable as distinct from a Christological pronouncement story).[23]

As noted earlier, an increasing number of studies have drawn attention to many significant aspects of the literary character that the Scriptures, at least certain books or pericopes, clearly demonstrate. We find, for example, numerous expertly interwoven genres and literary subtypes; elaborate image sets that are often related in various ways; a great density of figurative, symbolic, and multi-referential language; striking turns of phrase formed by syntactic shifts and ellipsis; many passages that are shaped by sound so as to appeal to the attentive ear; a preference for audience-engaging direct speech; and extensive allusions to and developments of earlier biblical texts. Finally, the Bible frequently manifests emotive, highly evocative discourse, coupled with a forceful rhetorical mode of challenging, even provoking readers and hearers alike with a vital *promissory*, life-death moral and theological message of utmost relevance both in the here and now and beyond.[24] In short, many detailed stylistic and structural analyses in recent years have convinced a majority of scholars that instances of excellent literature in the Scriptures, the prosaic as well as the poetic passages, are the rule rather than isolated exceptions.[25]

I am therefore working on the assumption that the diverse texts of the Bible, both Hebrew and Greek, over and above their obvious religious and moral content reveal a level of compositional excellence that is outstanding with regard to both the macrostructure and also the microstructure of discourse organization. Such high quality is clearly manifested in more texts than most people realize, from the skillful selection and combination of complete literary types and genres to the corresponding usage of

---

[23]A pronouncement story is "a brief story about Jesus that culminates in a short, striking saying (and possibly an action) and reveals something of his character and facility in repartee when challenged by others" (Bailey and vander Broek 1992:114). An example is in Mark 2:15–17. The final climactic saying typically enunciates some form of correction or commendation on the part of Christ. It is important to recognize the rhetorical nature and outcome of the argument that is either explicitly stated or clearly implied during the course of a pronouncement story; otherwise the point and purpose of the text will be missed.

[24]Thiselton (1999:231–239) cogently argues for the prominence of the speech act of promising in biblical writings as, for example, when he says, "[P]romise provides a paradigm case of *how language can transform the world of reality*" (ibid.:238, original emphasis).

[25]For a varied sample of such recent studies, see Breck 1994, Dorsey 1999, Harvey 1998, and Wilson 1997. It may be noted that critics who make a positive assessment of the literary quality of biblical literature, either as a whole or with regard to specific books, tend to adopt a broader perspective on the original text than most analysts. They thus carefully consider the larger discourse organization rather than just the surface structure (e.g., contrast Dewey 1980:29–39 with Turner 1976:11–44 concerning the Gospel of Mark). If Leviticus and Numbers have been convincingly shown to manifest a literary character (see Douglas 1999, 1993), can any other biblical book be excluded? On the literary (narrative) structure of the Pentateuch as a whole, see Sailhammer 1992:25–66.

figurative language, varied grammatical arrangements, subtly interwoven patterns of repetition, rhetorical features such as irony and hyperbole, vivid contrasts, ubiquitous intertextuality, and manifold phonaesthetic combinations. This claim may be supported whether one analyzes the discourse from a Semitic, a rabbinic, or a Greco-Roman stylistic perspective (or all three literary influences in the case of many New Testament texts).

Since many passages of the Bible arguably *do* demonstrate, by and large, a high literary standard,[26] they implicitly call for a correspondingly high quality of translation to maintain a relative balance in terms of functional equivalence, communicative effectiveness, "relevant similarity" (Chesterman 1997:69), or, more specifically, "aesthetic parity."[27] In other words, it behooves literary translators to at least attempt to approximate or match this overall level of stylistic *excellence* and rhetorical *effect* in the TL text,[28] to the extent that this is possible—that is, given their particular

---

[26]I recognize that the literary style and quality of the various books of the Bible differ from one book to another and "that different books of the Bible need different styles of translation....[W]hen the original is beautiful, its beauty must shine through the translation; when it is stylistically ordinary, this must be apparent" (Hargreaves 1993:48, 138). However, the "ordinariness" of the original must not be assumed or assessed too readily. Many biblical books supposed to be stylistically lackluster on the surface of the text reveal some complex, less obvious literary qualities, for example, complex phonological patterns or an elaborate underlying discourse arrangement—features that may have an effect even on the subliminal level, as several studies by Loren Bliese have shown (e.g., 2003). Therefore, given the great language-cultural barrier that present-day text consumers face when approaching the Scriptures, translators would seem to be justified if they incorporate some stylistic embellishments into their TL version as a means of reducing the level of difficulty with regard to text-processing, as well as increasing the cognitive and emotive benefits that they thereby derive from the biblical text.

[27]With regard to the translational goal of functional equivalence, de Waard and Nida state: "The translator must seek to employ a functionally equivalent set of forms which in so far as possible will match the meaning of the original source-language text" (1986:36). "Meaning," in turn, is not only informative in function; it is also expressive, affective, and directive. Concerning the issue of a translation's quality, Hatim and Mason propose that "one might define the task of the translator as a communicator as being one of seeking to maintain **coherence** by striking the appropriate balance between what is **effective** (will achieve its communicative goal) and what is **efficient** (will prove least taxing on users' cognitive resources) in a particular environment, for a particular purpose and for particular receivers" (1997:12). However, the matter of the translator's responsibility is also relevant here, that is, with respect to the communicative intentions and literary quality of the original SL text.

[28]"Any account of poetic effect or literariness must include an account of affective communication....The point of poetic effects and literariness more generally...is to broaden context, and make both thoughts and feelings richer, more complex and more precise with regard to actual situations or states of affairs" (Pilkington 2000:160, 161). It is imperative, therefore, that literary translators take the subtle but pervasive influence of verbal impact and appeal, as well as personal emotions and attitudes, most seriously in their task of text-conceptual transformation.

level of education, competence, experience, and commitment as well as the encouragement and support provided by their translation administrative committee and the community at large.[29] To do any less would represent a considerable *reduction* in the overall communicative *value* of the translation in relation to the original SL text. The Biblical literary critic Leland Ryken puts the case as follows (2002:162, 170–171):

> [I]f the Bible is a literary book, a translation of it needs to preserve the artistry of the original text....What's bad about an *un*literary Bible? It distorts the kind of book that the Bible is (mainly an anthology of literary genres). It robs the Bible of the power that literature conveys....What is the antidote to the problem of an unliterary Bible and the translation practices that produce it? ...This means, insofar as possible, retaining the concreteness, artistry, indirectness, subtlety, multilayeredness, and language patterns of the original. It is as simple as that.[30]

Thus the attempt to produce a sonorous and eloquent poetic rendering of at least certain portions of the Scriptures—those of undeniable literary quality to begin with—can be defended in principle, as long as there is a ready and willing receptor constituency that is either calling for such a translation, or who audience research suggests would presumably benefit from one. Translators must endeavor to do this, however, not by means of a mechanical feature-for-feature, passage-by-passage method, but rather in terms of larger chunks of text. This strategy would be carried out with respect to the dominant communicative functions that happen to be operative over those particular stretches of discourse in accordance with the literary genre concerned. If such a meaning-*full* signification cannot be reproduced in their language by means of the same literary devices and

---

[29]Is this a realistic goal to shoot for—"Is it realistic to expect great literature of one language to be re-presented artistically intact in another language?" (from the promotional text for the new [2003] book by Prof. Di Jin, entitled *Literary translation: Quest for artistic integrity*; on the website for St. Jerome Publishing, www.stjerome.co.uk). This academic, translator, and translation theorist definitely thinks so, and in this book he presents "a systematic delineation of a practical approach toward that seemingly idealist aim" (ibid.). I would certainly agree with such a proposal, but would qualify it somewhat by noting that there may be various degrees of tightness included in this goal of representing a text that is "artistically intact" in the TL.

[30]Ryken's statement "It is as simple as that" is undoubtedly ironic. Producing a literary translation is not at all simple, of course. I strongly agree with Ryken's critical evaluation of the Scriptures, that they are for the most part made up of excellently composed *literature*. However, I do not agree with him that it is not possible to produce a literary, as well as an accurate, translation following a "dynamic equivalent" approach to the task (see his criticisms in 2002:196, 228; see also the book's appendix by C. John Collins, entitled "Without Form, You Lose Meaning"). I hope that the present study will give some indication as to how a literary functionally equivalent (LiFE) rendition can be done using any translation methodology.

rhetorical techniques as in Hebrew and Greek, then it will have to be accomplished through the use of features that represent the biblical text's functional and connotative import in a way that is most nearly equivalent to the original as well as appropriate for the target audience and setting concerned.

1.7 Models: Important L-R methodologies

The following is a brief summary of some of the more important literary movements and schools that have influenced biblical studies, hermeneutics in particular, over the past half-century. They are listed chronologically, roughly in the order of their appearance, although there is much overlapping, especially in the case of the first two. One prominent practitioner of each method is mentioned.[31]

- *Rhetorical Criticism.* Analyzes the manner in which the author selected, structured, and shaped his text forms in order to carry out specific communicative objectives, especially that of persuasion, in relation to his intended audience. Two of its varieties are:
  a) *Classical:* Focuses on the use of ancient Greco-Roman rhetorical principles, categories, and techniques (Watson 1988).
  b) *Neo-Classical:* Focuses on the use of more contemporary methods of discourse and argument analysis (Trible 1994).
- *Formalism,* or New Criticism. Analyzes the text as a whole or alone in terms of its literary conventions and the artistic devices characteristic of a particular genre (following in the footsteps of Form Criticism), whether on the macro- or microstructure of text organization. Some of its several varieties in relation to biblical studies are:
  a) *Narrative* (Sternberg 1985): Focuses on narrative discourse in the Old Testament.
  b) *Poetic* (Alter 1985): Focuses on Hebrew poetry.
  c) *Linguistic* (Cotterell and Turner 1989): Focuses on special phonological, grammatical, and semantic features in the New Testament.
  d) *Canonical* (McCann 1993): Focuses on groups of related texts within a larger corpus, especially the Psalter.

---

[31]For more detailed surveys of these and other literary approaches and their relevance to Bible translation, see A. Mojola, "Scripture Translation in the Era of Translation Studies" (in Wilt 2002b, chap. 1) and G. Ogden, "Biblical Studies and Bible Translation" (in Wilt 2002b, chap. 5). Another handy survey is in P. House 1988:15–20.

- *Structuralism,* or Modernism. Analyzes the larger ideational form and the implicit conceptual arrangement of a text. Its most notable varieties are:
    a) *Semiotic* (Patte 1990a and 1990b): Focuses on a putative semantic "deep structure" of a biblical text according to abstract semiotic principles and formulaic procedures.
    b) *Thematic* (Brueggemann 1992): Focuses on various patterns of significant lexical and conceptual repetition in the discourse.
- *Receptionism,* or Reader-Response Criticism. Focuses on the creative activity of receptors as they interpret and apply a text in their real-life situation—often nowadays with an ideological bent, such as feminist, liberationist, postcolonialist, or Africanist critics. (For a useful survey of most of these see J. Green, ed. 1995, chaps. 15–17.)
- *Deconstruction,* or Postmodernism. Focuses on the idiosyncratic interpretive "play" of individual readers as they "encounter" and conceptually "transform" a biblical text (terminology of Adam 2000). With this method there is little or no concern for hermeneutical principles or the original communication setting (see Vanhoozer 1998, passim). An example of this view is S. Brayford (cited in Adam 2000:256), who says, "Postmodern theorists, challenging these modern assumptions [about language, equivalence, and meaning] ask what if the direction of dependence were reversed so that the meaning of the original text is dependent on the translation."[32]

There is an important shift in focus and emphasis with respect to the act of communication as we move from "modern" Rhetorical Criticism to that of "postmodern" Deconstruction. This theoretical and practical movement can be summarized as follows:

(Deconstruction)

INTERPRETER
_____   _____

////////////////////////////////\\\\\\\\\\\\\\\\\\\\\\\\\\\\\\\\

[AUTHOR ➜   **TEXT**   **⬅ READER]**

(Rhetoric)   (Formalism—Structuralism)   (Receptionism)

---

[32]There is a sense in which such a perspective is valid, for example, when comparatively evaluating the effectiveness of various contemporary interpretations of the Scriptures. However, the source of authority and ultimate standard of accuracy for most Bible translators is fixed and derives from a single, clearly defined source, namely, the original text; all translations (or interpretations) are dependent on this.

In other words, the hermeneutical perspective of Rhetorical Criticism is focused upon the activity of the real or implied author of the text. In the case of both Formalism and Structuralism interest centers on the text itself, which is viewed as an autonomous system of significant signs. Receptionism emphasizes the text's contemporary consumers (readers, hearers). And in Deconstructive-type studies, the interpreter or literary critic is primarily interested in his or her own personal reactions to the text at hand, regardless of either the original setting or the response of contemporary readers.

For many literary critics (such as those of the New Critical, or Formalist, school), the written text is all that matters; it is viewed as being the sole locus of meaning, independent from whoever wrote it and whoever reads or hears it. As has also been noted, other analysts take this approach a step further and designate the receptor as being the actual creator or originator of textual meaning. I do not accept such a radical reductionistic point of view; rather, I prefer an inclusive, interactive, context-sensitive, communication-based method of study: as a minimum, { S $\Leftrightarrow$ *M* $\Leftrightarrow$ R }, where a Message serves as a means of interaction between a Source (author) and a Receptor (target audience, whether singular or plural). In other words, verbal *forms*—all linguistic and literary signs, conventional as well as distinctive—are regarded as being conveyors and also contributors to a particular message's intended and derived significance. Meaning in its fullest sense then is a combination of *intent* (S focus) + *content* (M focus) + *judgment* (R focus), as it is systematically and progressively conceptualized, verbally represented, and subsequently perceived and understood in a given contextual situation.

The last mentioned variable is crucial. This textual and extratextual setting is manifold and very complex in its constitution. It consists of many intertextual resonances and interlocked linguistic levels as well as various nonlinguistic frames of cognitive, sociocultural, and situational influence. All of these converge to influence to varying degrees and with varied effects the individual mind-sets of the different participants in any communication event. The audience (or text consumers), both the originally intended ones and all subsequent eavesdroppers, also contribute to the activity of meaning generation and interpretation through their personal and group perspectives (private experiences and a corporate worldview—beliefs, values, presuppositions, goals, felt needs). Nevertheless, I consider the communicative process to be purposeful, hence directional, or *teleological,* in nature. Thus a "message" has to start or originate somewhere (i.e., within a specific human cognitive environment). It is then conveyed, or re-signified, by the source in relation to the intended receptor(s) and directly or indirectly back again, through feedback, both actual and also anticipatory. It seems necessary, at least to me, to adopt such an objective perspective on communication and meaning transmission, including its artistic and rhetorical dimensions, in order to provide the rationale for a functional component within the hermeneutical operation as a whole.[33]

Attention in an L-R approach centers then upon the distinctive or diagnostic (stylistic) *forms* of a particular text because these forms are regarded as having been deliberately chosen, crafted, and situated as clues or signals, whether on the macro- or microstructure of discourse formation. Therefore, they have the capacity, when considered together in dynamic interplay, to reveal (or at least suggest) how the original author intended his message to be perceived and interpreted by his primary

[33]This appears to be an increasingly unpopular perspective in contemporary scholarship (biblical studies, literary criticism, communication theory, and philosophy). Thus Douglas Robinson opines, "Translation in the West has traditionally, hegemonically, thus (almost) exclusively been defined as a process of communication: the transmission of meanings from one language to another. This is a rationalist bias, owing much to Plato and Aristotle" (1997:182). This conceptual-intellectual problem was exacerbated, according to Robinson, by "the Christian tradition [which] theorized translation as a channel of conversion [in which] the personal creativity of the translator had to be subordinated to, or subsumed in, the Logos, God's unitary Word" (ibid.). One struggles to follow the reasoning here. It is much more likely that the longstanding literalistic Christian approach to Bible translation developed either from a certain *mis*understanding of the nature of genuine communication, including its so-called *ritual* function, or from an overly reverential respect for the Word and warnings such as those enunciated in Rev. 22:18–19.

More helpful is Robinson's recycling of some of Cicero's notions concerning translation. Thus, the Latin "[e]xprimere literally means to squeeze out—a powerful image for the translation process as Cicero describes it, akin to giving birth" (ibid.:185). Furthermore, "[e]xprimere gives us the translator as mediator...as the artist who mediates between two forms of being [= text?], two modes of understanding, natural and plastic, material and verbal, matter and manner, source language and target language" (ibid.).

Now that is indeed a helpful way of imaging the translation process as it is carried out according to an L-R approach. But why does this not qualify as some distinct "mode" of communication? Whether these interlingual "mediators" (call them what you will) are literal or free in their methods, they are still "communicators"—conveyers, transmitters, revealers, and sharers of thoughts, emotions, and intentions involving one text-tradition-culture-context and another. Robinson's proposed translational antithesis between some supposed "Christian tradition" and the approved practice of Cicero is spurious at best (ibid.:186). For one thing, in recent years many "Christian" translators, such as Eugene Nida, have been equally active in "*removing a restriction*—in liberating the budding orator's [or translator's] verbal imagination from the prison of the original text" (ibid.)—namely, its lexical and grammatical *forms*.

However, there is one crucial respect in which all responsible Bible translators—even the most meaning-oriented and creative practitioners—willingly do remain "captivated," as it were, and that is to the sense and significance of the original sacred text, as determined by careful and complete exegetical procedures. In fact, it requires translators of much higher caliber to be both creative and captive in this way as they communicate the Holy Scriptures across diverse languages, cultures, literary traditions, the epochs of time, worldviews, and ways of life.

audience, based on their anticipated reactions. The more of these features that a complete literary work, or an integral portion of one, manifests, especially if they are comparatively novel or unexpected in nature and combination, the more dynamic (or "turbulent") the text is in communicative or rhetorical terms. As a result, a correspondingly more active "mediative" (freer) translation method will probably be needed to render it meaningfully (semantically, functionally, relevantly) in another language and culture (Hatim and Mason 1997:27–30, 147). Some applications of such a distinctly literary approach to the translation of biblical literature will be examined more closely in chapters 3–6.

1.8 Strategy: The importance of a project *Skopos*

The focus of the preceding discussion was upon the text—the "literariness" of the SL text and of the translated TL text. But that is only half of the translational equation. The other half concerns the extralinguistic setting of the overall transcultural communication event, namely, the contemporary audience or intended readership. Past translation theory and practice has usually noted the importance of this human component,[34] but often in a unilateral, even monolithic sort of way. That is to say, the act of communication is viewed as a message transmission in but one direction, where the author or translator contributes more or less everything, and the audience simply receives the text, interprets it, and then decides how to respond. Recent studies have shown that this is not the case at all—that communication is truly a *shared* process, in which an audience (as active "consumers" of the message) brings *to* a text their own distinct expectations, values, norms, biases, experiences, perspectives, and cognitive frameworks, all of which greatly influence—either to foil or

---

[34]The importance of the audience has also come into prominence in modern literary-critical and hermeneutical movements, beginning helpfully with what became known as "reception" or "reader-response" theory. This has unfortunately (to my mind) degenerated into the selectively egalitarian, iconoclastic, and ironically anticritical approach called postmodernism, based on the literary theory of Deconstruction. From this perspective, "every text is divided against itself" (Alter 1987:35), and hermeneutical practice becomes subjectively limited in scope to the free expression of one's personal introspection (see Vanhoozer 1998: 16–18, 30–31, 66–68). In other words, "[t]here no longer is anything that is distinctive and essentially literary to have a theory about" (Pilkington 2000:39). The unfortunate result is that the so-called theory of deconstruction "does not advance serious thought or inquiry but gives an impression of profundity and complexity without the effort and skill that would be required to make a substantial contribution to the understanding of the matter under discussion" (1989:7; also see the cogent criticism in Aaron 2001:81). As P. House observes: "In the study of the Bible the importance of the text must be stressed or the reader's understanding will not attain the level the literature itself intends. As Holy Scripture the Bible transcends the individual reader, though it does invite study and analysis" (1988:17).

to facilitate—the message that they perceive, understand, and ultimately react to.

The hermeneutical significance of audience input can be taken a step further. Here it concerns the translation project as a whole in that its planners and organizers cannot simply anticipate (or even ignore) their target group. Rather, they must make every effort to find out *beforehand* the specific nature of their listenership/readership—not only their perceived needs or desires, but their actual, expressed expectations and goals for the translation. In short, representatives of the target constituency must be integrally involved in all aspects of planning for the special type of version that is meant to serve their community within the settings where it will be used. This is not to say that the target group determines everything according to their personal felt needs, which may in fact be quite removed from an objective assessment of their real needs, based on the deeper exigencies and realities of their current, and possible future, life situation.

The importance of developing such an explicit operative framework has been greatly stressed in recent translation studies. This is known as the translation *Brief,* which explicitly sets forth "information about the intended target-text function(s), the target text addressee(s), the medium over which it will be transmitted, the prospective place and time and, if necessary, motive of production or reception of the text" (Nord 1997:137). The most important component of a *Brief* is the particular purpose, or *Skopos,* for which the translation is being made for its primary audience and setting of use in keeping with prevailing social and translational norms in the target society.[35] As H. Vermeer points out, "Each text is produced for a given purpose and should serve this purpose. The *Skopos* rule thus reads as follows: translate/interpret/ speak/write in a way that enables your text/translation to function in the situation in which it is used and with the people who want to use it and precisely in the way they want it to function" (translated and cited by Nord [1997:29]).

The whole preparatory stage of research and planning must therefore be fully interactive and freely negotiated between the proposed producer and

---

[35]The latter part of this statement deserves much more attention than I can devote to it in the present study. According to Lambert (1998:132), "all translation activity (whether it involves producing, using or commenting on translations) is guided and shaped by such things as the norms, value scales and models which are prevalent in a given society at a given moment in time. The study of literary translation therefore consists of the study of translation norms, models and traditions." Bible translation as a specific subset of such literary activity in a given language and culture will often have its own distinct set of norms, values, standards, traditions, and models (sometimes derived from a dominant language of wider communication in the region). For a detailed statement of some of the major issues and concerns here, see Wilt 2002a:43–58.

consumer groups. There must be a continual give-and-take dialogue in order to establish the objectives and working document for the entire project. A more complex *Skopos* is normally called for when it is "Holy Scripture" that is to be translated. The process must be both "source-oriented" and "target-oriented" (Hermans 1999:37). As to the latter, "[t]ranslation choices normally result from judgements by the translator—or whoever is in a position to control or override the translator—about perceived needs and benefits, audience expectations, personal and collective motivations." On the other hand, since an authoritative sacred text is being rendered, the translation is viewed "as a vicarious object, a substitute which must constantly be referred back to its source…[and] checked against the original for faults and shortcomings" (ibid.:39–40).

The official position statement, or *Brief,* then is what subsequently determines how the program will be carried out, and when and where and by whom (i.e., the type of translation staff, both official and auxiliary, required to get the job done in the most efficient and productive manner). Ideally, should the circumstances allow, this *Brief* ought not neglect the goal of producing a stylistically more creative translation, in certain key respects (e.g., to match the discourse markers, or the signals of emphasis in the biblical text). This would be a rendering that manifests at least some measure of general functional correspondence with respect to both the *rhetorical vitality* and *literary beauty* of the original text. As Jurij Lotman has observed, in a literary text "beauty is information" too (*Schoenheit ist Information,* cited in du Plooy 2002:267). If this is true, and it all depends on one's definition of *information,* this feature cannot be ignored in Bible translation.

1.9 A preview of things to come

The chapters that follow, though not light reading, will hopefully prove beneficial in terms of stimulating some new ideas with regard to both understanding and communicating the Word of God. In chapter 2 I present a more detailed treatment of what a specifically "literary" and/or "rhetorical" approach to the translation of the Bible is. Then an entire chapter is devoted to each of four major literary characteristics: tectonicity (chap. 3), artistry (chap. 4), iconicity (chap. 5), and rhetoricity (chap. 6). Each of these characteristics foregrounds a particular aspect of a given biblical text: *tectonicity* foregrounds its macroform (organizational structure); *artistry*, its microform (stylistic texture); *iconicity*, its content (ideational inventory); and *rhetoricity*, its communicative function (pragmatic motivation). These features are not, of course, realized in isolation in literary discourse; nor are they the only elements of literature that might have been investigated; furthermore, they are not dealt with exhaustively. Rather, they are presented more by way of illustration and as suggestions for future research. The separate treatment of these four features is provided as an initial framework for more fully exploring the basic principles and procedures of an L-R method. They undoubtedly are some of the more important literary attributes for translators to learn to recognize, analyze, and apply in their everyday practice of Bible translation. In the last chapters of this book some practical ways for doing this within the framework of a given project *Skopos* are then considered.

At several points in the Revelation, the final prophetic book of the Bible, we get a glimpse of one important long-range goal of all this effort aimed at more effectively communicating the Scriptures in earth's languages. For example, in Rev. 7:10 and 12 we read:

Ἡ σωτηρία	*Salvation—*
τῷ θεῷ ἡμῶν	**to our God**
τῷ καθημένῳ	*who is seated*
ἐπὶ τῷ θρόνῳ	*upon the throne*
καὶ τῷ ἀρνίῳ.	*and to the Lamb!*

Ἀμήν,	**Amen!**
ἡ εὐλογία	*praise,*
καὶ ἡ δόξα	*and glory,*
καὶ ἡ σοφί	*and wisdom,*
καὶ ἡ εὐχαριστία	*and thanksgiving,*
καὶ ἡ τιμὴ	*and honor,*
καὶ ἡ δύναμις	*and power,*
καὶ ἡ ἰσχὺς	*and strength*
τῷ θεῷ ἡμῶν	**be to our God**
εἰς τοὺς αἰῶνας	*forever*
τῶν αἰώνων·	*and ever!*
ἀμήν.	**Amen!**

Sometimes I wonder if communication in heaven will be carried out using prose or poetry, speech or song. I suspect that it is more likely to be poetry and song rather than prose and speech, given the nature of this divine locale. But in which language? Some totally distinct, heavenly dialect? From the immediate context of the preceding passages, another answer might be proposed: in every mother tongue that was ever spoken by believers on this earth, apparently uttered simultaneously as well as in mutually intelligible terms (Rev. 7:9). Babel unbound—Pentecost prolonged.

These would be words of praise to the King proclaimed in the most appropriate, artistically phrased and rhetorically pointed, "literary" language.

Until then, it makes sense to put in some serious practice towards that end by rendering the Word of the Lord accordingly in the various languages of the world—whether in prose, poetry, or an adjustable mixture of both. That is what this study is all about.

2

Defining the Parameters of a Literary-Rhetorical Translation

What do the following passages have in common? What can these words tell us about the compositional quality of the Scriptures that we study, learn, live by, testify to, and translate? Indeed, the nature of God's message is often characterized in the Scriptures by pointed and potent descriptive expressions such as "beautiful," "sweet," "powerful," "active," (energetic), "sharp."

רָחַשׁ לִבִּי ׀ דָּבָר טוֹב
אֹמֵר אָנִי מַעֲשַׂי לְמֶלֶךְ
לְשׁוֹנִי עֵט ׀
סוֹפֵר מָהִיר:

Beautiful words stir in my mind,
as I compose a piece for the king.
Like the pen of a *skillful scribe*,
my tongue is ready with a *poem*.
(Ps. 45:1 [v. 2 in Hebrew]—TEV, modified)

- -

מַה־נִּמְלְצוּ לְחִכִּי אִמְרָתֶךָ
מִדְּבַשׁ לְפִי:

How *sweet* to my taste are your words,
sweeter they are *than honey* to my mouth!
(Ps. 119:103—NIV, modified)

- -

καὶ δυνάμει μεγάλῃ
ἀπεδίδουν τὸ μαρτύριον οἱ ἀπόστολοι
τῆς ἀναστάσεως τοῦ κυρίου Ἰησοῦ...

Moreover, with *great power*
the apostles continued to testify
to the resurrection of the Lord Jesus...
(Acts 4:33a—NIV, modified)

- -

πῶς δὲ κηρύξωσιν   How then can they preach
ἐὰν μὴ ἀποσταλῶσιν;   unless they are sent out?
καθὼς γέγραπται,   As it stands written,
Ὡς ὡραῖοι οἱ πόδες   "How *beautiful* are the feet
τῶν εὐαγγελιζομένων   of those who *proclaim*
[τὰ] ἀγαθά.   the good news!"
                               (Rom 10:15—NIV, modified)

- -

Ζῶν γὰρ ὁ λόγος τοῦ θεοῦ   Indeed, living is the word of God
καὶ ἐνεργὴς καὶ τομώτερος   and *active, sharper* too
ὑπὲρ πᾶσαν μάχαιραν δίστομον than any two-edged sword...
                               (Heb. 4:12a—NRSV, modified)

The question is, Do these attributes, whether expressed directly or in figurative terms, refer only to the *content* of this Word of the Lord, or can they also be applied to the literary *forms* of the original text? And if the latter, what all is included, how can we determine this, and what are the implications for Bible translation? These are some of the issues that we will be exploring in this chapter.

2.1 The value of a literary-rhetorical translation

Why aim to produce a "beautiful" translation of the Bible?[36] Is it a stretch to claim that the Word is "powerful," not only in spiritual terms (e.g., Heb. 4:12) but with regard to its rhetorical forms as well? While biblical support does need to be explicitly demonstrated, and I hope to do that in subsequent chapters,[37] for the present I will simply assume that this premise is true—namely, that in the Scriptures we find many different texts

---

[36]I derive the quality of "beautiful" from Ps. 45:1 and also from the figurative reference to God's Word in Ps. 119:103 ('*sweet* honey' => *beautiful* message) as well as from the description of the gospel messenger's feet in Rom. 10:15 ('*beautiful* feet' => messenger => lips => words/message). Note that in Ps. 45:1 the terms אֹמֵר 'speaking' and לְשׁוֹנִי 'my tongue' also highlight the crucial oral-aural aspect of the biblical message that we read (in the original) and translate.

[37]Many recent scholars have come to the same conclusion, as noted in chapter 1. But the strongest, most credible support for this perspective comes from one's own individual study of the Scriptures. Indeed, the more we carefully investigate diverse passages of the Bible such as Ezra 4:15, John 5:39, and 1 Pet. 1:11 in a thorough, systematic fashion, the more the text itself convinces us. Both the content and the forms that represent and convey it in human language are divinely given, which is of course what the Bible also claims for itself. My point here is simply that a knowledge of the "creation"—the canon of Scripture as it has been received—also points invariably in the same direction, to the same Source.

that manifest both beauty and power in the presentation of their intended message. The issue at hand is this: Taking the artistic and rhetorical attributes of the Bible as a given, what implications does such a position have for its translators?

Information transmission is what most contemporary Bible communicators, including translators, see as their primary objective. We have to get the *content* of Scripture across to our constituency, they say. Certainly that task is daunting enough. But as we have already noted, "Beauty [too] is information." Now if our challenge is to include the original text's artistic beauty and rhetorical power, how can we even consider, let alone realize, success in this venture? The answer, of course, is, We cannot. As when dealing only with the "pure content" of the Bible, we are not able to succeed, either fully or completely. Something of the source-language (SL) text will *always* get altered—added, lost, distorted—in the process. Therefore, a deliberate choice has to be made: What aspect, area, or element of the original text do we wish to focus on—its forms (the ordinary as well as the exceptional ones), content, intent, impact, appeal? Because it is a sure thing that we cannot expect to represent them *all* in a single rendition— not even in a well-annotated version, or one that includes all sorts of "supplementary helps." My argument is simply that we need to take also the *artistry* and the *rhetoric* of the Scriptures seriously, so much so that even if we decide *not* to make any attempt at all to represent these features in our translation, then we clearly recognize the implications of what we have (not) done and the loss that is thereby involved.

But do we not have enough translation types to choose from already, especially in the languages of the world? And as for the so-called minor languages, would a literary version not be a luxury that cannot be seriously defended, or even proposed as a possibility? Consider the cost. A literary version would undoubtedly turn out to be very difficult and demanding in terms of time, finances, and human resources. In short, it would probably be too hard either to accomplish or to justify.

While these concerns are all valid, they are not necessarily determinative in every case. It really depends on the total setting: for whom, by whom, for what purpose, and in which situation the translation will be used. In today's world of extended and diversified communication options, the trend is for *greater* variety, not less, based on target-audience opinion (their desires, needs, and expectations) as determined by pre-project market research. More about this will be said later.

For now, I return to the basic premise: If—or better, *since*—verbal beauty and power were and are an integral part of the message of Scriptures, these dimensions *must* be dealt with in an appropriate, locally determined way in every Bible translation. Even if it is finally decided that such features cannot be handled due to inadequate resources, the issue still needs to be addressed. To do less would render the translators liable to the charge of incompetence or unfaithfulness. Indeed, one could argue that it is a matter of essential honesty with regard to the original text of the Scriptures. Whatever significance has been left out needs to be documented and the reasons for doing so clearly delineated. Usually, however, this subject is simply ignored, either out of ignorance or due to the lack of any suitable strategy for dealing with artistic verbal communication. Ironically, the argument here, as in the case of past debates in Bible translation studies, also concerns the *form* of the original text. In this instance, however, it is its *literary*, not linguistic, forms that are in focus—and with special reference to how their significance might be at least partially reproduced by capitalizing on some of the literary forms available in a given target language. Furthermore, it is not form for its own sake that we are concerned about—but distinctive form that also designates some definite aspects of "meaning" in the wider sense, whether informative, expressive, directive, aesthetic, or commemorative in nature.

The translation task in this regard is extremely complex and demanding. The quality of *beauty* involves artistic structure and style on all levels of textual organization, while the attribute of *power* relates to patterns of argumentation and rhetorical effects that aim to enhance the persuasive appeal and overall communicative impact of the text. This dimension of meaning is a given where outstanding literature is concerned. As one teacher of professional translators has observed:

> Approaching the complexities of translation from a literary theoretical angle makes sense when one keeps in mind that literature is regarded as the most complex form of language usage incorporating much more than semiotic meaning or signification. In poetic language all the aspects and possibilities of language are deliberately exploited to concentrate meaning, to achieve that density of meaning which Jurij Lotman...saw as the essence of the artistic text.... (du Plooy 2002:267)

So if it is a literary document that we have as a source to work with, surely one viable option as far as translational possibilities are concerned is to translate it as a literary text—a "value added" translation (Joubert 2002:34), as it were. Of course, the primarily theological nature and value of the Scriptures must never be lost sight of.[38] But even a cursory reading

---

[38]In this regard, the late Douglas Bush, a well-known professor of literature at Harvard for many years, makes the following interesting observation: "[T]he Bible is the grand proof in English that in the greatest writing literary beauty is not a main object but a by-product" (quoted in Linton 1986:25). My own comment is simply this: the preceding

of the Psalter, or any other poetic pericope, soon impresses one with the fact that these religious compositions were intended not merely (or even mostly) to inform the minds, but to move the hearts of their hearers—not by means of a silent reading to oneself, but by means of a public oral proclamation, or even a recital, of the text.

The aim of this chapter, which expands upon the preceding one, is to further define the parameters of a *literary-rhetorical* (L-R) method of translating the Bible.[39] This approach offers not only another option for rendering the Scriptures in another language, should circumstances allow, but it also makes a potential contribution to contemporary translation theory and practice. It may well be of interest and significance to the field of secular translation studies simply because of the great diversity of genres, text types, styles, and literary features that must be dealt with in translating the Bible. Certainly the scholarly exchange is fruitful from both standpoints, as the present chapter will show by surveying a number of prominent theories that relate to the subject of literary translation.

This is, however, a very limited treatment of a rather large topic. That is to say, although the field of literary study has expanded greatly in several directions over the past several decades, I will discuss in detail only those aspects that are of appreciable relevance to Bible translators or those engaged in teaching translators how to carry out their task. This selectivity accords with the book's ultimate aim: to encourage a formally more dynamic rendering of the dynamic Word in keeping with both accuracy of content representation and also an awareness of target audience preference—that is, a modern speech community who would appreciate hearing some or all of the Scriptures resound idiomatically in their mother tongue.

2.2 Background: The literary analysis of biblical literature

In the latter half of the twentieth century, there has been what Ryken terms a "quiet revolution" taking place in biblical studies as an increasing number of scholars—along with ordinary students of the Word—come to an ever greater awareness that the Bible is fundamentally literary in character. This has important implications for both interpretation and application. As Ryken states, "the methods of literary scholarship are a

assertion applies also in large measure to the original text of Scripture; furthermore, there exists the grand potential for it to be fulfilled in any world language.

[39]This compound term incorporates two distinct, but integrated perspectives on any literary text, not only the Bible, namely: (a) the *artistic*, which focuses upon the distinctive (marked) macro- and microfeatures of discourse (i.e., its *structural* and *stylistic* dimensions respectively); and (b) the *rhetorical*, which focuses upon the persuasive effect of discourse (i.e., the *affective* and *imperative* dimensions) and/or its structure of argumentation (see chap. 6).

necessary part of any complete study of the Bible" (1984:11). A problem exists, however, in the application of this insight to biblical studies. The difficulty, Wiklander observes, is that although "few scholars—if any—would seriously deny this basic premise...the extent to which it is allowed to shape exegetical work varies quite considerably" (1984:2). The present survey is intended to describe and illustrate several important applications of literary scholarship to a study of the Scriptures, whether in their entirety or in terms of a single book or a given pericope.

The discussion will further demonstrate the practical value of a literary-critical method in Bible translation. It also emphasizes the importance of carrying out a thorough examination of verbal art in the target language as a means of identifying possible functional "matches" that will prove useful in the transfer process. It is hoped that a careful consideration of this subject will serve as a springboard for further discussion and development of some of these preliminary ideas.

The modern scholarly movement promoting the analysis of Scripture as literature is frequently dated from 1969, when James Muilenburg's seminal essay "Form Criticism and Beyond" was first published. (It has since been reprinted in P. House, ed. 1992:49–69.) Muilenburg advocated the use of past and present literary methods, which he termed "rhetorical criticism" but perhaps better designated in his own words as "stylistics or aesthetic criticism" (ibid.:56–57), as a means to understand the various units and relations, structures and patterns, techniques and devices that effectively communicate the sense and significance of a complete biblical text. At the time, this approach involved a primary shift in focus from atomistic historical and genetic issues to holistic, artistic, and rhetorical concerns. In other words, the center of scholarly interest moved from a desire to learn how a text came to be composed to how it conveys meaning and purpose as it stands *already* composed, or simply, "how Scripture means what it says" (P. House, ed. 1992:9).

Petersen (1978:26) said of this perspective, "In literary studies the critic...became concerned with the things of which a text was 'made,' with how they 'worked' to make the text what it was or appeared to be, and with what literary works essentially 'were,' that is ontologically." The diverse methodologies whose primary aim is like this are generally referred to as "literary criticism." This is not to be confused with the earlier and very misleading use of this expression with reference to the historically focused but quite speculative study of the Scriptures known as "source criticism" (ibid.:10). Other terms often used to designate the whole or aspects of the practice of literary criticism are "stylistics" and "poetics," the latter referring to how literature is constituted, from the

Greek verb *poiein* 'to make' (see Preminger and Brogan, eds. 1993:928). The field of literary analysis now includes a wide range of specific methodologies, most of which may be applied to complement one another in providing a more accurate picture of the artistic richness and rhetorical depth of most biblical texts. I have selected a number of these approaches, those that seemed most profitable for Bible translators, in my overview of the subject that follows.

2.3 The crucial question: Can the Bible be classified as literature?

Many theologians, scholars, and commentators—especially those who come from a more conservative background—have a problem with calling the Bible literature.[40] This is largely due to their limited definition of literature, which always includes the components "fictional" and/or "creative," either of which in their opinion denies the additional and preeminent quality of divine inspiration.[41] As we shall see, however, the broader definition of literature employed in this book neither entails nor implies such a denial. In short, there is no essential opposition between the concepts of "scripture" and "literature." As P. House says, "Studying the literary nature of the Bible no more negates the binding nature of the Bible as holy scripture than does examining its historical components" (1988:18). In fact, it should be noted, a literary approach to the analysis and interpretation of the Bible is not really new; renowned theologians in the past have practiced it (in some cases wrongly, by modern standards), for example, Augustine, Jerome, and Martin Luther (ibid.:5). The great theologian Augustine writes:

> I could...show those men who cry up their own form of language as superior to that of our authors [of Scripture]...that all those powers [i.e., rhetoric] and beauties [i.e., artistry] of eloquence which they make their boast, are to be found in the sacred writings which God in his goodness has provided to mold our characters, and to guide us from this world of wickedness to the blessed world above. (cited in Ryken, ed. 1984:17)

---

[40]This matter was already considered in chapter 1, but due to its importance in terms of the rationale and the motivation for an L-R translation, it is taken up again as preparation for my overview of various theoretical approaches to the subject.

[41]The special literary character of the Scriptures, whether Hebrew or Greek, is also denied by those of a more liberal theological persuasion who consider it to be essentially an ethnic Jewish sacred mythology or a disparate early Christian sourcebook or compendium like any other held sacred by one or another of the world's major religions. Such critics have probably not taken the time (or do not possess the expertise) to carry out a thorough, unbiased stylistic and structural analysis and evaluation of the Bible's constituent writings.

Could anyone ask for a clearer affirmation of the functional importance of literary form? The later Reformer, Luther, is also worth quoting on this issue:

> I am persuaded that without knowledge of literature, pure theology cannot at all endure....certainly it is my desire that there shall be as many poets and rhetoricians as possible, because I see that by these studies, as by no other means, people are wonderfully fitted for the grasping of sacred truth and for handling it skillfully and happily....
> (cited in P. House, ed. 1992:25)

Here we have a fervent plea for a prominent literary perspective and procedure to be included not only in the study of systematic theology, but also within the scope of practical theology, which includes Bible translation in all of its stages of application.[42] It is in this spirit then that we confidently, if not always so skillfully, forge ahead with our consideration of how a literary approach can render assistance in the specific and complex task of an interlingual and cross-cultural message transmission of the Holy Scriptures.

One's understanding of the concept of literature will, to some extent, determine the nature and scope of one's investigation. For some, "literature" is restricted to "something written (as the Bible is basically a 'book')" (Maier and Tollers, eds. 1979:3). Sharlemann (1987:7) defines it similarly: "a [literary] text is a written work, in contrast to an oral performance." However, more recent studies draw attention to the "oral overlay" (Achtemeier 1990:3) or "auditory aura" (Silberman 1987:3) of ancient written documents and suggest that the distinction between the two modes of communication in these texts is not at all easy to maintain. This is because "in practice, interaction between oral and written forms is extremely common" (Finnegan 1977:160) in classical as well as contemporary literature (see also Finnegan 1970:18). Other scholars would limit the notion of literature to purely "imaginative" discourse "in contrast to expository writing," and by this definition "some parts of the Bible are more literary and other parts are less literary" (Ryken, ed. 1984:12).

But for many investigators there is no doubt that "[T]he Bible is literature, the kind of writing that attends to beauty, power, and memorability as well as to exposition" (Linton 1986:16). The case has been well put in general terms by the noted author and literary critic C. S. Lewis, who says, "There is a...sense in which the Bible, since it is after all literature, cannot

---

[42]As a specific instance of this translational implication, Luther once observed in a 1520 letter to a friend that "figures of speech and the liveliness of sentences and arguments [i.e., literary artistry and rhetoric] can be rendered in a free translation only" (cited in Hargreaves 1993:2).

be properly read except as literature; and the different parts of it as the different sorts of literature that they are" (1989:71).

But what does it mean to read the Scriptures as literature? How does the notion of literature per se affect reading and interpretation?

In short, reading the Scriptures as literature means that one approaches it with a conscious awareness of the *expressive, affective* (including the emotive and aesthetic), and *directive* dimensions of semantically signifi-cant and stylistically shaped verbal discourse. That is in addition to being aware of the cognitively oriented "information" being conveyed (i.e., theology).

Of course, when dealing with the Word of God, one does not wish to place too much of a central emphasis on the imaginative or creative element of the human author.[43] But Ryken (1984:14) draws attention to a valid application on the part of all perceptive listeners/readers: "[Literature] constantly ap-peals to our imagination (the image-making and image-perceiving capacity within us). Literature *images* forth some aspect of reality."

While this notion can certainly be taken too far (as frequently happens in the case of many frivolous postmodern brands of criticism), it is impor-tant for interpreters to consider those stylistic devices, such as metaphor, sarcasm, irony, or hyperbole, which strongly stimulate or appeal to one's perceptions, feelings, moods, and attitudes. By such devices, verbal art-ists, including now the various biblical authors, frequently exploit the cre-ative potential of language in order to present what the French literary philosopher Paul Ricoeur calls a "re-description" of reality—albeit from a divine perspective—one in which the world is not replicated but transfig-ured in the vision that poet and audience come to share. Such imagistic, highly expressive discourse is frequently coupled with and complemented by various forms of *phonic* pointing and highlighting (e.g., rhythm, rhyme, alliteration, assonance, word-/sound-plays) that attract and at-tune the ear to pay attention to particular areas and aspects of a given text. These devices are normally bound up with the key components of an author's theme and/or communicative purpose.

Many other more detailed definitions and descriptions of literature are, of course, available in standard textbooks on the subject. But for now it is enough simply to point out the most important characteristic of literature

---

[43]One needs to recognize the possibility (even likelihood?) that there are differences in literary quality among the various biblical books (e.g., 1 and 2 Samuel in comparison with 1 and 2 Chronicles; Mark with Luke; 1 Peter with 2 Peter). Often, however, I have discovered that the books regarded to be "less honorable" stylistically on the overt surface of discourse composition (including those just mentioned) reveal certain underlying features of the-matic development, structural organization, and/or rhetorical arrangement which are highly literary in nature.

from the standpoint of discourse analysis, namely, the predominant focus upon linguistic *form* (verbal shape or tectonic construction) that is typical of a superior literary composition. This, as already suggested, may be *aural as well as visual* in nature and effect. In particular, there is a special emphasis upon the artistic dimension of discourse—or what Roman Jakobson termed the *poetic function* of the text. According to this principle, "the two basic modes of arrangement used in verbal behavior, selection and combination," as they operate within both the paradigmatic and also the syntagmatic planes of textual organization (Jakobson 1972:95), are maximized through multiple application. The aim is to formally foreground and enrich salient elements of message content, thereby also heightening its interest value, emotive impact, and persuasive appeal.

The result of this artistic-rhetorical process, which may be realized in prose as well as in poetry, is normally a verbal text that is heavily *figured* (i.e., with many diverse rhetorical tropes represented), artfully *patterned*, permeated by a pervasive *intertextuality*, and provided with a manifold cohesion by many *recursive* syntagmatic and paradigmatic structures of various kinds (i.e., lexical, phonological, syntactic, semantic, pragmatic). This is manifested on all levels of discourse organization, from the word on up to the composition as a whole. Literature thus maximizes the "how" (or style) of the text in order to highlight the "what" (i.e., content) and the "why" (i.e., intent or purpose). This is done by means of such stylistic features as "pattern or design, theme or central focus, organic unity (also called unity in variety, or theme and variation), coherence, balance, contrast, symmetry, repetition or recurrence, variation, and unified progression" (Ryken, ed. 1984:23–24). In the process of analysis then, one seeks to demonstrate how diverse artistic forms and rhetorical strategies are utilized in order to persistently, progressively, and impressively shape the expectations of the readers/listeners. They are thus enticed and encouraged to direct their individual interpretive activities, whether implicitly or explicitly applied, in a specific direction with reference to a particular biblical theme or life situation.

Every art, trade, science, or technology has its own standards and criteria of excellence as well as modes of evaluation. So does the study of literature. *Literary* excellence thus calls for "a developed awareness of the conventions and workings of a given literary corpus and a consequent ability to discern what kinds of claims a given text within that corpus may be making" (V. P. Long 1997:89). A particular body of literature (whether the collection is that of an individual author, genre, or an entire people) may be viewed as having a distinct, analyzable discourse "lexicon" and "grammar" (Berlin 1994:15). According to poetics (the science of literature), any literary composition consists of a specifiable set of literary *units* (e.g., themes, motifs, topics, figures), *arrangements* (preferred or typical ways of combining the units), and *rules* (the principles and conventions by which the units and arrangements operate within a given text or corpus). These different aspects of analysis may be usefully joined in the notion of text type, or genre, each variety of which manifests a particular combination (selection, arrangement, and distribution) of elements. This sort of larger text study will be considered more fully in chapter 3.

If we aim to understand and translate the individual passages of a foreign literature such as the Old Testament or New Testament, which originated within the context of a time, place, and culture far removed from our own, it makes sense to learn as much as we can (limited though this may be) of its distinctive constitution, usage, and contextual setting. The effort to develop such competence is justified by the simple fact that "an increased appreciation of the literary mechanisms of a particular text—*how* a story is told—often becomes the avenue of greater insight into the theological, religious and even historical significance of the text—what the story means" (V. P. Long 1997:90).[44]

There are also some significant exegetical implications here. Paying attention to a biblical text's literary features, both structural and stylistic, often sheds considerable light on the meaning of a particular passage, especially an ambiguous or otherwise problematic one. Thus a literary perspective and the additional textual evidence that it marshals can shift the balance of interpretation regarding a controversial issue from one side to the other. In such cases, the supposedly optional embellishments of the original text are shown to be vital stylistic signals that point towards its author-intended meaning, whether this happens to be semantic or pragmatic (i.e., interpersonal) in nature.

In this regard one analyst notes:

> While keeping in mind the open-ended character of language by accepting that no interpretation can be absolutely correct, the

---

[44]To this, we might add du Plooy's provocative observation (2002:268–269): "Though this [literary] approach was used for all types of texts in the twentieth century, the attitudes expressed in these theories derive from the philosophical position of Immanuel Kant (1724–1804), who is primarily associated with the idea of artistic autonomy. Whether his ideas about *purposiveness without purpose* (*Zweckmässigkeit ohne Zweck*) are really compatible with the functions of mythological or religious texts, is a question which theologians will have to answer, but the close relation between artistic and religious texts is an issue which will have to be addressed in the argument. For Kant beauty and the experience of beauty (and I wonder whether one could here in a very careful way, for argument's sake, substitute faith for beauty), cannot be limited to conceptual thought, because the indeterminate experience of beauty cannot adequately be contained in thought or expressed in language...."

interpreter-translator is in the first instance confronted by the inevitable textual aspects of a text, the phonetic, semantic, syntactic and
narrative structures, the specific metaphoric style and a specific linguistic register which cannot be denied. These aspects of a text have
to be recognized as meaningful in themselves so that interpretation
is not completely arbitrary but permanently and irrevocably guided
by the determinants of the original text. Whereas interpretations in
classrooms and in literary essays and papers at conferences attempt
to impress people with their creativity in producing exceptionally
original or radical readings of texts, the translator does not enjoy
that much freedom. He does not have ownership of the text, he has
to respect the limitations imposed upon him by the text itself.
Umberto Eco...describes his view as follows: "A text is a place
where the irreducible polysemy of symbols is in fact reduced because in a text symbols are anchored to their context....thus many
modern theories are unable to recognize that symbols are
paradigmatically open to infinite meanings but syntagmatically,
that is, textually, open to the indefinite, but by no means infinite,
interpretations allowed by the context." (du Plooy 2002:274).

The authors of commentaries, study Bibles, and translator helps need to
pay greater attention to this vital dimension of hermeneutics, which is so
often ignored or passed over for lack of time or expertise. Translators too
must take the artistry of the original text into serious consideration, to the
limits of their ability, no matter what type of version they happen to be
preparing in their mother tongue. This is not an optional exercise. As Linton (1986:16) points out with regard to one prominent literary feature,
"[T]he style [of a Bible translation] must communicate (re-present) the
emotional environment of the original, for though content informs us,
feeling involves us and moves us."

2.4 Some theories of literary translation

It must be asked to what extent a manifestly excellent literary work is
fully translatable. Is the outstanding literature of one language really rep-
resentable or re-creatable in an alien idiom? Can there even be a credible
theory of literary translation? Then, if one adopts a positive approach to
this issue, how does one go about actually preparing a satisfactory translation of this nature? In what way(s) may the products of translation be
evaluated and their acceptability by the target audience be assessed?

   In sections 2.4.1–2.4.2 I will give an overview of the opinions of others
on the subject of a literary translation, beginning with some well-known
Bible translators and moving from there to more secular translational
studies. My treatment here is admittedly selective; certain theorists may

have been left out simply because I am unacquainted with them and others perhaps because I do not adequately understand or appreciate what they have written on the subject. I have restricted my consideration largely to book-length studies since these are most accessible and actually used by ordinary field translators and their teachers around the SIL-UBS world. In any case, this survey is intended to provoke some serious thought concerning the issues involved and also to lay the foundation for my own delineation of the task of literary translation.

2.4.1 Bible translation theorists

Quite understandably perhaps, the pioneers of meaning-based Bible translation studies did not say a great deal, if anything, about a specifically literary rendition during the decades of the sixties and seventies. Their emphasis was apparently focused so much upon conveying the basic content of the Scriptures in a natural, idiomatic way (in contrast to the prevailing formal correspondence method) that not much attention could be devoted to the refinements of this procedure. The aim was to break translators, who were increasingly mother-tongue practitioners, of their typical preference for a literal approach, opening them up to a freer methodology that directed their energies towards conveying the sense of the original by means of an appropriate style in the target language. Although many specific literary features of the biblical text are considered in the texts by Nida (1964, 1975),[45] Nida and Taber (1969), Beekman and Callow (1974), Callow (1974), and Larson (1984), their emphasis is on determining the meaning of these forms, primarily with reference to the microstructure of source-language discourse and with the goal of finding suitable equivalents in a given target language.[46]

William Wonderly was one of the first of the early Bible translation theorists to say much about a literary translation. He broadly defines such a

---

[45]In his early study, Nida notes that "[t]he influence of literary forms is found in two principal areas: (1) the occurrence of sound effects, e.g., puns, acrostic series, and rhyming and alliterative sequences, and (2) rhythmic speech utterances, whether rhymed or not" (1964:176). Indeed, this is where literary influence is first and most obviously manifested, and this is a good place to begin—but it goes much deeper than that.

[46]It may be observed that most recent studies that attempt to evaluate contemporary Bible translations also largely ignore the subject of literary translation. For example, in the essays edited by Porter and Hess (1999) I found the term only once, and that with little exposition. A standout exception in this regard is Hargreaves's discussion (1993) comparing the language of modern English Bibles.

rendition as follows—that is, in a context of comparing literary versions
to common-language and popular-language versions:[47]

> These [literary translations] are fully contemporary, are oriented to
> the general public (not just the Christian in-group), and vary from
> regular to formal in their [sociolinguistic] functional variety. They
> make free use of all the resources of the language at all levels which
> are considered acceptable for published materials, and are thereby
> not intended to be fully accessible to the uneducated reader.
> (Wonderly 1968:30)

Obviously a literary version so defined can be produced only in a linguistic community with a relatively long tradition of written literature. Its envisioned target group would be people who are comparatively well
educated, widely read, and who enjoy the challenge of wrestling with the
full range of lexical, grammatical, stylistic, and rhetorical usage in the
particular language concerned (see Nida and Taber 1969:31).[48]

Wonderly's definition above of a literary *translation* may be compared
with Nida and Taber's definition of literary *language* (1969:205):

> that form of language, sometimes but not always written, in which
> texts are composed and transmitted which are intended to be
> esthetically pleasing; characterized by careful, often elaborate use
> of words and grammatical and stylistic devices; in unwritten lan-
> guages, most closely resembles the FORMAL LEVEL of spoken
> language; often not understood by uneducated persons.

---

[47]A common language (CL) translation is a version that restricts itself more or less to
"that part of the total resources of a given language common to the usage of both educated
and uneducated" (Wonderly 1968:3). A popular language (PL) translation is more appropriate to a situation where the language in question is "spoken by people with little special-
ization along social, occupational, and literary lines" (ibid.), that is, in an oral-aural
society; in other words, it aims to reflect "the contemporary language in a form that is
shared by the entire population that speaks it" (ibid.). However, it is becoming increasingly
difficult to find such relatively uncomplicated sociolinguistic settings in today's world; thus
it may be helpful to qualify a PL translation as one that is oriented towards the *younger* generation (ages fifteen to twenty-five) with a style of language that tends to be the *spoken*
style, "regular-casual," whereas a CL version would be more mainstream in terms of a regu-
larized *written* style. (This is a modification of Wonderly's 1968 definition on pp. 14, 28–29,
41–46.) In short, a PL version is one that uses the full linguistic and literary resources of a
language, with the exception of youthful slang on the one end of the continuum and the archaic speech of court elders on the other. The central characteristic of both a CL and a PL
version is "dynamic equivalence," which is the receptor-oriented approach to Bible translation supported by the influential early manuals of Nida and Taber (1969) and Beekman and
Callow (1974). (See sec. 8.2 for further details on the features of CL and PL versions.)

[48]A *literary* version is not necessarily the same as a *liturgical* version, although the two
types are sometimes confused. A liturgical Bible is often quite traditional and literal in nature, hence not literary at all according to natural TL verbal norms. However, it may be regarded as literary as a result of long usage and official promotion by the user churches.

Such a definition appears to be rather narrow, in effect limiting literary language to the purely aesthetic function of communication and apparently linking understanding to educational level (see also de Waard and Nida 1986:50).[49] My particular emphasis on the importance of stylistic and rhetorical features in the analysis and translation of the Scriptures is not really a new development in the history of modern translation theory and practice. Indeed, the seeds for such a perspective were planted already in *The Theory and Practice of Translation* (Nida and Taber 1969). For example, it presents a "functional approach to style" as part of a consideration of the process of "restructuring" in a given receptor language (ibid.:145–150). This consists of a listing and description of sets of formal (grammatical) as well as lexical features that are designed to achieve either "efficiency" in verbal communication or certain "special effects." The latter category is of particular relevance to the topic of this chapter. It includes those stylistic devices that are "effective for enhancing interest, creating impact, and embellishing the message" (ibid.:146). The results, however, are somewhat disappointing since the viewpoint is rather too linguistically oriented and limited to forms that are non-usual in nature, as the following listing of features (paraphrased from Nida and Taber 1969:148, 150) illustrates: *grammatical*: lack of discourse markers, transition markers, non-parallel constructions, failure to mark participants, formal confusion; *lexical*: little-known words, infrequent words, unusual combinations of words, dated words. Nevertheless, an important beginning was made here and an initial foundation laid for the future. This perception was developed further in subsequent studies that took greater cognizance of both the presence and the influence of varieties of discourse types and the diversity of literary-rhetorical devices also on the macrolevel of textual organization.

Considerations of rhetoric, including issues of a literary-stylistic nature, play a much more significant role in de Waard and Nida's *From One Language To Another* (1986), where two central chapters (chaps. 5–6) are devoted to the subject. Here *rhetorical meaning* is very broadly defined as that which "is signaled by patterns of selection and arrangement" on the larger, "less rigidly rule-governed" levels of discourse organization (ibid.:78). Six principal "rhetorical processes" are described and illustrated in chapter 6, namely: repetition, compactness, connectives, rhythm, shifts in expectancies, and the exploitation of similarities and

---

[49] The linguistic and extralinguistic scope or range of my vision is much larger. That is, it includes the efforts to achieve genre-for-genre translational equivalence, where possible, and for an audience that is not restricted to the literate, well-educated strata of a particular society.

contrasts. These prominent literary forms are viewed as accomplishing "the rhetorical functions of wholeness, aesthetic appeal, impact, appropriateness, coherence, progression-cohesion, focus, and emphasis" (ibid.:86).

A wide variety of stylistic devices that would fall under my classification as being literary-rhetorical in terms of form and function are exemplified by de Waard and Nida (1986). In the category of "shifts of expectancy," for example, are included word order variations, anacolutha, play on meanings, paradoxes, irony, and different types of figurative language (ibid.:102–112). Larger discourse patterns of parallelism and chiasm are treated as instances of rhetoric involving the "exploitation of isomorphic features" (ibid.:112–119).[50] Their practical text-focused discussion leads to a classic formulation of the principle of *functional equivalence in Bible translation:*

> In treating rhetorical features it is often useless, and generally unwise, to attempt to match form for form. What one must try to do, therefore, is to match function for function, in other words, to attempt to discover in the receptor language the closest functional equivalent of the rhetorical structure in the source text. The particular set of forms used for different rhetorical functions is largely language specific, but the functions, as already indicated, are universals, and it is for this reason that one can aim at functional equivalence. (ibid.:119)

While de Waard and Nida (1986) present many helpful instances suggesting how this may be done in relation to specific passages of Scripture, the bigger picture is for the most part missing. Translators are not given much guidance as to how the complete texts of different literary genres may be meaningfully analyzed as wholes, either in terms of the SL text or their own language.[51] One of the aims of the present book is to offer several such sets of discourse-oriented investigative guidelines and heuristic procedures. Certain other studies that are helpful in giving similar direction and advice are also referred to along the way so that translators may try out these different L-R

---

[50]This discourse feature is termed "iconicity" when there is a "matching of form and meaning, so that the form reflects the meaning or the experience that is being described" (Chesterman and Wagner 2002:10).

[51]In a more recent short comparative study aimed at evaluating the relative amount of "creativity in [Bible] translating," E. A. Nida makes the following observations: "(1) the number and length of sentences or clauses is not as important as the manner in which they relate to one another, (2) ...what counts [in a translation] is the lexical effectiveness in impact and attractiveness, (3) monotony of sentence structure can be tiring, (4) unusual word order can highlight important features, (5) ...a translator should not hesitate to improve the stylistic awkwardness of the original" (2000:165)—*if* that is actually how the text would sound also in the TL if rendered more or less literally.

approaches and hopefully develop a field methodology which will work out effectively for them (see, for starters, de Regt, de Waard, and Fokkelman 1996; also Wendland 2002a).

2.4.2 Secular theorists

In this section I will survey[52] a variety of recent approaches that have been proposed, primarily by secular theorists, on the subject of literary (more specifically, literary-rhetorical) translation. My aim here is to determine how these diverse viewpoints might serve to inform and enrich the theory and practice of Bible translation. This is admittedly just a representative sample, but I do mention a number of recognized leaders in the field. I will comment only on what a particular specialist contributes specifically to our understanding of a literary rendition (however defined), not everything he or she has written on the broad subject of translation. Despite the limitations of space, I have tried, through direct quotations, to allow these theorists to speak largely for themselves concerning the different methods that they propose. Included here are the names of several scholars who have more recently become involved in Bible translating, for example, Alter and Nord. They work independently, however, not as members of some corporate translation agency. Furthermore, they come from a university or professional background of literary analysis and criticism that is not limited to Scripture and can, therefore, provide a helpfully different perspective on the task at hand.[53]

2.4.2.1 Literalist approach

The practitioner of a literalist approach makes a serious attempt to reflect the recognized literary style of the original text in the language of

---

[52]Mine is only a very selective survey of what is becoming a vast field of study (see also Wilt 2002a, chap. 2). For a more thorough examination and critique of the various approaches treated in this section, readers should consult works such as Baker 1998, Fawcett 1997, Munday 2001, Naude and van der Merwe 2002, and Shuttleworth and Cowie 1997.

[53]I am almost ashamed to admit that before 2001 I knew very little about most of the different translation theorists mentioned in this section (and many others in the secular field as well). My entire first draft was written with minimal reference to their critical and exploratory thinking. The present chapter, this section in particular, is an attempt to indicate how fruitful a mutual exchange of ideas can be in an effort to refine a contemporary approach to the theory and practice of Bible translation, including also its teaching to mother-tongue translators around the world.

translation—that is, "in English dress but with a Hebraic voice" (Fox 1995:ix).[54] The word *voice* in this quotation is important because it emphasizes the spoken word, both in its assumed original setting of communication and also in the corresponding contemporary context. As Fox (1995:ix–x) notes:

> This translation is guided by the principle that the Hebrew Bible, like much of the literature of antiquity, was meant to be read aloud, and that consequently it must be translated with careful attention to rhythm and sound. The translation therefore tries to mimic the particular rhetoric of the Hebrew whenever possible, preserving such devices as repetition, allusion, alliteration, and wordplay. It is intended to echo the Hebrew, and to lead the reader back to the sound structure and form of the original.

Thus Fox, "translating with an ear to the sound and [discourse] structure" of the original text (1995:xiii), tends to be very Hebrew oriented, which frequently results in a noticeably foreignized rendering in English. In effect, his is more a "translated literature" than a "literary translation" (Lefevre 1981:55).[55] He engages the biblical text primarily on the level of its distinctive language—the biblical form—and is not so much concerned about content:

> Rather than carrying across ("translating") the content of the text from one linguistic realm to another, I have tried to involve the reader [actually the listener!] in the experience of giving it back ("rendering"), of returning to the source and recreating some of its richness. (Fox 1995:xxv)

In order to effect an emphasis upon the oral-aurality of the original, Fox (1995) gives attention to three major translation techniques: setting the

---

[54]I take Everett Fox as the primary illustration of a literalist approach. (For a comparison with a capable colleague in this sort of SL-centered endeavor, see Alter 1996.) Another literalist practitioner is Peter Levy, whose translation of the Psalms, according to Hargreaves (1993:33–34, 86), "has tried to catch the spirit and idiom of the Hebrew Psalter....[F]or Levy the important idiomatic patterns of Hebrew poetry to be reflected in any translation are not only those to do with parallelism and with the skillful echoing and balancing of one clause by another, but particularly to do with rhythm and balance....[H]e implies that an English translation has to aim to achieve some terseness or economy....By far the commonest criticism leveled at the modern translations...comes from those who say that they miss the beauty and rhythm of language that the AV possesses." These same phonological qualities, along with the skillful selection and combination of words, would seem to be the minimum to aim for in any literary translation of the Psalms.

[55]The translation that results from such a literalistic practice may also be described as a "neoliteral" or "interliminal" text, which is "an attempt at colonizing the space in between two cultures" and languages, resulting in "an invented language where Hebrew structures in [English] show [English] as a transformation of Hebrew" (Klaus Reichert, cited in Gaddis-Rose 1997:88).

text out lineally in cola (basic utterance units), in lines that resemble free verse;[56] transliterating and explaining Hebrew names within the translation itself; and a strict reproduction of key thematic words, no matter how awkward this may sound in English. He also highlights a trio of minor devices that serve to accent "the Bible's spokenness," namely, wordplay, allusion, and repetition that is more restricted in scope to certain passages (xviii–xix). In this manner he seeks "to preserve not only the message of the text but also its open-endedness" (xx).

While the goal of message-preservation is undoubtedly out of reach by virtue of his literal methodology, in the latter effort he has surely succeeded. Thus a certain "open-endedness" of ambiguity is created due to the unnaturalness of the English that results from this formalistic approach. Furthermore, there is very little "literariness" that may be seen in the TL text, which has been foreignized at times to the point of unintelligibility for all but those who are already familiar with the Hebrew original. This is best demonstrated by an actual example from Fox's translation, Gen. 32:21–22 (reproduced below in its published format, but without verse numbers):

> You shall say: Also—here, your servant Yaakov is behind us.
> For he said to himself:
> I will wipe (the anger from) his face
> with the gift that goes ahead of my face;
> afterward, when I see his face,
> perhaps he will lift up my face!
> The gift crossed over ahead of his face,
> but he spent the night on that night in the camp.

Commenting on this particular rendering, Fox (1995:xi) asks, "What does the reader gain by hearing the literalness of the Hebrew? And what is lost by the use of its idiomatic meaning? As mirrored in [my] translation [i.e., in contrast to the NEB], it is clear that our text is signaling something of significance."

I would ask in reply, What is of greater importance to the present-day hearer/reader during this extremely overt (and awkward) signaling process—the form or the meaning of the SL text? And what is really conveyed

---

[56]While this may have been Fox's intention, in keeping with his personal "hearing of the text" (guided by the Masoretic accents, Aliviero Niccacci says in an online review of the Shocken Bible published at the SBL website, 11/1/01), it was not fully realized in actual publication, where the competing concern of presenting the text in a larger, more legible type size produces some unfortunate overlaps. We see this, for example, at Genesis 17:5c:

> ...for I will make you Av Hamon Goyyim / Father of a Throng of
> Nations!

For a discussion of this important issue of printed line formating, see Wendland and Louw 1993:78–82.

by it? To my mind, the marked repetition of *face* in English in fact distorts the intention of the original by focusing the audience's attention upon that particular lexical item at the expense of the message at large. Due to all this reiteration the hearer is indeed led to expect something "significant" to come out of it in terms of message content. But this expectation is frustrated, simply because *face* is not really that important to the dramatic account at this juncture, not in comparison with everything else that is taking place on the narrative stage. Thus the final clause beginning with *but* sounds rather anticlimactic after the many uses of *face* preceding it, the latter apparently but not actually building up to something big. In fact, I find the penultimate utterance almost unintelligible within this sequence ("The gift crossed over…"), as is the rather strange linkage of "idiomatic meaning" with Hebrew "literalness" in Fox's own comment on this passage.

A greater recognition of the importance—and *potential* literariness—of explicit recursion in the biblical text is indeed very necessary, and the prominence that it generates must surely be accommodated within an L-R approach to translation. However, there are certain limits that must also be respected, including some definite boundaries that need to be set with regard to the truly relevant formal possibilities in keeping with the artistic standards and rhetorical conventions of the TL. If the author-intended content *and* intent of the original are paramount, then these aspects of his message will have to be afforded a greater measure of consideration during the overall process of literary communication, and this includes the various features of meaningful sound that Fox and others call our attention to.[57]

2.4.2.2 Functionalist approach

It is interesting to observe that a fully functional approach to translation was being promoted and applied in the field for some years before the appearance of de Waard and Nida's 1986 popularization of this method for Bible translators (see also Wendland 1987a). This was a prominent aspect of the *Skopostheorie* school of translation pioneered by K. Reiss and H. Vermeer in the early 1980s and further developed more recently in the writings of C. Nord (1997 being one example).

---

[57]To this point, Landers (2001:53) adds: "A literal rendering of any world-class writer invariably makes that individual sound tongue-tied, as if he or she were speaking a foreign language, and poorly at that…[thus distorting] the TL reader's perception of the author. Why bother with a masterpiece from another language if it reads like a trot?" In 1680 John Dryden, the great English writer, made the following critical comment on this sort of a translation: "'Tis much like dancing on ropes with fettered legs…and when we have said the best of it, 'tis but a foolish task" (cited in Shuttleworth and Cowie 1997:104).

Functionalist writers naturally stress the purpose (normally referred to only in the singular) that a particular translation is designed to perform for its primary target audience within a given sociocultural setting. There appears to be a notable difference in focus, however, between this perspective and that of functional equivalence (FE) in the practice of Bible translation. For FE, the translators' goal is to "seek to employ a functionally equivalent set of forms which in so far as possible will match the meaning [i.e., functions] of the original source-language text" (de Waard and Nida 1986:36). Thus in Bible translation it is the communication functions (plural!) of the *SL* text which are preeminent and determinative, whereas in *Skopostheorie* the particular goal of the text within the *TL* setting will largely determine the manner and style of translating in accordance with the governing framework for the translation project as a whole. As we have seen (sec. 1.8), Nord terms this the translation *Brief*, which is a programmatic document that explicitly sets forth all the relevant details as to how, when, why, and for whom a specific translation project is being undertaken.

The two perspectives just referred to are not mutually exclusive, however. They may be harmonized, when so stipulated by the translation *Brief*, by means of a coordinated effort to convey the main functional priorities and implications of the biblical text through the appropriate formal means in the TL. That is easier said than done, of course, and a great many details relating to further principles and procedures need to be specified in a systematic manner within the scope of this broad framework of purpose.

Nord presents one of the clearest discussions to be found in recent literature on the subject of a literary translation (1997, chap. 5). She defines the notion of literariness in texts as follows (ibid.:82):

> Whether literariness is seen as a particular choice of subject matter, as use of a literary code, or as a relationship with language conventions (originality vs. conventionality), there is little doubt that a literary text can produce a particular aesthetic or poetic effect on its readers....[L]iterariness is first and foremost a pragmatic quality assigned to a particular text in the communicative situation by its users. Intratextual features are not marked 'literary' as such...but they do function as signals indicating the sender's literary intention to the readers. Receivers then interpret these features as literary in connection with their own culture-specific expectations, which are activated by certain extra-textual signals.

I would add that another important marker of "literariness" is the use of marked linguistic features in conjunction with each other, that is, in particular *combinations* and distinctive textual arrangements.

In contrast to the attempt to achieve a complete equivalence with re-spect to interpretation (the original sender's communicative intention), text function, understanding, and effect in the target culture, Nord offers four "suggestions for a purpose-oriented approach to literary translation":

> The translator interprets the source text not only with regard to the sender's intention but also with regard to its compatibility with the target situation.
> The target text should be composed in such a way that it fulfills functions in the target situation that are compatible with the sender's intention.
> The text world of the translation should be selected according to the intended target-text function.
> The code elements should be selected in such a way that the target text-effect corresponds to the intended target text functions. (1997:92–93)

These functions may be fulfilled by either a literal or a more idiomatic translation (a "documentary" or an "instrumental" version in Nord's terms) depending on the particular circumstances of communication at hand. As noted, the principal intentions of the original author are not ig-nored in this operation; however, in view of the impossibility of satisfying them all, they are evaluated for relevance in the light of the TL setting and then prioritized for application in the translation itself.[58] The crucial re-quirement in preparing a literary version is that the producers "justify their decisions in order to make others (translators, readers, publishers) understand what was done and why" (1997:91). Presumably, an explana-tory statement of this nature could be adapted from the project *Skopos* and made part of an introduction to the translation or published as a sepa-rate document.[59] Nord also tackles the troublesome issue of authorial intention (the so-called intentional fallacy) that often arises in criticism of a functional-ist approach with regard to interpretation as well as translation. She re-fers to this as "loyalty" (a nice alternative to the usual "fidelity"), which "means that the target-text purpose should be *compatible with* the original author's intentions" (1997:125, my emphasis). This is a more defensible position than the nondemonstrable criterion of being the "same as" what

---

[58]In most Bible translations, "the reader's presumed 'interest in an exotic world'...[might be] best satisfied by leaving the text world as it is and explaining strange details either in the text or in footnotes, glossaries and so on" (Nord 1997:93).

[59]Writing from the perspective of the secular literary translation profession, Wechsler calls attention to this same need for explanation on the part of translators: "What is rare is giving the reader background material and a context from which to better appreciate the translation, or discussing alternative ways the translation might have been done" (1998:283).

the original author intended. But how can even this less rigorous objective be accomplished when we have no direct access either to the author or his times? In fact, there are quite a *selection* of discourse features that can be used as "evidence" in such a quest, for example, the broad "conventional intentions linked with certain text types"; an analysis of *extra*textual factors pertaining to the original communicative setting that may be derived from *inter*textual and sociohistorical studies; and above all (in my opinion) "a thorough analysis of *intra*textual function markers...to find out about the communicative intentions that may have guided the author" (1997:125–126). Included in this last group would be detailed systematic and integrated studies that explore the structural arrangement (*tectonics*) and rhetorical argumentation (*forensics*) of the source language document.

On the other hand, a specification of the primary functions of the SL text is only part of the translator's task. Another challenge is to determine *which* of these communicative intentions are to be conveyed in the TL and *how* this is to be done, that is, by means of which stylistic devices and rhetorical strategies among those available in the TL according to the literary conventions that would apply to the genre and setting concerned.[60] We now recognize the impossibility of a goal that seeks to convey the *full* semantic and pragmatic value of the original text via any translation. A *choice* must always be made between those aspects of the message that the translators will at least attempt to convey and those they concede will probably be lost during the transmission process. Issues such as these will have to be thoroughly discussed and then spelled out within the project *Brief* and its central *Skopos* statement. It was interesting to observe that the translation principles and procedures developed by Nord and others within a functionalist framework correspond quite well with my own ideas as presented in this work, especially those having to do with a literary rendition of the Scriptures.[61]

---

[60]Nord also notes the translational implications of this last-mentioned variable (1997:88): "As a rule, literary codes include not only stylistic features such as rhythm, prosody, syntax, macrostructure, metaphors and symbols but also characters, ideas, expressiveness and atmosphere....[T]he relative familiarity of the text world plays an important role in achieving text effect....In literary texts...the author decides which elements of the literary code should go into the text. Further, since stylistic devices are culture-bound they are not the same for the source and target cultures, although there may well be a common ground in classical rhetorical devices [an important area for pre-translation research and evaluation]. Even so, traditional stylistic features often acquire new connotations and meanings when transferred to another literary environment." Indeed, the more distinct the two language-cultures are linguistically and culturally, the greater is the potential for novelty and/or mismatch in these crucial respects.

[61]In recent years Christiane Nord and her husband, Klaus Berger, have been engaged in a project to prepare a new translation of the New Testament in German. Their well-defined

2.4.2.3 Descriptive approach

A school of thought called "descriptive translation studies" (DTS) was developed in the early 1970s more or less in opposition to what its originators viewed as the prevailing "prescriptive" approach to translation. They rejected "the idea that the study of translation should be geared primarily to formulating rules, norms or guidelines for the practice or evaluation of translation or to developing didactic instruments for translator training" (Hermans 1999:7). DTS theorists attempt to be "diagnostic rather than hortatory" in their treatment with respect to two major objectives, namely, "to describe the relevant phenomena [that are manifested during the translation of texts], and establish general principles to explain and predict their occurrence" (ibid.:29). They are "product" rather than "process" oriented in their perspective (Gaddis-Rose 1997:9). Accordingly, the focus is upon pure research, which has a threefold emphasis—the description, explanation, and prediction of all sorts of translation-related phenomena, including the actual activity itself (i.e., how translators think and work). A major goal is to describe how translations operate in the wider context of society and more narrowly within a certain literary system.

Hermans (1999:32) offers a handy programmatic summary of the DTS approach:

> What they [DTS theorists] have in common is, briefly, a view of literature as a complex and dynamic system; a conviction that there should be a continual interplay between theoretical models and practical case studies; an approach to literary translation which is descriptive, target-oriented, functional and systemic; and an interest in the norms and constraints that govern the production and reception of translations, in the relation between translation and other types of text processing, and in the place and role of translations

---

translation *Skopos* focuses upon two principal aims: (1) "[T]o present a strange culture in a way that allows readers from a culture distant in time and space to understand and respect its otherness," (a *referential* function); and (2) "to show where these texts—in spite of their strangeness and ancientness—have something to say to people living in a modern culture" (an *appellative*, or affective, function). Nord refers to their goal as "otherness understood" since "it strives to make explicit what was left implicit in the [biblical] text because it was supposed to be part of the world and culture knowledge of the original addressees, without leveling the strangeness of the other culture, and at the same time to bridge the culture gap in order to allow modern readers to find analogies with their own world (where this is possible)" (from the abstract of an unpublished conference paper presented at the Similarity and Translation Conference, May 31–June 1, 2001, Bible House, New York City). Experienced Bible translators and consultants will be able to appreciate the magnitude, and perhaps also the impossibility, of this objective.

both within a given literature and in the interaction between literatures.

While this is important and certainly needs to be included as part of a comprehensive methodology of literary translating, we can observe that, due to their fear of being prescriptive, DTS theorists tend to produce studies that are not as helpful as they might be to Bible translators, except with regard to the essential follow-up research and testing needed once a translation has finally been published and distributed. But less capable translators who do not know the biblical languages require more guidance than DTS studies offer in the "how to" of carrying out their work efficiently and effectively. We might also add that in actual practice many "descriptions" that the DTS group produces turn out to be just as prescriptive as others since the various translation strategies that they draw attention to become in effect models of preferred performance or implicit goals to be achieved.[62]

One representative statement of a DTS approach to literary translation is found in the writings of Gideon Toury (e.g., 1995). Toury notes the fundamental ambiguity that the term *literary translation* presents: Does it refer to the translation of a text that is "regarded as literary in the *source culture*" or a TL product that is "acceptable as literary to the *recipient culture*" (1995:168)? In the case of the former, the translated product may not be regarded as literary in the TL; in the case of the latter, any SL text, literary or not, is transformed into a literary piece in the TL. My concept of an L-R translation combines both of these perspectives: a literary SL text (Scripture) is rendered in a distinctively artistic and rhetorical manner in the TL.

Toury appears to adopt a context-based, or "social," method (see sec. 2.5.1) in his definition of both literature and a literary translation:

> [L]iterature is first and foremost a cultural institution. Thus, in every culture (including different phases in the evolution of one culture), certain features, models, techniques (including modes of translation!), and—by extension—texts utilizing them, are *regarded as*, rather than *are* literary, in any 'essentialistic' sense. (ibid.:170)

This "essentialistic" sense undoubtedly refers to any sort of text-based (or stylistic) definition and assessment of what is more or less literary in stylistic terms. In other words, literature is what society says it is; and any text, no matter how clumsy or substandard in technique, may be declared

---

[62]This is evident, for example, in the list of strategies provided by Naude (2000:18–19) in his summary of the descriptive approach: transference, indigenization/domestication, cultural substitute, generalization, specification (explication), mutation (deletion, addition), transposition, and a combination of any two or more of these. These techniques are of course standard fare in all of the basic Bible translation handbooks and manuals.

to be literary if enough people say so. However, I would not like to generalize the notion of literariness solely in terms of such extrinsic (as distinct from intrinsic, text-based) factors, or seek to identify art merely on the basis of a popular vote, formal or otherwise. There would seem to be more to its essential origin, nature, and purpose than that.

Toury goes on to describe a literary translation in the following terms:

> [I]t involves the imposition of 'conformity conditions' beyond the linguistic and/or general-textual ones, namely, to models and norms which are deemed literary at the target end. It thus yields more or less well-formed texts from the point of view of the *literary* requirements of the recipient culture, at various possible costs in terms of the reconstruction of features of the source text. (1995:171)

It is not at all clear to me, however, how one can so easily divorce the "*literary* requirements" of a given language from "the linguistic and/or general-textual ones" (e.g., individual stylistic techniques or typical genre forms). Surely the latter are indispensable ingredients in any evaluation, even one carried out intuitively by a nonspecialist, concerning what constitutes literature (or indeed, orature) in the culture concerned. I would therefore suggest that the models and norms referred to above are not merely *deemed* literary by society—they *are* literary in the sense that they are constituted and hence characterized by sets of specific, popularly recognized linguistic and textual features, namely, those that happen to be associated with one particular (sub)genre or another. If this were not the case, then how could the following translational activity occur?

> Subjugation to target literary models and norms may thus involve the *suppression* of some of the source-text's features, on occasion even those which marked it as 'literary', or as a proper representative of a specific literary model in the first place [e.g., the acrostic pattern of certain Hebrew poetry]....It may also entail the *reshuffling* of certain features, not to mention the *addition* of new ones in an attempt to enhance the acceptability of the translation as a target literary text, or even as a target literary text of a particular type....[T]he added features may occupy central positions within the translation (when looked upon as a text in its own right), even serving as **markers of its own literariness**, despite their having no basis in the original. (ibid.)

This is, in fact, a very good description of what may well take place during the preparation of a full literary translation. The "suppression," "reshuffling," or "addition" referred to is not, however, an arbitrary, ad hoc exercise. Rather, it is carried out more strictly, for example, by means of a functional, speech-act approach (see sec. 6.2.4). The aim is to attain communicative equivalence in both general terms and also in specific respects to the extent that time and expertise will allow. Several examples of a poetic rendition of Scripture in the Chichewa language are given in appendixes A and B. These illustrate the truth of Toury's observation that "the potential gap between what translation of literary texts [SL text focus] and literary translation proper [TL text focus] gains in significance [is] in direct proportion to the distance between the source and target traditions" (ibid.:175). Such traditions, whether similar or different, are firmly founded upon genre-related linguistic and literary features in both SL and TL.

Over the years, DTS literature, including more recent translator "protocol" and "corpus-based" approaches, has performed a valuable service by calling attention to the importance of explicit as well as implicit social conventions and norms in translation practice (e.g., Hermans 1999, chap. 6; see also Nord 1997:53–59).[63] For example, product norms embody "the expectations of readers of a translation (of a given type) concerning what a translation (of this type) should be like" (Chesterman 1997:64). Process norms, on the other hand, "operate to regulate the actual work of translation in terms of accountability to the original author's intentions, a sufficient degree of intertextual similarity, and overall communication effectiveness" (ibid.:67–70; see also Hermans 1999:78). Such popularly recognized ideals and standards serve to guide translators in their work as they interact with their own culture and community, not only with respect to contemporary relevance (i.e., communicative efficiency and effectiveness), but also in terms of excellence and acceptability. The latter concerns would be especially important, of course, where a literary translation is being undertaken or evaluated.

2.4.2.4 Textlinguistic approach

The textlinguistic approach is represented by Hatim and Mason, whose theoretical studies (1990, 1997) provide many examples of how this methodology can assist translators in their text-transformation efforts. At a number of points their discussion is of particular relevance to those who are seeking to prepare some type of literary version. For example, they call attention to the difficulties that translators face when dealing with texts that are stylistically more dynamic, or "turbulent," in nature, as is characteristic of the literary texts my study focuses on. Such dynamic oral

---

[63]Kenny (2001) makes a detailed application of a corpus-based approach to "lexis and creativity in translation." Unfortunately, this book came to my attention when I was in the final stages of preparing my overview here. Therefore, I can only call attention to it as a potentially rewarding study. Kenny also provides a good summary of the DTS perspective (ibid.:49–50).

or written discourse consists of a higher incidence of novel or unexpected and unpredictable, "rhetorically marked," forms and "the use of language that essentially involves a motivated deviation from some norm" (1997:216).

The notion of "markedness" in literature can be defined from two inter-related perspectives: frequency and focus. The less *frequent* a phonological, lexical, syntactic, or textual form is, the more significance it has to the message; infrequent forms are less predictable or normal, hence more "in-formative" in their co-text of occurrence (see Hatim and Mason 1997:12). Such expressions may also manifest a more restricted or concentrated dis-tribution within a given text, thereby often creating special discourse pat-terns or arrangements of elements. From a more literary perspective, Jakobson says, "[m]arkedness entails the fact that in two choices, one is the more focused, the more narrowly constrained, the more concentrated than the other" (cited by Pomorska and Rudy, eds. 1985:160), as is so of-ten the case in the second (B) line of Hebrew poetic parallelism.

Such verbal creativity (a more favorable designation than "deviation"), whether effected by intention or intuition, is of course the essence of artis-tic as well as argumentative (or "evaluative") composition.[64] The two compositional functions of artistry and argumentation are often rhetori-cally combined in serious ideological literature (ibid.:181–183), which is what the Scriptures by and large embody. This sort of interactive dis-course contrasts with that which is mainly "expository," the latter being characterized by a more impersonal style that is less marked and more stable, usual, or expected in terms of the language that is used. The Bible includes texts that may be either more, or less, evaluative or expository in nature.

Hatim and Mason (1990:187) offer a rule of thumb that summarizes the translational implications of this relative linguistic-literary polarity:

> The less evaluative [i.e., stylistically/rhetorically marked] the text is, the less need there will be for its structure to be modified in translation. Conversely, the more evaluative the text is, the more scope there may be for modification.

In their later work on applying a textlinguistic methodology, they say (Hatim and Mason 1997),

---

[64]Hatim and Mason's (1997, chap. 6) discussion of literary discourse is rather disappoint-ing in that they limit their consideration to a study of specific register-related features such as tenor (level of formality), idiolect, and macrogenre. Similarly, no literary text is included in their grid display of "varying degrees of markedness" (ibid.:182–183), where only expo-sition, argumentation, and instruction are discussed. In their earlier book (1990), even less mention is made of the register of artistic literature.

> ...while an approach which tends towards the "literal" is likely to be appropriate and indeed sufficient for straightforward expository forms of texts (such as news reports [or simple narrative]), greater latitude may be needed in handling argumentation [or dramatic narrative] effectively. (pp. 181–182)
> ...where the text displays considerable degrees of dynamism, the translator is faced with more interesting challenges and literal translation may no longer be an option. (pp. 30–31)

I would express it even more strongly: When preparing a correspondingly dynamic (rhetorical) and/or attractive (artistic) rendition of a literary text, a strictly literal approach *cannot* be an option.[65] The compositional procedure must be suitably loosened up, at least phonologically, in order to allow gifted translators the freedom to more fully access and creatively utilize the stylistic and expressive resources of the TL.[66] As to the unavoidable all-pervasive factor of *culture* and its influence on a translation, there is an important principle that must be remembered: "The less culture-bound a text is, the less need there will be for its structure to be modified. Conversely, the more culture-bound a text is, the more scope there may be for modification" (Hatim and Mason 1990:188). What more culture-bound discourse could there be than the various genres and subtypes that we find in the ancient Hebrew and Greek Scriptures? Obviously, a considerable amount of formally innovative, but

---

[65]A more literal approach to translation may cause difficulties even in the case of narrative or expository discourse. The problems that can arise are not merely stylistic, but are often ideational as well. Thus a literal rendering of the biblical text into a Bantu language typically results in a version that is not only difficult to understand, but all too often is *mis*understood; that is, a different meaning (e.g., *Yehova* = the God of the white European colonialists) or zero meaning may be conveyed. Moreover, a more literal, foreignizing version cannot always prevent a transformative accommodation to the TL culture since virtually any formally correspondent expression within the text can unpredictably evoke within receptors an ethnocentric, uncomplimentary stereotypes of the SL culture (on this possibility, see Katan 1999:156).

[66] For a discussion of hearing the "translator's voice" in a translation, see Hermans 1996. This subject is gaining importance in secular translation studies. Charlotte Bosseaux (2001:73) points this out: "[I]t is possible to identify the 'other voice' of translation and the style of an individual literary translation and that in addition to the translators' strategies it is even possible to identify the kind of world that each translation has decided to recreate." (In the case of Bible translation, we might say "kind of theology" in place of "kind of world.") Wechsler adds: "The translator's ability to read and write at a professional level [in the TL] is what reviewers should be looking for" (1998:270). Proponents of a literalist method would like to diminish if not completely eliminate the translator's (or translation team's) voice in the TL text; but while this may be an admirable ethical objective, it cannot succeed in practice. To ordinary hearers/readers of a literal version, the translator's voice is still very much audible. The problem for them is that this translator—or the prophets and apostles being translated—simply do not speak the TL properly; the text lisps and has a strange, at times unintelligible, foreign accent.

semantically controlled modification may need to be introduced in order to duplicate in another linguistic and ethnic setting the artistic beauty, the depth of connotative feeling, and/or the rhetorical impact of these texts. At the same time, of course, translators must seek to accurately represent the essential theological content of the original author while preserving the measure of verbal decorum that may be needed in keeping with the primary setting of use in the TL setting.

In an early application of a textlinguistic approach to the translation of poetry, Robert de Beaugrande identifies and illustrates a number of "critical factors" that come into play during the analysis of the SL text and its subsequent transformation in a target language. He includes a number of helpful observations on the complicated nature of this twofold process:

> [A]ll great poetry is in some manner innovative, whether it derives from a native or a foreign source. But at the same time, innovation is only possible in some areas, not all at once. We conclude that a text is translatable [i.e., acceptably so] into a given language only if the resulting translated text fulfills at least some of the reader expectations in that language concerning the constitution and transmission of discourse [hence the crucial need for an explicit project *Brief* and *Skopos*]. The non-fulfillment of this stipulation can depend on the text itself, the foreign culture, or both. (1978:28; the material in brackets is my interpolation)

> [N]on-ordinariness and non-expectedness are significant stylistic qualities in poetic texts (and in many others). The degree of these two aspects which is manifested in a given alternative therefore serves as a standard for making appropriate choices and hence for reflecting the style of the work. The very nature and function of [the] poetic use of language demand that the translator seek non-ordinary and non-expected alternatives....The dense structuration typical of poetic texts [certainly in typical Hebrew parallelistic construction] leads me to believe that at least some equivalences and oppositions are recorded unconsciously and hence produce profound effects without the reader's [or hearer's] knowing just why. (ibid.:92)

> A translator, however skilled, cannot focus upon all such [problematic] aspects of translating at one time and produce a first version that fully represents the original text. If one focuses on only one or a few aspects each time, little progress can be made without a subsuming framework of priorities and procedures....In all cases where the total meaning of a passage was observed to be non-equivalent [i.e., from the specific perspective of a poetic use of language in the SL text, such as polyvalence or polyfunctionality, dense structuration, an expansion of ordinary grammar and lexicon, or the

non-fulfillment of reader expectations, whether of an inter- or intratextual nature], large numbers of additions, deletions, substitutions, and permutations were performed [i.e., in an effort to correct or compensate for these inequivalences in the TL text]....If we view translating as a progression, we can readily see that a poetic text characterized by [a] poetic use of language—language [densely structured and] inherently capable of multiple [or a manifold inter-related] interpretation—cannot be assigned a single "correct" translation....due to the language-specific nature of many such options and expansions of options, the perceptive [or communicative] potential of a poetic [or indeed a highly rhetorical paraenetic] text cannot be exhaustively rendered into another language. It follows that a commentary should accompany the text in order to account for losses and shifts [in terms of form and content] which cannot be averted. (ibid.:135–136)

If we had read and taken seriously advice such as this some twenty-five years ago, the study Bible movement in minority languages around the world might have been motivated much sooner than it was. Even now, however, as the preceding comment suggests, there is the need for at least some explanatory annotation also with regard to artistic and rhetorical matters in any translation. This is because the form of the text inevitably affects—in fact, constitutes—a significant aspect of meaning with respect to the original document as well as its representation in another language and culture.[67]

2.4.2.5 Relevance approach

The insights of Relevance Theory (see, for example, the work of Gutt 1991, 1992) are important to Bible translation, as has been pointed out[68]

---

[67]De Beaugrande also comments on the dilemma that faces translators when dealing with a literary text: "[F]orm-based procedures [in translation] have a certain appeal...[but] [t]he resulting text is usually not a very acceptable sample of the goal language....[These procedures] were generally applied to texts which enjoyed an especially prestigious status, such as religious and poetic texts. Translators hesitated to diverge from the most obvious features of the [SL] text, that is, the forms, in fear of being disrespectful. Content-based equivalence is much more difficult to measure and more accessible to intersubjective dispute. The more the unit of translation is enlarged from the word toward the entire context of communication, the greater are the possibilities for two translators to disagree about the 'best' rendering of a text. In addition, the widening of the unit demands much more complex and informed work habits than those used in word-for-word translating" (1978:96–97). Can there be any doubt that a literary type of translation, no matter what its scope and particular focus, demands the very best TL verbal artists available?

[68]Some significant theoretical criticism of this psycholinguistic approach is found in chapter 1 of Levinson 2000 and chapter 5 of Werth 2000.

by quite a few contemporary commentators and critics. Its foundation may be summarized as follows:

> The central claim of relevance theory is that human communication crucially creates an expectation of *optimal relevance,* that is, an expectation on the part of the hearer that his attempt at interpretation will yield *adequate contextual effects at minimal processing cost.* (Gutt 1991:20)

This principle, which is common sense, really, offers a good general heuristic with regard to effective verbal communication. Normally, serious speakers try to convey what they have to say in a way that is easiest for their hearers to understand (requiring low processing effort), yet also with a certain amount of communicative impact and appeal (resulting in high cognitive/emotive/volitional effects). Whether this is always true or not is debatable. In any case, this interactive strategy applies also to communication via translation, whether on the general level of policy (e.g., formulating a project *Skopos*) or more specifically with regard to actual translation principles and procedures (e.g., how to handle a particular metaphor in a given passage). In such instances, however, in order to make the necessary decisions and evaluations concerning communicative effectiveness, one also needs to adopt a *functional* perspective, as described in section 2.4.2.2. In other words, one needs to determine which communicative functions operate in a given case to make the transmission process most relevant for the audience (e.g., more informative versus more affective discourse).

Here we will consider how Relevance Theory would deal with the translation of literature and literary effects, based on the recent study of Pilkington. It will be helpful to begin then with a definition of literariness from this perspective:

> [L]iterariness should be defined in terms of cognitive events triggered in minds/brains by linguistic stimuli. It can be characterized in terms of a distinctive kind of mental process involving extensive guided exploration of encyclopaedic entries, which results in the marginally increased salience of a wide range of assumptions (and possibly original *ad hoc* concepts)...*together with* the evocation of intense subtly discriminated and precise qualitative states. (Pilkington 2000:189, 191)

This definition may be a precise and accurate description of what literature *is* or *does* in cognitive terms; however, it leaves us with the crucial problem of demonstration and assessment. How can we objectively determine or measure what goes on in an individual's brain in response to a given text, let alone the collective perception that leads to a certain work's meeting with a positive popular estimation and another with an adverse reaction? While it is reasonable to assume that excellent literary form stimulates a positive response (but only to a "marginally increased" degree), the question is, How does this knowledge help us to explain, evaluate, and/or apply the notion of literariness (or "poetics") any better than more overt structuralist, semiotic, and sociolinguistic methods?

Furthermore, why should we be interested at all in what goes on in the brain as it is processing a particular literary device, a metaphor, for example? Here is one possible explanation: If the nature of the conceptual and emotive effect that is stimulated by a certain literary feature can be satisfactorily specified, in more or less general terms, then translators would be encouraged to make an attempt at least to reproduce that same aesthetic experience and/or rhetorical impact via their rendering in the TL. On this issue Pilkington is quite helpful (using the case of metaphor by way of illustration):

> In the case of creative metaphors...the new concept is not derived from a subset of the properties of an existing concept, but it is constructed on the basis of an interaction between assumptions derived from two or more encyclopedic entries...the connection between which is neither well-established nor easy to achieve....A greater amount of processing effort is required: but the rewards in terms of contextual effects are correspondingly higher....The considerable processing effort involved in the search for relevant contextual assumptions is offset by the subsequently large range of implicatures weakly communicated....It is the range and indeterminacy of the implicatures which give the metaphor its poetic force....Contextual assumptions made accessible [in the text] prior to the metaphorical utterance itself help direct the search for relevant contextual assumptions from the encyclopedic entries of the concepts brought together in the metaphorical phrase or utterance. In this way, a good poem, by activating a wide network of contextual assumptions prior to the metaphorical utterance itself, may give greater direction to the interpretation of metaphors, enabling them to be read in a richer, more creative way than would be otherwise possible. The success of a poetic metaphor depends not only (if at all) on its originality, but in the creation of a [textual] context which encourages and guides the exploration of the encyclopedic entries of the concepts involved [ideally, as these are directly or indirectly related to the major theme or subthemes of the work as a whole]. (ibid.:100–103)

The problem here of course is that just as in the case of the semantic fields and associations of individual lexical items or figures of speech, so also these "contextual assumptions" and their conventional "networks" do not correspond between languages. This means that a translator has to create or evoke them either within the TL text itself (e.g., by means of some qualifying word or phrase) or, if that would be too difficult or semantically expansive, then by means of an appropriate footnote or some other supplementary device such as an illustration, a sectional heading, or some pointed cross-references.

A good example of the potential benefits of a Relevance Theory approach to biblical interpretation, and Bible translation in particular, is Stephen Pattemore's application of this interpretive framework to a study of the literary technique of *intertextuality* as manifested in the Book of Revelation.[69] He calls attention to the deliberate artistic use of intertextuality in the rhetorical figure known as *metalepsis*, whereby some definite "literary echo links the text in which it occurs to an earlier text,... [and] the explicit point of contact between [these] two texts can thus be a nexus for an implicit [but no less significant] flow of meaning between [them]" (2002:45–46). Defining intertextuality as a sort of communicative "relevance found within textually defined cognitive environments" (individual or communal conceptual perspectives), Pattemore then makes the following twofold distinction:

> An OT (or other source) text is *contextually evoked* if the audience needs to access the original context of the text, and add it to their cognitive environment, in order to optimise the relevance [as defined above] of the author's statement in their contemporary context. An OT (or other source text) is *used conventionally* if the audience can optimise relevance within the mutual cognitive environment of author and audience, without access to the original context of the embedded text. (ibid.)

An Old Testament text that is either "quoted" (more or less exactly), directly "alluded to," or merely "echoed" in a given New Testament passage (i.e., three degrees of perspicuity in intertextuality) will of course evoke its original context. It is therefore up to the current audience, whether those intended by the initial communicative event or all subsequent readers and hearers, to determine "optimal [hermeneutical] relevance" with respect to the two texts and contexts concerned by applying the cost versus gain principle of relevance to the situation. In other words, Which

---

[69] Pattemore, as well as the editor of *The Bible Translator Technical Papers*, in which his study will appear, have kindly given me permission to include the citations of the present section from a pre-publication version of this most helpful literary-translational study. The use of *intertextuality* in the New Testament is not of course merely a literary device; it is an essential exegetical, apologetic, expository tool in the overall rhetorical strategy of virtually all of the authors of the New Testament. This approach should find fuller treatment in Pattemore 2003, a copy of which I have not yet been able to obtain.

interpretation provides the greatest number of salient contextual effects (life- and theology-related meanings) for a minimum of processing effort? Pattemore applies this inferential methodology to several illustrative passages in Revelation on both the micro- and also the macrostructure of discourse, and comes to this important translation-related conclusion:

> Part of the task of translation must therefore be to pass on not merely lexical and semantic information, but also such information as will best help the audience to establish a mutual cognitive environment with the author....For a new audience to come anywhere near the understanding of the original audience, they must be able to optimise relevance by accessing the same prior scriptures.... First, the prior texts must be available to them....[S]econd, new audiences will probably not have the same "cognitive geography" as the original audience and will need to be given maps and sign-posts [such as explanatory footnotes and selected key cross-references] to direct them to the prior texts which are required to optimise relevance. (ibid.)

But this hermeneutical development needs to be taken a step further. Pilkington, in his 2000 study of poetic effects, has shown that prior Relevance Theory accounts of literary features and effects have been too restrictive, limiting their consideration to "what is communicated propositionally" (p. 141). What is one to do then with other key aspects of literary criticism, namely, those that deal with such affective notions as emphasis, emotion, and feeling? Pilkington views emotions "as complex states possessing cognitive, physiological, behavioral and qualitative properties" (p. 143). The cognitive properties of emotions may be analyzed "in terms of particular types of sets of beliefs and desires" (p. 143), while the other three categories may be studied as various "phenomenal" states which pertain to the human senses (p. 154). An overview of such an approach, which would apply also to the process of translating, is as follows:

> Affective states are communicated by setting up the belief/desire sets that correspond to the cognitive properties for a particular emotion. These states are heightened in the communication of poetic effects by contextual exploration which makes more of the appropriate conditions available and makes them more highly salient....[A]ttitudes as phenomenal state memories are triggered or evoked by rhetorical figures and verse features....It is the communication (or evocation/arousal) of such phenomenal [i.e., sensory] states that is central to poetic effects. Poetic effects are not relevant insofar as they communicate new information, but insofar as they communicate phenomenal aspects of experience....The point of poetic effects, and literariness more generally...is to broaden context, and make both thoughts and feelings richer, more complex and

more precise with regard to actual situations or states of affairs.
(ibid.:160–161)

The extent to which translators are able to take such phenomena into
consideration during their work depends on their level of expertise and
experience, the type of translation, the intended audience, and the relative size of the text portion concerned. The important thing to keep in
mind is that meaning involves more than propositional content. Diverse
feelings, emotions, attitudes, values, and other connotations are also present, more so in literary, especially poetic, discourse. Such communicative
significance must therefore be factored into the equation—either by
means of an explicit procedure or through an intuitive exercise of verbal
creativity aimed at attaining message equivalence—if justice is to be done
to the author's original intentions.

2.4.2.6 Interpretive approach

In a concise comparative overview of an interpretive approach to translation, John Delisle provides a helpful summary of "the characteristics of
literary texts" (1988:14–17):

- The expressive (emotive) function of language is predominant.
- Correspondingly, connotation—the power to evoke—plays a major role in the text.
- Literary form is important in and of itself; it manifests aesthetic
  qualities that enrich its referential content.
- Accordingly, the text is not limited to a single interpretation.
- Its message features a certain timelessness that needs to find periodic re-expression through translation in order to preserve its content and give new life to its form.
- The work reflects universal values and gives contemporary expression to ancient themes.

Serious Bible translators must, before they begin their work, consider to
what extent the Holy Scriptures manifest literary qualities such as the
above (or others), and what, if anything, can be done about this when
translating.

The interpretive method is not often mentioned in recent overviews
and anthologies that pertain to the field of translating. Indeed, Jan Sterk
(2001:3, fn. 4) asks, "Has this school and its insightful approach to

translation been overlooked by the English-speaking linguistic translation community?"[70] In essence, the approach may be summarized as follows:

> The interpretative theory...holds that the process [of translation] consists in understanding the original text by deverbalising its linguistic form, and in re-expressing in another language the ideas that were understood and the feelings that were felt....Crucial in the ESIT approach, therefore, is the finding that at a certain point in the understanding process [i.e., prior to translating], contact with the physical wording of the source text is abandoned and ideas take over. In text-to-text translation, the ideas (or the intent of the author...) that were abstracted from the words of the source text through the deverbalisation process, are re-expressed through the words of the target language. (ibid.:3–4)

It is interesting to observe how close this conception of translation is to Nida and Taber's:[71]

> The second system of translation [i.e., a deep-structure as opposed to a surface-structure method] consists of a more elaborate procedure comprising three stages: (1) analysis, in which the surface structure (i.e., the message as given in language A) is analyzed in terms of (a) the grammatical relationships and (b) the meanings of the words and combinations of words, (2) transfer, in which the analyzed material is transferred in the mind of the translator from language A to language B, and (3) restructuring, in which the transferred [conceptual] material is restructured in order to make the final message fully acceptable in the receptor language. (Nida and Taber 1969:33)

Much more is involved, of course, in analyzing an SL text and restructuring it in a given TL (e.g., with regard to many different discourse-based, genre-related, and rhetorically motivated features), and various translational strategies can be devised to account for these operations. However, it is the essential medial "transfer" stage that remains the focus of all the cognitively based methodologies. The question then is, What is to guide and control the elusive mental process of transfer, especially where the aim is to produce a literary rendition of a recognized literary SL text?

While the approach I propose, namely a combined relevance-functional approach (see sec. 2.7), is somewhat different from the interpretive method, it similarly recognizes the importance of this fact: The degree of

---

[70]The interpretive, or interpretative, method was first developed in conjunction with the teaching of live (simultaneous, oral-aural) translation. Later it was extended to written translation by the Ecole Superieure d'Interpretes et de Traducteurs (ESIT, Paris, France).

[71]Compare also Di Jin's fourfold "artistic integrity approach": penetration, acquisition, transition, and presentation (2003, chap. 3).

success in translation ultimately depends on the quality of the mind in which the conceptual transfer takes place. In other words, all other things being equal (SL/TL skills, practical experience, additional training), it comes down to this: the *literary* translator, like any artist, is born, not made. A translator must be born with the gift of interlingual communication; it cannot subsequently be created in an individual—only discovered, encouraged, and promoted where actually present.

Sterk, himself a practitioner of the interpretive approach to translation, points out the derived nature of this creative communicative competence:

> [T]he deverbalised ideas we filter out from a text, even an ancient one, will, under normal circumstances, not be our own. An objective, honest analysis of the source text, inspired by determined research and guided by common sense, will lead us onto the discovery of what the first author tried to impart through his/her words. If hard work is often needed, intuition will play its role too....The task of a re-expressor will not be a diluted one where everything is allowed, but it will need to be seen as the challenge of performing a creative act, fully comparable to the original one in its creative effort, but highly constrained in content. The ideas that should inspire the re-expressor should indeed not be his/her own, but those of the author. The re-expressor's goal is that of being relevant and meaningful to his/her audience...by re-creating the original process faithfully and respectfully, while keeping his/her own audience in view. (2001:7, 14)

Thus the production of a literary functionally equivalent version of any passage of Scripture requires translators who can empathetically immerse themselves in the text and sociocultural context of the biblical world, then allow the essence of the message to cross over to a contemporary setting and finally to emerge by an intuitively creative act of compositional transfer in the form of a linguistic representation that is a valid, relevant equivalent of the original text.[72] As Delisle (1988:110) says, "The most distinctive trait of human translation is its *creativity*, for translation involves choices that are not determined by pre-set rules." In short, Bible translation involves the *skill* of textual interpretation, based on a thorough knowledge of both the SL and also the TL literary and cognitive environments, coupled with the *art* of

---

[72]This is essentially what Walter Bodine, in an article in *Notes on Translation* (2000:43), says as he calls for "research that explores the Bible in pursuit of meanings that have been lost because of the vast distance in time and culture between ourselves and the peoples of the biblical world....Such research calls for prolonged and profound immersion in the biblical text in its original languages and in its historical context." Any artist-translator who hopes to produce an acceptable *literary*-equivalence version must have first had such a total text-context immersion experience.

re-expression that derives from a generous innate ability to communicate effectively.[73]

As to the process of translation, it is not just matching similar words ("transcoding"). According to Delisle, "translation is communicating an equivalent message" (Delisle 1988:55). He identifies "three stages in the development of…translation equivalence: comprehension, reformulation, and verification" (ibid.:53). This is a technique that is constantly interactive between the SL and the TL text. He goes on to define the three stages as follows (ibid.:53):

- Comprehension is based on decoding linguistic [and literary] signs and grasping meaning.
- Reformulation is a matter of reasoning by analogy and rewording concepts.
- Verification involves back-[translation] and choosing [the most appropriate solution in the TL].

Of special relevance for a literary approach is the notion of "analogy," which is a key aspect of the reformulation process, which in turn is based upon an accurate interpretation of the SL text. A thorough analysis of the original text, one that is both culturally contextualized and discourse-based, "sets off a chain of analogical reasoning in the translator's mind," according to Delisle, who goes on to describe this creative process in the following terms (ibid.:60–66):

> [I]n reformulating ideas, the translator continually shuttles between the de-verbalized meaning seeking expression and the linguistic forms through which it could be verbalized (*in the TL*)….[T]he translator reasons by analogy, probing the expressive [and rhetorical] resources of the target language through a series of associations and deductions, or inferences….Analogical reasoning is a process by which the imagination establishes similarities [in the search for translation equivalents]….Aspiring translators should therefore possess imagination and a sensitivity to parallels and connections between concepts in order to transfer the concepts contained in a text to another text….[They] explore, by analogy, the resources of the target language in search of linguistic signs capable of rendering those ideas….Sometimes an equivalent is discovered quite spontaneously. Inspiration strikes, and concepts are instantly matched….[T]he richer the translator's palette, the more colorful will be his rendition of the original. In other cases, however, reformulation is a more laborious process. Sometimes the mind has to be

---

[73]In a new book on the subject of literary translation, Prof. Di Jin refers to this process as "empathetic re-creation" (2003, chap. 5).

coaxed into producing an acceptable equivalent: analogies have to be "induced" and trains of thought more consciously followed.

Delisle's description resonates with my own experience of what actually goes on in the translator's mind during innovative, meaning-centered interlingual text transfer.[74] Can this method be taught? To a certain extent, yes, that is by learning to recognize and operate "the principles of language manipulation" as they may be applied both during an analysis of the original text and also during its re-expression in another language. Delisle calls attention to "four different levels of language manipulation" (ibid.:83, my own interpolations in brackets):

1. observing conventions of form [including those that pertain to literary genre];
2. performing interpretive analysis:
   a) transfer of monosemous terms [i.e., those having only a single sense];
   b) retrieval of standard equivalents from the [TL] linguistic system;
   c) re-creation in context;[75]
3. interpreting [and rendering] style;[76]
4. preserving textual organicity [i.e., cohesion and coherence].[77]

---

[74]"Paradoxically, it is a model of *unilingual* communication that best explains the translation process, because translation is in fact a particular form of interpersonal communication. In using language to communicate, one associates words with ideas, which are precisely what the translator does in translating" (Delisle 1988:78). In other words, it is by the process of analogical and associative reasoning, which is basically metaphoric and metonymic in nature (see Jakobson 1971; see also the Relevance Theory approach of "direct and indirect quotation across languages" of Gutt 1992:64–67).

[75]"To recreate a concept in context, the translator must attribute values to two unknowns: first he must establish the meaning of the expression in its original context, then he must explore the possibilities of the target language in order to construct an expression that semantically and stylistically balances the first one" (Delisle 1988:93–94).

[76]Delisle notes that "[a] measure of intuition and subjectivity inevitably enters into this type of stylistic adaptation....Translators do not all have the same linguistic sensibility, and opinions often differ as to the best way of conveying the spirit of a message. Their perceptions of the communicative aspect of a text vary" (1988:98). The best stylist is a verbal artist in the TL who can also analyze the SL text sufficiently to determine its essential content and thus more fully taste the particular flavor of its literary style and rhetorical power.

[77]Delisle (1988) suggests the following methods of helping to preserve textual "organicity" in a translation: redistributing the elements of information, concentration (i.e., condensing the textual form), implicitation or explicitation, and the use of transitions to link utterances (summarized from pp. 104–106). Obviously, other linguistic techniques could be added to this short list, such as the use of repetition/synonymy, demonstratives/deictics, and formal typographical devices such as text formatting, including section headings/titles, and a topical reference/index system. (For a more detailed listing of such optional and obligatory "textual strategies," see Chesterman and Wagner 2002:60–63.)

To be sure, many such strategies of translational practice can be precisely formulated, taught, and put into practice. In the end, however, it all comes down to a matter of skill—of being a master of comprehension and communication in two different languages and cultures. The more literary the original text and/or the translation being undertaken, the more necessary such mastery becomes in order to achieve success.

2.4.2.7 Comparative approach

The comparative approach to literary translation is less systematic in theoretical terms and correspondingly more ad hoc in its practical application than the other approaches that have been described. It differs from the DTS method (see sec. 2.4.2.3) in that along with being comparative (using the standard techniques of literary criticism) it tends to be more *evaluative* in nature. Also it devotes considerable attention to intercultural issues (similarities and differences) as reflected in the creative activity of translating.[78]

According to Gaddis-Rose (1997:88, 90), the general aim of a comparative approach is a "stereoscopic reading" that utilizes "both the original language text and one (or more) translations," whether literal or free in style, so as to assess the latter from an "interliminal" perspective. This refers to the initial adoption of an ideologically neutral point of view that hypothetically exists between two different languages and cultures. Thus, "[i]f we do not juxtapose a work and the translations it elicits, we risk missing many a [hermeneutical as well as affective] gift inside the [respective textual] borders" (ibid.:7). The desired goal of this relational process from the secular viewpoint of comparative literature is "to show how translating and translations make the reading of literary texts richer" (ibid.:75), that is, more complex, problematic, challenging, and thought provoking.[79]

---

[78]I attempt to apply the critical method in a more proactive and productive sense during the actual practice of translation as a method of helping compensate for translators' inability to access the original text of Scripture in carrying out their work (Wendland 2000b). For a detailed description of a functionalist approach to the comparative criticism of various translations, including those of Scripture, see Reiss 2000.

[79]Thus "reading literature with a translation will always ensure our collaboration with the author, and it will always add more to our experience of the work. A critical reading of literature entails a theoretical—analytical—approach to translation" (Gaddis-Rose 1997:73). The same experience will presumably also be gained if the literature in question happens to be found in the Bible. Further, "[t]he enhancement of literary experience by translation comes not only from what the author genially wrote and what the translator felicitously found but also from other words or ways they—or we—might have used instead" (ibid.:1–2). Indeed, this could be a provocative, yet also profitable way of conducting a group-oriented, interactive Bible study. Gaddis-Rose describes a literary translation quite

In biblical studies, on the other hand, this critical effort is usually channeled towards the pragmatic end of judging one translation of the Scriptures to be more or less correct or appropriate than another in terms of fidelity, accuracy, clarity, naturalness, and relevance. There are many books on the market that attempt to carry out such an evaluation. Most of them are written from a conservative theological position and view with considerable concern any contemporary translation that renders the text in a more idiomatic style.[80] Very few of them delve into the diverse literary aspects of Bible translation.

Of the few critical-comparative studies of Bible translation that do consider the artistic, rhetorical features of literary translation, one of the best in my opinion is that of Hargreaves. His 1993 book focuses on "a translator's freedom" and is filled with many insightful comments that highlight both the excellent literary characteristics of the biblical text and also the corresponding qualities of various English versions, ancient and modern, that have tried to duplicate these features. The value of his perceptive study can be demonstrated by citing a selection of his more salient observations concerning the artistic-aesthetic quality of the translations he compares. But first we should read what he says on the fundamental issue of the literariness of the Scripture. He is unequivocal:

> The Bible is literature, that kind of writing which attends to beauty, power and memorability as well as to exposition. It is like a rich chord compared to a single note....The Bible requires profound attention to style when it is translated....[W]hen the original is beautiful, its beauty must shine through the translation; when it is stylistically ordinary, this must be apparent. (ibid.:137–138)

Any translator who agrees with that assessment is immediately faced with a dilemma: What am I going to do about it in my own work? The fact is that in most cases relatively little time and attention is devoted to this aspect of the original text during the normal translation process—whether in preparing a formal correspondence or a functional equivalence translation.

---

broadly as one that involves "a transfer of distinctive features of a literary work into a language other than that of the work's first composition," pointing out (more helpfully) that "literary translation is also a form of literary criticism ...[which] helps us get inside literature" (ibid.:13). How many Bible translators would conceive of their task in that light?

[80]Often this concern is so great that it harshly criticizes any nonliteral version and assesses "accuracy [solely] in terms of formal equivalence" (Martin 1989:68). Even the moderately literal NIV fails the test and is thus deemed "not worthy of becoming the standard version of the English-speaking world" (ibid.:70). A much more thorough, balanced, and helpful recent evaluation of past and present English translations of the Bible is that of Wegner 1999. For a perceptive treatment of the subject of faithfulness in translation from the viewpoint of a secular editor and critic, see the chapter entitled "The Romance of Infidelity" in Wechsler (1998:65–104; also Di Jin 2003, chap. 2).

Hargreaves continues:

> "'[F]unctional beauty'...means that there must be an element of re-
> alism [i.e., according to the principal communicative functions
> expressed by the SL text] in the beauty of language fashioned for
> use in translation....Religion and beauty, religion and poetry, be-
> long together." (ibid.:147, 152)

In order to carry out his method of assessment in the most effective
way, Hargreaves, like Fox (see sec. 2.4.2.1), stresses the importance of the
oral-aural medium:

> Has there been much imaginative poetic freedom in style? And, in
> the combination of dignity and clarity that most of the modern ver-
> sions have aimed at, has there, in fact, been much dignity?...
> Perhaps I may recommend that the translations be read aloud, to
> test the effectiveness of the translation as spoken as well as written
> word. (ibid.:127)
>
> [The older English translations] eventually were recognized as hav-
> ing great beauty, being a merging not only of a biblical pattern of
> language but also a merging of the translators' lively use of contem-
> porary English idiom and poetic nuance with existing features of
> English literary style. (ibid.:133)

Such a mixed style of verbal expression would seem to be highly appropriate for every language that has an established literary tradition coupled
with a long history of Bible translation. As Hargreaves says, "[I]t is sensitivity to one's own language, not scholarly knowledge of the original, that
makes a translation permanent [due to its excellence]" (ibid.:135). This
has certainly been my experience with many Bible translators.

Hargreaves addresses the reasons why contemporary translations of the
Bible in English often fail to accomplish their objectives, let alone achieve
a high literary standard. With respect to the poetic quality of imagery, for
example, he says:

> It seems to be true, in relation to biblical translation for the modern
> cosmopolitan English-speaking world, that the more traditionalist
> translators stick too often to the precise and literal old, while more
> innovative translators, in moving on to something new, too often
> tend to discard any related imagery [i.e., the closest, natural figura-
> tive possibilities in the TL], and fall too easily into a generalized
> and paraphrased mode of expression....The difficulty here is to get
> English phrases that are both resonant and more than merely deco-
> rative, and also that capture the breadth of meaning [of the original
> text]....[This challenge] requires a poet to condense metaphor and
> meaning into a more dramatic compass. (ibid.:162–164)

> [T]he task of translating some biblical imagery in a way that takes
> the retention of metaphor and the communication of meaning seri-
> ously is a task still to be completed. (ibid.:173)

How can translators—in any language now—overcome this problem, if
their goal is to produce a rendition that will be recognized, by scholars
and ordinary readers alike, as being more, rather than less, literary in
terms of form, function, and effect? It certainly will not be easy, nor is it
the safe way to translate:

> [T]he translator's work involve[s] the taking of risks....It goes with-
> out saying that dangers cannot be avoided in any risk taking or
> imaginative moving along frontiers. The innovators' risk-taking, in
> the interests of clarity and directness of speech, can all too easily
> lead them into the sort of arrogant brashness of language that
> treads clumsily across intricate and sensitive areas of meaning. The
> traditionalists' type of risk-taking, in the interest of spiritual and po-
> etic resonance [an unusual combination of aims!], can too easily
> lead them into the sort of literary snobbishness that ignores the re-
> quirements of wide communication. (ibid.:191)

Thus both the literalist and the "colloquialist" must take care, and indeed can learn from each other, when they put their diverse principles
into practice during this "risky" endeavor:

> By and large, the aim in much modern translation has undoubtedly
> been to achieve living and lively equivalents of the original, rather
> than to achieve, through exaggerated colloquialisms, a superficial
> sense of modernity. And since idiom, and that which is idiomatic, is
> a main creator of vitality in language (it has been described as the
> sap of language), it is good idiom that one surely looks for in any
> translation and not primarily good colloquialism: the colloquial
> may be part of the idiomatic, and may overlap with it, but it is idi-
> omatic vitality that is entirely central. (ibid.:38)

This means that there must be "an emphasis on freedom from all that is
merely pedestrian and pedantic, and an emphasis positively on the use of
poetic imagination in the use of language" (ibid.:103).

How can this be accomplished? One helpful guideline is this: Capitalize
on the inevitable constraints to achieve a greater measure of creativity.[81]
It has always been recognized that translators, like original writers, must
operate under a number of limiting conditions or "frames of reference":[82]
sociocultural, political, literary (e.g., persistent traditions), linguistic

---

[81]This is the theme of the insightful introductory essay to the 1999 volume edited by
Boase-Beier and Holman.

[82]On the notion of "frames of reference" in Bible translation theory and practice, see Wilt
2002b.

(e.g., lexical inventory), media-related (audio, visual), and philosophical (e.g., Western versus Eastern modes of thought).[83] What is not often realized, however, is that some of these constraints actually open the door for certain creative impulses to be realized—for example, in terms of the various possibilities that a certain poetic genre makes available for use, whether adopted as is or in some creatively modified form.[84] Some genres by their very nature stimulate creativity, for example, the condensed linguistic style or ambiguous expression of many poetic forms, which "invites readers to fill gaps with their own knowledge" (Boase-Beier and Holman, eds. 1999:6). At times it may be the very fact of working in a box that spurs literary artists on. As they work "within the system," they can still manipulate the text at hand stylistically, enabling their audience to experience what lies beyond the givens. This has not been the normal procedure for Bible translators; they tend to limit their attention to either the bare form or the simple content of the original text; but I would like to raise this issue for discussion and trial, where possible, in order to open up some new possibilities of indigenous expression—and understanding—for the Word.[85]

---

[83]Scripture translators must also labor under the significant constraint of an authoritative, often revered religious text that serves as the touchstone against which their work will always be critically compared and evaluated. Sometimes this is accompanied by a superimposed "tradition" of Bible translation that further constrains the window of possibility as far as any formal (let alone semantic!) innovation goes. For this reason, the translators of Scripture cannot accept the position that "[t]here will always be compromise between faithfulness and freedom, between the need to be true to one's own and the author's voice" (Boase-Beier and Holman, eds. 1999:10), or that they may "presume to alter the content of the original in order to avoid causing offense to potential readers" (ibid.:16). It is not just any "author's voice" that Bible translators must reckon with; it is the voice of the One whom they revere as their God. The only "compromise" allowable, then, is the one forced upon them by the gap forged by an original text from a different time and place, language and culture.

[84]Boase-Beier and Holman also point out that a more literal, foreignized translation can produce a certain "creative stretching" of the target language *and* culture by introducing people to novel literary forms and significant new ideas. Since that has been more or less the norm in Bible translation, we would like to encourage such a "stretching" also at the other end of the communication continuum—that is, in terms of the full stylistic inventory and rhetorical resources of the TL, resulting in a text characterized by formal "glory" as well as semantic "clarity."

[85]"Clarity and glory [of style] have always belonged together, and do so today. It is becoming ever clearer that where there is true clarity, glory is never far away, and vice versa. The task of holding them together in biblical translation is an ongoing and unfinished task" (Hargreaves 1993:195). An exciting challenge is posed here for all those individuals and teams that would undertake a more or less literary (clear and glorious) translation of the Scriptures in their mother tongue.

2.4.2.8 Professional approach

Since I originally wrote this chapter, another important, and a rather distinct perspective on literary translation has come to my attention, namely, that of some hands-on practitioners, those who translate, edit, and critique translations of secular literature as their profession. It is helpful to read what they have to say on the subject since they are both author- and audience-centered in their approach; after all, they must produce "faithful" translations that *sell*, or are at least received well by critics. As one of them has said, "The goal of literary translation is publication" (Landers 2001:ix).

How does this strongly goal-oriented viewpoint and purpose affect their translation practice in terms of principles and procedures? I have selected as more or less representative a number of pertinent observations and exhortations from Clifford Landers, a professional translator. With a minimum of intervention on my part I will present his ideas here, along with several comments in the footnotes below by a literary critic and editor.[86] What they have to say is most insightful and has great relevance to any team that intends to produce a more or less literary rendition of the Scriptures, either as a whole or only as selected portions of the sacred text.

Clifford Landers is a professor of political science and a widely published translator of novels and shorter pieces of fiction from Brazilian Portuguese into American English. In a recent guide to the everyday work of a literary translator, Landers suggests the following steps for producing an acceptable rendering of a given selection of prose. His preferred principles of translation are implicit in this sequential listing of practical guidelines (2001:45–46, my emphasis added):

> (1) Read the entire work at least twice. For those who might contend that this is not actually a step in the translation process, *I argue that no translation can succeed without a thorough grounding in the SL text.* An unaware translation is *ipso facto* a bad translation; and 'unaware' means failing to have a firm grasp on the meaning of the work, both at the surface level (words, phrases, idioms, culture) and at the underlying level of deeper significance (...Subtext).
>
> (2) Determine the *authorial voice.* This will affect virtually every choice in the thousands of words to be translated. Note any shifts of tone from one part of the text to another.[87]

[86]"[A] translator has to be able to read as well as a critic and write as well as a writer" (Wechsler 1998:9).

[87]The importance of the original author is emphasized by most literary translators and critics. Wechsler feels that in order "[t]o determine an author's thought processes, where they go beyond the conventions of his language, a translator must also determine the author's intent....Suzanne Levine has written, 'An awareness of a book's intended effect on its

(3) Do the first draft, marking troublesome areas in square brackets and/or bold face for further attention. At this stage there is relatively less emphasis on smoothness and fluency and more on capturing the semantic gist of the text.

(4) *Consult* with an educated native speaker to clarify points that are still vague. For especially vexing items, consult the author.[88]

(5) *Revise* the manuscript, with emphasis on phraseology, fluency, and naturalness. At this stage *it should come as close as possible to reading as if it had been written originally in English.*

(6) Have a highly literate native speaker of English, *preferably one with no knowledge of the SL,* go over the manuscript and indicate any rough spots—i.e., parts that are awkward, stilted, 'translationese,' or that make no sense. Make any necessary changes.

(7) Go over the manuscript line by line with a native speaker of the SL who is also fluent in English. *Read it aloud while the other person follows in the SL text.* This catches mistranslations as well as inadvertent omissions...and *it focuses your attention on questions of sonority.* Unwitting homonyms, undesirable connotations, puerile constructions ('I see the sea'), unintentional repetitions of a word, and other infelicities are more likely to make their presence felt here than at any other stage in the process....[89]

(8) Make the final changes, run it through a spell check, and let it rest for a few days. Then *give it one last reading* (typos may have been introduced in the revision stage) and send it off.

As far as poetry is concerned, Landers (citing Clement Wood) is of the opinion that "[p]oetry cannot be translated; it can only be recreated in the new language" (2001:97). Furthermore, "[i]t must be recreated by a poet of like emotional power in the other language, if it is to survive as poetry" (ibid.:98). As to what this means in practical, personal terms, he says (ibid.:99):

---

original reader is obviously necessary in order for us to understand the difficulties of repeating that effect. The author's intentions, overdetermined by his or her own context, may or may not be verifiable, or even relevant, but the translator—like all interpreters—has to decide, within a given context, what function he or she is trying to fulfill' " (Wechsler 1998:139).

[88]Neither of these two recommendations (see point 7) is possible of course when the Bible is the original text. However, in place of an "educated native speaker" one could substitute a qualified fellow translator; instead of the author, one could consult recommended commentaries on the text at hand.

[89]"In translation, this ability is known as 'having a good ear.'...[I]t's having good instincts for what sounds or seems appropriate in a certain context...having a wide range of alternatives at one's fingertips...knowing the many ways in which words, sounds, and concepts interact: grammar, rhythm, and logic....Does this sound as right in the same way as the original...?" (Wechsler 1998:129).

> I am convinced that the translator must possess a poetic sensitivity,
> even if he or she had never written a line of original poetry. A po-
> etic sensitivity encompasses, but is not limited to, an appreciation
> for nuance, sonority, metaphor and simile, allusion; the ability to
> read between and above the lines; flexibility; and ultimately,
> humility.[90]

Landers states his guiding principle for literary translation in terms that are familiar to most Bible translators: "all facets of the work, ideally, are reproduced in such a manner as to create in the TL reader the same emotional and psychological effect experienced by the *original* SL reader" (2001:27).[91] He claims that this is "[t]he prevailing view among most, though not all, literary translators" and further that "[m]ost *translators* judge the success of a translation largely on the degree to which it 'doesn't read like a translation.' The object is to render Language A into Language B in a way that leaves as little evidence as possible of the process" (ibid.:49). Such an opinion differs from that of many translation theorists and critics, who "work a different side of the street" (ibid.:49). After all, "who other than scholars would want to read prose [or poetry] that bears the heavy imprint of foreign grammar, idiom, or style?" (ibid.:50).[92] In short, most professional literary translators would claim that one must be an artist in order to perform as an artist when carrying out their work.

But not only is expertise and excellence required. There is, in addition, an intellectual or professional price to pay:

---

[90]On this crucial dimension of "sonority" in poetry, Wechsler adds: "Rhythm and other aspects of sound, such as alliteration, assonance, and rhyme, are central to poetry. Often a translator has to give up exact meaning to preserve a sound component....[A] translator may also pick up vocal tones, intensities, rhythms, and pauses that will reveal how the poet heard a word, a phrase, a line, a passage....[W]hat translating comes down to is listening—listening now to what the poet's voice said, now to one's own voice as it finds what to say" (Wechsler 1998:131, 133). What a difference in technique if translators would approach the Psalms in this same attentively aural manner!

[91]One needs to add here that the translated text in and of itself will probably not be sufficient to provide a given target audience, no matter how educated, with enough of a frame of reference to contextualize and understand such culturally specific texts as those found in the literature of Scripture. This applies to the content of the original and even more so to its connotation ("the same emotional and psychological effect"). The hermeneutical background and perspective of receptors will therefore have to be expanded in certain relevant respects, for example, by means of appropriate descriptive and explanatory footnotes, in order to allow the process of interpretation to continue in a communicatively efficient and effective way.

[92]"[O]verly zealous applications of theoretical guides can wreak havoc with a translation," for example, "the doctrine known as 'resistance,' whose best known advocate is Lawrence Venuti" (Landers 2001:50). "I...have yet to meet a working translator who places theory above experience, flexibility, a sense of style, and an appreciation for nuance" (ibid.:49–50).

> The translator's problem is that he is a performer without a stage, an artist whose performance [ideally] looks just like the original.... Like a musician, a literary translator takes someone else's composition and performs it in his own special way. (Wechsler 1998:7)

Bible translators do not normally go solo like this. They work as part of a team and within the framework of a particular project *Skopos*. But a translator must be a genuine performing artist in order to do full, or even partial, justice to the literature of the Scriptures if an L-R version is the goal. There is much to learn about this subject from the professional practitioners themselves. It is profitable for Bible translators who happen to be engaged in a similar, but at the same time more controlled, endeavor to read about their experiences and take their words of encouragement and advice to heart.[93]

2.4.3 Evaluating the various theories

As a first step in evaluating the diverse translation methodologies of section 2.4.2, we should note the shift in focus that characterizes them. They range from the primarily author-focused ones (e.g., interpretive) to those with a target-audience focus (Relevance Theory, functionalist). Then there are the approaches that concern themselves primarily with the text, whether the SL text (e.g., literalist), the TL text (textlinguistic), or somewhere between or back and forth (e.g., critical-comparative, professional). These different perspectives are accompanied by varying emphases on certain

---

[93]A humorous example of such encouragement (with special relevance for Bible translators) and a good illustration of the literary craft of translation is Landers's own rendering (from Brazilian Portuguese) of the poem by Millôr Fernandes, entitled *La Dernière Translation*:

When an old translator dies
Does his soul, *alma, anima,*
Free now of its wearisome craft
Of rendering
Go straight to heaven, *ao céu,*
al cielo, au ciel, zum Himmel,
Or to the hell—*Hölle*—of the great
traditori?
Or will a translator be considered
In the minute hierarchy of the divine
(himmlisch)
Neither fish, nor water, *ni poisson ni l'eau*
Nem água, nem peixe, nichts, assolutamente
niente?
What of the essential will this
mere intermediary of semantics, broker
of the universal Babel, discover?

Definitive communication, without words?
Once again the first word?
Will he learn, finally!,
Whether HE speaks Hebrew
Or Latin?
Or will he remain infinitely
In the infinite
Until he hears the Voice, *Voz, Voix, Voce,*
Stimme, Vox,
Of the Supreme Majesty
Coming from beyond
Flying like a *birdpássarouccelopájarovogel*
Addressing him in...
And giving at last
The translation of Amen?

communicative functions to the exclusion or neglect of others, for example, a *literalistic* focus (=>*ritual* function) versus an *artistic* focus (=>*poetic* function). While the Bible translation theorist and practitioner can learn something from them all (from some more than others perhaps, depending on the particular project *Skopos* that is being followed), the textlinguistic, functionalist, and interpretive methods appear to offer the most insights and assistance. This will become apparent as I discuss my proposed literary approach further.

2.5 The ambiguity of the term *literary translation*

At this point, we need to recall the rather widespread problem that was referred to earlier, namely, the fundamental ambiguity connected with the term *literary translation*. This term may be understood as having at least four distinct senses: (1) a mechanically literal translation of a recognized literary SL text; (2) a literary rendering in the TL of a nonliterary SL original; (3) a fully literary translation (functionally equivalent) of a literary SL document; and (4) a selective literary rendering of certain marked literary features (structural and stylistic) of an SL text, such as balanced lineation, symmetrical syntactic parallelism, pleasing lexical collocations, condensation, imagery, figuration, rhetorical heightening, and intertextual allusion. I am here using *literary translation* with particular reference to a version of the third or fourth type.

Perhaps it would help if we recognize a distinction between two perspectives in the evaluation of the translational quality or relative compositional excellence of literature: a "social" perspective versus a "stylistic" perspective.[94] In the figure that follows, these two perspectives are roughly schematized in terms of form, content, and function:

---

[94]Some time after completing this study, I discovered that my twofold distinction with regard to "literary translation" had been anticipated many years earlier by E. A. Nida (not in so many words, but clearly enough): "The literary critic...restricts his interests to written texts regarded as belonging to a category of literature, either because these texts have stood the test of time (having attracted widespread and continuing interest) [i.e., a social perspective], or, in contemporary texts, have certain features of form regarded as aesthetically superior [i.e., a stylistic perspective]" (1975:25).

2.5.1 A social (popular) perspective

"Of course it's a work of art. It's in an art gallery," some say.[95] That's one way of defining art. Another is the passage of time. The aging process alone can put a mediocre piece of writing from the past in a much more positive, aesthetic light. Like an aged wine, it becomes tastier with age! Duthie recognized this: "Literary translations of the Bible include most older translations because of the connection between literature and the past in respect of language" (1985:68). Such a favorable characterization, whether unsophisticated or scholarly in origin, is usually based on widespread use, supported perhaps by a particular attraction for a more antiquated and familiar expression, in accordance with the whims of popular opinion. This is largely an emotive evaluation motivated by the *ritual and performative* functions of language, which tend to be activated in or by certain settings of sociocultural, including religious, significance, especially the formal liturgy of public worship.[96]

Nida and Taber point out another aspect of this progressive and cumulative *diachronic* development of a version's acceptance: "In many languages that have been reduced to writing within the last two or three generations there is a kind of 'literary' capstone…which may be regarded by many literate persons in the language as the only appropriate form to write the language" (1969:124). Thus, the designation *literary translation* is often closely associated with the relatively high educational standard of those who are able to read and who actually enjoy reading their own "sophisticated" version—that is, with special reference to its level of

---

[95] Pilkington (2000:3) attributes the quotation here to Damien Hirst (May 1994). This is how some people judge literature too; a certain text qualifies as literature if it happens to be found on the same bookshelf with recognized literary works. But what *does* certify a verbal message as being a literary work of art? I will be exploring answers to this question in the sections that follow. For many people, of course, the matter of whether the Bible is literature is a negative nonissue, since for them literature is by definition a *human* creation and hence could not apply to the Scriptures.

[96] It is possible therefore that an older, literal translation will become popularly regarded as "literary" in a given language and by a particular constituency as a result of a long liturgical use that creates an exotic, but valued compositional style within the tradition. More commonly, however, a *strictly* literal rendering (one that lacks, for example, the minimum of a euphonious manner of expression, attractive lexical collocations, or any phonological and rhythmic shaping) will turn out to be very unnatural according to TL norms (e.g., NASB). This is not to say that such a version will be rejected by its intended audience group, for the relative acceptability of a given translation is determined by a number of interacting sociolinguistic as well as religious influences. In addition, one must also consider the factor of relative *quality*; not every so-called literary version of the Bible is a good example of this translation type. The NEB is a possible case in point—it manifests occasional flashes of stylistic brilliance, yet these do not occur often or consistently enough and with enough duration for the translation as a whole to be rated very highly.

vocabulary and diction.[97] Not only is a certain period of time generally required for such a favorable professional and/or public assessment to grow with regard to a particular written work, but important and sometimes extremely complex sociolinguistic factors may be involved as well (e.g., extensive publicity, celebrity endorsement, political propaganda, large-church sponsorship). There are a number of examples of this type of popularly defined literary translation in Africa. They are the long-serving "missionary" versions.

This, however, is not what I have in mind in the present study. My notion of *literary* is not associated with age and long usage or with a particular "educated" dialect of a given language. Rather, I define it (in sec. 2.5.2) objectively and from a stylistic, technical perspective.

2.5.2 A stylistic (technical) perspective

A technical definition of literature, by which the relative literary quality of a certain written text can be assessed, is usually based upon a synchronic study that involves an analytical description and evaluation of a given work's harmonious integration of form, content, and function within an appropriate contextual setting. Experts in the field examine the text in question, whether an original composition or a translation, according to recognized universal (or in some cases, regional) literary features such as elaborately patterned repetition, rich thematic symbolism, novel figurative language, culturally resonant key terms, subtle phonic artistry, or the skilled use of ideophones and expressive exclamations (features of Bantu orality). They proceed to judge it with reference to these criteria along with traditional or locally favored aesthetic standards, codes of formality, and prevailing social conventions. They attempt to do so objectively, not influenced by the work's acceptance by the population at large. However, it may be expected that a creatively composed literary translation will, sooner or later, come to be regarded as literary in a popular, diachronic sense.

Thiselton refers to the "rich reading" that a genuinely literary text encourages due to its "multilayered coding": it is thus "open" or "productive" in terms of form and meaning and therefore either conveys or evokes varied "resonances, intertextual allusions, new perspectives, [and] transformed horizons" (1999:169–171). To a great extent such a stylistically marked text or semantically enriched translation is promoted by an emphasis upon what Roman Jakobson termed the "poetic function" of language, which activates

---

[97] In this respect we call attention again to the NEB "whose vocabulary includes 'purgation, ague, effulgence, miscreant, descry, bedizened, contumely, ministrant' " (Duthie 1985:68).

additional metaphorical and other associative relationships to augment the conceptual density of the discourse. According to Jakobson, this is effected by "[t]he verbal material [which] displays overall a hierarchical structure of *symmetries*, based on repetitions, regularities, and systematizations of various kinds" (cited in Pomorska and Rudy 1985:150). The result is a more intricate linguistic network or layering (i.e., than that normally found in "prosaic" texts) of formal parallels and verbal correspondences—contrasts as well as similarities—involving sound, sense, syntax, and text structure.[98] Such poetic structuration and stylistic embellishment are not gratuitous or self-serving, however. In literature of great cultural (including religious) significance, the artistry—including the requisite use of various rhetorical devices along with figurative and other image provoking language—is always utilized to enhance the intended message. Normally this would be manifested in some manner of thematic and emotive foregrounding or in the cohesive integration of various topical elements of the discourse at large.

Assuming then that we are beginning with an acknowledged instance of literature in the SL, it may be analyzed with special attention to either its form or its function. In the case of *form*, a stylistic study is undertaken, investigating the compositional organization and aesthetic features of the text on the macro- and/or microstructure of the discourse as a whole, usually in relation to its intended (source) or perceived (target) meaning. In the case of *function*, a rhetorical analysis is undertaken, focusing upon the argumentational dynamics and affective dimension of the discourse—that is, how the author shaped the text in order to move or persuade the intended audience to adopt a certain conclusion, opinion, perspective, conviction, or motivation (purpose) in relation to the message, whether as a whole or concerning selected portions. Both types of literary study are required to lay the proper foundation for a rendering of the same overall communicative effect in terms of both quality and quantity. This process must be repeated with respect to literature in the TL—first in general to determine the genre-based inventory and artistic resources that are available to choose from, and then with specific translational application to the text at hand.

2.6 Defining *literary translation*

I propose a systematic *global* technique to go along with the usual ad hoc *selective* artistic procedure applied in a literary rendering of biblical texts. The ultimate and ideal goal, where circumstances allow, is to effect a *genre-for-genre*, holistic transmission of the Scriptures, in terms of the Bible as a whole or of individual books and pericopes. This contextually

---

[98] On the continuing influence of Jakobson's structuralist-poetic approach to literary analysis, see Green's detailed study of the Beatitudes (2001:21).

conditioned methodology follows from the different approaches presented in section 2.4, combining elements of most of them.

As we might expect, to produce a literary translation requires a highly skilled, artistic, experienced, and biblically educated translation team. They must first apply all their knowledge and skill to a careful and thorough analysis of the SL text. They then endeavor to represent the original text in the TL, whether selectively or as a whole. In other words, they work either on a complete utterance-for-utterance or paragraph-for-paragraph basis, being always guided by the style of the TL genre that is the nearest functional equivalent to that of the SL text. The act of translation is automatically followed by a process of comparative text examination and evaluation (see sec. 2.4.2.7), as proposed by the "critical school" of translation studies. Such examination is with reference to the exegetical and literary features of the text, and the current draft is refined accordingly.

In order to achieve the objective, some type of "transformation-and-transfer" process is obviously necessary: The message originally conceived by a biblical author must be conceptually transported, as it were, across the formidable boundaries of time, space, language, thought, and culture, then verbally reconstituted and re-presented within a very different situational setting. The challenge is to carry out this cognitive activity in the most reliable (accurate) and relevant (efficient + effective) way possible.

2.7 Translation as a complex "mediated" act of communication

Meaningful translation, as opposed to *mechanical* translation, is a very specialized, complex, and manifold type of verbal communication. It involves an interpersonal sharing of the same text (an integrated arrangement of significant signs) between two different systems of language, thought, and culture. In other words, translation requires the *re-signification* and *re-conceptualization* of a text in one linguistic and sociocultural setting so that it is meaningful in another one.[99] This multilingual, intersemiotic, cross-cultural process of textual representation and cognitive reference may be variously defined and described, depending on a number of important factors such as the underlying theoretical

---

[99] A translation of the Scriptures imposes a greater constraint and responsibility upon translators to preserve the meaning (however defined) of the original text due to its perceived divinely generated, hence determinative and authoritative, nature for a particular religious community as well as for individual users. The religious nature or constitution of the biblical text thus greatly affects the expectations that a given target audience has about its translation into their language, including the level of verbal creativity that they would like to see or are willing to allow in "their" version of the Word of God.

model that one adopts, the designated purpose/*Skopos* of the translation in relation to the target audience, and the style in which the re-composition is carried out (e.g., relatively literal versus idiomatic). In the following definition (in italics on the left with further explanation in brackets), the process as a whole is broken down into a number of key components. Thus literary translation is:

a) *the mediated re-composition of*	[the translator acting as a conceptual bridge between two texts and contexts]
b) *one contextually framed text*	[context-sensitive: linguistically, socio-culturally, institutionally, situationally]
c) *within a different communication setting*	[the negotiated exchange of a verbal message in a new language + mind-set]
d) *in the most relevant,*	[the most cognitive-emotive-volitional effects with the least processing effort]
e) *functionally equivalent manner possible,*	[an acceptable, appropriate, and appreciable degree of similarity in terms of the meaning variables of
f) that is, *stylistically marked, more or less,*	pragmatic intent and semantic content as well as textual-stylistic form]
g) *in keeping with the designated Brief*	[specific *Skopos* aims, available resources, target audience, medium, etc.]
h) *of the TL project concerned*	[the overall communicative framework of the TL setting being determinative]

It is important to note that verbal translation of any sort is different from monolingual communication in that at least two different external settings and interpersonal situations are involved, and often three, if the translators cannot access the original text directly. "Translation is a type of communication which points, often explicitly, to a previous communication in another language" (Lambert 1998:132).[100] The formal and conceptual distance between these two (or three) contexts is variable, depending on the languages and cultures concerned. Generally speaking, the greater this distance, the more difficult the translation task and the more proactive mediation on the part of the translator is required if a meaningful, let alone a literary, version is being prepared.[101]

---

[100] "A translation is a type of [TL] metatext which serves as a substitute for another text ...and is the result of 'imitative continuity' with the [SL] prototext" (Shuttleworth and Cowie 1997:105).

[101] A more SL-form-oriented, foreignized translation of the Scriptures may be desired for various reasons, depending on the specific communicative situation (e.g., to facilitate the tradition-based ritual function of communication or to expand the literary categories and features of the TL) and/or the interpersonal setting concerned (e.g., the formal similarity of

Each distinct communication setting incorporates several interacting levels of extratextual influence that together affect all aspects of text representation—its production, transmission, and processing (factor *b* in my definition). Thus there are cultural, institutional, religious, physical or environmental, interpersonal (sociolinguistic), and personal (psychological/experiential) factors that affect the communication context either directly or indirectly. These variables all merge to form the respective collective cognitive frameworks of the SL or TL communities—and the individual viewpoint of each individual of which the group is composed.[102] The perspective and opinion of the current audience is then determinative (factor *h*) in drawing up an organizational *Brief* that defines the overall purpose *(Skopos)*, principles, and procedures of a given Bible translation project *(g)*.[103] In terms of my definition, the translation of a literary version is carried out according to the general principle of psychological relevance *(d)*, coupled with the *Skopos*-specific practice of functional equivalence *(e)*, which is applied with respect to the content and intent of the original text, but also in keeping with the genre-determined stylistic forms of the TL *(f)*.[104] Another type of translation—for example, a literal version for liturgical purposes—may be defined in much the same way, except for the qualifier of "relevant" (i.e., functionally equivalent as in *e*).

---

the translation to some familiar existing version in the TL or another accessible language). I also emphasize *form* in my study, namely the principal *literary* forms of the original text as well as those TL forms that are capitalized upon during the production of a similar poetic or rhetorical rendering. The degree of textual domestication is therefore considerable, but so are the potential positive contextual effects that an artistically aware and appreciative audience may derive from such an idiomatic expression of the Word of God in their mother tongue.

[102]I distinguish between the notion of "context" as an external, perceivable reality and "frame," which is one particular *cognitive* organization or representation of that reality. The sum total of frames that are relevant to the interpretation of a given text constitutes its conceptual framework. (This perspective stems from Gregory Bateson, as explained in Katan 1999:34.)

[103]I use the terms *Brief* and *Skopos* more or less as defined according to functionalist *Skopostheorie* (see Nord 1997:137, 140, chap. 3; Fawcett 1997, chap. 9; also secs. 1.8 and 2.4.2.2 of the present work).

[104]For a handy survey of Relevance Theory as applied to Bible translation, see Gutt 1992. The theory of functional equivalence (FE) is described and applied in de Waard and Nida 1986. I view Relevance Theory as being a useful way of conceptualizing the process of communication in general, but inadequate (if employed in isolation) when it comes to teaching mother-tongue translators the basic principles and specific procedures of Bible translation. For the latter, an FE approach, or some recent modification of this (e.g., Wilt 2002b, chap. 1; Maier, ed. 2000) is much more helpful in pedagogical terms (see also Nord 1997; Hatim and Mason 1997, chap. 11). The special type of translation that I have primarily in mind may be termed a "literary functional-equivalence" (LiFE) version (Wendland 2002b:227). In its fullest, genre-for-genre form of expression, LiFE could be termed a "literary equivalent translation" (LET).

But the translation would still need to be stylistically marked (*f*) in some discernible and appreciable manner, at least phonologically, for this is perhaps where a translation's style is most immediately perceptible. How the text reads aloud, and how it actually sounds, is a criterion of utmost importance for literariness.

Thus I have as my primary point of reference a translation that is literary throughout, one that manifests definite artistic qualities on all levels of linguistic structure in the TL.[105] This is normally produced within the framework of a TL genre that is a functional equivalent of the SL discourse being rendered, but with its own distinctive stylistic features that operate in concert to effect the principal communicative purpose(s) of the original text. However, I recognize that varied degrees of application are possible, depending on the intended audience and the *Skopos* that has been agreed upon for them. Thus a literary technique may be applied in a more restrained manner, that is, with respect to only *selected* features or portions of the biblical text.

It would appear, for example, that the *sound* structure would need to be modified as a first step in a literary direction. In other words, a literary translation would manifest a discourse that is aurally enhanced with respect to one or more phonic features such as balanced lineation, rhythm, rhyme, alliteration, assonance, and/or various kinds of word play (paronomasia). In order to produce this sort of euphony and rhythmic symmetry in utterance progression, certain preferred types of parallelistic syntactic construction, interclausal linkage, and lexical selection (diction) or collocation are often required. A more limited style of literary rendering would also seek to retain most of the evoked *visual* component of the original text—that is, its major images and metaphoric language. This would be modified only as needed to incorporate certain lexical cues or semantic clues to guide the reader/hearer's interpretation in the case of the more difficult or foreign figures of speech.[106]

---

[105]Nord would probably classify the ideal, or complete, sort of literary version on the continuum that I am proposing as a "homologous" translation intended to achieve "[a] homologous effect to [the] source text" (1997:52). She defines this as a rendering in which "the *tertium comparationis* between the source and the target text is a certain status within a corpus or system, mostly with respect to literary or poetic texts" (1997:52). This translation technique, the ultimate in linguistic "domestication," is also known in secular circles as "semiotic transformation" (Ludskanov) or "creative transposition" (Jakobson). It produces a translation which, like its original, should manifest a particular "aura" about it—that "ineffable affect emanating from any work of art that is sensed or felt but cannot be empirically described except by its effect upon...listeners, readers, etc." (Gaddis-Rose 1997:85).

[106]Thus I would agree with Linton's conclusion that the minimum features required to sufficiently distinguish a literary translation are "rhythm and figurativeness," for these elemental features of a poetic style "seem to be innate in the human sensibility, ready to respond when stimulated" by a text and therefore "mark the most ancient writings of

This possibility for allowing *degrees* of application with regard to a literary methodology results in a variable range of translational choices, choices which would be determined by the project *Brief*. This flexibility would, in turn, be reflected by a number of distinct translation types.

2.8 A continuum of translation types

The different styles of translation are frequently classified on the basis of how closely or loosely they retain the formal features of the SL text in the target language—how "literal" or "idiomatic" they are in linguistic-stylistic terms. An idiomatic version has the primary aim of reproducing as much as possible of the semantic content of the original message in the TL. But as noted above, recent secular and Bible-related theory has pointed out another, at times even more important, factor that needs to be seriously considered, namely, the intended major and minor communication functions of the various form-content units represented in the SL text.

A functional approach of this kind, guided by the principle of relevance, may be applied to a translation as a whole, that is, taking into consideration the text's intended purpose or prospective use within the TL community. This larger aim needs to be specified and guided by two distinct and not always congruent perspectives: that of the producers of the translation and that of the designated consumers (see the example in de Vries 2001).

Of course, no translation can reproduce all of the original document's elements of form, content, and function.[107] There is, rather, a variable continuum of possibilities in terms of selection, focus, and emphasis, ranging from versions that concentrate on the SL *forms* to those that seek to duplicate the principal communication (text-act) *functions* of the base document, but using forms that are natural and appropriate in the TL. The following figure represents this hypothetical continuum, giving English versions that are examples of each type-stage. Also represented is the

mankind and...endure unabated today" (1986:30). Linton adds that "these features are peculiarly susceptible to preservation in oral transmissions of culture over the centuries and are, indeed, important mnemonic devices" (ibid.).

[107]The SL message cannot be exactly reproduced or completely conveyed in a given TL because there will always be an appreciable loss or gain of semantic and pragmatic significance that occurs in the process of interlingual representation. Translators must therefore be selective, aiming to achieve the highest possible degree of parity. But this—whether the focus pertains to form, content, or function—can be done only with respect to certain aspects of the initial communication event or smaller portions of the SL text. Thus communication via translation is invariably only partial and imperfect at best: "a stewed strawberry" (Harry de Forest Smith), a "broken vessel" (Walter Benjamin), or the "wrong side of a Persian rug" (James Howell). At worst—and here is the real danger—it can also be distortive, misstating, or misrepresenting the message intended by the SL author.

relative degree of mediation (linguistic intervention in the form of TL textual adjustment) that is required to produce a particular translation style.
The figure is not intended to be a qualitative depiction, saying that type A
is better than B, but is merely a rough reflection of the amount of
translational modification involved.

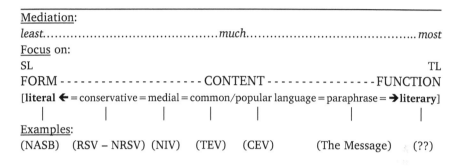

Mediation:
least..*much*.. *most*
Focus on:
SL   TL
FORM - - - - - - - - - - - - - - - - - - - CONTENT - - - - - - - - - - - - - - - FUNCTION
[**literal** ← = conservative = medial = common/popular language = paraphrase = →**literary**]
Examples:
(NASB)   (RSV – NRSV) (NIV)   (TEV)   (CEV)   (The Message)   (??)

I do not know of a single *completely* literary translation of the entire
Scriptures composed in contemporary English.[108] Such an ideal version,
whatever the language, would be one that generally succeeds in proxi-
mately matching the sequence of changing major and minor communicative (text-act > > speech-act) functions of the biblical text by the use of
suitable microforms (stylistic) and macroforms (genres) in the TL. Thus,
while a literary rendering, like a literal version, also stresses the importance of verbal form in translation, it is not SL form, but *TL form* that is
primary. This difference is considerable, but it is not always fully appreciated or acted upon. Therefore, certain translations officially designated or
popularly regarded as being literary may, in actual fact, not be so (e.g.,

[108]That is, *literary* in a technical, structural-stylistic sense (see sec. 2.5.2). This conclusion is partially supported by Norton's (2000) detailed, but selectively limited study. I grant
that other translation types, including a literal version (if composed by a master
wordsmith), might also manifest certain artistically marked or literary features from the
TL. However, such qualities would normally not be realized to the same degree on all levels
of linguistic structure (for a recent attempt, see Alter 1996). In the figure here in section
2.8, I show a literary version (i.e., a completely "trans-formed" version) as more functionally oriented than a "paraphrase" due to its emphasis on genre-equivalence in the TL and
the desire to achieve a correspondence with regard to *artistic*, as well as rhetorical, attributes, while maintaining an essential *semantic* equivalence with the original text. The key
representative translation types along the continuum roughly correspond to those proposed
from a secular perspective by Holmes in a 1968 conference paper (later published in 1988).
According to Hermans (1999:27), Holmes's types are those translations characterized by
"mimetic form" (= *literal,* e.g., rendering ancient Greek hexameter verse by corresponding
hexameters), "analogical form" (= *literary,* e.g., rendering Greek epic poems in English heroic couplets), and "organic form" (= *popular language,* e.g., rendering the classical epics in
a TL semipoetic form with an emphasis upon conveying the content of the original text).

NEB, JB)—at least not formally and not with reference to the text as a whole. Such an evaluation would need to be determined on the basis of recognized stylistic criteria of excellence with respect to a wide range of phonological, lexical, syntactic, and textual features of artistry and rhetoric in the TL. Furthermore, it is clear that such a critical assessment would have to be supported by practiced literary experts or experienced artists—not merely theologians, biblical scholars, or even a multitude of pious proponents of a familiar version revered by a certain religious denomination.

The easiest way to satisfy the preceding form-functional criterion, if the goal is a literary translation, is by means of a globally applied, *genre-for-genre* rendition of a complete book, text, or pericope. In other words, the translators move from a specific biblical text type such as a lament psalm into the nearest functionally equivalent vernacular genre, which in Chichewa, for example, is *ndakatulo* lyric poetry (discussed in chap. 10 and appendix B; see also chap. 3 of Wendland 1993). It is possible then for the stylistic and rhetorical quality of such a literary translation to be composed, perceived, and assessed *as a whole* according to the objective as well as subjective criteria that have been established for that particular TL genre.[109] Such a holistic, creative-compositional approach would seek to attain communicative *correspondence* (or sufficient *similarity*) at a much higher discourse level, rather than in terms of an attempt to match form-functional features on a one-to-one basis with regard to the microtext. Thus competent translators would seek to immerse themselves in the original message by thoroughly studying the SL text and its context. They would then with similar intensity search out the communicative resources available in the target language and cultural setting. The final step would be that act of creative *synthesis* whereby the biblical message is transformed in translation to reformulate it in the most relevant way for a particular contemporary audience.

Thus the measure of literariness or rhetoric manifested in a translation depends very much on the manner of text representation that was used to prepare it. Simply put, the more *concordantly* (woodenly) *literal* the rendering, the less artistic or rhetorical the TL version will normally be in terms of persuasive impact and/or aesthetic appeal. The less mechanically literal in style—that is, the more *idiomatic* and stylistically *accommodative* the translation approach is—the more rhetorical the TL text should

---

[109]The exegetical quality of the translation in question would have to be evaluated independently according to more semantically oriented analytical methods. It should be noted that I am using the term *literary* here in a broad sense to cover both oral and written texts of a distinctly artistic character, coupled also with a definite rhetorical motivation (see sec. 2.9).

turn out to be in terms of TL artistic norms and conventions, all other things being equal (e.g., given the same skill and experience of the translators). It also follows that a greater amount of mediation (creative hermeneutical and compositional action) is generally required on the part of its translators. In other words, it is necessary for them first to carefully analyze the SL document so that they can understand and interpret its rhetorical processes as well as its primary content (themes, subthemes, key concepts, etc.). As many as possible of these essential elements of original textual significance or contextual relevance would then be represented in the translation through the skillful exercise of personal intuitive artistry, both textually (in terms of TL structural and stylistic features) and extratextually (through footnotes, introductions, titles, glossary entries, illustrations, etc.).

However, as has been emphasized, a local translation *Skopos* may specify a version that is not so dynamic or idiomatic in nature. It may require a higher level of formal correspondence with respect to key structural and stylistic features of the biblical text such as its metaphoric imagery, parallelistic patterns, lexical combinations, instances of repetition, and consistency in key-term usage. Nevertheless, it would still be possible to render other aspects of the text in a pleasing literary manner, especially on the phonological level. From this perspective, then, *every* translation of Scripture can—and probably *should*—reflect a certain measure of the artistic style that is recognized in the TL as being appropriate for the genre being conveyed. In this case, the translation continuum in the preceding figure would manifest a + *literary* component at each and every stage along the way, with the differences among the respective versions being only a matter of degree, not completely different types of translation. That is the expanded vision of a "literary version" that I would like to see realized in all Bible translation work.

The question then would not be *if* a particular version is to be literary, only *how much* so-to what extent and in which respect(s) and where in the text. How much TL literary style or rhetoric can or should be reflected in a given translation, and which are the crucial determining factors in the local setting? What are the principal hermeneutical implications of this decision? These are important issues for any project to consider before actual translation work begins and the translators are selected. If the agreed-upon goal is to achieve a significant level of functional parity in the translation, the answer depends on the nature of the SL text being rendered: The more persuasive and vigorous the rhetoric and/or artistry displayed in the original document (i.e., with special emphasis on the *expressive, affective,* and *poetic* functions of communication), the more argumentative, evaluative, and evocative its rendition ought to *sound* in the TL.[110] However, these considerations will be influenced and modified by still another vital aspect of the translation event, namely, the composite human *setting* of communication. This *interpersonal* context encompasses the various sociocultural, ecclesiastical, institutional, and individual situations in which the translation will be transmitted, responded to, and utilized. All of these factors must be carefully investigated in conjunction with one another before a translation project gets underway because they will, or should, determine the type of version that is most suitable for the target constituency.[111]

---

[110]The terms *argumentative* and *evaluative* are from Hatim and Mason (1997:182–183). Such texts, they say, tend to be characterized by a higher incidence of *marked* linguistic forms (i.e., usages and expressions that are less expected or somehow extraordinary in terms of frequency, distribution, collocation, novelty, or impact). I have used the word *sound* in this sentence deliberately: The techniques of rhetoric are most obvious and effective when the discourse is either *oral* to begin with or composed to be presented orally (as in the case of most biblical texts). Rhetoric simply does not carry the same impact when it is read *silently* to oneself or when composed in the *idioms* of the SL text (see Fox 1995). I have added the qualifier *evocative* for stylistically beautiful, artistic texts, a dimension that Hatim and Mason largely ignore. In any case, as already suggested, the relative value of a recent translation may be assessed from two different viewpoints, that of the person or team who prepared it, for whom the minimum standard is "adequacy," and that of the community who will use it, for whom it is "acceptability" (see Hermans 1999:76, 162).

[111]I follow Hatim and Mason (1997:12) in defining relevance as communicative *efficiency* in relation to *effectiveness*, that is, relative ease of message interpretation in comparison with the degree of accomplishment of its pragmatic goals (see also John Searle 1969 and de Beaugrande and Dressler 1981:11). This value has more recently been popularized in different terminology within a psycholinguistic framework by the proponents of Relevance Theory (e.g., Gutt 1991:23–44; Pilkington 2000:58–83). The problem with using the "principle of relevance" as the *sole* criterion in the evaluative assessment of a given translation, as distinct from an original literary composition, is that it is often stated in terms that *appear* to give precedence to the text and context of the TL. For example, Gutt says (1991:42), "[I]f we ask in what respects the intended interpretation of the translation should resemble the original, the answer is: in respects that make it adequately relevant to the audience—that is, that offer adequate contextual effects. If we ask how the translation should be expressed, the answer is: in such a manner that it yields the intended interpretation without causing the audience unnecessary processing effort." How to balance these two potentially conflicting concerns in practice would indeed seem to be a subjective, even arbitrary, exercise.

In any case, the principle of *relevance* needs to be supplemented and employed in close conjunction with what may be termed the principle of *reliability*. The relevance criteria should be strictly applied also with respect to the original SL text-context so that there is in effect a fourfold set of limiting factors involved. In this interlingual communication effort, the notion of functional equivalence (or "parity," a better term than the visually oriented "resemblance") in terms of semantic content and pragmatic intent, including the discourse-determined features of impact and appeal, continues to be useful, despite some rather strong criticism (e.g., see Hermans 1999, chap. 4). Thus, the concerns of both relevance and reliability, whether complementary or competing in their operation or manifestation

2.9 Where to set the L-R parameters

My major premise is that a well-prepared, fully functionally equivalent translation of the Bible will normally turn out to be recognized as a literary text in the target language. This, in short, is *literary equivalence*, manifested on *all* linguistic levels, from indigenous text genres to significant local patterns of sound. In this respect, a literary-equivalent text might be characterized as being a stylistically "extended" and/or a rhetorically "enhanced" *popular-language* version (see Wonderly 1968:3). Therefore, if the original has been determined to be literature (and different degrees of artistic and oratorical distinction may be recognized with respect to the various books of the Bible), then its corresponding interlingual reproduction should be similarly regarded, in accordance with recognized standards of verbal excellence in the vernacular. A great deal of *dead* (i.e., nonfunctional in the TL) formal correspondence with the original text will inevitably be lost in this effort. But the goal is to gain pragmatic resemblance—"a [perceptible] similarity of communicative functions" (de Beaugrande 1968:94)—with respect to individual passages as well as the translation as a whole. *Live* formal correspondence in the TL will of course be retained wherever possible as a matter of policy.

Of course the practical implications of the decision to produce a more literary translation of the Bible need to be considered, and as has been supported by the different translation approaches surveyed earlier, the degree to which a more dynamic, domesticating approach to textual restructuring is generally applied will depend on the predetermined organizational *Skopos* for the project as a whole. Still, it is to be hoped that a high degree of situational and personal relevance for the intended audience can be achieved as a result of this disciplined exercise in artful text reconstruction.[112]

---

within a given translation setting, would have to be considered in the establishment and application of the project *Skopos*. More recent writing on the application of RT to biblical exegesis would appear to address my latter concern, for example: "Relevance Theory...gives access to the author's probable intentions, not as though they can be directly read off the text, but by assuming that the author has communicated ostensively and that human communication is guided by the quest for optimal relevance" (Pattemore 2002:53).

[112]As already noted, relevance refers to a bi-directional (SL ⇔ TL), situationally determined appropriateness with respect to *efficiency* (the least conceptual processing effort) on the one hand and *effectiveness* (the greatest cognitive gain or communicative impact) on the other. The principle of relevance is variously treated in different theories of translation. For some (e.g., Gutt 1992:24–25), it is the only concept and guideline that is necessary; for others (e.g., Hatim and Mason 1990:93–95), it forms just part of a much wider text and context-based, sociolinguistic and semiotic model of interlingual communication. (For more on this well-known "minimax concept," see de Beaugrande and Dressler 1981:11; Fawcett 1997:12; Shuttleworth and Cowie 1997:106–107; Pilkington 2000:73–75.)

A word of caution is in order here: Literary translators, seeking to produce a lyric version of a selection of psalms, for example, certainly do not
have the poetic liberty (or license) to *distort* either the original essential
meaning or its particular areas of thematic and socioreligious focus. A
clear measure of overall functional equivalence, including exegetical fidelity, must be maintained to the degree that this may be determined on
the basis of all available reliable evidence.[113] Critics and reviewers are
free to debate this or that specific usage as to whether the literary version
has gone too far in its artistry in an attempt to create rhetorical impact
and aesthetic appeal, but it should always be remembered that the basis
for such a comparative evaluation must be a careful examination and
analysis of the Hebrew or Greek original, not some translation.

On the other hand, one ought not to get tangled up in minor details of
form or interpretation when conducting an assessment of this nature. The
exegete's tendency to do so can easily muffle the poetic muse. In the case
of biblical poetry, for example, the Song of Songs (see Wendland 1995a),
it is often not the mere individual image or utterance that is important,
but the total conceptual, emotional, and sensory impression created by
the use of literary/oratorical language. It may well have been the primary
intention of the original author to activate the expressive, affective, and
aesthetic functions of communication to an equal or even greater extent
than the cognitive function that so many people mistakenly identify as being invariably paramount in the literature of the Holy Scriptures.[114] In any
case, the point is that there is a range of options. Degrees of application
are possible, with respect to both extension (*quantitative*—how many devices are included and how widely they are utilized) and also excellence
(*qualitative*—how skillfully and creatively these features are handled).
The appropriate proportion to be adopted will depend on the *Skopos* of
the project concerned.

Literary translation also presents some major implications in terms of
its overall relevance to a given TL community. This topic will be developed more fully in chapters 10 and 11, but the basic guiding principle, as
expressed by Gutt (1992:25), is this: "[W]henever a person engages in
ostensive communication, she creates the tacit presumption that what she

---

[113]Nord (1997) devotes an entire chapter to this crucial issue (chap. 8, "Function plus
Loyalty"). She explains: "The loyalty principle...induces the translator to respect the
sender's individual communicative intentions, as far as they can be elicited....[It] limits the
range of justifiable target-text functions for one particular source text and raises the need
for a negotiation of the translation assignment between translators and their clients"
(ibid.:126).

[114]Nord would designate the primary function in operation here as the "appellative,"
which is manifested in language that is specially crafted or designed to appeal "to the
reader's aesthetic sensitivity" (1997:42–43).

has to communicate will be optimally relevant to the audience: that it will yield adequate contextual effects, without requiring unnecessary processing effort." As to how these relevance principles apply to a translation project, it is a matter of weighing "cost" (sec. 2.9.1) against "gain" (sec. 2.9.2), in other words, evaluating the amount of processing effort that a literary translation project may require in relation to the communicated benefits to the intended audience.

2.9.1 Cost

In Gutt's definition of relevance, his focus is on the audience's conceptual *processing* of the text, but it is also true that there is a considerable cost to *producing* an acceptable literary version. Other types of translation would be much less demanding of the translation team. In fact, to prepare even a minimally literary version requires such great resources that at the very outset it may be overwhelming to a TL community. Even the mere proposal may be rejected out of hand. It is necessary therefore for the project's planning committee to "first sit down and estimate the cost" (Luke 14:28).

We begin with the *sine qua non*—namely, those communication and media experts who will make up the staff of the translation and review team. Are all sponsoring churches thoroughly committed to support (financially, educationally, spiritually) persons of such high intellectual and innovative caliber? The *team* nature of the endeavor needs to be stressed. It may be harder for individually gifted, artistically inventive staff to get along harmoniously. Yoke a creative artist together with a conservative exegete, and it is likely that the authoritative voice, with arguments based on the Hebrew and Greek of the original text, will always be able to drown out the opinions or protests of the more stylistically sensitive individuals. An additional cost is the larger committee needed: More than one team member of similar competence is needed to constructively criticize another's work, whether from an exegetical or stylistic perspective. It takes one (an expert) to know—and correct—one!

The next question is whether the receptor community is willing to pay the higher price of interacting with a literary rendition. It might be difficult, at least initially, for them to process a text that has been composed in a popular TL poetic genre. It will not be presented in the familiar, though often misunderstood words of the more literal version they may have had. Nor will the text be expressed in the simplified, perhaps restricted, linguistic forms of a common-language rendering.

An artistically poetic, yet also exegetically accurate translation will certainly require considerable effort for the translators to prepare and for the
intended audience to understand, appreciate, and apply, at least to start
with, as they get used to its novel stylistic forms or more elaborate discourse structures. The project management team may face a certain
amount of resistance and promotional difficulty when beginning their attempt to sell the constituency at large on the merits of an unconventional
translation. A great amount of proactive but gentle education—and persuasion—may be necessary to overcome the negative reactions that a dynamic literary version in the vernacular might provoke among certain
groups within the wider Christian community. The aim is not to force this
type of translation upon the receptor constituency, but simply to make
them aware of more possibilities in the area of style and format. They can
then choose the sorts of versions that they prefer from a wider range of options according to different targeted subgroups and their envisioned setting of use.

2.9.2 Gain

The costs of communication must of course be balanced against the potential
gains. The difficulties may well be offset by the actual (not merely prospective) benefits of a literary-rhetorical translation. But a practical assessment of
this sort may take some time to complete, as people gradually grow in their
understanding of the positive features of an artistically composed poetic or
prosaic text and how to use such a version and increase the personal and
communal "contextual effects" (Gutt 1992:22–23) to be derived from it.

    As noted earlier, a literary translation may not be acceptable, at least
initially, for general liturgical purposes in a public worship service. However, it will certainly possess some significant communication possibilities for particular audience subgroups in specific situations or special
settings—that is, in accordance with the guiding *Skopos* statement that
was prepared as an essential part of the initial project *Brief*. For example,
an oral-aurally attuned literary translation may be very appropriate for
members of minority ethnic-pride groups, anti-Western traditionalists,
popular entertainers, artists, and public performers, painters, sculptors,
musicians, dramatic players, actors, TV personalities, or well-known
sports figures. A literary translation may also be found to be highly suitable for use in certain nonprint media such as audiocassette or CD, especially when accompanied by background music or composed in a
popular-song style, and in mass-media broadcasting, audience-specific radio programs in particular.

There is one special gain in communicative effects that is more or less certain to be realized: the increased emotive, aesthetic, and memory-enhancing benefits for all who regularly make use of a literary translation, especially in close comparative conjunction with a more traditional literal or liturgical version. A poetic rendition could serve, for example, as a valuable devotional resource and a helpful means of renewing or expanding one's perspective as well as enhancing one's theological understanding by stimulating a greater awareness of and appreciation for the artistic, rhetorical, emotional, and connotative riches to be mined from the ancient texts of the Word of God. These passages would now sound more like genuine, contemporary literature in the local language—and in many more places than might formerly have been thought possible. We will have occasion to examine some of these texts more closely in the chapters that follow as we explore the possibilities of an approach to translation that is termed "literary functional equivalence," or *LiFE* for short.

Some time after getting into this study, as I neared the completion of this book, I happened to run across another one of those seminal thoughts on translation by Eugene A. Nida, one that well captures the essence of what I am trying to accomplish with a LiFE approach to the Scriptures:

> In addition to the lexical capacities of languages to speak about the total range of human experience, all languages possess certain devices for heightening the impact and appeal of a discourse. In other words, all languages possess [literary-] rhetorical devices that are important for contributing clarity, force, and beauty to verbal expression. These rhetorical devices, such as parallelism and emphatic order, *are all part of the meaning of a discourse.* They are also signs in a semiotic sense and have special significance. In fact, they are *often more important* in indicating intent, purpose, and urgency of a message than even the lexical forms. If "translating" means "translating meaning," then clearly one must take into consideration these important [literary-]rhetorical features. (E. A. Nida (1982) cited in Di Jin (2003:xvii); I have added the words in brackets and the italics.)

3

Tectonicity of the Scriptures

Tectonics being the art, or science, of construction, I use the term *tectonicity* here to refer to the meaningful organization or artful arrangement that is typically manifested in a literary text.[115] The essential compositional *unity* of the text under consideration is assumed in a literary approach, but this does not mean that one looks at a particular text from a uniform, monolithic, or undiscriminating perspective. Rather, it is viewed holistically as composed of a hierarchy of integrated structural levels and units.[116] The historical (diachronic) or editorial development of the discourse is not completely ignored, but is considered only where it can be clearly demonstrated and also shown to have some influence on interpreting either the text's final form or its content (e.g., in the case of pre- and post-exilic psalms, the "two books" of Samuel, LXX Jeremiah, or the Aramaic portions of Daniel). In general, however, a biblical book is analyzed just as it stands written (i.e., synchronically), and there is an emphasis upon explaining how its various pieces and literary devices fit together rather than on why they should be treated separately either in origin or in composition. Similarly, apparent stylistic anomalies are not automatically assumed to be foreign insertions, but rather as potential markers of some higher discourse function or rhetorical purpose. The assumption of unity also affects the analyst's methodology in its concern for the larger structure of a distinct book or pericope—how it is

---

[115]According to *Webster's New World Dictionary* (1988:1374), *tectonics* is "the constructive arts in general; esp. the art of making things that have *both beauty and usefulness*" (emphasis added). This definition would seem to apply very well also to verbal arts.

[116]For a helpful survey of various discourse-related aspects of linguistics in relation to Bible translation, see Ross 2002. For a more detailed discussion of some of the topics of chapter 3, see Wendland 2002b.

artistically and rhetorically fashioned in terms of *syntagmatic* (contiguous) and *paradigmatic* (analogous) units and their diverse formal and semantic interrelationships.

The presupposition of unity may be extended to include the corpus of Scripture as a whole, although that is a theological issue, not a strictly literary one. In support of this perspective are such important features as (1) the Bible's overarching *narrative design*, beginning in Genesis and ending in the climax of Revelation, a teleological arrangement that manifests a broad chronological progression as well as a clear peak in the story of Jesus' suffering, death, resurrection, and exaltation; (2) a central, sustained *textual focus* upon the nature, character, and activities of God in relation to humanity, especially in the person of the divine Messiah-Mediator, Christ the Savior and Lord of all nations; and (3) an elaborate and intricate system of *intertextuality*, including reiterated themes, motifs, and images as well as distinct key words and concepts, which relates the individual canonical books to one another both explicitly (by direct citation) and implicitly (through varied degrees of allusion).[117]

But while recognizing the unity of a discourse, we find it helpful to distinguish between the macro- and microlevels when examining its L-R characteristics. Although the macro- and microlevels operate together

---

[117]The unity of the Scriptures has recently been defended from a pragmatic (performative speech act) perspective by Dale Patrick (1999:205), who says, "The Scripture is designed to be synthesized—to be read as a whole." Along these same lines, David Jasper (1998:21–22) writes, "Within the canon of Scripture itself, in both Hebrew and Christian Bibles, an intricate pattern of cross-referencing establishes a web of intertextuality which promotes...the intrinsic relationships between and within the texts of literature. In the Bible, not only does this establish a theological as well as a literary coherence between the books of the canon, but it also makes possible a particular view of 'history' " (i.e., in relation to the NT fulfillment of OT prophecy). Writing from the perspective of discourse analysis and cognitive linguistics, Hilaire Paul Valiquette (1999:50) concludes "that the [biblical] text was *composed* as a unified whole and is to be read as a whole....To argue for disunity because of perceived 'inconsistencies' is...rather naïve. It is a far better approach to assume that the composer is using the 'inconsistencies' as a discourse device." Those of us working in non-Indo-European languages also realize that the so-called discourse inconsistencies perceived by Western scholars in biblical texts often turn out to be quite normal in other literary traditions as is the case for the varied panoramic in relation to scenic style of narrative presentations in Genesis (e.g., from the former to the latter in Gen. 1:1 => 1:2ff.).

A presupposition of the textual unity of individual books of the Bible constitutes one important aspect of the paradigm shift in the thinking of many biblical scholars that modern literary-critical studies helped bring about during the second half of the twentieth century (Baker and Arnold 1999:98–99). Three related features of this fundamental change in perspective are: (1) the movement from diachronic to primarily synchronic studies of the original text; (2) a focus on the larger, integrated units of discourse; and (3) a recognition of the pervasiveness and importance of intertextuality throughout the Scriptures, the Hebrew Testament's intertextuality being reflected somewhat passively within itself but more dynamically appropriated in the Greek Testament.

naturally in the transmission of the intended sense and significance of a certain message, they may be considered separately during analysis in order to simplify our perspective and enable us to focus in greater detail upon selected items of interest.

The emphasis in this chapter is on the macrolevel of textual organization, that is, on the larger (more inclusive or extensive) formal tectonic features in the Scriptures. However, there are several clear points of overlap and interaction with a microlevel linguistics-oriented analysis, as will be seen in later chapters. In chapter 4 some of the main subsentential artistic devices are in focus; in chapter 5 I overview the "iconic," or ideational, aspects of biblical discourse; and then in chapter 6 the dynamic "rhetorical" dimension of various stylistic forms will be considered.

The present chapter surveys text construction, or discourse design, from two different perspectives, first in relation to overt literary genres, and second with reference to a number of less evident structures and strategies. The use of both literary and linguistic techniques of analysis highlights the importance of an integrated interdisciplinary approach when investigating both the source language and the target language in preparation for carrying out a contemporary Bible translation.

3.1 Genres

The term *genre* may be defined as a "category of artistic composition...marked by a distinctive style, form, or content" (Soukhanov 1992:757). To this I would add definite communication function(s) in a given sociocultural setting. According to Barton, a genre is "a conventional pattern, recognizable by certain formal criteria (style, shape, tone, particular syntactic or even grammatical structures, recurring formulaic patterns), which is used in a particular society in social contexts which are governed by certain formal conventions" (1984:16).[118] "Form" here may be seen as denoting the larger structures and/or the rules of arrangement that characterize a recognized discourse type or even an entire corpus of texts. A given genre may be described with reference to different levels of specificity (*sub*genres) or to particular sociocultural settings in which certain types of text typically appear or are regularly performed. Here we are focusing upon *verbal art* in its various manifestations—oral and written, prose and poetry—but especially verbal art that has a pronounced religious character.

---

[118]A helpful, student-friendly, genre-based introduction to biblical interpretation is found in Stein 1994.

Thus genre, or discourse type, refers to a conventional stylistic code and literary template that enables one to anticipate, recognize, understand, and appreciate the compositional form, content, purpose, intended response, and in certain cases also the theological significance of a specific biblical book or pericope. The concept of *genre* is crucial to the analysis and interpretation of any passage of Scripture, large or small. In fact, it is generally the very first feature of a text that needs to be identified, whether on the macro- or microlevel of discourse organization (e.g., whether a complete wisdom psalm or an individual proverb).[119] Test yourself on the following selections. What are some of the primary visual, stylistic, semantic, and pragmatic characteristics that signal their genre?

> Teach me, O LORD, the way of your statutes, and I will observe it to the end. Give me understanding, that I may keep your law and observe it with my whole heart. Lead me in the path of your commandments, for I delight in it. Turn my heart to your decrees, and not to selfish gain. Turn my eyes from looking at vanities; give me life in your ways. (Ps. 119:33–37, NRSV)

> But be doers of the word,
> And not merely hearers who deceive themselves.
> For if any are hearers of the word and not doers,
> They are like those who look at themselves in a mirror;
> For they look at themselves and, on going away,
> Immediately forget what they were like.
> But those who look into the perfect law,
> The law of liberty, and persevere,
> Being not hearers who forget but doers who act—
> They will be blessed in their doing. (James 1:22–25, NRSV)

Misleading printed formats like those shown here should not confuse an experienced Bible reader with regard to the type and nature of the texts so displayed, even though they may well cause difficulties for an inexperienced

---

[119]"A text's genre is thus the key to its meaning....Genre studies not only illuminate a text...they also illuminate a reader. Good interpretation is dependent on understanding what a text is historically and structurally. Without this realization the reader's response is impoverished" (P. House 1988:28). House also provides a detailed listing of features that distinguish literary genres (ibid.:38). The importance of literary genre has more recently been reinforced from the perspective of cognitive linguistics: "Genre is essential if we wish to take into account the (cognitive) expectations of language users when they engage in a particular class of language use.... [L]anguage users never do any processing of language *in vacuo*, but always in some concrete situation, and they will have more or less detailed cognitive models and expectations about such contexts. I believe that the most important notion for the analysis of these cognitive models and expectations is the one of genre" (Steen 2002:285, 287–288).

reader.[120] Note that while the teaching conveyed by these two passages is relatively similar, the overall manner of expression and discourse structure is not. This difference in turn influences (to a greater or lesser extent, depending on the individual and society involved) how one reacts to the words of each emotively, and for some perhaps volitionally as well, that is, with respect to the degree of didactic or imperative force that is perceived. In this connection, it is important to note that the determination of genre in a particular instance will inevitably guide one's interpretation of any biblical text. In the practice of Bible translation, a team's re-composition of the message in the TL may similarly be affected stylistically. For example, if the Book of Jonah is construed as a literary parable analogous to a folktale instead of as narrative history, or if the story about the rich man and Lazarus in Luke 16 is taken to be history, it could well influence the translators' choice of a particular literary style in their language.

Similarly, an audience apprehends a selected discourse in their language, whether oral or written, with an acquired literary (as distinct from linguistic) competence that is based on learning and past experience. This enables them to discern and interpret the stylistic features present in specific types of text (see a fuller discussion in Barton 1984:11–19 and P. House 1988:23–29). The more experienced the readers or listeners, the greater is their active, critical competence. The recognition of genre and various expectations associated with it are a fundamental part of this ability. Genre involves a complex cognitive grid, an internal interpretive framework that facilitates an audience's processing and evaluation of a text's form (e.g., poetic devices), content, purpose, and significance. When a particular genre's norms are deliberately flouted, altered, or ignored, a certain element of surprise may be evoked, either disconcerting or enjoyable in overall effect.

The diverse codes and verbal conventions associated with different genres "are capable of different kinds of meaning and offer different kinds of information to a reader" (Tate 1991:64). However, such a significant meaning potential exists only in a virtual state until it is actualized by someone who is familiar with the formal system of linguistic and literary signals of the genre and related subgenres or tropes which the original author built into the text. Robert Alter (1981:46) describes the process thus:

> A coherent reading of any art work, whatever the medium, requires
> some detailed awareness of the grid of conventions upon which,

---

[120]This sort of visual misinformation occurs repeatedly throughout virtually every Bible that has ever been published, in some more than in others. (The formats in TEV and NIV are better than in most English versions.) This matter is of special concern to the literary analyst, who pays relatively greater attention to the organizing structures and patterns of verbal discourse (see Wendland and Louw 1993).

and against which, the individual work operates....an elaborate set
of tacit agreements about the ordering of the art work is at all times
the enabling context in which the complex communication of art
occurs. Through our awareness of convention we can recognize significant or simply pleasing patterns of repetition, symmetry,
contrast; we can discriminate between the verisimilar and the fabu-
lous, pick up directional clues in a narrative work, see what is
innovative and what is deliberately traditional at each nexus of the
artistic creation.

Knowledge of generic organization and stylistic operation can lessen
the likelihood of one's misinterpreting an artistic piece of literature that
contains metaphor, irony, paradox, and/or hyperbole: "The genre provides the literary context...and, therefore, partly determines what the
sentence means and how it should be taken....Genre thus enables the
reader to interpret meaning and to recognize what kinds of truth claims
are being made in and by a text" (Vanhoozer 1998:50). Ignorance of or
disregard for the formal and semantic norms associated with a given
genre can lead to what James Barr (1963:125) terms a "literary category
mistake": Failures to comprehend the literary genre lead to a use of the
biblical assertions with a wrong function.

> Genre mistakes cause the wrong kind of truth values to be attached
> to biblical sentences. Literary embellishments then come to be re-
> garded as scientifically true assertions.

Thus fictive devices may be wrongly construed as historical fact.

The converse is equally damaging, that is, when history is viewed as
some sort of figure of speech, as Long (in Baker and Arnold, eds.
1999:163–164) observes:

> What was written as utilitarian literature (history, legislation, lit-
> urgy, preaching, etc.) is read as pure literature (art for art's
> sake)....In other words, inherent in the literary approach is the dan-
> ger of losing sight of and interest in the historical truth claims of
> the text.

In this case, either a lack of literary sensitivity or an overemphasis on certain key literary categories and methods (e.g., in narrative: characterization, plot development, point of view) might lead to a misleading type of
reductionism. For this reason, a literary-rhetorical approach must always
be applied judiciously in conjunction with other discourse-oriented methodologies in order to produce a more balanced, objective account of the
data at hand.

It is clear that special attention devoted to both the generic and the specific literary-rhetorical forms of biblical discourse can direct one more

confidently along the path of a more meaningful and rewarding interpretation of such artistically composed theological literature. As P. House says, "The art form itself has intrinsic value" (1988:20). This is not merely a matter of structural identification, for the conventional form is merely the primary means to a more important end—namely, a better understanding of the author's message in terms of conceptual content and communicative intent as well. It is not surprising then that an accomplished secular translator and literary critic concludes that "recognition of genre and its rules is the translator's most important task" (Katan 1999:150).

Genre criticism, as a prominent component of literary-rhetorical analysis, involves the identification of those stylistic features, or "cues," that distinguish one popularly recognized type of writing (or speaking, in the case of oral discourse) from another within a specific sociolinguistic setting. As in the case of any linguistic form (not only verbal art), a basic classification in terms of distinctive similarities and differences is crucially important in this process of discernment, although the salient *differences* are generally more significant from a hermeneutical perspective. As Schökel says,

> [K]nowledge of the genre orientates the reader. It is also an excellent starting-point for comparing with other texts. When the common elements are realised, the individuality of the text is more clearly perceived. And in the last analysis the literature is made up of individual works, the primary object for contemplation and study. (1988:11)

It is important also to recognize the social or interpersonal as well as the communicative implications of genres. Thus a given genre (e.g., a psalm or a parable) acts like a literary contract between an author and his readers, promising that the text has been composed in a particular way for a specific purpose and that the readers must understand it accordingly. In other words, once they have ascertained the discourse type, they will automatically generate a set of interpretive expectations which are conventionally associated with that genre in its normal context of use. These include concepts that pertain to its textual structure, the artistic devices that it will manifest, and the function(s) of the message conveyed.

A skilled writer often includes different genres and styles within one text in order to promote interest and to prompt a distinctive sort of compositional unity. Within the Pentateuch, for example,

> [apparent] 'internal inconsistencies' should be treated in a manner analogous to disharmony in music, where the disharmony functions to provoke the ear of the listener and lead to resolution....The juxtaposition and ordering of different text types (narrative, songs,

legislation, and so on) broadly articulate the structure of the text (but not in a simple way), much like the different movements of a symphony....They [may] act as seams, joining disparate [or corresponding thematic] elements; they [thus] articulate the text, calling on listeners to make a connection between the [different] elements. (Valiquette 1999:48–49, 56)[121]

Therefore, despite the emphasis upon expected conventions and typical literary features, interpreters need to recognize that a biblical author may vary the composition and/or content of a certain genre in a novel way in order to create a special effect or convey an important underlying, often incongruent or contrastive message. The writer of Job, for example, creates an ironic "birthday song" in the style of a powerful curse, a bitter self-imprecation in fact (Job 3). Similarly, in Isaiah 5:1–7 a shocking, stinging rebuke of Israel composed in the form of a love lyric is featured. The author of Hebrews pens a forcefully apologetic sermon in the form of a letter, which gives it a more personal character and overtones of intimate concern. The Apostle Paul in his letter to the Galatians pointedly omits the pastoral-relational thanksgiving section that is typical of a Hellenistic letter in order to communicate his extreme displeasure over the Galatian believers' attitude towards him and his message (Gal. 1:6–10). Even the Gospel discourse form appears to have been a hybrid genre in terms of the literature of that age, being a combination of Hebrew historical narrative and Greco-Roman biography. It was thus "a new way of using [these literary forms] to present the [unique] story of Jesus" (Bailey and vander Broek 1992:15).

Unfortunately, the formal features of genre tend to be culturally specific not only with respect to form and content, but also regarding purpose, usage, and significance. The omission of a word of thanksgiving in a letter would have no significance for a contemporary reader. The poetic mode, for another example, is not commonly used nowadays in Western cultures to convey the sort of didactic discourse that we find in Psalm 119. Poetry has by and large lost its impact as a vehicle of religious instruction, except perhaps in a few restricted settings such as conservative Christian worship services and contemporary musical renditions. It would not, however, be out of place in a central African context where ancient traditional initiation rites for the youth occasionally employ a poetic form of

---

[121]Valiquette also uses several New Testament books to illustrate how seeming "disharmony...performs a discourse function in a unified composition"—for example, to overtly mark some point of structural and/or thematic significance within the work as a whole. For the structural analyst, then, "[t]he placement and ordering of disharmonious elements [e.g., spatial dislocation or acts of rebellion] is crucial" (1999:66).

discourse as a way of reinforcing the solemnity of this ancient and symbolic life-changing event.

Thus Bible translators face a formidable twofold task. First, they have to accurately determine the genre, along with the associated diagnostic characteristics, that constitutes a particular text in the original language. Second, they must then discover the appropriate L-R forms that will represent the intended message in a contextualized, functionally equivalent way in their own language.

Some other complicating factors that need to be taken into consideration when dealing with genre in relation to Scripture translation are: (1) the influence of *medium*, (2) the matter of *usage*, and (3) the nature of translations as *secondary* texts in the TL. (These three factors are discussed at length in de Vries 1999.) As to the first of these, while the medium may not actually *be* the message, as Marshall McLuhan proposed, it certainly greatly influences both the form and the content of a given message. An orally transmitted text will differ in a number of significant ways from a written one (see sec. 1.2). Thus the features of a certain oral genre in the TL may not be simply transferred into writing when preparing a translation. On the other hand, the characteristics of formal written discourse cannot be applied too slavishly because Bible translations are frequently transmitted orally rather than in print, especially in parts of the world where the functional literacy rate is low. Obviously, a certain amount of adaptation, testing, and revision needs to be done, after which the result may well be some form of literary hybrid that manifests the stylistic features of no other genre in the verbal tradition of the TL.[122]

In regard to *usage*, we must remember that the various social situations in which the Bible is used tend to be very different from those of other types of TL discourse, whether oral or written. Take the typical "performance tradition" (de Vries 1999:29) of most Christian communities, where the text is publicly read aloud, with greater or lesser degrees of fluency and formality and often in a fragmented fashion. The norm is for relatively small portions to be selected, which may or may not be topically related to one another and the socioreligious setting. Each reading is

---

[122]The Chichewa (see fn. 129) *ndakatulo* genre is an example. It originated as a concise impromptu form of intensely expressive oral poetry in which an individual singer or declaimer would comment publicly on local social issues concerning the family, clan, or village. This developed in more recent years into a popular *written* style of critical verse, one that is intended to display the verbal virtuosity of the poet as well as draw attention to some outstanding personal complaint, social cause, or political issue. The question is whether this genre can now be adapted still more in terms of form and function to serve as an acceptable translational equivalent for some (if not all) of the psalms; certainly, a great deal of audience testing will be needed to determine the answer (see the example of a *ndakatulo*-ized Psalm 23 in sec. A.1.8).

usually accompanied by some form of didactic comment or exposition that attempts to explain or apply the passage in question. This scenario is quite different from the popular usage of most secular genres of literature, especially those that are transmitted in oral form, where connectivity and context are factors of utmost importance.

That the literary texts of translated Scripture are *secondary texts* must also be borne in mind. They are "secondary in the sense that each biblical text represents another text, a source text from a different world,...the strange world of the ancient near east" (ibid.:30). While the extent to which a given cultural group regards the biblical setting as different from their own may be debated (and a great deal of careful research needs to be carried out in order to determine this),[123] the point is that translators need to anticipate all areas of potential misunderstanding or zero understanding and deal with them proactively, whether in the text itself or in the accompanying paratext (footnotes, glossary, cross-references, section headings, and illustrations). These include all references to culturally unfamiliar referents as well as imperceptible presuppositions and implicatures associated with the source text. One's hermeneutical concern in this respect must be extended, however, to include those literary and rhetorical usages of the biblical text that may be more or less alien to the target language (e.g., divine passives, sudden pronominal shifts, concentrated clusters of event nouns or prepositional phrases, certain metaphors and similes, indirect and embedded speech, the preferred type of participant reference, and relative sentence/utterance length).

The notion of genre in relation to a given literary or oral tradition may be explored from either an *emic* or an *etic* point of view, the emic perspective being language-culture specific and etic the universal perspective. Emic categories will be discussed in section 3.1.1 and etic categories in 3.1.2.

3.1.1 Emic categories

Emic distinctions are those that are made *within* a given language and literary tradition. Language-specific terms for different genres help us in

---

[123]While I would agree that the "perceived authenticity" of a Bible translation on the part of the target constituency is an important factor to consider, I would not automatically value it more highly than stylistic naturalness or semantic clarity, as some, such as Anderson 1998, propose. Perceptions can be modified, as Anderson points out, through "a gradual re-education of the receptor audience" (ibid.:9), and this would include adequate instruction concerning the "literary" (artistic/rhetorical) nature and purpose of the original text, which complement its *actual* authenticity as "Scripture." Furthermore, popular perceptions may be *wrong* as well as right—based perhaps upon some exotic interpretation derived from a wrongly construed, hence misunderstood, literal translation.

distinguishing emic categories since they represent an "internal," indigenous perspective on the literary phenomena concerned. In the case of the Bible, however, such terms are not often explicitly used to describe the different types of literature. Even when an explicit designation is given, the terms are usually difficult to define due to their generality or our lack of information concerning them. Schökel concludes that "[t]he Hebrews show awareness of different literary genres, but they are not clearly differentiated" (1988:8).

Our difficulty in defining many of the specific literary terms applied to different psalms is well known, for example, *maskil* (מַשְׂכִּיל) in Ps. 32:1, *miktam* (מִכְתָּם) in Ps. 16:1, *shiggaion* (שִׁגָּיוֹן) in Ps. 7:1, and the enigmatic "song of ascents" (שִׁיר לַמַּעֲלוֹת) in Ps. 120:1. Other terms are broadly inclusive and give little help. For example, *mashal* (מָשָׁל) may be used as a generic reference to various kinds of wisdom discourse such as a proverb (1 Sam. 10:12), a derogatory epithet (Ps. 69:11), an oracle (Num. 23:7–10), a taunt song (Isa. 14:4–21), a parable (Ezek. 17:2–10), a lyric ode (Num. 21:27–30), a didactic psalm (Psalm 78), and ethical maxims (Proverbs 10).

The Greek παραβολή 'parable' is not much easier to pinpoint in meaning and is rendered variously as "parable" (Luke 13:6), "proverb" (Luke 6:39), "symbol" (Heb. 9:9), "figure" (Heb. 11:19), and "comparison" (Mark 4:30). Despite the problems of definition, however, such technical emic terminology must certainly be noted wherever it occurs in the biblical text, if for no other reason than as a stimulus to see what competent biblical commentators have to say on its possible literary and exegetical significance in the particular co-text concerned.

3.1.2 Etic categories

Many universal, externally derived systems of etic analysis have been proposed for classifying the various kinds of literature to be found in the Scriptures. Their key components are combined and presented in this section. One must also recognize the presence of a dynamic, flexible literary *poetry* ⟺ *prose* continuum of stylistic features and the fact that many biblical books exhibit texts of mixtures or degrees between the two putative poles of genre "purity." Thus in many cases a particular text will be *both-and*, rather than *either-or* in this respect. Finally, if one wished to distinguish the various emic and etic literary categories, one might refer to the emic category as "genres" (proper), and to the etic category as discourse "types."

3.1.2.1 Poetry

There are a number of literary features which, taken together, distinguish Hebrew poetry from relatively more prosaic texts.[124] These features include (1) composition in the form of comparatively short (average three "words"), balanced, rhythmic utterances (*cola*) that normally occur in parallel linguistic patterns and/or coupled as sense units; (2) a tendency for a progressive heightening (e.g., intensification, specification, dramatization) of expression as the text is developed on all levels of structural organization; (3) a greater incidence of phonological foregrounding; (4) direct speech as the preferred mode of communication; (5) a higher concentration of imagery and figurative language; (6) lexical-syntactic condensation (e.g., lack of transitional markers such as the *waw* copula in a second parallel line, particles indicating a direct object or relative clause, nominal ellipsis, verb gapping); (7) obvious variations from normal narrative word order (e.g., "insertion," A—*X*—B); (8) a generally wider semantic range of vocabulary with a heavy concentration in the religious terminology of worship, repentance, prayer, and restoration; and (9) a fuller manifestation of larger, often symmetrical discourse arrangements, including overlapping, concentric (chiastic), and acrostic structures.[125]

[124]For a brief description of the difference between prose and poetry in Biblical Hebrew, see P. House 1988:29–36. The great Russian linguist and literary critic, Roman Jakobson, summarized what was for him the essence of poetry in the following dictum: "The poetic function [of literature] projects the principle of equivalence from the axis of selection into the axis of combination" (cited in Pomorska and Rudy 1985:147). Thus in poetic discourse, various types of equivalence (or similarity, whether phonological, lexical, or syntactic) constitute the essential organizing principle according to which a given text is composed. Waugh (1985:150) says, "There is, in other words, a radical parallelistic reorientation of all the verbal material as it relates to the building of the sequence....Moreover, such parallelisms create a network of internal relations within the poem itself, making the poem into an integrated whole and underlining the poem's relative autonomy." In biblical literature such structured patterning serves to define text boundaries and to highlight certain features of content in keeping with the author's communication intentions for the message at hand.

[125]There are, of course, other more sophisticated and specifically literary techniques that could be noted (see Wendland 2002a, chap. 5). One is the apparently widespread use of text-structuring by means of extended patterns of "metrical chiasm" (based on lineal word counts) and numerical arrangements (based on symbolic numbers such as 3, 7, 10, 17, 22, 26, and their multiples). Three other examples are the placement of divine names within a book or pericope; the frequency and distribution of certain key words; and breaks in parallelism and rhythmic sequences (see Bliese 2003). Since my primary interest is with the biblical text as it was presumably *aurally* apprehended by original and subsequent *audiences*, I do not consider devices of such literary intricacy in my analytical approach.

One could ask, "Who was the intended audience for these elaborate literary patterns?" They would not be hearers of the text, since the system requires the counting of written letters. Possibly the poet/compiler wanted to enhance the aesthetic beauty of the biblical text and therefore used whatever techniques were available within a community of educated

These poetic devices operate in varied combinations to perform certain *functions*, such as (1) to broadly organize and arrange a given text; (2) to pinpoint and highlight certain structural and thematic elements within it; (3) to express with greater or lesser degrees of intensification the author/speaker's emotions, moods, and attitudes and evoke corresponding feelings within the audience; (4) to forcefully impress upon listeners, by means of the very language that is used, the importance of the message being transmitted, including its particular moral imperatives and religious instruction; and (5) to bring the faithful psychologically and spiritually into the presence of the God whom they are worshiping (especially via the familiar phatic forms of liturgical language). Clearly, it is an essential part of the translation task to convey this same level of communicative significance—including connotative as well as denotative aspects—in the TL, selecting from the inventory of linguistic and literary resources that are available there. As part of this exercise of determining functional matches or correspondents in the TL, it may be necessary also to differentiate types of poetry, especially if these happen to be associated with disparate communication settings and purposes in the target culture.

Four principal etic types, or macrogenres, of biblical poetry may be posited, although these often appear in close combination or in mixed form:

- *Lyric*—for panegyric, liturgical, expressive, and evocative proclamation (e.g., Psalms).
- *Didactic*—for conveying moral instruction and religious information (e.g., Proverbs).

---

readers who could appreciate such patterns. However, features such as the center of metrically chiastic structures, twenty-six-letter lines, and rhythmic breaks are not mere stylistic embellishments, being posited as markers of prominence in poetic discourse (ibid.:131–133).

Problems for exegetes and translators then arise in cases where analysts using different approaches differ also in their opinion of where instances of prominence occur within a given book (as in Amos) and what they signify, that is, what the key points of structural form and/or thematic content are (see Wendland 1988). Who is the translator to believe and follow, and according to what criteria can translation decisions be made? These are some of the issues that have restricted the great potential usefulness of literary and rhetorical studies in Bible translation. Perhaps this dilemma will never be solved and translators will be left to adopt an eclectic method, as in the past, or to resort on a case by case basis to majority opinion. While perhaps acceptable from a technical or practical point of view, such a textual approach is aesthetically unsatisfactory, tending to diminish or downplay the unity of the artistic whole. I therefore strongly second Jan de Waard's call (in de Regt, de Waard, and Fokkelman 1996:251) for "a handbook on Hebrew [and Greek] rhetoric for translators."

- *Hortatory*—for pastoral reproof, criticism, consolation, and encouragement (e.g., Amos).
- *Predictive*—for visions or oracles revealing future events, +/– explicit warning or comfort (e.g., Ezekiel 38–39).

We find all four of these poetic types in the Book of Hosea, for example, 7:1–10 (hortatory), 14:8–9 (didactic), 11:8–9 (lyric), and 14:4–7 (predictive). The question then arises, Is it possible to convey these distinct lyrical styles (with or without the various formal aspects involved), along with their essential functional and contextual implications, by means of similar distinctions in the language of translation? If not, how great is the loss in terms of meaning equivalence, and how might this deficit of overall message significance be at least partially replaced or compensated for?[126]

Literary analysts normally subdivide the preceding four general categories of poetry into a number of subtypes according to form and/or function, for example, whether segments of narrative (as in epic) or dialogue (as in drama) are included (see P. House 1988:39–44). In the Psalms it is useful to distinguish the following etic types in terms of their major function and manner of liturgical expression (see Wendland 1998a, chap. 2), these often being combined in various ways within a single text and being further differentiated into *individual* ("I") and *communal* ("we") psalms. The illustrative quotations that follow are taken from the NRSV:

- **Petition** (*lament*), in which a definite request is made for help from God in a time of great danger, testing, or need.
  Rescue me, O my God, from the hand of the wicked,
  from the grasp of the unjust and cruel. (Ps. 71:4; see also Psalm 70)
- **Thanksgiving** (*eulogy*), in which God is thanked for assistance or deliverance received during some past situation of deprivation, illness, or threat.

---

[126]The notion of equivalence is not easy to define. For my purposes, Nord's attempt (following Reiss) is quite satisfactory: " 'Equivalence'...is a static, result-oriented concept describing a relationship of 'equal communicative value' between two texts or, on lower ranks, between words, phrases, sentences, syntactic structures and so on. In this context 'value' refers to meaning, stylistic connotations or communicative effect" (Nord 1997:35–36). The assessment of "values" in relation to verbal texts must be determined sociolinguistically on the basis of a text's interaction with its context, including those who are participating in the communication event. The notion of translational equivalence applies then to the meaning relationship between two texts, with primacy of reference directed towards the original and normative source text. In the case of a function-oriented approach to translation, a special concern for the target language might be better termed "functional appropriateness" rather than "functional equivalence."

He delivered me from my strong enemy,
and from those who hated me;
for they were too mighty for me. (Ps. 18:17; see also Psalm 30)

- **Praise** (*hymn*), in which the person, character, and behavior of God is praised in terms of his greatness, goodness, and glory.
  Praise the LORD!
  How good it is to sing praises to our God;
  for he is gracious… (Ps. 147:1; see also Psalm 100)

- **Instruction** (*homily*), in which people are taught how to live a life pleasing to God in thought, word, and deed, often in contrast to the wicked.
  Fools say in their hearts, "There is no God."
  They are corrupt, they commit abominable acts;
  there is no one who does good. (Ps. 53:1; see also Psalm 1)

- **Profession** (*creed*), in which the psalmist expresses his complete trust in God as the unfailing provider and protector of his life and entire being.
  God is our refuge and strength,
  a very present help in trouble.
  Therefore we will not fear… (Ps. 46:1–2a; see also Psalm 23)

A literary classification such as this encourages translators to think more precisely in terms of form and function, both as they analyze the biblical text and also while they are rendering the passage meaningfully in their target language. The psalms are not "all the same"; certainly they are not nearly as similar in nature as many people think. Rather, there are many shades of compositional diversity, the obviously different hues as well as those that are more subtle. These divergences in style and content are associated with corresponding changes in setting and communicative purpose. This concerns information—or better, semantic significance—which needs to be conveyed in the TL, whether via an available genre of poetry or some form of poetically heightened discourse. The goal is to ensure that the translated message carries an equivalent level of impact and appeal, of power and beauty.

Having recognized the five broad types of psalmody, translators may move on to consider thematic and functional subcategories. (Many of them are discussed in commentaries and study Bible notes.) For example, there are passages as well as larger pericopes that may be labeled with the subsidiary notions of *remembrance* (historical), *retribution* (imprecatory), *liturgical* (ritual), *repentance* (penitential), and *royal* (panegyric). The following quotations (from the NRSV) illustrate these subcategories:

Our ancestors, when they were in Egypt,
did not consider your wonderful works;
they did not remember the abundance of your steadfast love,
but rebelled against the Most High at the Red Sea.
(Ps.106:7, *remembrance*)

Let them be put to shame and dismayed forever;
let them perish in disgrace.
(Ps. 83:17, *retribution*)

It is he who remembered us in our low estate,
for his steadfast love endures forever;
and rescued us from our foes,
for his steadfast love endures forever;
who gives food to all flesh,
for his steadfast love endures forever.
(Ps. 136:23–25, *liturgical*)

Against you, you alone, have I sinned, and done evil in your sight,
so that you are justified in your sentence and blameless when you pass
    judgment.
(Ps. 51:4, *repentance*)

Then he will speak to them in his wrath,
and terrify them in his fury, saying,
"I have set my king on Zion, my holy hill."
(Ps. 2:5–6, *royal*)

Is it possible to convey moods, emotions, attitudes, and overtones such as these in languages other than Hebrew? Surely it can be done—but translators commissioned with this challenging theological, as well as literary, task first need to be cognizant of what is actually present in terms of overall significance in the SL text. Second, they must be actively aware of the full store of poetic resources available to choose from, whether in the original or modified form, in their mother tongue.

A similar study of common generic types and subtypes, including a diversity of mixed genres, can be profitably made for the *sapiential* and *prophetic* poetry of Old Testament literature.[127] While such an exercise cannot be carried out properly within the confines of the present study, several points of special literary interest may be noted with regard to the prophets. The first is that, as primarily divine proclamation (God to

---

[127]Berry (1995) provides an excellent overview of wisdom poetry in the Hebrew Bible. For a summary listing of the various prophetic genres from a form-critical perspective, see Sweeney 1996:512–544. Another instructive survey is found in Aune 1991:88–101. Note that "prophetic" poetry may be distinguished from the "lyric" poetry of the Psalms by means of stylistic features such as parallelisms that are less strict, prosaic insertions, a predominance of cause-effect relations, scatological and other types of shocking imagery, and the prevalence of criticism, rebuke, accusation, and warning (see Wendland 2002b:207).

people), prophetic discourse is more aggressively imperative or prescriptive and less expressive or affective than the psalmic genres are (people to God). The prophet-poets are also much more concerned with individual as well as corporate issues of judgment and its outcome, whether denunciation or deliverance. Furthermore, in the predictive passages of prophecy, there is also a future referential aspect (national, messianic, or eschatological), which is not often found in the poetry of prayer, praise, and worship.

Another notable feature of poetic prophecy is its explicit marking of words of divine origin. An "oracular formula" typically announces the onset of a new speech or thematic/pragmatic segment and, less frequently, the close of such a unit. Even a medial passage of special importance may be similarly signaled. Among such structural and emissarial indicators are the following familiar expressions: "Hear the word of the LORD" (Isa. 10:1); "Go and say to..." (Isa. 7:3–4); "Thus says the LORD" (Isa. 44:6); "The word of the LORD that came to..." (Mic. 1:1); "This is what the LORD God showed me" (Amos 7:1); "On that day" (Hos. 2:16); "then you/they will know that..." (Ezek. 33:33); and "says the LORD God" (Amos 4:8). Appropriate formulaic, discourse-marking equivalents need to be discovered, or carefully created, in the TL and then appropriately placed in the translated text in positions that signal the beginning, ending, or peak of a prophetic discourse segment, whether major or minor. The various levels of quotative embedding that often occur with such prophetic formulas must also be marked in an appropriate, unambiguous manner, as at the beginning of the Book of Zechariah (1:1–4).

There is yet another major diagnostic principle worth mentioning, one that is also structural or organizational in nature: Many of the prophets' "pronouncements" or "sermons" (which are two possible ways of characterizing their speechwriting), whether for weal or woe, frequently fall into a basic two-part pattern that needs to be clearly distinguished in translation. Thus there will be a promissory or minatory *declaration* from Yahweh, either of future blessing or of present condemnation, preceded by one of the previously mentioned formulas and often accompanied by some other conventional utterance(s). This divine declaration uttered through his prophet is supported by a corresponding *reason*—usually a forceful word of accusation for past or present sins committed in violation of Yahweh's gracious covenant with his people (indictment). Alternatively, the pronouncement may take the form of lavish praise for religious loyalty or, more often, a pastoral enunciation of the pure mercy of God. These two principal discourse functions, declaration and reason, may appear in either order, first or second, even within the same book. An example is seen in Isa. 43:1, which is a typical "salvation oracle":[128]

But now thus says the LORD,	[FORMULA]
He who created you, O Jacob...	[DIVINE ATTRIBUTION]
Do not fear, for I have redeemed you...	[REASSURANCE]
When you pass through the waters, I will be with you... when you walk through fire, you shall not be burned...	[PROMISE OF **BLESSING**]
Because you are precious in my sight, and honored, and I love you...	**[REASON]**

In contrast, a "judgment oracle" sounds like this, in Isa. 1:21, 24–25:

How the faithful city has become a whore!	**[REASON]**
She that was full of justice, righteousness lodged in her— but now murderers!...	
Therefore says the Sovereign,	[FORMULAIC TRANSITION]
the LORD of hosts, the Mighty One of Israel:	
Ah, I will pour out my wrath on my enemies,	[PREDICTION OF **JUDGMENT**]
and avenge myself on my foes! I will turn my hand against you; I will smelt away your dross as with lye and remove all your alloy.	

Such functionally complex passages, consisting of a divine declarative assertion coupled with its associated rationale, permeate the literary-religious discourse of the prophets. Another common pattern is the "disputation speech,"

---

[128]More detailed procedures for analyzing the literature of Hebrew prophetic discourse are presented in Wendland 1995b along with extensive exemplification Hosea and Joel. Seven common thematic components occur in prophetic writing (normally accompanied by characteristic formulas and stereotypical language). According to P. House (1988: 113–115), these are, in the order of usual occurrence, (1) certification (a speech of *YHWH*), (2) covenantal obligations, (3) human rebellion, (4) divine judgment, (5) divine compassion, (6) divine deliverance and restoration, and (7) human testimony. There is a general movement from religious ruin to renewal in the works of the prophets, though the detailed outworking of this is often quite complex, both thematically and structurally, as, for example, in Zeph. 1:2–3:8 → 3:9–20, an overall development that manifests a number of twists and surprises within a basic sequence of divine pronouncement followed by prophetic reflection (e.g., 1:2–6 → 7, 1:8–13 → 14–16, 1:17–18 → 2:1–3...).

which generally consists of three basic elements: (1) a religious (theological or moral) *thesis* put at issue by the people, (2) the divine *counter-thesis* for which the prophet argues, and (3) the elaborated *argument*. The Book of Malachi has a recurrent pattern of this kind (see Wendland 1985). Translators must pay special attention to these SL text types so that both the rhetorical impact and the perlocutionary implications of the message may be clearly and naturally reproduced in the TL. If this is not attended to, at least some measure of skewing will probably result.

It is important to keep in mind that although some debate the presence of pure poetry in the New Testament (except for LXX quotations), poetic discourse *is* undoubtedly manifested there to a greater or lesser degree. This is especially evident in the artistically crafted, rhetorically toned segments of prose that can appear without warning in the discourses of Christ or the hortatory writings of his apostles. One of the outstanding instances of artfully composed theology is Paul's paean to love in 1 Corinthians 13, as illustrated by vv. 1–3 (NRSV, reformatted):

> If I speak in the tongues of mortals and of angels,
> > but do not have love,
> > > I am a **noisy** gong or a clanging cymbal.
> And if I have prophetic powers,
> and understand all mysteries and all knowledge,
> and if I have all faith, so as to remove mountains,
> > but do not have love,
> > > I am nothing.
> If I give away all my possessions,
> and if I hand over my body to be burned,   [CLIMAX]
> > but do not have love,
> > > I gain **nothing**.

It cannot be denied that 1 Corinthians 13, if not actually composed in a Greek poetic meter, is about as close as prose can come to purely expressive lyric. In other words, it is "poetic prose." The rhetorical effect is naturally more prominent in the *original* language and when the text is expressively read, recited, or chanted *aloud*. The euphonious, balanced, and rhythmic literary form clearly contributes to the ultimate transmission of meaning here, not only in terms of this panegyric piece itself, but also with respect to the epistle as a whole. In fact, a good case could be made for viewing chapter 13 as constituting the thematic and stylistic epitome of the entire letter.

We can ask ourselves, then, how this climactic section of 1 Corinthians measures up in our local translations. How close or comparable is the overall effect of the text as expressed in the vernacular versions that we happen to be translating or are presently using? To be sure, even the best efforts will undoubtedly be found wanting from an L-R point of view when weighed against the original. However, that does not absolve translators of the obligation to at least consider an attempt to reproduce certain aspects of this dimension of artistic apostolic significance.

3.1.2.2 Prose

The general stylistic quality of Hebrew prose, or of the more prosaic texts, is perhaps most effectively defined by a *minus* description-by a relative *reduction* in the incidence of those features that constitute poetry in the Hebrew Bible. Accordingly, we would expect to see in prose a decrease in number of measured, rhythmically and symmetrically shaped bicola or larger units; less phonological embellishment; fewer concentrations of imagery; not as much abbreviated syntax and ellipsis; and less lexical diversity. Conversely, we would expect to see an *increase* in the so-called prose particles (the sign of the direct object, the definite article, the relative pronoun, and various prepositions), and we would see more standard word order (Verb-Subject-Object being the norm for Hebrew narrative discourse). This is not to say that poetic features do not appear in prose. It is simply a matter of frequency—fewer of these features occur than in poetry and in doses that are not as dense or diverse.

Four frequently interrelated etic functional macrotypes are seen in the prose texts of the Bible:[129]

- *Narration*—presents a chronologically arranged sequence of character-based speech and action events, at times incorporating one account or quotation within another, and often overlapping one story or report with another (e.g., the "Patriarch cycle" of Genesis).
- *Exposition*—explains how or why something is said or done, sets forth an ordered set of facts (e.g., genealogy, census), enunciates a series of laws or directions, or instructs concerning a particular moral or theological topic.
- *Exhortation*—offers criticism (rebuke, reproof, admonition, warning) or edification (commendation, encouragement, comfort, confirmation) in the form of commands and advice to a specific audience or receptor group with regard to their attitudes and behavior (e.g., the speeches of Ezra and Nehemiah).

---

[129]Compare these four to Longacre's basic quartet of narrative, procedural, behavioral, and expository discourse (described in Dooley and Levinsohn 2001:4). His "procedural" text is similar in some respects to narrative, but it lacks a character focus and there is generally no tension (climax) involved. Prophecy is a type of future oriented ("projected") exposition or narrative.

- *Description*—verbally visualizes a scene in order to stimulate or evoke a mental image of some character, event, object, scene, or setting. (Pure description is normally included as part of one of the preceding three types.)

Most vernacular literatures or oral traditions will have instances of these four major prose types, with narrative undoubtedly being the principal one within the complete corpus of verbal art forms, as it is also in the Bible. However, the general inventory of TL stylistic elements and their usage may well differ. That is, the stylistic features that characterize each TL prose type will vary from those found in the Scriptures, for example, with respect to the amount of direct speech incorporated, the manner of personal address, tense/mood usage, or the incidence of nouns as opposed to pro-forms. There may also be differences with regard to the primary communicative purpose or social situation in which the discourse is used. This is the case in the Chichewa language,[130] where traditional narrative is primarily fictive and didactic in nature and told in a setting of a public oral performance.

Narrative is clearly identified in Hebrew by the *wayyiqtol* verbal construction for reporting a sequence of past events and in Greek by the multitude of *kais* linking the main action verbs of any given pericope. Of course, many of the other features that typify narratives around the world are also present in most cases, such as an implied *author/narrator* with a distinct *point of view* (third person, omniscient and omnipresent, but usually unobtrusive);[131] an implied *audience* (normally unmentioned); an episodic sequential *character sketch* with the focus on character(s), not events; a climactic *plot structure* (initial situation=>inciting incident [conflict/controversy] => progressive development => eventive/emotive climax => [partial/temporary] resolution); various *characters* (flat, round, agents, or props); and a prevailing *setting* (geographical, temporal, social, historical).

---

[130]Chichewa (also known as Chinyanja) is a southeastern Bantu tongue spoken as a first or second language by some twelve million Chewa people in Malawi, Zambia, and Mozambique. I have included many Chichewa illustrations in the present study because they have been actually used in Bible translation, either in published versions or those of an experimental nature.

[131]There are certain exceptions and variations in the corpus of biblical narrative with regard to the different features mentioned here—the active implied "narrator" of Nehemiah, for example, or the degree of omniscience allowed in an account, the number of subplots included within a given book, or the amount of background information that is supplied. These generally do not involve issues that concern the translator. A clear exception, however, is the presence of parenthetical intrusions into the narrative by the author, for these need to be appropriately marked in a translation (as in Gen. 32:32; Josh. 5:4–7; 1 Sam. 19:24).

Of greater importance to Bible translators than these general features is the nature of the artistry and rhetoric found within a specific text (see sec. 3.2.3). According to many scholars, Old Testament narrative may also be broadly characterized by the presence of five important literary attributes: (1) verbal *repetition* or various types of synonymy; (2) analogous or antithetical *event sequences* and parallel patterns; (3) dramatic *dialogue*, frequently contrastive in nature, used for both characterization and thematic development; (4) the deliberate *omission* or withholding of nonfocal supplementary details, producing at times a rather bare account; and (5) *irony* and understatement.[132] These are features that may be manifested to a greater or lesser degree in most of the oral and literary traditions of the world. In cases where the disparity between SL and TL is significant (e.g., in the relative incidence of direct speech or exact repetition), then some extensive modifications will have to be made during translation in order to preserve a natural style in the TL.

Narration is the principal prose type of the Old and New Testaments not only because it is the most commonly occurring type but also because it is the one that most readily incorporates any of the other three kinds, either in the occasional narrator comment (for explanation or evaluation) or, more often, in the direct speech of the various characters. The Book of Ruth is undoubtedly the purest narrative in the Hebrew Bible, displaying a masterful combination of the "hallmarks of effective historiography," namely, selectivity, simplification, and suggestive detail (V. P. Long 1994:73). The extended family histories *(toledoth)* of Genesis, on the other hand, are very diverse in terms of including an assortment of other genres, but well-formed and connected nonetheless.

Exposition plays a large role in Old Testament juridical and legislative discourse (e.g., Leviticus, Deuteronomy). It is also prominent in the New Testament Epistles, where it normally precedes or alternates with portions of paraenesis or exhortation as in Romans and Hebrews.

Description is most common in the primarily directive accounts of the establishment of the Israelite system of worship (e.g., Exodus 25–40). It is also prominent in the visionary or apocalyptic genres (e.g., Ezekiel 40–48, Revelation).

Within these four principal types there are, of course, a variety of minor genres, not necessarily prosaic in nature; and in the Bible, as in other literature, we often see them co-mingled. Ryken and Longman (1993:367)

---

[132]For more on these basic attributes of biblical narrative, see Alter 1981:179–184, also Ryken and Longman, eds. 1993:76–78. The most detailed description of Hebrew prose narrative—its literary qualities and rhetorical workings—is found in the magisterial work of Meir Sternberg (1985). A discussion of irony in specific relation to prophetic discourse is in chapter 6 of Wendland 1995b.

observe, "Considered as literature,…what most characterizes the New Testament is the mingling of literary convention and innovation." For example, in the variegated "narrative" (διηγησις) of Luke, we find, along with the central ideologically toned biographical account, such diverse items as a parable (e.g., 8:5–8), its explanation (8:11–15), enigma (5:34–35), didactic oration (6:20–49), directive instruction (9:3–5), diatribe (7:24–35), proverb (4:23), prophecy (quoted, 3:4–6; new, 21:25–28), genealogy (3:23–38), and hymn (1:46–55). A similar well-composed mixture occurs in Samuel and in the quasi-narrative apocalyptic discourse of Revelation. In composition of this nature, the recorded events often serve merely in a transitional role, for example, to get Christ from one setting and situation to another, or as an introduction to a portion of foregrounded direct speech. In this respect the prose of the Gospels can be very complex in literary and functional terms, as we see in Mark 2:23–28:

> One sabbath he was going through the grainfields; and as they made their way his disciples began to pluck heads of grain. [**narrative**—setting the scene] The Pharisees said to him, "Look, why are they doing what is not lawful on the sabbath?" [**direct speech: accusation/challenge** vis-à-vis ethical legality] And he said to them [onset of the **rebuttal/riposte**], "Have you never read [indirect **citation** of authoritative Scripture] what David did when he and his companions were hungry and in need of food? [referential narrative **analogy**] He entered the house of God, when Abiathar was high priest, and ate the bread of the Presence, which it is not lawful for any but the priests to eat, and he gave some to his companions." [casuistic **example**—of a great ancestor] Then he said to them, "The sabbath was made for humankind, and not humankind for the sabbath [relevant religious **maxim**]; so the Son of Man is lord even of the sabbath." [climactic **conclusion**—spurious accusation parried, basic theological principle established]

As this passage illustrates, "only half of the content of the Gospels is narrative material. The rest is sayings, discourses, parables, and didactic conversations" (Ryken and Longman, eds. 1993:367; see also Bailey and vander Broek 1992:8). These literary forms may need to be overtly differentiated from each other and marked in translation. This can be done extratextually by means of the typographical format (e.g., a new paragraph, indention, separate lines for distinct utterance units) or a well-positioned section heading. It is also necessary in a translation to distinguish the discourse textually—hence audibly—by whatever means available in the TL. Ways of doing this include: initial formulaic or conventional expressions (e.g., "There once was a man who…" in Luke 8:5); discourse transitional indicators (e.g., "Jesus began to teach them saying..." in Luke 6:20); and a verbal style that is natural and appropriate to the genre based on accepted vernacular literary standards (e.g., tense/aspect usage, the mode of participant reference, the degree of explicitness or implicitness, and distinctive vocabulary). This last is especially important when two or more distinct genres are juxtaposed within the same literary context, such as the dramatically contrastive "blessings" and "woes" of Luke 6:20–26.

New Testament epistolary literature is quite complex in terms of its generic constitution. Many long articles and monographs have been written in the attempt to differentiate one genre, stereotyped usage, or rhetorical device from another. But for our purposes it is sufficient simply to note this diversity of form in order to make translators aware of its presence and implications for their work. As part of any message of apostolic instruction and pastoral exhortation, for example, we find incorporated conventional Jewish or Hellenistic genres such as diatribe, midrash, apocalyptic segments, *topoi*, vice and virtue lists, the "household code," liturgical fragments, hymn portions, and, on occasion, selected techniques of Greco-Roman argumentation (see sec. 6.2.2). Observe, for example, the varied forms of appeal that are concentrically combined within the diachronic development of the discourse to comprise the forceful argument of the short Epistle of Jude:

Letter *Opening* and *Benediction* (1–2)
| *Exhortation*—Purpose of the epistle (contend for the faith, 3)
| | *Motivation*—Threefold accusation concerning "intruders" (4)
| | | *Reminder*—Warning via 3 analogies of evil from the OT Scriptures (5–7)
| | | | *Application*—Accusation renewed, in triple form (8)
| | | | | *Example*—Historical contrast to the intruders (Michael, 9)
| | | | | | *Description*—Accusation renewed, in triple form (10)
| | | | | | | ➔*Warning*—"woe" oracle + 3 examples (11)
| | | | | | *Description*—Metaphoric accusation, 2 x 3 (12–13)
| | | | | *Example*—Historical prophecy of the intruders (Enoch, 14–15)
| | | | *Application*—Accusation renewed, in triple form (16)
| | | *Reminder*—Warning via predictions from the apostles (17–18)
| | *Motivation*—Threefold accusation concerning the intruders (19)
| *Exhortation*—Purpose of the epistle (build yourselves up in/on the faith, 20–23)
Letter *Closing* and *Doxology* (24–25)

Whether or not one accepts the proposed chiastic arrangement of this brief letter,[133] one must be impressed by the degree of literary diversity that it displays, including a basic midrashic manner of composition that often employs a notable biblical example or allusion plus a current

---

[133]For a more detailed, comparative discussion of the intricate composition of the Epistle of Jude, see Wendland 1994b.

application (see Bailey and vander Broek 1992:42–43). The letter clearly reveals a meaningful thematic unity despite its stylistic variation—with a structurally highlighted paraenetic focus upon the central prophetic ("woe"-full) warning. It would seem important then that certain aspects, at least, of this functionally significant formal organization be manifested in a contemporary translation somehow, along with the main textual and all pertinent intertextual connections.

I have given special attention to the subject of genre here because of its crucial importance to the entire enterprise of Bible analysis and translation. If the various genres of Scripture, along with their major subtypes and related discourse conventions, are not recognized and adequately dealt with, then it is quite unproductive to proceed with a literary-rhetorical approach. It is genre study that establishes the form-functional framework and foundation for everything else. From this broad perspective of the literary whole and its constituent parts we can then proceed to study a closely related—in fact, normally integrated—aspect of unified compositional tectonicity, namely, the varied textual patterns and structures that will be discussed in section 3.2. This leads to a consideration in chapter 4 of the major microstylistic devices and techniques that create the textual "artistry" of biblical literature and in chapter 5 of the different "archetypes" that contribute to the overall "iconicity" of the Scriptures. In chapter 6 is an overview of the varied means for generating the prominent "rhetorical force" that appears throughout much of the canonical corpus. However, these subjects will be treated in less detail, with special mention being made only of the literary features that appear to be of direct relevance to creative Bible translators interested in communicating more of the functional, including artistic, significance of what they find in the original text.[134]

3.2 Structures

The discourse arrangement of a literary text normally displays the unity of a particular discourse "design," though with varying degrees of

---

[134]As was already noted, the inclusion of an explicit literary component within one's overall translation strategy, or *Skopos* (see sec. 1.8), requires staff of a certain minimum level of intellectual, technical, and practical competence, both to comprehend the significance of this technical aspect of the biblical message and then to apply this knowledge skillfully and consistently in their work. Where the necessary degree of expertise and the corresponding level of commitment in terms of time and resources are absent or wanting, it may be advisable for a translation supervisor to omit a literary concern from the translation program *(Brief)*. It would probably prove to be too complicated or confusing and therefore be misapplied in practice.

clarity.[135] This verbal framework is constituted by the interaction of several compositional forces within a given text as a whole, each of which manifests a particular structure or pattern that is relatively more regular and predictable. Such organizational devices are distinct from the use of conventional genres, which results from a deliberate holistic choice on the part of an author. They are, probably, for the most part the product of a given author's intuitive skill in terms of artistic compositional strategy and technique. The different aspects of textual architecture need to be considered both individually and also in combination during any discourse analysis whether of a book, section, or pericope. These design features serve to identify the principal *units* of a given text, the *spatial arrangement* of these units with respect to one another, and the *semantic relationships* they have to each other as well as to the composition as a whole. After a brief definition of each type of structural variable, I will attempt to show how they interact in the realization of a familiar biblical passage known for its outstanding literary-rhetorical quality—that is, its power of aesthetic attraction, emotive expression, and persuasive appeal.

The chief elements of discourse design, or textual tectonics, may be categorized for ease of reference into four processes and four techniques. The four distinct but interrelated compositional *processes* (functions) are segmentation, connection, projection, and progression (sec. 3.2.1). The stylistic *techniques* (forms) are recursion, interruption, concentration, and condensation (sec. 3.2.2). Each of the processes (which, taken together, normally characterize a well-formed literary text) is effected by the application of one or more of the techniques. This occurs either sequentially or in combination during the creation—or subsequent translation—of an artistic, affective verbal composition.[136]

---

[135]"Every literary analysis needs to deal with structure, since themes, images, ideas, and actions must be revealed through a literary framework" (P. House 1988:55). Furthermore, "one must discern the intent of a structure before making statements about it" (ibid.:56), for example, the manner in which the Book of Zephaniah is structured thematically around the notion of the Day of the LORD—its present relevance and future implications.

[136]A literary approach to discourse analysis as proposed here is rather different from a strict linguistic methodology, but I would expect the respective results to correspond and converge in a number of important areas. The occurrence of any clashes or contrasts may mark points that require further study from one perspective or the other. No single method is sufficient to analyze a literary text completely, accurately, and relevantly; the most credible and helpful study normally involves a combined approach that selects and applies the principles and techniques of several different modes of analysis. Notable examples of a helpful linguistic procedure applied to biblical discourse include, for the Old Testament, Longacre 1989 and Wiklander 1984 and, for the New Testament, Guthrie 1994 and Levinsohn 1987.

3.2.1 The four processes of discourse design

The four processes of discourse design are defined as follows:

- *Segmentation* refers to the explicit and implicit demarcation of a text into a hierarchy of discrete but interrelated and diachronically organized compositional units from beginning to end, as well as inclusively from top to bottom, from the most to the least extensive structural segments.[137]
- *Connection* refers to the internal bonding of a text in terms of varied spans of cohesion (formal junction), stretches of coherence (semantic and pragmatic linkage), and points of greater or lesser transition (the junction between and among different structural units).
- *Progression* refers to the tendency for the semantic significance of a well-composed literary discourse to be teleological in nature, that is, purposefully forward-moving (goal-oriented) and cumulative in its overall development, with subsequent syntagmatic (contiguous) and paradigmatic (analogous) elements building resonantly and relationally upon those that have preceded them in the text (intra- and intertextuality).
- *Projection* refers to the formal highlighting and marking of larger "areas" and foregrounded "points" of particular structural importance ("peak," narrative or nonnarrative), emotive prominence ("climax"), and thematic salience (e.g., "topic" or "focus"), either within a part of the discourse, or with respect to the text as a complete whole.

These four processes, which merge in the construction of any verbal text, may be shown diagrammatically (in a very idealized and schematic fashion) as follows:

---

[137]The earliest (pre-Mishnaic) effort to segment the Hebrew text appears to be by means of intratextual markers to initiate longer and shorter sections, petuah or *peh* (פ) and *setuma* or *samek* (ס) respectively. This ancient system forms the basis for the new "pericope series" of structurally oriented commentaries, for example, Korpel 2001.

([|] = segmentation, [----] = connection, [➔] = progression, [#] = projection)

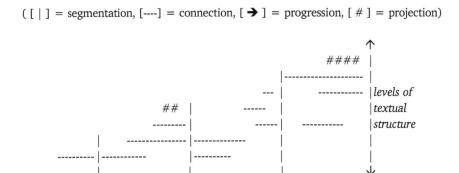

3.2.2 The four techniques of discourse design

The four techniques of literary discourse design are defined as follows:

- *Recursion* has to do with the various types of verbal reiteration—complete or partial; synonymous, contrastive, or antony-
  mous; phonological (e.g., rhythm, alliteration), grammatical (e.g.,
  a repeated syntactic frame or verbal tense), and lexical (e.g., a key
  term or opening formula)—that occur on a significant scale locally
  or globally within a given text. It includes the repetition of items selected from the same set of semantically related words, concepts, or
  topics as well as of formal elements that create extended discourse
  linear or concentric patterns.
- *Interruption* is the opposite of recursion in that it involves a clear
  disjunctive break of some sort in the flow of forward discourse
  movement. A novel element (or feature set) may be introduced, or
  there may be a shift in an existing component such as a new topic,
  imagery, point of focus, logical move, time, place, character,
  speaker, mood, or text type/genre.
- *Concentration* involves a conspicuous convergence, juxtaposition,
  or piling up of similar or diverse stylistic features (e.g., figurative
  language, intensifiers, rhetorical questions, repeated items, formulas, vocatives, or direct speech) intended to mark a compositional
  peak or border at a particular place in the discourse.
- *Condensation* is a deliberate deletion or shortening of overt text material (e.g., ellipsis, asyndeton, nominalization, pronomina-
  lization, allusion, summary) intended to create suspense, enigma,
  rhythm, or some special pattern of elements. It may also be employed as a marker within the larger discourse (e.g., to signal an

initial or final compositional boundary) or used for stylistic purposes in keeping with a particular genre or subgenre (e.g., poetry > lyric > lament > penitential psalm).

The presence and operation of any of these techniques is established, described, and assessed with greater credibility and consequence on the basis of the criteria of quantity and quality. In this respect, *quantity* refers to the sheer number of compositional features that are present in a given text; by *quality* is meant their relative objectivity, diversity, compatibility, perceptibility, and novelty.[138]

There are also a number of important structural *markers* in biblical literature that along with the recursion patterns help us to identify the organization of a particular text. These appear with significance at the following points of compositional prominence:

- Initial *aperture*, exemplified by typical opening formulas and expressions, intensifiers (vocative, rhetorical question, imperative), a preview summary or thematic orientation, asyndeton, contrast, change in setting, scene, subject matter, or major linguistic or literary form;
- Final *closure*, exemplified by a concluding saying, maxim, formula, summary-conclusion, emphatic utterance, transitional expression (i.e., transitioning to the next topic or unit of discourse), and the ending of a particular linguistic, literary, or rhetorical pattern;
- Internal *climax*, exemplified by vigorous action, a "crowded stage," direct speech, a concentration of key terms, figurative language, theological focus, or some significant repetition of form or content, this last being the most usual.

---

[138]The application of any individual or combination of these, recursion in particular, serves to create symmetrical arrangements and significant patterns of textual material such as parallelism, alternation, terracing, inclusio, exclusio, chiastic transposition (from the A-B-A "ring" to much longer element inversions), anaphora, anadiplosis, epiphora, and refrains. These different tectonic devices may be represented in formulas as follows (the brackets designate a discrete structural unit): *parallelism* = A+A', B+B', C+C' ...; *alternation* = A+B, A'+B', A"+B" ...; *terracing* = A+B, B'+C, C'+D...; *inclusio* = [A ... A']; *exclusio* = A [...] A'; *chiasmus* = $A+B+C$ ... $C'+B'+A'$; *anaphora* = [A...] + [A'...] + [A"...]...; *anadiplosis* = [... A] + [A' ...]; *epiphora* = [... A] + [... A'] + [... A"].... A refrain is similar to either anaphora or epiphora, but does not necessarily occur as part of a given structural unit. (For further explanation and illustration of such markers, see Dorsey 1999, chap. 2; Wendland 1995b, chaps. 2–3; and Wendland 2002b:208–210.) Other, more specific linguistic markers should also be noted, for example, the occurrence of progressive, pragmatically determined variations in main topic and central focus throughout a given text, as in ancient Hebrew narrative by means of a NP + *qatal* clause (see Heimerdinger 1999:261–263).

A thorough architectural analysis of the Scriptures is essential for both exegesis and translation. Not only does it contribute to a better understanding of a given biblical text, but it also makes possible a more accurate representation of the original message in any TL (whether by textual or extratextual means). A case in point is the value of discovering the pattern of synonymous transitional refrains in Matt. 7:28, 11:1, 13:53, 19:1, and 26:1 ("When Jesus had finished saying these things..."). This pattern suggests "a five book pattern that pays tribute to the Pentateuch and to Jesus as the new Moses" (Wilson 1997:42–43). Thus each "book" consists of an initial narrative and a subsequent discourse, for example, 3:1–4:25 (narrative) and 5:1–7:28 (discourse). Similarly, Guthrie's detailed study (1994, chap. 6) of key-term-constituted transitional constructions in the Book of Hebrews uncovers several major and a few minor patterns that help explain in a credible way the intricate and meaningful (motivated) discourse structure of this seemingly repetitious and disconnected pastoral document. These different types of transition play a key role in functionally interrelating the blocks of exposition and exhortation that alternate throughout most of the text of Hebrews to embody the Christological macrotheme: "God has spoken to us in [his] Son" (ibid.:144). Guthrie concludes, "The author of Hebrews was a highly skilled individual, a 'Mozart' of oratory, and his discourse a 'symphony' of form" (ibid.:147).

Any systematic, comprehensively applied L-R study will reveal many more of these "musical" passages of the Scriptures, from the one-line motifs to the full-score overtures. Hopefully it will also motivate translators to make them resound more audibly, even beautifully in their mother tongue.

Thus the skillful application and varied combination of such literary processes and techniques (including overlapping, enclosed, and interlocking structures) has the potential to accomplish a variety of important text-rhetorical *functions*. These include the creation of discourse unity (harmony, wholeness, etc.), textual shaping (symmetry, balance, etc.), aesthetic appeal, emotive impact, stylistic appropriateness, semantic movement or transition ("interlude" as in Job 28), a progression to climax or resolution, topical focus (similarity or contrast), thematic emphasis, and message memorability.[139] In other words, a biblical author (whether viewed as real or implied) utilized these design features in order to carry out certain communicative (interpersonal or "pragmatic") purposes in

---

[139]Closely related to this final motive is *synopsis*, that is, skillfully condensing a much longer literary discourse down to its essentials for effective reporting, as in Paul's sermon at the Areopagus. In this case, each clause or key word probably represents or is abstracted from a paragraph or more of actual speech (Acts 17:22–31).

relation to his intended audience and the exigencies of the particular rhetorical situation in which they are living, which in turn elicited the message at hand (see sec. 6.1). More specific, speech-act functions may then
be designated according to the content and context at any given point in
the discourse, for example, to instruct, warn, encourage, rebuke, inform,
or console a text's primary receptors as well as a more general readership
or audience.

In this connection, David Clark (1999) raises a number of interesting
and important questions concerning the relationship between structural
features and rhetorical intentions.[140] First of all, he asks, "[H]ow can we
derive the latter (relatively subjective conclusions) from the former (relatively objective data)?" While I feel that such broad functional processes
as segmentation, connection, projection, and progression are rather
clearly indicated by the selection and deployment of prominent L-R forms
within a given text, I would admit that the analysis becomes more subjective and speculative the more specific that one tries to be—for example, to
posit such intentions as warning, encouragement, and instruction, or such
emotive overtones as anger, sorrow, joy, and frustration. In fact, I do not
think that it is really possible to *directly* associate form and function in this
manner. The best one can do, then, is to objectively demonstrate on the
basis of textual data, including the actual content currently being conveyed, how a certain L-R device (e.g., a chiastic construction) may serve

---

[140]Clark's comments come as part of an in-house review of a 1996 work by de Regt, de
Waard, and Fokkelman. The subject of authorial intention has become rather controversial
in this age of "reader-response" and postmodern literary criticism. Who cares about the author, whether real or implied, anymore? Most serious communication-oriented theorists
still *do*. As David Katan (1999:126) says, "The idea that one needs to understand the underlying intention of a writer to translate effectively has been a cornerstone of translation theory." Katan further demonstrates how "the analysis of the three universal modeling
processes of generalization, distortion and deletion can increase the understanding of the
cultural and experimental worlds behind the original act of speaking or writing. As a consequence, we can more definitely point towards the psychological intentions of the originator of the message" (ibid.:95). These procedures would complement a careful study of the
author's presumed intentional or intuitive usage of the various stylistic and rhetorical resources of his language. It seems that many professional secular translators and translation
critics would agree (e.g., Wechsler 1998:109; Landers 2001:53).

Recent oral-aural studies of the Scriptures also presuppose the presence of a creative
author within the text. Lou Silberman puts the issue this way: "What if the text is vocally
constructed [as he proposes]? Can the author's voice be silenced [implied answer, 'Definitely not—not even for the skeptical Postmodernist!']" (cited in Wendland 1994a:19). As a
translation theorist of the functionalist school, Christiane Nord affirms that "As a rule, the
translator has to infer the sender's intention from the source text, interpreting the textual
features and consulting secondary sources.... [T]here are ways and means to interpret the
sender's intention, consciously and unconsciously, from the linguistic, stylistic and thematic markers in the text." Nord goes on to point out that "what is actually translated is not
the sender's intention but *the translator's interpretation of the sender's intention*" (1997:85).

to distinguish, intensify, or foreground a particular aspect of meaning, whether denotative or connotative. An example of the design function of stylistic technique may be seen in Paul's paean in praise of the energetic qualities of Christian love in 1 Cor. 13:4–13 (see sec. 3.2.3).

Clark (ibid.) also asks whether these "rhetorical intentions [are] more language-specific or culture-specific." In reply I would say that whereas the different functions mentioned above would tend to be more or less universal in literature, the particular ways (formal means) of marking or highlighting them are language- and culture-specific, perhaps also author- and even text-specific. But as Clark rightly observes, future research is needed for these matters, starting with studies of living authors who might be willing to provide feedback concerning their rhetorical and artistic intentions in a given literary work.[141]

3.2.3 An example of discourse design in the Scriptures—1 Cor. 13:4–13

An instance of rhetorically motivated text structuring can be seen in 1 Cor. 13:4–13. Where such a clear instance of discourse design appears (as confirmed by complementary analyses), one may expect to find others within the same document, as further studies of 1 Corinthians show.[142]

It will be helpful to display the Greek text of 1 Cor. 13:4-13, which exhibits both linear and concentric patterning, in order to demonstrate features that do not appear in a translation. This example illustrates the fact that the phonological structure can also be integrally involved in artistic arrangements, as here where there is a prominent rhythmic progression of short utterances.

Ἡ ἀγάπη μακροθυμεῖ,   X   (4)
χρηστεύεται ἡ ἀγάπη,

   οὐ ζηλοῖ, [ἡ ἀγάπη]   Y
   οὐ περπερεύεται,
   οὐ φυσιοῦται,

---

[141]I made an attempt to do this when preparing my dissertation (Wendland 1979). I spent many hours in the home of Mr. Chongo, questioning him in detail about the particular functional aim of the many different stylistic features of his popular stories. I would record such interviews and later refer to them when writing up my analysis of his artistry. This turned out to be an informal educative process that was just as beneficial as my formal academic one, at least with respect to the Nyanja language and literature.

[142]This is a modification of the pressure of symmetry principle in phonological study, that is, the "pressure of frequency." I made such an analysis in an unpublished paper, "The Rhetoric of Repetition: A Discourse Analysis of 1 Corinthians 8–16."

οὐκ ἀσχημονεῖ, (5)
οὐ ζητεῖ τὰ ἑαυτῆς,
οὐ παροξύνεται,
οὐ λογίζεται τὸ κακόν,
οὐ χαίρει ἐπὶ τῇ ἀδικίᾳ, (6)
συγχαίρει δὲ τῇ ἀληθείᾳ·

πάντα στέγει, X' (7)
πάντα πιστεύει,
πάντα ἐλπίζει,
πάντα ὑπομένει.

Η ἀγάπη οὐδέποτε πίπτει· A (8)

εἴτε δὲ προφητεῖαι, καταργηθήσονται· B
εἴτε γλῶσσαι, παύσονται·
εἴτε γνῶσις, καταργηθήσεται.

ἐκ μέρους γὰρ γινώσκομεν C (9)
καὶ ἐκ μέρους προφητεύομεν·
ὅταν δὲ ἔλθῃ τὸ τέλειον, (10)
τὸ ἐκ μέρους καταργηθήσεται.
ὅτε ἤμην νήπιος, D (11)
ἐλάλουν ὡς νήπιος,
ἐφρόνουν ὡς νήπιος,
ἐλογιζόμην ὡς νήπιος·
ὅτε γέγονα ἀνήρ, D'
κατήργηκα τὰ τοῦ νηπίου.

βλέπομεν γὰρ ἄρτι δι᾿ ἐσόπτρου ἐν αἰνίγματι, C' (12)
τότε δὲ πρόσωπον πρὸς πρόσωπον·
ἄρτι γινώσκω ἐκ μέρους,
τότε δὲ ἐπιγνώσομαι καθὼς καὶ ἐπεγνώσθην.

νυνὶ δὲ μένει πίστις, ἐλπίς, ἀγάπη, B' (13)
τὰ τρία ταῦτα·

μείζων δὲ τούτων ἡ ἀγάπη. A'

Love is patient X (4)
and kind;

love is not jealous Y
or boastful;

```
it is not arrogant
or rude.                                                    (5)
Love does not insist on its own way;
it is not irritable
or resentful;
it does not rejoice at wrong,                               (6)
but rejoices in the right.
```

```
Love bears all things,                          X'    (7)
believes all things,
hopes all things,
endures all things.
```

```
Love never ends;                                A     (8)

    as for prophecies, they will pass away;     B
    as for tongues, they will cease;
    as for knowledge, it will pass away.

        For our knowledge is imperfect          C    (9)
        and our prophecy is imperfect;
            but when the perfect comes,              (10)
            the imperfect will pass away.

            When I was a child,                  D   (11)
                I spoke like a child,
                I thought like a child,
                I reasoned like a child;
            when I became a man,                 D'
                I gave up childish ways.

        For now we see in a mirror dimly,        C'  (12)
            but then face to face.
        Now I know in part;
            then I shall understand fully,
            even as I have been fully understood.

    So faith, hope, love abide,                  B'  (13)
    these three;

But the greatest of these is LOVE.              A'
```

Even a relatively literal translation such as the RSV fails to duplicate the
linguistic unity manifested in the Greek text, and it leaves the design of
the discourse flawed or at best blurred in English. This is especially

apparent with respect to sound symmetry and rhythmic progression. In any case, a study of the Greek text reveals that this passage is an exceptional example of the four compositional processes of segmentation, connection, projection, and progression operating in harmonious functional interaction. The pericope as a whole is clearly demarcated into three subunits, vv. 1–3, 4–7, and 8–13. (Only the last two subunits have been quoted in full here; the first was formatted earlier in sec. 3.1.2.1.) Moreover, there are various formal and semantic threads of connectivity running throughout the entire pericope (e.g., the thematic topic of love) as well as some of its constituent units (e.g., the references to faith, hope, and love in vv. 7 and 13 that link the two principal sections). Finally, we note the two internal progressions that build up to a minor peak in v. 7 and a climactic major peak in 13b for the pericope as a whole.[143]

We also have some excellent examples in this passage of the four literary techniques of recursion, interruption, concentration, and condensation.[144] The many instances of recursion are obvious; this device is clearly the most evident, hence prominent, throughout the text (as it is in biblical discourse generally). Through Paul's skillful use of selection and arrangement, the various types of iteration—phonological, syntactic, and lexical—combine with some deliberate interruptions (e.g., the sudden introduction of 'prophecies', 'tongues', and 'knowledge' in B) to produce several important instances of conformation (text-patterning). For example, there is the simple chiasmus involving the placement of 'love' in v. 4a (obliterated in the RSV);[145] the parallelism of sound, sense, and syntax in v. 6 (to mark the close of its subsection); the 'now'–'then' alternation of v. 12; the simple contrastive X-Y-X' ring composition that structures vv. 4–7; and the prominent inversion that spans vv. 8–13 (A-A': inclusio based on love; B-B': three passing charismatic gifts versus three ever-remaining Christian graces; C-C': the partiality of our present knowledge in comparison with what it will be "then"; and the dramatic contrast between a

---

[143]The movement towards an ultimate "end stress" in this case is confirmed by the larger chiastic organization: When such a reverse parallel arrangement features an odd number of panels, the peak normally occurs in the middle, with a reinforcing or lesser emphasis at the end. In the case of an even numbered sequence, as we have here, the major focus is upon the text's conclusion in v. 13b.

[144]For a useful overview of this pericope based on Classical rhetoric, especially the use of examples and antithesis to highlight the theme of *agape*, see Mack 1990:64–66. (In sec. 6.2.2 of the present work is a summary of Classical rhetoric.)

[145]The overall structural pattern displayed in 1 Corinthians 13 would support a text-critical decision to include the third occurrence of 'love' in the *third* clause of v. 4 (which in the fourth edition of the UBS Greek text is bracketed).

childish and an adult spiritual state in D-D').[146] Instances of condensation
and concentration are less apparent, but they do occur, as with, respectively, the repeated ellipses of 'love' in vv. 4–6 and the juxtaposition of
figurative imagery, parallel phrasing, conceptual contrast, referential
shift ('we' => 'I'), wordplay, and a concluding aphorism in vv. 12–13.
   First Corinthians 13 is truly an outstanding instance of a literary-
rhetorical-shaped discourse. The crucial question again for translators is
this: how well—or comparable—does this text turn out in their rendition?
First of all, there is the artistically composed poetic style to consider.
Would the translation be evaluated in similar terms using the appropriate
TL criteria of excellence? In addition, it is important that translators take
care to reproduce the verbal parallels as closely as possible so that they
may act as perceptible clues (visual and/or aural) to the text's structural
arrangement in their version. Finally, translators might try, depending on
the nature of their version, to present an overt display of the corresponding ideas of the original text by means of the typographical format on the
printed page.[147]

---

[146]Obviously, some measures of control are necessary to substantiate the validity or
credibility of these larger textual patterns within a given pericope. The following eight criteria, in relatively decreasing order of importance, are helpful in this regard: (1) *closeness*,
in terms of the lexical repetition between presumed parallels, that is, the more exact, extensive, perceptible, and unit-specific the reiteration, the more persuasive the pattern being
proposed; (2) *inclusiveness*, meaning incorporation of or accounting for the entire pericope
within the suggested pattern, not excluding certain significant elements; (3) *essence*, meaning that the pattern covers a discrete discourse portion, one whose external boundaries may
be established by other means; (4) *parallelism* of conceptual content, for example, synonymous, antithetical, cause-effect, reciprocal, and positive-negative parallelism; (5) *relationship*, meaning that the points of emphasis within the proposed structure reinforce or
correspond with the theme of the composition as a whole; (6) *balance* in the relative verbal
size of the corresponding units; (7) *augmentation* of the primary pattern through the parallelism of syntactic structure or in sound similarity; (8) *plausibility* based on the pressure of
symmetry, where an element that seems to fall outside the pattern can be shown to fit in a
looser, but arguable way or else to manifest a deliberate aberration in order to highlight its
specific content.

[147]A smaller text portion, whether a single chapter or a short book such as the Song of
Songs, would probably be more amenable to the use of specially formatted discourse displays. Of course, the publishers, perhaps a local Bible Society, would first have to be convinced of their value in relation to the probable ability of the intended readership to
perceive and correctly interpret them. No doubt a word of introduction would be necessary
in the case of longer arrangements in order to explain the purpose and significance of the
novel format. However, there should be no problem in the case of a shorter passage like Isa.
55:8–9:

For my *thoughts* are not your *thoughts*,	A
neither are your *ways* my *ways*, says the Lord.	B
For as the *heavens* are higher than the *earth*,	C
so are my *ways* higher than your *ways*,	B'
and my *thoughts* than your *thoughts*.	A'

3.3 The importance for biblical interpretation of perceiving literary structure

I will conclude this survey of some key aspects of the tectonic arrangement of discourse with a brief example that highlights the importance for biblical interpretation of literary studies. Many illustrations could be cited here, but we will look once again at 1 Corinthians 13, especially in terms of its textual context. How does this pericope lauding Christian love connect with 12:31, on the one hand, and 14:1, on the other? This question involves several problems of interpretation that a literary approach is able to clarify in favor of one reading over another. I will not undertake a complete exegesis of this portion of the letter. My aim is much more limited in scope, namely, to show how a literary-rhetorical perspective may be applied as one tool among many others in the text analytical process and, moving from there, in a meaningful translation.

To begin with, we look at the matter of genre. What is the text type that chapter 13 exemplifies? All commentators view this passage as an integral discourse unit, but they differ over what to call it: "Various interpreters have labeled it poetry, chiasm, or encomium" (Bailey and vander Broek 1992:18), but note that these are *not* mutually exclusive categories of genre. Some view it as a sort of "meditative hymn" (ibid.:79). Probably "encomium" is the most precise designation, for this chapter is clearly intended as a high tribute to love. It is "written in praise of an abstract quality," Ryken says (1992:293),[148] yet these words cry out for personal embodiment in every believer.

The elaborate literary patterning has already been pointed out. In addition, we observe the significant appearance of text elements in triads throughout the passage. The encomium begins (vv. 1–3) with three parallel conditional statements that build to a climax in the third (whether one reads 'burning' or 'boasting' here). The next poetic segment (vv. 4–7) leads off with three descriptive clauses, each of which includes explicit

---

Here the conclusive simile that confirms the Lord's case is positioned in the focal center of this minor tectonic structure, following K. Bailey's " 'Inverted Parallelisms' and 'Encased Parables' in Isaiah and their Significance for OT and NT Translation and Interpretation" (in de Regt, de Waard, and Fokkelmann 1996:15). Bailey recommends that these structural parallels "be seriously considered for formatting in a manner that allows the reader to identify [correspondences] when they are clearly the conscious intent of the original writer." But he also notes in this regard that translators need to be "appropriately cautious and thereby prudently wait for some [scholarly] consensus before proceeding" (ibid.).

[148]An encomium may also be used to praise a "general character type" (or, I would add, a specific personage); examples are Psalms 1, 15, and 119 (multiple); Prov. 31:10–31; Isa. 52:13–53:12; John 1:1–18; Col. 1:15–20; and Hebrews 11 (see Ryken 1992, chap. 12).

mention of the topic, 'love' (ἀγάπη), which does not appear again in vv. 4–7.[149] The third and final panegyric segment features a contrast in vv. 8–9 between three spiritual gifts that appear to have been much sought after in the Corinthian congregation (prophecies, tongues, knowledge) and, in v. 13, three more-substantial Christian life qualities: faith, hope, love. But of these three, one stands supreme, love, as the placement of ἀγάπη shows. This is an illustration of the tectonic device of locating a particular thematic emphasis at the end of a unit. The lyric literary quality of this entire pericope may also suggest an underlying level of symbolism of number—that is, the recursive threes and their multiples (e.g., nine occurrences of ἀγάπη) pointing to a Godlike love.

Thus "whether the parallel elements function in terms of comparison or contrast (or have some other relationship), knowledge of the chiastic form allows the exegete to grasp more effectively the meaning the author intends to convey" (Bailey and vander Broek 1992:52). This is true also on the macrostructure of text organization, namely, with reference to the larger section covering chapters 12–14 (from περι δε in 12:1 to γνωριζω δε υμιν in 15:1). The elaborate inversion of 13:8–13, coupled with its central placement in the unit as a whole foregrounds its primary thematic significance overall. Thus a proper evaluation and application of love enables Christians to put into a proper perspective the varied spiritual gifts that are manifested in the body of Christ (according to chap. 12). Such knowledge serves in turn to contextualize Paul's pastoral admonition and advice concerning one *charisma* in particular that had provoked such an unfortunate controversy within the Corinthian congregation (according to chap. 14).

When the importance of the placement of chapter 13 is recognized, namely, as the central core of an even larger A–B–A' block ring construction, several other hermeneutical issues are clarified. Thus segment A' (chap. 14) carries on the argument that was broken off at the end of A (12:31) with the transitional utterance 'Best of all, however, is the following way' in 13:1. The verb ζηλουτε 'earnestly desire' in 12:31 is therefore better understood as an imperative, rather than an indicative (as in *The Message*), corresponding with its parallel in 14:1, which is an instance of structural exclusio: (... A) + (B) + (A' ...), where B = chapter 13. Furthermore, the double δε construction in 14:1 must be translated in a manner that takes both its resumptive nature and also the focal message of chapter 13 into account, for example, "Make love your aim; but be eager, too, for spiritual gifts, and especially for

---

[149]This interpretation requires an acceptance of the bracketed third occurrence of 'love' and a re-punctuation of the UBS Greek text, fourth edition. For a clear discussion of the textual options here, see Fee 1987:635–636.

prophesying" (NJB).[150] Thus the two δες appear to mark a double contrast here—the first more general, that is, between love and all other gifts, while the second concerns the particular charismatic pair at special issue in Corinth: "proclaiming God's message" and "speaking in strange tongues" (TEV). While an argument from discourse design, like an argument from literary artistry (see chap. 4), cannot be regarded as final or sufficient to prove a given case in and of itself, it does constitute some important text-based evidence, the weight of which might possibly be great enough to tip the scales of interpretation—and translation—in one direction or the other.[151]

---

[150]Contrast the NJB rendering with those that are ambiguous or confusing due to either inaccurate connectives (e.g., ...NRSV's "Pursue love, *and* strive for the spiritual gifts, *and* especially that you may prophecy"...) or inadequate marking (e.g., CEV's "Love should be your guide. [asyndeton] Be eager to have the gifts that come from the Holy Spirit ...").

[151]David A. Dorsey (1999:42–44) notes the following ten potential contributions of a literary-structural analysis to biblical study: appreciation of literary artistry, identification of unit boundaries, discovery of the rationale behind a unit's overall layout, clarification of the relationship of the parts to the whole, accounting for repetition, accounting for apparently misplaced units, clarification of a unit by comparison with its match, a check on redaction-critical theories, discovery of a unit's main point, and discovery of a composition's theme.

4

Artistry of the Scriptures

A literary-rhetorical approach to the analysis of Scripture promotes a holistic, integrative perspective on the original text. That is, the text is viewed as a composite, hierarchically shaped unity consisting of a diversity of larger structures and their enclosed compositional units. While this point has already been stressed, it is particularly important in connection with the topic of this chapter.

In considering the artistry of the Scriptures, our focus is on the *micro*structure of discourse—on those stylistic devices that serve to embellish and at the same time highlight or sharpen the texture of the text. It is a form-functional emphasis that encourages a clear perception of the lower-level artistic features, devices, and techniques of biblical discourse. This is different from the older historical *"behind*-the-text" studies and also from the contemporary vogue, reception criticism (*"before*-the-text" studies), in that it adopts a primarily *"in*-the-text" interpretive viewpoint. The question is, How do the microfeatures of the text serve to complement the larger structural tectonics that were discussed in the preceding chapter to enhance the communication of the biblical author's intended message?

Each one of the eight artistic compositional techniques that will be discussed in this chapter may be viewed as consisting of a number of different devices.[152] However, they are not neatly differentiated features but are often found in mutually complementary interaction within a literary text. Furthermore, there is a great deal of overlapping among them, and

---

[152]In chapter 6 of Wilt 2002b, I present a more detailed discussion of these different artistic features in a somewhat different format and with illustrations from the book of Jonah.

different strata of textual organization or discourse function are perhaps involved in their use as well. In any case, these stylistic features constitute some of the major aspects of what is termed biblical artistry, which combines considerations of stylistic excellence (or "aesthetics") and rhetorical power (or "dynamics").[153] They thus form the heart of what I am proposing as a practical, text-oriented literary methodology applied to Bible translation.

Other types or subdivisions could undoubtedly be proposed, but the ones described here seem to me to be some of the most important for the religious literature found in the Scriptures. These artistic devices (as exemplified in most biblical books) are found in varying proportions along the prose ⇔ poetry continuum of written discourse. It is essential to consider them in the analysis of a given biblical text and in the search for translation equivalents. The recognition and application of stylistic technique is also an important part of training translators how to carry out their task more effectively in terms of communicating the original message in the target language (TL).

Of course, these artistic features are well-recognized aspects of any literary approach and therefore it is not necessary to describe them in the same degree of detail as those that pertain to compositional tectonicity. However, the extent to which they are actually manifested in the texts of Scripture may not be so well known. Therefore, after a short overview of eight of the more common stylistic devices, we will see how the Joseph Story of Genesis 37 illustrates them. This will show how important such features are in biblical discourse and what they contribute in combination to the overall communicative significance of a particular text. (Some other illustrative examples are in Appendix B.) There is a definite need for translators to be able to discern and delineate this aesthetic dimension of the source document so that they may in turn recreate it in their own language.

4.1 Artistry in relation to Scripture

Many people mistakenly associate "artistry" with "fiction" (see sec. 1.4) and are therefore reluctant to apply the term *artistic* to the Holy Scriptures. But as has been shown, not all artistically composed literature is

---

[153]The term *literariness* encompasses both aesthetics and rhetoric. It is used by many contemporary literary critics to denote the object of their practice, which is the study of what distinguishes creative literature from other types of written discourse. *Poetics* is the "science devoted to identifying the defining quality of the literary work" (Preminger and Brogan 1993:697) by means of detailed text-centered analyses.

fiction. Take Genesis 1, for example.[154] No perceptive critic, religious or secular, will deny the fact that this first chapter of the Bible has been most artfully crafted in all respects—verbally shaped to serve an eminent theological purpose. So the question of whether creative artistry can coexist with theology—beauty with import—has an unavoidable answer. It is the same whether one interprets this highly structured, poetically phrased account as literal, historical fact (e.g., six twenty-four-hour days) or as an ordered liturgical and/or symbolical reflection concerning the divine origin of all things. Literalists who equate artistry with fiction thus encounter a major hermeneutical problem: Since Genesis 1 is clearly literary in quality, how can it also be historical in the sense of being true to the facts being reported? The only solution is to allow the two characteristics to coincide and recognize that the Bible *is* well-crafted "literature."

This assumption is important for the interpretation of the Scriptures for another reason:

> ...it is impossible to avoid completely the implications of literary analysis when speaking of the Bible. To do so would ultimately rob the Scriptures of much of their dynamic significance. In fact, an appreciation of the literary qualities of the biblical texts can only lead to a greater appreciation of their relevance. (Nida et al. 1983:157)[155]

The Bible stands as "literature" because it deals with momentous themes of continued existential and eternal relevance, and also because this content is "effectively structured so as to provide both impact and appeal for important insights on various levels" (Nida et al. 1983:153), theologically, spiritually, and morally. Not only is cognition affected, but also human emotions and volition as well. Indeed, one could argue that excellent artistic technique is absolutely essential for the effectual communication of religious subject matter, which by its very nature as the Word of God requires a distinctive, unconventional, captivating, and convincing method of communication in terms of genre and diction, if not style as well: "Any attempt to relate infinite realities to finite experience almost inevitably calls for figurative language, since there are no natural models which combine infinite and finite elements" (ibid.:154).

Thus the artistic features discussed in this chapter contribute a great deal to the penetrating manner of expression found in the "two-edged

---

[154]The final chapter of the Bible offers another good instance of the application of the literary-rhetorical technique in the communication of a profound theological message. For a survey of some of the artistic patterns that characterize Revelation 22, see Wendland 1990.

[155]Nida et al. 1983 is another important precursor of the sort of literary-rhetorical approach to biblical analysis advocated here, and once again we note the influence of Eugene A. Nida in this significant early initiative in translation studies.

sword" of the Scriptures, divine content unsheathed in human language (Heb. 4:12). The very character of the Bible as literature is a testimony to God's ultimate desire to communicate as effectively and efficiently—that is, as relevantly—as possible with people, no matter what language they may speak in the world. The implicit imperative for *translating* this corpus in a corresponding manner—as *literature* (appreciable as well as appreciated verbal art)—is unmistakable. Should not at least some of our translations be thus "seasoned with salt" (Col. 4:6)?

In sections 4.1.1–4.1.8, then, certain key stylistic devices found in the literature of Scripture will be summarized, particularly those that concern the surface structure of the biblical text. Most of them fit into one or another of the eight categories listed here (although there are others as well):

Figuration	=>	imagery, figures such as metaphor/metonymy $(+/- symbolism)^{156}$
Documentation	=>	intertextual citation—reference—allusion $(+/- clustering)$
Repetition	=>	exact/synonymous, contiguous/remote recursion $(+/- patterning)$
Compaction	=>	ellipsis, asyndeton, cryptic/concise expression $(+/- enigma)$
Deviation	=>	with respect to form or content, e.g., RQ, irony, hyperbole $(+/- novelty)$
Phonation	=>	phonological decoration and/or signification $(+/- dissonance)$
Evocation	=>	stimulating sensory impressions through evocative diction $(+/- synesthesia)$
Dramatization	=>	a preference for direct quotation and direct discourse $(+/- embedding)$

The point here is not merely to classify but rather to enable us to better understand these devices and their role in a biblical discourse so that closer artistic and rhetorical equivalents may be found in the language of translation. The question is, To what extent is it possible to verbally represent the story and the theology of Scripture with a corresponding measure of beauty and power, impact and appeal in another language?

---

[156]The terms in parentheses refer to one prominent way in which the intensity, frequency, artistry, or diversity of the designated category may be augmented.

4.1.1 Figuration

Since figuration is one of the most widely recognized and discussed aspects of literary artistry, there is no need here to elaborate. Suffice it to say that the term *figuration* refers to the use of various types of graphic language, whether literal or nonliteral, direct or indirect (allusive). It is image-evoking, with the purpose of creating a vivid visualizable conceptual background, spotlighting certain portions of the text, rendering the discourse in a more memorable manner, and/or describing new (especially religious) experience—including an "expression of the inexpressible" with reference to the attributes and actions of God.

Figures of speech (or "tropes") are manifested most commonly as words or phrases that are figures of *comparison* (simile, metaphor, personification, anthropomorphism, antithesis) and figures of *substitution* (synecdoche, metonym, euphemism). But they also appear at higher levels of discourse, as an utterance (e.g., proverb) or even a complete text genre (e.g., parable).[157] Figurative language is an important element in the poetry of any literary tradition (including that of the TL), especially in a love lyric like the Song of Solomon (see Wendland 1995a). But imagery and the common figures feature prominently in rhetorical prose as well, as in the speeches of Christ (e.g., Matthew 5–7) or in the Epistles, an example being the concentration and diversity of figures in the didactic Epistle of James.

4.1.2 Documentation

Documentation, or cross-text referencing, may be of four intersecting types: active or passive in terms of degree of explicitness in the text, and past or future with regard to temporal reference. *Active* documentation is the deliberate citation of prior texts in exact, paraphrased, or adapted form for the purposes of authorization, explanation, or illustration in a

---

[157]For a simple definition of a number of these figures of speech with an application to translation, see chapter 5 of Wendland 1987b. More precise and extensive definitions are found in Heinrich Lausberg's exhaustive 1998 tome. A still useful work is E. W. Bullinger's *Figures of Speech Used in the Bible* ([1899] 1968). A handier guide to the subject is Richard Lanham's *A Handlist of Rhetorical Terms* (1968). A helpful reference work on New Testament metaphoric imagery is Williams 1999, which identifies twelve metaphoric "fields," namely, those dealing with life in the city, life in the country, family life, providing for physical needs, slavery and freedom, citizens and courts of law, manufacturing and marketing, the business world, travel, warfare and soldiering, cultic observances, and public shows and sporting events. It includes many exegetical insights useful for translators. For example, when Paul says that he "did not run or labor for nothing" (2 Tim. 4:7), Williams says that "[i]n this context 'labor' should be understood as a metaphor of the athlete's training" (p. 268). (For an overview of Old Testament "images of God" and "images of humanity," see Gibson 1998, chaps. 6–7.)

present text. Such "intertextuality" contributes an important additional dimension of theological and moral significance to the richly textured unity of the Scriptures and therefore plays a vital role in its interpretation. This is especially true with regard to understanding the New Testament in the light of the Old (note the prominence of quotations from the Old Testament in the Gospel of Matthew, for example, or in the Epistle of Hebrews).[158] But intertextual resonance and interaction is important in the Old Testament also, whether the sense remains essentially the same, as in the so-called "covenantal correlates" (e.g., Exod. 6:7, Deut. 7:6 => Ezek. 11:20, Hos. 2:23) or in some modified form as we see in the many semantic reversals that occur in the prophecy of Joel (Wendland 1995b:242–253).

Passive documentation consists of more informal, less direct references that point to earlier texts (*flashback*),[159] to subsequent ones (*foreshadowing*), or to the extratextual historical, sociocultural, and religious setting (*contextualization*).[160] The recurrent Exodus deliverance motif, for example, runs throughout the Hebrew poetic and prophetic corpus, providing a constant reminder of God's steadfast protection and provision for his people. Such passive allusions, including the more covert "echoes," whether past (*memorial*) or future (*predictive*) in temporal direction, may serve the same purposes as active documentation, but the process is less conspicuous and involves a greater dependence upon the presupposition of shared knowledge with regard to the pertinent texts. Implicit intertextuality may also be manifested simply to preserve the canonical character or to support the credibility and authority of a current document through the use of a familiar style and conventional religious terminology (e.g., a

---

[158]These Old Testament references pose a special problem for translators when the LXX citation differs considerably from the Hebrew MT. Readers may be puzzled by a cross-reference to a passage that seems to bear little resemblance to the New Testament text, such as Phil. 1:19=>Job 13:16 and 2 Tim. 4:16–18=>Psalm 21. (I owe these references to Philip Towner, who discusses them in an article to be published in *The Bible Translator*.) Perhaps the best solution in such cases is to provide a footnote in which a translation of the LXX text is given. A more novel and perhaps controversial interactive device would be to incorporate a marked note containing the pertinent intertextual references at the point where it applies within the biblical text. Two recent studies that detail the structural and hermeneutical significance of New Testament intertextuality with Old Testament are Aageson 1993 and Soards 1994.

[159]Foreshadowing, or literary "anticipation," is an especially important factor in religious texts like the Bible that are read and re-read. In a book that manifests a recursive style, such as John's Gospel, crucial themes resonate semantically both progressively and retrogressively as they are encountered, thus enriching the discourse and rendering it conceptually deeper, or at least apparently so.

[160]For an insightful survey of the last-mentioned "nonscribal" dimension of intertextuality, see Robbins 1996, chapter 3.

"Septuagintal Greek" style of writing, as in Mark).[161] One fact is certain: the importance of the various degrees of documentation will undoubtedly increase for biblical studies in general and translation in particular as more and more credible examples are discovered and applied with reference to their textual location and purpose.

4.1.3 Repetition

Verbal recursion with reference to textual patterning on the macrolevel of discourse structure is very important in biblical literature (see sec. 3.2.2).[162] The significant correspondences and parallels are usually positioned at some distance from one another, that is, at distinct boundaries or peak points within the text at large. Likewise repetition is prominent within the *microstructure* of a text, where immediate, more randomly placed instances of exact, synonymous, and contrastive reiteration may be found. Repetition of sound, sense, and syntax constitutes the backbone of the lineal parallelism of Hebrew poetry (see Kugel 1981). It is also common in the prose discourse of both the Old and the New Testaments. For example, lexical repetition creates the topical background against which selected areas of the text may be foregrounded through the use of certain distinctive stylistic devices as being noteworthy aspects of information, emotion, and/or volition.

The Greek orators identified a host of specially formed repeated forms that were regarded as exhibiting an artistic, rhetorical style in oratory. The same is true of Greek written discourse. Examples include *anadiplosis* (repetition of the last word of one line or clause at the beginning of the next), *anaphora* (repetition of the same word at the beginning of successive clauses or verses), *epistrophe* (repetition of a closing word or words at the end of several clauses, sentences, or verses), *polysyndeton* (use of a conjunction between each clause in a series), *auxesis* (a series of words or clauses placed in climactic order), and *isocolon* (repetition of phrases of equivalent length and often corresponding structure as well). These terms

---

[161]For a discussion of such a "Septuagintal" or "Semitic" Greek style, see Turner 1976:1–4.

[162]It is not surprising, therefore, that repetition, given its prominence in biblical literature, confounded—and continues to mystify—the "source critics" (as the comment in Gibson 1998:38–39 illustrates), especially those who have no acquaintance with the stylistic techniques of oral art forms and non-Indo-European literary traditions. To more experienced literary critics, on the other hand, such varied recursion, particularly when coupled with periodic points of notable variation, appears to be one of the most common—and significant—characteristics of the storyteller's art (or the orator's or poet's or epistle-writer's). This constitutes a vital means of structuring as well as shading (foregrounding/ backgrounding) his or her discourse, especially when transmitted oral-aurally, with respect to both the explicit and also the implicit message that it conveys.

are not important, but their possible forms and functions are, especially where they have been convincingly identified in the New Testament epistolary literature (see, for example, Watson 1988 and 1991, also Nida et al. 1983:174–181) Thus the different types of repetition, in both the source and target languages, need to be carefully studied by translators so that they can achieve a suitable degree of functional equivalence in the TL text, in keeping with the conventions of their literary tradition.

It should be noted that deliberate contrast, or *antithesis*, is an important variant or subcategory of repetition whereby a given concept is highlighted through a pointed reference to its negative or opposite. Such a device, when utilized in conjunction with exact or synonymous repetition, may be developed into an important thematic strategy in certain hortative books such as Proverbs or 1 John.

4.1.4 Compaction

Compaction corresponds to "condensation" in the macrostructure (see sec. 3.2.2), but with application to the lower, microlevel of discourse organization. Since recursion is such a common feature of biblical discourse, any shortening of compositional form is probably obvious and forceful when it clearly does occur.[163] However, since this device depends upon the reader or hearer's being able to "fill in the gaps," both formal and semantic, it may not be as effective for receptors of less literary sophistication, especially when found in written texts. Thus it is of special relevance for translators, who in most cases must work with and attempt to represent an often unfamiliar message in print. What then can be done to help the target audience to correctly fill in those gaps?

Compaction may be realized by either omission or abbreviation. Examples of strategic *omission* include *apocope* (omitting the last syllable or letter of a word), *syncope* (omitting letters, sounds, or syllables from the middle of a word), *asyndeton* (omitting normal conjunctions between words, phrases, clauses, or sentences), *ellipsis* (omitting a word that is implied in the linguistic context), *zeugma* (the use of one word to govern several congruent words or clauses), and *aposiopesis* (a sudden break that leaves the utterance unfinished). Compaction sometimes operates together with repetition to create a particular *rhythm* of discourse, whether in a relatively constrained form as in the Psalms, or more freely as in 1 Corinthians 13. These features tend to be manifested with the greatest

---

[163]"[P]oetic style in the [Hebrew] Bible often works by omitting those little words and particles that otherwise would make explicit the relationship between adjacent clauses" (Kugel 1999:193).

frequency in Old Testament poetic literature, the Epistles, and the didactic discourse of Christ.

A terse, abbreviated manner of expression characterizes biblical discourse in general, prose as well as poetry. But since the text tends to adhere rather closely to the religious topic under consideration, any deliberate instance of abbreviation is difficult to demonstrate. However, Gen. 25:32, Matt. 25:9, and John 2:18–19 are relatively clear examples. (Bullinger 1968:47–51 gives other possible instances; see also Nida et al. 1983:181–183.) Abbreviation is a device that is typical of concentrated formulaic statements and summaries of a theological or ethical nature (e.g., the pious but ironic assertions of Jonah 1:9, 4:2, and various Pauline creedal, doxological, and epistolary formulations as in Eph. 2:4–9, 3:20–21, 5:25–27, and 6:23).

The nominalization of event expressions (e.g., "a *baptism* of *repentance* for the *forgiveness* of *sins*" in Mark 1:4) is another form of compaction (more in the nature of semantic *concentration* than omission). Often seen in biblical didactic discourse or narrative summaries, such nominal composition is expected and an efficient way to communicate. The opposite is true in many other languages, however, where a verbal style is much preferred; hence a literal translation turns out to be unnatural as well as overly marked. Nominalized prose is frequently facilitated or accompanied by the use of associated linguistic structures like the passive voice, prepositional phrases, "of" constructions, and "pro-forms" (pronouns in place of nouns and pro-verbs in place of verbs). Some of these abbreviating features may be found also in certain poetic texts, as in Luke 1:47–55 and 68–79, where the pronominal reference system in the Greek text is very complex. In all cases of compaction, it is frequently necessary for translators to "unpack" and rephrase the expressions so that their content and intent is stated more naturally and in a manner that can be readily apprehended aurally. This unpacking may be done by means of a more explicit, active verb-based style, for example, or by introducing some redundancy into the text through the synonymous repetition of some key concepts.

4.1.5 Deviation

A deviation is a marked departure from a given norm or a shift in expectancy. There is a wide and diverse range of literary devices that fall into this category (see Nida et al. 1983:183–185). Changes in the expected order of words, phrases, and clauses within a sentence are quite common and important in biblical literature. An example of this is *anastrophe*, that is, front-shifting for the purpose of topicalization or back-shifting for the purpose of emphasis or focus. Such changes of word order cannot often be duplicated in translation with the same effect, and the function must be reproduced in some other way (e.g., by a deictic word or an intensifying particle or affix). In the case of *hyperbaton*, to mention another prominent example of syntactic dislocation, words that normally belong together are noticeably separated. Morphological deviation, which is called *enallage*, involves the substitution of one case, person, number, tense, or mood for another. It typically presents translational problems, especially when pronominal reference suddenly changes as so often happens in the prophetic literature.

Other deviations affect the flow and meaning of the text more directly, presenting the translator with even greater difficulty. These kinds of deviation include *parenthesis* (digression), *anacoluthon* (broken syntactic construction), *paradox* and *oxymoron* (apparent contradiction, conceptual or lexical), *irony* (contrast between apparent and intended meanings), *hyperbole* (deliberate exaggeration), *litotes* (understatement), and *cataphora* (forward- instead of back-reference). Such rhetorical techniques are very powerful in their impact, but they also present some of the greatest challenges in biblical literature for interpreter and translator alike. The multifaceted irony that pervades Jonah, for example, creates a second, underlying level of meaning and significance for the entire book. This is best dealt with extratextually in an introduction to the book. The periodic irony that appears in an epistle like 1 Corinthians, however, would in many cases have to be marked somehow in the text in order to prevent misunderstanding (e.g., 1 Cor. 4:8–13).

In this category of the relatively novel and unexpected we should also include the important devices of *rhetorical question* (one used to make a strong assertion, evaluation, criticism, etc.) and *leading question* (one that serves to introduce a new topic and/or section in the discourse as in Ps. 121:1, Song of Sol. 5:9, Matt. 3:7, and Rom. 6:1). *Idioms* also are a special type of deviation, either with regard to the idiosyncratic grammar (as in Revelation) or the lexical-semantic system, so that the expression as a whole cannot be understood in terms of the meanings of its constituent elements, as in the Semitic "children of ___" phrases (e.g., Matt. 9:15). Deviations of this type, if translated literally, will usually not mean anything in the TL or they will suggest a wrong meaning. In such cases translators must attempt to reproduce their functional effect by means of familiar rhetorical forms and artistic devices from their oral or literary tradition.

4.1.6 Phonation

Phonation, or "phonological aesthetics," is an artistic process whereby an author distinguishes his discourse through various techniques of sonic ornamentation. Consonance, assonance, alliteration, rhyme, rhythm, and punning are examples. They are overtly decorative in nature and occur mainly (though not exclusively) in poetic and highly dramatic texts. They depend upon some form of audio recursion (see sec. 4.1.3): repetition of consonants, of vowels, of consonants or vowels in word-initial position, of utterance-final syllables, of measured sequences of stress, accent, or tone, and of sound similarities in words of different senses. In biblical literature such oral-aural embellishment typically performs a higher communicative function as well, namely, with regard to the lexical items so distinguished. Therefore phonation needs to be examined with the possibility in mind of its being a means of semantic highlighting or emphasis, the signal of a discourse transition, or an aid or stimulus for the memory.

The potential for meaning enhancement that the sound structure offers is often overlooked, if not by the commentators, then surely by many Bible translators, who either do not perceive its presence in the original text (if they cannot access it) or do not know how to deal with it even if they do recognize its presence. The device of punning (technically known as paronomasia) is especially important because it frequently serves to reinforce or subtly modify the text's thematic meaning. This may occur with respect to the different senses of the same key term, or to the variously related senses of two different expressions that are linked by some sort of sound similarity, for example, to foreground the significance of many proper names in relation to the surrounding narrative of Genesis. A similar example is in the poetic judgment oracles of Amos 1:3–2:5.

4.1.7 Evocation

A concern for the artistry of a given text includes a study of the emotive and sensory effects that rhetorical devices produce in the TL audience. According to Robbins (1996:29–30), "the sensory-aesthetic texture of a text resides prominently in the range of senses the text evokes or embodies (thought, emotion, sight, sound, touch, smell) and the manner in which the text evokes or embodies them (reason, intuition, imagination, humor, etc.)." It is important to pay attention to this less obvious *synesthetic* dimension of discourse because it contributes a great deal to the ongoing interpretation as well as the overall "feeling," or impression, that one experiences when processing a literary work, or a distinct portion of one.[164]

Of course, this turns out to be a very hypothetical and subjective exercise when it is oriented away from the tangible here-and-now and directed towards a totally different historical, ecological, sociocultural, and religious setting, such as that which pertains to the original texts of Scripture. However, several literary analysts, notably those who practice so-called social-scientific criticism (e.g., Elliott 1993) or anthropological exegesis (e.g., Malina 1993), have begun to develop a methodology that is somewhat more objective in nature. Robbins (1996:30) describes one possible approach along these lines:

> One way to search for sensory-aesthetic texture and pattern can be to identify and group every aspect of a text that refers to a part of the body (like eyes, ears, nose, etc.) and to actions or perceptions related to a part of the body (like seeing, hearing, smelling, etc.)....Another way is to identify "body zones" in the discourse....Thus, humans consist of three mutually interpenetrating yet distinguishable zones of interacting with their environments: the zone of emotion-fused thought, the zone of self-expressive speech, and the zone of purposeful action.

In implementing this approach, the analyst would seek to record and categorize the various activities that pertain to each of the three bodily zones of sensation within a given text and note any special accumulation that pertains to each one (along with its principal lexical markers) as well as any obvious progression from one to another as the discourse unfolds. All three zones of interaction find expression in the second half of the Sermon on the Mount, for example: "eyes-heart (Matt. 6:19–7:6), mouth-ears (7:7–11), and hands-feet (7:13–27)" (Malina and Rohrbaugh 1992:227).

Since speech and action predominate in most biblical narrative, any unusual concentration of affective-emotive infused language may well be significant both in the interpretation of the text and also when translating it into another language. The evocation of sensual imagery is the central feature of many of the love lyrics of the Song of Songs. A similar poetic example of thematic relevance occurs in the psalm of chapter 2 of the Book of Jonah, as we experience the sensation of God's prophet sinking to the bottom of the sea (especially vv. 3–6). Jonah's prayer of thanksgiving

---

[164]Obviously, there is a close connection between evocation and the other features that have been presented in this section, figuration in particular (4.1.1): "Imagery is 'any verbal appeal to any of the senses; a stimulation of the *imagination* through sense experience' " (W. Guerin, cited in P. House 1988:74). The richer the imagery, the more resonant and important the sensory synthesis becomes—for example, the jarring combination of theophanic and military scenes in the judgment oracle of Zeph. 1:15–16.

here acts as a lyric structural interlude and a thematic foil within the organization of the book as a whole. Another important, highly contrastive
concentration of emotion occurs in 4:6–8 just before the conclusion of the
work's prophetic argument (ironically directed by Yahweh *against* his
chosen prophet). Here we can almost feel the cooling shade over Jonah's
feverish brow, giving him a bit of joy in his sulky state, as this is transformed overnight into a searing heat that matches his jaundiced attitude
not only towards the detestable Ninevites but also towards his merciful
God (4:10–11).

In order to translate such sensory-appealing (or -repugnant, as in Isa.
66:24) portions of the Scriptures, translators must practice imagining
themselves in analogous situations and circumstances of their own culture. Their aim would be to empathize with the biblical setting in an attempt to stimulate a similar mood through their choice of appropriately
connotative and evocative expressions in their language. In Bantu languages, for example, this would mean using familiar idioms or well-
chosen exclamations and ideophones).

4.1.8 Dramatization

In dramatization direct speech is used in the text ('I' and 'you', rather than
a third person reportative mode). This device would seem to be so common in the Bible as to not warrant its mention as a distinctive artistic feature. Alter brings this out with respect to Hebrew prose: "narration in the
biblical story is...oriented toward dialogue" (1981:66).

The way dialogue is used can be quite diverse as well as discriminating.
The general function of dialogue in discourse, whether in narrative or
prophetic texts, is to advance the action and/or theme, characterize the
speaker and those spoken about, give the impression of naturalness and
realism, and focus attention upon what is being said. Even a character's
thoughts (including the reflections of God in Genesis and elsewhere) are
frequently presented in the form of direct speech.[165]

Translators need creative imagination when they deal with this common feature of biblical discourse. They must have the ability to situate
themselves mentally in analogous conversational and oratorical settings
in their own culture, because, as a rhetorical device, dramatic speech
gives a highly personal *scenic* viewpoint, focusing on what is immediate

---

[165]P. House (1988) considers the direct speech of *YHWH* and his prophet to be key elements in the "drama" of Zephaniah. A closer examination of this prophetic text, however,
reveals not true dialogue, but rather an extended divine monologue, interspersed with responses by Zephaniah to what the LORD has just spoken, much in the manner of an ancient
Greek chorus (e.g., *YHWH*—3:9–13; Zephaniah—3:14–17).

and close up in contrast to a more detached *panoramic* (distant) narrative perspective.

A variant of direct discourse is *semidirect* speech, which features a combination of direct and indirect references to the speaker and his addressees or the inclusion of such features of direct speech as exclamations and deictics of immediacy. Semidirect speech is common in Hebrew poetic texts, often conveying a subtle shift in perspectives. In Psalm 84, for example, the psalmist worships God using both second and third person singular forms at the close in vv. 10–12 (2—3—3—3—3—2—2), thus moving from nearer to farther and back again in his words of praise. On the other hand, in Zech. 12:1–9, an oracle of Yahweh is presented in which God initially speaks in the first person, as would be expected (vv. 1–6); then he shifts to third person references to himself at the prophecy's climax where the "salvation" of Judah, David, and Jerusalem is highlighted (vv. 7–8); and finally he concludes in the first person again (v. 9).

Some extremely delicate variations in perspective, as well as in the degree of directness with respect to a person's speech and/or thought, can be achieved in Hebrew prophetic discourse through different stylistic means, one being levels of embedding in the formulaic speech openers (e.g., "This is what the LORD says...") and another being the complex forms of "metarepresentational" discourse introduced by the particle *kiy*. This word is typically glossed as 'that, because, for, indeed' according to the context, but it really designates a diverse range of author-manipulated viewpoints that must be contextually specified. For example, in 2 Sam. 6:6, we read, "Uzzah reached out and took hold of the ark of God, because [*kiy*] the oxen stumbled" (NIV). In other words, from Uzzah's (pre-death) perspective the oxen's movement was about to cause the holy ark to 'drop down' to the ground (the real meaning of the Hebrew verb [*sh-m-t*] here), and so he acted—perhaps for the best of reasons, but with the worst of results.[166]

Most Old Testament poetry as well as the New Testament Epistles is composed in the formal style of direct discourse. The Psalms, for example, have been prepared for oral articulation as prayers and praises during worship. The prophetic and apostolic literature is "speech" intended to be read aloud in a verbal representation of the personal presence of its author. As even a cursory reading reveals, the direct discourse in the Scriptures is *dramatic*—designed to mimic actual human speech in a vivid albeit conventionalized way (e.g., inclusive of personal exclamations and expressive interjections). It is also *determinative*—determining those aspects of the overall message that an author deems important and thereby

---

[166]I owe this example and its explanation to an unpublished paper by Carl Follingstad (2001b); for the details, see Follingstad 2001a.

wishes to highlight. In any narrative, for example, *who* actually speaks, *when, where, how often,* and *why* are all significant. They are factors that need to be noted for their underlying implications with regard to character, plot, and theme in addition to the content of what is actually said. In poetry, which already stands in a "direct" mode, any additional insertions of actual speech are particularly noteworthy, as in the Psalms where we may find emphasized direct discourse of the psalmist (e.g., Ps. 73:15), God (e.g., Ps. 46:10), and even one's enemies (e.g., Ps. 64:5–6).

Finally, it should be noted that direct discourse may be further dramatized by *incorporation,* that is, through the use of any of the previously discussed artistic features, including the embedding of segments of speech within itself. This renders these texts doubly dramatic—that is, inherently dramatic and also dramatic through stylistic insertion. We frequently find this sort of elaborate layering in the prophetic literature, where the messenger of God is commanded to speak "the word the LORD" to such and such a person or group. At times there are several levels of speech embedding, as in Isa. 49:8–9. Because in many languages such stratified speech is too complicated for audiences to follow; it must be unraveled to varying degrees in translation.

4.2 Functions of artistry in biblical discourse

The eight artistic devices just described perform one or more of eight functions in biblical discourse. But such rhetorical intentions can be posited only on the basis of a careful study of the text (form + meaning), context (textual + situational), and "pretext." This last term refers to how an author either consciously or unconsciously deletes, modifies, and generalizes his verbal representation of reality so that it better fits his audience's culturally conditioned "map of the world" (Katan 1999:94).

The eight functions of the various artistic devices are as follows:

- *Intensification*—expressing a specific concept within an utterance (or clause) in a vivid, dramatic, extensive, and/or superlative manner.
- *Unification*—connecting one part of a text with another (*intra*textuality) and also with prior discourse(s) of a formally or semantically related nature (*inter*textuality).
- *Conceptualization*—facilitating the communication of crucial, new, foreign, and/or difficult principles, experiences, values, goals, and ideas.

- *Attraction*—rendering the discourse in an aesthetically appealing and emotively compelling way, making it clearly recognized and valued as verbal *art.*
- *Accentuation*—highlighting or emphasizing certain similar or contrasting concepts in relation to others on the (sub)sentence/(sub)paragraph level of discourse structure.
- *Structuration*—arranging phonological, lexical, and syntactic elements within the sentence or paragraph (e.g., in extended patterns and at strategic positions) in the most effective manner with respect to the main message being conveyed.
- *Memorization*—enabling certain aspects of a message to be more readily recalled, even verbatim (e.g., through mnemonic, rhythmic-poetic, or sense-specific expressions), so that it can be personally transmitted and/or applied in future.
- *Familiarization*—domesticating the discourse so that it sounds idiomatic and at home in the TL, linguistically at home, as distinct from the text's content, which may still seem foreign due to differences presented by the original historical, sociocultural, and religious setting.

Often these literary functions are, like the devices that express them, concentrated within a discourse at certain points (such as at its climax or peak) for structural-thematic purposes. This is an important compositional characteristic that must be evaluated on the basis of *quality* as well as *quantity*. In other words, what counts is not only how many instances of a given feature there are but also how diverse, novel, unexpected, appropriate, or symbolic the feature is and with how many different devices it co-occurs. Such an artistic selection and arrangement contributes also to a text's larger discourse design (see chap. 3) and the level of "rhetoricity" or persuasiveness (chap. 6). The functions need to be first carefully analyzed in context and fully experienced or conceptualized in relation to the original message; they must then be reproduced in the TL, to the extent possible, using carefully selected stylistic forms that are the closest available and appropriate functional "matches" in terms of overall message equivalence and communicative relevance (see Zogbo and Wendland 2000, chap. 4).

4.3 The Joseph Story: Biblical artistry in context

Some outstanding examples of the eight artistic devices and their functions will now be illustrated from part of the Joseph Story in Genesis 37.

Due to the limitations of space I cannot examine all the details of the intensive and extensive interaction of these features as they occur both in combination and sequentially throughout this intensely dramatic text (for more details see Wendland 1984). I will note only a representative selection, but hopefully enough to demonstrate the importance of artistry in the narrative form of biblical literature.

4.3.1 Examples of figuration

Several graphic figures of speech and images occur in Genesis 37, especially in direct speech. To begin with, the great love that Jacob had for Joseph is quaintly depicted in the expression 'son of his old age' (v. 3). This stands in sharp contrast to his brothers' malevolently jealous opinion of him, as reflected in their epithet 'this lord of (the) dreams' (v. 19). Reuben advises his brothers not to 'shed blood' or 'lay a hand' upon Joseph (v. 22). Judah later follows this warning with a similar admonition concerning their 'flesh [i.e., 'brother']' (v. 27): do not 'cover his blood' or 'lay a hand' on him (v. 26). Death is the implicit topic of the euphemism that Jacob employs with reference to Joseph's untimely demise: 'Joseph has truly been torn!' (v. 33). In the end, the bitterly bereaved father closes the dialogue of chapter 37 with another poignant euphemism that simultaneously alludes to his own death and that of his beloved son: 'I will go down to my son' (v. 35). Vividly contrastive imagery highlights the shocking difference between the sweet-smelling merchandise of the Arabic traders—'spice and balm and myrrh' (v. 25)—and the human cargo they were about to take along, courtesy of Joseph's hard-hearted brothers (vv. 27–28). Just prior to this we are presented with a stark contrast in scenery: poor, robeless Joseph languishes in a well without 'water' while his remorseless brothers eat 'bread' (vv. 24b–25a). This is an example of narrative compaction (see sec. 4.1.4) as well as figuration.

4.3.2 Examples of documentation

In Genesis, the head of the canon of Scripture, obviously there are not as many instances of intertextuality as in subsequent books.[167] However, several examples do appear. Most notable is the covenantal promise of blessing pronounced by Yahweh upon Abraham and his descendants (e.g., Gen. 12:3, 18:18, 22:18, 26:4, 28:14). This series of passages may also be regarded as an instance of *intra*textuality, depending on one's perspective, since it occurs within the same book.

---

[167]Genesis provides a number of important *pre-texts* that resonate in passages of later biblical literature.

As far as Genesis 37 is concerned, we are told that 'Joseph dreamed' (v. 5)—just like his father Jacob had done so many years before (28:12), an experience which further establishes him as the paternal favorite and heir apparent, despite the unpopular content of his dreams. The seriousness of the state of affairs between Joseph and his callous brothers is indicated in an implicit expression of their hatred: 'they were not able to speak [to] him for peace [*shalom*]' (v. 4), which reflects the common Hebrew social greeting 'Peace to you'. (In v. 14 we read 'go see about the welfare/peace of your brothers'—what irony!) The deception that his deceitful sons practiced upon Jacob ('the Deceiver'), especially the important role of a slain goat, recalls (again, with considerable irony) the momentous event in which Jacob and his mother tricked his father, Isaac (Gen. 27:5–13).

Most of the literary documentation of this chapter is future oriented and expressed in the *allusive* predictions voiced in Joseph's two dreams, which of course later come true (e.g., Gen. 42:6; 43:26; 44:14; cf. Deut. 33:16). There is also a more subtle prefiguring that underlies the price that Joseph was sold for, 'twenty pieces of silver', which was the price that later was set as the value for redeeming a young man who was 'dedicated to the LORD' *(Lev. 27:5).*[168] It is probably no coincidence, either, that the word *bor* 'pit' referring to the pit into which Joseph was thrown is subsequently used by him to refer to the prison in which he was incarcerated in Egypt (40:15).[169] Another example of allusive, anticipatory documentation, now involving an ironic reversal, lies again in the use of a goat as a sign of recognition during a critical act of deception. Thus just as Judah was a ringleader in tricking his father with a dead goat (37:31–33), so Judah was himself deceived with a goat by his daughter-in-law Tamar (38:17, 25–26). A more positive, forward-looking reversal involves a repetition of the word 'go down': Jacob feared that Joseph's apparent death would surely bring him 'down' in sorrow to the grave (v. 35; cf. 44:31); then some years later he sends all of the brothers who were involved in this cruel plot 'down' to Egypt to seek deliverance from this same lost son (42:2–4); and finally Jacob himself—accompanied by God—'goes down' in search of renewed life (45:9–10; 46:3–4).

---

[168]For a discussion of some additional thematic significance that is associated with the sending of money between Canaan and Egypt during the Joseph narrative, see Alter 1981:139, 172.

[169]His use of the word 'pit' for his prison may have been an implicit claim to innocence and simultaneously a complaint regarding the injustice of his second imprisonment. Paradoxically, God transformed these places of pain and punishment into a means of preservation as far as Joseph's life was concerned.

4.3.3 Examples of repetition

The words of Gen. 37:1, which are transitional, form a structural link with the previous mention of Jacob in 35:27 (*exclusio*). This is followed by 'This is the story [*toledoth* 'descendants'] of Jacob's family', the recursive formula that partitions the Book of Genesis as a whole into ten sections. This is the tenth and last occurrence of this formula (cf. 36:1, an instance of sequential structural *anaphora*).

In vv. 5–8 we have a good example of the Hebrew reduplicative narrative technique in which a panoramic summary preview (v. 5) is followed by a more scenic telling of what happened (vv. 6–8). (Likewise, the summary statement in v. 18 is followed by a scenic explication in 19–22.) The reverse of this also occurs, namely, where the contents of a segment of direct speech are summarized at the end, as in vv. 6–8a + 8b, 9b–10 + 11, 21b–22b + 22c, 35c + 35d, v. 35 also acting as a contrastive inclusio for the entire chapter (cf. 3a). Thus the essential content of a given scene is in effect reported twice, in greater or lesser detail.

The reiteration of *hinneh* 'Look!' functions in dramatic fashion both to foreground the various elements of Joseph's two dreams and also to convey his own personal excitement in reporting these wonderful events to his family (vv. 6–7, 9)—a strangely unreceptive lot. Thus in contrast to Joseph's naive enthusiasm, his brothers' growing 'hatred' recurs as an ominous refrain in the first part of the story (vv. 4, 5, 8).

A more subtle and focused repetitive technique is manifested in direct speech at the beginning of v. 19, where the brothers exclaim, 'Look [lit., 'behold'—again!], here comes that dreamer!' They use words that ironically mimic their complaint concerning Joseph, as in v. 6: 'this dream that I dreamed—Behold...' (cf. v. 9). A similar device effects even greater irony when Jacob exclaims, upon seeing the bloody robe of Joseph, 'An evil beast has eaten him!' (v. 33)—here using the very expression that the brothers had spoken in their original plotting (v. 20). He thereby unwittingly confirms the complete success of their immoral plan without their having to verbally plant the possibility in his mind. This pathetic utterance is also transformed into an effective metaphor of characterization through its indirect reflection back upon the 'evil report' that Joseph had been making about the brothers to his father (v. 2).

An important connective *leitmotif* that runs throughout the chapter is created by the repeated references to the ornamented/embroidered/multicolored 'robe' (vv. 3, 23 [twice], 31 [twice], 32 [twice], 33 = eight times) that was the concrete symbol of Jacob's love for Joseph and his brothers' hatred for him. A less obvious iterative element is the syntactic construction *family relation noun + pronominal possessive suffix*, as exemplified by 'his brothers' and 'their father'. This type of nominal expression appears nearly forty times in Genesis 37 alone, frequently where it is unnecessary for referential purposes—an implicitly ironic suggestion perhaps of what should have been a close-knit family splitting apart at the seams.

Finally, again in the prose of direct speech, we see several instances of poetic parallelism. An example is in v. 8, 'Will you really reign over us—will you truly rule over us?!', which also manifests rhyme and syllabic balance in Hebrew (cf. 10b). Also in v. 8 are two instances of the intensive iterative verbal cognate construction 'to reign will you reign—to rule will you rule?' (cf. v. 33).

A topical instance of lexical repetition-in-reverse distinguishes the unhappy ending of this first stage of the Joseph Story. The chiasmus (vv. 34–35) constitutes an ironic isomorphic structural reflection upon the striking reversal in the young man's fortunes so dramatically recounted in this chapter (see also the transitional v. 36) even as it reinforces the intense expression of his father's lonely love for him (end stress at A') despite the presence of all his siblings (v. 3):

> A And Jacob ripped his clothes [in grief],
> B and he put sackcloth on his body [a funerary sign],
> C and he mourned
> D for his son many days.
> E All his sons and all his daughters arrived to comfort him,
> _____
> E' but he refused to be comforted,
> D' and he said, "Surely I will go down to my son
> C' mourning
> B' to Sheol [the grave]."
> A' And his father wept for him.

4.3.4 Examples of compaction

'Jacob's history' (Gen. 37:2a) begins abruptly, without any sort of transitional expression, not even a *waw*. The name 'Joseph' (2b) is a topicalizing construction that immediately suggests his unexpected importance in the account to follow. This initial portion of the turbulent experiences of Joseph, like Hebrew narrative in general, features a very terse style of reporting. Only the most important details are mentioned; everything else is eliminated. For example, there is no explanation of what sort of 'mischief' (lit., 'evil') Joseph's older brothers were up to (v. 2) or why he, not Benjamin, happens to be the favored son of Jacob (v. 3). Even the customary greetings are dispensed with in the scene involving an unnamed stranger (vv. 15–16), seemingly to get right to the point. This sort of condensed storytelling style produces many *enigmas* (plot-oriented puzzles) in the account. The most important of them are resolved, while many others are not. One wonders, for example, why Reuben did not speak up when his brothers were negotiating the sale of Joseph, if he really wanted to rescue him (v. 22). This question is not answered until it is later reported (v. 29) that Reuben was absent from the scene during the actual sale—why, we are not told.[170] In any case, there is an obvious gap in the narrator's sudden aside regarding Reuben's motivation: ' "Don't lay a hand on him." [Reuben said this] in order to rescue him from their hand' (v. 22). The dialogue also features a number of idiomatic ellipses to imitate (presumably) the typical stylistic compaction of actual speech, for example, 'What profit [will we have] if we kill our brother' (v. 26).

4.3.5 Examples of deviation

A relatively large number of non-information-seeking rhetorical questions (in effect, emphatic assertions or criticisms) punctuate the dialogue of Genesis 37. In addition to their content, these forceful mock-queries convey a variety of crucial attitudes and intense emotions as in "evocation" (see sec. 4.3.7), for example, 'Will you really rule over us?!' (v. 8—angry pique; cf. v. 10); 'What this dream that you dreamed?!' (v. 10—irritation); 'What gain by killing our brother?' (v. 26—pity and concern); and 'Where can I go now?!' (v. 30—sadness and shame).

Many textual shifts and emphatic placements with regard to word order are also seen in the dialogue of Genesis 37 since such a feature increases the oral idiomaticity or verisimilitude of direct speech. For example, there is syntactic regression ('See the lord of dreams *this!*' in v. 19); syntactic advancement ('*This* [coat] we have found' in v. 32); and lexical-syntactic reversal ('I will go down [a] to *my son* [b], mourning to *Sheol* [a'] in v. 35).

An unusual instance of repetition occurs in v. 22 as a new and complete quote margin breaks into Reuben's speech, perhaps to emphasize its content (i.e., the first kind word spoken by a brother about Joseph). Another departure from the normally lean Hebrew narrative style appears in v. 28–36, where the pathetic fate of Joseph is reported at length: Joseph's

---

[170]It later turns out that Joseph did not accept his forced captivity in silence as the account here seems to indicate. This detail is omitted in chapter 37 (due to condensation) and only revealed later, for greater dramatic effect, when his brothers unknowingly confess their guilt before Joseph in the land of Egypt (42:21).

name is explicitly mentioned four times in this passage (but surprisingly not with reference to 'the robe' in v. 31).[171] Two important parenthetical digressions from the story line are employed for explanatory purposes in Genesis 37. The first stresses (by means of a parallelism) the fact that the cistern into which Joseph was thrown was dry (v. 24b); the second reveals what the Midianites did with Joseph when they arrived with him in Egypt (v. 36; cf. v. 28). We also have the interesting example of what appears to be an ironically conceived missed prediction as Reuben is credited with delivering Joseph from the hand of his brothers (v. 21), when in fact this attempt ends in an embarrassing failure (vv. 29–30).

4.3.6 Examples of phonation

A prime manifestation of phonation as a rhetorical technique is punning. A pun on the name of Joseph with thematic implications is found in both v. 5 and v. 8 of Genesis 37: the brothers 'increased [*yosiphu*] hating Joseph [*yoseph*]'. In 4b and 5a they could not speak 'peace [*sh-l-m*]' with him because of all his 'dreaming [*ch-l-m*]'.

Another play on similar sounds involving 'Joseph' occurs in v. 33, where it serves to heighten the expression of Jacob's great grief as he mourns the loss of his son: *taroph toraph yoseph*. In v. 30 repetition is combined with similar sounds to express Reuben's guilty anguish over the loss of Joseph: *wa'aniy 'anah 'aniy ba'* 'As for me, where [can] I go?!'. In v. 20 harsh assonance accents the heinousness of the brothers' proposed lie to their father: *chayah ra'ah 'akhalathehu* 'A wicked wild animal has wolfed him down!'. Rhyme, on the other hand, ironically emphasizes their fake affirmation of fraternal affection for Joseph in v. 27: *achiynu besarenu hu'* 'our brother our flesh he [is]'.

These examples are good evidence that the sound structure of literary discourse is closely connected with personal emotion and characterization as well. Phonation is therefore an essential part of the message that is represented in the original text, just waiting to be reproduced in another language.

4.3.7 Examples of evocation

In the Joseph Story are a number of complex thought-speech-action combinations that serve to heighten or foreground the emotive tension of the

---

[171]This omission may well be meaningful: in fact, Joseph *was* no more the owner or possessor of that hated robe. In Hebrew narrative all apparent, seemingly anomalous additions or deletions need to be carefully investigated for their possible implicit significance.

account. First, in v. 2, there is the graphic clash of feelings and attitudes that Joseph's report regarding his brothers provokes. This is juxtaposed in v. 3 with the lavish outpouring of love by the father towards a beloved son, love objectified in a multicolored robe of distinction. This same robe becomes a symbol of fraternal animosity and the sign that occasions a murderous reaction when it next appears on the scene—namely, as the brothers see Joseph from afar coming to meet them (spy on them?) in the sheep fields of Dothan (v. 18). Without the protection of his father, the naive Joseph becomes easy prey to the malicious design of his callous brothers. All his authority over them is swiftly lost, as signified by an ignominious public divestiture (v. 23). Finally, the hated robe, now torn and soaked in goat's blood, becomes the means of a cruel deception, as Joseph's fate is seemingly sealed by his exile into slavery at the hands of foreigners (vv. 26–27, 31). So salient is the symbolic evocation of sin and guilt here that the report of this heinous deed is prolonged in a climactically shocking display of heartless cruelty and fabrication (v. 32), coupled with the heartbroken verbal and physical expression of a father's anguish of soul (vv. 33–35).

4.3.8 Examples of dramatization

At least half of the complete text of Genesis 37 is composed as direct speech. The characters are thus conceptualized for the audience not only by their actions, but more importantly by their own words—for example, first the frustration (v. 10) but finally the inconsolable grief of Jacob (v. 35) over what happens to Joseph, the central character. Another example of such dramatized discourse is Joseph's simple naiveté (vv. 6, 9) in contrast to the calculated hatred of his brothers (e.g., vv. 19–20), though not quite all of them, at least not to the same degree (e.g., vv. 21b–22a, 26–27).

These dialogues seem to get rather colloquial at times as shown, for example, by the incorporation of Hebrew idioms (e.g., in v. 13, 'Here I am', meaning "I am ready!" [TEV], and in v. 30, 'where [am] I-going', meaning "What am I going to do?" [TEV]), exclamations (e.g., in v. 35 an asseverative *kiy*, 'For sure [i.e., despite what you say to comfort me]!'), imperatives (e.g., in vv. 13–14 'Come/go!'—the same verb), emphatic demonstratives (e.g., in v. 19 the pejorative 'this', meaning Joseph), pronouns (e.g., in v. 32 'it', meaning the robe), negatives (e.g., in v. 32 'or not' ['*im loo*']), and discourse particles (e.g., in v. 7 a climactic *gam*, and in vv. 6, 14, and 32 the imperative ameliorative *na*', and in v. 20 the instigating temporal adverb 'now').

The only instance of embedded speech occurs in v. 17. Presumably it is intended to support the veracity of the information that the stranger gave to Joseph (confirmed through repetition of the place name 'Dothan' at the end of the verse). There is also a good example of verbalized thought, positioned at a key juncture in the account: Reuben comes to secretly deliver Joseph only to discover—'Look, there's no Joseph in the pit!' (v. 29). This could also be seen as a case where the narrator dramatically merges his viewpoint—and that of the audience—with the perspective of a character on the scene.

4.4 The implications of artistic devices

To conclude, we must ask ourselves, What are the implications of what we have discovered hidden beneath the surface of the original text of Genesis 37? What is the real communicative significance of the special convergence of artistic techniques in this complete pericope, both in terms of itself and with reference to the surrounding episodes (in this case, Genesis 36, 38, 39)? What part do these devices play in the author's overall or underlying narrative argument? How does the message's form (actually many interrelated forms) serve to heighten or enhance the intended content in these varied respects? Furthermore, how does one go about translating a masterful discourse such as this so that much of the same literary effect can be recreated in a given TL, along with its principal semantic and pragmatic intent?

Obviously, the detailed and sustained artistry of the SL document contributes a great deal to the progressive and cumulative meaning (conceptual plus emotive, hence also *affective* impression) that the original text ultimately conveys. It must also be admitted that this is an aspect of meaning that has not often been either fully considered or adequately responded to during the translation process. We are left, therefore, with some larger questions: Shall this always be so? Must real literature—verbal art—remain restricted to the realm of secular discourse in language X? The importance of this literary layer of signification within the original text is clear. What relevance does this have, then, for serious Bible translators in terms of the processing costs versus communicative benefits of the version that they are currently preparing in their language?

Of course, questions such as these can be answered only within the framework of an actual project scenario and the particular *Skopos* that has been discussed and approved by qualified representatives of the target audience. One thing is certain: The adoption and application of a literary approach to Bible translation inevitably requires a large commitment in terms of time, talent, treasure, and training before the challenge can be taken up and an appropriate response be made to such issues, whether in relation to the text as a whole or only in part (meaning applied only partially, or only to a selected—perhaps a featured—text portion or pericope), as determined by the project's guiding *Skopos*. However, a careful examination of the Word of God in the original text should convince us that such an objective is worth at least considering. This would be worthwhile even if it means merely calling attention in footnotes to the most important stylistic features and rhetorical functions that have not found equivalent expression in the TL translation.

5

Iconicity of the Scriptures

The term *iconicity* refers to the Bible's characteristic imagery, cultural symbols, ideal models, and conventional (generic) figures of speech.[172] It is the discourse-level equivalent of figuration in relation to the microstructure (see sec. 4.1.1). The nature and purpose of the iconic features are closely related to the medium of communication in which they are typically employed for facilitating and enriching the message-transmission process.

---

[172]The word *iconic* is defined as that which has the nature of an icon, "an image, a figure, a representation"; it also refers to something "done in a fixed or conventional style" (*Webster's New World Dictionary* 1988:668). Such imagery is much more significant in semiotic terms (salience and scope) than the various figures of speech considered in section 4.1.1. It should be noted that I am here using the terms *iconic* and *iconicity* in a literary, not a linguistic sense. From the latter perspective "iconicity principles" are those "which govern natural form-function correlates" in language grammar (Givon (1984:33). Thus in instances where "the coding relation between structure and function in syntax is non-arbitrary, or in some sense iconic, ... one could proceed to infer common function from common structure." Furthermore, "to the extent that an isomorphism can be demonstrated between code and message, one is entitled to call the relation iconic" (ibid.). I employed this linguistic sense in chapter 3 when referring to the possibility of having an isomorphic equivalent of a text, for example, one manifesting a chiastic construction, being represented as to its structural organization in some appropriate visual or oral representation. Boase-Beier and Holman also apply the term *iconicity*, "the mirroring of meaning in form," to the lexical aspect of literary creativity, where "words or word-patterns are actually to mimic what they denote" (1999:6–7; see also Chesterman and Wagner 2002:10). Such is the case with onomatopoeia, of course, and, in a deeper semantic sense where African ideophones are used (see appendix B).

Iconicity is a quality that is normally manifested in its most dynamic and dramatic form in oral discourse designed to make a lasting impression on the minds of a listening audience.

> Oral conventions evolved to provide the storage systems for organized remembering, and as [oral and written literature] developed it appropriated those conventions to provide common frames for the listening audience. The shape of each mnemonic container predicted its contents in the same way that one would not expect to find milk stored in a gasoline can or sugar in a ketchup bottle. (Wilson 1997:24)

The preceding characterization, in my opinion, does not sufficiently allow for creative artistry and generic flexibility in the typical oral compositional event (which was often a public performance); nevertheless, it does draw our attention to the prominence of conventional forms in this process. Such forms include the use of recognized genres and hybrids (see sec. 3.1) along with major tectonic arrangements like the inclusio, chiasmus, terrace pattern, and refrain that feature a significant recursion of elements as well as balanced, often symmetrical and layered, patterning based on parallelism (see sec. 3.2). Literary-rhetorical devices of this nature provided an ancient audience with an aural "grammar of orientation" (ibid.:35), enabling them to distinguish the external and internal boundaries of a composition, to discern its points and areas of special salience (especially in the center or at the end of discrete units), to mentally process and organize the unfolding message, and also to remember and be able to repeat its thematic and topical essence themselves.

In this chapter I will focus on the importance of the principal images and their recurrence in the biblical literature with several examples of iconicity provided from the Epistle of James.

5.1 Archetypes

In a literary approach the characteristic of iconicity is often equated with the study of archetypes, which may be defined as follows:

> Generally speaking, an archetype is an original pattern from which copies are made, or the most essential characteristic trait shared by the members of a class of things....In poetry [and prose], an archetype may be any idea, character, object, institution, event, or setting containing essential characteristics which are primitive, general, and universal rather than sophisticated, unique, and particular. (Preminger and Brogan 1993:95)

Archetypes, that is, major conventional icons, convey an extra measure of communicative significance by virtue of the fact that they function as signs within two distinct, but interrelated systems of meaning—namely, the linguistic structure of the language and also the literary (oral-written) tradition and system of conventions of the society concerned.[173] Instead of novelty, which is often in focus where artistry is concerned, the iconicity of archetypes features the creative dimension of *familiarity*, where a well-known image resonates with the many texts and social contexts in which it has been used in the past, thus stimulating a deeper reflection that is nourished by one's memory.[174]

Archetypes are the basic building blocks of human conception and imagination. Due to their characteristic recurrence, whether in explicit or modified (e.g., metaphoric) form, they contribute not only to the unity of a given oral or literary work, corpus, or tradition, but certain prominent instances also serve to connect a particular text with what is universal (more or less) in world literature, considered as a whole.[175] They are the typical images, illustrations, examples, pictorial elements, and patterns that appear in a great many, though not necessarily all, verbal traditions, no matter how disparate the languages and cultures concerned. Certain archetypes and their combinations may occur more frequently in one region of the world than another. For example, some archetypes that are common in the literature of the Ancient Near East as well as the Scriptures include the benevolent king, an oppressive opponent, a fruitful garden, a barren wilderness, valuable jewels, fragrant spices, burning sulfur, joyful singing, mournful weeping, a sacred temple, and a polluted tomb.

Two other important distinctive features of archetypes are their *concreteness* and their *contrastiveness*, as the preceding list from the Ancient Near East illustrates. Archetypes normally refer to entities, events, places, or situations that can be readily evoked verbally and easily visualized—that is, *if* one is sufficiently familiar with the pertinent local

---

[173]The older structuralist notion of connotative semiotics offers a helpful way of viewing the additional significance involved in literary iconicity. Thus "the first system [of denotative significations]...becomes the plane of expression, or signifier, of the second system..., the plane of connotation" (Barthes 1967:89).

[174]Such meaningful resonance is an instance of the literary creativity that may arise despite the constraint that has been imposed by some formal rule, norm, or social tradition (see Boase-Beier and Holman 1999:7).

[175]Text- and tradition-specific images and motifs also effect compositional unity in terms of cohesion and coherence when they are repeated throughout a work (e.g., a body + its parts in 1 Corinthians 12). The focus in this section, however, is upon images of a more general or widespread nature. Frye, one of the recognized pioneers in archetypal criticism, is of the opinion that the deeply significant, recurrent imagery of the Bible makes it "the most systematically constructed sacred book in the world" (1957:315).

setting.[176] In the Scriptures this is true even when certain archetypal images or themes from religious mythology are mentioned or alluded to in demonstration of Yahweh's all-surpassing superiority,[177] most notably in the graphic divine Warrior scenes and events that depict the Lord's awesome theophany against the enemies of his people (e.g., Hab. 3:3–15; cf. Ps. 18:7–15, 68). Furthermore, many prominent positive archetypes have their negative counterparts, although these are less commonly utilized in the Bible. In any case, their referents also fall under God's sovereign governance of the universe, for example, the primordial 'deep' of Gen. 1:2, or 'pestilence' and 'plague' in Hab. 3:5 (see Ryken, Wilhoit, and Longman 1998:xviii–xx).

Such corresponding, contrasting, and complementary iconic recursion is very evident, for example, in Revelation 21–22, where we observe a great deal of allusion to the Genesis 1–2 account of creation along with the expected eschatological embellishment. There are references to "a new heaven and a new earth" (21:1), God dwelling among his people (21:3), a perfectly formed city of glory (21:10–21), a pervasive bright light with no need there for "the sun and the moon to shine" (21:23; cf. 22:5), a river containing the rejuvenating "water of life" near which is planted the restored "tree of life" (22:1–2), with the spotlight of attention being focused upon the divine Being who controls "the Beginning" as well as "the Ending" of all creation (21:6, 22:13). Also present in this vivid visionary climax of the canon is a prominent element of pastoral imagery, which throughout the Bible is used to depict the loving, caring relationship between God and his people. Note, for example, the repeated mention of the Lamb in 21:9, 22, and 22:1 and 3. This kind of study of

---

[176]This caveat is crucially important. A given target audience simply cannot completely or correctly perceive and understand what they have no experience or education about. Inadequate knowledge of the biblical background is undoubtedly the greatest conceptual barrier that people face as they read or hear the Scriptures; it is more of a barrier than a poor translation. The current rush to produce various types of study Bibles is an attempt to address this great need, but such a version helps only Bible *readers*. What can be done for Bible *listeners*—audiorecorded notes, special expository and descriptive programs broadcast on Christian radio stations, "hypertext" computer programs? (But then how many nonliterates own a computer?) The great need for such contextualizing information about the total biblical setting offers a serious challenge to contemporary Scripture communicators worldwide.

[177]With reference to the mythological archetypal allusions to be found in Ezekiel 1–24, L. E. Boadt observes, "To combat this rebellious and stubborn rejection of [the people of Judah's] own God, Ezekiel summons up all the myth-making powers at his disposal to counter their claims and establish the divine kingship of Yahweh" (1996:230). Gibson (1998, chap. 5, "The Rhetoric of Hebrew Myth") presents an informative survey of ancient mythological allusions and motifs (although he includes rather too much within their range of possible biblical reference); his material on allusions associated with Satan and the Lord of Hosts is helpful.

prominent topics, key terms, central concepts, characters, and their various interrelationships within a certain text is an important part of any literary analysis, namely, in the plotting and projection of discourse *cohesion* (formal surface level connectivity) and *coherence* (an underlying congruence in ideational and ideological notions).[178]

As we can see, archetypal analysis helps to reveal in ever-increasing detail the great dependence of the New Testament upon the Old. This debt of imagery and iconicity—along with the more obvious quotations, allusions, and specific references to the Hebrew Scriptures which permeate the writings of the evangelists and apostles (a demonstration of intertextuality)—is so substantial and significant that one really cannot adequately comprehend the New Testament without at least some knowledge of the Old. The nature and importance of this conceptual debt is nicely stated by Wilson (1997:62):

> The gospel writers may add different shading to their story of Jesus, but they are unified in that they see in Jesus not a new thing but the complete fulfillment of an old thing. At every turn images are resurrected from the old covenant and brought to life in the new. In Matthew the spotlight is often full on, with rich passages full of prophetic voice lifted straight from the Old Testament. "It is written," says Matthew; again and again: "It is written." Matthew uses the Old Testament in the New...like patches in a quilt. The references are bold and clear. But Luke uses the Old in a more allusive way, not as a quilt, more like subtle weavings in a blanket. So, too, do Mark and John. [So it is that] a host of images come to mind that are born in the Old Testament and given life in the New.

The unity of *archetypes*, however, goes far beyond this Scripture-internal harmony of plan, plot, perspective, and purpose. It also concerns the conceptual, emotional, and sensory "resonance" that the books of the Bible have with other works of world literature, both religious and secular, in reference to significant symbols, images, or figures that occur in the literary traditions and verbal lore of cultures around the world or within a large region and epoch, such as the Mediterranean Middle East at the time of Christ. Some examples are sun, moon, light, darkness, angel, demon, initiation, beatification, prodigal, prince, mountain, and valley. "These master images are the building blocks of the literary imagination—the forms to which the imagination gravitates when it organizes reality and

---

[178] "[T]he coherence of a text is, in essence, a question of whether the hearer can make it 'hang together' conceptually, that is, interpret it within a single mental representation.... COHESION...[is] the use of linguistic means to signal coherence....Signals of cohesion indicate how one part of the text with which they occur links up conceptually with some other part" (Dooley and Levinsohn 2001:27).

human experience" (Ryken 1992:26). One noted archetypal critic asserts that "some symbols are images of things common to all men, and therefore have a communicable power which is potentially unlimited" (Frye 1957:99). Another claims they "make up the groundwork of the human psyche" (Jung 1953:47).

The concentration of these archetypes in the various books of the Bible is yet another reason to classify them as literature. However, the primary relevance of archetypal study for translators lies in its potential to unlock the disparate localized connotative overtones and symbolic values as well as the actual significance of much of the imagery of the Scriptures. A recent dictionary on the subject states,

> Many of the images and motifs discussed in this dictionary are archetypes. They recur not only throughout the Bible but in literature generally, and in life. Being aware of them will help us draw connections—between parts of the Bible, between the Bible and other things we have read, between the Bible and life. (Ryken, Wilhoit, and Longman 1998:xvii)

As already noted, archetypes are frequently paired in a dialectical, often hyperbolic pattern of contrasts, polarities, or opposites that graphically portray human nature and behavior as either the social ideal or its corrupt antithesis. Other animate beings, the physical universe, and the supernatural world are similarly depicted and categorized. The following selective examples from Ryken (1992:26–28) are merely suggestive of this common understanding of the universe that permeates also the diverse writings of Scripture (see also Ryken, Wilhoit, and Longman 1998:xviii–xx):

The Supernatural (+): God, angels, heavenly beings, ancestors/patriarchs, miracles

(–): Satan, demons, evil spirits, idols, monsters, evil omens

World of Nature (+): spring/summer, sun/moon/stars, light/day, gentle rain, farm, fertile fields, lush grass, vineyard, fruit, tree of life, spring/fountain/river/pool

(–): autumn/winter, eclipse, night/darkness, storm, drought, wilderness, desert, thorns/thistles, unproductive plants, decay, chaff, dry stream, mirage

Human Relations (+): community life, tribe, friendship, faithfulness,
love, marriage, festal meal, family, covenant,
freedom, peace, relatives
(–): tyranny, anarchy, isolation, treachery, slavery, torture (cross), war, riot, divorce, feud,
familial discord, betrayal, foreigners

While there will be sociocultural variations due to a people's particular
geographical and ecological setting, their oral or written literature is
bound to include items similar to those included in such archetypal inventories. Their other graphic art forms, such as painting, architectural deco-
rations, weaving, and pottery, will also depict universal images, as will
their diverse musical compositions.[179]
The parables of Christ are especially prominent in terms of their archetypal constitution and significance, particularly with respect to their
contrastive personages. This wealth of cross-culturally relevant symbolism
undoubtedly contributes to their worldwide popularity, even in translation
where their succinct, vivid, and incisive style needs to be duplicated if at all
possible. The language of the Psalms and the Old Testament prophets provides another rich lode of ancient Near Eastern archetypes. In the relatively
short prophecy of Joel, for example, we find graphic and diverse imagery de-
picting destructive locusts, drunkenness, drought, fasting, divine theophany,
military siege and conquest, a darkening of sun and moon, propitiatory sacrifices, wedding night allusions, life-giving rains and abundant harvest, "inspiration" in dreams and prophecy, celestial portents, eschatological judgment
day and retributive justice, and the fertile holy mountain versus a desolate
wilderness. Observe also the abundance of fantastic apocalyptic archetypal
imagery in Revelation 12, which features a semidivine pregnant woman giving birth, a malevolent dragonlike creature bent on oppression and destruction, spectacular heavenly calamities that mirror deep spiritual antagonism,
a stark wilderness sanctuary, a cosmic battle pitting angelic against demonic

---

[179]With regard to the positive and negative connotations and associations suggested here
(and elsewhere) it is important, in the context of a given receptor culture, for Bible translators to determine where possible mismatches occur. For example, with regard to the semantic field of human relations, are all blood relatives viewed positively, or does such an
evaluation depend upon the circumstances? Is it the same in times of stress and calamity,
when threats of witchcraft or sorcery abound? How are one's work mates, colleagues, or
comrades in arms evaluated when danger or death is near? And what about ethnic "foreigners"—are they all regarded as wicked, dangerous, or at least suspicious and unreliable? The
answers to questions such as these are important when exploring the underlying significance and implications of a book like Jonah, for example, where such considerations become an important aspect of the narrative account as well as its underlying thematic
development.

forces, and a defeated serpentine foe seeking vengeance upon the earth via a cataclysmic flood.

Such unifying elements, even those linked by antithesis, must also be investigated in terms of their culturally and religiously specific manifestation within the Holy Scriptures, especially where some anomaly or variation from the norm is concerned. For example, it is crucially important for interpretation (in this case, to perceive the text's underlying irony) to note that the behavior of Jonah represents the negative inverse of what would be expected of the typical prophet of Yahweh. Jesus too was a marked contrast to what would be expected of his closest contemporary cultural equivalent, namely, a Jewish rabbi or itinerant teacher. In that he taught and ministered with great spiritual insight and authority, he conducted himself very differently from the religious leaders of his day (Matt. 7:28–29); the common people, especially the socioreligious outcasts, both observed and benefited from this (Matt. 7:28–29; Luke 4:14–15; 15:1–2).[180] The same is true of the Apostle Paul whose manner of teaching contrasted with the popular religious philosopher-orators of the ancient Mediterranean world (see 1 Cor. 1:17; 2:1, 4). These and many other types and archetypes or their opposites thus need to be thoroughly examined with regard to their historical and sociological setting by serious exegetes and translators as part of a complete discourse study of the biblical texts.

Another prominent archetypal contrast, one that is especially notable in our postmodern times, is seen in the depiction of Hebrew women of the Old Testament. They frequently stand out for their drive, determination, and common sense in contrast not only to comparatively weaker and duller male personages, but also with respect to contemporary ancient Near Eastern cultural stereotypes. Some examples are Sarah (vs. Abraham, Genesis 12), Rebekah (vs. Isaac, Genesis 27), Moses' mother (vs. her husband, Exodus 2), Rahab (vs. the spies, Joshua 2), Deborah (vs. Barak, Judges 4), Jael (vs. Sisera, Judges 4), Jephthah's daughter (vs. Jephthah, Judges 11), Delilah (vs. Samson, Judges 12), Ruth (vs. Boaz, Ruth 2–3), Hannah (vs. Elkanah and Samuel, 1 Samuel 1), Michael (vs. David, 1 Samuel 19), Abigail (vs. Nabal and David, 1 Samuel 25), and the medium at Endor (vs. Saul, 1 Samuel 28).

---

[180]Observe how markedly the ethical and spiritual principles so boldly enunciated by Jesus in the Beatitudes differed from the values, ideals, attitudes, and aims embodied in the thinking, teaching, and practice of Jesus' contemporaries. For example, the "blessings" pronounced upon the "poor in spirit" and "meek" are in dramatic contrast to the prevailing personal desire to preserve one's honor and control others (Pilch 1999:5; see also Pilch and Malina 1993:139–142).

As far as Bible translators are concerned, such archetypes are important, first of all, in terms of their reference, especially in cases where the imagery and its associations are alien to the local TL setting (e.g., the notion of a sabbath), or where they appear in culturally unfamiliar situations and combinations (e.g., the practice of infant circumcision). The additional conceptual connections and emotive overtones that these images always convey should also be considered. Thus a careful study of the *denotative* content of the preeminent figures must always be complemented by a corresponding examination of their respective *connotative* significance. ("Connotation" refers to the emotions, attitudes, and values that tend to be typically associated with certain words and phrases, especially those bearing a special symbolic import.) Connotative overlays may be positive or negative along the lines of the antithetical archetypes previously mentioned. This is an area in which intercultural conceptual "interference" may be considerable. For example, while angels, connotatively, are regarded as positive and demons negative in the biblical literature as well as in the teachings of the mainline churches of south-central Africa, in the syncretic ancestral possession cults the demon spirits (*mademoni*) are often viewed much more favorably, functionally speaking.

The problem for translators is that a word's connotation, like its denotation, is culturally perceived and defined, hence not always so easy to convey, even partially, in another language. As in the aforementioned case of 'demons', the connotation, in contrast to the literal sense of a term, may be different in the social setting of a particular target audience from its associative significance in the biblical setting. Such differences will therefore need to be clarified, whether in the text or a footnote. This is important too in the case of important archetypal antitheses (e.g., a dry/dead versus a green/living tree, drought versus fertility, day versus night, war versus peace), for these often introduce an explicit or implicit contrast or emphasis into the message of a text, as 'light' and 'darkness' do in 1 John 1:5–2:11.[181]

Some of the important biblical archetypes (sheep, shepherd; fig, oak, olive, and palm tree; vineyard, wine; bread; hill, mountain [e.g., Mt. Zion]); cornerstone; eagle; bridegroom; firstborn son; green grass; milk; honey; olive oil; prophet; rainbow; ring; shade; throne; symbolic numbers such as seven, ten, and thousand; and the names of famous persons, such as Abraham, Israel, David, and Solomon) can usually be translated more or less literally into a Bantu language, for example, with roughly the same referential sense. However, the positive connotation that these archetypes have in Scripture,

---

[181]Thus when items, events, or attributive features are designated in such a way that they fall outside the poles of two opposites, this abnormality emphasizes them (e.g., the quality of lukewarmness in Rev. 3:16).

which tends to be more difficult to deal with than the negative, is largely lost in the conceptual transfer process. Other seemingly innocuous key terms may turn out to communicate quite different and often unwanted connotations to the Christian community due to their past and present association with African traditional religion. For example, 'horn' may suggest sorcery and witchcraft; 'root', magical substances; 'salt', menstrual taboos; and 'spirit', ancestral veneration. Clearly, a great deal of research and testing is required on the part of translation teams to be able to handle major areas of connotative signification. They are issues that are potentially very sensitive, perhaps even controversial as well.

Four different aspects of iconicity, or varieties of archetype, may be usefully distinguished: symbols, character types, type scenes, and literary-cultural categories.[182] These iconic features will be considered separately in sections 5.1.1–5.1.4 for the purposes of description, though they often merge and overlap in a given literary text and tradition of oral and/or written literature.

5.1.1 Symbols

Certain important images and image-clusters that are reiterated within a given work or corpus gain the status of *symbols* when they begin to convey a multiple and/or magnified referential and emotive import. In other words, both the literal meaning and one or more nonliteral meanings, including their respective connotations and other nonreferential implications, are significant. A symbol functions conceptually like either a metaphor or a metonym (see sec. 4.1.1). The difference is that a symbol is more extensive in its field of conventional, culturally based associations, more evocative in its range of semantic linkages, more pervasive with regard to intertextual connections, and more compelling in terms of its perceived rhetorical force.

A well-known image may be just as powerful in sacred literature as in nonsacred usage, and perhaps more so, due to the added religious dimension. For example, in Psalm 23, short as it is, we conceptually encounter the rapidly shifting scenes of a shepherd and his sheep, a well-watered pasture, a dark and dangerous canyon, anointing a visitor's head with oil,

---

[182]D. Northrop Frye's 1957 *Anatomy of Criticism* provides a much more elaborate development of this subject. In this book, he discusses the field of "archetypal criticism" in terms of four major categories: "modes" (fictional, tragic, comic, thematic); "symbols" (literal and descriptive, formal, mythical, anagogic); "myths" (comedy, romance, tragedy, irony/satire); and "genres" (epos, prose, drama, lyric). This sort of a "wide-angled" approach certainly increases one's awareness of and appreciation for the importance of imagery and symbolism in literature. But the reader must beware of its universalistic, reductionistic tendency—that is, a preference for neat patterns and wholes, often at the expense of the novelty, complexity, and detail of a culturally particular tradition.

welcoming an honored guest to the banquet table, and life in a loving father's residence. The concentration of symbolic imagery makes a deeply
moving, lasting impression that greatly enriches the central theme: the
steadfast covenantal relationship between a gracious God and his faithful
people. Such an effect is realized, however, only in the case of those who
understand, appreciate, and can empathize with the imagery. The mutually involving and obligating bond of a lifelong covenant, for example, is a
key biblical concept that is quite foreign to most Westerners.

A symbol's aesthetic appeal, emotive impact, and spiritual inspiration
can therefore vary a great deal depending on the TL audience's familiarity
with it as well as with the tradition in which it occurs.[183] References in the
Bible to an olive tree or olive oil, a fig tree or ripe figs, vineyard or wine,
milk and honey, grain or bread, a stronghold set on a high hill, and a
house built on a solid rock meant a great deal to devout Jewish people; on
the other hand, these references have little or no special significance for
average Christians living in south-central Africa.[184] As a result, an appreciable amount of meaning, along with the literary artistry involved, gets
lost, diluted, or distorted in translation.

What can be done to lessen this semantic loss? First, there is the matter of
initial *perception*. Translators have to be made aware of exactly how much
meaning is at stake in any given instance. (In addition to the standard commentaries and handbooks, a scholarly tool that should prove helpful in this
regard is Ryken, Wilhoit, and Longman's 1998 *Dictionary of Biblical Imagery*,[185] which includes articles on character types, plot motifs, type scenes,
rhetorical devices, and literary genres.) Think how much cognitive and emotive significance lies beneath the surface in the story of the prodigal son.
What, for example, does the forgiving father's ring symbolize, and what is

---

[183]The possibility of specialized symbolical usage within a given text also needs to be explored, for example, the presence of "anti-language" in John's writings (see Malina and
Rohrbaugh 1998:46–48).

[184]Certain figurative references may convey the exact opposite of what was intended due
to cultural and contextual conditioning. In Africa, for example, only an ignoramus would
construct his pole and thatched grass "house" upon a stony site, let alone a large rock (Luke
6:48), or plant a crop simply by throwing his seed into the air where it could easily fall on
clearly unproductive ground (Luke 8:5–6).

[185]Williams (1999) has a similar treatment of the metaphors found in the Pauline writings. The footnotes of his study are very informative for Bible translators. However, one
must always be prepared for scholarly differences of opinion. For example, interpreters differ concerning the symbolic significance of 'salt' in Matt. 5:13. The standard interpretation
calls attention to the seasoning, preserving, and/or purifying function of salt (so Ryken,
Wilhoit, and Longman 1998:752). Pilch (1999:4–6), on the other hand, makes an interesting case for understanding salt as a catalytic agent that was essential to ignite the dried
dung used as fuel in an earthen or clay oven. In his view the focal function of salt in Matt.
5:13 is to promote burning, which is in turn a metaphor for enhancing, revealing, or defending the honor of the Father (Matt. 5:16).

the full implication of his giving the ring (plus a new suit and dress shoes) to his unworthy son in a great public display of forgiveness and affection? Often, as in this story, Jesus seems to tell two (or more) stories at the same time—one that is readily apparent on the surface of the text, but which represents another that is implied or understood within the cultural and religious framework of an ancient Near Eastern society.

Second, there is the matter of *selection*. Translators need to find out just how much of this highly connotative biblical imagery can reasonably be included—or at least suggested—in the TL version. Any special significance may be signaled in different ways, of course: It may be built into the text itself through local form-functional equivalents (when available), displayed visually with an illustration placed near the pertinent passage, and/or explained in a footnote.

Finally, a great deal of *testing*, with a view towards possible *revision*, needs to be carried out with respect to the symbolic dimension of message transmission. This is simply to ensure that, at the very least, the inevitable cross-cultural disparity of significance, including any underlying implications, does not result in confusion or misunderstanding on the part of the intended audience (a case in point being the wisdom that is attributed to serpents in Matt. 10:16).

5.1.2 Character types

Not a great deal needs to be said about the important iconic affinity that the Bible has with other great world literature when it comes to character types. Certain typical personages, "characters," activate the accounts, whether fictional or historical in nature and intent, just as in a great many indigenous narrative traditions.[186] Like the symbolical archetypes already noted, these personages and their associated roles tend to reveal a prominent pattern of opposites—heroes and villains, loyalists and traitors,

---

[186]The presence of certain common literary conventions and techniques does not mean that the Bible is fictional or imaginary in nature. It simply indicates the extent to which its authors were willing to go in order to communicate with their intended audiences. They accommodated themselves to the shared assumptions and expectations of the contemporary people about how such information should be effectively composed or packaged in verbal form—how it needed to be selected, arranged, embodied, and shaped to obtain the best results. As T. S. Elliot observed, "It is the function of all art to give us some perception of an order in life, by imposing an order upon it" (1957:93). The story of Ruth, for example, manifests a great many motifs and plot elements that are common to both popular soap opera romances and also to everyday accounts of wooing and wedding a spouse (see Ryken, Wilhoit, and Longman 1998:xvi). How one happens to tell the story does not of itself render it fictive, or, for that matter, factive either. This caveat applies to all of the literary and rhetorical features that I discuss in this book. The use of artistry is not incompatible with either veracity or historicity (credibility or authority, either).

benevolent rulers and terrible tyrants, wise people and fools, brave warriors and cowards, rich and poor. Of special interest are the various *fantastic* beings and bestial creatures, both good and evil, that appear in apocalyptic literature. Since these eschatological figures (e.g., the lion, lamb, and dragon of the Revelation) are typical of a genre that few today are familiar with, some background information may need to be supplied in footnotes to the text in order to clarify their meaning, at least where the textual and extratextual context allows.[187]

A distinctive feature of the Scriptures as a whole is the fact that not even major personages such as Moses, David, Solomon, John the Baptist, Peter, and Paul are characterized or repeatedly referred to simply in order to chronicle their own individual development or achievements. On the contrary, in keeping with the discourse feature of condensation (sec. 3.2.2), they are given a part to play in the biblical account only for the sake of the larger story, the record of God's salvation history as this is carried out in the lives of individuals, of nations (beginning with Israel), and ultimately of all peoples, the fitting climax being symbolically depicted in John's Apocalypse.

Furthermore, seemingly just, benevolent, courageous, and holy human characters are not painted in perfection; rather, they are realistically portrayed, warts and all, in speech as well as actions. Thus there is really no extensive dualistic polarity that corresponds exactly to the antithetical categories of saints-and-sinners or heroes-and-villains.[188] The acceptable or favored individuals are, like their negative counterparts, all measured or evaluated according to a single divine standard, namely, their faith and life in relation to Jesus the Christ, the "chief character"[189] of the Bible.

---

[187]A good question for translators is whether the names of certain indigenous mythological "monster" types can be utilized to render (whether referentially or comparatively) terms such as Leviathan, Rahab, or the beasts that John saw in his vision. The answer no doubt depends on accepted ecclesiastical usage as well as the local connotation, which may be decidedly negative if such creatures happen to be closely associated with traditional religious beliefs. An example among the Chewa people (Malawi) is a huge subterranean serpent named *Napolo*, which is believed to cause earthquakes and other natural disasters.

[188]We know virtually nothing about the lives of the male saints referred to in the Scriptures—Enoch, Melchizedek, Joseph of Arimathea, Stephen. Surprisingly, more is revealed about the female heroines—Deborah, Hannah, Ruth, Abigail, Mary mother of Christ, and Mary sister of Lazarus.

[189]There is at least one major character type in the Bible that is not filled true to form, the Messiah figure. This lack of fulfillment caused no end of uncertainty and confusion among the people in Christ's time. The Son of Man (also Son of God) did not realize either the character (personality) or the role (office) that was expected of the divinely appointed long-prophesied Messiah. Jesus Christ did not come as a mighty warrior-king to liberate Israel from all social, economic, and political oppression to establish a new world order on behalf of the nation. Rather, his kingship and kingdom were not of this world (John 18:36–37).

This pervasive honesty of reporting runs right throughout the corpus—from Noah, Abraham, Jacob, Moses, David, the singer of Psalm 73, Solomon, Hezekiah, Peter, Paul, and on to entire groups (characterized in terms of the majority), such as "Israel/Judah" (e.g., in the Book of Hosea), "Jerusalem" (in Matt. 23:37–39), the "Galatians" (in Gal. 3:1–2), and the seven churches of Asia Minor (Revelation 2–3). Along with the attributes that make them role models for God's church of modern times, the foibles and failings of these persons and groups are also revealed. The point is that the depictions of their inconsistent or incontinent behavior need to be rendered in a manner that does justice to the intention of the account in the biblical text without euphemism or downplaying prominent character flaws such as Noah's drunkenness, the dissembling of Abraham, Jacob's trickery, Judah's prostitution, David's adultery, the thunderous temper of James and John, Peter's denial, John Mark's desertion, and Saul's preconversion anti-Christian zeal.[190]

5.1.3 Type scenes

Type scenes are composed of archetypal "plot motifs," those prominent action elements ("moves") or situational states that recur in the world's oral and written narrative traditions. When these motifs are arranged in a general pattern, then a type scene is formed—that is, a sequence of events that tends to manifest itself in stories in a more or less fixed, predictable fashion.

> [These] conventional forms spin through the fabric of Scripture in the form of battle reports, birth announcements, commissioning stories, sea storms, "murmuring" stories, and even stylized reactions to bad news. They are called type scenes because each type represents a specific social situation. Both the *form and the general content of a type scene are relatively stable,* as the betrothal convention illustrates. (Wilson 1997:25)

At times the expected sequence of eventive and dialogic elements is made more concrete by the presence of various correspondences in actual vocabulary (which of course need to be matched in translation). We notice such prominent "narrative parallels" (Wilson 1997:27–28), for example, in the

---

[190]A good example of such translational skewing may be seen in renderings that describe Peter's shameful public compromise of biblical principles in Gal. 2:11: "was clearly in the wrong" (NIV), "to be blamed" (NKJV), "clearly wrong" (GNB), and "wrong" (CEV). The Greek verb καταγινωσκω that Paul employs here is considerably stronger than such mollifications would suggest—more along the lines of "condemned" or "convicted" (see Bauer, Arndt, Gingrich, and Danker's lexicon). It is for this very reason that Paul had to take a vigorous "stand against" (ανθιστημι) such behavior and the attitude that motivated it.

accounts of the banishment of Ishmael (Gen. 21:8–21) and the offering of Isaac (Gen. 22:1–19), where Abraham is the common character who is thereby foregrounded in these two "yoked episodes" (Wilson ibid.:29). Another patent, hence highlighted, instance of type scenes occurs at the beginning of the New Testament narrative in Luke 1:5–2:40: the respective announcements and birth narratives of John the Baptist and Jesus the Christ (Wilson ibid.:31). These narrative parallels have an important thematic implication. They indicate that John was the divinely appointed, prophetic forerunner to the Messiah and the fulfillment of another aspect of God's salvific plan of intertestamental interlocking (see also Luke 3:1–20 / Isa. 40:3–5; Mark 1:1–8 / Mal. 3:1, Isa. 40:3; Matt. 3:1–12 / Isa. 40:3).

Parallels in narrative can be considered analogous to the cumulative progression of the functional constituents in a text of a nonnarrative genre. An example is the familiar psalm of lament, the constituents of which typically exhibit the following movement: general invocation/appeal => description of problem/need => specific request => personal defense/confession => profession of faith => promise/vow => praise/thanks (Wendland 2002a:34–36). Where narrative parallelism occurs, whether in obvious or less apparent form, there is always a theological lesson to be learned or a moral point to be made as the sequence of corresponding panels unfolds (as in Gen. 12:10–20, 20:1–18, and 26:6–11, the story of the patriarch's cowardice in a foreign land). No doubt many of Christ's parables followed motifemic sequences that were by and large familiar to his audience from the Jewish rabbinical tradition. Playing off the known, he would typically highlight his own distinctive message by means of an unconventional and challenging, often shocking twist at the end, for example, in the parable of the great banquet where a rabble of socio-religious outsiders replaces all the honored invited guests. (For a detailed literary-rhetorical study of this parable in Luke 14:16–24, along with some translational implications, see Wendland 1997.)

Whether in poetry or prose, then, what we have is a "set of *conventions*— ingredients that recur so often in similar situations that they become familiar expectations in the minds of writers and readers [or listeners] alike" (Ryken, Wilhoit, and Longman 1998:xv). Some common literary motifs to be found in dramatic narrative, including that of the Bible, are: a crucial quest, a difficult preliminary initiation/testing, a journey to a far-away place, a strong temptation (resisted or succumbed to), a timely rescue or provision, death and rebirth, trials of the suffering servant, a rags-to-riches or ignorance-to-illumination progression (Ryken 1992:50).

More interesting and informative are the cases when these motifs combine to form a recurrent type scene. The following cycle, for example, is common in the Book of Exodus: crisis=>the people complain=>Moses appeals to God => God provides/delivers => God rebukes and/or punishes the people. This is similar in turn to a set that reappears later in the Book of Judges: the people sin => God sends an enemy to oppress them => the people appeal to God for help => he sends a deliverer to rescue them. In the Gospels a familiar pattern recurs: a Sabbath healing => confrontation with religious leaders => Christ's exposé and refutation of legalistic attitudes. The early chapters of Acts also feature a recurring sequence: the apostles preach the gospel and perform mighty works=>crowds converge and many people are converted => this sparks antagonism and persecution on the part of the Jewish religious establishment=>God protects and delivers the apostles => the church grows or spreads.

At times these recurrent patterns are quite specific in terms of narrative detail, for example, in the scenario of two strangers, a man and a woman, meeting at a communal village well, which Ryken, Wilhoit, and Longman (1998:xv) describe as follows:

> the arrival of the man from a foreign land, the appearance of the woman at the well to fetch water, a dialogue between the man and woman, the drawing of water from the well by either the man or the woman as a gesture of thoughtfulness toward the other, the woman's running home to tell her family, and inviting the stranger into the home of the future betrothed in an act of hospitality and welcome.

This portrayal of what Wilson (1997:25) calls the "betrothal convention" is probably a little too precise, for we see that with a few adjustments the original reference in Gen. 24:10–6 may be generalized to fit a wider range of situations, both near (e.g., Gen. 29:4–12) and far (most notably, the account of Christ's meeting with the Samaritan woman at Jacob's well in John 4).[191] Once again, it is not necessary to assume that such typical, recurrent patterns imply complete or partial fictionality (so Alter 1985:46) or a distortion of the facts. Rather, it is a matter of the author's selecting and highlighting from the disorganized detail of human history those elements that happen to conform to sequences that are

---

[191]With regard to this last-mentioned episode, Wilson (1997:241) claims that "like John's *signs* [*semeia*] the story becomes a metaphor far larger than its immediate context.... What is particularly remarkable is that this [betrothal] convention should have been woven into *this* story of the woman at the well. And while it is not apparent to the modern reader, the convention would have been as obvious to many in John's audience as a newspaper wedding announcement is to us. Nevertheless, this would have been a startling scene to John's early audience, as it was to the disciples on their return (John 4:27). After all, the event is located in despised Samaria and involves an outcast woman....It would be virtually impossible for a traditional Jew in Jesus' day to imagine a person of lower human standing."

conventional within a given literary/oral tradition. His aim, presumably, was to communicate efficiently and more effectively—that is, with greater relevance, impact, appeal, and memorability.

Yet while there surely is meaning in a recursion of expected elements, even greater significance is conveyed by the additional specific *details* or *variations* that appear within a particular story in comparison with others. How important is it, for example, that Christ met with a notoriously immoral woman at the well and not some innocent virgin? One must also consider the connotative implications that are possibly present due to cultural norms and expectations. For example, how would people of Christ's day regard his being found alone with a woman in an isolated location? Similarly, we see in Jonah the great importance of the technique of irony that pervades the account. Irony is suggested at the very beginning of the narrative when Jonah acts in dramatic contrast to what would be expected in accordance with the type scene of the prophetic call: the "word of the LORD comes," instructs God's chosen prophet, and he immediately sets out on his divine mission (Jonah 1:1–3; cf. 3:1–3).

Such literary devices do not have a great effect on the translation process since it is content, not form, that is primarily involved. But it would be helpful to footnote and/or cross-reference those instances where a major, hence meaningful, variation in the standard pattern occurs, or where a vital element of contrastive intertextuality is present, or where some clash with cultural or literary conventions occurs, examples being the unexpected initial response of Jonah to his divine call and Christ's royal entry into Jerusalem riding upon a lowly donkey (Luke 19:28–38; cf. Zech. 9:9). Furthermore, the distinctive narrative elements in the overtly analogous accounts in the Bible are significant and must therefore be preserved lexically in translation. An example of this last consideration is in the parallel accounts of Gen. 12:10–20 (the narrative of Abraham's shameful expulsion from Egypt over his duplicity concerning his relationship to Sarai) and Genesis 20 (in which account a friendship pact is established with Abimelech as a result of similar circumstances twenty years later). A similar procedure is followed in the case of the many "parallel passages" of the Gospels.

5.1.4 Literary-cultural categories

In contrast to specific archetypal symbols (figures/images), character types (persons/roles), and type scenes (events/states), a literary-cultural category is a more inclusive, higher-level iconic feature that gives meaning and depth to good literature. A given oral-literary tradition, and distinct genres within that tradition, will normally have a recognized or preferred inventory of such topical fields, or conceptual domains, pertaining to primary values, attitudes, and modes of behavior that orators and authors alike will draw upon as they compose their works.

To be sure, an individual verbal artist will generally have his own characteristic preferences too. Thus his typical pattern, frequency, and range of selection is a means of describing his personal corpus and differentiating his work conceptually from that of others, for example, the prophecy of Isaiah as distinct from that of Ezekiel, or Mark's Gospel from that of Luke.[192] To be more specific, in Luke, we find a particular emphasis on certain religious macro-concepts: salvation for all people; the lost and disreputable in society who especially need such deliverance; the poor, needy, and disadvantaged who received their Messiah's message gladly; the operation of the Spirit of God who converts and empowers his people; and the efficacy of prayer coupled with the need for praise of God. Bible translators will have to carry out a systematic, comprehensive, and continuous program of lexical-semantic analysis coupled with pragmatic research to investigate these diverse literary-cultural categories in their language. How do the TL groupings and combinations relate to the corresponding fields of meaning found in the Scriptures with respect to denotation, connotation, and cognitive association?[193]

During the past several decades a number of prominent biblical socioanthropologists have developed some helpful methods of identifying and analyzing such cultural categories (often referred to as "norms" or "values") on a multigroup, comparative basis. Commonly known as "social-scientific criticism," this methodology is also useful from a literary standpoint: It provides one with an analytical perspective for viewing the broader conceptual-iconic framework of the Hebrew and Greek Scriptures, both in terms of individual books and also more generally as complete corpuses (see, for example, Malina and Rohrbaugh 1992).[194]

---

[192]These compositional differences are usually accompanied by those of a linguistic nature—that is, in a particular author's style of writing.

[193]Nida and Louw's 1992 work, which provides the rationale for their *Greek-English Lexicon of the New Testament Based on Semantic Domains* (Louw and Nida 1989), is a helpful overview of how such a research program might be carried out in terms of contextualized componential analysis procedures, illustrated by a survey of New Testament vocabulary. Their basic methodology is currently being revised in the light of developments in the field of cognitive linguistics and applied to the Old Testament by a team of scholars under the leadership of Reinier de Blois (see, e.g., R. de Blois 2000).

[194]As far as the Hebrew Scriptures are concerned, some of the most insightful studies of this nature are by Mary Douglas, somewhat surprisingly of Leviticus (1999) and Numbers (1993). Douglas demonstrates how key Mosaic cultural-religious categories play an important role in establishing the literary structure of each book. Examples of her categories are: rules concerning defilement (profane), purification (holy) and associated sacrifices; the

The crucial topics of investigation are often grouped into larger headings (frequently paired or multiple conceptual headings), such as honor-shame; in-group/out-group relations; temporal and spatial categories; patron-peasant economies; social stereotypes and surrogates; the religious hierarchy; the notion of "limited good"; crime and punishment; clean versus unclean foods, persons, or objects; and the "three-zone personality" (Malina and Rohrbaugh 1992, 1998, passim).[195] Of course, it is always necessary to double check the findings and conclusions of these scholars with regard to their proposed "reading scenarios" (Malina and Rohrbaugh 1992:16), for they may be rather controversial and hence occasion some important differences of opinion both among themselves and also with other biblical scholars concerning the "correct" interpretation of the relatively limited data at hand. An example is Malina and Rohrbaugh's proposed reading scenarios for the Beatitudes (Matt. 5:3–12); if this set of utterances were placed within the sort of discourse that is typical of an honor-shame society, they would recommend a translation of "how honorable" in place of "blessed"—and a corresponding "how shameless" in place of "woe to" in Matt. 23:13–31 (1992:47). Another proposal concerns the Ancient Near Eastern practice of sorcery; this scenario, when applied to the Bible, would greatly modify one's perspective on the words of Christ in Matt. 20:15, "Is your eye evil because I am good?" Of this, Pilch (1999:120) says, "When the first hired in the story realize that the last hired are being treated with favoritism, they cast an evil eye on the owner of the vineyard. This is serious, a matter of life and death. Jesus' audience would be horrified to hear him include it in the parable." Obviously, if his construal is true, it would affect the translation of this expression and perhaps require an explanatory footnote as well (see also Mark 7:22).[196] Even where there is scholarly disagreement, however, translators are at least alerted to the possibility of greater meaning significance at these

construction and layout of the tabernacle; annual Israelite feasts and festivals; and the classification of animals. R. Bascom (2002) has a good socioanthropological survey in relation to Bible translation.

[195]For a dictionary-type arrangement and discussion of such categories, see Pilch and Malina 1993.

[196]Most versions have something like "are you envious...?" (NRSV, NIV). *The Handbook on the Gospel of Matthew* (UBS Handbook Series) does not mention the possibility of sorcery being involved. Malina and Rohrbaugh note the connection: "The evil eye is a serious matter in Mediterranean societies. It is the eye of envy, and one must be on constant guard against the damage it can cause. Amulets and gestures of various kinds...are intended to provide protection" (1992:125). An evil eye is also associated with curses and sorcery in a number of Bantu language-societies. Note the contrastive reference to eyes at the end of Matthew 20, where Christ brings blessing instead of cursing by healing two blind men (21:33–34).

points in the biblical text. Such areas of controversy concerning prominent culturally resonant categories encourage us to carry out additional
linguistic, literary, and sociocultural investigations that will hopefully resolve the outstanding issues and further suggest how these affect both the
theological interpretation and a literary-rhetorical evaluation of the discourse at hand. A more confident application to translation, including the
footnoting of valid alternatives, can then be made.

5.2 The iconicity of the Epistle of James

The Epistle of James is a good example of an intensely iconic, inductively
developed hortatory discourse. That is, it is a text in which at least one
manifestation of each of the following stylistic-rhetorical features occurs:
(1) a progressive movement from specific, life-related facts to a general
conclusion, prohibition, or exhortation; (2) concrete, sense-related examples, illustrations, stories, proverbial lore, traditions, analogies, figurative
language, and personal anecdotes; (3) a preference for colloquial direct
speech and dialogue; (4) language that appeals to the listener, having the
special characteristics of oral-aural communication; and (5) a focus on the
target group in terms of their worldview, values, hopes and fears, problems, and failures and successes. It is these features that make the epistle
so highly dramatic and challenging to the lives of its audience.

James appealed to the imagination and everyday experience of his addressees by using the contextualized, inductive devices of provocative,
human-oriented illustrations (e.g., 5:17); graphic figures of speech (e.g.,
1:6); vivid contrasts (2:2); lists (3:7); repetition (4:11–12); quotations
(1:13); authoritative Scripture citations (4:5–6); maxims (2:13); vocatives
(2:1); imperatives (2:12); rhetorical questions (2:14); hyperbole (5:4);
irony (2:23–24); and contemporary allusion (5:1–3). The abundance and
diversity of these strongly affective features suggest that this epistle
was consciously composed for public proclamation to a listening
congregation.

Though James connected these inductive stylistic techniques rather
loosely with each other, all are strongly linked as a cohesive group to the
letter's central theme: *True trust in God is demonstrated in how you treat people.* The varied examples and illustrations thus move forward in a circle
(or a recycling spiral) around this principal thematic core, as different
tests of faith and faithfulness unfold and the text gradually builds James's
paraenetic case up by sheer cumulative progression. It is therefore difficult to discern a single peak of prominence, or climax, in the discourse as
a whole, except for the simple end stress on the final pericope of 5:19–20.

Perhaps we are to see here that winning back an erring brother or sister is the ultimate instance of the faith-in-action that characterizes real Christians, especially in times of social, economic, and religious testing.

To relate James's communicative strategy to the subject of this chapter, we need to take note of the many examples of iconicity that are packed into it. The reader/listener ideally experiences (not merely perceives) an alternating succession of vivid pictures, symbols, figures of speech, character types, type scenes, and culture-based stereotypes intended to evoke powerful sensations and feelings and accordingly summon a strong positive or negative personal reaction. Despite its predominantly visual appeal, the imagery is most effectively stimulated aurally, that is, by being heard as it is read aloud.

A recommended exercise for a translation team is to test the overall exegetical relevance and translational importance of these literary-rhetorical features by, first, selecting the most prominent and potent icon, image, or symbolic item in each paragraph of the epistle and, next, analyzing each one, briefly indicating what appears to be its primary denotative and connotative significance in the original text and situational context. The team should then determine what a literal rendering would most likely mean to an average TL audience in their sociocultural setting. Finally, in cases where a miscommunication is highly probable, the team might suggest how to re-express the concept with a functionally equivalent literary technique in the TL, one that preserves the essential author-intended meaning, including the text's overall beauty and impact. The following is a brief illustration of such an exercise, considered with reference to the Chichewa language and culture:

text: 1:6   image: like a wave of the sea driven and tossed by the wind

SL: 'Wave of the sea' is a poetic redundancy. Further superfluity ('driven by wind and tossed all about') serves to highlight the deliberate excessiveness of the watery imagery. Most of the original listeners would have been acquainted with maritime scenery and the instability as well as the danger depicted here in a minatory metaphoric description of a doubting disciple.

TL: Many speakers of Chichewa (also called *Chinyanja* 'language of the lake') know what 'wind-blown waves' are and thus understand the sense of this simile, even though it is not indigenous to the traditional orature. However, the use of water as an image of instability is familiar from proverbial lore, so it is unlikely that James's point will be missed. The two descriptive participles ἀνεμιζομένῳ καὶ ῥιπιζομένῳ, both meaning much the same thing, are duplicated with similar sonic and semantic effect in Chichewa: *amavunduka ndi kuwinduka.*

text: 1:8   image: a double-minded man, unstable...

SL: A 'double-souled' (δίψυχος) person is someone who utterly lacks single-mindedness with respect to his or her thoughts and values. (The soul was regarded as the seat and center of a person's emotions, desires, and will.) This is a person who cannot make up his mind or maintains a divided loyalty concerning the key issues and persons of life. The description 'unstable' (ἀκαστάτος) suggests that the indecisive thinking of such an individual reflects itself in corresponding behavior—that is, wavering, unable to walk a straight line or keep to one course.

TL: In Chichewa there is a similar idiom that conveys the idea of δίψυχος: a person 'of two hearts' (*wamitima iwiri*). Then an ideophone (*wosakhala khazike!*) is used to reproduce the impact of the qualifier ἀκαστάτος and the /s/ alliteration in the sounds of -ψυχος 'soul' and ἀκαστάτος 'unstable'. The overall communicative correspondence here is thus quite close—the nearest functional equivalent in several respects.[197]

A similar comparative study in culturally conditioned literary iconicity could be made with reference to the Old Testament, in particular the conceptually colorful, paraenetically powerful language of Isaiah, beginning from chapter 1 and proceeding all the way through to the end in 66. This prophecy is permeated with picturesque rhetoric in artful service of the prophet's straightforward, life-shaking message on behalf of the Sovereign Yahweh (יהוה), as in Isa. 5:16, 6:3, and 57:15, who earnestly desires to maintain a personal covenantal relationship with an obedient people who serve him in righteousness (Isa. 1:26, 3:10, 60:21).

5.3 The value of studying the iconicity of the Scriptures

A careful study of the archetypal iconicity of the Bible—its symbols, character types, type scenes, and literary-cultural nodes—gives translators, first of all, a better grasp of its literal meaning, which is essential for understanding the text's pervasive, polyvalent figurative level of significance. This in turn enriches their cognitive understanding of and affective response to the Scriptures, both as a whole and with specific reference to key passages under investigation (see Ryken, Wilhoit, and Longman 1998:xx). Archetypal analysis also contributes much to our interpretation and communication of this diverse but complementary corpus of biblical literature, consisting of distinct compositional unities, yet each, along

---

[197]Other passages in James that could be discussed and analyzed with reference to their iconicity as well as figurative language and rhetorical technique are 1:8, 10, 11, 12, 14–15, 18, 19, 21, 23–24, 26, 27; 2:2–4, 6, 15, 21, 25, 26; 3:2–4, 5–6, 7–8, 9, 11, 12, 15, 17–18; 4:1–2, 4, 8, 9, 12, 13, 14; 5:2, 3, 4, 5, 7, 8, 11, 12, 14, 17–18, 20.

with the canon in its entirety, manifesting a comprehensive cohesion, structure, and forward progression.

As was noted earlier, proposing a literary analysis does not presuppose a fictional object of attention. Nor does it suggest that the Scriptures are imaginary in any respect. It simply highlights the artistic, skillfully crafted character of these texts from a technical and critical point of view. The Bible displays a diverse panorama of visualizable images and down-to-earth scenes in which the drama of personal and corporate faith is played out in realistic human situations for the purposes of relevant contemporary appropriation and application.

Finally, where a close comparative examination reveals that the archetypal allusion and symbolism of certain biblical passages are not readily apparent to, or understood by, people today, translators are alerted to the need to explain them by means of supplementary helps, such as footnotes, glossary entries, and illustrations. Such an extratextual strategy, supplemented by pertinent cross-references (to probe all pertinent intertextually related verses), is an effective means of preserving the basic semantic function of these literary techniques. Judiciously applied annotation may also be necessary either to correct or to reinforce a particular target group's overall perception of the sacred corpus as consisting of a polysemous harmony of interconnected parts and wholes—that is, in terms of its imagery as well as its more straightforward referential content.

6

Rhetoricity of the Scriptures

The focus of the previous chapters was on the major stylistic features of biblical form and content. We now move on to the topic of rhetoricity and literary purpose or, more broadly, communicative function. Rhetoricity is the characteristic of literature that pertains to the manifestation of various forms of argumentation ("rhetoric") in oral and written texts. The biblical corpus embodies a diverse collection of *purposeful* discourse—writing with a point, often a sharpened one. In other words, it is not simply "art for art's sake." Its tectonicity, artistry, and iconicity are all designed to persuade the audience to adopt a certain theological and moral position in relation to the God of sacred Scripture. This introduces a prominent functional focus into our discussion of style and structure.

In this chapter, I will define rhetoric, then explore several of the principal ways in which rhetoric has been applied in the study of biblical literature. This will include a number of practical examples to illustrate different types of rhetorical analysis. I am treating this subject in rather more detail than the earlier ones of tectonicity, artistry, and iconicity because its importance has not always been fully recognized in exegetical studies or applied in Bible translation.

6.1 Defining rhetoric

With origins that go back to the influential Greek philosopher Aristotle,[198] the compositional discipline of rhetoric (or "literary pragmatics") may be defined as the verbal art and craft of persuasion. Such discourse is intended to persuade or motivate an audience either to change or to remain steadfast in terms of their thinking and/or behavior with regard to a particular issue. As an "art," rhetoric is innate, an inborn ability, but as a "craft" it may be learned and perfected like any other technique or trade. There are two basic streams of rhetorical study, depending on whether one happens to emphasize the art-craft or the persuasion-argument side of the definition, that is, *aesthetic* (structural) or *directive* (argumentational) rhetoric.[199] Experienced practitioners tend to include both aspects in their analyses, a procedure that I recommend for the practice of Bible translation and related activities. We are therefore concerned about matters that pertain to both literary style (including discourse structure) and communicative purpose when analyzing the Scriptures in order to better understand the text's overall intended meaning. Here in this chapter we want to pay special attention to the *functional* component of rhetoric since the formal dimension of artistry on both the macro- and microlevels of compositional organization has already been considered in the three preceding chapters.

Rhetoric may be further described as a study of the skill of persuasive argumentation or, more generally, of *effective* communication, with the message conveying also a certain perceptible impact and appeal.[200] In

---

[198]There was also a strong tradition of style and rhetoric (with normative principles, procedures, and standards) among the ancient Hebrew verbal artists, although there does not seem to be a specific term to designate such activity. Perhaps נבא 'prophesy' (see 1 Chron. 16:7–9, 25:1–8; Ps. 45:1, 17)? In any case, the practice of rhetorical argumentation with respect to the Scriptures was extensively developed into a formal compositional system and hermeneutical strategy by the Jewish rabbis (see Lane 1991:cxix–cxxxv).

[199]If a more precise distinction between these two approaches is needed, one might designate the study that emphasizes literary *form* as "poetics" and that which focuses upon literary *function* as "rhetoric" (proper). Some analysts have emphasized the *oral-aural* nature of biblical rhetoric—in particular, the audible "thematic and structural markers and mnemonic pegs which have been used by the composer" (Davis 1999:60; cf. Wilson 1997, chap. 2). These analysts seek to show how oral-aural "principles affected the form, style, diction, scope and interrelationships of the literary (or oral) units" of the diverse works of Scripture (Davis 1999:11). But most other aspects of their methodology are similar to those applied to written discourse.

[200]There are of course good, poor, and mediocre instances of rhetorical technique in literature. Thus the process of *evaluation* must also be involved—an assessment of the comparative quality, merit, and value of a given literary piece in relation to others. Such an evaluation is best carried out according to explicit techniques of analysis and criteria of excellence (or inferiority).

other words, a given text (pericope, verse, or device) may be evaluated on the basis of the degree to which it satisfies the intended purpose or goal that motivated it. Although the theory of rhetoric (*what it is*) and its practice (*how to do it*) was undoubtedly applied in its classical setting to oral discourse ("oratory"), the pertinent standards, models, and principles came to be viewed in relation to written texts also, certainly by the time that the New Testament was composed. The major issue over which scholars disagree is the degree of rhetorical influence; some argue for more and others for less. It is probably best to adopt a middle-of-the-road approach and seek a balanced perspective when carrying out any functional investigation of this nature.

Such caution is especially necessary in view of the great deficiency—at times complete lack—of information that limits our understanding of the precise situational setting of virtually all of the biblical books (the so-called "rhetorical exigency"). Similarly, our literary-based assessment of several of the more useful *styles* of rhetorical analysis, which we will be considering shortly, is also restricted: We realize that we do not know for sure the extent to which any one of these approaches reflects or is able to reveal the actual communication dynamics in the original context of message transmission.[201] If the analyst of a biblical discourse should posit a different place, author, exigency, receptor group, and/or time (e.g., with regard to the Book of Jonah, whether it is pre- or post-exilic, or with regard to the Epistle of Jude, whether its date of composition is first or second century), a different analysis will invariably result, one that is likely to contradict the hermeneutical understanding of some prior study.

As we shift our attention now to the pragmatic end of the form-content-function translational continuum, we will be exploring several distinct approaches to the issue of authorial intention in literature. *Pragmatics* investigates the overall effect of the contextual setting and the interpersonal situation on the production of discourse. It considers the linguistic choices available as well as the formal and semantic constraints that may apply in a given set of sociocultural circumstances. From a more strictly defined, literary perspective, pragmatics is defined as a systematic study of all pertinent aspects of the "close relationship between author and audience that affects the composition of the text" (Wiesemann

---

[201]A rhetorical motivation may also be detected in the redactional development of a given book or pericope. For example, the "misplaced" passages of Exod. 11:4-8 and Ezra 4:6-23 presumably have a point and a purpose exactly where they happened to be positioned in the final form of the Hebrew text. Thus, it may be argued that these "interruptive insertions" perform a strategic contrastive function in the discourse in order to highlight an underlying ideological, theological, or polemical argument. (This possibility was brought to my attention in a 2003 paper by Lénart J. de Regt.)

n.d.:11).[202] The pertinent questions that pragmaticians ask are, Why was this particular text written? What goals did the author (whether real or implied) hope to achieve in relation to the intended audience? What did the author expect to gain from the act of communication with regard to "relevance"—that is, what benefit in terms of significant cognitive effects and emotive stimulation?

The fact that the author's message includes implicit information and connotative meaning—including aesthetic meaning—raises some additional questions: What information (and how much) could the original writer assume his readers/hearers would know, so that the information could be left implicit? What is the primary communicative intent behind specific artistic expressions of form and content? Of course, in the case of the Bible, since we are so far removed from the original event, any reconstruction or postulation based on our presuppositions and inferences will be very tentative and conjectural, but should nevertheless be seriously attempted because the original text does contain pragmatic meaning that must be signaled in translation to the extent possible.

While we cannot consider the complex field of pragmatics in all its ramifications, a brief discussion of some of the principles and procedures of rhetorical composition may help us to better understand how it was applied in biblical discourse. This will enable us to bridge the temporal and cultural gap presented by a translation of texts with a greater measure of certainty.

6.2 Methods of rhetorical analysis

Most rhetorical studies of the biblical literature have been carried out on the Epistles, which are in effect written sermons verbally shaped and crafted to persuade their intended addressees how to think and act with regard to various theological and moral issues. But the prophetic books too are strongly hortatory in nature, hence amenable to some form of rhetorical analysis (as demonstrated by Gitay 1991 and also a number of

---

[202]According to Levinson (1983:14), pragmatics studies the total "communicational content" of utterances in context, which includes a consideration of such constituent aspects as truth conditions, deixis, conventional and conversational implicatures, presuppositions, felicity conditions, speech acts, and inferences based on the dialogic structure of a given discourse. Relevance Theory provides a helpful (but at times reductionistic) unifying perspective that enables the analyst to link and interrelate these different discourse features—that is, according to the communicative *principle of relevance* (and its corollaries). This involves the "tacit assumption" that whatever a person has to communicate "will be optimally relevant to the audience: that it will yield adequate contextual effects, without requiring unnecessary processing effort" (Gutt 1992:25). In other words, a text is deemed relevant if it proves to be conceptually worth the mental effort needed to process it (interpret, understand, and apply it).

essays in de Regt, de Waard, and Fokkelmann 1996). The same thing is, in fact, true of a majority of the Scripture texts that have been composed either as direct speech or some other representation of interactive, interpersonal discourse in prose or poetry, such as the Psalms.

A number of distinct, but often interrelated or mutually compatible methods have been applied to an analysis of the rhetorical structure and style of selected texts and books of the Bible. The rest of this chapter is devoted to some of the most important of these: the rabbinic/Christic technique (sec. 6.2.1); the classical Greco-Roman method (sec. 6.2.2); the epistolary method (sec. 6.2.3); speech-act analysis (sec. 6.2.4); and argument-structure analysis (sec. 6.2.5).

6.2.1 The rabbinic/Christic technique

The rhetoric of the Jewish rabbis—appropriated and uniquely developed by Jesus the Christ—represents a sort of midway point between the literature of the Old Testament and that of the New. The discourses of Christ, as they have been recorded and edited in the four Gospels, have a lot in common with the prevailing literary style of the Hebrew prophets as well as that of the teachers and preachers of his day (see Osborn 1999, chap. 9, for an overview of this last group in relation to Christ).[203]

In sections 6.2.1.1–6.2.1.7 seven of the main artistic and rhetorical features of "Jesus speak" will be identified and described. These features will

---

[203] Jesus of Nazareth went considerably beyond his prophetic predecessors as well as his rabbinical contemporaries, not only in terms of content (i.e., speaking as God himself), but also in terms of style and rhetorical dynamics (although this is a debatable issue). There is a big controversy in biblical studies today concerning the degree to which the Gospels preserve the actual *ipsisima verba* of Christ. The elaborate (and to my mind extremely eccentric) efforts of the Jesus Seminar scholars notwithstanding, I do not think that it is possible to be conclusive on this issue one way or the other. My position is simply to accept the testimony of the Greek New Testament when it claims to quote the direct discourse of Jesus, give or take some possible variation if his words are being translated from an original Aramaic base. This point makes little difference to my present argument, which is basically descriptive in nature, even if we are dealing with a particular Gospel writer's "representation" (compilation, reorganization) of Christ's speeches, debates, or informal conversations. The question is, How did the original (or implied) author wish Jesus' words to be understood and assessed in relation to their textual and theological context? I believe it is possible to carry out a literary-rhetorical analysis on that basis, certainly with regard to a practical application to Bible translation.

be illustrated with selections from the Gospel of Matthew (see also section B.2 of appendix B).[204]

6.2.1.1 Authoritative demeanor

Christ spoke with full divine authority as the Son of God. This rhetorical ethos is most clearly reflected in his utterance of categorical blessings and curses; in his many imperative, legislative, judicial, revelatory, and predictive assertions; in his performative pronouncements (e.g., healings in Matt. 8:3 and miracles in 4:39); in his reinterpretation of the Old Testament Scriptures (in opposition to conventional rabbinic teaching); and in his usage of certain expressions appropriate to his messianic person and role. Some examples are: "I have come not to abolish but to fulfill" (Matt. 5:17); "You have heard that it was said to those of ancient times.... But I say to you" (Matt. 5:21); "Truly I tell you" (Matt. 11:11); "no sign will be given to [this evil and adulterous generation] except the sign of Jonah" (Matt. 16:4); and "Have you not read that the one who made them in the beginning 'made them male and female' " (Matt. 19:4–9). His use of the formula "Amen, I say to you" was yet "another way of expressing his authority within the framework of a teacher-student relationship" (Aune 1991:165); and in the manner of rabbinic *midrash* he frequently cited, paraphrased, and alluded to the Scriptures to support and contextualize his proclamation.

Thus, in addition to his own authority, Christ appealed to that of the divine Word that he came not only to reveal and elucidate, but also to fulfill, as he said in Matt. 13:13: "This is why I speak to them in parables: 'Though seeing, they do not see....' " By means of this familiar midrashic model, he contemporized the Old Testament and made it live in the current moral and spiritual setting of his hearers, frequently in connection with some sort of critical reproof or call for repentance, as in Matt. 15:7–8a, "You hypocrites! Isaiah was right when he prophesied about you: 'These people honor me with their lips....' " Similarly, Christ at times employed a typological method of interpretation and application, for example, in his use of the story of Jonah with reference to his own coming death and burial (Matt. 12:39–41).

---

[204]These are largely characteristic of an *inductive* didactic style. However, Christ also employed *deductive* techniques in his argumentative discourse, for example, the ad *hominem* (Matthew 24), a *fortiori* (Matt. 6:30, 7:11), and *reductio ad absurdum* (Mark 3:23–26) techniques. For a discourse-oriented exploration of Jesus' persuasive manner of teaching, see Wendland 1996a; for a classical Greco-Roman perspective, see Kennedy 1984, chapter 5; for a more literary-based overview, especially with reference to John, see Ryken 1992, chapter 17 (also Robbins 1984, chap. 1, and Witherington 1994, chap. 4). Aune (1991, chaps. 6–7) documents in detail the prophetic characteristics of the discourses of Jesus.

6.2.1.2 Prophetic style

Christ preached and taught like a Hebrew prophet of old. This is evidenced by his stern calls to sincere repentance in order to avoid future divine judgment (e.g., the woe oracle of Matt. 11:21–24); his reverence for, devotion to, and emphasis upon "the word of the LORD" (reinterpreting the Scriptures with a gospel-oriented focus, e.g., in Matt. 9:12–13); his blunt condemnation of hypocrisy as in Matt. 10:34, "Do not think that I have come to bring peace," and Matt. 15:6–7, "So, for the sake of your tradition, you make void the word of God. You hypocrites!"; and his gracious invitation to enter the kingdom of God in both its present and future manifestations (Matt. 11:28 and 24:34–36).

Christ's prophetic manner of speaking includes his frequent use of ironic and satiric discourse directed against all ungodly folly, vice, or error. Such talk was usually intended to reprove, correct, and/or counter verbal attacks by contemporary religious leaders whose hermeneutical system and legalistic lifestyle he was undermining (by pointing out its fallacies as well as futility) and overturning (by offering the people something better). Examples of this are: "You are wrong, because you know neither the scriptures nor the power of God..." (Matt. 22:29); "The scribes and the Pharisees sit on Moses' seat; therefore, do whatever they teach you and follow it; but do not do as they do, for they do not practice what they teach" (Matt. 23:2–3); and the whole of Matthew 23. Christ's discourses, although firmly situated in the everyday present of his hearers, made the kingdom of God relevant for people of his day and of today. His instruction also made significant reference to the future manifestation of God's kingdom at the great eschatological day of judgment, as we see in Matthew 24–25 with its many apocalyptic allusions.

6.2.1.3 Wisdom tradition

The speeches of Christ reveal significant influence from the sapiential, or "wisdom," school of ancient Hebrew theology and rhetoric. Thus his verbal style, which is characterized by a simple directness of expression and concrete, picturesque, down-to-earth language (see sec. 6.2.1.5), nevertheless deals contrastively with the deep issues of life and death, goodness and evil, right and wrong, and God and man. He uses questions, both real and rhetorical, and evocative analogies, often expanded into narrative parables. The wisdom tradition's predilection for comparison, antithesis, hyperbole, the maxim, and other forms of aphoristic utterance is especially evident.

We see a number of these features in Matt. 5:14–15: "You are the light of the world. A city built on a hill cannot be hid. No one after lighting a lamp puts it under the bushel basket, but on the lamp stand, and it gives light to all in the house." Christ frequently employed this manner of discourse to counter and correct traditional Jewish religious principles that had been distorted and misapplied by the teachers of his time (e.g., concerning the reappearance of Elijah the prophet). Often, to sharpen his point, he would utilize a memorable "antithetical aphorism" (Tannehill 1975:52) that could neither be denied nor ignored by his opponents, as in Matt. 7:2–5. Another common feature of Christ's didactic sayings is "a two-part structure in which the first part is related to the present and the second to the future" (Aune 1991:166), as in Matt. 23:12a, "For whoever exalts himself will be humbled."[205]

6.2.1.4 Dialogic technique

The rabbinic style of teaching favored dialogue, especially interaction with the audience by means of question and answer, or question and counter-question. Jesus apparently became skilled at this mode of rhetorical discourse early in his lifetime, even before he chose to put it into practice in his public ministry (see Luke 2:46–47). Indeed, it is somewhat ironic that the verbal technique of the boy Jesus that so impressed the Temple teachers was effectively utilized some twenty years later to expose their gross religious hypocrisy and false teachings.

In the honor-shame world of the Mediterranean Middle East, any rabbi worth his salt had to be a good speaker; and frequently his teachings, especially if they were in any way novel, controversial, or subversive of the religious status quo, had to be both demonstrated and defended by means of the method of debating now known as "challenge-and-riposte" (see Malina and Rohrbaugh 1992:306–307). Any verbal *challenge* that sought to test or undermine the honor, credibility, authority, or status of another person had to be responded to in a way that either silenced or satisfied the initial assertion. Often the respondent would then go on the offensive with a counter-challenge, that is, *riposte*. Such challenges could be either positive (e.g., praise, compliment) or negative (insult, accusation, innuendo). To refuse to respond would result in a serious loss of face. "In the Synoptic Gospels Jesus evidences considerable skill at riposte and thereby reveals himself to be an honorable and authoritative prophet" (Malina

---

[205]Aune (1991:166) points out that there is often an "eschatological polarity in the sayings of Jesus" that manifests "an ethical or existential dimension in addition to a temporal dimension." In this way "eschatological expectation [is used] as the basis for a hortatory or paraenetic purpose."

and Rohrbaugh 1992:188, also 42).[206] The ultimate "challenge-riposte" sequence in the Gospels is in Matt. 4:1–11, where Christ is tempted by Satan. Most of Christ's controversies with the scribes and Pharisees (or with skeptical crowds) are initiated by such an exchange, for example, in Matthew 12: picking grain on the Sabbath (vv. 2–3), healing on the Sabbath (vv. 10–11), exorcising a demon (vv. 22–28), seeking a sign (vv. 38–39), and the identity of Jesus' mother and brothers (vv. 46–50). This type of dialogue sometimes is a springboard for a parable, as in the case of the Parable of the Good Samaritan in Luke 10:25–37.

6.2.1.5 Speaking in specifics

The discourses of Christ are permeated with specific, life- and people-related imagery. His figures of speech, especially simile and metaphor, are based upon the local environment and everyday experience of his hearers. On one occasion, when discussing greatness in the kingdom of God, Jesus utilizes a handy object lesson—a small child who happened to be on the scene. He also clarifies his call to genuine humility by means of figurative references to a stumbling block, a millstone, the Great Sea, a person's hands, feet, and eyes, hell fire, the angels in heaven, the "face" of the Father God, and a shepherd rejoicing over a lost sheep that has been found (Matt. 18:1–14). Such imagery appeals not only to one's sensory impressions (e.g., drowning in the sea or burning in fire as in Matt. 18:6 and 8), but it also strikes deeply into the emotions as well.

Christ often uses a "focal instance," that is, an "extreme example" (Tannehill 1975:53) in which a certain shock value is conveyed (see, e.g., the series in Matt. 5:39–42). These verbal depictions are frequently extended to form the complete setting and scene of a picture-parable as in his teaching about the need to forgive an enemy "seventy times seven," which is transformed into the sad story of the unforgiving servant (Matt. 18:21–35). Jesus' criticisms are never leveled in the abstract but are normally accompanied by brief, dramatic "case studies" designed to drive home his point along with the underlying spiritual principle; for example, when practicing piety "do not sound a trumpet before you…in the streets" (Matt. 6:1–2). The same is true of his words of encouragement, an example being his words about "the need to pray always and not to lose heart," which introduce the parable of the widow and the unjust judge (Luke 18:1 and 2–8). In this skillful and insightful manner of speaking, Christ "contextualized" his teachings, using the inductive method, to illumine the minds and hearts of his hearers. Thus the kingdom of God as he

---

[206]Mark 2:1–3:6 is a structured sequence of such "challenge => riposte" episodes (see Dewey 1980).

portrayed it was not something purely conceptual and distant; rather, it was an immediate living experience for all who entered in (Matt. 5:3; 12:28; 18:2–3; 21:31–32; also Luke 17:20–21).

6.2.1.6 Audience appeal and involvement

As several of the features already noted indicate (the dialogic method in particular), Christ was communicatively very close to his audience—so close in fact that on occasion he had to put some physical space between himself and them in order to project his voice to a larger group (e.g., Matt. 13:2). His use of questions was a prominent aspect of this style of instructive engagement. He often used rhetorical questions, which were a standard rabbinical tool (e.g., "What do you think?" in Matt. 18:12). He also used "real" questions at times to find out their thinking on particular issues: asking what people were saying about him (Matt. 16:13); clarifying a controversial position such as taxation (Matt. 17:25); developing a catechetical lesson (Luke 10:26–27); or allowing one of his critics to incriminate themselves by their answer (Luke 10:36–37) or by a defeated silence (Luke 14:4).

Jesus was a master in the art of enigma and indirection too. However, when avoiding specific details, he would replace the particular not with the abstract or general, but with audience-appealing allusion. The audience could then fill in the blanks or paint the full picture in their own minds, creating a conceptual background for his message, whether from Old Testament history (e.g., about King David in Matt. 12:3–4), or from the surrounding environment (e.g., a mustard seed in Matt. 13:31), or from daily domestic, economic, political, and religious life in Palestine (e.g., bread making in Matt. 13:33, fishing in Matt. 13:47, a besieged city in Matt. 12:25, and local "prophets" in Matt. 13:57). Christ's enigmatic sayings would certainly test the thinking, opinions, attitudes, and level of commitment of his listeners, even those who, like the Twelve, were closest to him; for example, concerning the demands of discipleship (Matt. 8:22), his ministry to sinners (Matt. 9:13), his future departure (Matt. 9:15), the nature of death (Matt. 9:24), the character of his teaching (Matt. 12:42), and the reason he used parables (Matt. 13:11–17).

Also undoubtedly attractive to Jesus' audiences were the touches of humor—sometimes subtle, sometimes hyperbolic—that often tinge his teachings. The following are a few examples: an obscuring plank in the eye of a critical beholder (Matt. 7:3–5); a blind guide that leads others into a ditch (Matt. 15:14); a financially foolish builder (Luke 14:28–30); straining one's soup to remove a gnat and then swallowing a camel (Matt.

23:24); well-tended white tombs with decayed, polluting corpses inside (Matt. 23:27).

6.2.1.7 Poetic composition

Christ was a poet as well as a theologian. In his discourses he utilized the many minor stylistic features of imagery, figures, hyperbole, repetition, questions, wordplays, parallelisms (synonymous and contrastive as in Matt. 7:7–8 and 23:12), and cadence.[207] He frequently spoke poetically with rhythmically balanced, phonically patterned sense and sound units, an example being the contrastive admonition concerning treasure in Matt. 6:19–20: "Do not lay up for yourselves—treasures—on earth / where—moth—and rust—consume / and where robbers—break in—and rob // but lay up for yourselves—treasures—in heaven / where neither moth—nor rust—consumes / and where robbers—do not break in—nor rob." Such larger structural arrangements characterize a great many of his didactic sayings. It is for this reason no doubt that Luke describes Jesus' words as being exceptionally "pleasing," words of *charis* (Luke 4:22), and as showing amazing "power/authority," words of *eksousia* (Luke 4:32; see also Matt. 7:29).

Pleasing and powerful would be a good characterization of the nature and effect of literary rhetoric in general, but it is especially apt for describing the proverbial sayings and provocative parables of Christic discourse. A study of them in the original text shows that clearly Christ's masterful speeches surpassed the prevailing standards of his day, as in Matt. 7:24–27, the challenging conclusion to his hillside discourse:

Πᾶς οὖν ὅστις ἀκούει μου τοὺς λόγους τούτους καὶ ποιεῖ αὐτοὺς,
    ὁμοιωθήσεται ἀνδρὶ φρονίμῳ,
        ὅστις ᾠκοδόμησεν αὐτοῦ τὴν οἰκίαν ἐπὶ τὴν πέτραν·
            καὶ κατέβη ἡ βροχὴ
            καὶ ἦλθον οἱ ποταμοὶ
            καὶ ἔπνευσαν οἱ ἄνεμοι
            καὶ προσέπεσαν τῇ οἰκίᾳ ἐκείνῃ,
            καὶ οὐκ ἔπεσεν,
                τεθεμελίωτο γὰρ ἐπὶ τὴν πέτρα.

---

[207]According to C. H. Dodd, "the poetic character of [Christ's] sayings [stood] in contrast to rabbinic teaching and [was] reminiscent of the style of the prophets of old" (cited in Aune 1991:160).

καὶ πᾶς ὁ ἀκούων μου τοὺς λόγους τούτους καὶ μὴ ποιῶν αὐτοὺς
ὁμοιωθήσεται ἀνδρὶ μωρῷ,
    ὅστις ᾠκοδόμησεν αὐτοῦ τὴν οἰκίαν ἐπὶ τὴν ἄμμον·
    καὶ κατέβη ἡ βροχὴ
        καὶ ἦλθον οἱ ποταμοὶ
        καὶ ἔπνευσαν οἱ ἄνεμοι
        καὶ προσέκοψαν τῇ οἰκίᾳ ἐκείνῃ,
    καὶ ἔπεσεν
    καὶ ἦν ἡ πτῶσις αὐτῆς μεγάλη.

Every one then who hears these words of mine *and does them*
    will be like a *wise* man who built his house upon the *rock*;
        and the rain fell,
            and the floods came,
            and the winds blew
            and beat upon that house,
        but it did not fall,
        because it had been founded on the rock.

And every one who hears these words of mine *and does not do them*
    will be like a *foolish* man who built his house upon the *sand*;
        and the rain fell,
            and the floods came,
            and the winds blew
            and beat against that house,
        and *it fell*;
        and great was the fall of it!

There can be little doubt about the artistically conceived and rhetorically motivated construction of the preceding passage, for the second,
contrastive half is a mirror image of the first, except for the several corresponding, hence highlighted, points of antithesis. Graphic imagery, balanced structural symmetry, a compelling, forward moving rhythm,
end-stress climax (with variation)—it is all concentrated in this emphatic
closure to Christ's discourse which outlines the required behavior in his
radically new kingdom (Matt. 5:3, 10). The very literary form of the text
serves to foreground its implicit, twofold religious exhortation—for some
a comforting encouragement, for others a dire warning. It is no wonder
then that the crowd on hand responded as it did with utter amazement
(see Matt. 7:28).

A fair question in response to this is, How do people react when they hear
Matt. 7:24–27 in our current translations? Is the overall communicative

effect anywhere near the same? If not, what can be done to increase the level of functional equivalence between the original and its contemporary reproduction? Literary "text-total" translators are charged with the responsibility of faithfully conveying not only the referential significance, but also the dynamic, nonreferential aspect of biblical meaning. At the very least they must do everything possible to prevent unnaturalness, zero meaning, or an erroneous understanding on the part of listeners. But more than that, every attempt should be made to retain the provocative, persuasive, precise, and poetic character of Christ's rhetorical style in contemporary renditions of his life-changing message.

This challenge perhaps reaches its limit when dealing with a pericope like John 6:48–58, which on the surface of the text seems to be just so much repetition, albeit nicely put. On closer examination, however, we detect an intricately constructed chiasmus that displays the height of artistic compositional technique and enhances a provocative message coupled with a strongly rhetorical motivation. The diagram on page 202 of its concentric structure is adapted from Breck (1994:211–212):[208]

The horizontal line indicates the point of an interruption of the unfolding sequence by a skeptical question from Christ's audience. It occurs just prior to the central structural-thematic peak of the passage in H-H'. Then in vv. 53–54 there is an instance of antithetical parallel patterning—with one exception, a single line that falls outside the arrangement and is thereby highlighted (shown in boldface). The "eternal life" that Jesus was continually referring too is not just so much talk; on the contrary, it involves a final resurrection of the believer's body (see v. 39). Thus similarity is deftly interwoven with contrast throughout the discourse, its very symmetry and balance serving to reinforce the certainty of the promise being made to all who spiritually feed on Christ. What a powerfully persuasive passage—but it is one that raises a corresponding dilemma for the serious translator. How can its attractive artistic design and rhetorical force be captured in another time, text, and context (perhaps also another medium of transmission) for the benefit of a totally different group of needy receptors?

---

[208]This is another example of message-enhancing artistic text tectonicity (chap. 3). Whether one attributes this particular verbal arrangement to Jesus himself or to John, his spokesman, is irrelevant to the functional-equivalence translator, who is commissioned to transmit the text's *fullest possible* meaning (content + intent + the connotations of literary form) as it stands, especially those formations that have been illuminated and supported by a variety of scholarly studies, ancient and modern.

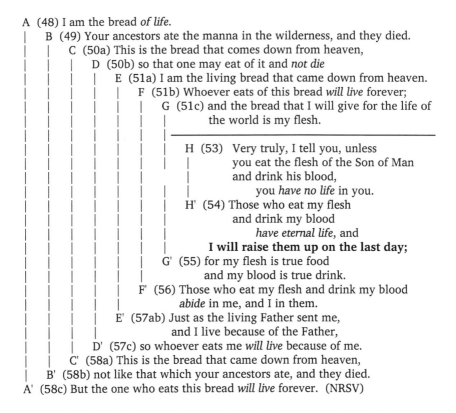

A (48) I am the bread *of life.*
| B (49) Your ancestors ate the manna in the wilderness, and they died.
| | C (50a) This is the bread that comes down from heaven,
| | | D (50b) so that one may eat of it and *not die*
| | | | E (51a) I am the living bread that came down from heaven.
| | | | | F (51b) Whoever eats of this bread *will live* forever;
| | | | | | G (51c) and the bread that I will give for the life of
| | | | | | | the world is my flesh.
| | | | | | | _____
| | | | | | | H (53) Very truly, I tell you, unless
| | | | | | | | you eat the flesh of the Son of Man
| | | | | | | | and drink his blood,
| | | | | | | | you *have no life* in you.
| | | | | | | H' (54) Those who eat my flesh
| | | | | | | | and drink my blood
| | | | | | | | *have eternal life,* and
| | | | | | | | **I will raise them up on the last day;**
| | | | | | G' (55) for my flesh is true food
| | | | | | | and my blood is true drink.
| | | | | F' (56) Those who eat my flesh and drink my blood
| | | | | | *abide* in me, and I in them.
| | | | E' (57ab) Just as the living Father sent me,
| | | | | and I live because of the Father,
| | | D' (57c) so whoever eats me *will live* because of me.
| | C' (58a) This is the bread that came down from heaven,
| B' (58b) not like that which your ancestors ate, and they died.
A' (58c) But the one who eats this bread *will live* forever. (NRSV)

6.2.2 The classical Greco-Roman rhetorical-oratorical method

A great body of literature is available concerning classical Greco-Roman rhetorical style, which has been practiced for well over two millennia now with regard to both speech (oratory) and written discourse. I will not go into either the history or the theory of this discipline (for that, see Kennedy 1984), but will simply summarize some of the main analytical categories and procedures, with special reference to their implications for Bible translation and the study of the Scriptures as literature.[209]

There are five basic steps in this analytical method, each one of which consists of a number of subprocesses:

---

[209]Although most rhetoric-related analysis has been carried out on New Testament texts (the Epistles in particular), a number of similar studies of Old Testament literature are also available (e.g., Duke 1990; Trible 1994; Davies 1999, and Wendland 1998a). The relevant aspects of such materials for Bible translators need to be abstracted and made available in some convenient format.

- First, delineate the overall scope, or textual span, of the pericope to be analyzed with respect to its external boundaries, that is, its beginning and end points. This is the "rhetorical unit." If part of a larger work is being considered, then this demarcation process must be carried out with reference to the surrounding portions of the discourse.
- Second, describe the "rhetorical situation," or contextual setting, of the pericope to the extent possible based on whatever historical and sociocultural evidence is available. This background information would include all of the relevant factors, personal as well as impersonal, which together appear to influence the text in question. More specifically, the rhetorical situation pertains to the particular crisis or stimulus ("exigence") that motivates an appropriate human response in the form of a verbal discourse, oral or written.
- Third, determine the outstanding problem or issue ("stasis") that underlies the text, along with its principal type, or "species," of rhetoric: (1) *judicial*, concerning accusation (wrong) and/or defense (right) with regard to some case or crisis that has already occurred; (2) *deliberative*, dealing with either persuading or dissuading an audience with regard to the expediency or danger of some future course of action; or (3) *epideictic*, connected with the celebration (praise) or condemnation (blame) of current social and moral values and/or evident character traits and behavioral attributes.
- Fourth, analyze the text in terms of the three rhetorical "canons" of invention, arrangement, and style.[210] Invention (*inventio*) concerns the choice of various conventional proofs, topics, and commonplaces (maxims) to best support the case being argued, whether according to *ethos* (credibility/reliability/authority of the orator/author), *pathos* (emotions and attitudes of the audience), or *logos* (inductive or deductive mode of reasoning). Arrangement (*dispositio*) deals with the compositional structure of the discourse on the basis of its ordered primary constituents, such as the *exordium* (introduction), *narratio* (initial statement of the issue), *probatio* (main body of the argument), and *peroratio* (conclusion). Matters of style (*elocutio*) then pertain to the specifics of how a particular speech is put together in a pleasing

---

[210]There are two other canons of rhetoric, namely, memory and delivery (*pronunciatio*), but due to their relative inaccessibility (in most cases) these are rarely considered in analysis. I did pay special attention to the canon of delivery in connection with a study of Chichewa sermons (Wendland 2000b). Perhaps more thought ought to be given to this phonological feature in Bible translation, taking the oral/aural medium into consideration (the medium by which the text is most often transmitted and processed). Surely it ought to be discussed in any project *Skopos*.

and persuasive way by selection from a large inventory of available stylistic devices, such as distinctive diction, varied forms of repetition, syntactic transformations, and a diverse assortment of figures of speech.

• Finally, a full classical Greco-Roman analysis concludes with a critical positive or negative evaluation of the various rhetorical devices and techniques manifested in the pericope at hand. How well do these features succeed or fail in meeting the postulated exigence and in resolving the outstanding issues? What are the chief implications of the discourse as it has been created, delivered, and/or transmitted? What revisions need to be considered in order to compose and communicate a more "relevant" (conceptually accessible and practically applicable) text?

To be sure, many important questions may be raised concerning the validity and current utility of these classically based principles and procedures. For example, to what extent may they be applied to written texts if their original domain was largely public oratory? But as was already noted, the Epistles were composed orally and in anticipation of their eventual oral transmission,[211] so why should such rhetorical techniques *not* have been used in their formation, at least in modified or adapted form?

Problems are also presented by either the generality of some of the analytical categories posited (as is the case with the three "species" of rhetoric) or conversely, their over-specificity. Just about every possible topic or turn of speech in a text may be assigned some technical designation, it seems, for example, *alloiosis* (breaking a subject down into alternatives), *antanagoge* (balancing an unfavorable subject with a favorable one), and *enumeratio* (any sort of recapitulation).[212] Related to this difficulty is the tendency of some Greco-Roman analysts to mechanically classify and label a complete pericope or letter entirely in terms of these detailed features. They analyze it to pieces, but do not show clearly how all the individual devices fit together to form an integrated whole, or how they combine to heighten the overall appropriateness, impact, and appeal of the discourse, or how they advance the author's main theme or argument. Most scholarly assessments of the rhetorical technique when applied to

---

[211]Aune observes that "[t]he Greek word *epistolee* ('epistle') originally referred to an *oral* communication sent by messenger" (1987:158). He later states, "By the first century B.C., rhetoric had come to exert a strong influence on the composition of letters, particularly among the educated. Their letters functioned not only as a means of communication but also as sophisticated instruments of persuasion and media for displaying literary skill" (ibid.:160).

[212]For a handy synopsis of these and other rhetorical terms, see Lanham 1969:125–128.

biblical texts turn out to be quite favorable, usually on rather impression-istic grounds that are not explicitly related to the intended message being conveyed. In addition, an undiscriminating application of a classical Greek model can blind the analyst to other possible perspectives on the textual data at hand. Thus the considerable influence of the artistic and rhetorical patterns of the Old Testament (LXX) on the literary style of the writers of the New Testament may not be given the attention it deserves when translators interpret and evaluate the form and function of the bibli-cal text.

Nevertheless, it is helpful to be familiar with the essentials of this type of rhetorical study because it is very text based and form/function oriented. Thus, when judiciously applied and selectively combined with other ap-proaches, the classical method—or certain aspects of it—often produces some useful insights into the structure, style, and communicative purpose of many biblical passages, and even complete books, especially those that are largely didactic, apologetic, or paraenetic in nature. As an example, the fol-lowing outline (adapted from Mack 1990:61–62) reveals the intricate construction of Paul's apostolic defense in 1 Corinthians 9, a line of argumen-tation that is punctuated throughout by the repeated use of incisive rhetori-cal questions and varied examples:

Introduction: Paul asserts his Christ-designated position in implicit contrast to the claims of his detractors and ironically appeals to the very presence of believers at Corinth as irrefutable living testimony to this fact (1–2).

Demonstration: Four judicial aspects of a specific case study—*the right to personal support* (3).

First Issue (of *law*): What are the legal requirements involved in this matter?

Thesis: An apostle has the right to support from those whom he serves (4).

Arguments:
Paradigms: the apostles, brothers of the Lord, Cephas (5–6).
Examples: soldiers, vintners, herdsmen (7).
Citation: Moses said: Do not muzzle the ox (Deut. 25:4) (8–9).
Interpretation The plowman and the thresher expect a share in the crop (10).
Application: The preceding is applied to the case of Paul and Barnabas.
Comparison: Spiritual benefactors can expect more assistance than
                 material ones (11–12a).
Example: Temple servants receive their food from their service (13a).
Example: Temple priests share in the offerings brought (13b).
Command   The Lord enjoined this same principle (see Luke 10:7–8) (14).
Conclusion (implied: Paul too has the legal right of support.)

Second Issue (a point of *fact*): Did Paul accept this support from anyone?

Assertion: Negative—Paul chose not to accept support (see 12b) (15a).
Clarification: Paul is not writing in order to obtain such support (15b).
Reason: Paul *does* not want to remove his grounds for boasting (15c).

Conclusion: (implied: Paul does indeed have a reason for boasting.)
Enigma: What sort of boasting is Paul referring to?

Third Issue (of *clarification*): What exactly did Paul do to establish these grounds?

Thesis 1: Paul was compelled to preach the gospel (16).
Reason: partially implied: The Lord called Paul to preach
(see Acts 9:1–16, 26:16–18) (17b).
Thesis 2: Paul was free to give up his right to support and to preach
voluntarily (17a).
Proof: Paul willingly relinquished his right to support (15a, 18).
Assertion: Voluntary preaching brings its own reward (17a).

Conclusion: That Paul did not expect any support for preaching the
gospel is therefore a valid ground for boasting or reward
(18). (The potential enigma is clarified by a paradox.)

Fourth Issue (of *quality*): Why did Paul do this?

Assertion: Preaching the gospel freely, unconditionally, might win
more converts (19–22).
Example: Paul himself—he made himself a "slave" to others.

Assertion: Preaching the gospel freely, no matter what the hardship,
brings a personal *spiritual* blessing, the reward previously
referred to in 17 (23).

Thesis 3:   Enduring hardships for the gospel's sake helps one to serve the
Lord more fully, which will be rewarded with a crown in
heaven, while lazy service disqualifies one from such a
spiritual reward (24b, 25b, 27b). (See also 3:10–15.)
Example: a runner and a boxer—*positive* (24a, 25a, 26–27a).
Example: Paul himself—*negative* (rhetorical surprise!) (27b).

While this analytical proposal needs to be complemented by others of a
linguistic and literary nature, it does make a noteworthy contribution to
our understanding of Paul's skillful manner of argumentation. It shows
how he makes an indirect, but effective defense (*apologia*) of his apostle-
ship (1 Cor. 9:1–3; see also 1 Corinthians 2–4) by vigorously demonstrat-
ing his judicial and religious right to the personal support of those whom
he was serving with the gospel (9:4–27). The ultimate "proof" of Paul's
elaborately argued case is twofold: he gave up his right to physical assistance so as not to hinder the preaching of his saving message (9:12, 15,
18), of which the Corinthian congregation was the ultimate beneficiary

(9:1–2), and also, paradoxically, to gain spiritual blessings through personal deprivation (9:23–27).

Translators need to be aware of these diverse verbal techniques and tools of argumentation, the larger structures as well as the individual stylistic devices, for they can provide a possible etic framework or inventory to guide a thorough investigation of the original message. This methodology would apply not only to the biblical text, but it could also serve to inform a corresponding study of the rhetorical resources that are potentially available in the TL and its oral or literary tradition.

Furthermore, such analyses, when conducted by competent scholars,[213] may shed some hermeneutical light upon certain more complicated instances of logically composed exhortation, such as we often find in the Epistles. These texts frequently manifest rather complex (such as abbreviated, combined, and/or sequentially extended) instances of the use of the rhetorical syllogism, which typically sets forth, whether in explicit or implicit form, a major premise, a minor premise, and a conclusion. For example, the following outline summarizes Paul's argument concerning the spiritual blessings that are received by faith, without works (Gal. 3:6–9):[214]

Thesis: All believers (the *attribute*) are justified (the *blessing*) by God (the *agent*), just as Abraham was (the *example*).

[Note: This thesis follows upon the proof by citation of the assertion made in vv. 2 and 5 that only believers in the promises of God receive his blessings, especially the Holy Spirit]

Concerning the *attribute*: "Abraham believed God
Concerning the *blessing*: and it was reckoned to him as righteousness" (Gen. 15:6). (6)

Enthymeme 1: Concerning the attribute
Major Premise: True children manifest the attributes of their fathers.
Minor Premise: You believe God's promises (as Abraham did).
Conclusion: You (believers) are the (spiritual) children of Abraham. (7)

Enthymeme 2: Concerning the blessing
Major Premise: God blesses people, like Abraham and his spiritual children, who trust his promises.
Minor Premise: You believers are the spiritual children of Abraham
Conclusion: You too will also receive God's blessing. (9)

---

[213]To coordinate such an essential, but possibly debatable, evaluation process, it would be helpful for an editorial team of scholars to prepare a handbook of recommended, "translator-friendly" literary, structural, and rhetorical analyses, along with a list of preferred options in cases involving some controversy.

[214]For an alternative rhetorical analysis of this passage, see Mack 1990:70. Note that my analysis supports a format in which Gal. 3:6 is part of the preceding paragraph, 3:1–6, as supported by the Greek text and the sentence-initial conjunction καθως, but not most English versions (e.g., NIV, GNB, NRSV, NEB, NJB).

Specification: The people who will be blessed by God through faith are
                     not limited to Jews;
                     God's promise of justification applies to all peoples on earth.
Proof—Citation: "All nations will be blessed through you" (Gen.12:3). (8)

In some languages, in order to clarify the direction of Paul's line of reasoning here or prevent any misunderstanding, it may be necessary to reverse the order of vv. 8 and 9, as shown above. This would also put into prominence, by means of end stress, the new information that the Gentiles, too, are included in God's promises of blessing (see also v. 14, an instance of *epiphoric* structural parallelism).

It should also be noted that in hortatory ("paraenetic") discourse, such as we find in the Prophets and Epistles, the "conclusion" of a certain enthymeme is frequently stated in the form of an appeal. This may be stated in varying degrees of mitigation, ranging from a direct imperative to a muted imperatival participle or infinitive (Wendland 1998c:59–64). For example, Gal. 5:1 may be outlined as follows:

Major Premise: God wants all believers in Christ to be free from spiritual slavery.
Minor Premise: Religious legalists continually try to enslave believers (again).
Command: Do not allow them to do this! (Freed Christians must oppose
                   legalism: stand *fast* in your faith, resist their attempts.)

Here, the "minor premise" leads to a concluding "command" (lit., "Do not submit again to a yoke of slavery"). It may need to be stated in a more explicit fashion, as in the *New Living Translation*, "don't get tied up again in slavery to the law," or *The Message*, "Never again let anyone put a harness of slavery on you," or, combining them, "Never again allow anyone to harness you in slavery to the law." The aim here is not to transform the target audience into nascent rhetoricians, but simply to enable them to follow the basic contours of a Pauline argument without getting completely lost or missing the main point that he is trying to make.

6.2.3 The epistolary method

The epistolary method of analysis is closely related to the Greco-Roman oratorical-rhetorical method, and the two are often practiced together, at least to a certain extent. The epistolary method, however, is more specifically applied to the written discourse of letters. It is also influenced to a greater degree by form-critical studies, which emphasize the structural organization of a complete text and its relationship to the sociocultural setting in which it originated.

Letters were a significant means of formal and informal communication in the ancient Mediterranean world. They acted as a *dialogic* mode of message transmission between people who were spatially separated.[215] They were quite flexible in terms of both style and content, although conventional compositional norms were usually followed. Stowers (1986:15–16) provides the following list of some of the important purposes served by letters in that age, many of which find a place in a typical Pauline epistle:

> Order or request provisions
> Elicit a virtue or promote a habit of behavior
> Initiate a relationship with another person or group
> Maintain a relationship with a person or group
> End a relationship with a person or group
> Restore a relationship with a person or group
> Praise someone
> Cause someone to be sorry
> Give orders (a superior to a subordinate)
> Give a report of events
> Cause a group to share a common hope
> Elicit capacities for social bonding
> Threaten someone
> Console someone
> Mediate between individuals or groups about a certain matter
> Give advice
> Request advice
> Express thanks
> Give honor

Stowers (1986:7–8) proposes a generic functional classification grouping Greco-Roman letters into six broad and somewhat overlapping categories (the examples added parenthetically are my own):

1. Letters of friendship (certain commonplaces are present as in 1 Thess. 3:6–10)
2. Letters to family (family members to be greeted are listed as in Romans 16)
3. Letters of praise/blame (thanksgivings may be included as in Philem.1–4; 'love' is praised in 1 Cor. 13)
4. Letters of exhortation and advice
   a) Letters of exhortation or dissuasion or both (observe the alternation in Hebrews)
   b) Letters of advice (e.g., Paul as a model for imitation in 1 Corinthians 1–4, 9)
   c) Letters of exhortation to newness of life (e.g., 1 John 3)

---

[215]Greco-Roman letters tended to include three basic elements: (1) a commitment to the friendship that existed between the writer and addressees; (2) an anticipation of their reunion after a period of separation; and (3) a discourse aimed at renewing their mutual fellowship and communion (see Aune 1987:172).

   d) Letters of admonition in diatribe style (e.g., Rom. 2:1–5, 17–29; 11:13–25)
   e) Letters of rebuke (e.g., Gal. 1:6–10; 3:1–5; 4:8–10)
   f) Letters of reproach (e.g., 1 Thess. 2:6–7)
   g) Letters of consolation (e.g., 1 Thess. 4:13–18)
5. Letters of mediation (e.g., Philemon)
6. Letters of accusation, apology, accounting (e.g., Paul's apology in Gal. 1:11–2:14)

To the six categories of Stowers, Aune adds a seventh, "Ancient *official* letters" (1987:162), an example being Acts 23:25–30. He goes on to point out that all these types of epistle may be mixed in their composition as well as more or less "literary" (or, I might add, "rhetorical") in style.

In keeping with their form-critical background, epistolary analysts, as they examine the functional development of any specific instance, look for typical formulas and other general stylistic conventions. These may be summarized as follows (see Aune 1987, chap. 6):

- *Opening formulas*—to initiate the communication, including mention of the participants (sender/receivers), a formal salutation (e.g., "Grace to you and peace"), and frequently also a prayer of thanksgiving (e.g., "I give thanks to God always for you").
- *Closing formulas*—to conclude the communication, including a *charis* benediction preceded by one or more optional elements such as a peace wish, request for intercessory prayer, secondary greetings, "holy kiss," and/or autographed greeting.
- *Internal transitional formulas*—to link one major section with another, for example, "I want you to know, brothers"; "I do not want you to be ignorant"; "I appeal to, or beseech, you, brothers"; "Now concerning"; and various expressions of confidence.
- *Epistolary topoi*—certain common types of content *such* as conventional topics and standard motifs concerning letter writing, health, business, domestic activities, future reunion, and government affairs, two particularly important categories being "virtue and vice lists" (e.g., 1 Cor. 6:9–10; Gal. 5:19–23; 1 Thess. 4:3–7) and "codes of household ethics" (e.g., Col. 3:18–4:1; Eph. 5:21–6:9; 1 Pet. 3:1–7).
- *Liturgical forms*—religious texts over and above those used at the opening or close of a letter, including blessings (e.g., 2 Cor. 1:3–4; Eph. 1:3–14; 1 Pet. 1:3–9), doxologies (e.g., Phil. 4:20; 2 Tim. 2:18; Heb. 13:21; 1 Pet. 5:11), hymns or hymn fragments/adaptations (e.g., Phil. 2:6–11; Col. 1:15–20; Rom. 11:33–36), short confessions (e.g., "Jesus is Lord" in Rom. 10:9; "God is one" in Rom. 3:30); longer

confessions (e.g., 1 Cor. 15:3–5; Rom. 4:24–25; 2 Tim. 2:11–13; 1 Pet. 3:18), and sacramental segments (e.g., 1 Cor. 11:23–26; Rom. 6:3–4).

- *Autobiographical references*—to establish or promote the upright moral character and conduct of the writer (his *ethos*), which in Paul's case was normally connected with his efforts to defend his gospel from attacks by opponents (e.g., 2 Cor. 1:12–2:17 along with 7:5–16).
- *Travel plans*—sometimes called, with reference to the Epistles, the "apostolic *parousia*" (e.g., Rom. 1:8–15; 15:14–33; 1 Cor. 4:14–21; 2 Tim. 4:6–18; Heb. 13:18–19, 22–23).
- *Concluding paraenesis*—prominent sections of ethical advice, exhortation, instruction, and admonition, often coming towards the end of an epistle (e.g., Rom. 12:1–15:13; Gal. 5:1–6:10; 1 Thess. 4:1–5:22), but not always, as in 1–2 Corinthians, James, and Hebrews.

We should also include LXX citations in any listing of the typical features that were important in the composition of theological and moral argument in the Epistles. Hebrews, for example, is filled with Old Testament quotations that form an important part of the author's argument. Lane lists a number of other rhetorical features that the writers of certain letters derived from "contemporary rabbinical practice in treating biblical texts" (1991:cxix). These are as follows, with examples from the Book of Hebrews, plus some modification (ibid.:cxix–cxxiv):

- *Clarification*—the addition of an explanation to clarify a potentially confusing or ambiguous use of the Scriptures (e.g., Heb. 2:8b–9 with reference to 8a, which is a quotation of Ps. 8:6b).
- *Reinforcement*—the use of a passage of Scripture to strengthen or validate an exhortation (e.g., Heb. 10:37–38, a conflation of Isa. 26:20 and Hab. 2:3–4, here used to underscore the need for steadfast perseverance in the faith, which is the topic of the extended exhortation of 10:19–39).
- *Expansion*—drawing out the contemporary implications of an Old Testament text that has been cited as part of the argument (e.g., Heb. 8:13, which reflects on the notion of "new" in relation to the covenant referred to in Jer. 31:31–34 and quoted in Heb. 8:8–12).
- *Literal focus*—an interpretation based upon the literal sense of a word or phrase from a cited passage (e.g., 'today' quoted in Heb. 3:7 from Ps. 95:7 and developed in 3:12–15 and 4:7–8).

- *Verbal analogy*—building an exposition upon the relationship between words that are the same (or cognates) in two or more different Scripture passages (e.g., the play on 'rest' in Heb. 4:3–11 based on *katapausin* from Ps. 95:11 and *katepausen* in Gen. 2:2).
- *Chaining*—stringing together a number of biblical quotations on the basis of common catchwords as a means of lending scriptural support to the theological or moral argument at hand (e.g., Heb. 1:5–13, which consists of three pairs of linked quotations—Ps. 2:7 + 2 Sam. 7:14, Deut. 32:43 + Ps. 104:4, and Ps. 45:6–7 + Ps. 102:25–27—and a concluding thematic citation from Ps. 110:1).
- *Listing*—a series of examples from Scripture to encourage the audience to avoid wickedness or pursue virtue (e.g., the heroes of faith in Hebrews 11).
- *Typological application*—showing that an Old Testament type is fulfilled by a recent antitype (e.g., Heb. 3:15–19, where the Israelite wanderers at Kadesh, based on Ps. 95:7–8, serve as a negative example applied to contemporary skeptics).
- *Homiletical midrash*—interpreting an Old Testament passage in terms of its current relevance for the author's target audience (e.g., Heb. 10:5–10 concerning the issue of Christ's universal sacrifice in relation to all the sacrifices and offerings of the Mosaic code, based on Ps. 40:6–8).

D. Watson (1997) offers a helpful comparative summary of the epistolary and the Greco-Roman rhetorical methods in relation to Paul's letter to the Philippians:[216]

> Epistolary analysis has the problem of determining the significance of a multitude of epistolary formulae and transitional elements [and] describing the function of the parts of the letter within the whole (especially the body middle)….Rhetorical analysis moves beyond epistolary analysis in determining the significance of the parts of the letter and their function within the whole….However, rhetorical analysis can be accused of arbitrary demarcation of units and identification of their function, and is more convincing when it can be shown to have a corresponding epistolary analysis. (ibid.:426)

This supports a principle that I have recommended throughout the present study, namely, that the complexity of most biblical discourse is

---

[216]One must read Watson's entire 1997 article in order to see how these different analytical distinctions are used. While I do not entirely agree with Watson's results, they do offer a basis for comparison with a structural-stylistic or a textlinguistic study of this epistle (see also Davis 1999 and Reed 1997).

such that more than one type of literary analysis is absolutely essential to correct and confirm one's conclusions with regard to a given text's formal arrangement, stylistic operation, and communicative dynamics. The results of diverse studies will generally complement and reinforce each other. But when apparent conflicts or contradictions appear, then it is time to reanalyze the material or reassess one's results in order to ensure that the deviations are genuine. Another option is to explore the possibility that a certain deviation pertaining to style or structure signals the presence of some more elaborate or sophisticated artistic technique or rhetorical function.

According to D. Watson, "rhetorical [analysis] and epistolary analysis are complementary, and together they present a strong case that Philippians is a coherent and unified letter" (ibid.). The results of such an analysis indicate where certain major breaks in the letter are *likely* to occur. This is illustrated by these two different outlines of Philippians:

Rhetorical Outline of Philippians	*Epistolary Outline of Philippians*
Letter Opening (1:1–2)	Letter Opening (1:1–2)
Exordium (1:3–26)217[217]	Thanksgiving (1:3–11)
Narratio (1:27–30)	Body Opening (1:12–30)
Probatio (2:1–3.21)	Body Middle (2:1–3:21)
First Development (2:1–11)	Transitions at 2:1–2
Second Development (2:12–18)	Transitions at 2:12, 17–18
Digressio (2:19–30)	Transitions at 2:19, 28, 29
Third Development (3:1–21)	Transitions at 3:1, 17–21
Peroratio (4:1–20)	Body Closing (4:1–20)
	Transitions at 4:1, 8
	Transitions at 4:10
Letter Closing (4:21–23)	Letter Closing (4:21–23)

These major breaks, if confirmed by an independent analysis such as a text-structural or literary-rhetorical analysis, are points that will need special attention during the translation process so that the same compositional framework and manner of discourse development can be maintained in the TL.

---

[217]The Greco-Roman rhetorical approach has its own special inventory of technical terms. Following Kennedy (1984:23–24) we can define these in their sequential order: In the *exordium* a rhetor seeks to gain the audience's attention and good will or sympathy toward his person. The *narratio* gives any necessary background or introductory information and summarizes the central purpose (*propositio*) of the letter. This leads to the *probatio* in which the speaker's main case is developed by means of various deductive or inductive proofs and their elaboration. This argument is normally divided into several subsections and may include a *digressio* or two in which underlying motivations and attendant issues or circumstances are examined. In the *peroratio* the author finally summarizes his argument and also tries to arouse the emotions of his audience to make judgment or take action.

Although spelling out the textual features and structural schemata may seem rather obvious or even superficial, it does offer some valuable (though not necessarily conclusive) insights into the organizational contours of a particular epistle as well as its main line of thematic progression. However, it is important to couple a preliminary investigation of these stylistic devices with a thorough literary-rhetorical analysis of the sort described earlier, which may possibly correct or modify it. Translators would then have a functional overview of the discourse as a whole—a "top to bottom" analytical approach giving a rough-and-ready idea of the general arrangement of the author's epistolary argument—before they begin to tackle a verse-by-verse rendering. It will also be necessary for translators to take note of the formulaic, discourse-marking operation of these epistolary schemata so that corresponding devices can be found to perform a similar purpose in the TL text.

6.2.4 Speech-act analysis

The functional implications of viewing rhetoric as some manner of persuasion should be clear by now. However, having defined rhetoric more broadly as the study of effective communication, we can proceed to consider a narrower range of discourse purposes during the process of message transmission. This perspective is perhaps best illustrated by "speech-act analysis," which is a popular mode of pragmatic investigation (i.e., the study of a text in relation to its interpersonal and situational context). First developed by the philosopher J. Austin as a "speech-as-action" approach in the early 1960s, this method of analyzing texts (especially direct discourse) was refined and elaborated upon by another philosopher, J. Searle, about a decade later, and subsequently by a host of other scholars, including those such as Hatim and Mason who have incorporated this functionally based system into their text-linguistic approach to the field of translation studies (see Hatim and Mason 1990, chap. 4; also Austin 1975 and Searle 1979).[218]

The term *speech act* refers to the interactive intention for which a segment of discourse, whether a complete text or only part of one, is manifested either orally or in writing (the latter domain being an extension of

---

[218]In Wendland 1985, chapter 5, I make use of a simple speech-act methodology in an analysis of John 4 with an application to Bible translation. More recently Kevin J. Vanhoozer (1998, especially chap. 5, "Resurrecting the Author: Meaning as Communicative Action") has made a cogent and innovative application of speech-act theory to the field of biblical hermeneutics in defending the validity of the notion of textual meaning, that is, referential content as an aspect of the communicative intentions of the original authors of the Scriptures.

the methodology).[219] It is commonly described as consisting of three aspects: the *locution*, which is the overt act of verbal representation (utterance/sentence, form + content); the *illocution*, which refers to the primary functional force or communicative aim of the speaker/writer's words (e.g., to promise, warn, console, instruct); and the *perlocution*, which designates the actual effect or outcome of the discourse (e.g., persuade, surprise, offend, strengthen). This last aspect, "the extent to which the receiver's state of mind/knowledge/attitude (+ /– behavior!) is altered by the utterance in question" (Hatim and Mason 1990:60), often cannot be fully specified in the context, especially in the case of literary communication. Alternatively, it is assumed to be more or less the same as the illocution (e.g., "encouragement" as intended or effected). Therefore, perlocution does not play a major role in most analyses. Since the form of a text (the "locution") is quite distinct from its function (the "illocution"), for all practical purposes one may identify the latter with the designation "speech act." A coherent, delimited sequence of speech acts is called a "speech event," which may be described in terms of its relational structure and one or more predominant functions ("text act[s]").

Speech acts (or their illocutions) may be described with varying degrees of specificity. The following eight generic types are perhaps the most useful for analyzing the segments of direct speech that occur in the Bible. They are found mainly in narrative portions and text that is locutionary in nature (i.e., consciously composed in anticipation of oral articulation as with prophetic, poetic, and epistolary writing). Each of these types of speech act will be defined and then illustrated by an utterance or two selected from the dialogues of Genesis 37 and the prophecy of Ezekiel 37 (all quotations are from the NRSV, except where noted):[220]

- *Informative*—a speech act in which the speaker/source (S) seeks either to reinforce the target audience's present *cognitive* state or change it in some way by supplying some information or denying a certain state of affairs: declare, describe, refuse, explain, assert

---

[219]When applied to written discourse, *communicative acts* would probably be a better term than *speech acts*. Thiselton (1999:151) calls attention to the theological significance of communicative acts: "According to the central traditions of the Old and New Testaments, *communicative acts of declaration, proclamation, call, appointment, command, worship, and most especially promise are constitutive of what it is for the word of God to become operative and effective*."

[220]For an illustration of this sort of rhetorical analysis as applied to a New Testament epistle, see Wendland 1998c. Normally in biblical narrative only two speakers or speaker-groups (e.g., 'the brothers') are active during any given dialogic exchange, and a spokesman will speak on behalf of the group, as Reuben or Judah did for the brothers of Joseph.

(e.g., Gen. 37:7, "Suddenly my sheaf rose and stood upright; then your sheaves gathered around it, and bowed down to my sheaf"; Ezek. 37:1, "the LORD set me down in the middle of a valley; it was full of bones").

- *Directive*—a speech-act intended to modify the *behavior* of the target audience, in particular to move them to do something for S, including providing some desired information: ask, command, urge, exhort, advise, forbid (e.g., Gen. 37:14, "Go now, see if it is well with your brothers...and bring word back to me"; Ezek. 37:9, "Come from the four winds, O breath, and breathe upon these slain, that they may live").

- *Expressive*—a speech act that aims to verbalize the feelings (sensory) and emotions (psychological) of S and/or to correspondingly influence the *emotive* state of the target audience: various types of exclamation and expressions of joy, grief, anger, affection, and frustration (e.g., Gen. 37:30, "The boy is gone; and I, where can I turn?"; Gen. 37:33, "Joseph is without doubt torn to pieces!"; Ezek. 37:11, "Our bones are dried up, and our hope is lost; we are cut off completely!").

- *Aesthetic*—a subsidiary, supportive speech act (perhaps a subtype of expressive) that pays special attention to how the discourse is encoded and formulated. It includes all forms of artistic, poetic expression used to reinforce, highlight, or embellish other types of speech act (e.g., Gen. 37:7 [my rendering], "Look-we are binding sheaves...and look-my sheaf arose...and look-your sheaves bowed down...!"; Gen. 37:21–22, "Let us not take his life....Shed no blood"; Ezek. 37:22, "Never again shall they be two nations, and never again shall they be divided into two peoples"; Ezek. 37:24, "My servant David shall be king over them; and they shall all have one shepherd").

- *Evaluative*—a speech act that renders a particular judgment, assessment, criticism, opinion, or attitude: condemn, rebuke, commend, praise, disparage (e.g., Gen. 37:10, "What kind of dream is this that you have had?"; Gen. 37:19, "Here comes this dreamer"; Ezek. 37:3, "Mortal, can these bones live?"; Ezek. 37:23 "They shall never again defile themselves with their idols and with their detestable things").

- *Commissive*—a speech act that commits S to some future course of action in relation to the target audience or some other group: promise, vow, pledge, plan, plot (e.g., Gen. 37:13, "Come, I will send you to them"; Gen. 37:20, "Come now, let us kill him...and we shall see what will become of his dreams"; Ezek. 37:12, "I am going to open your graves...and I will bring you back to the land of Israel"; Ezek. 37:27, "and I will be their God, and they shall be my people").

- *Performative*—a speech act that actually carries out or verbally effects the particular action that it refers to:[221] bless, curse, baptize, ordain, marry, dedicate (e.g., Gen. 37:35, "No, I shall go down to Sheol to my son, *mourning*"; Ezek. 37:9–10, a directive followed by an indirect report of a direct performative speech act, "*Prophesy* to the breath...and *breathe* upon these slain that they may live" => "I *prophesied* as he commanded me, and the *breath* came into them, and they lived").
- *Interactive*—a speech act that serves to open, maintain, mark, or close a larger speech event. This category includes phatic speech: the language of greetings, small talk, farewells, vocatives, and reciprocal ego-stroking. Interactive discourse may also reflect the sociocultural discourse of power or solidarity in its use of honorific, deferential, and "royal" terms and expressions. Also included in this category are such formulas as "Here I am" (Gen. 37:13); "O LORD God, you know" (Ezek. 37:3); and "Thus says the LORD God" (Ezek. 37:21). "Ritual(ized)," or "commemorative," communication belongs here, that is, formalized speech uttered to evoke, establish, recall, or celebrate some memorable setting, event, experience, or relationship—as in liturgical worship.

Informative, directive, evaluative, and expressive speech acts are the most important in biblical literature both quantitatively (in frequency of occurrence) and qualitatively (in terms of their functional significance). Commissive assertions are prominent in predictive prophecy (as in Ezekiel 37) and in discourse that conveys a prominent eschatological implication (as in Matthew 24–25).[222] An aesthetic motivation distinguishes all poetry and poetic-type discourse. Performative speech acts are always noteworthy whenever they occur, especially in Old Testament "divine discourse," where they immediately enact God's own commands, promises, blessings, and judgments.[223] Interactive speech acts are relatively

---

[221]In the following examples the performative is in italics.

[222]Thiselton (1999:237) argues that illocutions of the commissive type, promise in particular, are "paradigmatic or 'strong' [because] they (1) *entail serious obligations on the part of the speaker;* (2) *presuppose serious institutional facts*...and (3) *achieve transformative effects not by causal perlocution but through institutional illocution.*"

[223]Patrick claims that "[w]hen God speaks, the illocutionary force is generally of a performative character" (1999:205). Rhetoric is involved here because "[t]he promises, commandments, and judgments of God are designed to persuade the audience of the truth of what is communicated" (ibid.:204).

rare in written narrative texts; but where present, they contribute a great deal to the naturalness of the composition. Formulaic interactives, however, are common in the responses to be found in liturgical psalms (e.g., Psalm 136) as well as in prophetic literature, where they frequently serve to demarcate and punctuate the text with regard to its overall topical structure and thematic development.

These different speech acts usually occur in combination, both sequentially and simultaneously, to form speech events. In other words, any given utterance (spoken) or sentence (written) may often be analyzed as consisting of two or more distinct types. As was pointed out, the aesthetic variety is normally superimposed upon any of the others as a means of heightening their impact and appeal, especially in poetry and other forms of artistically fashioned speech. Many portions of the commissive discourse of Ezekiel 37, for example, are distinguished by such a poetic overlay. A good illustration of this is also in Jacob's expression of surpassing grief on seeing the bloody coat of his beloved Joseph (Gen. 37:33). Another instance of speech acts in synchronic combination is seen in Gen. 37:8: "Are you indeed to reign over us?" (= *expressive* [anger] + *evaluative* [a negative opinion of Joseph] + [non]*informative* [i.e., a denial of Joseph's preceding implicit prediction of leadership]).

It is important for translators to be aware of this pragmatic feature of biblical discourse so that they can attempt to duplicate the main speech acts (or "illocutions") of the original text in an effort to reproduce the rhetorical dynamics of the Scriptures in their translation. Such an analysis may be carried out to any degree of detail, depending on the time available and the translators' technical skill, but some minimum level of correspondence is essential if a functionally equivalent rendering is to be achieved with regard to this important dimension of the text.

6.2.5 Argument-structure analysis

Argument-structure analysis is a development of the "structure of argumentation" approach applied by L. Thuren (1995) to 1 Peter (for an attempt to simplify Thuren's methodology see Wendland 2000c). Two helpful texts that present a cross-cultural approach to the analysis of argumentation are Hatim 1997 and Kennedy 1998.

Though rather complex, this method is attractive, especially with reference to the paraenetic (hortatory-admonitory-minatory) texts found in the Prophets and Epistles, because it takes into consideration a relatively large number of textual as well as contextual factors. The key extralinguistic elements explicitly or implicitly involved in a formal paraenetic argument may be displayed in dynamic interrelationship with each other and the sole verbal constituent (the "appeal") as follows:

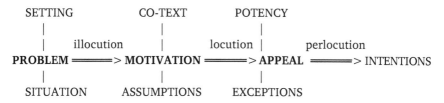

According to this approach, the ten components of a hortatory "argument" operate as an integrated communication system within the framework of the broader theory of speech acts (illocution => locution => perlocution) as discussed in section 6.2.4. They may be briefly defined and illustrated with reference to Paul's letter to Philemon as follows:

- *Setting*—the general historical, cultural, social, political, religious, and environmental milieu in which the written act of communication takes place, as this concerns both the author and his addressees/audience. Paul presumably wrote his letter to Philemon from a Roman prison (or while under house arrest) early in the second half of the first century C.E. (v. 1). Philemon was apparently a wealthy Greek Christian living in Colossae, a market town located in the prosperous Roman province of Asia (v. 2). This was an age when commercial and domestic slavery was widely practiced and recognized as an important economic institution. It was also a time when many slaves were being converted to Christianity.
- *Problem*—the particular spiritual or moral lack, fault, failing, need, test, or trial that the author wishes to discuss and deal with in his text, whether an entire book or only a portion of one. In Philemon, Paul had the problem of how to reconcile the runaway slave Onesimus with his master Philemon without the benefit of a personal talk or the opportunity to bring the two together. It is interesting and important to note that neither Onesimus' flight nor his apparent theft (see v. 18) is mentioned overtly anywhere in the letter. This could be an essential aspect of Paul's argument strategy— a rhetoric of silence, that is, by not suggesting any sort of wrongdoing on the part of Onesimus.
- *Situation*—the human events or interpersonal interaction that occasioned or provoked the problem; the set of circumstances (rhetorical exigence) that calls for a verbal response from one or more of the parties concerned. By escaping from slavery, Onesimus had

committed a capital offense. If ever identified and caught, he would be subject to death under Roman law. In the meantime, however, Onesimus had somehow come into close contact with the Apostle Paul in Rome and was converted to Christianity (v. 10). Not only that, he had risked his own life by faithfully ministering to the prisoner Paul (v. 11). Now Paul was sending Onesimus back to his master with this letter of intercession (Col. 4:8–9).

- *Appeal*—the specific verbal exhortation, command, rebuke, or warning that either promotes or prohibits a certain way of thinking and/or behaving in keeping with biblical teaching and its associated lifestyle. In the Epistle to Philemon, Paul makes two direct appeals: first, that Philemon "receive" (i.e., forgive) Onesimus, whom Paul is sending back as a Christian brother ("free" in Christ); second, that he charge any of Onesimus' debts (such as those due to stealing or lost service) to Paul's own account (vv.16–18). The first appeal entails an associated behavioral consequence, namely, that Philemon would *not* punish Onesimus in any way, either personally or through the public legal system.

- *Intentions*—the desired results in terms of either new or reinforced thinking and behavior that may be expected to materialize, sooner or later, if the addressee(s) fully comply with the appeal. As a result of his passionate entreaty on behalf of Onesimus, Paul is hopeful that Philemon "will do even more than I ask" with regard to the case in question (v. 21). It is reasonable, or at least arguable, that the main intention here (or implicature, considering the text in relation to its interpersonal context, as discussed in sec. 6.3) is that Philemon would go beyond what Paul requests on the surface and would read between the lines, so to speak, in order to do something even greater to "refresh the apostle's heart" (v. 20). This would undoubtedly be to give Onesimus his freedom so that he might return to Rome to assist Paul (vv. 13–14, 21). Whether or not this implicit personal aim of Paul is applicable, the potential impact of this master-servant crisis and its outcome for the Christian community was indeed great. Onesimus was a test case for the Colossian house church. If its leader, Philemon, would act in loving forgiveness towards his errant slave, he would not only confirm his status in the congregation, but would also establish the unity of the body and set an example for other Christian slave owners (5–7). Some commentators feel that the presence of this letter in the canon maximizes the likelihood of the perlocutionary outcome that Philemon did in fact grant the manumission of

Onesimus so that he could serve in Paul's mission outreach and stand as a living testimony of the power of forgiveness.

*   *Potency*—the relative degree of linguistic strength with which the text's main appeal and supporting motivation(s) are expressed (i.e., its overt level of directness, urgency, and authority) or the relative degree of mitigation and indirection. An imperative verb, for example, would manifest the least mitigation while an implicit request would convey the greatest mitigation. Paul's approach, as he develops his personal petition to Philemon, is very low key. He issues no direct command in connection with Onesimus (v. 8), and although he refers in different ways to his special request, he nowhere orders Philemon even to forgive Onesimus, let alone release him for service to Paul. The intention of the entire argument is developed by subtle implication and is based primarily upon Paul's relationship with Philemon, on the one hand, and that which exists between Christ and his church on the other (vv. 1, 5–6, 16, 17, 19–20, 21, 22). It is a masterfully constructed argumentative discourse aimed at fraternal persuasion for the common good of the larger fellowship.

*   *Exceptions*—any potential objections to the central appeal or imperative. Exceptions are conveyed by such devices as contrast, antithesis, counter-case, opposing evidence, or a likely rebuttal and are generally anticipated by the author and dealt with in the discourse, whether directly or—to avoid calling too much attention to them—indirectly. Since exceptions are often implicit rather than stated, their postulation in the analysis must be tentative. As part of his plea to Philemon, for example, Paul takes care of the likelihood of Onesimus' having stolen from Philemon by offering to make restitution on the slave's behalf (vv. 18–19a). The significant financial loss that the release of Onesimus would mean for Philemon is gently handled by a reference to the unrepayable debt that Philemon owed Paul for his spiritual deliverance (v. 19b). Anticipating Philemon's possible tardiness, reluctance, or even refusal to deal with this sensitive issue, one that could bring him into sharp criticism (along with considerable "shame") within the secular community if he acquiesced, Paul makes a pointed promise to visit Philemon in the near future (v. 22), at which time, he certainly implies, he will be able to see for himself how the matter has been resolved.

*   *Motivation*—the various types of reasoning offered in support of the author's appeal(s). These may be either deductive (e.g., cause-effect, general-specific, lesser-to-greater) or inductive (e.g., proofs,

maxims, syllogisms, testimonies, examples, analogies, case studies). Both kinds of reasoning relate to content (*logos*), emotion (*pathos*), and/or the speaker's personal credibility, reliability, and
authority (*ethos*). In my view, the Epistle to Philemon consists of a
string of interconnected motivations of varied potency that extends throughout the entire text, from the salutation to its valedic-
tion. This seminarrative thread of largely implicit importunity
builds progressively to a climax in v. 21b. The principal elements
may be summarized as follows: Philemon's love and faith are well
known in the community of believers; thus he stands as a prominent model to follow (5–6)=>Such Christian behavior has greatly
encouraged Paul, a beloved coworker in the kingdom work (1, 7,
17) => Paul prefers not to command his "elevated" colleague
Philemon (1) as to how he should act (8) but wants him to do the
righteous thing voluntarily (14)=>Paul is currently living in dire
circumstances (9)=>Formerly "useless" Onesimus is now a fellow
believer and most "useful" to and loved by the imprisoned apostle
(11–12)=>Paul wished to keep Onesimus with him in Rome to assist in the gospel ministry (13)=>Onesimus is in a position to serve
Paul on Philemon's behalf (16)=>Philemon owes his present spiritual state as well as his future eternal life to Paul (19)=>Paul could
use some extra personal "refreshment" from Philemon (20)=>Paul
is most confident that Philemon will "obey" and do "even more"
than what he is overtly requesting (i.e., a brotherly welcome for
Onesimus), namely, release him from slavery for evangelistic service (21) (this being the culminating climax of Paul's line of motivation)=>Paul will visit Philemon as soon as possible to wind up
the case of Onesimus in person (perhaps receiving him as a personal aide (22) (this being a possible denouement)=>Paul is once
again "encouraged" by Philemon's manifestation of brotherly
"love" (7).

• *Co-text*—all texts that are either semantically or pragmatically related to the discourse under consideration, whether syntagmatically (i.e., intratextually, as part of the same document) or
paradigmatically (i.e., intertextually, from different but somehow
related discourse-oral or written). Since the Epistle to Philemon is
a short document, intratextual influence is not a significant factor.
As for external influence, the greatest influence comes from the
Epistle to the Colossians, which was written and sent at about the
same time (see Col. 4:7–9). In addition to the same names of those
being greeted by Paul (see Col. 1–2; 4:10–14; Philem. 1–2, 23–24),

there are some important thematic similarities: praise for the clear manifestation of the recipients' "faith in Christ Jesus" and "love for all the saints" (Col. 1:4; Philem. 5); the call for believers to forgive one another (Col. 3:13b; Philem. 17); and a strong appeal to demonstrate the qualities that promote spiritual unity in the church (Col. 3:12–17; Philem. 6, 15–17). There are also a number of lexical parallels between Paul's exhortations in Philemon and those of Ephesians (e.g., Eph. 4:2–3, 12–13, 16, 32; 6:9).

- *Assumptions*—the various ideas, values, attitudes, and feelings that a writer shares with his readership. A writer takes it for granted that his own presupposed viewpoint (including a wider worldview) will be understood and applied to the text at hand by his audience according to the principle of relevance. When they share knowledge, it does not need to be made explicit in the text, though it may be stated for special effect, as in the case of Paul's reminder to Philemon in v. 19 that Philemon owes his life to Paul. Some other important assumptions underlie the argument of the epistle: In early Christianity the institution of slavery was accepted (without defending or promoting it) with the idea that it could be ameliorated through a spiritual change in the persons involved. Forgiveness between fellow Christians of diverse social statuses was essential to the unity of all believers in Christ and to the church as a religious fellowship (see vv. 1–3 and 23–25). Philemon is a genuine Christian and sincerely desires to be of assistance to Paul, and he has the legal power and wealth to enable him to commute Onesimus' potential sentence. Paul has the religious authority to command Philemon (v. 8). The congregation at Colossae, to whom this letter is also addressed (v. 2), will support Paul's appeal that Philemon forgive Onesimus. Paul will keep his promise to visit shortly and take up the case if it has not yet been satisfactorily resolved. Onesimus has become a believer and a disciple of Paul; he has also personally demonstrated his repentance by returning to his master despite the potential danger of doing so. Paul truly loves both Philemon and Onesimus as brothers in the Lord.

The primary rhetorical-argument line, this triadic cause-effect sequence of *problem + motivation => appeal* and its various transformations, constitutes the essential backbone of any hortatory argument in the Bible, whether more specifically minatory, admonitory, consolatory, advisory, motivational, or inspirational in nature. The surrounding situational factors flesh out the central appeal, so to speak, in terms of related and relevant presuppositions, assumptions, implications, implicatures, and other contextualizing background information. Translators would do well to keep these ten interactive variables in mind when analyzing a paraenetic text in preparation for transmitting it meaningfully in their language. (Of course, most books are far more difficult in this respect than Philemon.) Much pertinent material, such as the setting, situation, or assumptions, may have to be relegated to footnotes or a book introduction. But in order for the basic thrust of the discourse to be accurately conveyed and conceptualized, the crucial interlocking series of *problem-motivation-appeal* must be clear, or at least easily inferred from the text.[224] Otherwise, the translation cannot be deemed a success.

6.3 The implicit dimension of rhetoricity

As we have seen, implicit information is very important in all oral or written communication. Three closely related pragmatic notions will help us to explore this subject in somewhat greater detail: presupposition, implication, and implicature.[225] These must always be taken into consideration, along with the principle of relevance, when analyzing the rhetoric of speech acts in the biblical literature.

Presupposition refers to the unexpressed shared assumptions that surround any text. This information, whether denotative or connotative in nature, is assumed by the writer/speaker to be already known to the audience or derivable from the total situational setting—the historical, geographical, political, social, and cultural context, including a people's worldview and value system. In the interest of communicative economy and efficiency (i.e., reduced text processing effort), it is not necessary for such content to be stated explicitly. The author takes it for granted that this information is conveyed along with the message as written. In the case of a Bible translation, however, this cannot be done due to the different languages, cultures, and temporal eras that are associated with the respective SL and TL documents. Therefore, any presupposed information that is absolutely required for a given TL audience to correctly understand the biblical text should be included in the footnotes of a translation, if it is known to scholars today.

---

[224]Another simple (and incomplete) example is the Book of Jude: *Problem* = false teachers (4); *Appeal* = 'contend for the faith!' (3) + 'remain faithful and full of brotherly love' (20–21); *Motivation* = examples cited of the Lord's severe judgment contrasted with the joys of eternal life for true believers (21, 24).

[225]For a helpful, if somewhat dated, linguistic description of these notions, see chapters 3–5 of Levinson 1983. My definition of them is, hopefully, an adequate, common-sense simplification of their more technical application in pragmatic analysis.

Examples of contextual presuppositions in Genesis 37 would include information about the physical nature of "the land of Canaan" (v. 1), what was involved in the work of "shepherding the flock" or what Joseph's role as a pastoral "helper" was (v. 2), the social significance of Joseph's "long robe with sleeves" (or "coat of many colors") and the fact that it was given by Jacob to him instead of to an elder brother (v. 3), or, indeed, the importance of dreams (v. 5) and their interpretation in Ancient Near Eastern society. In Ezekiel 37 such presuppositions would involve knowledge concerning what constituted "the whole house of Israel" (v. 11), the nature of "graves" and how they could be "opened" (vv. 12–13), why "the mountains of Israel" were important (v. 22), what sort of illicit practices were referred to by "idols," "vile images," and "offenses" (v. 23), or, contrastively, what it meant to "follow the laws" and "keep the decrees" of Yahweh (v. 24).

Presupposed information that an author does not need to explicitly mention in his text must be distinguished from content that he *chooses* not to reveal, whether for dramatic purposes (the generation of suspense or enigma) or simply for the sake of compositional efficiency, both of which are instances of compaction (see sec. 4.3.4). Examples of such withheld information in Genesis 37 would be the sort of behavior that occasioned Joseph's "bad report" of his brothers to his father (v. 2), how it would be possible for the sun, moon, and stars to bow down to Joseph (v. 9), or where Reuben was when the brothers were selling Joseph (v. 29). In Ezekiel 37 the prophet does not tell us if the bones referred to were those of men, women, and children (v. 1), what "the rattling sound" signified when the bones were put together (v. 7), or what kind of "stick of wood" is prophetically envisioned (v. 16).

Implication is information that is linguistically implied, or "implicated," by the particular lexical selection, syntactic arrangement, and/or linguistic context of the original text. It is legitimate to express this kind of meaning in a translation, if need be (as generally determined by the project *Skopos*), in order to approximate a natural style of discourse or enable the receptors to ascertain the correct meaning. The following are a few simple examples (the implicated material is in italics): "gone to graze their flocks near *the city of* Shechem" (Gen. 37:12); "*Let us capture/grab* Joseph *and* throw him into this pit here in the wilderness" (Gen. 37:22); "saw a caravan of Ishmaelite *traders/merchants* coming from *the region* of Gilead" (Gen. 37:25); "The hand of the LORD was upon me, *Ezekiel*" (Ezek. 37:1); "These bones *represent* the whole nation of Israel" (Ezek. 37:11); "and *the new/second* David my *chosen* servant will be their *leader* forever" (Ezek. 37:25); "Then *all the other* nations *of this world* will know that..." (Ezek. 37:28).

Implicature is information that is conveyed by the semantic content of a text in conjunction with its pragmatic context. More specifically, a significant implicature is said to result when one of the "Gricean maxims" of conversation is deliberately deviated from, or violated, or exploited during the text-transmission process (termed "flouting").[226] The distinct sociolinguistic "felicity conditions" (Grice's term) of this "cooperative principle" involve the basic maxims of "quantity" (concerning truth), "quality" (concerning informativeness), "relevance" (concerning appropriateness), and "manner" (concerning perspicuity, brevity, and orderliness).[227] The validity of the notion of flouting such maxims has recently been challenged as being too linguistically limited (limited to Indo-European languages) and ethnocentrically biased (in favor of Western culture). Nevertheless, the approach might be salvaged if deemed desirable for translational purposes by extending the possibility of flouting (i.e., intentional pragmatic innovation or deliberate nonconformity with respect to a conventional mode of communication) to both the SL and TL. In other words, whether or not a given speech act happens to violate the norms of Hebrew or Greek discourse (often a difficult matter to prove one way or the other), it will be regarded as generating an *unwanted* implicature if the *literal* textual form does in fact sound strange, unnatural, or skewed in relation to TL standards of speech usage within a specific sociolinguistic and situational setting (namely, the one depicted or suggested by the passage at hand).

With regard to translation practice it would be justifiable for a team, when preparing a literary version, to convey the intended implicatures both explicitly and in an idiomatic manner in order to reproduce the rhetorical dynamics of the original text and also to prevent ordinary readers or hearers from misunderstanding the biblical message.[228] That is to say,

---

[226]Thus the term *implicature* refers to "the exophoric linking that a hearer needs to form to make an utterance relevant" in the sociolinguistic and situational setting in which it is spoken (Katan 1999:128).

[227]For an elaboration of these concepts, see Levinson 1983:101–102 (I have not had a chance to explore a possible update in Levinson 2000) and also Hatim and Mason 1990:62–63. Among other things, the cognitive-inferential approach known as "Relevance Theory" boils these four maxims down into one—the "principle of relevance," which determines the following "condition of communicatability": "An intended interpretation [i.e., meaning] is recoverable not just in any context, but *only in a context where the requirements of optimal processing are fulfilled*, that is, where there are adequate contextual effects, without unnecessary processing effort" (Gutt 1992:28). Hatim and Mason apply a similar notion to translation using the terms "effectiveness" and "efficiency" (ibid.:93–94). Fawcett (1997:76) attributes this "minimax" concept of communication to the Czech translation theorist Jiri Levy—later taken up by Wolfram Wilss.

[228]Katan notes that "one of the greatest problems in cross-cultural communication is the fact that speakers and writers assume that the surface language refers the reader or listener to the same semantic base" (1999:93). Translators often make the same assumption.

irrespective of whether or not this sort of implicit meaning is actually an aspect of the rhetorical strategy of the original text, it would essentially be treated as such during the process of interlingual message transmission so as to preserve an overall parity or correspondence of communicative value. Thus this operation would be carried out under the assumption that many similar techniques employed by the biblical authors have either gone unnoticed or have proven impossible to recreate in the translation. In a sense this is simply a corollary of the principle of functional-equivalence translation, but now the procedure is being applied more consciously and precisely in terms of norms, values, techniques, and strategies that are indigenous to the TL sociological and literary context.

The following examples from Genesis 37 illustrate implicatures and some possible ways of translating them. The first one is in v. 8: "Are you indeed to reign over us? Are you indeed to have dominion over us?" (NRSV). In some languages this would sound extremely redundant or verbose; Joseph's brothers' use of the double question form to convey their displeasure may violate the maxim of "manner" in addition to that of "quantity." CEV communicates both the intended sense and the connotative overtones of the Hebrew using a single question: "Do you really think that you are going to be king and rule over us?" The interrogative is maintained also in Chichewa and Chitonga, but with rhetorical particles included to indicate the hostile attitude of the brothers in their response. Another example in which a literal rendering would contradict a norm (in this case the conversational norm of relevance) is Joseph's phatic reply, "Here I am" (v. 13), which is unnecessary to say in most languages since Joseph was visible to his father as he stood there in his presence. The better rendering would be an idiomatic (hence rhetorically appropriate in literary terms) indication of agreement, as in Chichewa, "Good, Father!"—or in Tonga, "I am already on the way." The NLT has "I'm ready to go." Still another example is in v. 15, "What are you seeking?" In a Bantu language to ask this of an obviously needy stranger would be a gross insult—a flouting of the maxim of "manner" (i.e., of politeness, a necessary addition to the list of maxims). In Chichewa the way to say this would be, "Say, is it well around here?" This indicates that the speaker is willing to offer help, if needed, without making the addressee beg for it, thus losing face.

Then there is Reuben's cry, "Where can I turn?" (v. 30), which to render literally would in many languages lack relevance in the same way as "Here I am" in v. 13. Why would Reuben want to physically turn anywhere at this critical juncture? Where did he wish to go (if motion away is implied)? The Tonga rendering of this exclamation is the idiomatic "Now as for me, what can I do?"

And how does one render a lie (which is a violation of "quality") so that it is understood as such? A literal rendering of 37:32 would hide the devious, despicable character of the brothers. In Tonga it is rendered as a self-incriminating question: "Say, could it be that this is the coat of your son, which we happened to find just like that?" Jacob's reply, if translated literally, sounds much too composed and restrained: "It is my son's robe. A wild animal has devoured him; Joseph is without doubt torn to pieces" (v. 33). The logical form with which Jacob seems to speak here would contradict the highly emotive content. In Chichewa some extensive rephrasing is required to express Jacob's shock and grief: "Ha! It's his indeed! [Tonga has "It's the very one!"] A beast has killed my child. Woe to me, Joseph has been torn to bits!" The amount of attention paid to these subtle aspects of direct speech can make or break a translation with regard to idiomaticity—or just plain naturalness. Either way, the rhetorical impact of the text is inevitably affected.

6.4 The importance of understanding the rhetoricity of TL literature

In addition to an adequate grasp of the rhetorical dynamics of a biblical passage in its situational context, translators must also have a good idea of how arguments and appeals are made in the TL and the local sociocultural setting (see chap. 8). It may well be that the TL has an assortment of literary devices, structures, and strategies available, such as particles, word order, verbal mood, formulas, and preferences for propositional sequence (e.g., reason-result), both to express the appeal and also to mark the various stages and aspects in the development of what would generally be regarded as a convincing or convicting composition. Once discovered, it would be important for translators to apply these logical (inductive or deductive) arrangements and techniques of argumentation in the TL translation, where appropriate, so that both the nature of the discourse as well as its overall impact and appeal may be effectively represented. The rhetorical argument of a biblical text, a hortatory one in particular, is a vital part of its intended communicative significance. The question for translators is, How persuasive does this passage sound in the TL?

7

Literary-Rhetorical Analysis Techniques

In this chapter, we will consider a methodology for preparing a text-oriented, literary-rhetorical analysis of a biblical pericope in preparation for translation. (The same techniques are summarized in sec. 1.5 omitting the illustrations.) Certainly, many other helpful methods are available, some of which may be found in the literature of the bibliography at the end of this book.

The purpose of presenting these techniques is to enable translators to compare them with their own analytical procedures and apply them, in greater or lesser degree, with modifications as preferred, to any type of biblical text, whether poetic or prosaic in nature.[229] (Since every teacher or translation consultant has his or her own preferred way of doing things, I will not go into very much detail.)

The twelve techniques in section 7.1 are especially helpful when dealing with a *nonnarrative* text (e.g., poetic, prophetic, epistolary discourse).

---

[229]For a specific application of these guidelines to the Psalms, see Wendland 2002a:204–209. My guidelines may be compared with Davis's recommendations (1999:55–60) for analyzing literary structure according to the principles of "oral biblical criticism." Mine do not include a proposition ("kernel-sentence") or semantic-structure level of analysis. While such a method may usefully complement an L-R approach, it is not essential to it. The same applies to various aspects of discourse analysis as outlined by Dooley and Levinsohn, such as the charting of text constituents, thematic groupings, and patterns of participant reference (2001:44–47, 128–134), or to a text's nominal and verbal systems, interclausal relations, information types and their sequence, and highlighting devices such as substitution, stress placement, left/right dislocation, addition or deletion (Wiesemann n.d., passim).

The four groups of sample questions in section 7.2 relate to the study of *narrative* text. In section 7.3 is a selective application of these procedures to the Book of Obadiah.

7.1 L-R analysis techniques for nonnarrative discourse

Twelve steps will be described here as a general methodology for examining nonnarrative texts. They are intended to be applied to complete *textual* units, whether an entire biblical book or a clearly defined portion of one. Although the same steps could easily be adapted for use with narrative discourse, the nonnarrative focus is adopted here because it is not as frequently discussed as a specific method of analysis in preparation for translation, especially as this relates to the prophetic and epistolary writings.

7.1.1 Step 1: Study the complete textual, intertextual, and extratextual context

By *context* is meant all information that affects the interpretation of a given passage or pericope in terms of form, content, or any other related information. The pertinent passages and/or complete pericopes that come immediately before and after the passage in focus are the textual context (or "co-text"). These can generally be determined by comparing the textual arrangement of several standard versions, especially those that pay more attention to the larger features of organization (e.g., TEV, CEV, NIV). Look for similarities—or significant contrasts—in content and discourse type between the passage under study and its textual context in terms of specific wording or general content. If there are any, does this shed light upon the interpretation of the passage as a whole or even a key term within it?

A careful study of the total context often helps to reveal the various types of *implicit* meaning in the biblical text. As was noted in section 6.3, semantically or pragmatically crucial content (necessary for a correct understanding of the discourse) that is directly implied may have to be expressed *explicitly* in a translation in order to achieve a functional equivalence with respect to certain desired aspects of the intended message.[230] This would include information of a structural, connotative, artistic, or rhetorical nature.

Assuming for the moment (to be checked again in the next step) that the pericope being studied is clearly demarcated with respect to its outer borders, one must determine the larger discourse unit of which it is a part (unless it happens to constitute a complete book or a principal section on its own). It may help to compare the standard versions, looking for a major section heading or paragraph break on either side of the focal section and observing the flow of thoughts, feelings, and intentions across these larger compositional boundaries. What governs or characterizes the movement of one text segment to and from another, and how do the adjacent units seem to be related to each other in terms of form, content, and purpose? What then appears to give the section under consideration its discrete unity?

Next, the *wider* textual context of the focal pericope must be investigated: Carefully investigate all cross-references to related passages in an annotated Bible, a study edition, or some similar reference work. Most of these citations will turn out to be only loosely connected with the section at hand, but it is usually worth the effort to carry out this exercise in any case. Are there any passages found elsewhere in the Bible that are noticeably similar to the one being analyzed, especially in their use of key theological or technical terms and expressions? Scripture is its own best interpreter; therefore major correspondences of form, content, or function in other texts can help us to understand a difficult passage. Is it possible that another text (e.g., in the Old Testament) may have influenced the section under study in some way? If so, how? In this process of *intertextual* comparison it is important to pay attention to significant differences as well as similarities between the two passages and what they mean for interpretation.

---

[230]Ellis Deibler's *Index of Implicit Information in the Gospels* (1993) and *Index of Implicit Information in Acts–Revelation* (1999) are manuals designed to assist translators in the difficult area of implicit versus explicit information. Each includes a brief but helpful introduction to the subject as well as an appendix that summarizes the different types of implicit ⇔ explicit procedure often needed during Bible translation such as the author-reader communication situation information ("implicatures"), author-reader information ("assumed information"), TL requirements ("explication"), plus various types of semantic management with regard to deictic reference, ellipsis, event-based "arguments," and other information associated with "events," figures of speech, and argument structure. While the operation of implicit ⇒ explicit tends to be more common, it may also be necessary for certain material that was explicit in the biblical text to be implicit in the TL, for example, redundant information that would make the translation sound unnatural or even obscure due to all the detail. This is especially true in poetic discourse, in which brevity of expression often produces greater impact.

Finally, there are reference works (commentaries, study Bibles, Bible dictionaries, encyclopedias, and other specialized helps) that are helpful in connection with the *extratextual* context or conceptual background of the pericope being studied.[231] They can shed light on the situational setting, that is, on the total historical, political, ecological, economic, sociocultural, literary, philosophical, and religious environment of the time when the passage was most likely written and also on specific topics such as personal names, places, peoples, parties, geography, flora/fauna, customs, worldview, way-of-life, nonbiblical beliefs, and worship rites.[232] What light does such investigation shed on the passage at hand? In recent years, the hermeneutical school of social-scientific criticism has contributed a great deal to this effort to reveal the overall environment in which the biblical books were composed, transmitted, and understood in relation to the postulated cultural perspective and practices of the originally intended audience (see, for example, Malina and Rohrbaugh 1992 and 1998; Walton, Matthews, and Chavalas 2000; and Keener 1993).

The importance of this first step—*conceptual contextualization*—cannot be overemphasized. Sadly, it is often ignored in the rush to get to the words of the text itself. But shortcuts only make for incomplete and inadequate exegeses.

7.1.2 Step 2: Read the entire text and determine its genre and subgenres

A repeated reading of the text is vital to analysis. This is often taken for granted, but not often done. It is very important to do it *aloud* (even if you are alone) and *in the original language*, if possible. Visualize a familiar setting and a typical audience sitting before you[233] and for whom you are orally reciting the passage on a specific occasion. Do this several times for

---

[231]Secular translators and theorists, too, recognize the importance of reading both the text to be translated and anything related to it, as well as the translation itself as it is being produced. Baker (1998:129) says, "An essential preparation for the translation will be careful reading and re-reading and accompanying research of source text and other work by the author....[A]ny translation is ultimately the product of multiple reading and drafts which precede and determine the shape of the final draft delivered to the publishers....Repeated reading and research enable the translator to identify...[rhythmic, lexical, figurative, structural, and symbolic] patterns [in a source text]."

[232]"The cultural context is...a world vision that links together the members of a social group and distinguishes them from others. In other words, it is a set of cultural predispositions (conventions, beliefs, values and assumptions) internalized in the mind of the individual but socially determined. The interpretation of a text therefore becomes the product of a social (or inter-subjective) practice" (Megrab 1999:61).

[233]Use of "you" in these guidelines (implied also in the imperative forms) may be taken as singular or plural—that is, directed either to an individual draft translator or to a team working on the text together.

variety, with a different mood, perspective, or emphasis each time. *Listen* to the text. Allow it to stimulate the ears as well as the eyes. Certain prominent *oral-aural* stylistic and structural devices (especially those based upon sound) will become apparent through this attentive listening exercise.[234] This will give a general idea of what the portion is about and what type of a Scripture text it is. Make a tentative summary in a sentence or two of the main thoughts of the section as they occur as well as the main theme or themes. This may change after you have analyzed the pericope in more detail, but at least you will have a topical framework for your study as you continue to develop it in different ways.

It is important to specify the particular genre, or functional type, of text that you are dealing with, for this basic literary impression will guide you in further analysis of its form and content (see sec. 3.1). Is it a prosaic or a poetic discourse, and what particular category or subtype of either one—for example, for *prose*: narrative, prophetic, epistolary, genealogical; and for *poetry*: lyric (lament, hymn), apocalyptic, hortatory, didactic? Where do instances of "type mixing" occur, and for what apparent purpose? On a more specific level, for example in the case of a prophetic discourse, should it be classified as an oracle of judgment, of salvation, of assurance, of admonition, of divine self-disclosure, of "woe," or as a judicial speech or an apocalyptic-eschatological prediction (see Aune 1991, chaps. 4–5)? Within a Gospel narrative, does the text at hand appear to be a miracle story, a pronouncement passage, a biographical account, a parable, prophecy, disputation, or a homiletic midrash (see Aune 1987:50–54)?

The wider genre classification determines both the hermeneutical expectations that one brings to a text in terms of form, content, and function as well as the method of analysis and interpretation that is most appropriate for that particular type of discourse.[235] Once the nature of the whole has been thoroughly investigated by means of a study of its larger structural arrangement and communicative purpose, it will be easier to understand the individual verses—the constituent parts. Decisions as to genre and subgenre will affect how you treat the pericope in the process of translating it, especially if a corresponding genre or text type is not part of the TL oral inventory or literary corpus.

---

[234]The important structural implications of ancient oral "typesetting" by means of transitional formulas, repetition, parallel patterning, etc. are set forth in detail in the works of Davis (1999) and Harvey (1998).

[235]From a linguistic perspective, Wiesemann (n.d.:94–104) notes the importance of employing different analytical techniques for different types of discourse; for example, to narrative (procedural) she adds also "expository" and "behavioral" texts.

7.1.3 Step 3: Plot all occurrences of recursion/repetition in the pericope

A thorough analysis of the various types of verbal recursion present in a text is necessary, whether one's interest is primarily linguistic or literary. This is especially true in the case of the Holy Scriptures due to the sheer abundance and variety of phonological, lexical, syntactic, and semantic reiteration—it is present in virtually every passage. Thus it is necessary to make a detailed examination of any kind of repetition that appears, whether of content or form.[236] To do this, first note the sameness of any feature within the section or distinct subsection, for example, a continuance of time, place, participants and props, action line, topic, or genre/subgenre. Then examine the actual words or phrases and their order, placement, or arrangement within the section. Is any particular idea, expression, or syntactic construction repeated, and is such repetition exact, synonymous, or contrastive in nature? If possible, it is best to do this using the original Hebrew or Greek text or an interlinear version, since that is the only way in which the same or similar sounds—as in alliteration, assonance, or punning—can be detected. If that is not possible, a literal translation like the English RSV or NASB will have to do.

After noting all the instances of lower-level repetition, search for any *patterns* of recursion that are developed in the larger discourse, whether local or global in size and scope. In a poetic text, identify the different types of *parallelism*. (Such parallelisms—coupled lines—also occur in prose, especially in direct speech.) These parallel utterances may be found right next to each other (*adjacent*) or at some distance away (*separated*) as in inclusio, exclusio, anaphora, or epiphora (see definitions in sec. 3.2.2 and 7.1.6). When the second member of a parallelism is distant from the first, the B line often appears at a strategic compositional point such as at a structural boundary or a thematic peak. Lexical recursion also contributes to the *cohesion* (referential connectivity) of the text as a whole as well as of the distinct portions ("spans") that are included within it, creating, for example, participant chains, event sequences, temporal-spatial extensions, and topical threads. All deictic forms (pronouns, pro-verbs, demonstratives) are important in this regard, whether forward or backward directed (i.e., cataphoric or anaphoric), as is the significant continuity that is manifested by any other formal feature of the discourse (e.g., tense-aspect, mood-tone, person-number, speaker-addressee, text type).

Once the whole text has been examined with respect to all occurrences of exact, synonymous, contrastive, or associative (e.g., cause-effect)

---

[236]I sometimes distinguish the reiteration of form and content on the microstructure of discourse (*repetition*) from that on the macrostructure (*recursion*). An analysis of the former gives one a picture of the latter.

reiteration and it has been determined whether or not these are instances of random repetition or patterned recursion, observe how they all fit together to support the author's intended message. Can any explanation be given for the variations that appear? For example, are they due to a different co-text, one that is revealed by a shift in subject or style (see step 4)? It may be helpful as part of this general exercise to join any obvious or probable correspondences by means of arrows or to mark prominent parallels by underlining or highlighting them with felt markers of the same color. Then see if you can fit the similar instances and related thoughts together under a general topic such as blessing, punishment, righteousness, wickedness, good works, God's nature, promises, commands, and warnings. Key concepts of this kind may be written down as they occur individually or in combination on a separate piece of paper. Then after re-reading the text, you may decide to rearrange the listed categories, adding to them, or deleting, conjoining, separating, or renaming them. Perhaps it will turn out that a certain idea that is highlighted by repetition in the pericope under study has been important also in other portions of the larger document (or will turn out to be so later as the discourse is developed).

7.1.4 Step 4: Find all instances of disjunction within the discourse

In step 3 we saw how the various types of repetition effected textual *continuity* (i.e., cohesion and coherence) within a pericope. In contrast, the technique of disjunction highlights the obvious points of *discontinuity*, meaning some sort of a new beginning in discourse. These points are usually created at the beginning of larger compositional units, especially of paragraphs or their equivalents (in poetry, "strophes"). Disjunction is effected by a noticeable shift in the linguistic form (e.g., changing from past to present tense, from narrative report to direct speech, from third person to first person point of view) and/or content (e.g., moving from one scene, time setting, cast of characters, sequence of events, topical focus, or argument line to another).

Changes of this nature are sometimes seen combined with an appropriate *formula* that either opens or closes a distinct discourse unit to signal either "aperture" or "closure" respectively. Examples are "Then the word of the LORD came to me saying…"; "And it came to pass in those days…"; "The time is surely coming, says the LORD, when…"; "So the land had rest X years"; "While he was saying this"; "Now concerning …"; "Come now, you who say …"; "Next I saw …"; and "Praise the LORD!" A formula of this kind, which is especially common at the beginning of a section, often occurs in conjunction with the syntactic operations of *topicalization* (i.e., introducing a new topic into the discourse) and *focalization* (i.e., marking certain information as being of special salience within the clause/sentence). In oral texts, intonation and pause are normally utilized in this process, while in written texts the marker is often a full noun phrase +/– some form of dislocation in the word order (i.e., a "front shift" or "back shift" of the topical information).[237]

However, modifications in form, arrangement, content, tone, or perspective and the use of transitional expressions are not the only indicators of disjunction. These devices may be accompanied by a discourse marker of another kind, which increases the disjunctive effect. These other types include vocatives, imperatives, redundant demonstrative indicators, information concerning the interpersonal setting (e.g., Ezek. 14:1), and explicit references to time, place, or circumstance (e.g., in Ezek. 8:1, 7, and 9:1 "In the sixth year..."; "And he brought me to..."; "Then he cried in my hearing..."). A more literary type of disjunction may be incorporated into the discourse by means of special forms that involve an overt or covert shift in expectancy, or some other variation from the conventional norm such as a change in some sequence of parallelism or a prevailing metrical pattern; an elliptical, inserted, interrupted, or broken syntactic construction (anacoluthon); a rhetorical, deliberative, or leading question; the use of hyperbole, irony, sarcasm, or an unusual figure of speech; and the use of a parenthesis, a dramatic antithesis, or a striking instance of paronomasia (punning).

7.1.5 Step 5: Isolate the areas of stylistic concentration

Another marker of disjunction besides those mentioned in section 7.1.4 is an unexpected or unusual concentration of literary devices. It is useful, however, to consider this feature as a separate step in L-R discourse analysis, since such a stylistic concentration, whether "pure" or "mixed" in character, may serve to mark not only a compositional boundary but also a peak point in the text.[238] An example of a *pure* concentration is a cluster of related figures, especially simile-metaphor; another example is a passage of extended imagery that functions to foreground a certain segment or subject within the pericope as a whole. A *mixed* concentration may be

---

[237]For some helpful comments on topic and focus in Hebrew narrative, see Heimerdinger 1999, passim. See chapters 1 and 6 of Levinsohn 1992 for a discussion of topic and focus in New Testament discourse.

[238]Another purpose for a general stylistic analysis of a text to be translated has been summarized by Baker (1998:173): "[A] stylistic analysis can help the translator establish priorities in the decision-making process on the micro-level. Such an analysis is often carried out unconsciously or intuitively by experienced translators and sensitive readers." It is helpful, however, to make this an explicit step in the set of procedures that Bible translators regularly put into practice.

composed of any number of different features, for example, an initial rhetorical question encoded as direct speech that repeats some important element mentioned earlier in the text and includes a play on words, a hyperbole, or some other type of emphatic, idiomatic, or colorful language.

Poetry, being a form of discourse that is compact and condensed, is characterized by an extra measure of stylistic concentration. It is frequently marked in Hebrew by such features as rhythmic and balanced line-coupling, ellipsis (e.g., omission of the verb in the B line of a parallel couplet), conjunctive asyndeton, a reduction in the number of prose particles (definite article, sign of a direct object, prepositional prefixes, relative pronoun), predication through the use of nominalized verbals (gerunds or infinitives), and gnomic, proverbial, or conventional utterances of a religious nature. Conceptually concentrated passages appear in the Epistles on occasion in order to highlight a particular theological thought or communicative purpose (e.g., in 1 Tim. 3:16 to focus upon the saving mystery about Jesus Christ; in Heb. 4:12 to accent the power of his Word; in 1 John 2:12–14 to encourage the faithful; and in Jude 12–13 to warn readers of the grave danger of false teachers). In narrative discourse, we sometimes see a "crowded stage" (many participants) or a beehive of activity (many events in close succession) signaling the peak of the account (e.g., in Exod. 14:19–29 Israel's crossing of the Red Sea in advance of the Egyptian army; in Isa. 66:15–24 the eschatological last judgment to close the book of prophecy; in Luke 23:44–49 the crucifixion of Jesus Christ; in Acts 27 the storm that almost ended Paul's sea journey to Rome; and in Rev. 19:17–21 the final defeat of the beast and his armies at the end of time).

After the presence of such a concentration of features has been identified and analyzed, its particular placement and purpose within the text must be contextually evaluated. Some examples of a carefully positioned concentration of stylistic devices can be seen in the following passages from Daniel: the doxology of Darius, which ends the narrative and begins the prophetic half of the book (6:26–27); Daniel's intense prayer of confession and intercession (9:1–19), which divides the apocalyptic portion in two; and the awesome vision of a universal world tribulation followed by a resurrection and day of final judgment, which highlights the prophecy's concluding portion (12:1–4).

7.1.6 Step 6: Identify the major points of discourse demarcation and projection

Based on the results of steps 1–5, step 6 can now be carried out. The aim here is to provide an overview of the discourse organization of the pericope or book being analyzed. This is done first of all with regard to the text's external and internal boundaries (its "demarcation") and then any areas of additional emphasis ("projection"). The latter may be either major or minor points of importance (above or below the paragraph level) in relation to the development of message content and the realization of its primary pragmatic intent.

Obvious occurrences of separated recursion (see sec. 7.1.3) often indicate a structural break in the textual movement from one poetic paragraph (strophe or stanza) to another. In other words, they may signal a compositional border either within or at the extremities of the text. The more frequent the incidence of recursion and the greater its quality (degree of formal correspondence), the more diagnostic it is as an architectonic marker. Some of the most common discourse-framing techniques are *inclusio* (a parallel beginning and ending of a unit), *anaphora* (parallel unit beginnings), *epiphora* (parallel unit endings), and *anadiplosis* (unit overlapping or transitional parallelism).

Sometimes separated recursion of form or content, instead of signaling a break, signals a place of special significance within the composition as a whole. In most cases this sort of projection occurs somewhere near the close of a pericope, though in poetry it may be sometimes be found near the textual midpoint. Separated recursion may signal a point of prominence or culmination in other genres as well, for example, in relation to either the central action of a narrative account ("climax"), the main theme of an exposition or exhortation ("peak"), or in the development of the author's feelings and intensity of emotive expression ("apex"). However, lexical recursion on its own, unless it happens to be very exact and/or extensive, is not sufficient evidence to postulate a major discourse break or peak. Therefore, the case for a break or peak is strengthened if lexical recursion is found to occur in conjunction with a significant shift (see sec. 7.1.4) in time, place, speaker, or topic (+/– focus marking) and/or an unusual concentration of poetic features (e.g., figurative language, rhetorical question, direct speech, hyperbole). The more literary evidence that can be marshaled in support of a given structural hypothesis, the more credible it is and the easier it is to defend it in the face of alternatives.

Thus, with these signals in mind, the analyst should, as step 6, record all posited breaks and potential peaks in the original text. This could be done using different marking colors to indicate the points of closest semantic correspondence. Then the breaks and peaks can be related to one another in terms of their topical content and major or minor importance. This forms the basis for step 7.

7.1.7 Step 7: Outline the compositional structure of the entire pericope

After a thorough consideration of the structure-related information derived from step 6, the analyst will be able to discern the larger textual contours of the entire pericope, including all of its internal segments. The material now needs to be outlined and given summary subject headings according to the various form-content divisions, fitting them together into a hierarchical framework of discourse organization. During this exercise it is helpful to consult some other structural outlines, such as those proposed in study Bibles and translation handbooks, but this should not be done before your own analysis and outline have been completed. The major and minor section headings of the TEV, CEV, and NIV are also useful with respect to larger discourse patterns and arrangements. Finally, time permitting, the outlines given in recognized exegetical commentaries may be examined and evaluated by the translation team.

Next, consider the smaller groupings (paragraphs or strophes) into which the various published versions divide the text under study. You may later decide to disagree with some of their postulated sectional divisions, but at least they give you a basis for comparison with your own results.

More experienced translators can then go on to carry out a propositional analysis of the complete pericope, or perhaps only certain complex portions of it, in order to arrive at a more precise indication of how the discourse is organized.[239] A structural-thematic outline of the kind prepared in this step provides a necessary conceptual framework that permits a more accurate assessment of the full artistic beauty and rhetorical power of all the literary devices that the text at hand incorporates. Artistry and rhetoric must always be viewed in terms of the salience and significance of the larger compositional whole as well as the major functional aim(s) that the original author wanted to achieve in relation to his intended audience (based on the study of their most probable setting of communication in step 1).

---

[239]For a recent overview of discourse analysis procedures, see Dooley and Levinsohn 2001; for a simplified presentation based on the Psalms, see chapter 3 of Wendland 2002a.

7.1.8 Step 8: Prepare a complete semantic (word/symbol/motif) study

Having established the overall segmentation and internal structure of the passage under study, you are ready to give some attention to the details of its semantic texture and cognitive construction. Begin by underlining, or otherwise marking, all the primary theological concepts and other re-peated expressions in the discourse. These key terms and thematic motifs (the latter being derived from the larger document or from the Scripture at large) will consist of nouns, verbs, and sometimes adjectives—or, in se-mantic terms, entities, events, and attributes (e.g., 'holiness/sanc-tify/holy'). In the case of poetry, any prominent word pairs should also be noted (e.g., 'love-mercy', 'rock-fortress', 'cry-call out', 'clean-pure'). You may already be well acquainted with these significant words and phrases, but a review of their distinct senses and range of meanings is necessary so that they are correctly understood as used specifically in the text under consideration and according to their individual literary contexts. For a ba-sic understanding of such terms the notes and cross-references of a good study Bible or the pertinent book in the UBS Translator's Handbook or the SIL Exegetical Summary series may suffice, but more difficult expressions and concepts require the use also of Bible dictionaries, topical encyclope-dias, analytical commentaries, and, if possible, biblical language lexicons, especially those based on semantic domains (e.g., Louw and Nida 1989, de Blois 2000).

Such a detailed analysis of essential vocabulary, including all figurative or symbolic language, will enable you to reconsider the structural-thematic outline you formulated in step 7. Some revisions may now be necessary. The main thing is to recognize the larger *unity* of the composi-tion— how all of its parts fit together and all of its L-R devices operate in harmony to convey the essential theological or moral content and com-municative purpose of the whole. Of course, exceptions and anomalies do occur, and these should not be ignored or smoothed over. Review any ap-parent conceptual gaps, conflicts, and other outstanding points of diffi-culty or opacity to see if your plan for the complete discourse can assist in the interpretation of the remaining problem areas. It may well be that these are features of deliberate disjunction (see step 4) intended to signal some key juncture or idea of special importance within the larger pericope.

7.1.9 Step 9: Analyze any remaining linguistic and literary features

Step 9 takes care of the "leftovers." All of the stylistic devices and compositional techniques that were not fully considered during the preceding structural and thematic studies are now to be analyzed in relation to what has already been discovered. For example, the various significant literary forms that occur in the pericope might now be studied in terms of their quality, quantity, distribution, location, and semantic interaction. In addition, some unusual or heretofore unexplained linguistic usages or arrangements may turn out, on closer examination, to be clearly rhetorical in terms of their particular communicative purpose. Again, the emphasis should be upon discovering form-functional unity within diversity. The point is not to simply provide neat literary labels for each of the different devices that are present, but rather to determine the extent to which they have been effectively utilized in order to enhance their individual and cumulative effect in the discourse at large. It may be possible then to show how style serves to reinforce the central message being conveyed by the complete pericope as well as by its constituent parts—that is, in accordance with the text's organizational outline (step 7, which may or may not require further revision at this stage).

This would also be the time to carry out any special investigation that relates to the structure, style, and (proposed) pragmatic operation of different types of discourse, such as poetic, predictive, narrative, or hortatory/paraenetic texts. With regard to this last category, which includes the prophetic or apostolic writings, you could apply the argument-structure model described in section 6.2.5. In the case of narrative discourse, you would want to pay closer attention to such important features as plot structure and development, character depiction, dramatic dialogic interaction, point of view, and the influence of the contextual setting on the account (see further below). Poetry, of course, requires a different set of investigative methods in terms of type and focus (e.g., procedures pertaining to parallelism, condensation, concentrated imagery, sound plays, liturgical language, and rhythmic diction). Other discourse types and subtypes—from complete apocalypses (e.g., Ezekiel 38–39) to individual parables and proverbs (as in the Gospels)—would each call for its own specific literary perspective and analytical approach to supplement the more general guidelines described here.

7.1.10 Step 10: Note the major speech functions and their interaction in the discourse

The total meaning package of a biblical text includes not only its content (information), but also its expressions of emotion, attitude, preference (value), and purpose. The original writer carefully chose his structure and style—the "artistry" of discourse—in order to communicate these vital aspects of a life-related message. They must not be ignored in any exegetical or literary study, whether or not a translation is the ultimate aim.

For example, although it is a psalm's principal religious function that determines its genre (step 2), the principal communicative aim of some of the included strophes (stanzas) may be different. This is because the successive structural units of poetic discourse often refer to different situations ("speech events," each composed of a sequence of interrelated "speech acts") as far as the interaction of the psalmist with his (implied) audience is concerned. Consequently they express different aspects of his involvement with them, hence also of his message to them. The individual speech acts are best analyzed in terms of rhetorical purpose, what the speaker/writer intended to accomplish by means of his words (i.e., the utterance illocution as discussed in sec. 6.2.4). One frequently finds passages of encouragement, promise, warning, rebuke, commitment, consolation, and condemnation in the psalms, and these motives are frequently accompanied by expressions of the appropriate emotion, such as joy, sorrow, fear, pain, trust, despair, and hope. The same sort of intentional, volitional, and connotative diversity occurs in other types of biblical discourse, particularly where direct discourse (as in narrative) or its equivalent (as in the Epistles) is involved. Oftentimes various combinations, mixtures, or degrees of overlapping may be discerned in terms of communicative function as the discourse progresses from one context to another.[240]

All of these functions and feelings, whether major or minor in scope and importance, are an important part of the author's assumed intention as he composed the original message. Thus they need to be identified at their point of occurrence in the text. These connotative features must be noted along with the various literary and rhetorical devices (e.g., rhetorical questions, exclamations, intensifiers, repetition, syntactic displacement, phonological embellishment) that help to reveal and highlight them. In particular, the analyst needs to record any special concentration of such

---

[240]Fawcett's warning applies to any functional analysis: "This is one of the most frequent criticisms of function-based translation taxonomies: they assume a monolith where there is really multifunctionality. Although the overall aim of a text is important, we still have to concentrate on the mosaic of subtextual functions" (1997:108).

devices, for this may serve to mark an emotional apex within the development of a discourse or one of its integral constituents. This sort of emotive-attitudinal mapping is important: it ensures that the apparent *interlocutionary dynamics* and *argument arrangement* of the pericope under study will be functionally reproduced, to the extent possible, during the translation process.[241]

To determine the personal interaction underlying the discourse of a particular psalm, it would help to view it as a dramatic dialogue in some cases or as a prayer-conversation between the psalmist and God. Sometimes other participants enter this sacred speech event, either as speakers or addressees (e.g., the psalmist's enemies, detractors, or his fellow worshipers in the house of God). How do these different groups interact with one another in terms of their speech patterns as the psalm progresses? Who is speaking to whom, under what circumstances, for what purpose, and with what sort of mood, emotion, viewpoint, or bias? An even greater challenge in this respect is presented by the prophetic writings, which are notorious for their various levels and diverse combinations of speaker-addressee engagement.

Another question is whether an overall plan, or pattern of speech acts or illocutions, is manifested in the discourse (the "text act"). There may be a distinct structure of this kind that either dominates or complements the organization of a text's thematic content.[242] The more fully that you the translator (or consultant) can imagine yourself engaging as an active partner in the dialogue of the larger discourse, the more accurately you will be able to understand the writer's communicative situation and then dynamically convey his intentions in the TL—or be able to advise other translators how to do so. Interactive role-playing (e.g., modeling that between Christ and his disciples, Christ and the Pharisees, Christ and the surrounding crowd, or between the key participants of a parable) can also help a creative team analyze these various text-internal speech acts and their illocutionary interrelationships.

---

[241]"[A]s part of their understanding of how a text is constructed and functions, translators should be able to recognize not just the specific functions of cause, reason, time, etc., but also the more general functions of elaboration (restating or clarifying), extension (adding to or modifying) and enhancement (extending by specification)" (Fawcett 1997:97).

[242]See Dooley and Levinsohn 2001:4–6, 97–101 for an overview of this sort of "conversational analysis" intended to reveal the structure of dialogic discourse, for example in terms of speech "turns" and "moves."

7.1.11 Step 11: Do an L-R comparison for possible form-functional matches

To this point in the analytical process, the focus of attention has been upon the SL and the original biblical text. Now translators must turn to the TL and its literature, both secular and religious, oral and written. The same kind of "mining" investigation that was done with respect to the original text will now be done in order to discover, assemble, categorize, and evaluate the verbal resources available in the TL for rendering the Scriptures as poetically or rhetorically as possible. The goal, as always, is to accomplish this task in a functionally equivalent manner in selected relevant respects, including now literary artistry as well as primary semantic content and communicative intent. Indigenous poetry and prose will have its own inventory of texts, contexts, and linguistic features (phonological, lexical, syntactic, and discourse-related) to be explored, and there can be no shortcuts when seeking to discover and document these for use in translation.

The TL features that must be investigated include the distinct genres and subtypes, traditional as well as modern; discourse structures, markers, and arrangements; stylistic devices in terms of their form and function, denotation and connotation; rhetorical techniques and their application within complete texts and included portions; typical vocabulary, formulas, and figurative language; shifts in "register" (i.e., typical speech variations according to language *medium, user,* and *use*);[243] and finally, all of these features in relation to specific settings of oral performance and social distribution or use. These disparate aspects of poetic and prosaic composition will each have to be carefully tested for its suitability or appropriateness for translating the Scriptures. If people are not accustomed to dynamic literary language in the Bible (perhaps due to the influence of an existing literal version), then the testing must be precede by some explanation and language-specific illustration. This will shed some light on how, or if, a literary rendering will be received. But once it is understood that the original biblical books are artistic and rhetorical as well as theological in nature, receptors usually respond positively to skillful, yet sensitive, attempts to make them sound that way also in their mother tongue. Thus the stage is set for the final, indeed the climactic,

---

[243]Fawcett provides a helpful summary of some of the principal sociolinguistic aspects of register as these relate to translation (1997:74–84). He points out (p. 83) that "all translators should be able to perform a register analysis...in order to have an understanding of the text they are translating which goes beyond the simple level of denotation and allows them to choose the appropriate register in the target language...."

step in this whole set of heuristic procedures, namely, the actual translation process itself.

7.1.12 Step 12: Prepare a trial translation and test it against other versions

Once a pericope or book has been analyzed following the previous steps, a translation in the TL may now be composed. (This assumes some preliminary interlingual transfer of ideas and experimentation with literary forms having been done along the way.) First, prepare a *literal* rendering of the piece, unless such a version already exists in the language. Base it on the SL text or an interlinear version of the SL text with English or some other language of wider communication. This will give you a general sense of the text's original *form* and essential *content* (i.e., its fundamental lexical and conceptual inventory). Then if there are any well-done meaning-oriented translations in the lingua franca of your region, assess their potential value as models. Also look at the vernacular versions that exist in a language related to your own, whether good or bad. They too can be helpful for comparative purposes.[244]

These model versions, considered together with the SL-to-TL analysis that was completed during steps 1–11, will enable you (as an individual or a team) to move on now to produce an idiomatic, oral-aurally sensitive rendering of the biblical text in the TL. The careful comparative process is intended to provide you with an understanding of the essential meaning of the original message and suggest some possible ways of expressing this in your language. As you work, remember the important communication principles of *efficiency* (current ease and economy of expression), *accuracy* (with regard to original content and purpose), *effectiveness* (immediate discourse impact and appeal), and *relevance* (in terms of the contemporary sociocultural, literary, and ecclesiastical setting). The goal is to represent in the TL the closest literary-functional equivalent—a fully natural and contextualized correspondent—of what you have determined to be the heart of the message conveyed by the biblical text.

As we see, Bible translation must be a rigorously *analytical* and a systematically *comparative* text-based exercise.[245] A close parallel examination of a

---

[244]If linguistically competent, bilingual staff are available, have them prepare a back-translation into the TL of a good vernacular version in a closely related language, if there is one. This would provide another excellent model, one that might be even more helpful than a version in a language of wider communication that the translators "know" but are not really very competent in. If the vernacular model is too literal and not "literary" enough, its text could be modified in the TL as the translators proceed.

[245]In Wendland 2000a I present some explanatory notes as well as an illustration of this sort of a practical text-comparative exercise.

number of versions, especially those in related languages, shows you how others have understood and expressed the aspects of meaning presented by the same text that you are dealing with. It is particularly important to pay special attention to the *differences*, both large and small (the latter quickly add up to make a great disparity), that appear among the several versions consulted. Be able to specify what these differences are in terms of linguistic form and what stylistic or functional effect they have on the respective texts. In many cases, the diversity is simply a reflection of the languages involved or of different methods of translation, whether literal or idiomatic. But at times the variants will be more significant. One or another may represent a failure to convey the intended meaning (content + intent) or even an obvious error such as an addition, modification, or omission.

Finally, it is important to extend this comparative method to the TL constituency, using various formal and informal testing methods. In many settings, this will require the development of oral-aural assessment procedures, not only written ones. The purpose is to gain enough feedback— both corrective and suggestive—so that when the translation is published, whether as portions or in its entirety, it will be met with the widest possible acceptance.

A careful comparative examination of texts, together with the insights gained in testing the early drafts with TL speakers in various settings of use, will surely reveal problems. All of the exegetical and translational difficulties that come to a translator's attention during this process need to be discussed, corrected if necessary, and perhaps also evaluated in terms of how they originated. This is also a good time to consider the *medium* of communication with regard to producing a more readable (legible) or hearable (intelligible) translation in terms of its intended format of presentation.

7.2 L-R analysis techniques for narrative discourse

The aim of the preceding twelve steps has been to suggest the importance of following an explicit strategy of comparative analysis with respect to the distinctly *literary* and *rhetorical* character of the original message of the Scriptures, that is, in addition to a thorough exegetical study. Thus the SL text must be carefully compared in this respect with its present expression in the translator's mother tongue or the language of the project that one is overseeing as a translation officer.

In section 7.1 the focus was on poetry. Now we turn to the analysis of narrative texts. In this section we will consider some sample sets of investigative questions that are particularly applicable to the   analysis of narrative texts as part of preparing to translate them adequately and acceptably.

The arrangement of these questions is according to the basic framework of a dramatic (plot-built) account:

[*PLOT* = *initial state* ➜ *complication* ➜ *build-up* ➜ *climax* ➜ *resolution* +/- *transition*]

PLOT/EVENTS ⇔ Action Progression (via the text's primary event backbone)
CHARACTERS ⇔ Participant Tracing (via noun/pronoun spans or stretches in a text)
SETTING ⇔ Background Information (e.g., word order variations, verb tense/ aspect)
RHETORIC ⇔ Feature-Focus (i.e., to highlight key aspects of the text's structure or function)

7.2.1 Questions concerning events

- Is there a *key event* (or core set of events) that appears in this episode? If so, how does this seem to be marked in the SL text by linguistic features? (This may be discernible even in a translation.) Is there a strong *event line*? If so, where does it lead? How should this event line be marked in the TL, and how may it be broken up into distinct, readily identifiable stages or scenes? (This sort of application to the TL and its oral or literary conventions must be made as a matter of course with regard to all of these questions.)
- Is any type of significant *reversal* introduced into the primary sequence of events? If so, what is the larger significance of this in relation to the whole account?
- How does the key event (or core set of events) compare with other events in the narrative? Is it the most important of all—a major *turning point*? Or is it simply a logical result or outcome of something that happened earlier in the story? What is the evidence for your conclusion?
- How is the *sequence* of main action events reported? Are the events reported in chronological order or are there significant temporal shifts either backward (flashback) or ahead (flash forward)? If so, how is this disruption of the event line signaled in the text, and what seems to be its dramatic purpose?
- What is the *tempo* of narration? Are the events recorded in slow motion or with a rapid pace?

- Are the main actions reported in summary fashion or in great detail? In other words, is this *panoramic* or *scenic* narration? Are there any obvious variations in this respect, and what seems to be the significance of this in terms of the overall plot—or purpose—of the account? How does the proportion of the scenic or panoramic technique affect the reader/hearer's perception of time?
- Are any events referred to more than once? If so, do these *reiterations* have the same level of prominence? For example, do the different references appear in nominal or verb form, and are the verbs finite or nonfinite? What seems to be the main reason for the repetition?
- How are the *backgrounded* events indicated, and what sort of actions or states do they record? In view of the condensed nature of biblical narrative, why are these events reported at all (e.g., for contextual information, explanation, previewing future events, or reviewing past ones)?
- What elements of *conflict* are apparent in the events being reported? Do any of these stand out? If so, in what way and how are they distinguished? Does the conflict build up to a *climax*? How is this part of the story distinguished? Is the conflict resolved in the present episode, or does it carry on in the next?
- Does the sequence of main events lead to a *conclusion* of some kind, or does the story line continue to be developed in another episode? If there is a clear break in the narrative at the end of the present episode, how is this point of closure marked—by what indicators?
- Where does *dialogue* or speech occur in the narrative, and what is the significance of this? In other words, why are these particular words put into direct speech at this specific point in the account? Do they seem to be of special theological or moral importance? What do the dialogue portions reveal about the character of the speakers? Do any of the speeches express a lot of emotion? If so, of what kind and why?
- From whose *point of view* are the events and situations of the episode reported? The narrator's, whether first person or third person, or a participant's? Is there any noticeable *shift* in point of view? If so, where does it occur and, in terms of plot or purpose, why?

7.2.2 Questions concerning characters

- Who are the *principal* characters (usually there are only two per scene or episode)? What part do they play in the account? Is some one character *dominant*? What is the significance of this to the story as a whole? Is the principal character distinguished linguistically in the text? If so, how is this done?

- How are characters *introduced*? Do any special linguistic devices mark their appearance? What is the preferred way of *referring* to characters once they have been introduced? Is there any difference in this respect between major and minor characters?
- If there are *minor* characters, what *role* do they perform in the dramatic movement of the story? Do any of them appear earlier, or are they introduced here? What is their function in the larger discourse?
- Is there any special significance to *where* in the account individual characters are brought into the narrative or where they are removed?
- What does the narrator tell us about the chief characters? Do we learn about them from their own actions, speeches, and reported thoughts or from what others in the account say about them? In other words, from whose *point of view* do we learn about the chief characters?
- How many characters tend to be active in the *dialogue*—two, or more? Do some characters speak on behalf of a group? Which narrative players do not speak and what is the possible significance of this?
- Are the characters *round* (fully described), *flat* (only partially revealed), or *stock* (conventional or typical) in nature? What are the reasons for the particular amount and manner of characterization in relation to the dramatic action of the plot?
- If *God* (*YHWH*, Christ) is one of the major characters on the scene, how is he distinguished (if at all) in formal terms? What role does he play? What does this account reveal in particular about the divine nature, purpose, and will?
- Are there any important *props* in the account—that is, conventionalized nonhuman creatures (e.g., ravens, doves) or objects (e.g., thirty pieces of silver)? If so, what is their narrative purpose or possible symbolic significance?
- Does the *narrator* intrude upon the story to comment or provide descriptive or background information (e.g., in the Gospel of John)? Is (or was) the narrator or implied narrator a participant in the action being reported (e.g., Luke in the Book of Acts)?
- Which characters are most *empathetic* and why? Which ones are most *antipathetic* and why? Has the account been composed so as to move the audience to see these characters from this perspective? Is

there perhaps some difference between the ancient and contemporary point of view with regard to such characterizations?
- How are characters depicted in *connotative* terms, that is, in a positive, negative, or neutral light? Which specific stylistic devices contribute to making this particular impression?

7.2.3 Questions concerning the setting

- What is the *spatial, temporal,* and *social* setting for the episode at
hand? Is there any difference in place, time, or interpersonal situation in comparison with the previous scene?
- *How much* information pertaining to the setting is included in the
account and *where* is this introduced, if not at the beginning of an
episode?
- How are the place settings in the narrative described—up close
with much detail (a *scenic* perspective) or from a distance with only
a summary of the high points (a *panoramic* perspective)?
- What is the relationship in the account between "natural time" and
"discourse time," that is, between a strict chronological order and
the order in which the narrator presents the events or episodes?
How do these literary constructs relate in turn to the actual time
that it takes to read the text aloud—is there a close correspondence
at certain points in the narrative and, if so, what is the dramatic
significance of this?
- Is information pertaining to the setting introduced into the account
as foregrounded material or backgrounded? What are the linguistic *markers* of this, if any? How do the foreground-background indicators of Hebrew narrative (devices such as frontal displacement
that signal topic" or focus) differ from the corresponding TL indicators? (See Heimerdinger 1999 and van der Merwe, Naudé, and
Kroeze 1999:344-350 for a discussion of these devices in Hebrew;
also see Levinsohn 2002.)
- Are verbs in a setting passage different from event-line verbs in any
way? Do they differ in terms of tense, aspect, mood, voice, or any
other feature?
- Are there any ways in which the setting of the episode under study
is distinct or even unique in relation to the larger narrative
account? What is the significance of this distinction? What does it
reveal about the author's wider purpose in presenting this particular episode?

- What is the overall psychological *mood* of the current setting? Is it optimistic or pessimistic, joyous or sorrowful? What is it that contributes to this atmosphere? (It could be such things as narrator comments, character speech, and/or the main sequence of events.)
- How much *sensory* description is in this particular scene (e.g., cold/heat, crowded/lonely, foreign/home)? Do the sensory impressions come from the characters or the narrator (e.g., through the narrator's backgrounded commentary)?
- Is the setting, or some distinct aspect of it, conventionalized, that is, some form of literary stereotype, and what is the significance of this (e.g., forty days, wilderness, Temple precincts, River Jordan)? Does there seem to be some deeper *symbolic* import to any of the physical or natural features that are described, or briefly referred to, as the account unfolds (e.g., some mountain, plant, animal, sun, desert region)? If so, what does this latent meaning contribute to the overall message (e.g., in the story of Satan's temptation of Christ)? How do such iconic implications compare to what these same features would mean in the sociocultural setting of the TL audience?
- Are the characters' spatial *movements* (e.g., fast or slow, up or down, in or out, towards or from some place or goal) noteworthy for any special reason? Is there any additional importance attached to the particular *time* of the events in this account (e.g., the time of year, coincidence with a religious festival, the reign of a king or other ruler, the activity of a prophet or apostle)?
- What is the specific *cultural context* within which the story occurs? How do such situational and circumstantial features affect the characters, their words or actions, and the interpretation of the details selected for inclusion in the account?
- What contextual information pertaining to the temporal, spatial, or sociocultural setting is left *implicit* in the SL text because the author assumes it to be known by his intended audience? Which parts of this implicit material need to be made explicit so that people today can correctly understand the biblical message? Of special importance (since it is often overlooked or ignored) is information concerning ancient social and political institutions, class structures, economic systems, religious rituals, culturally distinct customs, and conventions of politeness.

7.2.4 Questions concerning the rhetoric of the text

There may be rhetorical features in the text under consideration besides those that have already been described that are worthy of special attention. Be alert to literary techniques that increase the impact, appeal, beauty, appropriateness, acceptability, and persuasiveness of the narrative. These include figurative language, irony, hyperbole, allusion, paradox, and symbolism.

- Are any of the rhetorical devices in the passage used in an unusual manner? Are any of them especially difficult to perceive and interpret?
- Do rhetorical devices (or one certain type, such as metaphors) appear to be *concentrated* in a particular portion of the discourse, perhaps at its plot peak or climax, or in relation to a particular person to aid in his or her characterization? What do such features reveal about the values, presuppositions, priorities, preferences, and communicative aims of the biblical author? Would they carry the same implications in the TL?
- What larger patterns of *repetition* appear and how do these serve to *demarcate* the discourse? Which *disjunctive* devices are present to help segment the text (e.g., into action-based paragraphs or episodes)? How is *cohesion* effected or manifested within and between the segments? Is there *internal* connectivity within the pericope under study? Is there *external* connectivity in relation to the surrounding pericopes/episodes?
- What *speech (or text) acts* are performed or enhanced through the use of the varied stylistic and rhetorical features of the narrative text? Which speech acts are prominent in the dialogue portions? What seems to be the overall effect that the biblical author seeks to achieve upon the intended (or implied) audience by means of his written message, in this case, the particular account that he is narrating?
- Point out any possible *oral-aural* elements that are especially evident in the discourse. Is there any particular significance that may be attached to their location within the text? What effect would they have most likely had upon listeners? Do such audio-oriented features appear to be prominent enough to suggest that the text was originally presented orally or that the author composed it with oral articulation in mind? What implications does this have for translation?

- What part do these rhetorical features play in the communication of the narrative's principal message with regard to content (meaning) as well as intent (function)? Do they suggest another level of interpretation (symbolic interpretation), as may be the case with the prevalent use of irony in Jonah to criticize prejudice among God's people, especially the clergy?

7.3 Applying the twelve procedural steps to the Book of Obadiah

In this section the twelve procedural steps of section 7.1 will be applied to the Book of Obadiah, which is the shortest book in the Hebrew Bible but often said to be the most difficult in relation to its size. This is not a complete analysis, only a brief discussion of selected examples to see how the recommended guidelines may work out in practice. (For further details, see Wendland 1996b and 1996c.)

7.3.1 Textual, intertextual, and extratextual context

Since the discourse under consideration is a whole book, there is no co-textual influence of a linguistic nature that applies. It is interesting, however, although perhaps coincidental, that the preceding prophetic book in the canon—Amos—includes two important references to Edom, *YHWH*'s ostensive addressees in Obadiah. Amos's first-mentioned topic, toward the beginning of the document, is judgment (Amos 1:11; cf. Obad. 14). The second, at the end of Amos, is a prophecy of blessing for Israel at the expense of Edom (Amos 9:11–12; cf. Obad. 17–21). Some scholars see a certain compositional significance in the position of Obadiah within the so-called "Book of the Twelve" (see Nogalski and Sweeney 2000:3–87).

As to specific intertextual ties, there are strong links between Obad. 1–9 and Jer. 9:7–16, as well as some important connections with Ezekiel 35. This makes a supposition regarding the extratextual setting of Obadiah more plausible, namely, that the prophecy was written down (after being presented orally) sometime shortly *after* the destruction of Jerusalem by the Babylonian armies in 587-586 B.C.E. (cf. Obad. 11).[246] If that is indeed true, then the prophet is proclaiming his message from "the Sovereign LORD" (v. 1) either to a remnant of the Jews still left in their devastated homeland or, more likely, to a people who had been forcibly removed into

---

[246]A cogent case can be made for a pre-exilic date of composition, that is, in response to a bloody rebellion by the Edomites during the reign of Jehoram (2 Kings 8:20–22; 2 Chron. 21:8–10). For details, see "Obadiah" by J. Niehaus (1993:495–541). However, both the internal textual evidence and the most likely postulated purpose for the book appear to favor an exilic date.

exile. In either case, the main purpose would be consolation and encouragement, the same as the purpose of Ezekiel and Jeremiah, that is, to reassure the presently oppressed and depressed people of Israel that God is
still in control of world events and will one day bring about a just retribution upon all enemies and a glorious restoration for his faithful flock (vv.
17–18).

7.3.2 Genres and genre subtypes

The author of Obadiah entitles his text a "vision" (*chazon*), indicating its
general prophetic and poetic character. Some commentators have suggested that the final three verses, 19–21, are written in prose. While this
may be phonologically correct, the elaborate repetition and parallelism of
this section certainly points to a poetic manner of composition, varied
from the preceding text here at the end for special effect perhaps. In general terms, then, Obadiah falls into the conventional generic category of
the "oracles against the nations" (e.g., Isaiah 13–23, Jeremiah 46–51,
Ezekiel 25–32 + 35).

More specifically, Obadiah may be analyzed as an adapted "covenant
lawsuit address" (Niehaus 1993:507) consisting of an optional setting, the
"scene/setting of judgment" (v. 1); a "speech by the divine Judge" against
the covenant violator, which is a declaration of the verdict or sentence
(2–10); and an "accusation" plus a judicial "pronouncement of guilt"
(11–14). Normally a pronouncement of guilt occurs first, so this reversal
may be a deliberate move in the interest of rhetorical effect by the author
(but note the included indictments of v. 3 and v. 10a). If it is, there is a significant modification in that this lawsuit is leveled against Edom, not
Yahweh's covenant people, as is usually the case in the Old Testament
(e.g., Hos. 4:1–3, 12:2–14; Micah 6:2–16; Isa. 6:13–26). Moreover, the accusation and judgment are extended from Edom to all pagan peoples at
the eschaton (15–16), and there is included a "promise of restoration/vin-
dication" to the covenantal victims of the violators' oppression, namely,
the "brother" of Edom, Israel-Judah (17–21). Certain commentators also
note some genre subtypes, such as a "taunt oracle" (vv. 2–4), an eschatological "judgment of reversal" prophecy (15–16), and a "salvation oracle"
(17–21).

7.3.3 Random and patterned repetition

As in any Hebrew poetic text, the diverse forms of repetition abound in
Obadiah. A parallel syntactic construction, a double rhetorical question

with an included exclamation, closely knits the content of vv. 5–6 together into a protasis => apodosis construction, in which each of the utterances highlights the coming judgment of Edom. This is preceded by a chiastic arrangement of logical elements that foregrounds the reason for Edom's fall, namely, pride: A = consequence (2), B = cause (3a), B' = cause (3b), A' = consequence (4).

Reiterated references to Edom punctuate the verdict announced in vv. 8–9, while a graphic verbal depiction of Edom's crime is accented by the reduplicated, cohesion-fixing temporal phrase 'in the day of' (11–14). Although Edom ('*edom*) is not mentioned by name in this section, its reference is indirectly reinforced by the wordplay alluding to "their disaster" ('*edam* in v. 13).

The final two strophes (the last third of the book) are linked by repetitions of key thematic terms: 'mountain' (five times), 'house' (five times), 'possess' (five times), 'Esau' (= Edom, four times), 'Jacob/Joseph/Israel/Jerusalem' (five times), and the prophetic temporal indicator 'it will be' (six times).

There are exact, synonymous, and contrastive recursions that, in addition to their cohesive function, also serve to demarcate the main internal boundaries of the book. Examples include the divine declaratory formula 'utterance of the LORD' in 4b and 8a; the inclusio 'you stand' ('*-m-d*) in vv. 11 and 14; references to the eschatological day, speaking, and ruling in 15a, 18e, and 21b; and mention of the mountains of Esau in 19a and 21a.

7.3.4 Disjunction: Breaks and formulas

Several disjunctive formulas have already been noted. The beginning of the Book of Obadiah is announced by the prophetic pronouncement "Thus says the LORD...," as is typical of prophetic book openings. The prophecy is segmented into three parts by an implicit interchange of speakers to form an A—B—A' "block ring construction," namely, 1–10, 11–14, and 15–21. There are two divine discourses each having a *future* time orientation (A/A'): The first is directed (overtly) towards Edom; and the second, to the real recipients, the dispossessed of Judah. The two discourses are separated by B, a denunciation by Obadiah in which he castigates Edom's traitorous treatment of Judah during the *past* siege of Jerusalem. (Note the progressive specification of Edom's crime as this section develops.) The divine verdict that is announced for Edom in A is followed by the judicial reason for it in B, which is an accusatory indictment having reference to Judah's disastrous day of despoliation.[247] From this there is a sudden shift back again to a future day of deliverance for Judah and judgment upon Edom.

An interesting transitional piece occurs in vv. 15–16, where God is clearly speaking once more, but now to the heathen nations concerning a future punishment to be inflicted on behalf of Judah-Israel (v. 17). Major and minor forms of disjunction also occur to signal the peak in vv. 10, 17, and 21 (see sec. 7.3.6).

7.3.5 Stylistic concentration

Peak passages are normally marked compositionally by a concentration of literary-poetic features. For example, at the close of A (part 1) in v. 10, we have a cluster of key terms, including a reference to Edom's specific crime (i.e., 'violence'), his punishment ('cut off'), its personal impact ('shame'), and his fraternal victim ('your brother, Jacob', which is the very first mention of God's people in this prophecy). The armies of Edom will be 'cut down' (*k-r-th*) in the same way that *they* cut down the people of Jerusalem who were attempting to flee the city's destruction (vv. 10 and 14, a case of *epiphora* and an ironic *lex talionis* pairing). The book's twin thematic peak (vv. 17 and 21) is distinguished by the only references in the book to Mount Zion and an ultimate deliverance. The blessed inheritance to be received by God's people contrasts markedly with the punitive judgment that will befall 'all the nations' (vv. 15–16), in particular the 'house of Esau' (v. 18). Included in the inheritance are, surprisingly, those very 'mountains of Esau' (v. 21). Significant too is the fact that Yahweh's reign (v. 21) will not be characterized by military, political, or economic might, but by moral and religious 'holiness' (v. 17), a purity effected by Yahweh himself.

7.3.6 Demarcation and projection

As has already been shown, the L-R devices of repetition (step 3), disjunction (step 4), and concentration (step 5) operate in analytical progression to identify both the book's structural organization (demarcation) and also its points of major emphasis (projection). This tentative structural-thematic framework must be checked out now, step 6, in order to coordinate and test the results and then synthesize them in the form of a unified compositional whole.

---

[247]These words of B, apparently uttered by an eyewitness, could be attributed to Yahweh. The distinct temporal shift on either side of this portion (i.e., from 10 ⇒ 11, and 14 ⇒ 15) still clearly segments the book into three sections.

The analyses of other commentators will be helpful here. Where do the main differences lie? Can these be resolved or explained in some way? In the case of Obadiah, the main question will be the number of the book's principal parts, whether two or three. Most scholars prefer two—that is, roughly, 1–14 and 15–21 (as in the TEV and *NIV Study Bible*). My argument for a threefold division (1–10, 11–14, 15–21) has been suggested in section 7.3.4. It hinges upon one's structural construal of v. 10: Does v. 10 follow from v. 9 as a climax to part 1, or is it included within the larger section—whether as the beginning of a new unit (TEV) or not (NIV)? This issue is of some consequence because it affects not only the text's typographical layout (e.g., paragraphing and a possible section heading), but more importantly it guides the reader in interpreting the book's overall content.[248]

The accurate demarcation of a literary discourse includes an adequate, explicit textual marking of its peak(s) of development, but this is where virtually all versions miss the mark. They do little or nothing that is constructive or creative. Beginning a new paragraph at v. 17 (with or without a section heading) would help, and setting the final verse (Obad. 21) off by itself does present some natural prominence on its own, but is this sufficient for the reader, let alone the hearer of this pericope? Solutions to this problem will vary according to the TL setting and constituency. Perhaps the simplest highlighting device would be an explanatory footnote. Also, the two related passages, vv. 17 and 21, could be printed in the same typeface, whether italics or boldface. Additional stylistic markers would be needed of course to alert listeners to the importance of these two special prophecies of blessing.

7.3.7 Outline of compositional structure

The result of an L-R discourse analysis based on steps 1–6 would be a structural-thematic outline of the Book of Obadiah in the putative format of a prophetic "covenant-lawsuit address." It would be more or less as follows:

A. *Introduction* (1a)
B. *Setting*: a divine summons to battle, the occasion a judicial repudiation of Edom for fraternal covenant violations (1b)

---

[248]The demarcation of the TEV (second edition, 1994) is more accurate than that of the NIV, but is badly marred by the proposed "Outline of Contents": "The punishment of Edom" (1–14) and "The day of the Lord" (15–21). This omits the "good news" and makes no reference to God's people. My own literary-rhetorical and structural-thematic argument concerning the placement of v. 10 in the larger format of the book is presented in Wendland 1996c:31–32.

C. *Judgment:* three sentences of punishment upon Edom (2–10, with increasing severity)
   1. Edom's overweening pride will be undone by the LORD (2–4)
   2. Edom's land will be devastated and the nation betrayed by its former allies (5–7)
   3. Esau will be completely destroyed for violence done to Jacob (8–10)
D. *Indictment:* a series of crimes committed by Edom against Judah (11–14, announced with an increasing specification of Edom's perfidy)
E. *Vindication:* of the victim, Judah/Jerusalem (15–21, a reversal recorded with increasing detail)
   1. All of Judah's enemies will be punished in divine retribution (15–16)
   2. The victorious "holy fire" of Jacob will consume the wicked of Esau (17–18)
   3. The exiled remnant of Judah will take possession of their "inheritance" (19–21a)
F. *Conclusion:* "And the [whole] kingdom will be the LORD's!" (21b)

It is important that the pericope being analyzed not only be correctly demarcated, but also appropriately outlined, that is, in accordance with an accurate perception of the discourse's thematic movement. Poorly worded headings can be very misleading, especially for readers who depend upon section headings for an understanding of the progression of a book's content. A case in point is the TEV's section heading for vv. 17–21, "The Victory of Israel," which obscures the source and nature of this victory. In fact, it was Yahweh who worked this mighty deliverance on behalf of his covenant people. It was not at all a result of their own fierce fighting skills, but rather a reception of a graciously granted inheritance.

7.3.8 Word and motif study

In steps 1–7 the larger compositional framework of a particular discourse was the focus. Step 8 involves looking more closely at the included, less obvious stylistic characteristics of the discourse's lexical-conceptual inventory, including figurative language and other stylistic devices. There is a focus upon "key terms" and the paradigmatic strings of related, thematically important words that extend through the portions of the text.

Among the terms in Obadiah that need to be investigated because of their prominence in the Hebrew Bible as a whole are the following: 'Sovereign LORD' (*'adonay yhwh*, 1), 'the nations' (*goyim*, 1 and 15—note the reversal in the connotation of this word), 'pride' (*zidon*, 3), 'wise men' (*chakhamim*, 8), 'violence' (*chamas*, 10), 'your brother' (*'achikha*, 10), 'shame' (*bushah*, 10), 'forever' (*le'olam*, 10), 'survivor' (*sarid*, 14 and 18), 'rescued' (*peletah*, 17), 'holy' (*qadeshiy*, 17), 'fire' ('*eesh*, 18), and 'saviors' (*moshi'im*, 21). There are also several prominent series of associated conceptual recursion. They include: clefts of the rock—heights—soaring aloft—nest among the stars (3–4); Edom—Mount Esau—Teman—Mount Esau (8–9); day of his misfortune—their ruin—distress—their calamity—his calamity—distress (12–14); house of Jacob—Jacob—Joseph (17–18); Negeb—the Shephelah—Benjamin—Halah—Sepharad (19–20); Philistines—Ephraim—Samaria—Gilead—Phoenicia—Negeb (19–20).

But the thematic sequence of greatest significance within the book as a whole is undoubtedly the one that incorporates the various references to Edom/Esau as contrasted with Judah/Jacob and their respective 'mountains' (preeminently Zion), which are in turn connected with the blessed 'inheritance' that the remnant of Yahweh 'will take possession of' during the Messianic Age. All of these interrelated ideas provide the short text of Obadiah with its distinctive texture, cohesion, coherence, and prominence within the prophetic corpus.

7.3.9 Other literary-rhetorical features

Several other stylistic features in addition to those already mentioned need to be pointed out as distinctive elements of the artistic rhetoric of the Book of Obadiah. Most obvious perhaps is its striking imagery, which at times is hyperbolic. For example, the pride of Edom is described as 'soaring aloft like the eagle' and 'building its nest among the stars' (v. 4), and Edom's malicious behavior against their ethnic relatives is likened to 'casting lots for Jerusalem' (v. 11). This will one day be avenged when the 'fire of the house of Jacob' will 'burn and consume [the Edomites] like stubble' (v. 18).

Often these graphic figures function to foreground the book's prominent element of *irony*. Instances of irony are in v. 7 (Edom will be undone by its former allies, 'those who ate your bread') and vv. 9 and 14 (Edom's soldiers will be cut down just as they themselves cut down the army of Judah, the only difference being that Edom will lay fallen 'forever'). Several rhetorical questions heighten the effect, like the one in which Edom indirectly taunts God in direct speech: 'Who will bring me down to the ground?!' (v. 3). Closely related to these devices is the prediction of an ironic "reversal of fortunes" that characterizes not only Esau's fate, but also that of every enemy of God's people. One day they all will be forced by the covenant Lord to 'drink and gulp down' a terrible punishment that sees their wicked 'deeds returning upon [their] own heads' (vv. 15–16). Even the Hebrew sound system is enlisted in the service of the larger irony of Yahweh's acts of judgment, as in the following paronomasia: Edom's 'misfortune' (*nakro*), v. 12, will be brought about by 'foreigners' (*nakrim*), v. 11; thus in the end the descendants of Esau 'will become as though they had never been!' (*wehayu kelo' hayu*), v. 16.

The small, but forceful biblical text of Obadiah presents the translator with a considerable challenge. In order to reproduce the dynamic impact of such difficult microlinguistic literary techniques as hyperbole, irony, and wordplay, in addition to the normal inventory of figuration, a careful study of the SL text and an in-depth understanding of the TL inventory of literary devices will both be required.

7.3.10 Speech-act functions

The discourse macrofunctions of the Book of Obadiah follow the typical tripartite prophetic pattern: a strongly indicting *denunciation* of human sin; a stark *declaration* of divine judgment (these two are textually reversed in Obadiah, basically vv. 11–14 => vv. 2–10); a consolatory *prediction* of righteous retribution (15–16) and glorious restoration for the faithful remnant (17–21). The text of course incorporates a number of minor speech acts and their respective individual illocutionary forces. Some examples of these are: *summons* to battle ('Rise up!' in 1c); *warning* ('you shall be utterly despised' in 2b); *reproach* ('you should not have gloated over your brother!' in 12a); *promise* ('But on Mount Zion there shall be those that escape' in 17a); and *proclamation* ('and the kingdom shall be the LORD's!' in 21b). The interesting, but typically prophetic discourse feature of this compact prophecy is the multileveled nature of the speech events of which it is composed. At least four distinct discourse strata may be identified (each corresponding to a distinct speech event; S = "speaker" and A = "addressee"):

S1	=	YHWH's envoy	A1	=	the nations
S1'	=	Edom (personified)	A1'	=	any enemy of Edom
S2	=	YHWH (Obadiah)	A2	=	the Edomite nation
S3	=	YHWH (Obadiah)	A3	=	the people of Judah
S4	=	YHWH (Obadiah)	A4	=	any future receptor

The first level (S1) is subdivided because it includes all *embedded direct quotations* that are employed by the author for some special rhetorical effect, for example, to dramatize the message for a listening audience. Level 2 (S2), although it too is a literary device (*apostrophe*—a divine/prophetic address to an absent Edom), is noted because it is so prominent, not only in this book, but also in many of the other oracles against the pagan nations (e.g., Jeremiah 49). The disparate and potentially limitless fourth level (S4) takes us up to the present day. Level 3 (S3), Yahweh's proclamation through Obadiah to his fellow citizens of the devastated kingdom of Judah, constitutes the primary *horizon of interpretation* according to which the message as a whole must be read and understood, both exegetically and for the purpose of translation.

7.3.11 Corresponding TL devices

Before the individual literary-rhetorical devices of the original text can be dealt with in terms of their TL functional equivalents, the genre of the text as a whole must be determined. Can an approximate genre-for-genre rendering be attempted, poetry for poetry, or does some formal (language-related) or situational (project-related) factor prevent this? A poetic recreation in Chichewa, for example, would have been most effective and appropriate, but the translation team did not have the time necessary to devote to such a sophisticated literary endeavor.

The Chichewa *ndakatulo* genre of lyrical poetry features an intricate combination of ideophones, graphic imagery, balanced-rhythmic lineation, unusual syntactic movements, condensed expression, intensified diction, extensive affixal modification, dramatic direct speech, semantic reiteration, and sound symbolism. (Samples of this vigorous literary style are presented in sec. 7.3.12 and 8.4.)[249] There is, in fact, as an investigation of Chichewa discourse reveals, a relatively close communicative match between Hebrew and Chichewa in this regard, for *ndakatulo* lyrics may be employed for critical, corrective admonition as well as for poetic messages of hope and encouragement. But in the end, the Chichewa translation team had to settle for rendering Obadiah in the form of a rhetorically heightened "poetic prose," using only some of the characteristic features of the *ndakatulo* genre.

Another important operation to keep in mind when translating with a literary-rhetorical orientation is *compensation*. This means that translators attempt to utilize natural stylistic features in the TL text whenever contextually appropriate in order to make up for those that are lost due to formal nonequivalences that appear during the message transfer process.[250] For

---

[249]In the widely-accepted translation typology of James Holmes, a literary, genre-based poetic rendition would be termed an "analogical translation," in which "a culturally corresponding form is used" in the TL (1988:25).

[250]Compensation is "the technique of making up for the translation loss of important ST [source text] features by approximating their effects in the TT [target text] through means other than those used in the ST" (Shuttleworth and Cowie 1997:25). Of course, in the case of a literary Bible translation one would also try to approximate the original stylistic "means" as well, but that is not often possible when a genre-for-genre rendering is being attempted.

example, they may replace a Hebrew metaphor or hyperbole with a Bantu ideophone (see the example below).

7.3.12 Trial translation and testing

An application of step 11 produced the following rendering of Obadiah 5 in a Chichewa ndakatulo lyric-poetic form:

Pajatu mbala zikabwera usiku,	As you well know, when thieves come at night,
zimangotengako zimene afuna.	they take away only what they want.
Okolola akamathyola zipatso,	When field-harvesters pluck fruit,
mwina amangosiyako zinazake.	at times they just leave some of it there.
Koma inuyo, adani anu, basi—	But as for you, your enemies, finished—
ha! adzakupululani pululu!	ha! they're going to strip you completely BARE!

I will not elaborate on all the form-functional similarities to, and differences from, the Hebrew text that we see in the Chichewa text (see Wendland 1996b:77–81). One major difference, however, in addition to the generally balanced lineal poetic structure, is obvious: the Chichewa text shifts the Hebrew exclamatory 'Oh how you will be pillaged!' from the middle of the verse to the end of it in order to increase the overall dramatic effect. This is augmented by the exclamation *ha!* and the ideophone *pululu!* in an effort to match the shock value of the interruptive character of the original Hebrew utterance.

The main general translational concern is that the referential content and illocutionary intent remain the same, corresponding in the vernacular as closely as we can tell to the original text. That essential aspect of the interlingual communication process must always be double-checked by the translators after they have completed their initial draft. As for reactions to the text's artistic style and an assessment of its rhetorical, oral-aural impact, these will have to be determined by careful audience-testing procedures specifically designed to investigate such features (see chap. 10).

7.4 Summary

In summarizing a possible L-R analytical methodology as applied to Bible translation, I would call attention again to the four basic features of literary discourse that need to be considered: *segmentation, connection, direction,* and *intention.* These are important both as individual form-functional components and also as interrelated elements of a single meaning-generating process.

First of all, after determining the principal genre or genre-complex of a text, one attempts to *segment* a text into its constituent parts. The individual lines (bicola/tricola) or sentences normally cluster to form the smaller portions, the strophes and paragraphs. These clusters in turn combine to create larger units, the stanzas and sections or episodes, which are related both sequentially (syntagmatically) and by analogy (paradigmatically) to form the organizational hierarchy of a complete composition. A careful documentation of the distribution of repeated key words and phrases as well as characteristic transitional formulas that occur on the proposed structural-thematic boundaries, together with all significant indicators of aperture or closure, is an important aspect of this initial delimiting and defining operation.

Second, one looks for additional types of verbal repetition involving the sound, sense, syntax, or subgenres that pertain to the poetic and prosaic structure of the text, whether uniform or diverse. The purpose of this is to establish (more firmly now) the principal discourse conjunctive bonds (not only its boundaries). Such features provide the text with *connectivity*. The analyst's aim is to reveal how the various compositional components are linked together, that is, given formal cohesion and conceptual coherence, both in relation to one another and also within the work as a whole. The distinctive larger patterns of recursion (e.g., inclusio, exclusio, anaphora, epiphora, anadiplosis) function together to help define the major and minor borders of a text. But one must also examine all forms of random lexical repetition for their relative connective value.

The next step is to discover the various *directive* cues and stylistic clues that the writer has built into the text either intentionally or unconsciously. These features serve as oral-aural or visual indicators that assist the audience to discern the high points of the text, whether the development is primarily emotive (with an *apex*), directive (with a *climax*), informative (with a *peak*), or a combination of them. Here we find the biblical author skillfully utilizing the stylistic, especially the clearly poetic and rhetorical, resources of the Hebrew or Greek language for designative purposes. These literary devices are typically employed in disjunctive, marked, attractive, or unusual combinations—that is, as a means of accenting certain vital, message-bearing portions of the discourse, whether these pertain to its general theological theme or to its specific ethical implications.

Finally, taking all of the preceding evidence into consideration, one is able to determine the author's most likely *intention*, that is, the functional significance of the entire composition as it was communicated in its presumed initial context. Biblical style is not merely ornamental—though it does serve to beautify the language and increase its emotive impact and aesthetic appeal, especially in poetic discourse. On the contrary, verbal style (or artistic form) is always employed in the service of religious content to more effectively carry out a wide range of interpersonal, proclamatory (didactic, motivational, and hortatory) objectives.

In particular, the analyst must take notice of any special concentration of literary-rhetorical features such as compaction (e.g., ellipsis), graphic imagery (including that of a military, apocalyptic, and eschatological variety), irony and sarcasm, hyperbole, nuanced and patterned lexical reiteration, reversals of form and content, intertextual allusion and citation, dramatic direct address (apostrophe), intensifiers (e.g., vocatives, imperatives, exclamations), and the characteristic rhythmic and balanced line-forms of biblical poetry. Certainly these stylistic devices do not exist for their own sake. Rather, they have been carefully chosen, positioned, and combined in order to make the author's point with greater forcefulness and clarity in relation to his principal subject matter as inspired by God.

By applying an appropriate analytical methodology, one can learn to investigate the biblical text more thoroughly and more systematically in order to understand more fully which sorts of compositional forms are present and how they were intended to mark and convey special significance for the initial audience. After analyzing the formal features of discourse, the next consideration is even more important: the "what" (content) and "why" (purpose) of the biblical message. God's chosen prophetic and apostolic messengers were carrying out several larger pragmatic purposes through their characteristic literary-poetic style, its rhetorical argument in particular. The goal was to communicate more effectively—to persuade the hearers and readers in a more convincing and compelling manner. The paramount purpose of the diverse and distinctive literature of Scripture was to forcefully attract, convict, influence, encourage, and warn their readers and listeners alike, both primary and secondary, to faithfully follow along the path of discipleship in total covenantal loyalty to Yahweh and his promised Messiah.

It is this same contextually conditioned significance that translators seek to creatively re-present today through their vernacular texts. When called for by the communicative setting and its associated translational *Brief*, this goal (*Skopos*) may be accomplished by means of a more dynamic method of analysis and a more daring manner of recomposition designed to interact in appealing, yet also challenging, ways with a specific audience and contemporary context of communication. This requires a careful investigation of the TL linguistic and literary resources (the textual dimension) to the degree that they are appropriate for use in Bible translation (the social dimension), a subject that will be investigated further in the next chapter (an implementation of step 11, sec. 7.1.11).

8

Determining the Stylistic and Rhetorical Features of TL Literature

The target language (TL), more accurately termed consumer language,[251] has already been referred to, particularly in describing the analytical procedures of chapter 7. In this chapter the literature (and orature) of the TL will be the main focus. If a team desires (in accordance with the project *Skopos*) to apply a literary-rhetorical approach during the translation process, whether wholly or only in certain selected relevant respects, then it is vital that they understand the stylistic and rhetorical features of TL

---

[251]The term *consumer* emphasizes the conceptually active role that the intended readers/listeners play in the communication process. They are not passive receptors, not merely an inert target to be shot at with the translated text. Rather, they significantly influence, even as they are normally influenced by, the ultimate message that is transmitted. I retain the commonly used term *target language* (TL) simply to follow the current convention. The importance of the consumer audience in contributing to the ultimate "meaning" of a given text properly receives great attention in contemporary translation studies, even if at times too much. The following comment regarding this new perspective by C. Tourniaire is typical: it is "a view of translation as a relative rather than an absolute process, subject to changes, inevitably biased, and addressing a specific audience (at the risk of alienating other readers);...[with] a reliance on the audience as an active participant, encouraging them to explore possible meanings and leaving them to consider, or indeed to reject, potential alternatives" (from "Bilingual Translation as a Re-creation of the Censored Text: Rhea Galanaki in English and French," cited in Boase-Beier and Holman 1999:80). The question to be asked is, In which respects and to what degree do these observations apply to Bible translation?

literature. More research of this kind will be necessary than for other types for translation.

In section 8.1 I propose eight guidelines with regard to the question of how to analyze vernacular verbal art. In section 8.2 the discussion has special reference to an oratorical model of communication. In section 8.3 I address the importance of a rigorous comparative procedure. In section 8.4 I go on to illustrate the application of these procedures in the production of a literary-rhetorical translation of Ezek. 37:1–10 in Chichewa. In the concluding sections (8.5–8.6) I deal with some of the practical implications of this discussion for Bible translation.

8.1 A literary-rhetorical analysis and application of TL verbal art forms

How one carries out an analysis of the literary-rhetorical (L-R) features of a given target language and applies these features appropriately in a Bible translation is an issue of considerable practical relevance (already touched upon briefly in sec. 7.1.11). It involves eight important steps. More could be said concerning these procedures,[252] but the description here will suffice for the present—mainly as a reminder of the importance of this TL-focused task, which, ideally, should be presented during the initial, translator-training stages of a project and then reinforced periodically thereafter.[253]

The eight basic steps that will be discussed in sections 8.1.1–8.1.8 are as follows:

1. *Constitution*—putting together the right team: competent, compatible, committed, gifted!
2. *Collection*—gathering the TL data, oral and written, secular and religious, standard and dialectal.
3. *Classification*—analyzing the collected material as to form, content, function, setting of use, and users.
4. *Comparison*—comparing the TL stylistic resources with the inventory of L-R features of the SL text.

---

[252]See, for example, Wendland 1981a and 1981b. I discuss the nature and purpose of such an oral-aural oriented version in Wendland 2000d.

[253]Although it is probably true that master translators are born, not made, there is a great deal to be said for providing them with an adequate theoretical and practical (formal and informal) training program—both to sharpen the skills of the rare artist that comes along and also to develop and improve the artistic sensitivity of the rest. In a sense, then, "the 'art' of translation comes from the accumulated experience of enriching and applying the 'science' of translation" (Fawcett 1997:52).

5. *Compensation*—devising creative strategies for dealing with mismatches of form or function, stressing the latter over the former in the interest of intended meaning.
6. *Creation*—verbally reconstituting the essential message in the TL by informed intuition and insight.
7. *Check-examination*—assessing the draft by informal testing procedures, followed by revision as needed.
8. *Criticism*—evaluating the translation by explicitly comparing it with the original SL text.

8.1.1 Step 1: Constitution

The first, and perhaps most important, step involves the selection and training of a team that is well experienced, instructed, practiced, and manifestly gifted in the art and skill of literary analysis with respect to both SL and TL discourse. Hopefully some literary-rhetorical assessment criteria can be incorporated into the testing of would-be translators and reviewers.[254] An opening workshop, consisting of individuals who have been specifically recommended for such creative interlingual work, should be organized and conducted so as to reveal those who have the greatest flair and appreciation for this vital aspect of communication. Really gifted artists or stylistic experts are few and far between, but at least one member of the translation team should be someone who can readily recognize what a good, popularly acknowledged literary-rhetorical style is in various genres (e.g., not an archaic, esoteric, or overly colloquial style) and can make concrete recommendations in this regard while the translation is being prepared and later revised. Also needed is a corps of well-trained reviewers who possess a certain level of stylistic competence in vernacular composition.

8.1.2 Step 2: Collection

A qualitative, discourse-oriented investigation requires that all genres of TL texts—oral and written, prose and poetry, sacred and secular—be collected and categorized. The works of several recognized authors or orators should be included because it is not just any sort of style or rhetoric

---

[254]"It is generally acknowledged today that a translator should have 'a real talent for writing in his own language'... [for] 'if a translator does not have a mastery of his own language and is incapable of writing well, his translation is bound to be poor, however well he may understand the [original] text' " (Sir Stanley Unwin, cited in Reiss 2000:11). Frye makes the same point with reference to the Bible in *The Great Code*: "[I]t is sensitivity to one's own language, not scholarly knowledge of the original, that makes a translation permanent" (cited in Hargreaves 1993:135).

that we wish to reproduce in the Scriptures, but the most worthy exemplars possible in keeping with the nature of the literature concerned—the Word of God. Artistic radio productions need to be identified and recorded as well, since these programs, if well done, may offer a helpful model of composition for Bible translation, being works that are produced in *written* form but intended for *oral* elocution and reception. I have found that certain popular radio preachers can provide some excellent examples of powerful hortatory rhetoric. They know how to effectively exhort, reprove, console, or argue a case in the vernacular (see Wendland 2000b). Several diverse recorded texts may be transcribed and translated into English (or another lingua franca) as a means of getting the translators to think more deeply, broadly, and creatively about their language. These texts should then be discussed and mutually critiqued in order to gain a more analytical understanding of the complex concepts of genre and style as they apply in particular to the TL in relation to the SL (or to a major lingua franca of the area).

8.1.3 Step 3: Classification

Classification involves a sorting out of the different texts that have been collected in step 2. The different *emic* genres and subgenres that are present in the TL corpus must now be identified, analyzed, and categorized in terms of their distinctive features of form (text), function (co-text), and typical setting of use (context). The stylistic and rhetorical devices that are characteristic of each genre and subgenre should be listed and described along with some outstanding representative examples. It is important to include accurate reference numbers so that the specific examples may be reexamined later, if necessary, in their original textual context and according to their principal genre. The translation team and invited participant-experts then discuss and agree upon the various feature selections and descriptions in order to create an inclusive L-R stylistic template. Extensive descriptive and explanatory notes need to be taken by a qualified recording secretary who has been chosen for this purpose. The secretary's notes may be duplicated for each member of the committee, with revised editions issued periodically as further research and the translation work itself is subsequently carried out.

8.1.4 Step 4: Comparison

The various TL literary-rhetorical features identified in step 3 must now be compared with those that are prominent in the poetic and prosaic books of biblical literature, as determined by prior study. A careful search is made for any and all functional matches with reference to both larger and smaller discourse units. The closer they match in form as well as function, the better the case will be when the translation is evaluated later. The results of this comparison should be recorded for future reference. Text comparison will be carried out again in step 7 once a draft has been completed and circulated for critical reaction. The purpose at every stage is to check for accuracy not only with respect to semantic content and communicative function, but also concerning the respective levels of rhetorical dynamism and literary artistry between the SL and TL texts.

8.1.5 Step 5: Compensation

The possibility of compensation should be considered whenever it has not been possible to find a TL form-functional match for a certain SL literary-rhetorical feature with respect to either a particular Scripture text or the overall inventory of biblical stylistic devices. In general, where mismatches involve *both* form and function, then as a general rule the aspect of form will have to give way in the interest of communicative function, especially where a literary version is being prepared.

Compensation usually involves compositional quantity as well as quality. Thus, a given device (e.g., a pronominal intensifier) may be used with greater frequency in the TL text than its formal correspondent in the SL text because it is needed also to compensate for some other SL literary feature that occurs infrequently if at all (e.g., enallage). Similarly, a completely different TL form may be used as long as the textual function is close enough to that of the original (e.g., an ideophone for a graphic, but unfamiliar SL metaphor). In all cases of compensation, it should be remembered that even though the semantic content of the biblical text and the translation may correspond closely enough, there may still be some measure of message loss in the translation due to the nonequivalence of artistry and/or rhetoricity.

Sometimes meaningful compensation involves spatial position or strategic text location. For instance, if a stylistic match cannot be made at one foregrounded point in the text, it may be possible to achieve its functional effect somewhere else in the immediate co-text, thereby maintaining a relative balance in the overall communicative "value" of the original message as represented in the TL. In other words, a solution of this nature is necessary in order to maintain a greater level of textual equivalence (preserving the L-R dynamics overall) and/or contextual relevance (i.e., cognitive-emotive-volitional efficiency and effectiveness).[255]

8.1.6 Step 6: Creation

Creation is the most vital step in the compositional process. It is perhaps better called re-creation, or re-composition, since the goal of Scripture translation, of a literary-rhetorical version at any rate, is to accurately and effectively reproduce the essence of the central message of the SL document using the appropriate linguistic and literary forms of the TL.[256] Thus, having carried out a detailed analysis of both the SL original text and various TL stylistic models according to the preceding guidelines, the production team, or a selected member thereof, now prepares a draft version for joint consideration.

In cases where serious consideration is being given to verbal style and the L-R factor, writing the draft is probably best done by a single, gifted individual so that his or her poetic impulse is not stifled, diminished, or dissipated by too much discussion.[257] Content-based corrections and modifications with a view towards greater exegetical accuracy can always be made later. Some teams, on the other hand, may operate more efficiently by working closely as a unit to produce a basic, semantically equivalent, if lackluster, draft which they can subsequently either polish up together or

---

[255]Boase-Beier and Holman (1999:12) present some useful observations on the subject of translation matches and mismatches and the strategy of compensation: "[T]he constraints of mismatch are legion: cultural, linguistic and political,...also genre-determined, stylistic, historical, philosophical, psychological, pragmatic....Translation decisions will depend to a great degree on the dimension of the entities: temporal, spatial, cultural, within which a match is sought, of what is thought of as 'the text'....[There are] different levels of compensation and therefore...different possibilities of matching texts and realizing their different potentials....[C]ompromises always have to be found...[and] solutions will necessarily depend on the translator's individual estimation of the different levels of perception and preparation in the SL and TL audiences."

[256]Some might prefer the term *reconstruction*, which would refer to the contextualized (or "framed") verbal/textual product (TL) of the "cognitive creation" of a "virtual text" that is derived from a setting-sensitive analysis of the original SL document (Katan 1999:125). I am using the expression *essential meaning instead of virtual text*, but both terms refer basically to the central meaning-significance of the original message. This is what must be reconceptualized during the course of the medial "transfer" stage of the translation process (Nida and Taber 1969:33; cf. the misrepresentation in Katan 1999:123).

[257]"[T]he translator of poetry must be a competent poet....[T]he translator's knowledge of and poetic competency in the host language count for very much more than his knowledge of and poetic competency in the language of the original" (Preminger and Brogan, eds. 1993:1305). In sec. 7.1.12 I suggest that a more literal rendering should be prepared first just to fix the content of the biblical text in one's mind before producing a LiFE version. Teams will have to experiment a bit to see which compositional method works best for them.

submit to one or more recognized TL stylists to give it vernacular naturalness and literary character. Either way, it will be necessary to experiment with novel genres and various stylistic selections and combinations in the TL in order to convey the basic semantic content of the original text along with its associated pragmatic intent (communicative function) and rhetorical impact (in terms of both aesthetic and emotive significance).

8.1.7 Step 7: Check-examination

Once the translation team is satisfied with its initial draft, whether produced immediately together or in sequential interaction, the reaction of those for whom the version is intended must be sought. This step is not nearly as straightforward as it may seem, nor is it easy to include within a team's budget of temporal and financial resources. In any sort of a pinch, it is the testing program that usually gets cut first. However, *testing is indispensable*, especially in the case of a version that is intended to be a dynamically equivalent rendering, corresponding more fully in selected relevant respects to the original with regard to literary artistry and rhetorical quality. The problem is that a translation of this kind will be much further away from the biblical text in terms of its overt form than a literal translation, and this is often what inexperienced critics first look to as they make comparisons. Any testing is therefore best preceded by a clear explanation and illustration of the nature of translation—its principles, procedures, alternatives, critical assessment factors, and limitations.

The check-examination is normally of two types, both of which focus on the language of translation: The first involves recording a sample audience's reactions, whether an individual's or a group's, in order to determine whether the translation is grammatical, natural, idiomatic, fluent—or not, and in which respects. The second type is a systematic comparison of the TL text with one or more model versions in another language such as English, French, Spanish, or Swahili.

Any L-R version needs to be evaluated according to audio criteria as well as visual, text-based ones such as page format and typography. The testing also needs to take into consideration the more technical issues of semantic and pragmatic equivalence to ensure that both the semantic content and the functional intent of the biblical text have been satisfactorily communicated. Examination-checks will inevitably lead to many revisions in response to the feedback, whether indirectly through observing someone read the text aloud, for example, or whether directly by means of different types of qualitative questions regarding form, style, content, impact, appeal, preference, and appropriateness.

8.1.8 Step 8: Criticism

Criticism takes the process of evaluating a translation a step beyond the more informal check-examination of section 8.1.7. As Reiss (2000:9) says, "No critique [is possible] without a comparison with the original."[258] But to compare the TL text to the original biblical text requires critics who are competent, even expert, in both the SL and TL: "when translations are criticized there should always be a proposed remedy,... alternative translations, substantiated with convincing evidence" (ibid.:5, 15). This "would rule out judging a translation solely on the basis of its faults" (ibid.:15).

The criteria and categories for critical evaluation should be based on the translation principles and procedures outlined in the project *Skopos*. Although it will not be possible for most Bible translation teams to conduct critical inquiries and formal assessments that require a high degree of expertise, this is an ideal goal to aim for, especially in the case of versions in a language of wider communication that can serve as "models" for other translations.

8.2 The difference between literary and oratorical text

In the early 1960s, in order to provide an alternative or a complement to the then-prevailing literal type of Scripture translation, the United Bible Societies (UBS), the Summer Institute of Linguistics (SIL), and associated agencies initiated a new strategy and style of translation. It was oriented more towards conveying the *meaning* rather than *forms* of the biblical text. Versions in this style were often called "common-language," "popular-language," or simply "idiomatic" translations since they were intended to speak the natural language of the ordinary Scripture consumers. (For definitions of these types of translation see sec. 2.4.1, especially fn. 47.) Such versions had features that promoted readability and intelligibility and

---

[258]The importance of comparative text criticism is such that it really needs to be made an essential aspect of the initial translator-selection process: "[T]he translator needs also, as Dryden points out, to be 'a nice critic in his mother tongue before he attempts to translate a foreign language' [e.g., the language of the Bible, whether the original text or a translation]....this statement finds justification in the view that *translators are privileged readers whose interpretation of the text is the version of reality that will reach the masses.* It is essential that they should be very careful in handling matters such as the meaning of the text both propositionally and expressively" (Megrab 1999:65). The significance of the italicized portion applies regardless of the nature of the translated text, that is, whether it happens to be more or less literal in style. The point is that the translation team (or their qualified project associates) need to determine exactly what is "the version of reality" that most consumers derive from the text as it has been rendered, first in draft form, so that any necessary adjustments can be made where outstanding deficiencies are noted.

were content/context-sensitive. These features included a selectively limited vocabulary (e.g., fewer archaic, figurative, colloquial, translational, or technical terms); reduced grammatical range (e.g., fewer genitives and compound prepositional phrases); a preference for relatively short, noncomplex, active sentences; a greater tendency to express implicit information explicitly in the text (e.g., making pronominal referents and noun classifiers explicit); the use of redundancy to prevent conceptual overloading; a reduction in the number of event nouns (transforming them into verbal constructions); the avoidance of unusual or highly idiomatic lexical/syntactic constructions; and the clear marking of sentential and discourse transitions (see Wonderly 1968:75–78).[259]

In discussions concerning common (or popular) language versions in relation to others, a literary type was also mentioned. Wonderly pointed out that literary translations "make free use of all the resources of the language at all levels which are considered acceptable for published materials, and are thereby not intended to be fully accessible to the uneducated reader" (ibid.:30). Obviously a literary version in this sense can be produced only in a linguistic community that possesses a relatively long tradition of written literature. Its envisioned constituency, or target group, would be people who are comparatively well educated, widely read, and who enjoy the challenge of wrestling with the full range of lexical, grammatical, stylistic, and rhetorical usage in the particular language and society concerned. (In chapter 2 we considered the implications of this and other approaches to the translation of secular as well as biblical literature.)

As was noted in section 1.2, literary translation as defined by Wonderly does not apply in the case of a language group that does not have a tradition of literature and whose members communicate predominantly by oral-aural means. This is the situation in most societies in Bantu Africa as well as in many other regions of the world. For them the closest equivalent might be termed an *oratorical* text—that is, verbally distinctive oral discourse that accesses the complete inventory of genres and styles in the spoken language to convey a message that is widely regarded by listeners as being impressive, persuasive, and beautiful. Such semiformal, oral-rhetorical usage would, of course, exclude youthful jargon and foreign-based colloquialisms (e.g., English borrowings and calques). It would also exclude widely unintelligible archaisms or specialist in-group technical argot (e.g., vocabulary pertaining to specific occupations or activities like

---

[259]Wonderly illustrated the application of these techniques with extensive reference to the Spanish *Versión Popular*. They are also very evident in its English counterpart, *Today's English Version* (TEV), and more recently in the *Contemporary English Version* (CEV).

hunting, fishing, house building, herbalistic medicine, or traditional initiation ceremonies).

Nowadays, such an oratorical style is manifested in the main by popular singers, public speakers, and radio broadcasters, including skillful oral performers of ancient verbal art forms as well as Christian evangelists and revivalists.[260] Thus many recognized models of excellent oratory do exist; however, they must be carefully collected (often by audio-recording for later transcription), analyzed, published and distributed (or broadcast) in order for standards of popular and specialist assessment to develop to the point where they may be effectively applied in written literature. Of course, the medium of print itself requires certain compositional modifications to be made during the transposition to a published text. For example, it may be necessary to modify the text for less repetition; a more explicit expression of content (to counteract the lack of an extralinguistic situational context); compensation for suprasegmental, intonational, and elocutionary (phonological) significance (e.g., inserting commas to represent dramatic pauses); more precise conjunctive and transitional devices ("function words"); and a lower incidence of informal or colloquial diction.[261]

The use of these oral models and stylistic techniques is particularly appropriate for translations of the Bible, which are much more frequently accessed by the ear than the eye.[262] Furthermore, recent research has tended to confirm the hypothesis that the various documents of the Scriptures were in large measure composed aloud or were written down with an oral-aural transmission and reception of their message in mind (see

---

[260]I present the results of an extensive study of an outstanding representative of the last-mentioned group in Wendland 2000b. These texts may provide good models that can serve in the development of an oratorical style of rendering the paraenetic texts of the Bible, such as we have in prophetic and epistolary literature.

[261]Compare the set of audio-oriented features noted in Sundersingh's 1999 study (p. 170). I would heartily support Sundersingh's appeal that "[t]he media scene of today's world demands that we be sensitive to the needs of non-literates and non-readers by way of providing them with biblical Scriptures in media other than print" (ibid.:315). These two human categories overlap, but are not the same, and therefore their respective "needs" must be determined separately.

[262]The preface to the ABS's CEV(1995) states this point well: "Languages are spoken before they are written. And far more communication is done through the spoken word than through the written word. In fact, more people *hear* the Bible than read it for themselves. Traditional translations of the Bible count on the *reader's* ability to understand a *written* text. But the *Contemporary English Version* differs from all other English Bibles—past and present—in that it takes into consideration the needs of the *hearer*, as well as those of the reader, who may not be familiar with traditional biblical language." This final claim concerning its uniqueness may be somewhat of an overstatement, but for our purposes the point is simply this: An oratorical version is meant primarily to be *orally* read, to be clearly understood *aurally*, and to make its artistic-emotive impression upon an audience through the message as it is being *heard* by them.

Achtemeier 1990 and Sundersingh 1999, chap. 6). Consequently, "[s]ince the acts of both writing and reading were normally accompanied by vocalization, the structure [and style] of text was marked by aural rather than visual indicators" (Davis 1999:11).[263]

This fact has important implications for both the analysis and transmission of the biblical text via translation. Most notably, such prominent aural sonic, stylistic, and structural indicators—the "rhythmic envelope" of discourse, including its audio-punctuation devices—need to be reproduced by means of functionally equivalent techniques in a translation as well as in special text-formatting that promotes readability. The latter would include meaning-based lineation, no end-of-line hyphenation or justification, a single column, and a legible print size and style. This oral-elocutionary dimension of meaning—"the spokenness of the Bible," Fox (1995:xv) calls it—is a particularly important consideration in the case of any specifically oratorical version, meant primarily to be heard rather than read.[264] For many literary critics and stylists alike, the crucial phonological factor is simply the *rhythm* of the text—pleasing recurrent patterns of textual sound:

> Why does excellence of rhythm matter? One answer is aesthetic: Good rhythm is beautiful, and bad rhythm is grating and ugly.... Second, good rhythm is essential to any text that is uttered orally.... Thirdly, good rhythm is an aid to memory as well as to oral performance....Finally, rhythm is the natural concomitant of impassioned and heightened speech (J. L. Lowes, cited in Ryken 2002:268).

It would seem then that an attractive rhythmic flow is the least that any translation, no matter how formal or free, should aim to achieve. Certainly it is the *sine qua non* of any oratorical version.

However, a possible objection to an oratorical, or even indeed a literary, translation needs to be considered. This concerns a stylistic comparison and evaluation with respect to the original texts of Scripture. Some might claim that an artistic-rhetorical manner of composition is a

---

[263]Davis's observation here regarding the NT literature readily extends to—or better, is founded upon—OT literature. Dorsey writes: "[A]ncient texts were written primarily to be heard, not seen. Texts were normally intended to be read aloud....To study structure in the Hebrew Bible, then, requires paying serious attention to verbal structure indicators" (1999:16). Such aural indicators would include features such as rhythmic lineation, phonic accentuation, verbal patterning, prominent discourse demarcative devices, lexical recursion, direct speech, graphic diction, and vivid imagery (to promote topical-thematic recall).

[264]For a discussion of these concepts in relation to a poetic translation of John 17:1–9 into Chichewa and Chitonga (Bantu languages), see Wendland 1994a:19–43. Newman proposes that "a truly *contemporary* translation must be 'ear-oriented' and focus upon such considerations as (1) oral readability, (2) aural comprehension, and (3) aesthetic appeal, both to the reader and the hearer" (2001:9).

distortion of—in this case, an intentional "improvement" upon—the supposed vernacular "common-language," or *koine*, style of the New Testament documents.[265] Are we perhaps in danger here of *over*translation? To what extent *are* the biblical books themselves literary (or oratorical) in nature? Are they, or are they not, of recognizable, demonstrable excellence with respect to their thematic, structural, and affective qualities? Furthermore, how would the results of such a compositional assessment if carried out today compare with an evaluation carried out within the original setting? Obviously, no direct comparison of this kind can be made, and to provide a credible and convincing answer to such questions would require a much more extensive study than I have space for here.[266] Moreover, such potentially controversial issues need to be considered in relation to a specific translation text, audience, intended occasion, purpose (*Skopos*), and setting of use.

My own conclusion, as argued in the preceding chapters, is that the various books of the Bible give abundant evidence of a high literary standard. Translators must therefore endeavor to reproduce this stylistic quality in their work, to the extent possible, in order to achieve a basic communicative parity in relation to the message at hand (see sec. 1.6). Perhaps they cannot effect this on all levels of discourse throughout the translated text, due either to their lack of artistic competence in the TL or to certain restrictions presented by the proposed setting of use (e.g., a formal meeting for public worship). But there is always *something* that can be done linguistically to improve the translation with respect to its literary character such as the use of idiomatically equivalent figurative language, appropriate word choice and placement, naturalness of internal sentence syntax and external sequencing, and, above all, the creation of a euphonious text that will attract the ears of a listening audience.

Translators should approach their task with this special compositional goal in mind and then consciously and continuously put it into practice in the course of carrying out their creative work on the text, not leaving it as a hopeful patch-up job afterwards. It will not take long for them to learn to appreciate and apply a particular TL poetic technique more widely, even discovering in the process other previously unrecognized features in their language that will enable them to better match the power and beauty of the original text of Scripture.

---

[265]A stylistic assessment of the Hebrew Scriptures is of course more difficult to make due to the limited corpus of texts, religious or secular, on the basis of which an adequate analytical comparison may be made (even in cognate literatures). However, the diversity and abundance of "universal" Semitic literary features that are manifested in many Old Testament passages greatly reduces the doubt concerning this issue.

[266]The essays in Ben Zvi and Floyd 2000 strongly presuppose the literary character of the prophetic corpus.

8.3 The importance of comparing the literary features of SL and TL texts

It is important to apply the same rigorous analytical methodology to the oral and written literature of the TL as to the text of Scripture, and also carefully compare the corresponding SL and TL literary genres in order to discover potential functional matches. Such an ongoing investigation, although it is often overlooked or omitted for various reasons, is an essential aspect of a fully integrated approach to Bible translation, whether or not a translation team intends to attempt a fully literary rendering. Research of this nature would include giving attention to such structural and stylistic qualities as macro- and microgenres, figurative language, forms of recursion, degree of dialogue, and the appropriate use of rhetorical devices.

A number of suggestions in this regard have already been made, and the topic summarized (in sec. 8.1.4). Here we will explore the possibility of developing a systematic set of procedures for comparative text analysis aimed at producing a more effective interlingual representation of the Scriptures.

With regard to literary features and translational equivalence, we need to identify some of the principal factors involved when making a comparative evaluation of the SL and TL. In other words, given feature A in the SL document, (whether a stylistic device or a complete genre), what needs to be investigated in the TL context as one searches for an appropriate correspondent, B? The following characteristics are suggestive of some of the potentially significant interlingual considerations:

- The communicative function and/or intended effects of the proposition that contains A or B, plus its "illocutionary force" in terms of speech and text acts.
- The primary sociolinguistic setting of A or B when used normally, either in oral or written discourse, and the common scenes and situations that are evoked by A or B in isolation.
- The density or frequency of A's usage in the SL vis à vis that of B in the TL, also its usual position in a text, if determinable (e.g., at the beginning, peak, or ending of a discourse).
- Typical emotions, attitudes, and moods that co-occur with A or B's usage (its connotation).
- The usual subject matter in which A or B appears.
- The usual type of discourse, genre, or literary structure in which A or B occurs.

- Other literary features that tend to occur in texts where A or B is found.
- Possible collocational restrictions in the usage of A or B (i.e., literary or lexical features that are not, or only rarely, found where A or B is).
- The different subtypes or literary relatives of A or B as classified and used in the SL/TL.
- The relative social register or level of formality that is associated with A or B's usage in literary discourse.

To carry out a detailed literary and sociolinguistic comparison of this nature on a selected pericope, let alone a complete book, would be beyond the ability of all but the most qualified and best-funded translation teams. It is more realistic to suppose that such concerns would have to be considered and applied by translators only partially and more intuitively —but even then only after they have received thorough instruction and sufficient practice in dealing with the various, sometimes competing, issues involved and the conflicts or nonequivalences that would inevitably manifest themselves.[267]

A systematic illustrated documentation of the available corpus of TL verbal art is a vital aspect of the effort to produce an equivalent literary translation. Such an approach employs a situationally framed, genre-for-genre procedure that emphasizes functionally oriented renderings (the closest, natural communicative correspondents). This would incorporate the examination of all extant discourse types and subtypes—oral and written, prose as well as poetry (e.g., etic "tale-types" and "motif index," emic or indigenous folk morphologies). The text studies of larger scope would need to be complemented by detailed microstructural stylistic analyses in order to obtain a relatively complete inventory of what is available in the language and literature concerned. Important local literary techniques must be described with reference to form, function, and—if oral in nature—also the primary sociocultural setting of use. Pertinent text samples from diverse contexts should be recorded for the sake of concrete illustration and future reference. In this exercise, the main difficulty might not be the initial collection and analysis of indigenous linguistic data, but rather writing the material up in a way that is easily accessible by the translation team and also presents the

---

[267]For an illustrated consideration of some of these issues in the context of preparing a relatively "poetic" translation of biblical poetry, see Zogbo and Wendland 2000, chapters 4–5.

functionally corresponding features of the original biblical discourse in comparative terms.

There are a number of difficulties that present themselves in doing a comparative analysis. How does one determine what is literary or natural in the case of the Scriptures? And what if one is not an expert in biblical languages, let alone their literature? Obviously, most translation teams will have to depend on study Bibles (e.g., *The NIV Study Bible*) and reliable commentaries (e.g., the *Berit Olam* series) that keep the literary dimension and larger discourse organization in mind.

Another difficulty: How can one discern what is artistic or excellent in the local language when there is not a large corpus of secular literature to use as the basis for comparison and assessment? Furthermore, how does naturalness in *oral* texts relate to the corresponding quality in *written* discourse, especially in cases where a tradition, standards, and models of literature have not yet been firmly established or even written about? Finally, how is form-functional proximity to be ascertained during an interlingual stylistic analysis—what criteria and methods should be employed?

While it is not possible to be as precise or certain as one would like to be during this sort of contrastive exercise, nevertheless a competent and committed translation team, given the necessary consultant guidance and direction, can make significant progress towards developing a workable literary approach over the years. Once an excellent L-R version is prepared in a widely used language of the region, it can become a model for other translation projects. It may be necessary when budgeting project time to add a year or more at the end for the entire translated text to be read through and revised with the stylistic factor specifically in mind. It is assumed, of course, that by this time (when they are about ready to finish their work) either the team as a whole, or one member with special artistic gifts in local language composition, has at long last reached the peak of both competence and performance abilities in this crucial skill.[268]

Such an intensive familiarization and educative program conducted with regard to the language of translation needs to begin *before* actual translation work is undertaken. Then it must be continued, perhaps on a more informal basis, until the project is brought to completion. There will always be *new* literary features to investigate along the way, but with growing experience

---

[268]On the controversial issue of whether skilled literary translators are born or made, I must conclude on the basis of personal experience that both are true. Unless a translator has some essential artistic competency to begin with, all the teaching in the world will not impart the techniques required. On the other hand, even artists need a considerable amount of training to help them control their creative inclination and preserve the referential sense of the sacred text that they are dealing with.

translators should be able to identify, analyze, assess, and apply the results accurately with greater independence, confidence, and ultimate success in relation to the immediate sociological and communicative context. Naturally, the extent and depth of this sort of vernacular-oriented training depends on the linguistic abilities and translation skills of the personnel involved, the functional focus of the version's *Skopos*, and the external support provided by the project *Brief* that was established at the onset.

8.4 An L-R oratorical version illustrated: Ezek. 37:1–10 in Chichewa

The Chichewa rendition of Ezekiel's dry bones vision that follows illustrates certain aspects of the nature and purpose of a literary-rhetorical, or oratorical, translation.[269] This composition represents a specially prepared semipoetic, rhetorically motivated rendering of the pericope, formatted in what I consider a readable design[270] and presented with its English back-translation. It is followed by a summary of its main stylistic features and a comparison with two other versions: the older, literal *Buku Lopatulika* (see sec. 10.7.1) and a recent common-language translation, *Buku Loyera* (see sec. 10.7.2).

---

[269]I chose this portion of Scripture on account of its general popularity, theological significance, stylistic verve, and rhetorical power—and because I had recently analyzed the original Hebrew text in detail in preparing another publication, Wendland 1999. The Chichewa rendition is the product of a joint effort involving my seminary Psalms class. (I served as the final text "redactor.") The translation, which was prepared according to the principles outlined in section 1.5 and the procedures in section 7.1, reflects the pure lyric style called *ndakatulo*, the main features of which are ellipsis, reiteration, ideophones, exclamations, emphasizers, demonstratives, independent pronouns, figures of speech, idioms, phonological accentuation, punning, and modifications in the normal prose word order.

[270]Newman has some pertinent things to say about audience-sensitive Bible text formatting: "[The text should be]...crafted to be read aloud without stumbling, heard without misunderstanding, and listened to with enjoyment....Most readability formulas focus on sentence length and choice of vocabulary, with others including such factors as sentence structure. Unfortunately, these measurements tend to be mechanical and do not take into consideration the *interest* level of texts: Is the text appealing to the eyes? Is it easy to read aloud? Does it make for easy listening? Are the words and sentence patterns familiar? Does it capture and hold the reader's interest? Are the thoughts easy to follow and understand?" (2001:19).

Chauta aukitsa mafupa oumatu

The LORD raises dried-up bones

Dzanja lamphamvu la Chauta lidandigwira—
    gwi!
Nyamu! Mzimu wa Mulunguwu
    wandinyamulatu,
nukandiika pakati pachigwa chachikulu
    chotakaka.
Chinali chodzaza ndi mafupa okhaokha ali
    mbwee!

[1] The mighty hand of Chauta
    grabbed me—tightly!
Up and away! The Spirit of
    God picked me up,
and put me in the middle of a
    large, broad valley.
It was filled up completely
    with bones all scattered!

Uku ndi uku Chauta ankandiyendetsa
    m'chigwa umo.
Pakati pa vibade vija ndinkazungulira pali
    ponsepo,
ali ochulukadi mafupawo nga' mchenga
    wapagombe.
Onsewo anali gwaa! pansi mu chigwa
    choopsacho.

[2] Here and there Chauta moved
    me inside that valley.
In the midst of those skulls I
    circled all around there,
the bones were so numerous
    like sand on a sea shore.
All dried out! hard on the
    ground in that awful valley.

Adandifunsa Chauta kuti, "Iwe mwana wa
    munthu,
kodi angakhalenso m'moyo mafupa ouma
    onsewa?"
"Ha! ine ndingadziwe bwanji munthu
    wapadziko ine?
Koma inu nokha, Ambuye, popeza
    mukudziwa zonse."

[3] Chauta asked me, "Say you,
    child of somebody,
can all of these dry bones
    become alive again?"
"Ha! how can I know, a person
    of this earth like me?
But you alone, O Lord, since
    you know everything."

Adandilamula Chauta nati, "Ulalike
    kwa mafupa awa,
uwauze kuti amvetse mau onse amene
    ndidzalankhula.
Ambuye Mulungu ali ndi uthenga wofunika
    kwambiri.
Iwo achere khutu, amve bwino zomwe
    ndifuna kunena.

[4–5] Chauta commanded me,
    "Preach to these bones,
tell them to listen to the words
    that I will speak.
The Lord God has a very
    important message.
Let 'em lend their ear n' listen
    to what I want to say.

"Mafupa oumanu, nazi zimene ine Chauta
    n'dzachita:
Ndidzakuuzirani mpweya, mudzapumanso
    wefuwefu!
Ndidzakuikirani mitsempa ndi mnofu, ah!
    khungunso.
Apo mudzazindikira kuti ine Chauta ndilipo
    ndithu!"

[5–6] Y' dry bones, now here's what
    I Chauta'm going t' do:
I'll blow breath in you, you'll
    breathe again puff-puff!
I will put tendons and flesh on
    you, ah! skin as well.
Then you'll realize that I Chauta
    I really do exist!"

Nanga ine n'kukana kodi? Ndidayambo-
    lalika mau,
monga momwe adandilamulirawo Chauta
    Mulungu.
Pamenepo panalidi phokoso lingoti
    gobedegobede!
Taonani, mafupa onse ouma aja adachito-
    lumikizana!

[7] So how could I refuse? I began
    t' preach the words,
just exactly as those he com-
    manded me, Chauta God.
Right then there was a big
    noise like clatter clatter!
Just look, all those dry bones
    acted t' join together!

Ndili chiyang'anire choncho, n'dapenya
    zodabwitsa:

[8] While I'm staring there thus, I
    saw s' amazing things:

Pa mafupa oumawo paoneka mitsempha ndi
  mnofu,
kudzanso khungu pamwamba, zonse zili
  bwino *nde!*
Koma muli *zii!* Munalibe mpweya m'kati
  mwakemo.

On those dry bones appear
  tendons and flesh,
and also skin on top, everything's
  just alright *ready!*
But inside is *emptiness!* There's
  no breath in there.

Adandilamula Chauta nati, "Ulalikire
  mpweya tsono,
iwe mwana wa munthu, uwuze mau a ine
  Ambuye:
'Bwera kuno, mpweyawe, dzawauzire
  ophedwawo
kuti akhalenso m'moyo pamaso panga monga
  kalelo.' "

[9] Chauta commanded me, "Now
  preach to the breath,
child of somebody, tell it the
  words of me the Lord:
'Com 'ere, you breath, breathe
  into these killed ones
so that they become alive in
  my presence as before.' "

Izi zonse ndidachita monga adandiuzira
  Chauta.
Mpweya udangoti *fiku!* n'kulowa mwa
  mitemboyo.
Pomwepo onse aja adasanduka amoyo
  naimirira *njii!*
Panali chinamtindi cha anthu m'chigwa
  chonsecho!

[10] All these things I did just
  exactly as Chauta told me.
The breath *arrived!* n' entered
  right into those corpses.
Immediately they all revived
  and stood up *upright!*
It was a huge crowd of people
  in that valley there!

There are seven principal stylistic features that distinguish the Chichewa poetic version of Ezekiel 37 from this passage in the *Buku Lopatulika* (BL) and *Buku Loyera* (BY).[271] Since my focus here is on the literary-rhetorical text, and the differential overview that follows will be carried out from that particular perspective:

• The oratorical poem rearranges the ten verses of the traditional version into nine stanzas of four measured lines each. These are roughly equal in length for rhythmic purposes, including several "ballast lines"—those which reiterate certain aspects of content or its main implications (e.g., 'The Lord God has a very important message' [4–5]). This, if printed in the preceding format, would presumably be a much easier text to articulate aloud in a public reading than the others. For example, it could be expressed in a more dynamic mode of oral intonation such as recitation or declamation.

• Nine ideophones and two exclamations accent the dramatic character of the discourse in the L-R rendition versus only two ideophones and no exclamations in the other versions. Thus even

---

[271]For the special purposes of this short illustration, I will not consider exegetical issues, matters of text structure and format, or terminology, such as the difference in the rendering of the Tetragrammaton, יהוה: *Yehova* in BL versus *Chauta* in both BY and L-R, *Chauta* being the name-title of the supreme Creator God in Chewa religion (see Wendland 1998b:115–121).

the lack of an overt action may be highlighted thereby (e.g., 'But inside is *emptiness!* [*zii!*] There's no breath in there' [8]).
- The average sentence length is the shortest in the L-R rendition; it is longer but still normal in BY; it is unnaturally long and grammatically complex in BL (the problem here being compounded through the overuse of semicolons). Thus the L-R text is the easiest to comprehend as it is being uttered aloud, since each line is meaningful as it stands and can be recited as such.
- The literary style is the most idiomatic in the L-R text, both lexically and syntactically, with many colloquial pronominal, demonstrative, and intensive affixes; word order variations; graphic diction; and rhythmic expression. The literal BL is the least idiomatic, hence difficult to understand; on the other hand, BY manifests the clearest, most natural and straightforward manner of speaking, in both direct and reported discourse. The BL is almost unintelligible in places. For example, right at the beginning in v. 1, 'The hand of Jehovah rested on me, and he went out with me in the spirit of Jehovah' (a literal back-translation) suggests that Jehovah had a physical hand and Ezekiel was accompanied by his own personal spirit, which could be sent out on special missions.
- There are several lexical-semantic replacements and additions in the L-R rendition. They embellish the language, fill out certain poetic lines, and avoid too much exact repetition, for example, in v. 1 'a large, broad valley' to accommodate the many bones that a multitude of people would produce; in v. 2 'those skulls', a more picturesque term than 'bones'; in v. 3 'a person of this earth', stressing the divine messenger's human nature better than 'child of a person'; in vv. 4–5 'let 'em lend their ear' replacing the simple 'hear'; in vv. 5–6 'you'll breathe again *puff-puff!*', which is a more climactic predication than 'you will live again'; in v. 7 'all those dry bones' in place of the unadorned 'those bones'; in v. 8 'everything's just alright *ready!*', bringing out the cumulative implication of the awesome description at this point; in v. 9 'alive in my presence as before', emphasizing Yahweh's implied personal relationship to all the dried-up, dead bones; and in v. 10 'entered those corpses' in place of the pronoun 'them'. This style suggests a *ndakatulo* lyric in Chichewa, which is characterized by vivid, emotive, highly evocative imagery intended to stimulate the listening audience to experience a dramatic scene and the associated physical sensations and psychological feelings.

- The dialogue portions of the L-R rendition are more extensive than those of BL and BY (some being refashioned out of narrative report). They are also more natural, even colloquial at times, in their manner of expression as in vv. 5–6, 'Y' dry bones, now here's what I Chauta 'm going t' do.' This crucial feature makes the account more immediate, personal, and verbally familiar.
- The L-R rendition includes a number of impressive phonological devices: wordplay, rhyme, alliteration, and assonance as in v. 1: *Nyamu! Mzimu wa Mulunguwu wandinyamulatu—nukandiika pakati pachigwa chachikulu chotakata—chinali chodzaza ndi mafupa okhaokha.* Such selective, purposeful sound shaping enables the poet to highlight certain similarities, contrasts, or high points within the text. The conceptual and connotative content being conveyed is correspondingly that much more dynamic and sensual—hence more memorable as well.

A word of caution is in order here. Translators of a lyric version of a given biblical text certainly do not have the liberty to distort either the original essential meaning or its particular areas of thematic focus. Neither are they free to gratuitously embellish the biblical text in a display of artistic virtuosity. A clear measure of functional equivalence, including exegetical fidelity, in relation to the text of Scripture must be maintained to the degree that this may be determined, keeping the envisaged audience and venue of use in mind (in this instance, a public recital in a nonworship setting). While critics and reviewers may debate this or that specific usage or claim that the L-R version has gone too far in the attempt to create rhetorical impact and aesthetic appeal, it should always be remembered that the basis for comparative evaluation must be the project *Skopos* and a careful analysis of the original source text, not some translation in English or another language.

On the other hand, one ought not to get tangled up in minor details of form or interpretation when conducting a critical assessment of this nature. The exegete's zeal for precision can easily stifle the poetic muse. In the case of biblical poetry and prophecy such as Ezek. 37:1–10, it is often not the individual image or utterance that is important, but the total conceptual, emotional, and sensory impression created by the literary/oratorical language. This may well be the primary purpose of the original writer, namely, to activate the expressive, directive, affective, and aesthetic functions of communication. This compound intention, in such a case, is at least equal to or even greater than the informative function that so many people mistakenly identify as being invariably paramount when it comes to the literature of the Scriptures.

8.5 Different translation styles for different types of consumer groups

Each of the three versions mentioned in section 8.4 was either composed for, or may be most comfortably received by, a different segment of the larger constituency of Chichewa speaker-hearers. *Buku Lopatulika*, the old, literal Chitonga version, is still the most popular despite the unnatural archaic awkwardness of its language. This is because it is the version that the majority of Protestants have grown up with in church, learned by heart, and become devoted to. The problem is that for so many people many passages are either unclear, ambiguous, misunderstood, or not understood at all. The words may be familiar through long exposure, but the content of the text, whether individual passages or occasionally a complete paragraph, is not well comprehended. All too often ordinary receptors are forced to reply, when challenged, as the unnamed Ethiopian official of the Acts account did: "How can I understand unless someone helps me?" (Acts 8:31).

For this reason, the meaning-oriented popular-language version *Buku Loyera* (BY) was prepared by mother-tongue speakers of the language, not to replace the *Buku Lopatulika* (BL), but to be used alongside it, as a meaningful alternative. The purpose was, and is, to provide readers and hearers alike with a more intelligible, complementary text to turn to, if need be, for clarification. It is also used with audiences of younger people, new Christians and non-Christians, and even second-language speakers of Chichewa. For these people it is high time that the dry bones of the existing literal version be resurrected as a text that finally makes more sense—both overall as well as in a host of passages that simply did not communicate to them before.

In contrast to the BY, which was prepared to be *complementary*, the oratorical L-R version was prepared as a *supplementary* text. It was intended not so much for general use, but for selected purposes (e.g., a day of public worship and praise, a tract publication, an audiocassette series),[272] particular audiences (e.g., youth choirs, school Bible-study groups), and special events (e.g., a public drama performance, a radio broadcast). It is

---

[272]The great potential of audiocassettes and radio broadcasts for mass-communicating the Scriptures needs to be more fully exploited, especially in areas of the world where access either to the Bible itself or to sophisticated means of message transmission (e.g., TV, video, computers) are limited, and/or where the majority of the population are not literate. For a helpful comparative survey of the possibilities as well as the limitations of cassette and radio communication, see Sundersingh 1999:138–150.

a matter of which version best fits the specific need and situational setting at hand. Of course, some explanation, education, and illustration is needed to facilitate the mutually supportive use of these different translational types. In many areas of Africa today, that is indeed the lesser problem; the far greater challenge is to provide people with more than one reliable version to choose from in the first place.

8.6 Some implications for Bible translation in Bantu Africa

Four major implications for Bible translation arise from the various vernacular-oriented issues that have been discussed in this chapter, especially in connection with south-central Africa. However, they would seem to apply in similar settings elsewhere in the world as well, at least in part.

1. Concerning *transmission strategy*. Local Bible societies, national churches, and mission agencies need to plan together and budget for the preparation of different versions that will serve diverse audiences within the total population, often by means of nontraditional media and modes of transmission to match a more dynamic style of translation (e.g., a specially formatted and illustrated publication, a "narrativized" audiocassette version, a video selection, a dramatic or musical stage production, an electronic hypertext multimedia program).[273]
2. Concerning *translation style*. Some of these versions will necessarily manifest important stylistic variations in several dimensions and on a number of distinct linguistic levels, such as the amount of formal correspondence or functional equivalence that is demanded, desired, or allowed; the degree of artistry and/or idiomaticity that is encouraged in order to promote an oratorical reading of the discourse; the application of TL literary/oral genres for (novel) use in Scripture translation; careful textual adaptations for a primary oral-aural medium; and the amount and kind of extratextual "reader's helps" provided (e.g., footnotes, section headings, illustrations, cross-references, book introductions, and a glossary of key terms).[274] In all cases a particular vernacular style needs to be

---

[273]Sundersingh, in his survey of the Tamil people of India with respect to the most effective mode of audiocassette production of a selected Scripture portion (in this case Mark 1:21–28), found that a multivoiced drama format won out over both a story format with modulated intonation and a straight reading format (1999:290).

[274]It is possible to provide "reader's helps" in an oral/audio text (or any other nonprint medium), although the helps would of course need to be carefully distinguished from the words of Scripture. This could be done by an aside by a different speaker or by a sound signal such as a bell or music.

specified on the basis of a thorough study of the target language and its literature (or orature).

3. Concerning *translator training.* Translating a nontraditional, audience-specific version—certainly a literary-rhetorical rendition—demands higher standards of quality. Production teams must include more competent and creative (oratorically "artistic") personnel, whether as exegetes, stylists, drafters, illustrators, formatters, media experts, educators, literacy advisors, or promoters. The translators of today not only require more intensive biblical training, but also supplementary courses in a variety of specialized fields that target their own language, such as traditional oral-art forms, mixed media technology, indigenous literary-poetic studies, and cross-cultural communication.

4. Concerning *audience testing.* A detailed and extensive research survey of the receptor group must be carried out nowadays *before* an expensive translation is embarked upon. Financial resources are too limited to waste on educated guesses or subjective, provincial preferences. A thorough sociolinguistic, religious, and aesthetic testing of the target audience should also be conducted *while* a given project is underway to ensure that it is hitting the mark, especially with regard to their "felt needs" and desires in the area of idiomatic style. How does it actually sound to *them* in *their* Scriptures? Finally, a sufficient amount of survey work is necessary after publication in order to determine the version's relative success in achieving the goals that it set out to accomplish in relation to its primary user group. Hopefully, past mistakes can then be avoided and successes repeated in future TL translations.

While these points relate more or less to all types of Bible translation, they especially apply to a literary-rhetorical (oratorical) version because of its relative novelty in relation to the envisaged audience and the difficulty of composing a text of this level of stylistic quality in the target language. Despite the potential problems, we are motivated to excellence by the great potential of a vernacular poetic rendition to convey a fuller measure of the original communicative dynamics and lyric style of the Book of Psalms, for example. In addition, a recognizably artful—yet also semantically faithful—interlingual recreation of this nature has the inherent verbal power to make a cognitive and emotive impact on people who probably never realized or expected that the Word of God could speak to them so idiomatically, beautifully, and powerfully in their mother tongue.

This is not to suggest that such a communicatively more dynamic translation is the only way to go. I have stressed the point that the type of translation style that is appropriate for a given speech community must be determined on the basis of a thorough investigation of the entire sociocultural and religious setting in which the proposed version will be received and used. An L-R text is but one possibility among many; however, it is a translation type that seems not to have been seriously considered much in the past, perhaps for good reasons, such as the quality of translators needed to do a good job of it or simply the time available for the project. On the other hand, if the production of such versions has been hindered merely for financial reasons that relate to the poor economic base of the primary target audience, then the problem is much greater than the linguistic or translational difficulties. Then the issues become ethical, even theological, in nature, effect, and implication.

9
Teaching a Literary-Rhetorical Approach

While a few specific pedagogical applications were mentioned in chapters 7 and 8, we will now focus on the more general features of teaching a literary-rhetorical approach to Bible translators. It is assumed that we are agreed on the need to pay more attention to the artistic, oral-aural dimension of the text with respect to both the biblical pericope that we happen to be analyzing as well as the translation that will result. What then is the best way of introducing translators to the compositional issue and the communication implications involved? In other words, how might we incorporate a contextually-framed, discourse-oriented, and style-sensitive methodology into our teaching programs, in both formal courses and on-the-job training techniques?[275]

I begin in section 9.1 with seven guidelines to orient us to the important task of translator education.[276] These will be followed by a discussion in section 9.2 of several specific issues that pertain to the training of translators from the perspective of a literary-rhetorical motivation and methodology. In section 9.3 I will emphasize high-quality training, and in section 9.4 preparation for ongoing testing.

---

[275]Specific suggestions with regard to *poetic* discourse are outlined in Wendland 1998b:225–236. See also Hatim and Mason 1997, chapter 11.

[276]Further guidelines that might possibly be helpful from a translator-training perspective are found in my elaboration of the base-model translation technique (Wendland 2000a; see also Wendland 1982). For a broad perspective on the teaching, research, and status of literary education in Western universities, see Bush and Malmkjaer 1998.

Let me precede this discussion with the following caveats, written by two professional secular translators, on the possibilities of training a skilled literary translator:

> [M]ost literary translators are largely self-taught or have learned informally at the feet of experienced translators or editors who have critiqued their work. (Wechsler 1998:168)

> It is unfortunate that there is no mentorship program for literary translators, and precious little training is available for would-be literary translators...As a result, most literary translators have to be self-taught; making mistakes along the way, they gradually evolve a *Fingerspitzengefühl* that serves them well once they have surmounted the initial barriers that may deter all but the most dedicated or tenacious. The good news is that very few successful literary translators learned their craft through courses of formal study. (Landers 2001:28)

Despite these cautions, I still feel that in the case of Bible translation we need to put forth at least a serious effort to prepare personnel for the task that we expect of them, especially if this involves a literary rendition of any sort, whether more or less in terms of its style or scope.

9.1 Laying the groundwork for the training of translators

How does a translation consultant begin to organize a project that will implement at least certain aspects of a literary-rhetorical approach? It is by planning for *the teaching* of an L-R approach to the translators. Some general considerations relating to this will be presented in section 9.1 as follows:

1. Building a strong L-R emphasis within the project *Brief* (sec. 9.1.1). The desire to produce a version with a literary focus must be incorporated within the *Brief* of a translation project's guiding terms of reference. This perspective, including the nature and purpose (*Skopos*) of the translation needs to be made clear to all project participants from the very beginning, even before the nuclear team begins its work.
2. Conducting an intensive L-R-oriented analysis of the SL text (sec. 9.1.2). A systematic L-R analysis of the biblical text as discussed in chapter 7 complements and augments the normal discourse-based exegetical interpretation of it.
3. Determining the L-R stylistic resources available in the TL (sec. 9.1.3). An L-R translation will be possible only if an adequate

study has been made of the oral and written stylistic and rhetorical conventions and resources that are available in the TL for the various existing genres of verbal art (see chap. 8).

4. Translating a trial L-R version (sec. 9.1.4). After the preceding three concerns have been completely and successfully addressed, a draft translation is now prepared under the eye of a competent supervisor who helps the team apply all the relevant procedures to the biblical text at hand, particularly with respect to the search for suitable L-R functional matches.

5. Assessing the equivalence of the SL and TL texts (sec. 9.1.5). An assessment of the degree of equivalence of the SL and TL texts is carried out with respect to those discourse features that have been specified in the project *Skopos*. Generally, the focus is on a dynamic representation of meaning (i.e., the biblical text's semantic content plus its functional intent) by means of L-R forms appropriate to the particular TL setting and the projected situation of use. This is a comparative exercise and also an intuitive one.

6. Testing and revising the draft translation (sec. 9.1.6). There is a certain amount of informal testing and revising that takes place during the translation process, but once the team has completed a good draft, it must be examined and evaluated according to procedures that are systematic, complete, and conducted by well-trained staff.

7. Reviewing and documenting the lessons learned (sec. 9.1.7). Periodically the translation team together with the project committee analyzes, re-evaluates, and, if necessary, revises the translation principles and procedures that were specified in the original *Brief*. A way of doing this is by using a logbook to record the discussions and decisions made in the course of the work, especially with regard to issues that pertain specifically to the preparation of an acceptable L-R version in the TL.

9.1.1 Building a strong literary-rhetorical emphasis within the project Brief

A *Brief* is the guiding teleological framework, an explicit statement of the communication strategy, for the translation project as a whole. Included in this operational blueprint are the project's primary goals in relation to the proposed target audience (see sec. 1.8).[277]

The *Brief* for an L-R translation project should include a specification of the following elements:

1. The precise nature of the translation, that is, its communicative purpose (*Skopos*) as well as its clearly defined position on the putative form ⇔ functional stylistic continuum, which ranges from a very literal version through a common-language version and on to the other extreme of a fully literary rendering in the case of languages that have an established tradition of what constitutes good (or bad) "literature" (see sec. 2.8);
2. The type of publication envisaged, whether a full Bible, a New Testament, individual portion, special audience selection, or new media production;
3. The means for conducting a sufficient amount of preliminary linguistic, sociolinguistic, literary (oral), and distinct target audience-oriented research;
4. The minimum qualifications necessary for translation personnel to enable them to successfully undertake a L-R version;
5. A reasonable (achievable) temporal framework for the project, including the time needed to carry out testing and revision work;
6. Establishment of an effective organizational and administrative structure;
7. A plan for acquiring the total resources needed to complete the project within the proposed time frame; and
8. The kind and amount of training required for all staff and how this will be carried out within the scope of available project resources.

---

[277]My understanding of the term *Brief* is basically the same as Nord's (1997:27–31). (Hatim and Mason [1997:11–12, 126] do not clearly distinguish the concepts of *Brief* and *Skopos*.) If a literary approach like the one I propose here were being applied to a translation for distribution through nonprint media, a different *Brief* and *Skopos* would be needed than for a print publication. Much the same kind of SL text analysis would be needed, however, although the features of special semantic and pragmatic significance once identified would need to be matched in the TL in a medium-sensitive manner. This is an important area of concern within the worldwide intercultural and cross-technological program of Scripture communication, one that requires a more specialized treatment than I am able to offer here.

In the case of an enhanced popular-language version,[278] one that utilizes most of the commonly recognized linguistic and literary-oratorical
resources of the TL, the stylistic dimension would be a crucial factor to
consider and specify in concrete terms (with illustrative examples) at the
outset of the translation program. This would need to be done not only for
the benefit of the translation-review committee, but also for the enlight-
enment of church leaders and the general constituency for whom the new
version is intended. In developing a *Brief*, remember that a fully L-R version would not be the first translation for a given constituency; rather, it
would be a subsequent version, prepared to meet a specific need as a complement to the other translations already available in the language.

9.1.2 Conducting an intensive L-R-oriented analysis of the SL text

From the very beginning of a project the translators need to be
trained—preferably on a day-to-day, on-the-job, inductively oriented apprenticeship basis—to carry out the fundamental analysis integral to an
L-R approach.[279] This involves the following (which is a summary of secs.
7.1.1–7.1.12):

1. *Identification* in the SL text of the meaning-bearing L-R features,
   this in addition to those that are normally examined in a detailed
   exegetical analysis.[280] Translators must learn to discern what is really significant in terms of literary form (plus associated content
   and function) in the biblical pericope under consideration. Such
   assessment with regard to stylistic import and impact may be the
   hardest part of the whole procedure. They also need to develop
   the ability to spot those stylistic devices that will be most likely to
   cause difficulties when searching for the closest functional

---

[278]I am extending Wonderly's original conception of *popular language* (see 1968:3–4) to
include this concern for a popular style that makes use of diverse literary and rhetorical devices (oral and/or written). These artistic features may not be found in the oral *parole*-per-
formance of most speakers, but they are a recognized and appreciated part of their aural
langue-competence.

[279]Fawcett (1997:142–143) discusses this sort of method (geared to problem solving) as
part of a wider basic translation strategy.

[280]"Significance," or communicative value, in literary discourse is related in large measure to the notion of "markedness." In this respect, a certain linguistic form may be evaluated as being more or less *marked* (significant) on the basis of criteria such as frequency,
relative novelty, intertextual (including possible symbolic) relevance, complexity, and distribution (place of occurrence in the text, whether on an individual or global basis). Such
significance with regard to any specific literary feature can be determined only after the
completion of a comprehensive comparative stylistic study of a sufficiently large corpus of
related texts.

equivalents in the TL. Only individuals with a sufficient amount of technical training, analytical skill, and practical experience will be able to carry this out well. They would have to be able, for example, to recognize the various markers that distinguish a particular L-R genre and style in Hebrew and Greek (with regard to purpose, means, and result), such as repetition, disjunction, concentration, cohesion, and accentuation, along with the more specific devices included under these major compositional techniques.[281]

2. *Explanation* of the L-R feature(s) that have been identified, that is, explicitly defining and analyzing them, then telling how they function to convey special significance (with or without emphasis) or to modify the overt or implicit meaning of the biblical text (e.g., the use of direct imperatives or their equivalents versus covert implicatures). This sort of explanatory exercise must be carried out in a systematic, holistic, and text- or context-specific manner, that is, in terms of how one device interacts with, complements, and possibly also alters the effect of another within the discourse as a whole.[282]

3. *Application*, that is, making a preliminary conceptual transfer of the knowledge gained during steps 1 and 2. The transfer must be based on a prior extensive, form-functional analysis of the TL and its literature/orature. Such a study seeks to identify the genre-specific characteristics as well as the more general L-R devices available in the TL, that is, at the particular stylistic register which has been specified for the translated text. Translators would thus learn to anticipate how various prominent SL artistic and rhetorical features

---

[281]Follingstad (2001b), in his comprehensive study of the particle יכ, demonstrates how important such an exercise is, not only in terms of content and structure, but also with regard to important expressive, connotative, rhetorical, and perspectival aspects of the biblical message. He says, "With respect to יכ, translations need to be evaluated as to **how they translate the perspective taken on a particular utterance—the viewpoint on the content contained in it**—and not only the transfer of the ideational/referential propositional content information packaged within the clause" (pp. 7–8). Translators who cannot access the original text are at a particular disadvantage, for they may be easily led to repeat the mistakes of a version in a language of wider communication, when their mother tongue may operate very close to the original in this nonreferential, stylistic dimension (ibid.:5).

[282]It would be helpful to translators if specially prepared translator's handbooks or exegetical guides (e.g., on the Pentateuch, prophetic books, OT poetry, Gospels, Epistles) could be developed to point out and discuss the various structural and stylistic L-R features—instances of tectonicity, artistry, iconicity, and rhetoricity—as they appear diachronically in the books of the Bible. Even just one comprehensive handbook, presenting a sample of the most important devices and techniques, should be enough to give translators an idea of what to look for and how to analyze them.

might be rendered on an individual or combined basis with similar impact and appeal in the target language.[283]

9.1.3 Determining the L-R stylistic resources available in the target language

The analysis of the L-R features of the target language was considered in detail in chapter 8, and readers are referred to the various procedures outlined there (especially 8.1.1–8.1.8). The need to *train* the translation team in the application of these procedures is the focus in this chapter.

9.1.4 Translating a trial L-R version

While preparing a trial L-R version, translators put everything together conceptually and compositionally from their previous exegetical study of the biblical text and their research into the L-R resources in their mother tongue.[284] Here is where they now exercise their creativity (i.e., via their informed artistic intuition and experience-based expertise).

In practice it may turn out best if a single member of the team, someone skilled in various modes of TL stylistic expression, is chosen to produce the basic draft.[285] Just as great literature is not authored by committee, so also in most instances a popular-language version probably cannot be effectively composed by a number of translators working closely together. Rather, the most gifted individual may have to be given the freedom (yet within the confines of the authoritative SL text) to follow the inner leading of his or her own literary genius to recreate the biblical text. Thus this designated verbal craftsman or -woman should be allowed to work unhindered according to his or her unique artistic inclination and inspiration while endeavoring to transmit the Scripture's essential sense and significance in a genre-natural, verbally idiomatic manner in the TL. If the necessary degree of competence, confidence, and/or experience is

---

[283]See Zogbo and Wendland 2000, chapter 4, for some guidelines when investigating the possibility of finding translational matches in the poetic discourse of a given TL.

[284]Translators, in order to stimulate and channel this intuition in the right direction, must try, according to Linton (1986:19), "to absorb the original writer's total message, personality, character, circumstances when writing, historical and cultural environment, and distinctive stylistic tendencies. It is like living in intimate contact with an individual before writing a biography of him." Only after such an all-out effort to "know" a given biblical author will a translator be prepared to render the essential dynamics of the original text's form and meaning in a literary-equivalent manner in the TL.

[285]It is a definite advantage, of course, if such a stylist-composer (drafter) has acquired some prior biblical or theological training so that his or her work will not be later called into question, debated, and possibly denigrated on the basis of SL exegetical issues that are unrelated to stylistic excellence in the TL.

deficient,[286] it might be beneficial to have the drafter work closely with a recognized TL verbal artist for a period of time. It may also help in some situations to do the drafting orally. Certain genres, like the ones used for the poetry of the Psalms, could probably be more easily composed in oral form and recorded for later transcription.[287]

I have emphasized the point that an L-R approach may be applied in different *degrees*. It is not necessary to fully reproduce a biblical subgenre by its closest equivalent in the TL. While that may be the ideal, it is done only where the situational circumstances allow—which is probably the exception rather than the rule. For example, if the guiding project *Skopos* specifies that the version under preparation is to be used in public worship, it cannot, in the interest of decorum, be overly dynamic; rather, a judicious selection of L-R features that will fit the style to the primary setting of use will have to be made. A minimum selection would normally involve some significant modification of the *phonology* of the text with a view towards promoting its sonic beauty along with improved readability, including such aural features as general euphony, lightly rhythmic utterances, natural lexical collocations and pleasing diction, and sound enhancement in keeping with the norms and genius of the language concerned (e.g., selective alliteration, assonance, gentle rhyming sequences, or some paronomasia).

It would be extremely helpful to the translation team if a good L-R version in a closely related language were available as a model. I have found that this is perhaps the most important factor in getting translators (as well as all their associates, supporters, and sponsors) to recognize the purpose and advantages of having an L-R version in their mother tongue. Such a model version also provides abundant access to concrete examples that they can understand, appreciate, and hopefully emulate. Making one available in the languages of wider communication of many regions should therefore be a top priority in terms of wider Bible translation strategy. Truly "popular" renditions are needed especially in situations where the only text that currently exists is an older, literal one. While it is a great challenge to produce one where no related L-R version exists, it is well

---

[286]Fawcett makes a pertinent observation in this regard: "As translators become more experienced and acquire greater control over their mother tongue, so the translation strategy moves more toward the sense-oriented approach based on larger translation units with checking for style and text typology" (1997:143).

[287]There is a helpful set of procedures for carrying out such an exercise in chapters 15 and 16 of Klem 1982. Several other articles on this subject are Bartsch 1997, Noss 1997, and Wendland 1994a:27–30.

worth the effort, for it will not only serve its target audience, but will also stimulate the creativity of translators in related languages.[288] There is one other critical factor for success in producing a literary version: It is absolutely necessary to have a sympathetic supervising translation consultant who possesses considerable technical knowledge of the SL as well as sufficient practical ability and experience in the TL (or a related language). This person would have the primary responsibility for on-the-job training and guiding of a team of translators to compose a suitable L-R version in the TL. He or she would of course need a sufficient amount of time to devote to such a project, especially during its initial formative stages.

9.1.5 Assessing the equivalence of the SL and TL texts

Now the team is ready to evaluate the initial trial draft that has been produced. To do this they can work individually or as a group. Their evaluation will take the form of a complete discourse-comparative exercise looking at form, content, emotion, and function in relation to the biblical text (ideally in the original language). The goal is to produce in the TL rendition the *closest, natural, contextualized, functional* equivalent of the SL message.[289]

Each of these qualifiers—*closest, natural, contextualized,* and *functional* —is significant and must be carefully considered during the translation (and evaluation) process. The qualifier *closest* has reference primarily to the biblical message's meaning (denotation plus connotation), but secondarily also to the original forms of its expression, to the degree that such literary imitation is possible during the interlingual transfer

---

[288]An extended variant of this procedure is to have a skilled, bilingual translator transform a good vernacular model text into a related TL. Ideally this would be done in a manner that accommodates to the TL's distinctive manner of expression, including its artistic and rhetorical features, in order that it may serve as a base text for another language. Then the TL translation team, advised by a committee of reviewers, would be able to polish up this transferred text both exegetically and stylistically.

[289]The concern for translational equivalence is by no means restricted to Bible translators. It is "[a] term used by many writers to describe the nature and the extent of the relationship which exists between SL and TL texts or smaller linguistic units" (Shuttleworth and Cowie 1997:49). Fawcett devotes an entire chapter to this notion in his 1997 work and concludes (p. 62) that (despite certain problems inherent in this approach) "the notion of equivalence and the techniques for achieving it continue to be used in the everyday language of translation because they represent translation reality....[Equivalence taxonomies with reference to denotation, connotation, social register, genre, functional goals, poetic style, and discourse structure] are based on observations of what actually happens in translation."

process.[290] The qualifier *natural*, on the other hand, focuses upon the text's relative idiomaticity in terms of TL stylistic norms and the larger goal of producing a popular-language version. The qualifier *contextualized* takes the entire communicative situation and setting of the target constituency into consideration. More specifically, contextualization is concerned with the most "relevant," that is, the most efficient and effective means of conveying the biblical message in this particular mother tongue (Gutt 1992). A variable, relevance-determined balance must be maintained between efficiency (relative cognitive ease versus effort during text-processing) and effectiveness (the product of textual appropriateness, impact, and appeal). Thus in translating a literary version, communicative effectiveness will normally be favored over efficiency. When translating a common language version, on the other hand, conceptual efficiency comes to the fore.

Last but not least is the qualifier *functional*. This factor needs to be evaluated in relation to both the larger and smaller units of discourse—that is, the whole of the message and also its constituent parts. The main motivational and re-creative intentions involved in Bible translation activate the informative, expressive, affective, imperative, relational, and artistic (poetic) functions of communication. This last-mentioned one is of special interest in a translation that makes an effort to duplicate the literary-rhetorical dynamics of the biblical text within the linguistic framework of a particular vernacular.

Of course, it is impossible to produce a functional equivalent with respect to *all* the pertinent features of the original text. Therefore a *priority rating* needs to be made in accordance with the principle of relevance in relation to the intended audience and the primary aims of the project *Skopos*. It will undoubtedly take some time and a considerable amount of guided practice to teach translators how to assess and apply these complex criteria in their everyday work.

---

[290]I still subscribe to the "premodern" opinion that there is such a thing as a relatively objective (author-intended) meaning (content + intent) residing—that is, linguistically and literarily encoded—within the various documents of Scripture. Nord defends such "loyalty" to "the original author's intentions" and capably deals with a number of "criticisms" of it (1997, chap. 7, also pp. 125–126). For a theological perspective on this important hermeneutical issue, see Vanhoozer 1998, chapters 2–4. This meaning is of course relative to the extent of our technical understanding of the linguistic and literary nature of the text and its sociocultural, including religious, context. However, it is "objective" in the sense that this meaning is determinable using the accumulated knowledge and analytical techniques at our disposal, as informed by the mainstream hermeneutical tradition of Christian scholarship. The alternative—namely, disparate relativistic and existentialist theories of solipsistic "meaning"—to my mind in effect renders the task of translation obsolete and unnecessary: You simply access your own mind and experience the text in "postmodern" fashion, thus composing your own Scripture—one that is "right" and "works" for you. What "loyalty" to the original author exists in such cases?

9.1.6 Testing and revising the draft translation

An extraordinary translation, which a literary-rhetorical version might turn out to be in some local settings, will require a corresponding amount of care during the text-testing process. Many people may be negative or suspicious with regard to the draft at first, especially if they are familiar with a well-established formal-correspondence translation. Therefore, it is important for translators, or designated specialists on the review committee, to *try the new version out in varied contexts and on different audiences* —different, that is, in sociolinguistic terms such as age, denominational affiliation, sex, and situation of use. Some people may turn out to be more immediately receptive to a meaning-centered, idiomatically expressed message in their mother tongue than others are. For example, I have found young people (such as youth choir members), and educated Bible study groups to be more open.

A helpful thing for translators (or their representatives) to do prior to the *formal* testing procedure, is to *thoroughly explain and exemplify* the nature and purpose of the new literary-rhetorical translation. The importance of this must be highlighted in their training and not be left to chance. Receptors should be reassured that the new version is not intended to replace their more literal or liturgical version, if one exists, unless there is no longer any appreciable demand for it. The aim, it should be explained, is to provide a text that accurately presents the Word of God and does so in a manner that more fully duplicates its original artistic beauty and rhetorical power.

During the testing process itself it will probably be necessary to assess audience reaction to specific L-R features, particularly in cases where they might initially react negatively but are unable to explain exactly what they do not like about the new translation. What they object to may not be the dynamic or idiomatic style as a whole, but only a few of its components such as the way selected key terms have been expressed, or the overuse of ideophones, or a few overly graphic figures of speech, or dialogue that sounds too colloquial. Perhaps it will turn out that while the text is acceptable in written form, concerns arise when it is read aloud in a setting of public worship.

Once the more specific objections have been discussed and resolved by successive stages of revision, the general estimation of the new version may change. People may even turn into strong supporters of the project when they notice how ready the translators are to hear their personal opinions and do what is necessary (within limits) to satisfy their stylistic preferences.

The process of testing a draft translation will include yet another careful comparison of the translation with the standard versions, and if possible the original text, to make sure that all of the essential units of content and aspects of intent are fully represented. Comparing the texts ensures that no skewing or avoidable loss of meaning has occurred. This is a process that translators need to be trained to do on a step-by-step basis. Many published texts are available that can be adapted for use in teaching some explicit principles and procedures for this purpose (e.g., Mossop 2001, with its useful summary on pp. 149–154).

It is also essential to test the *oral-aural* character and quality of the translated text, for as has been mentioned, most people receive it in spoken form (see Newman 2001:9–11). This kind of testing is often done, in many parts of Africa at least, using audiocassette recordings. The tester, perhaps a chosen member of the translation team, must be adequately trained in the techniques of presenting the material and writing down the responses so that they can be evaluated later by the translation team as well as the main editorial or review committee or specially appointed "research" office. Literary evaluation is not a job for novices, no matter how eager and willing they may be.

Another means of oral-aural testing is via special radio programs. For example, a weekly segment of a regular Bible Society program broadcast on AM, FM, or short-wave radio could feature sample readings of the trial translation from different genres.[291] These could even be read in alternation with the corresponding passages from the older version(s) accompanied by an explanation of the basic principles of functionally equivalent, L-R translation. Listener feedback on a particular text or topic could be elicited as well as the reasons for the listeners' opinions and suggested improvements. In view of the current competition among both religious and secular radio stations in some parts of the world, many station managers or program producers, especially at a new station, are often more than willing to offer some free or reduced-rate program time to the local Bible Society or a mother-tongue translation group for a program of this kind.

---

[291]Rev. Salimo Hachibamba, the then-coordinator of the New Chitonga Bible Translation Project, prepared and presented such a series of programs on national radio (Zambia Broadcasting Services, vernacular department). This program generated a lot of interest in the new common-language version along with some helpful feedback, which was used to prepare additional broadcasts. Christian radio stations, formerly shortwave but increasingly FM nowadays, are springing up all over Africa as well as in many other parts of the world. They offer a good opportunity to Bible Societies and specific translation projects to "advertise their wares" and encourage meaningful interaction with interested members of the TL constituency.

9.1.7 Reviewing and documenting the lessons learned

Producing a new, dynamically worded translation that pays special attention to the diverse literary and rhetorical features of both the biblical text and the TL literature is no easy task. It requires translators and consultants of the highest caliber—and a suitably educated constituency that knows what such a version is all about and is prepared to receive and use it. An initial practical program of instruction for translators and key reviewers carried out according to the original project *Brief* and its *Skopos* would be just the beginning. This has to be followed up by continuing education and task-related assessment sessions to monitor both the developing compositional skills of the translators in the use of the L-R approach and also their primary receptors' reactions to it. If the general responses are found to be consistently and widely negative, this would call for a modification of the methodology at the level of its operational details. At this point even the broad guidelines and goals set forth in the project's governing *Skopos* would need to be reconsidered.[292]

All decisions of this kind, both great and small, need to be recorded in writing, with explanations, for possible future consultation by the translation committee (whether the original production team or a subsequent responsible group). While the team should not abandon their efforts to produce a more dynamic, meaning-centered translation just because of some initial resistance and occasional unfavorable comments, they certainly cannot force their target constituency to accept a version that the majority is opposed to, no matter how unreasonable or unenlightened such a response may seem. Above all, the translators must never push ahead and attempt to publish a text that they know in advance will be extremely controversial and liable to rejection by significant portions of their church commissioners and supporters.

Extensive research and testing may reveal at the outset that the people at large are not yet ready for a popularly styled idiomatic version. In this case, the more dynamic L-R features of the translation will have to be toned down and sometimes replaced by more literal or neutral renderings as agreed upon by compromise. A partial reversion to formal correspondence is likely to be called for with reference to the better-known prose passages of the Bible, especially those regarded as being key or even

---

[292]The importance of getting translators to view their task from the wider perspective of an overall, continually monitored and modified guiding strategy statement is underscored by many secular translation theorists. Fawcett (1997:143), for example, says, "[P]rofessionals make better use of what is called top-down text processing, working from general concepts and objectives down to precise goals, rather than bottom-up processing, working from data, which, in translation, means the specific words on the page" (see also Wilt, ed. 2002b, chap. 2).

doctrinally "diagnostic" verses by one church body or another. In the less familiar poetic portions, however, it may be acceptable for the translators to be more dynamic and creative, rendering a poetic text in a more condensed poetical style. Perhaps if a few selections composed in a genre-sensitive literary form of this kind were to be published in advance, it might help prepare the way for freer, more artistically composed translation at a later date.

It is possible that positive prepublication exposure to sample portions or text selections, coupled with ongoing educational workshops and informational seminars,[293] might gradually awaken the target constituency's awareness of the importance of a literary version as a viable option among the different styles and models available to them. Such awareness may further lead them to a greater appreciation of the implications of an L-R translation for communicating the Word of God more effectively to certain segments of an increasingly complex and diverse contemporary society. In the end, a significant number of Bible users may finally see that the literature of Scripture is indeed unique, being both numinously religious and dynamically artistic. The challenging message of the biblical text (whatever the genre), along with its inherent beauty and power, must therefore be given a chance at least to strike a responsive chord and resonate rhetorically in their own language. Such an endeavor is necessary not only for the sake of fidelity to the aims of the original documents, but also for the sake of fidelity to the vast communicative potential presented by the literary resources of the target language.

9.2 The relation of an L-R approach to translation theory and practice

There are a number of issues to be considered when applying an L-R approach to Bible translation. Some of them will be discussed here with special reference to the training of the translators who will implement the L-R methodology, hopefully in an appropriate, audience-sensitive manner.

---

[293]Such extension workshops and educational seminars would seem to be an essential aspect of the translation task (*Skopos*) whenever a meaning-oriented version of greater or lesser degree is being prepared. This is true especially in situations where an older, literal version already exists. To my knowledge, an extensive promotional program of this kind is being carried out only in Spanish in South America (see Omanson 2001:9–10). If there are others, the various translation agencies would do well to document and share resources in this communicative endeavor.

9.2.1 The uniqueness of Bible translation

It is important for translators to recognize the special nature of Bible translation. Its uniqueness should be periodically, if not continually, impressed upon all translation staff and their associates, as this affects both theory (the underlying principles and assumptions) and practice (the procedures that arise from these principles). What makes Bible translation distinctive is a complex of eight factors. Together they distinguish it from all other types of literary translation, necessitating a coherent, comprehensive, and contextualized theory as well as a corresponding methodology to support it in practice. These eight attributes are:

1. The preeminently religious character of the biblical text (of divine origin, hence authoritative for many segments of the TL constituency), which requires an extra measure of intentional fidelity to the original documents.
2. The beautifully artistic and often dramatically presented nature of much of biblical discourse, though not necessarily of all portions.
3. The pervasive intertextual influences seen throughout the canonical corpus, which is a compound, but unified work.
4. The significant level of possible external influence in the form of other translations of the Bible, either in the same language, a related language, or some language of wider communication that speakers of the TL may be familiar with.
5. The overall rhetorical function of the Scriptures, which are intended to convince, persuade, convict, motivate—not merely inform or edify or, least of all, entertain.
6. The implicit aural-oral dimension of the text, which was by and large composed to be read *aloud* (recited, chanted, intoned) and heard in public by a congregation.
7. The text's multifarious compositional nature, with many diverse literary genres, languages, and rhetorical styles, but always of deep theological and ethical significance.
8. The considerable length and diversity of the corpus of the Old and New Testaments, which nevertheless must always be considered and analyzed as a complete, integrated, progressively developed, mutually reflective whole.

Some of these eight factors (1, 3, 4, 8) would tend to lead translators to be rather conservative in their handling of the sacred text. The other factors (2, 5, 6, 7) should stimulate translators to be more daring as they endeavor to render the Word with greater communicative impact, appeal, and relevance in their mother tongue.

9.2.2 Putting the theories into practice

The development of a specific translation theory is dependent upon the particular point of view that one adopts with regard to the task at hand. When the point of view is changed or expanded in significant ways, this will result in a modified proposal as far as a statement of the theory is concerned. These considerations in turn affect Bible translator training programs.

There are a number of older schools of literary-critical criticism that translators could be introduced to for useful background on theory and practice, namely, the Genre, Rhetorical, Formalist, Speech-Act, and Social-Scientific methodologies (see sec. 1.7). There are also a variety of more modern secular theories that can educate and assist Bible translators in their challenging task (see sec. 2.4.2). The most helpful of the latter retain a major interest in the actual text (form and function) and situational context of the original message. Certain underlying literary/theological presuppositions determine the philosophy and practice of each of these methods, however, and some of them are definitely more applicable and teachable than others as far as Bible translation is concerned, the approach of functional equivalence in particular.

In systems where the surface-text forms of the Scriptures (or any piece of literature) are largely irrelevant (as in Structuralism), or are regarded as conveying a fluid, indistinct, or subjective meaning (as in Postmodernism), some serious hermeneutical problems are bound to arise. For example, if the original meaning is more or less indeterminate or subjectively appropriated, why worry so much about its accurate representation in a translation? A deliberate divorce of the contemporary reader/hearer from other elements of the communication event (most notably, the sociocultural and historical setting of the SL documents) characterizes certain of these methods. This is true also where the focus is on "art for art's sake" (see Powell 1990:91–98). Related to this is the modern hermeneutical approach, such as radical "reader-response" criticism, that overly favors the (projected) setting of the today's receptors and their "reading" (i.e., interpretation or, more accurately, intuitive reflection). But any such communicatively unnatural separation ultimately denies or disregards the need for fidelity in translation, overlooking any responsibility to convey the essence of the (implied) author's intended meaning.[294]

Another difficulty in some approaches is the adoption of an outmoded source-critical methodology (à la J-E-P-D) that seeks to identify the different constituent "documents," "fragments," or "interpolations" within a given biblical book. Such an effort, no matter how considerable, always turns out to be inconclusive and frequently contested as well. It is also quite unnecessary as far as Bible translation is concerned, which is an exercise aimed at communicating the final, "received" form of the text. A more serious concern is a perspective that views the Scriptures as "ordinary" literature—the creative, fictive product of the human imagination, hence subject to all the defects and deficiencies of any secular work of art, albeit ostensibly religious or somehow spiritual in nature.

Therefore, the translation teacher needs to review with the trainees some of the potential *dangers* of an improper application of a secular literary approach to the analysis of the Scriptures. They must be advised of these problems and learn to recognize them by means of relevant comparative examples involving different analytical techniques. Responsible Bible translators should be trained to adopt a flexible context-centered, two-horizon (SL/TL), literary-critical perspective on the biblical text. Such a complex, but integrated and holistic viewpoint is required in order to better understand the original documents, though there will always be a certain degree of approximation and probability involved in this endeavor. Any text that is more fully comprehended in terms of how its various stylistic forms have been utilized to convey various types of meaning will, all other things being equal, be more completely and correctly translated—content-for-content, function-for-function, genre-for-genre—into a contemporary target language.

The four characteristics that serve to define a literary approach to textual analysis (tectonicity, artistry, iconicity, and rhetoricity) may be useful also in assessing the value of the different theoretical perspectives in relation to translator training. The observations that follow regarding these four characteristics apply first of all to a study of the SL text; however, they should be extended also to a thorough examination of TL literature and orature in the effort to discover an inventory of potential form-functional matches for maximum or limited use (depending on the *Skopos*) in equivalence-oriented Scripture translation.

- **The tectonic dimension.** Bible translators normally treat each of the canonical books as a unity and analyze them accordingly. That is,

---

[294]For a thorough systematic defense of a meaning-based approach to text analysis, see Callow 1998, especially Part 1.

they consider every text to be a verbal construct consisting of a hierarchical organization of interrelated parts that make up a complete, coherent whole. Their focus is therefore on the finished, authorized and established literary product, not its compositional or editorial history, except in cases where the latter concerns have definite, demonstrable exegetical implications. It is important to teach inexperienced translators how (and when) to adopt a wider (macrostructural) discourse perspective as well as a narrower (microstructural) sentence point of view, that is, a top down as well as a bottom up approach, interpreting the included parts in view of and on the basis of the whole and vice versa. A holistic, genre-based, multifaceted method of exegesis and translation helps translators not only to better comprehend the overall message of a particular biblical text or pericope, but it also encourages them to pay closer attention to its constituent literary forms. In other words, they must learn to analyze the various stylistic devices typically found in a particular genre both for their artistic and/or rhetorical value and also as clues to areas of special or concentrated, explicit or implicit communicative significance, whether in terms of thematic content, connotative import, or pragmatic intent.

- *The artistic dimension.* Translators should be able to identify and perhaps also describe the diverse artistic devices within a given work or pericope in terms of form and function. When they are able to do this, they may then proceed to point out how such features contribute both singly and collectively to the SL text's impact and appeal, hence also to its evocative effect and ultimate memorability. If the team members do not have enough educational background, experience, or expertise to analyze the original documents on their own, they should at least be capable of accessing and assessing commentaries and translation guides that provide this information. During the step of re-creation, translators, whether as an individual specialist assignment or as a team effort, seek to reproduce in the TL draft the same textual effects (i.e., sense and significance, including feeling, force, and beauty) that are manifested in the original text. The aim is to represent all the crucial message-bearing, structure-marking elements, both major and minor, that have been identified there. Naturally, this effort can be successful only if they also devote themselves to a corresponding study and documentation of the tectonic and artistic resources of the TL.

- **The iconic dimension.** Translators ought to have a reasonable command of the conventionalized, intertextually resonant aspects of the archetypal content of the Scriptures. As noted in chapter 5, these Near Eastern archetypes include the various symbols, character types, type scenes, and culture nodes that tend to recur in different books of the Bible as well as in portions of the same text. The question to ask is how this corpus of significant imagery compares in referential constitution and connotative evocation with the nearest equivalents available in the TL literature (or orature) and sociocultural setting. Where there are important differences or even contradictions, the team must be trained to recognize, evaluate, and resolve them in a manner that best suits the competency, needs, and desires of their primary target group. This may be done either in the text (e.g., by carefully controlling vital areas and aspects of lexical-semantic correspondence) or through some supplementary, extratextual means (e.g., descriptive or explanatory footnotes and glossary entries).
- **The rhetorical dimension.** Finally, translators require considerable training in the functional, pragmatic area of literary communication. This includes a mastery of the principles and techniques of various kinds of deductive and inductive argumentation (in biblical texts intended for encouragement, exhortation, dissuasion, reproof, etc.). They need to be able to detect the different rhetorical features of the Scriptures and how these all interact to make a given biblical pericope more persuasive, compelling, authoritative, credible, and relevant in relation to its major communicative intentions as well as less prominent illocutionary aims. They must then endeavor to create in their TL text the same overall power and pointedness, along with the more specific but equally important message functions, using the appropriate literary devices and larger textual strategies. This would include the effort to preserve communicative equivalence on the level of the major speech acts of a given document—how to analyze this dimension of meaning in relation to the biblical text and how to ascertain whether or not this has been maintained in the translation.

Obviously, what is not discerned or correctly analyzed in the original document—with regard to genre, structure, artistry, archetypes, emotion, or rhetoric—cannot be duplicated in the translation. It is imperative, therefore, that translators be provided with all the training necessary to enable them to carry out, with both confidence and effectiveness, the most important and productive aspects of the impossible communication task that they have been entrusted with by fellow members of the TL community.

9.2.3 An L-R perspective in relation to functional-equivalence translation

The theory, practice, and teaching of functional-equivalence Bible translation may be refined and productively developed in an important new direction by means of a contextually framed, literary-rhetorical approach to the SL text and its re-presentation in another language-culture. It is a major premise of this book that an artistically fashioned source document calls for a more daring method of rendering it in another language, at least as one principal option.[295] The aim of a more mediated, domesticated rendering of this kind would be to preserve a greater measure of the overall communicative value, including the artistic attractiveness and theological impact, of the biblical text. This contrasts with a more conservative (hence easier to implement), foreignizing approach that expects the target audience themselves to carry out both a semantic analysis and a functional analysis on the spot and on their own as they read or hear the translated Scriptures.[296]

Another way of saying this is that L-R translators carry out more textual intervention in the interest of preserving communicative efficiency and

---

[295]In this connection E. A. Nida (2000:165) observes: "[D]espite the worshipful attitude that many people have toward the Greek of the New Testament, a translator should not hesitate to improve the stylistic awkwardness of the original—something that almost all good translators normally do." Some insights from the perspective of a renowned secular translator may also be instructive in this regard: "[Ezra Pound] seems instinctively to have understood...that the translation of poetry is an art, but at its best only a partial and inevitably a somewhat derivative art. He saw that we not only do not but cannot translate *words*, if living poetry is the desired result....In linguistic terms Pound intuited that the essence of the translation process was not a single-stage transposition, original into translation, with the focus on either words or on information and ideas, but rather a complex, organic, and multistage procedure in which, first, the original is disassembled and then, often more or less laboriously, reassembled—but reassembled within the constraints of the host language and the conventions of its poetic culture" (Preminger and Brogan 1993:1304).

[296]On the debate over L. Venuti's distinction between "foreignizing" versus "domesticating" methods of translation, D. Robinson (1997, part 3, chaps. 8–11) has some incisive critical observations, as does Katan (1999:156, 164). In the application of an L-R translation strategy, the content of the original message may still turn out to be quite "foreign" in relation to the norms and traditions of the target culture, but every effort would be made to state this in the most "domesticated," familiar way possible in terms of text structure and style, that is, based on TL literary conventions and popular norms.

effectiveness.[297] When applying a dynamic literary-rhetorical translational strategy, there is more occasion for "functional compensation,"
even with respect to the text (genre) as a whole, as translators seek to
maintain the SL text's overall level of impact and appeal in the TL text. At
all times the emphasis is on using the contextually most natural stylistic
forms of the TL in order to convey the principal semantic and pragmatic
(including rhetorical) intentions of the SL document or pericope, whether
on a global, text-inclusive basis or in accordance with some specific selective procedure (utilizing only an approved set of TL literary features).

In section 2.7 I proposed an expanded definition of translation within a
functionalist framework that lends itself well to a literary-rhetorical version. There are a number of salient features of this model that translators
need to be trained to recognize and apply. In the first place, a literary-
critical approach to the Scriptures serves to more fully reveal the great
semiotic and iconic density of the original discourse. Biblical texts generally tend to be "thick" both conceptually (in terms of religious and other
socially specific references) and also formally (in terms of the variety of
stylistic devices and techniques that are regularly used in both Hebrew
and Greek to convey the intended message). A functionally focused methodology, guided by the more general principle of interpersonal relevance,
is therefore very helpful in presenting the essentials of a meaning-
centered translation procedure. It is a strategy that aims to achieve an acceptable degree of correspondence, or significant similarity, with respect
to communicative value between the two literary texts concerned.[298] This

---

[297]See Hatim and Mason 1997:12, 30, 114–116, 123, 125, 147, 151–153, 161–162, 181,
217; also Hatim and Mason 1990:188, 127, 129, 223ff., 236. In E. A. Gutt's terms these
equate to less "cost" for greater "gain" in terms of cognitive (add emotive and volitive)
"contextual effects." Kathleen Callow terms these the "three imports" of verbal message
transmission: informational, volitional, and expressive (1998:100–123). She differentiates
between expressive import, which "communicates feelings and attitudes," and emotion,
which is "a heightening of feeling" that can accompany any kind of utterance, even information or a command (ibid.:124–125). I probably should have observed this distinction
more strictly in my own various analyses and discussion.

[298]It should be stressed once again that *complete* meaning equivalence (semantic, pragmatic, connotative, text-based, etc.) is impossible in any translation. Only partial equivalence, in varying degrees of cognitive and emotive parity, is possible. This is especially true
in the case of Bible translation due to the great disparity between the two settings involved.
The best that translators can do is to approximate to a greater or lesser extent depending on
a complex of relevant factors as many aspects of the original message significance as possible, in accordance with the established *Skopos* for the particular project concerned. I have
certainly been guilty in earlier writings of offering an overly optimistic assessment of what
it is possible to do right in the translated text itself. The addition of supplementary helps,
such as footnotes, illustrations, and glossary can assist in this manifold communication
challenge, as can the teaching ministry of local churches, but all these efforts will inevitably
fall short of conveying the fully intended meaning and associative significance of the original text.

involves the evaluating and monitoring of semantic-pragmatic "function" with respect to an established priority rating during the overall meaning-exchange process. At the same time, the translation team must always be sensitive to what is both appropriate and acceptable to the intended audience.

The basic set of functions to be taught to the translators include the following (the relative order of importance here being variable, of course, in relation to the nature of the specific biblical passage in view):

- *informative*—with a focus upon the accurate, clear transmission of semantic content
- *imperative*—with a focus on behavioral change, reinforcement, or modification
- *expressive*—with a focus on conveying personal feelings, values, and attitudes
- *textual*—with a focus on reproducing appropriate macro- and microstructures in accordance with the type of discourse (genre) and sociocultural setting involved
- *artistic*—with a focus upon utilizing the various stylistic (linguistic/literary) devices in order to embellish specific areas and points of the discourse as well as more generally to create message impact and appeal (in service of one or more of the other communicative functions)
- *interactive*—with a focus on maintaining a sociolinguistically "natural" channel of communication in terms of formality, politeness, dialect, conventions of opening and closing, etc.
- *ritual*—with a focus on traditional, formulaic, liturgical language that evokes a great deal of connotative meaning deriving from the use of well-known and greatly loved texts in familiar sociocultural and religious contexts

As the course of training progresses, these broad functional motivations and implications may be refined in terms of a rhetorical perspective. A speech-act and/or argument-model approach may be introduced to enable the more precise identification of the pragmatic goals realized during the communication event, that is, the "illocutions" (intended) and "perlocutions" (achieved). In fact, even further refinement or specification is needed so that the SL message can be seen as *framed* or *contextualized* in terms of its varied and variable situational setting—physical, interpersonal, and conceptual.

The functional "priority rating" that would act as a working plan to guide translators as they attempt to re-present (re-signify) the source text in their mother tongue is dependent upon a number of different contextual factors:

- the nature of the biblical text, that is, the *text type or genre* (e.g., where it is situated along the prose ⇔ poetry continuum)
- the *discourse* structure of the SL text (especially prominent patterns or arrangements of form and content)
- the *stylistic* dimension of the SL text (how diverse, concentrated, or extensive the L-R features are in their overall manifestation)
- the immediate *co-text* of the SL passage (its macro- and microstructure)
- *intratextuality* (appreciable linguistic and literary influence from within the same document)
- *intertextuality* (substantial influence from external texts, oral or written)
- the primary extralinguistic *setting* (historical, political, ecological, institutional, sociocultural)
- the intended *medium* (audio, print, visual, electronic, or a combination)
- the *Skopos* in relation to the nature of the translation desired (literal ⇔ free) as well as the manifest needs, abilities, desires, and experiences of the TL community
- the general level of *competence* and *experience* of the translation team and their support group (reviewers, etc.)

These ten variables (and no doubt others) then need to be factored into the development of a *functional profile* for the text under consideration. This would be explicitly written out as an assignment when translator trainees analyze a particular biblical text. It should influence the method of production as well as the intended linguistic shape of the translated text, not only with regard to referential content, but also in terms of the major noncognitive, connotative aspects of meaning, including all prominent implicatures, which also need to be conveyed. A psalm of praise, for example, would normally not manifest the same functional mix and measure as the didactic portion of a Pauline epistle, since the informative component would not be as prominent when rendering a lyric psalm. Thus a consideration of purpose alone, when assessing the desired degree of meaning correspondence, is insufficient. The complete communication setting for any text must also be fully analyzed, as a team exercise, in the effort to achieve *contextualized* functional equivalence—or perhaps, to state the aim more realistically, simply *"func-tional* adequacy" (Chesterman and Wagner 2002:21).

This is not a completely new theory; it is simply a more sharply focused, clearly delineated elaboration of the model that translation theorists have, in the main, been working with for the past decade or so. It is one that gives as much consideration to the situational setting of a translation as it does to the style of the TL text.

At this point I might reiterate the proposal in chapter 2 regarding setting the goals of Bible translation in accordance with a manifold, contextually framed, functional-equivalence, style-sensitive approach. In this light, *every* translation should be rendered in a literary-rhetorical manner to a lesser or greater extent in specific relevant respects, that is, from a partial, selective application to a full literary version.[299] If this is done even minimally, the TL text should manifest certain recognized artistic devices, whether in the area of phonology (e.g., balanced, rhythmic utterances), vocabulary (e.g., local figurative language), syntax (e.g., grammatical parallelism), or discourse (e.g., a vernacular poetic genre). Just how "partial" the application of L-R features will be depends on the skill of the translators and the desires of the target community, as expressed in their project *Skopos.*

Despite all the efforts applied to understanding and communicating the sense and significance of a particular text, there will always be a certain "gain" in meaning. This is due to the need to overspecify, underspecify, or recategorize information in the TL text, inevitably chunking the SL concepts down, up, and sideways. On the other hand (and perhaps more often), we also have a considerable amount of "loss," or leakage, of meaning in comparison with what is actually present in the original. Part of this is expected—there is bound to be unavoidable semantic and connotative loss. But in addition there is invariably also a reduction with respect to the literary and rhetorical dimensions of the original. All of these potential problem areas need to be worked through systematically and consistently in mutual consultation as the translation team learns how to recognize and deal with them as a group, capitalizing upon the particular analytical, compositional, and text-critical resources that each member brings to the joint task.

It is clear, then, that an L-R approach to translation requires that the translators first be *taught* a dynamic and interactive, communication-event method of translating. Then, when applying the approach, they must strive to analyze each biblical document in its specific situational

---

[299]There are thus only three basic types of translation: *null* literary (a "gross" literal version), a *full* literary (a complete genre) transformation, and *partial* literary application (manifesting at least some obvious artistic and rhetorical features in the TL text).

context within a general Ancient Near Eastern setting, which consists in turn of a distinctive set of enveloping frames, or communicative levels (e.g., textual, cognitive, medium-related, experiential, institutional, and sociocultural). The first objective here is to determine the essential *meaning package* (form + content + function, including any and all significant L-R features) of the message that the original author conveyed to his intended audience. Next, the translators attempt to anticipate the particular manner in which the Scripture message will be perceived and understood by *their* audience in their particular "conceptual environment," a cognitive contextual framework that will always be different, sometimes radically so, from that of the original biblical setting.

But how far does the team need to go in reconstructing this text in their language? For example, how much extratextual help (such as notes, illustrations, glossary, section headings, and cross-references) should they provide in order to supplement what cannot be conveyed in the text? How can they best compensate for contextual differences in the setting of message reception and for conceptual interference (e.g., if the audience is illiterate or uneducated) and for any possible noise in the environment of transmission? Answers to questions such as these depend on the project *Brief* and the target constituency that it was designed to serve. The team might want to set the more limited goal (*Skopos*) of rendering the text so that the consumer community would regard it as idiomatic only in certain prominent formal respects. This would be a "partial" L-R version. On the other hand, they might want to set the more challenging goal of rendering the text, or selected portions thereof, so that it is widely recognized and acknowledged as an acceptable, perhaps even excellent body of literature in the TL.[300] This would be a "full" L-R version.

What difference does it make, relatively speaking? Is it worthwhile to seek a greater degree of equivalence with respect to the situational as well as stylistic aspects of message transmission? The answer, no matter what type of version is being prepared, literal or literary, is yes. Translators need to be instructed how to pay greater attention to the contextual factors in translational communication. These factors are the *components, frames,* and *functions* that pertain to the complete event of interlingual text re-signification. There are, for example, mutually influential inner and outer levels of circumstantial framing that are operative during any act of communication as well as distinct, but overlapping contexts that influence, and sometimes impede, the producer- and also the consumer-supplied contributions to the interactive message transmission process,

---

[300]"A good poet is no more like himself in a dull [i.e., literal] translation, than his carcass would be to his living body" (Dryden, cited in Preminger and Brogan 1993:1304). The same applies to Bible translation.

including, for example, various "special interest" groups, government language and orthographic policy, local culture-awareness organizations, competing ecclesiastical constituencies, interethnic rivalries, and so forth. Such situational competition, incongruence, or even opposition must be counteracted, compromised, or compensated for in some way, whether textually or extratextually, and the techniques for doing this practiced on a regular basis by the translation team, with the guidance of local experts in the respective fields of controversy. In short, translator training must be extended to include the area of communication "diplomacy."

Finally, a training program should be geared to help translators realize that the difference between a formally correspondent version and a literary functionally equivalent (LiFE) version is not simply a matter of choosing just one set of principles and procedures or the other. They need to understand that there is a broad continuum (extended now by literary factors such as those mentioned above) between the poles of literal and idiomatic and that there are many possibilities of modification between them. If the emphasis is to be upon an artistic-rhetorical rendering, this would suggest a goal of what has been termed a stylistically enhanced "popular-language" version, that is, a contemporary rendering designed for a relatively homogeneous society without an extensive literary tradition using the discourse fashion of the younger generation (so Wonderly 1968:28–29). A translation of this kind in which the range is stylistically extended, in contrast to a more linguistically restricted common-language version, would appear to be more amenable to the inclusion of an artistic-rhetorical dimension, to a greater or lesser degree, if warranted by the overall situational setting.

9.3 The necessity of high-quality translator training

High-quality translator training is the *sine qua non* for the whole L-R translation enterprise. Its importance to the methodology being proposed in this book calls for a few further observations here.

It is clear that the effort to apply a literary-rhetorical, LiFE approach during the translation process requires staff of the highest caliber who are equal to the task, that is, competent and capable in terms of prior education, training, aptitude, experience, *and* desire. Indeed, only accomplished TL verbal *artists*, proven literary (oratorical) stylists, will do.[301]

---

[301]"If at all possible a stylist should be a professional writer. It is not even enough that he be an editor or a corrector of other people's writing. He should have creative writing abilities himself, for in the process of providing stylistic help for a translation he must do more than spot awkward sentences; he must be able to provide the creative assistance which is so

Their instructors, project coordinators, review specialists, and translation consultants must also be exceptionally competent in order to effectively teach such an intensive and TL-sensitive approach, especially if they are not very familiar with the vernacular. An artistic version simply requires the best, most highly qualified available personnel in every respect and with regard to all aspects of the work.

A translation team cannot be expected to carry out what it has not been adequately trained to do. This applies to a literary-oriented methodology in general, whether used in exegesis or translation. Translators must be fully prepared to examine the complete biblical text in an accurate and discerning manner. They must also be able to assess the significant forms that they find there with respect to their relative artistic quality and rhetorical impact. This would include evaluating the contribution that the respective features make to the overall meaning of a given passage or larger pericope.

The translators then need to study their own language and literature and/or orature applying the same procedures. They should be able to provide valid and reasoned TL alternatives for every stylistic option that is manifested in the biblical text. However, the intuition of a mother-tongue speaker is not enough to equip a person to identify and describe the crucial linguistic and stylistic features. The translators must therefore be carefully trained, largely through inductive and interactive didactic methods, before they can carry out such analysis and research, especially the manifold, multipurpose comparative studies noted in section 8.3.

The target audience too must be educated to a certain critical level of competence in order to appreciate the type of version being prepared for them. They also will need instruction in the use of the supplementary aids and the principles of Bible study so that they can grasp the intended message of any passage of Scripture in terms of its textual co-text and extratextual context.

---

essential" (Nida and Taber 1969:157). The problem is that "[t]he really first-rate stylist usually does not survive as a member of a committee, for his job is an aesthetic type of contribution, and aesthetics is something many theologically trained persons simply do not understand" (ibid.:158). The only possible solution (where it is possible) is to select a recognized, well-educated, and experienced stylist as an integral member of the translation team and also provide the other members with sufficient training in L-R principles and techniques to appreciate the stylist's work and evaluate his or her professional contribution with a sympathetic mind. The ultimate success of any genuinely literary-rhetorical version would certainly depend upon the quality and quantity of the stylist's contribution to each and every draft translation. Unfortunately, in the effort to produce common-, even popular-language translations, the option of literary excellence seems to have been largely forgotten. (See Nida and Taber 1969:157–162, 186, for a valuable treatment of style and the stylist; see also de Waard and Nida 1986:194, 204). In the case of any L-R, LiFE rendition, the contribution of an expert stylist will be indispensable.

An L-R version will certainly not be appropriate for every setting, even if the goal is only a limited application of artistic technique. In fact, it is probably safe to say that only a minority of projects in today's world are currently up to such a demanding task. In many, if not most instances this is not due to the translators' lack of abilities; rather, it is a matter of a suitable training program and sufficient resources for providing sustained guidance. But even if an L-R version is not the primary goal, all practical courses of instruction and the associated translation procedures should incorporate a greater literary-critical component than most do at the present time in order to serve those translators who can confront, albeit partially, this significant comparative dimension of discourse organization in the SL and TL texts.

It is important for teaching methods at any level of expertise to be carefully adapted to the preferences of the culture concerned. For many societies, for example, less formal inductive techniques coupled with more reality-based examples and practical on-the-job or apprenticeship training are much more effective than institutional programs and procedures.

Finally, it is only fair to suggest that seriously substandard teams—that is, in terms of education, experience, and expertise—should probably be advised not to undertake an L-R translation. A project that aims to produce a functionally equivalent literary version is much more demanding than any other type. It is potentially more controversial as well, given the relatively low level of understanding of most target constituencies with regard to the compositional quality of the Scriptures, let alone the practice of Bible translation.

9.4 Training for ongoing testing

It is one thing to train a competent corps of translation staff and produce an adequate draft of a LiFE version but quite another to ensure that it achieves the goals that were set for it within the communicative setting at hand. Even without the literary dimension it is hard to get translators to regularly review and test their work, revising it consistently and systematically in accordance with feedback from the community using it. How will it be when the L-R dimension is incorporated along with the complex interacting features of stylistic excellence and audience acceptability with respect to clarity, naturalness, and the text's perceived authenticity or authority as the Word of God? Continual assessment will be more important than ever, and special tests will have to be devised that can assess the nebulous psychological factors of rhetorical impact and aesthetic appeal in literature. Such factors must be carefully distinguished. They also need to be related to the fundamental issues that pertain to theological and other types of biblical content, which considerations also need to be made an integral part of any complete program for translator training.

Periodic text evaluation is a must. This is particularly true in the case of a literary-rhetorical version. A public qualitative assessment is an essential aspect of the entire production process at every stage along the way. The goal is to accurately determine what constitutes consumer preferences with regard to factors such as semantic *fidelity*, conceptual *clarity*, verbal *idiomaticity*, and formal *proximity*. (These criteria will be discussed further in chapter 10.) It is difficult to carry out such a program with respect to the more concrete aspects of message content, let alone one's affective reaction or connotative evocation in response to the text. To what extent, then, is it really possible to determine how effective the results of our research are when actually applied in Bible translation, especially with regard to literary features such as quality, idiomaticity, and rhetoricity? These are questions that require much more research and actual case studies in diverse languages and translation situations before confident answers and advice may be given.

My own limited experience in this area indicates that as far as south-central Africa is concerned the testing method that holds the most promise is a personal (face-to-face), interactive (group setting), and oral (dialogic) method. A community-centered exercise, coupled with a certain amount of audience instruction and training concerning the nature and purpose of a literary version, appears to work well. Such a program serves to increase the cognitive and emotive benefit for both the version's testers, including any new translator trainees, and those tested, the Scripture consumers themselves. All actively involved participants seem to derive a much greater appreciation for the great rhetorical power and depth of the artistic resources that convey the dynamic message of the Scriptures, as expressed now more vibrantly and vigorously—more "literarily"—in their mother tongue.

10

Assessing a Literary-Rhetorical Translation

The subject of translation testing and evaluation, as Hatim and Mason observe (1997:197), has not received a great deal of attention in field studies. The present chapter addresses this overlooked matter, taking a tentative first step in one possible direction of interest through a selective stylistic-comparative analysis and assessment of four different translations of Psalm 23 in Chichewa, a Bantu language of south-central Africa (also called Chinyanja). The four translations are the *Buku Lopatulika* (BL), which is an older and relatively literal version; the *Buku Loyera* (BY), a recent popular-language version (see Wendland 1998b); a specially composed poetic rendering (PR) in the modern *ndakatulo* genre; and finally a well-known hymn version (HV). The basis for a critical comparison of these significantly different versions is the original Hebrew Masoretic text of Psalm 23.

The particular objective of the assessment model that I have applied has been motivated by three areas of concern: *literary artistry, aurality,* and *acceptability.*

Literary artistry, which I view as distinct from but fully compatible with the notion of semantic fidelity, is my principal focus here (as it has been throughout this book), since it is so often neglected in the process of Bible translation. The basis for this chapter was a rather detailed comparative survey of the artistic domain of poetic composition in terms of the three discourse dimensions of linguistic form, denotative content, and pragmatic purpose as manifested by the salient similarities and differences among four Chichewa versions in comparison with the original Hebrew text.[302] However, only the most prominent aspects of this comparison will be presented. These mostly have to do with the *ndakatulo* version with respect to a simplified set of the five major communication functions of informative, expressive, directive, aesthetic, and relational (see sec. 10.8.2).

Aurality, which was the second area of concern in my research, is important because most receptors throughout history have accessed the biblical text via the spoken word. Moreover, significant portions of it were probably composed originally in oral form. Aurality is particularly important in south-central Africa where functional literacy for both men and women remains at considerably less than 50 percent. For their sake a translation of the Scriptures must be rendered in a form that facilitates aural reception, mental processing, in some cases memorization, and public elocution. Because reading aloud is quite different from silently reading a text,[303] the test for aurality included assessing two different printed formats (both with the same typeface) in order to identify some priorities in the combined visual-audible dimension. The predominantly oral-aural environment of the target audience meant that most of my comparative testing had to be conversational and interactional in nature. However, several auxiliary procedures were also carried out to obtain reactions to the printed samples as well as to a musical rendition of the psalm (which was presented first as a written text like the others). Most personal opinions were elicited orally and given orally; the only additional written responses received were requested from a class of seminary students.

Acceptability, the third area of investigation, is not measurable solely, or even primarily, by means of an analytical comparison of linguistic and literary features. Far more important is the subjective, informal response of the key receptors, those for whom the Bible translation is ultimately intended. Average, nonprofessional readers and hearers were enlisted to evaluate a well-known text of Scripture on the basis of a complex mixture of both verbal and nonverbal factors. These less tangible elements differ of course from one person to another depending on such things as dialect or register preference, medium of transmission, denominational influence, the perceived ability and credibility of the translation team, level of

---

[302]My earlier comparative analysis of Hebrew and Chichewa lyric poetry (Wendland 1993) is the basis of my estimation of the literary artistry of the four translations of Psalm 23 in Chichewa that I will describe in this chapter.

[303]Klem (1982, chap. 16) conducted similar research, though his was much more extensive and elaborate than mine. It involved a very different type of biblical discourse (Hebrews 1–6). He focused particularly on receptor comprehension and memorizability, that is, an oral-aural method in comparison with standard educational, literacy-type of learning (see also Sundersingh 1999:317–318).

literacy, biblical background knowledge, setting, prior experience with the Bible as a whole, and familiarity with the pericope in question. It is necessary to try to isolate, neutralize, or compensate for the influence of such factors on the testing process.

Accordingly, I tried to determine the relative extent (quantitatively) and degree (qualitatively) of the acceptability of the *ndakatulo* lyric version in particular. This was done in relation to the three other versions as a comparative control and with regard to the following seven important text qualities: *intelligibility* (clarity of content in relation to the correctness with which one hears or reads the text), *readability* (legibility of the print and format), *sonority* (aural aesthetics, including the musical setting of one version), *idiomaticity* (stylistic naturalness and colloquial appeal), *rhetoricity* (dynamic message impact), *authenticity* (as the written Word of God), and *memorability* (of both form and content). These are admittedly overlapping and interdependent variables, and it is not very easy for unsophisticated respondents to distinguish them, especially where several different texts are being evaluated. Nevertheless, during the course of my investigation I attempted to establish at least a rough priority rating for these seven factors, with reference to being "*more* acceptable" or "*less* acceptable" to a given individual, audience, or the entire receptor group.

In less literate face-to-face societies research and assessment are primarily conducted by means of personal dialogue. But in the Chichewa experiment the preference for communal discussion had to be restricted at first to preliminary matters of explanation so as to avoid homogenizing or popularizing the test results. A group session was occasionally arranged then to see if it would result in any sort of consensus in terms of the respondents' aesthetic appraisal of the several styles of translation.

Due to the public and dialogic nature of the testing process my operating range as a researcher was considerably limited. I therefore made it a priority to first test, then train a number of student assistants from the theological seminary where I teach in how to carry out a basic set of objective and subjective investigative procedures and write up the results. This helped expand my database considerably. It also introduced a greater measure of variability, but I hope that the wider survey, which enabled us to obtain a clearer impression of the diverse aspects of popular opinion, compensated for this.

The first and principal aim of this small, informal research project was to ascertain the degree to which a more verbally artistic translation of the Scriptures—specifically, a clearly *poetic* portion—was understandable and acceptable to, as well as aesthetically appreciated by, a listening audience.[304] Also, there was the question of how different the reactions to a poetic rendering would be versus reactions to a prose version of the same passage.

A secondary aim was to determine the influence of some informal audience education on the testing process. How would the results of the testing be affected when a certain amount of explanatory information was provided regarding the form and function of the original text and the nature of the Bible translation process? Would the effort to cognitively contextualize the overall procedure lead any of the initially negative receptors to change their opinion about the communicative or religious value of a more poetic, genre-for-genre rendering of certain key pericopes?

A third aim was to assess not only the medium, but the mode of text transmission. We did this by revealing to the testees which one of the texts being tested was a hymnic version. We wanted to know what difference it would make in the Chichewa-speaking audience's aesthetic evaluation of it if they realized that they could actually sing this particular version of Psalm 23.

Then, with all the testing done and the results tabulated, we asked ourselves what the main implications of this limited experiment were. How might this test's outcome possibly affect Bible translation and its wider assessment in Africa (and perhaps elsewhere) as we move forward in this media-rich new millennium?

In considering these issues I do not give much space to a discourse or stylistic analysis of the individual texts under study. It is the popular reaction to these different translations and how to appraise the differences in the reactions that will be the focus of my attention. Textual features will be surveyed only where needed to provide some essential background information. The emphasis in this chapter is upon practical, receptor-oriented assessment—translation in relation to a diverse target audience group as they respond in particular to an artistically fashioned poetic text.[305]

---

[304]For a cogent argument encouraging more extensive use of the Psalms in hymnic Christian worship, see Godfrey 1999, in which is included an excellent English poetic rendition of Psalm 22 set in an 8:6 common meter. A *ndakatulo*-style rendering of Psalm 22 in Chichewa may be found in Wendland 1993:187–194. A well-known, century-old lyric translation of Psalm 23, originally approved by the Church of Scotland for use in public worship, is available in a reprint edition (see Barbour 1995:50–51). It is reproduced here in section A.1.2 of appendix A.

[305]Source-oriented assessment involves a comparative evaluation that focuses upon the exegetical and stylistic relationships between a translation and the original text (see sec. 9.1.5).

Since what we learn from this exercise might prove helpful in conducting future, more comprehensive testing in the subjective area of literary poetics, the particular manner of research itself will also be evaluated. What are some of the main problems that we encounter when attempting to isolate and elicit personal verbal aesthetic reactions to religious discourse? Does this experiment point to any possible solutions to methodological difficulties? Let me add that my results, as presented here, are highly tentative and, though suggestive in several respects, need to be followed up and possibly corrected by more intensive and extensive research efforts.

10.1 Translating the literary artistry of the Scriptures

Before undertaking the assessment exercise several issues need to be reviewed. The first is whether or not the corpus of Jewish and Christian sacred writings known as the Bible does in fact contain recognizably excellent, artistic literature and, if so, can it be translated equally artistically.

10.1.1 Can artistry survive its transformation into another language?

Artistry is a factor that is frequently overlooked in assessing translations. According to Hatim and Mason (1997:197), it tends to be ignored when assessing translations of secular literature. This is certainly true of Bible translations, perhaps because the diverse texts of the Judeo-Christian Scriptures are mistakenly regarded as not being all that artistic, or literary, to begin with. Or perhaps artistry, like style, is seen as being so nebulous or subjective a feature (lying only in the eye of the beholder) that evaluation cannot be attempted. In any case, the primary emphasis in the practice of Bible translation, depending on the specific purpose of the project at hand, has usually been upon reproducing either a close formal equivalent of the biblical SL text or the closest natural equivalent of the conceptual content (see, e.g., Nida and Taber 1969:22–24). In recent years the more sophisticated criteria of functional equivalence and cognitive relevance have been promoted as ideal translation goals, but the means for determining whether or not they have been achieved have not been clearly delineated (see de Waard and Nida 1986:119, 204–206, and Gutt 1991:180–190).

While a positive view of the compositional artistry of Scripture is not difficult for many past and present Christian scholars to accept, it may raise a few questions for lay people, even those who read and study their

Bibles. They probably have never thought about the Scriptures in this literary way. Can the Word of God be described as being "of recognized artistic value," as the *American Heritage Dictionary* (1992) defines literature? This brings up several more questions of equal importance: What constitutes literary artistry? How may this be determined for a given work? Who does the evaluation?[306]

This matter was already addressed in sections 1.4 and 2.3. Here I will simply restate my conviction that the Bible—including Psalm 23, to which we will give special consideration—demonstrably does consist in large measure of compositions that are highly literary, verbally artistic and structurally well-formed, over and above their inspiring and authoritative religious content. Three primary features of the Scriptures would lead one to this conclusion:

- They manifest many different literary *macroforms* (i.e., types or genres), both major and minor, such as narratives, poems of all kinds, prophetic speeches, proverbs, parables, and letters.
- They manifest various literary *microfeatures*, or stylistic devices, such as figurative and imagistic language, rhythm and other sound plays, recursive verbal patterning, direct speech, rhetorical flourishes, syntactic innovation, lexical elaboration or condensation, and distinctive vocabulary.
- They manifest the principal *functions* of literature, including—in addition to the cognitively informative—the poetically oriented expressive, the affective, and the aesthetic varieties.[307]

In answer to the question of whether artistry can survive its transformation into another language there are two extremes: *No,* simply forget about the artistry of the original text and do what you can to transfer the basic sense or merely the literal linguistic forms. *Yes,* but you must completely redo the work, including "transculturizing" (hyperdomesticating)

---

[306]The literary school of biblical criticism has been gaining some ground in recent years. Witness the publication of an increasing number of books and articles that adopt a more or less literary perspective on the Old and/or New Testament (e.g., Alter and Kermode, eds. 1987; Ryken and Longman, eds.1993). Valiquette notes and supports this tendency in his insightful 1999 study.

[307]The aesthetic, or "poetic," function was highlighted by the well-known literary critic Roman Jakobson in his many scholarly writings (see Pomorska and Rudy, eds. 1985). Jakobson defined this as language that has a special emphasis on the linguistic *form* of the text. This occurs in particular where the two basic modes of compositional arrangement used in verbal behavior—namely, *selection* (paradigmatic) and *combination* (syntagmatic) —are utilized in maximal relation to one another in order to foreground certain key aspects of the message being communicated and also in order to heighten the text's interest value, emotive impact, and persuasive appeal.

its content if necessary. The first alternative clearly follows the path of least resistance, but it may in fact be the only thing that most translation teams are equipped or prepared to do anyway. The second is unacceptable in the case of the Scriptures, the Word of God, where the original message's intended *meaning* is central and must be preserved to the fullest extent possible.[308] This whole issue of message survival or message transformation is extremely complex and raises several important questions concerning the motives and methods of Bible translation.

10.1.2 Types of translation

In the specialized field of Scripture translation, a basic continuum of translation types may be identified (see sec. 2.8). TL versions may be characterized with respect to how the texts relate to the original SL document in terms of form, function, and content in accordance with recognized community-established norms and their desires as expressed in a formal project *Brief*.[309] Between the two poles—that is, between a fully literal and a fully literary version—we may posit a putative shift that moves from a desire to transmit the basic linguistic *forms* of the biblical text to the goal of conveying its presumed communicative *functions*.[310] The medial translations represent versions where the transmission of SL *content* to a contemporary TL audience has general priority.

---

[308]It is clear that my concept of meaning derives—in a somewhat more flexible, modified form—from a traditional conservative understanding of the term in Bible translation circles (e.g., see Beekman and Callow 1974:19–20, 24–25). A more recent pragmatic ("speech-act") hermeneutical development within this tradition is found in Vanhoozer 1998. For some interpreters, the term *content* has more specific reference to what is known as propositional/referential/ denotative/cognitive meaning. Other types or aspects of message meaning may then be distinguished, for instance, "connotative" (emotive/ attitudinal), "encyclopaedic" (associative), "pragmatic" (interpersonal, sociolinguistic, functional), "textual" (i.e., the meaning of a certain linguistic item within a given text—as modified by its distinct syntagmatic and paradigmatic co-text), "contextualized" (i.e., a text's semantic significance as perceived from the perspective of a particular worldview and value system, most notably that of the source culture as distinct from that of a given target culture), and perhaps also "figurative" meaning, which incorporates several of the preceding types.

[309]The importance of extratextual and textual *norms* in translation theory and practice is emphasized by the so-called Descriptive Translation Studies approach. "Professional norms," for example, govern or guide "the accepted methods and strategies of the translation process" (Chesterman, cited in Shuttleworth and Cowie 1997:132). There are three main types of professional norm: the "accountability" (ethical) norm, the "communication" (social) norm, and the "relation" (equivalence) norm (ibid.:132–133).

[310]This observation requires some qualification. While a literary version undoubtedly does put the priority upon communicative function (i.e., expressive, affective-aesthetic), it accomplishes its intended effect(s) with a special emphasis on one or more (usually more) features of discourse form in the TL—whether phonological (e.g., rhythm), syntactic (e.g., parallelism), lexical (e.g., repetition), and/or textual (e.g., versification).

Each kind of version has its primary purpose and therefore also its proponents and opponents, since each has advantages and disadvantages. A
literal version, for example, provides its receptors with a good idea of how
the original SL text was worded and arranged (not completely, of course,
but useful enough for concordance work and similar studies). However,
since these wordings and arrangements usually turn out to be unnatural
in the TL, a translation of this type is often very difficult for ordinary read-
ers/hearers to understand and appreciate. A *literary* rendition, on the
other hand, which is intended to have considerable impact and appeal in
the TL, is always in danger of achieving these receptor-oriented effects at
the expense of the conceptual content of the biblical text. Furthermore,
any meaning-oriented version, certainly one that aims to achieve an artistically appealing style, can accomplish its goals only through extensive
translational mediation, that is, through significantly altering or even
completely changing many of the forms found in the SL document in favor
of a more natural TL linguistic and textual environment.

The translations tested in the Chichewa experiment are located on this
continuum as follows: The old Chichewa Bible (1922), *Buku Lopatulika*
(BL), is a good example of a literal version[311]; the new 1998 Bible, *Buku
Loyera* (BY), is an interconfessional popular-language translation; the poetic *ndakatulo* rendering of Psalm 23 (PR) is a literary—perhaps better
termed oratorical—version (see sec. 8.2); and the Psalm 23 hymn version
(HV) falls somewhere between the last two.

10.1.3 How artistry is transformed during the translation process

It should be noted that there are *degrees* and *levels* involved in the artistic
"transformation" process as a text passes from one linguistic system and
literary tradition into another. Change in one respect or another is inevitable since two different genre frameworks, stylistic inventories, and their
associated sets of aesthetic norms or values are involved. While it is often
possible to retain the artistic forms on the higher strata of discourse organization (retaining the macrogenres of prose and poetry and some of their
principal subtypes such as narrative, exposition, exhortation or poems of
lament, praise, and reproof), the task of preservation becomes increasingly difficult as one moves down the ladder of linguistic/literary

---

[311]The *Buku Lopatulika* is a translation that was prepared by and intended for Protestant
Christians. The Roman Catholic version of 1966, *Malembo Oyera* 'Holy Letters/Writings',
which is also a relatively literal translation composed by an expatriate missionary, is a popular text among that religious constituency (see Wendland 1998b, chap. 1), but was not included in my research because of its literal nature, which was already represented in my
corpus by the BL version, and so as not to make the testing process any more confusing than
it already was with four different texts under consideration.

specificity. It is not only difficult but frequently impossible on account of syntactic, morphological, and phonological incompatibility as well as incongruity of word order, lexical choice, and paronomasia. Poetry is especially difficult due to the great extent that phonology is tied up with the stylistic effects being conveyed by a lyric or some other type of poetic text.

Despite the formal disparity on the microstructure, however, it *is* possible for skilled, creative translators to reproduce the essential content of the original text along with a great number of its functional effects. The literary devices and techniques used to achieve this in the TL may be different, sometimes radically so; nevertheless, the various communicative intentions of the SL text, the major ones at least, can for the most part be duplicated.

Of course, it will not help us to discuss this matter in the abstract. The issues involved must be demonstrated and illustrated with some actual text material as well as some real-life audience responses. That is one of the purposes of the receptor-oriented experiment involving Psalm 23 that is presented in this chapter. It will give readers an opportunity to make their own assessment some of the major communicative problems and possibilities, just as did the Chewa[312] respondents who participated in the initial testing of the various versions of Psalm 23 in our field survey.

10.2 The literary artistry of Psalm 23

We will begin with an overview of how the three characteristics[313] of biblical literature—many literary forms/genres, many artistic features, and many communicative functions—are realized in the Hebrew text of Psalm 23. (Psalm 23 in the Masoretic Text and RSV can be seen in sec. A.1.1.)

10.2.1 The macrostructure of Psalm 23

The Hebrew text of Psalm 23 revolves around a distinct medial utterance that acts as a prominent area of transition dividing the compositional structure (including the traditional title in line 1a) into two relatively

---

[312]Strictly, speaking, Chichewa is the name of the language; the Chewa are the people who speak it, though the latter is often used as a shorthand reference to the former.

[313]For a good discussion and illustration of the main communicative functions that occur in biblical literature, see de Waard and Nida 1986:25–32.

equal halves.[314] This structural turning point and topical hinge (symbol-ized as ‖) is found at the midpoint of the second line of the unusual tricolon that constitutes v. 4: ‘not = I-fear evil ‖ for = *you* [are] with-me’. There are twenty-nine Hebrew "words" (disregarding *maqqeph*/hyphens) before this break (‖) and another twenty-nine after it. Each half builds up to a final thematic and pragmatic climax in the semantically inverted ex-pressions "*you* are with *me*" in the middle (4b) and "*I* am with *you*" (lit., 'and I shall dwell in the house of the LORD forever') at the end (6b). The transitional introduction to the second major division is highlighted by the initial emphatic expression 'for *you*' (*kiy-'attaah*), which features a ma-jor shift from third to second person singular references to *YHWH*.[315] This divine covenantal name appears at the beginning (1b) and the end (6b) of the psalm (and only at these two points) to form a bounding inclusio. The borders of the poem are also less ostensibly marked by the reiterated *loo'* 'not' in 1b, 4b, and by the same Hebrew consonants (לֹא) in 6b, that is, in the word *le'oorekh* 'for the length/span of'.

10.2.2 The microstructure of Psalm 23

A variety of typical poetic devices supports both the binary compositional structure and the encouraging theological message of Psalm 23. The text's parallelism, though quite apparent, especially in the final bicolon, is not particularly strong,[316] but this relative looseness serves to create a pro-gressive movement towards the poem's minor and major peaks in v. 4b and v. 6b respectively, near the close of each structural half. A gradually increasing line length distinguishes this progression from beginning to end. It is further punctuated and provided with a rhythmic flow by the asyndeton (i.e., no *waws*) that is found from start to finish—all except for

---

[314]Biblical Hebrew poetry is distinguished by a basic compositional sequence consisting largely of conjoined, variously paralleled two-line units (i.e., utterances featuring phono-logical, lexical, and/or syntactic parallelism) that function within a larger structural and thematic whole. These measured poetic lines (3 [–/+] "word-units" each) are often re-ferred to as "cola" (one "line" being a "colon"). Occasionally, and then significantly, nonnormal three-line (tricolon) and single-line (monocolon) units appear.

[315]"One thing that is often crucial in the psalms is the moment when the speaker turns from the somewhat more distant, and formal, third-person way of speaking *about* God to the direct, second-person 'You' (or sometimes, the reverse)" (Kugel 1999:195).

[316]But there are some subtle connective and contrastive touches, for example, the posi-tioning of the four first person singular suffixed words in vv. 2–3 (i.e., in v. 2 line-final 'he-leads-*me*', in v. 3 line-initial 'soul-*my*', the latter item being a key noun instead of a usual verb form).

the climactic affirmation at the very end: "*And* [ascensive, or asseverative, meaning *Indeed*] I will dwell...."[317]
The rich symbolic imagery of Psalm 23 portrays two inviting, highly
evocative scenes—namely, a caring shepherd and his trusting sheep in
part one and a gracious banquet host and his specially welcomed guest in
part two. The allusive references to a 'valley of deep/deadly darkness' in
4a and to 'my enemies' in 5a introduce some contrastive tension on either
side of the break between husbandry and hospitality. Two verbless, possibly accentuated clauses highlight the corresponding apertures of each of
the psalm's halves: '*YHWH*—my shepherd!' in 1b and 'for you-with me' in
4b. Similarly, emphatic particles perform a demarcative function at their
respective areas of closure: 'even when' (*gam kiy*) in 4a and 'surely' ('*akh*)
in 6a. (Note also the semantically contrastive idiomatic expressions in
these two lines: 'valley of dark-death' and 'for the length of days'.) And finally, we hear (!) several instances of the phonological decoration that
characterizes classical Hebrew poetry, such as consonance in 5b (*sh/שׁ*,
perhaps suggesting abundance); alliteration of silent gutturals ('/א and
'/ע) coupled with reiterated *a* vowels (sound-stress) in the structurally
central transitional line of 4b; and some internal rhyme in v. 2
(...-*owth*...-*niy* ‖...-*owth*...-*niy*).

10.2.3 The multifunctionalism of Psalm 23

Psalm 23 is normally classified as a "prayer of trust." This description is
well supported by the poem's overall *form* (e.g., diverse but related imagery), *content* (a description of the relationship between a believer and his
God),[318] and *tone* (reverent and resolute reliance). As an instance of lyric
poetry, hence an example of the aesthetic function (see sec. 9.2.3), the
text does not evince a great emphasis on cognitive content in the informative sense, although there is certainly a prominent commemorative, almost celebrative, intention that is present in relation to the steadfast,
ever-faithful goodness and mercy of *YHWH* (6a).
   In contrast to the typical "lament psalm" (e.g., Psalm 25), there is little,
if any communication of a directive nature. Not a single imperative or

---

[317]Kugel, noting the touch of irony that precedes the psalm's final peak in 6a, renders it
as "My only pursuers will be goodness and kindness" (1999:194). Kugel also has some interesting comments on the possibility of the last line's being a reference to life after death. After a brief survey of several pertinent Old Testament passages, he concludes: "[T]he idea of
an afterlife, if it is not stated in Psalm 23, is certainly to be found elsewhere in the Hebrew
Bible. In many of the passages cited it is as plain as day" (ibid.:210).
[318]I use the masculine pronoun here and elsewhere since the original author of Psalm 23
was most likely male, and—quite arbitrarily now—so am I. This is a stylistic decision, and
no offense is intended thereby.

appeal appears in the entire piece, nor is there an explicit word of thanksgiving to God for blessings received. However, such direct, divinely oriented motivation is replaced by a pervasive manifestation of the expressive (emotive) function as the poet quietly pours out his heart to and about God in varied articulations of confident trust and assurance. Thus one may also posit here a strong realization of the so-called phatic (relational, interpersonal) function of communication since the psalmist clearly employs the words of his poem (along with its abundant artistry) to reinforce and reassure himself of the personal presence, provision, and protection that he enjoys from his divine shepherd (1b) and heavenly host (6b). In addition, as in much deeply religious discourse, Psalm 23 includes a prominent ritualistic element. That is, it is a text which, when recited in unison, surely stimulates a sense of communal solidarity in the realm of the sacred.

10.3 A stylistic comparison of Psalm 23 in Hebrew and in Chichewa

Comparative analysis, which is imperative in stylistic study (see sec. 8.3), will be illustrated in his section by applying it to a description of the Hebrew text of Psalm 23 (see sec. A.1.1) and its poetic rendering in Chichewa. Any assessment of artistry, like the more inclusive notion of literary style, inevitably involves some kind of objective comparison, for artistry is a highly relative quality. That is, the TL text may be *more* artistic, or *less* artistic, or not really noteworthy either way. But the question arises, Which text or corpus is compared with which? And what are the criteria of evaluation that apply in this exercise? In fact, a stylistic norm must be established for each of the two languages and traditions of verbal art being analyzed. In our exercise the two are Biblical Hebrew and contemporary Chichewa, an important Bantu language and lingua franca of southeastern Africa.

Since an extensive comparative examination is beyond the scope of this study, I will, when necessary, simply refer to previously published research on the subject (e.g., Wendland 1993, chaps. 2–3). Therefore, our focus here will be largely on the Hebrew text of Psalm 23 (MT) and its Chichewa poetic rendering (PR). Three other versions will be referred to occasionally: *Buku Lopatulika* (BL), *Buku Loyera* (BY), and the hymn version (HV), which can be seen in secs. A.1.4, A.1.5, and A.1.7.

In my 1993 study, I compared Hebrew psalmic poetry with the Chichewa lyric genre of *ndakatulo* verse in terms of ten major stylistic features: balanced rhythmic lineation, vivid imagery (including ideophones), phonesthetic appeal (including paronomasia), syntactic transposition (front- or backshift), referential (including deictic) specification, formal and semantic condensation (e.g., ellipsis) or expansion (e.g., reiteration), lexical (including affixal) intensification, dialogic dramatization (incidence of direct speech), and discourse structuration (text patterning). Each of these generic qualities was found in both Hebrew poetry and the *ndakatulo* genre , but the various stylistic forms utilized to realize them were naturally quite different. I carried out a separate comparative analysis (1993, chap. 4) with respect to the functional properties of each genre. These too, while more divergent (*ndakatulo* poems are mainly secular in character), were found to be sufficiently close to warrant further exploration of the possibilities of using Chichewa lyric verse to translate the Psalter.

The following example is the product of a TL literary-rhetorical analysis of the sort proposed in sections 8.1.1–8.1.7, but with the focus on step 6, "creation." It is a re-creative, L-R composed translation of Psalm 23 in the genre form of a Chichewa *ndakatulo* lyric poem.[319] After presenting the text of this particular rendering and its back-translation into English, I will give a few evaluative comments that pertain to its main stylistic differences from the original Hebrew text. This would constitute the first phase of the process of check-examination (sec. 8.1.7), which needs to be followed up then by an extensive assessment prepared on the basis of various audience responses.

Wanga Mbusa ngwokoma mtima.
   Herdsman of mine he's so good-hearted.
Chauta ndi dzina lake lochukadi.
   Chauta is that most famous name of his.
Mwa iye, ine kusowa kanthu ayi.
   In him, as for me—I lack nothing, not at all.
Gonee! pa zobiriwira andigonetsa.
   DOWN! on fresh greens he makes me lie down.

Malo opumulirako n'kumadzi odikha,
   [My] resting place is at quiet waters,
Moyo ine amanditsitsimutsa komweko.
   My life he always revives it right there.
M'njira zolungama amanditsogoleramo,
   Along straight paths he leads me in them,
Malinga n'dzina lake lomveka—Chauta!
   According to his well-known name—Chauta!

---

[319]For more information about the *ndakatulo* poetic style and an application of it (to John 17:1–9), see Wendland 1994:29–30, 39–41. Two other helpful articles are Schrag 1992 and Neeley 1996.

M'chigwa cha mdima bii! n'kayendamo,
   If in a deep dark valley BLACK! I happen to walk,
Mantha onse balala! poti Chauta alipodi.
   All [my] fear GONE! since Chauta is right there.
Inu Abusa, muli pafupi n'zida zotetezera,
   O Herdsman, you're close by with weapons for defense,
Ine mtima pansi phee! nthawi zonsezo.
   As for my heart, it's completely QUIET! at all times.

Kunena chakudya, ha! ndine mwana-alirenji,
   Talk about food, ha! I'm a what-can-the-child-cry-for
Mwandikonzera phwando, adani angoti tong'oo!
   You've prepared me a feast, my enemies can just STARE!
Chiko changa cha madalitso chiri nde-nde-nde!
   My cup of blessings is full-up BRIM-BRIM-BRIMMING!
Kwanu inu mwandilandiradi ndi manja awiri
   At your home you've welcomed me with two hands.

Indetu, zokoma za chikondi chanu chosasinthika,
   Yes indeed, the good things from your unchangeable love,
Zimandilondoladi m'moyo wonse wa pansi pano.
   They really follow after me [my] whole life down here.
M'nyumba yanu yoyera, inu Chauta, sindichokamo,
   From inside your holy house, Chauta, I don't leave it,
Nchito yanga n'kukutumikirani mpaka muyayaya!
   My work is to serve you right up until FOREVER-EVER!

The principal formal text variations between the preceding Chichewa
PR version and the original Hebrew text and the communicative/func-
tional implications of these may be summarized as follows:

- In Hebrew the number of lines (cola) varies, namely, at the midpoint in v. 4, where a tricolon appears in place of the usual bicolon,
  whereas in the Chichewa text the number of lines remains constant,
  that is, four lines in each stanza. The Hebrew lines (line 1 includes
  the psalm title) differ greatly from one another in length (based on
  word counts), whereas in the Chichewa version their length is relatively constant (based on the number of syllables). However, the
  average line length is noticeably greater in the Chichewa poem's
  second half, as is the case in the Hebrew original.
- The Chichewa text has only five stanzas whereas the Hebrew has
  six "verses." In the vernacular version the basic content is relo-
  cated somewhat, but it is essentially reproduced. The climax at the
  conclusion is highlighted by means of a redundant manner of expression, including several idioms (e.g., 'My work is to...', meaning

'I am constantly engaged in...') and a poem-final ideophone, *muyayaya*!

*   In the Chichewa text there is no pronominal shift back to a third person reference to Yahweh at the end (in v. 6; cf. v. 3); it is replaced by the direct vocative expression. The initial shift to a second person pronominal reference in the Hebrew of v. 4b, which signals the midpoint of the psalm (with twenty-nine words on each side of the divide, just before כי־אתה 'for-you'), is marked at the following line ('O Herdsman, you...'). However, the break itself is just as pronounced in Chichewa as in the Hebrew since the vocative is immediately preceded by a reference to God in the third person (*Chauta*). The middle of the *ndakatulo* version (i.e., ten lines preceding and ten following *Inu Abusa*) is a transition point, emphasized on either side by ideophones (*bii! balala!—phee!*) and sound similarity (*poti...alipodi—n'zida zotetezera*).

*   The Hebrew psalm's middle line (i.e., 'For = *you* [are] with-me; your-rod and-your-staff *they* they-comfort-me') is distinguished by two emphatic pronominal forms that occur nowhere else in the Hebrew text ('you', 'they'). This midpoint is preceded by four lines (bicola) of six words each, and it is followed by four lines (cola) of four to six words each. In the Chichewa the midline is not really highlighted as such. However, the forces of danger on either side of the break are foregrounded by ideophones (e.g., 'If in a deep dark valley BLACK! [*bii!*] ‖ my enemies can just *stare!* [*tong'oo*]').

*   In the Chichewa text additional emphasis is placed on the name *Chauta* 'Lord' since it is accorded an additional poetic line (2) at the beginning and repeated via a vocative in line 11 at the onset of the poem's second half. This results, however, in the loss of the original inclusio that is formed by the psalm's initial and final mention of *YHWH* (vv. 1b, 6b).

*   In the Chichewa text the brisk, progressive style of the Hebrew suggested by the asyndetic sequence of cola is reproduced except for the final, climactic *waw* in 6b. The subtle focusing force of *waw* is duplicated in the Chichewa by a repetitive line.

*   The juncture between the two basic image sets of this psalm is marked by the shift from rural to urban imagery (i.e., shepherd/sheep vs. house/banquet). The shift is indicated rather more forcefully in the Chichewa version at the onset of stanza 3 by means of a transitional expression, 'Talk about food', which is a fronted, topicalized phrase (*casus pendens*).

- The use of Chichewa ideophones (e.g., *gonee!* = lying down/sleep-ing, peacefully, at ease) to complement the psalm's picturesque language makes for a more direct, dynamic, emotive, and vividly imagistic presentation in the TL. This is strongly characteristic of the *ndakatulo* genre.
- Certain important implications of the Hebrew are made explicit in the Chichewa version: God's good-heartedness (stanza 1); that the psalmist lacks nothing (stanza 4); that he serves the Lord in his 'holy house' (stanza 5). On the other hand, there are several appar-ent semantic reductions in specificity, such as the Chichewa 'weap-ons for defense' in place of the Hebrew 'rod and staff' and no explicit mention of 'evil' in stanza 3, though evil is certainly im-plied.
- Several culturally motivated contextualizations are introduced in the Chichewa rendition, for example, 'herdsman' for the Hebrew 'shepherd'; 'Chauta' (the High-Creator God of the Chewa people) for *YHWH*; 'what can the child cry for' as part of the festive banquet imagery; 'welcome with two hands' for anointing the head with oil; and the graphic images implied in ideophones such as *balala!*, meaning completely scattered in all directions (in stanza 3) and *tong'oo!*, meaning to stare or glare fixedly with eyes protruding (in stanza 4).

What then is the effect of these differences in terms of comparative functional equivalence? Is it possible to assess the relative degrees of mes-sage correspondence where two diverse literary-artistic compositions, traditions, and sets of aesthetic values are concerned? This is probably im-possible on the microlevel of discourse organization, that is, comparing a Hebrew device to a TL equivalent used to render it. However, in terms of the respective texts as functional, semiotic-pragmatic wholes, some sort of an evaluation should be possible. In fact, such a comparison *must* be made as part of the overall translation process (see sec. 8.3). Thus, for ex-ample, does the personal expression and attitude of confident trust that is so much a part of Psalm 23 in its original form come through sufficiently in the re-created version, or does something seem to be missing? Worse, does the vernacular version convey quite different emotions or connota-tions? This may turn out to be a problem in the case of the *ndakatulo* text, which due to its verbal vigor, graphic imagery, and rhetorical pointing might be construed as evoking a more aggressive emotive and attitudinal stance, even a more defiant sort of faith, than the original expresses.

It must be noted that lyric poetry of the *ndakatulo* genre is by its very nature highly expressive Chichewa discourse. Consequently it is well suited to the transmission of deep spiritual feelings and indeed great literary beauty as well. Its heightened verbal rhetoric is regarded as typical of the genre as a whole and hence not really overdone for evocative, hortatory religious purposes—at least not with respect to individual stylistic devices. Perhaps a distinction in the setting of use may need to be made. The *ndakatulo* version may not be entirely appropriate for recitation in formal public worship services but would be very effective anywhere else, especially in a choir's musical rendition or as part of a drama production. In situations like this, where personal preference—what one has become used to—is so important, only some serious text-testing among various audiences will tell the full story.

10.4 The importance of aurality

Before we begin a consideration of the method and results of poetic text assessment it will be helpful to review what was said earlier about the interrelated notions of orality and aurality (secs. 1.2 and 8.2). Both orality and aurality figure prominently in the SL setting. Recent studies (Niditch 1996, chaps. 1 and 8; Davis 1999, chap. 1; Sundersingh 1999, chap. 6) tend to confirm the hypothesis that most, if not all, of the original Hebrew and Greek Scriptures were either initially authored in oral form or were written down with subsequent oral articulation and aural apprehension in mind.[320]

Orality and aurality are important in the many preliterate, postliterate, or partially literate societies of the world.[321] In fact, most people of today's world *hear* the biblical text during message transmission rather than read it (de Waard and Nida 1986:199). A translation for them must therefore be rendered in such a way that oral elocution and aural comprehension are

---

[320]See my analysis of these aspects of a biblical text's "rhythmic envelope" in relation to the oral-elocutionary structure of John 17:1–9 (Wendland 1994, esp. pp. 20–21), a study of the Greek text and two Bantu language translations, Chichewa and Chitonga. One must take note of such features in order to produce a valid structural or stylistic analysis. It is equally important to ensure that the aural indicators of the SL text are built into a translation to the degree possible.

[321]Sundersingh seems to overlook the great phonological potential of poetry in presenting Scripture texts when he says, "An audio medium lends itself to narrative genre much more effectively than other forms of discourse....Audio is good at dialogue and weak at linear monologue" (1999:100). A dramatically "prayed" or "sung" psalm can be just as compellingly presented by an audio medium, including radio.

facilitated.[322] Depending on the genre, this would call for certain text-adaptive measures. Overall syntactic length and complexity must be reduced. A greater measure of textual explicitness may be called for in terms of both content (e.g., by providing the classification of certain proper nouns and technical terms) and form (e.g., by providing transitional expressions). A more colloquial style of diction may be needed and more redundancy built into the message (e.g., through repetition, exact and synonymous). Prominent audio factors such as rhythm, periodic pause points, and general all-around euphony should be included.[323]

In some cases, it is easier and more natural for a drafter of the text, a poetic passage in particular, to compose it in oral form, whence it is recorded, transcribed, and revised according to the meaning of the original SL document and the conventions of writing in the TL. Most *ndakatulo* poems, for example, if not originating in oral tradition, are oral-aurally created. That is, the author utters or sings the text aloud during the process of composing it. Perhaps this manner of composition needs to be tried out more widely in Bible translation, especially where poetry is involved.

In such cases it is essential to test the aural quality of a translation as it is actually heard aloud. If people are asked just to read the text silently and respond to it in writing, the test results will be skewed and inaccurate. Reading and writing are for many people in the world today an unavailable, unnatural, or infrequently used mode of communication. Thus in the experiment described in this chapter the primary *medium* of message transmission, namely, the oral-aural channel, affected my choice for both the *object* of testing (several psalm texts heard while being read aloud)

---

[322]Translations that are more readable-hearable are becoming increasingly important in many (post)literate Western societies, at least in certain settings. The preface to the 1995 CEV brings this out: "The *Contemporary English Version* has been described as a 'user-friendly' and a 'mission-driven' translation that can be *read aloud* without stumbling, *heard* without misunderstanding, and *listened to* with enjoyment and appreciation, because the language is contemporary and the style is lucid and lyrical." A contemporary translator, Eugene H. Peterson, has this to say (1994:6): "I started paraphrasing the Psalms into the rhythms and idiom of [spoken] contemporary English. I wanted to provide...access to the immense range and the terrific energies of prayer in the kind of language that is most immediate to them, which also happens to be the language in which these psalm prayers were first expressed and written by David and his successors." (See Peterson's paraphrase of Psalm 23 in sec. A.1.3 and judge how successful it is in terms of sound and how effective in its attempt at sociocultural contextualization.)

[323]TL text-adaptation during translation is not an arbitrary or purely intuitive procedure, however. It must always be based upon a thorough analysis of what might be termed the implied "audio profile" of the original SL text. As Kenneth Thomas (1990:2) points out, "A study of the oral features in the receptor language must be matched with an examination of features in the biblical text which indicate various aspects of meaning. This then leads to a consideration of how those features in the biblical texts can be translated for oral renditions."

and also the *manner* of testing (a personal, dialogic, question-and-answer, verbal-nonverbal interactive method).

10.5 Measuring acceptability

Before undertaking an assessment of a Scripture translation, one must be clear about the notion of acceptability since it governs both the formulation of the test questions and the evaluation of the answers. The very term *acceptability*, though it allows for a range of possibility, may seem to imply only a minimum level of quality. "Acceptable" is not usually thought of as a high standard compared to "good," "superior," "excellent," or "outstanding." In fact, a rating of "acceptable" may seem uncomfortably close to "(barely) tolerable," nothing to get very enthusiastic about. Therefore, during the questioning of the respondents I endeavored to go beyond a determination of mere acceptability to an expression of higher levels of literary appreciation, where warranted. But this could not be done using precise critical terms—the interrogation had to be more informally comparative in nature and dependent upon subjective aesthetic reactions as expressed in the vernacular.

Recognizing the subjective nature of the culturally-conditioned exercise in which I was involved, I endeavored to lessen the inevitable skewing that would result. One way to compensate for *qualitative* subjectivity is through *quantitative* means, namely, by getting the verbal and extraverbal reactions of a sufficient number of respondents. But even this is not entirely objective, for the process also depends on whom you pick for your sample. Moreover, this factor was not really applicable to the present experiment, which was conducted on a relatively small scale and an informal basis.

Another problem to consider was the politeness of the respondents. Very few would be so blunt as to say that a biblical text, even qualitatively speaking in terms its style, was not good, let alone unacceptable, whether in part or as a whole. To detect a contrary appraisal, the tester would have to be alert to subtle negative reactions, both verbal and nonverbal. The same is true of trying to determine relative degrees of acceptability. The tester has to move up or down the scale of excellence by noting the precise nature of the evaluative remarks and the respondents' overt level of enthusiasm versus their lack of interest and excitement. It is also important that all those involved in the testing process be well instructed as to methodology and agreed on how to record the results.

To help overcome the ambiguities involved in assessing acceptability, the assessment of a particular translated passage of the Bible should be done in terms of specific criteria.[324] The four principal criteria are shown in the diagram that follows. They relate to each other within a framework composed of two basic parameters: on one plane the focus is on either the source language (SL) or the target language (TL); on the other the focus is on either textual meaning or form (see Wendland 1991:8–10; Larsen 2001:40–42). These are the factors that determine the relative degree of the translated text's acceptability. The criteria are numbered in order of their relative priority in the case of a Bible translation that is intended to be a literary functionally equivalent (LiFE) version.[325] (Other types of translation would require a reordering or a reweighting of the four criteria.)

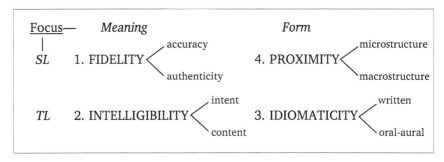

10.5.1 The criterion of fidelity

Factor 1, fidelity to the meaning of the SL message as intended by the original author, is the paramount concern in most, if not all, translations

---

[324]Carl Gross (2003) argues that "another principle…tends to take precedence and to displace the commitment to accuracy of meaning, clarity and naturalness on many occasions in the translation process. This principle is that of "acceptability", in which the acceptability of the translation to the receptor culture…becomes more important than whether the translation conveys the meaning of the original "faithfully", i.e., accurately, clearly and naturally."

[325]Wonderly's (1968:3–4, 28–29) description and illustration of a popular-language type of Bible translation remains the best (cf. Wendland 1998b:42–47). Chesterman and Wagner (2002:92–93) propose "four general norms [that] give us four positive quality criteria for the translation product." They are: appropriate target language fit (*acceptability* norm), relevant similarity of the TL text to the original (*relation* norm), optimum intelligibility (*communication* norm), and manifest loyalty to the parties involved in the translation (*accountability* norm). Of the second norm they observe that "[t]he necessary degree and kind of similarity therefore depends on what is relevant—relevant to the purpose of the translation, to the situation in which it has been requested" (ibid.:93). They also list a useful set of evaluative queries involving intended function, form, content, style, naturalness, text status, medium, and other criteria (ibid.:50–51).

of Scripture, regardless of whether this ideal is achieved in actual practice or not.[326] However, problems immediately develop here with regard to how meaning is to be defined. As far as the literalist is concerned, the given linguistic form of the original text is a key aspect of its meaning (see sec. 2.4.2.1). For most communicators, on the other hand, the semantic content and pragmatic intent of the biblical message is of much greater importance than the verbal signs in which it was expressed, except in those instances where the artistic shape of the original text contributes to its literary significance.

In any case, the criterion of fidelity may itself be factored into two important aspects: *actual* fidelity, or accuracy, and *perceived* fidelity, or authenticity. *Accuracy* is a quality that may be more or less objectively assessed through various analytical means that relate the SL and TL texts in comparative terms.[327] However, this must not be considered solely in terms of the propositional content of the Scriptures, for the dimension of message meaning also includes important affective, imperative, poetic, and relational aspects. *Authenticity* is a more subjective property. It is based upon a particular individual's or target group's expectations about Bible translation and thus depends on their estimation of the degree to which the translated text, no matter how accurate or intelligible, is

---

[326] It is in fact *impossible* to be 100 percent "faithful" in communicating the intended meaning of a given text—including all of its significant, author-intended implications and implicatures—even within the same language, let alone via translation into another language. In other words, no translation can ever "say the same thing" as the source text on which it is based and from which it derives. Only relative degrees of success are possible, that is, with respect to certain designated aspects and features of the original text. For complete communication to occur, the entire message context—cognitive, literary, cultural, environmental, interpersonal—would have to be conceptually accessible to the TL audience and also actually apprehended by them in their various verbal interrelationships (Gutt 1992:65, 67). The more disparate the languages, cultures, and settings, the greater the problems involved in conveying the desired message.

Fidelity, like intelligibility, is a relative notion, dependent upon a host of textual, interpersonal, and situational factors. The formal criteria of idiomaticity and proximity are less variable in this respect. As noted earlier, I am operating with a more traditional notion of meaning, which for many has been eclipsed, or "deconstructed," in this postmodern age. I will not argue my case here; suffice it to say that I am not convinced by the contemporary alternatives being proposed. To me they essentially proclaim the death of the translator. Why translate at all if there is no objective, intentional "meaning" to begin with, or end up with, except that which is subjectively created by, for, and of oneself? The Hebrew philosopher-poet who composed the ancient text of Job dealt with this controversial issue several millennia ago in Job 28 (substitute "meaning" for "wisdom") and came up with what is to my mind a most satisfying answer in Job 28:28 (cf. Eccles. 12:13).

[327] This analytical assessment is ideally carried out by mother-tongue speakers of the TL who are also skilled exegetes with reference to the biblical languages. If the evaluation of accuracy is made by second-language speakers, they should have nearly mother-tongue fluency in terms of text-processing competence (e.g., discourse stylistics), if not actual speech *performance*.

viewed as representing the genuine Word of God. Is it "a trustworthy version of the original message" (Andersen 1998:1; see also Larsen
2001:42–43)? It may well be that the Bible as a whole (at least the current
vernacular version of it) is popularly regarded as constituting a
macrogenre *sui generis*, having distinct literary characteristics and standards of form as well as content that relate to its unique religious function
and at times ritual usage, such as the reading of discrete pericopes according to a church's particular "performance tradition" of public worship
(see de Vries 1999:29).

10.5.2 The criterion of intelligibility

The second most important factor in any popular-language Bible translation is intelligibility. Like fidelity, the factor of intelligibility pertains not
only to the propositional content of the original text, but also to its main
pragmatic intent. In other words, it concerns what the original author desired to *do* with his message, whether consciously or intuitively, in terms
of communicative function (including the implication of all constituent
"speech-acts") in relation to his presumed audience. What conceptual, volitional, and emotional effect did he wish to achieve in and by the words
that he wrote with respect to rhetorical impact (e.g., encouragement, admonition, consolation, warning) and affective appeal (e.g., the expression
or elicitation of joy, anger, disappointment, sorrow)?
    The violation or nonrealization of either the factor of fidelity or intelli-
gibility would make any translation of the Holy Scriptures "unacceptable." No distortion of the essential meaning of a sacred theological text
(as determined by scholarly as well as popular and community-based consensus) is tolerable, no matter how innocently or how ignorantly perpe-
trated. When detected, any communication failure ("break-down") of this
nature must be corrected, either textually or extratextually (e.g., in an explanatory footnote).
    On the other hand, no matter how correct the message may be from an
exegetical point of view, it will profit little in communicative terms if the
message is not clearly conveyed to ordinary receptors. It would serve no
purpose other than religious ritual in which the text is a verbal icon of
pure symbolic or emotive value. We must remember that Koine Greek
(and presumably the basic style of Old Testament Hebrew) was chosen as
the principal mode of expressing God's Word on account of its general linguistic clarity to the masses. An accurate translation should aim to
achieve a corresponding effect with regard to its overall perspicuity and
understandability.

10.5.3 The criterion of idiomaticity

Idiomaticity (factor 3) and proximity (factor 4) largely concern the form of the text, not so much its meaning. They are therefore more or less optional elements in the measurement of translational acceptability. However, they must not be overlooked or ignored by serious Bible translators. Idiomaticity pertains to the *naturalness* of the translated text as expressed in the TL with respect to the diverse linguistic signs used in its transmission—phonological, morphosyntactic, lexical, as well as those devices employed on the discourse level of composition. A translation may be relatively intelligible, but still not sound natural compared with the normal patterns and conventions of everyday speech or the oral and written genres that people are familiar with. In some cases this "foreign accent" may be so strong as to threaten the fundamental clarity of the text. This applies in particular to the more subtle aspects of discourse structure such as participant reference, tense/aspect sequence, conjunctive-transitional devices, and foreground-background distinctions. It also applies to the sociolinguistic dimension of language such as dialect, register, level of formality or familiarity, and degree of politeness.

Educated receptors will probably be sophisticated enough to realize that a document originating in ancient times and in a very different ecological environment and cultural setting will not sound the same as contemporary local discourse. Even so, any disparity with respect to general intelligibility should be limited to that caused by the basic content and concepts of the biblical message (e.g., terminology pertaining to the Jewish religious system in the Pentateuch or the heavy Christocentric theological instruction of the Epistles). However, there should be no awkward, unfamiliar, or misleading usage with regard to the stylistic form of the TL version—such as the undue use of long, complex sentences, event nouns, genitive constructions, and conjoined prepositional phrases. Furthermore, the idiomaticity, or naturalness, being referred to here must be oriented primarily towards the *spoken* form of the target language since this is how the majority of people will be receiving it, just as those in the original communication event did. This is especially important to remember in settings where a distinctly formal written style is present and often advocated for use in official or important documents.

10.5.4 The criterion of proximity

Factor 4 in the assessment process is proximity. This may be the least important of the four factors, yet it, like the others, involves the issue of procedural integrity with respect to the original divinely inspired text. In other words, there is a general principle that obligates Bible translators to stay as near as possible not only to message content, but also to the distinctive textual forms of the SL document.[328] However, this transformative process must be carried out according to whatever priority scale and set of guidelines have been set up for the translation (e.g., to render poetry as poetry, or prose as prose, or to maintain the same relative degree of artistic-literary quality or rhetorical power). Formal closeness, whether on the macro- or the microstructural level of discourse organization, should definitely *not* be retained where it would result in a reduction in semantic fidelity, intelligibility, or situational appropriateness (e.g., in a setting where poetry is deemed suitable only for children).

There may be some—perhaps considerable—debate, however, when attempting to adjudicate between the demands or preferences of idiomaticity on the one hand and proximity on the other. Such decisions can be made only with reference to a flexible form-functional continuum applied within the particular framework of text and context (message and medium) that has been established as part of the organizational *Brief* regarding the purpose, or *Skopos* (the guiding principles, procedures, and policies), for the translation project as a whole (Gutt 1992:70; Hatim and Mason 1997:11–12; Wendland 1991:10–11).

The type of translation that has been officially designated for a target community is also a crucial factor in this discussion. A common-language or popular-language version will usually rank idiomaticity over proximity, whereas a middle of the road translation will reverse this order. The specific sort of biblical discourse that is to be translated also needs to be considered, for example, a lyric psalm of praise versus a Pauline epistle. In the figurative language of a psalmic or prophetic pericope, it would normally be necessary to allow a greater measure of idiomaticity with regard to certain lexical designations in order to achieve a functionally equivalent or appropriate rendering. But in a historical narrative, such as we have in the Gospels, the translation would have to remain relatively more

---

[328]Thus it would seem preferable to render the Hebrew term רֹעֶה in Ps. 23:1 by a TL generic equivalent such as 'herdsman', rather than the semantically more specific (and familiar) 'cowherd' in societies where cattle play an important role in the culture. This decision would be supported by the overall importance, both denotatively and connotatively, of 'shepherds' and 'sheep' in the Bible. A local colloquialism such as English *cowboy* would of course be completely inappropriate due to its connotative coloring. Because lexical consistency is especially important when dealing with certain key theological terms, it is a recommended procedure to render such words as *grace, sin, cross, heaven, sacrifice,* and *law* in the same way whenever they happen to appear in similar semantic contexts (e.g., the Psalter or the synoptic Gospels).

proximate to the referential forms of the text, even the more difficult ones, in order to uphold the preeminent criterion of fidelity to facticity.

10.5.5 Criteria of acceptability in application

As we have seen, the four factors of assessment closely interact (and also conflict in certain situations) when they are applied in an actual translational setting, and it is not easy to give a recommended answer or a standard strategy for achieving acceptability in every eventuality. This pervasive reality of Bible translation calls for staff of the highest competence, aptitude, and experience. It also draws attention to the need for a carefully planned, wide-ranging audience testing program to ensure that the project remains on target as far as the will of the majority (or at least the project's principal supporters) is concerned.

The artistic *ndakatulo*-style version of Psalm 23, which is the focus of my study, falls toward the more mediated, functionally oriented end of the translation continuum given in section 2.8. During the process of its composition there was a definite priority or preference that placed contemporary colloquialness (focus on TL form) over textual proximity (focus on SL form). But how would audiences react to this relatively high level of formal flexibility, which conflicts with all the other Chichewa versions that they are familiar with (except the hymnic version)? Would impact and appeal win out over a stipulated or even subconscious desire to remain more proximate to the biblical forms in the interest of religious authenticity? Would the high degree of idiomaticity of the lyric text detract in any way from its general intelligibility or even integrity (e.g., decorum)? And if so, how would this affect the majority receptor response?

These are some of the factors that I wished to investigate more fully, at least in a preliminary sort of way, by means of my little audience-testing experiment. It was designed to explore the nature of a diverse popular assessment of a translation's textual *creativity* ("literariness") as distinct from its textual *content* ("literalness"). In other words, we wanted to assess *acceptability* in relation to artistry on the one hand and authenticity on the other.

10.5.6 Other measures of acceptability

Relevance theory (RT) offers a more general way of evaluating the acceptability of a given translation. In the terminology of RT a text is deemed "optimally relevant" (or fully acceptable) if it provides "adequate contextual effects" for the audience with respect to their current "cognitive environment," yet "without requiring unnecessary processing effort" (Gutt 1992:24–25).

Hatim and Mason (1990) express a similar notion with regard to satisfying a text producer's communicative intention, which involves a balanced fusion of new, evoked (or old, presupposed), and inferable information. They see this process as being "regulated by the principles of *effectiveness* (achieving maximum transmission of relevant content or fulfillment of a communication goal) and *efficiency* (achieving it in the most economical way, involving minimum expenditure of processing effort" (p. 91, emphasis mine).

According to the preceding "minimax principle" (Shuttleworth and Cowie 1997:106–107), efficiency is clearly related to intelligibility (see sec. 10.5.2). Effectiveness, on the other hand, is more complex and must be determined on the basis of a person's, or group's, perception and evaluation of a given text's fidelity, idiomaticity, and proximity within a specific context of use. Such a critical judgment—whether carried out formally or informally, consciously or subconsciously—is based in turn upon their expectations of how the translation should read/sound in terms of style (form) as well as their intentions with regard to how they propose to use or apply it (intended function). It is clear that the only way to determine whether a certain translation manifests the desired "effects" along with an appropriate level of efficiency is through some rather sophisticated and extensive testing techniques. The adequacy of my more informal method of textual assessment through interrogative interaction or investigative dialoguing, with an actual sample of the potential audience needs to be tested further.

Hatim and Mason also have some pertinent things to say about the difficulties that translators face when dealing with a text that is stylistically more dynamic (or "turbulent") in nature (see sec. 2.4.2.4). This refers to an oral or written discourse that consists of a higher incidence of unpredictable, rhetorically marked forms and "the use of language that essentially involves a motivated deviation from some norm" (1997:216). That is, of course, the essence of artistic as well as argumentative (or evaluative) composition, two motivations that are often combined in serious ideological literature, such as the Scriptures (ibid.:181–183). This sort of discourse contrasts with discourse that is mainly expository in nature. Expository discourse is characterized by a style that is less marked and more stable, usual, or expected in terms of the language used. Such texts usually do not require as much restructuring in translation as does an overtly evaluative or literary discourse (ibid.:187). Restructuring is especially necessary when preparing a "dynamic" and/or "artistic" rendering of a literary text. Texts that are more "culture-bound" normally require a greater measure of translational mediation as well, as Hatim and Mason observe, if they are to be represented accurately in a given TL (ibid.:188).

The two polarities of relative "evaluativeness" (i.e., artistry) and "culture-boundedness" (i.e., non-alienness) may be combined to suggest a gradient of translation difficulty.[329] The main factors that determine degrees of translation difficulty are indicated on the diagram that follows. (In the diagram the symbol [+] means relatively *more*, while [-] represents relatively *less* textual artistry in terms of stylistic form or cultural alienness with regard to situationally specific content, especially features foreign to the TL sociological setting.)

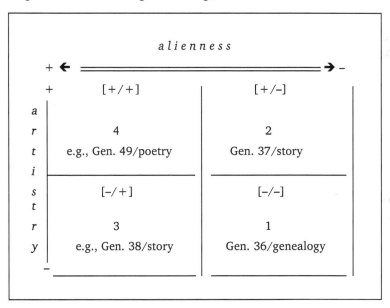

Based on this model the genealogy of Genesis 36 (situation 1), to give a simple example, would tend to be the easiest (-/-) to translate into another language,[330] while the poetry of Genesis 49 (situation 4) would be the most difficult (+ / +). Not only does the latter present translators with much more textual turbulence, but the notion of a father's deathbed

---

[329]Overall linguistic disparity between the SL and TL also affects the relative difficulty of translation; for example, with respect to interlingual transfer, it is easier to render Psalm 23 in Arabic than in English. But this factor is general and does not relate to specific texts.

[330]A Hebrew genealogy is the unadorned prosaic equivalent of what is known as "royal praise poetry" in a Bantu tradition of artistic oral performance.

prophetic blessing on all of his sons is quite foreign conceptually and socioculturally to many people, certainly to the matrilineal, matrilocal Chewa people of south-central Africa. In other words, all other things being equal (e.g., the relative affinity of the TL to the SL, use of the same translators, the generic literary inventory of the TL), situation 1 would require the least translational intervention in terms of formal linguistic and semantic modification, whereas situation 4 would require the most, primarily on the microstructure of textual organization (see Hatim and Mason 1997:30).[331] In addition, the important cultural and religious dynamics underlying the text of Genesis 49 would call for a number of extratextual footnotes, and even an illustration or two, to handle problems of meaning that could not be taken care of within the translated text itself.

Situations 2 (+ /–) and 3 (–/ +) bear an interesting relationship to one another: A stylistically more artistic but less alien (or socially specific with reference to the SL text) narrative like the Joseph story of Genesis 37 should be more difficult to translate in a functionally equivalent manner, but it would undoubtedly be easier for a given TL audience to conceptually process (e.g., with regard to the serious interpersonal tensions that can arise also in a rural Chewa polygamous family setting). The reverse would be true for the less artistic but more alien Judah-Tamar story of Genesis 38—easier to render, but more difficult to understand due to the culturally unfamiliar marital and sexual practices that are reported: a father arranging for his son's marriage, a brother refusing to fulfill the levirate custom, sending a widow back to her father's house because the traditional bridewealth had been returned to her father's village, and incest between a man and his daughter-in-law. In the matter of incest here, discourse meaning, or intelligibility (see sec. 10.5.2), is involved, not discourse "form," or idiomaticity; therefore the level of *textual* (as opposed to *translational*) difficulty is regarded as being somewhat higher. Consequently, any assessment, or testing, of one version in comparison with another, where several different texts are concerned, would have to take these variables into consideration in an effort to isolate the factors causing the difficulty (i.e., compositional artistry versus cultural incongruity). No such case was involved in my evaluation of Psalm 23, the text of which

---

[331]The following definition by R. Taft (1981) may be helpful at this point: "A cultural mediator is a person who facilitates communication, understanding, and action between persons or groups who differ with respect to language and culture. The role of the mediator is performed by interpreting the expressions, intentions, perceptions, and expectations of each cultural group to the other, that is, by establishing and balancing the communication between them" (cited in Katan 1999:12). Any communicative translator is, of course, a "cultural mediator."

would be classified as " + artistry / – alienness" in terms of the diagram and with specific reference to southeastern Bantu Africa.

10.6 Assessing a specific translation

The activity of assessment is in focus in this section—specifically, the evaluating of the effects of artistry or the lack thereof. Four different Chichewa translations of Psalm 23 were assessed according to the framework presented here. The methodology and results of my initial research will be summarized. During the course of the testing, the procedure itself was continually assessed and modified as necessary in order to improve its overall efficiency and effectiveness.

10.6.1 The testing methodology, a contextualized problem-shaped approach

The attempt to estimate an audience's reactions to literary artistry presents the investigator with several significant problems that need to be considered in any methodology that is applied. First of all, how does one sufficiently isolate the criterion of *creativity* (artful idiomaticity) from the other principal criteria of evaluation in relation to Bible translation, *intelligibility* in particular (see sec. 10.8.2)? In other words, how can a tester determine whether a testee is reacting positively or negatively to the Psalm 23 poetic rendering (PR) based on its rhetorical impact and stylistic appeal as distinct from its clarity or understandability (found also in the popular-language version, BY)? Secondly, to what extent is it possible to factor out some of the other possible influences upon audience reaction, especially their probable familiarity with the older, more literal *Buku Lopatulika* (BL) or the semipoetic hymn version (HV)?[332] Finally, how can we deal effectively with the sociocultural problem that arises due to the communal nature of the particular consumer group being tested? That is to say, how does one obtain an honest answer in a face-to-face, "high context,"[333] shame-conscious society, where people typically try to give an

---

[332]The hymnic version is classified as "semipoetic" because it manifests only some of the principal features of *ndakatulo* lyric verse, and then only in limited concentration, for example, the relative amount of ideophones, figurative language, syntactic movement, phonological enhancement, and semantic redundancy.

[333]A "high-context" society is one in which people tend to depend more on the nonverbal interpersonal and situational setting in order to gain information relevant to any given act of communication; a "low context" society, on the other hand, is one that prefers to have such information explicitly coded within verbal texts (Katan 1999:177–194). Most central African speech communities have the former communicative preference, while Americans generally have the latter.

honored or respected person the "right answer," the one they think is expected?

Because of this last problem, it was necessary to involve others in the testing program, despite the apparent additional subjectivity that this would introduce into the procedure. It was assumed that respondents would tend to be more honest and open when replying to questions put by an African seminary student instead of a white missionary professor. As for the other difficulties posed by our effort to focus as much as possible upon artistry in the text, we had only one practical option available in view of the largely nonliterate, oral-aural community that we were dealing with. This was the traditional method of informal *dialogic interaction.* The aim was to progressively channel the discussion and present the nature of the assessment process in credible terms in order to get more or less straightforward opinions (even if indirectly expressed). In most cases this required us to give the testees a certain amount of explanation to clarify the purpose of the experiment as well as the distinct parameters involved (e.g., fidelity, accuracy, clarity, intelligibility, artistry, and idiomaticity).

Furthermore, we wanted the investigation to reach beyond an assessment of acceptability alone to a determination of the level of genuine aesthetic appreciation for a text (the PR of Psalm 23) that was stylistically quite distinct from the others. A certain amount of flexibility therefore had to be allowed during the process of questioning in order to probe more fully where needed and elicit an adequate expression of a testee's feelings. The questions were formulated in such a way that they could not be answered with a simple yes or no, but required some measure of evaluatory explanation or an expression of personal opinion. This necessitated a prior discussion of the appropriate "diagnostic language" to be used in Chichewa for descriptive and classificatory purposes. In addition, it was made clear to the testers that they were free to modify or supplement the standard questions (which are presented in sec. A.2). However, they were requested to record in writing any such adjustments in the interest of a future development of the testing technique. As a result, the set of core questions was adjusted several times during the experiment in response to various exigencies that arose or improvements that were discovered along the way.

10.6.2 Training the testing team

The first step in the process of artistry assessment was to train some capable assistants to help in the testing process. I took advantage of the fact that I happened to be teaching an exegetical-translational course on the Psalms and enlisted the thirteen members of my second-year seminary class. They became my colleagues in this practical research project.[334] An initial joint training exercise was held to introduce some consistency and uniformity into the procedures that would be followed in the field. The students learned not only how to analyze the various types of psalms, but they also tried their hand at composing several examples according to the *ndakatulo* genre of Chichewa poetry (or a corresponding poetic form in their own language).[335] This was to remind them of the main artistic techniques and rhetorical devices of their own language as well as teach them about the corresponding features of Hebrew poetic discourse. The emphasis was upon finding suitable stylistic "matches" to serve as functional equivalents for use in a genre-for-genre translational approach. It seems to help students better understand what is going on communicatively in the biblical text if they can associate the SL features with the common devices that are available in their own oral and written literary tradition. They also come to appreciate their indigenous verbal art forms and can therefore be more effective when appraising the responses of other people to them.

My students were the first ones to be tested, both orally and in writing, with regard to the four renditions of Psalm 23. During this familiarization procedure we also discussed the various problem areas and how to handle them when they would go out to conduct their own investigations. Together we evaluated the set of test questions (see sec. A.2), and a number of revisions were made. Thus they became joint owners of the project from the very beginning. As seminary students, these men (all mature married persons) have weekend pastoral assignments in local congregations in both rural and urban areas of Lusaka, the capital city of Zambia (the wider population being some three million people). Their churches offered a diverse proving ground for carrying out our cooperative program of artistic assessment. Each student was given the assignment of testing and writing up a survey report concerning at least one person per week.

---

[334]The Lutheran Seminary students who participated in this research project are as follows: David Baloyi, Edward Bangwe, Philip Chikwatu, Bright Munthali, Sylvester Mwanza, Simon Mweete, Lambulani Mzalule, Lackson Nkhunje, Amin Phiri, Lucius Renard, Cappy Shamwanga, Tuesday Shubi, and Fainos Tarisayi. I wish to express my appreciation to these men for all their help, without which the testing program could not have been conducted in a satisfactory manner.

[335]The workbook that I use as the basis for this course (Wendland 2002a:237–251) provides information in its appendix (pp. 225–236) on how to encourage students or translators to compose psalms in the genres of their mother tongue.

The thirteen students began the testing process with their own wives and/or a teenaged child to get used to the procedure and note any potential difficulties. I included several local pastors in my own research outreach. This program was continued for a period of roughly ten weeks. A total of ninety individuals were sampled (see sec. A.3). In addition, the students were asked to carefully observe and report on the dynamic interaction that occurred when several other, larger groups were tested as wholes to see how this would affect the assessment process. For example, would a joint sample session foster the development of a consensus of aesthetic opinion, and if so, how was this facilitated and accomplished? How would the result of a group assessment compare with the tests of individuals questioned in isolation?

Each student report had to be written up and turned in to me for collation and evaluation on a weekly basis. (A separate recording notebook was supplied for this purpose.) We would then discuss the results of the week's testing together in class and make any necessary improvements in our methodology. All these measures were intended to provide a greater degree of objectivity to what was clearly a very subjective process. Thus, although our testing procedure was changed somewhat during the course of our research (with regard to some of the content and wording of the questions asked), such modification served to improve its overall effectiveness. That is, it enabled more precise and reliable feedback. In this way, in addition to qualitatively evaluating the four texts of Psalm 23, the method of assessment was itself assessed, and revised as needed.

10.6.3 Testing the text for readability and legibility

The activity of silent reading did not play a major role in our text-testing process. This was because, as already pointed out, most receptors in central Africa access the biblical text by means of hearing a public reading during a worship service or some sort of Bible study. Thus the opinion that most people might form concerning the relative acceptability, or indeed the level of artistry, of a given translation will be based upon their *aural* apprehension of it—how clear, beautiful, and powerful the text sounds to them. Therefore the majority of testing was aimed at individuals or groups who *listened* to the Word being read and subsequently answered oral questions about their evaluation and related opinions. For some, this included the memorization of certain passages to determine the quality of a specific translation in this regard, which is an important consideration in areas of limited functional literacy.

Despite this oral-aural emphasis, I found it necessary to make at least some effort to judge the several translation samples of this study with respect to their degree of "readability." This was for two reasons, the first being the importance of oral reading, even though few do it. A text that is not very intelligible due to unnatural syntax, word usage, and discourse construction (as in the literal *Buku Lopatulika*) is more difficult to read aloud; the reader fails to anticipate what is going to come next in the text. Expectations are frequently frustrated, and the result is mistakes, mispronunciations, wrong intonation, and hesitations as it is read aloud. In view of this, the most understandable translation, namely, the popular-language BY version, is likely to be the most fluently and accurately read in public.

The second aspect of the testing process was to determine the impact of artistry on readability. Would the artistic poetic rendering (PR) turn out to be difficult to articulate on account of the greater amount of idiomatic language, stylistic embellishment, and structural shaping that it includes? For this assessment three types of lector (poor, average, and good) were identified in terms of the quality of their public elocution of the sample portions. Again it was the seminary students who were the first to take this readability test.

There was another factor related to reading that needed to be tested as well. While it was rather minor in relation to the experiment as a whole, still it was worthy of some consideration. This concerned the legibility of the text as displayed on a printed page. Bible translations are generally quite poor in this respect, even though such things as small print, lack of white space, errors, an unfamiliar typeface, and lack of paragraphing can adversely affect many public readers' performance. The problem is that when a passage of Scripture is not well read, it will be that much harder for an audience to understand as they hear it. Every mispronunciation or mistake breaks the audience's train of thought and throws the interpretive process off track, making the passage as a whole incomprehensible. The more errors there are, even minor ones, the "harder of hearing" a passage becomes.[336]

Some typographical features that make reading easier include a ragged right margin (nonjustified), no end-of-line hyphenations, shorter utterance units, and line breaks at meaningful points within a sentence. Under the right circumstances (for trained and practiced readers), certain important suprasegmental sounds can be signaled typographically, for example,

---

[336]For a more detailed discussion of this subject, see Wendland and Louw 1993. Eugene Nida (2000:156) observes that "the [printed] format of the text...has an important bearing on readability and the highlighting of stylistic features, especially those that relate to its larger discourse organization."

by smaller print (for soft articulation), capital letters (FOR LOUD SPEECH), repeated letters (for vooowel elooongaaation), and italics or boldface (for *stress, intensity,* or **focus**).

One of the tests we conducted was comparing the legibility of two different formats of the Chichewa popular-language version—one printed in an ordinary two-column, efficiency-programmed "Bible style" of publication the other realigned for greater legibility. (These two layouts may be seen in sections A.1.5 and A.1.6). We concluded that careful formatting procedures are indeed helpful if the aim is to promote the forceful, dynamic, and compelling oral recital of the Scriptures, no matter what the style of the translation itself.

10.6.4 Applying the testing methodology

A question-answer, dialogic technique formed the heart of my audience-testing procedure. It was based upon (but not necessarily limited to) a set of sample queries prepared in advance and discussed first with my student testers (see sec. A.2 for the original questionnaire). The aim was not only to elicit answers to these prepared queries, but also to encourage the expression of personal preferences or dislikes and the reasons for them from respondents with regard to the various oral text samples.[337] The "personal background" questions are rather straightforward in nature; however, the "practical assessment" questions are not so regular and thus allow for greater flexibility with regard to situational modification and expansion or deletion as needed. The student testers recorded all of the responses, even in those rare cases where the respondents had the ability to write them themselves.

Several respondents who reacted negatively to the poetic *ndakatulo* version were chosen to receive some additional instruction or explanation regarding its nature and purpose to see whether it would make any difference in their opinions. The results of this special assessment were noted separately.

During the interrogation process an informal attempt was made to distinguish seven specific focal features that pertain in some way to degrees

---

[337]A further way perhaps to encourage a more objective testing procedure would have been to tape-record the different text samples being read by a single competent lector and then play these recordings for each of the individuals questioned. However, my available funding was not sufficient for this. On the other hand, a "live" reading by the student testers would probably have been a more effective method anyway in view of the testees' background as members of an interactive, face-to-face communal society. Another method of standardizing the assessment more fully would have been to tape-record all the audience responses for later analysis. This would have provided greater consistency in how a given individual's answers were reported.

of acceptability with particular reference to intelligibility and idiomaticity (see the diagram in sec. 10.6.2). The special emphasis of each is
summarized below and a key question (KQ) given as an example, along
with the Chichewa equivalent of the critical term:

- *intelligibility* (clarity of form and content)—KQ: What part of this
  text sample in Chichewa was most 'difficult' (*Chichewa chovuta*) for
  you to understand and why? Which specific words caused problems
  for you?
- *readability* (print/format legibility)—KQ: Which of the sample texts
  is 'easiest' (*chapafupi*) to read and why do you say so? At which
  points in these texts did the reader make an obvious mistake of
  some kind?
- *sonority* (pertaining to aural aesthetics)—KQ: Which text and verse
  sound the 'sweetest' (*chozuna*) and most 'beautiful' (*chokoma*) and
  why do you say this? Give an example of an expression which
  'sounded like a song' (*chomveka ngati nyimbo*).
- *idiomaticity* (stylistic naturalness and verbal appeal)—KQ: Which
  text and verse sound the most 'salty' (*chamcere*), 'twisted'
  (*chokuluwika*), or 'hidden' (*chophiphiritsa*)? Give a specific example
  from the text.
- *rhetoricity* (dynamic message impact)—KQ: Which text and verse
  had words which sound the 'strongest' (*champhavmu*) or which
  'pulled the heart' (*chichewa chokoka mtima*)? Give an example of
  this from any sample text.
- *authenticity* (accuracy in representing the Word of God)—KQ: Is
  there an expression in any of the sample texts that seems to be 'a
  little mistaken' (*cholakwika pang'ono*) or 'inappropriate'
  (*chosayenera kwenikweni*), for example, or perhaps too 'youthful'
  (*chachinyamata*) to use in a translation of the Bible?
- *memorability* (pertaining to both form and content)—KQ: Which
  text would be the easiest for you to memorize or 'enter into [your]
  heart' (*kuloweza pamtima*), and why do you say this?

These questions (all of them, or sometimes fewer, sometimes more, depending on the respondent)[338] were asked on three different levels: each

---

[338]The testers were free to eliminate one or more of the question sets if they thought that
a respondent was being confused by too much detail. But this reduction, along with any additional explanation needed for clarification, had to be noted along with the reason. The
testers could also re-phrase these questions in order to illuminate their content or intent.

text considered on its own, then each text compared with the others, and finally with regard to a set of three selected passages (see j in A.2.2). Of course, these assessment questions do not fully cover the subject. Moreover, some of the questions are rather too general or might elicit answers that fit several different categories. The testers were therefore encouraged to follow up on any question that elicited a response that was insufficiently specific or perhaps not properly understood. But they were only to clarify the question, not try to influence the respondent's reply. Any supplementary questions or added explanations were to be written down in their official notebooks where possible, at least in summary form, for future reference.

10.7 The results of assessment

A report of the most important findings of the investigation of the four translations that were evaluated is presented in sections 10.7.1–10.7.5. One of the versions, the popular-language *Buku Loyera* (BY), was evaluated in two different text formats, hence the five sections. A statistical summary of the results of the assessment is given in section A.3.

My methodology was broad, diffuse, subjective, and uncontrolled with respect to certain key variables, and therefore I can hardly claim statistical reliability. The percentages noted are approximate and rounded off to the nearest 5 percent. Thus only the most prominent trends, preferences, dislikes, and related opinions recorded here are valid enough to be worth noting. The tentative conclusions of the investigation as presented here have special reference to the aural assessment of artistry in the poetic *ndakatulo* rendering as compared to the other versions. For the sake of interest, I have reproduced a number of the most significant quotations of audience opinion, but have not included the names of the investigator, whether one of my assistants or myself, who actually recorded it at the time of testing.[339]

10.7.1 The literal version Buku Lopatulika (BL)

The *Buku Lopatulika* text, a sample of which can be seen in section A.1.4, was clearly the most difficult translation to understand, hence also the hardest for people to memorize. This was the opinion of roughly 70 percent of those interviewed, irrespective of their mother tongue. As a result,

---

[339]It should be noted that in most cases the quotation marks of this section distinguish the actual words spoken by the various respondents, which have been back-translated from the original Chichewa into English. A few answers were given originally in English, mainly those of the seminary testers when questioned by me.

this version was for most respondents not considered the most "beautiful" or "idiomatic," although many (45 percent) found its language to be the most "powerful," which is perhaps significant in view of the fact that people had difficulty in understanding it. The style was widely recognized as being "old Chichewa," even though the text was familiar to many through long exposure in the church. A few considered this style to be "real Chichewa," hallowed over time and by repeated religious usage. This comment was typical: "I am used to it since I became a Christian." On occasion, just in order to clarify the distinction between intelligibility and familiarity for the relatively few who initially considered the *Buku Lopatulika* text to be the "easiest to understand," we simply asked them to explain the meaning of a few choice expressions (e.g., v. 5, "You spread out a square platform before my eyes in the seeing of my enemies"). That was usually enough to demonstrate the difference, although it certainly did not lessen their reverence for and devotion to this beloved Chichewa "King James version." On the other hand, many respondents would agree with this confession by a young man: "I don't read the [*Buku Lopatulika*] Old Testament because I am not able to understand the language."

10.7.2 The popular-language version Buku Loyera (BY)

The *Buku Loyera*, a sample of which can be seen in section A.1.5, was widely regarded by the respondents as the "easiest" translation to understand and also to read (65 percent) due to the natural style of language in which it is expressed. A factor in this opinion was the relatively high proportion of second-language speakers of Chichewa among those interviewed (about 75 percent). One of them said, "It is written in a way that a Zambian person can understand." Another nonmother-tongue speaker commented, "BY is a simplified version because it uses words in current Chichewa; some words are almost the way we speak in my language [Tumbuka]." Still another noted that "this Chichewa is modern [*Chichewa chamakono* 'Chichewa of these present days'];...even children nowadays can understand it." It is not surprising then that a significant number of people (40 percent) considered this version to be their favorite, second only to the hymn version, no doubt because more of the text was readily intelligible, hence immediately applicable to one's life. One person even proposed that the BY text should be transformed into a hymn form (*nyimbo*) in order to increase its popularity and memorizability.

There was one controversial issue that affected our test methodology. We had to try to isolate (and sometimes diffuse) this point of contention whenever it arose. It had to do with the name *Chauta* that had been introduced by BY for the Hebrew 'LORD' (יהוה). *Chauta* is different from the traditional *Yehova* used in the literal *Buku Lopatulika*.[340] In cases where a respondent's devotion to the BL seemed to be affecting his or her response to the various topics in the questionnaire, we had to step in to clarify the point that this particular divine name was not what we were testing in this experiment.

10.7.3 The hymn version (HV)

In the course of the early testing of the hymn version (see sec. A.1.7 for this text), when the seminary students were tested for their response to it, the very first result to be revealed was the powerful aesthetic and emotive attraction that a musical rendition carries for virtually all respondents. As in the case of the popular-language text (BY), the recommendation was made that it would be a good idea if the entire Bible could be translated in a hymnic manner. Some suggested that it would also be a good idea if the whole Bible could be printed in such short but meaningful lines, which make the text easier to read. Thus HV was easily the most appealing version—90 percent said so when it was presented in its sung form. For this reason we adjusted our procedure to test it like the others, as a spoken text, at least at first. (As a spoken text it came in second in popularity to the popular-language version, BY.) Only later, as the last of the assessment questions, was it revealed to be a text from their hymnbook. In cases where the HV was immediately recognized as a well-known hymn, I recommended that it be treated separately and not evaluated with the other three texts in the main sequence of questions. The hymn version was also considered to be the easiest to memorize (if not already learned as a hymn) since the words and lines tend to be "short" and "simple." It can be tied to a familiar melody and a fixed rhythm and line length (in terms of syllables). This particular version had a surpassing advantage in the minds of many since they already "sing it all the time in church."

10.7.4 The ndakatulo poetic version (PR)

The poetic rendering (PR), presented in section 10.3, was selected by 40 percent of those interviewed as the "most beautiful" or "sweetest" to listen to. This was the largest percentage for any version; 60 percent considered it the "most idiomatic" as well. Respondents of all types—men, women, youth,

---

[340]In Wendland 1998b:115–121 I present the rationale for this significant alteration of the name of God.

mother-tongue speakers, and second-language speakers—gave this response. The ideophones seemed to be the single most popular (albeit sometimes opaque) stylistic element—"words like *gonee, balala,* and *nde-nde-nde,*" which are "expressions we use in our daily lives." The idiomaticity of the PR, however, also meant that it was perceived by 20 percent as being rather difficult to understand, but this was a distant second to the old *Buku Lopatulika* version. Thus for some second-language speakers, the style was "too deep" or "too twisted"—even at times "confusing"—and certain words "too big" (i.e., too long), which is the result of a more conjunctive type of orthography. In contrast, some respondents picked this version as being the "easiest to memorize" precisely because of its interesting idiomatic style.

There were a variety of reasons that people—mother-tongue speakers in particular—gave for their attraction to this poetically restructured text. It was especially in subsequent discussion with respondents that its general popularity was revealed, as the following sentiments indicate: "we studied this [dynamic, literary] style of writing at school"; "those who know Chichewa are happy if somebody speaks idiomatically like this to him"; "the idiomatic language makes me learn some new words in order to understand the text"; "I like the *ndakatulo* version because of its emphasis on [certain] words here and there"; "it shows that a person is speaking [the language] with complete freedom [*ali omasuka*]"; "the words strike my heart" and "create a picture in my mind"; "this style is new [hence attractive] to me"—"this is my first time to see such kind of writing"; "it is a poem and therefore keeps one attentive" because one "does not get tired when listening to it"; "it raises the appetite to continue reading"; "I like to read the Bible as poetry like this"; "the youth especially enjoy *ndakatulo* writing so this will help them learn Psalm 23"; "these words remind us of our mother tongue" and "our traditions," such as "oral narratives"; "it sounds like modern Chinyanja [the Zambian dialect of Chichewa]." One experienced pastor exclaimed: "Every line and verse sounded like a song to me!" Another of the student surveyors noted, "They asked me to read it again and again and explain it [i.e., the idiomatic usages]." One student noted that the person being tested "showed a feeling of happiness" as he read the poetic text—"he favored *ndakatulo* the way I was observing his face." Some people felt that while this lyric, expressive style may not be appropriate for use throughout the Bible, it certainly fits the poetic character of books like Job, Psalms, Proverbs, Ecclesiastes, and Song of Songs.

Nevertheless, the negative opinion of a small number of respondents needs to be considered and investigated more fully in further studies. This is especially important with regard to the issue of the PR's lively style of language—its distinctive "English," as one young man described it. Is it too idiomatic, too "youthful," to be appropriate for reading or recitation during public worship services? One thing is clear in this regard: the solemn, introspective, meditative mood of the original Hebrew text has been transformed in Chichewa to reflect a viewpoint that is rather more vigorously optimistic and outgoing. The original poet's somewhat passive faith now sounds a good deal more active, in its emotional attitude if not in concrete action. Yet the thematic focus, as in the original, remains fixed upon the plenteous provision and protection of Yahweh.

10.7.5 The reformatted popular-language version Buku Loyera (BY)

There was no doubt that the easiest text to read aloud (excluding the hymn version) was the reformatted popular-language version, a sample of which is in section A.1.6. This was the opinion of 70 percent of the respondents. Nearly all respondents appreciated the way in which the lines were typographically "straightened out [*yoongoka*]" and the individual verses separated. The optimum length of line, however, is a matter that clearly requires further extensive testing (i.e., testing the format in sec. A.1.6 in comparison with the format in sec. A.1.5).

In contrast, the many overlapped lines and hyphenations in the *Buku Lopatulika*, as well as its small print, caused its readers major difficulties, especially the poorer readers and those with vision problems); it was hard for them to follow the text easily or correctly. As for the poetic *ndakatulo* rendering (PR), most of the mistakes that were noted when it was read seemed to occur as a result of word length; the poetic style favors the use of many smaller verbal affixes that often add several syllables to a given stem (e.g., *mwandilandiradi* 'you-have-really-received-me-well'.)

10.8 The practical and theoretical implications of this study

What can be learned from this and similar studies about assessing a Bible translation in general and its literary artistry in particular? I believe others can benefit from the experience we gained in the process of testing these versions in an oral-aural, group-oriented community, especially with respect to the subjective aspects of the test that pertain to personal preference. However, there are some other considerations that need to be noted as well. These are summarized in the sections below.

10.8.1 The implications for the test methodology

During the course of the assessment experiment my student assistants and I held weekly consultations concerning our practical methodology. We discussed what went wrong, or right, and what this teaches us, not only about the several translated texts being tested, but also about the testing procedure itself. These regular feedback sessions alerted us to certain problems and enabled us to take remedial action. As a result, we could improve our techniques for gaining the subjective information that we wanted.

Ongoing modifications meant that the later groups of testees were not examined for their aesthetic opinions in exactly the same manner as those who were tested first. However, we felt that the possible loss that this inconsistency caused for our goal of producing a final homogeneous statistical report was more than compensated for by the development of an improved mode of investigation. It was not only more appropriate for those we questioned, but also more accurate in terms of the answers that we received. If people do not know exactly what it is that they are being asked (or why), they cannot be expected to give satisfactory, or even correct, responses, no matter how hard they may be trying. Wrong responses can result from trying to please the tester (see Larsen 2001). Before we had finished, the entire evaluatory process had become more flexible and audience-sensitive, and this in turn made it more instructive for the testers themselves.

The observations expressed in our weekly meetings follow:

- By far the greatest procedural problem that emerged during the course of this study was the inclusion in the testing of nonmother-tongue speakers of Chichewa (68 out of 90 persons tested). In fact, the respondents comprised sixteen different ethnic groups. This put the *ndakatulo* PR version at somewhat of a disadvantage, because many Zambians—the young in particular—were not familiar with the "deep" Chichewa idiomatic usage spoken in Malawi and were unable to fully appreciate its special diction and stylistic features. Despite this limitation, it was our hope that enough of the artistry would become apparent even to second-language speakers to allow them to make a fair evaluation of the PR in relation to the others.
- The problems that arose when interviewing nonreaders were greater than anticipated. Thirty-seven persons revealed that they were nonliterate, but the rate of *functional* illiteracy is no doubt

even higher. Even in the case of those who *could* read, it was difficult to get answers to specific questions involving the four different versions because they often did not have the pertinent text in front of them. Consequently, the entire test sample usually had to be repeated a number of times in order to help people focus on the words of a given version so that they could remember more precisely what they had liked or disliked.

- We found that it was advantageous to give the respondents a brief overview of the type of questions that they would be asked before beginning the part of the questionnaire that is in section A.2.2. This helped the respondents focus more fully as they listened to specific aspects of the sample texts being read to them. Along with the overview we explained that we were *not* trying to eliminate any particular translation, or elevate one over another. We simply wished to see whether there was a way of making better use of the versions that were available or might be produced in the future.[341]

- In cases where the respondents were literate, they were sometimes given a copy of the sample texts to read through at home in advance. Familiarity with the four portions enabled them to answer questions about their preferences and opinions more confidently. Future testing should include a larger percentage of formally educated persons. This would help the testers obtain more precise, explanatory responses to questions about stylistic differences and their effect on a given evaluation of the text samples.

- The length of the original test seemed to present difficulties for some people. It was too intensive for people with little formal education to deal with all at once. Therefore, it was decided to make several questions optional (namely, questions *i–m* in sec. A.2.1 and *b* in sec. A.2.2). These were the questions the research group determined to be either peripheral or too technical. It may be noted, however, that several testees *were* capable of providing very helpful responses to some of these questions, for example, in regard to the potential lexical-semantic confusion between *mbusa* 'herdsman' (the Protestant 'pastor') and *busa* 'pasture' in vv. 1–2 of *Buku Lopatulika* (BL).

---

[341]It is important to explain to people, at least in general terms, *why* such testing is being carried out so that they can participate more fully as partners cooperating towards the completion of a particular objective that will be of benefit to the Christian community as a whole. As Sundersingh observes: "The non-literate is not accustomed to thinking in generalizations, and new information [such as that supplied in a testing program] must demonstrate its importance and relevance to his everyday life" (1999:184).

- Except for the student wives and a few other congregational leaders, women could not be interviewed individually without others being present. This was a matter of cultural propriety. According to traditional mores, no man, no matter how respected and religious, converses alone with an adult woman who is not his wife. Though this stricture is being loosened somewhat nowadays in many urban situations, even here it always generates a certain amount of suspicion among casual observers and can further lead to harmful rumors. In addition, since women are traditionally taught to act very modestly in formal public settings, they are reticent to give answers to a questionnaire of the type that we were presenting. For this reason, most of our women participants were tested in small groups of two or three. One was designated as the "principal" respondent (about whom the personal data would be recorded), and the others were "assistants." The latter were free to consult with and advise the principal testee about a given question and/or her evaluative reply. This arrangement permitted us to get an accurate sample of general public opinion in the most appropriate manner possible.
- With quite a few respondents it was not easy to elicit a single choice as to which sample from among the four versions was the "most difficult" or "easiest" or "most beautiful"; to obtain a number 2 choice was even harder. Some felt the difference between the first and second choice was too arbitrary or difficult to distinguish (e.g., in the case of questions *a* and *c* in A.2.2). On such occasions this follow-up question was therefore dispensed with.
- It was essential that the testers be allowed to dialogue with those being tested in order to encourage a nonconfrontational atmosphere. Dialoguing also helped ensure that the questions would be answered honestly, not just to please the interviewer. This undeniably introduced a rather large subjective component into the procedure, even though the testers were carefully instructed to try not to influence people to favor one version over another. Subjective or not, this was the only way in which we felt the testing process could be conducted with any depth of detail, especially in view of the prevailing "high-context" sociocultural setting and the fact that

all the participants were well known to each other, precluding a
cold, personally detached manner of testing.[342]

- We found that, generally speaking, some post-test explanation concerning the nature and purpose of the *ndakatulo* rendition (PR) enabled a significant number of nonmother-tongue speakers of
Chichewa to revise their originally neutral or even negative opinion of it. Although most second-language speakers still were not
able to completely understand the text due to its idiomaticity, they
came to appreciate the communicative goal of a poetic version,
and some even began to relate its outstanding stylistic features to
similar features in their mother tongue (e.g., ideophones, graphic
images, exclamations, syntactic mobility). It can be hoped that this
understanding will prepare such individuals to respond positively
to a poetic rendering that might some day be prepared in their own
language.

- It was interesting to observe the group dynamics when several
samples were tested with a larger audience. Our practical problem
was how to obtain any divergent opinions that might be present
among the group. We needed to overcome the conformity-seeking,
consensus-preferring, shame-avoiding tendencies that typify a
communal society. Neither an oral *inde* 'aye' or *iyai* 'nay' nor voting
by show of hands really worked. In fact, I think we were unable to
fully counteract this significant problem. People preferred to debate the issue or to vote with the majority in an effort to form a
common group viewpoint, seeking the best text for all concerned.

- As for the overt enthusiasm factor, it definitely favored the
ndakatulo version. In most cases where those tested really understood this poetic text and recognized some of its vibrant stylistic
usages (ideophones in particular), they responded in an open
extralinguistic manner with hand, head, and/or body movements,
smiles, affirmative exclamations, and even ululation (a shrill

---

[342]As noted earlier, a *high-context* society is one in which people depend a great deal
upon the sociocultural setting and interpersonal network as a framework for
contextualizing verbal discourse. Background information therefore does not have to be explicitly verbalized during normal discourse. A *low-context* society, on the other hand, is one
in which speakers prefer to textually express these vital aspects of context, rather than leaving them implicit or presupposed (see Katan 1999, chap. 10). Larsen (2001:44–45) points
out several related factors of a sociocultural nature that need to be considered during translation testing, namely, a "declarative" versus an "interrogative" educational system and a
"prestige ascribed" versus a "prestige achieved" society. People who represent an interrogative educational system and a prestige achieved society would "find it easier to accept new
ideas," as manifested for example in a more meaning-oriented, dynamically rendered translation of the Scriptures.

female cry of delight and celebration). Further testing is needed, however, to determine whether such demonstrations of gusto would or could be expressed during public worship and, if so, how appropriate they would be in the eyes of the elders of certain more conservative denominations.

- A testing procedure that is temporally and geographically more extensive and demographically more diverse than the experimental testing we undertook is obviously required. It may also be possible to devise a test that is more objective, yet still suitable for an audience that is largely nonliterate, oral-aurally inclined, interpersonal-relational, and community-based. Different models and methods of assessment need to be developed and tried out to see how the results would compare with those that I have reported. For example, in one model a single tester could be used; in another, multiple testers; and in still another, the nonverbal indicators of feeling or attitude could also be recorded. The experimental use of other such methods would tell us how reliable the informal, interactive, dialogic approach employed in the present study is in comparison with the alternatives. An expanded program of evaluation would do well to pay more specific attention to the medium of communication (e.g., silent reading tests for the literate) and cater to the distinct audience segments with different sets of group-specific questions (e.g., urban versus rural, older versus younger, literate versus nonliterate, and mother-tongue versus second-language speakers).

10.8.2 The implications for publishing, funding, and staffing

The focus of our test was to ascertain ordinary lay people's reactions to varied styles of the translated Scriptures. The test itself featured an artistic, poetic rendering (PR) in comparison with several other types of translation in Chichewa. The versions that were compared to the PR were (1) an older but revered literal version, *Buku Lopatulika* (BL); (2) a recent popular-language version, *Buku Loyera* (BY); and (3) a familiar hymn version (HV). The main finding was that there is a significant aesthetic attraction for the poetic rendering in terms of impact and appeal, even among second-language speakers. This finding has some definite implications for future publications and funding.

From a more technical, but also rather subjective perspective, I also conclude that between the *ndakatulo* poetic rendering and the original Hebrew text there exists an approximate parity in terms of five major communication functions (informative, expressive, aesthetic, textual, and relational). Furthermore, with regard to the four aspects of acceptability that were considered earlier (in sec. 10.5), the following diagram summarizes the results of our assessment with reference to the PR text in comparison with the Hebrew (with [+] representing appreciable equivalence, and [–] representing lesser equivalence):

Fidelity: accuracy [+], authenticity [–]	} —with respect to textual *meaning*
Intelligibility: intent [+], content [–]ᵃ	

Idiomaticity: written [+], oral-aural [+]	} —with respect to textual *form*
Proximity: macrostructure [+],ᵇ microstructure [–]	

ᵃThis does not mean that the PR text is hard to understand, but it is presumably more difficult in this respect than Psalm 23 was to its Hebrew hearers.
ᵇThe poetic rendering (PR) is rearranged, but the basic structural features are preserved vis à vis the Hebrew original text.

These observations, albeit tentative, would tend to encourage a move by the Bible Societies and other translation organizations to conduct further research into the potential of poetic translation to satisfy the stylistic preferences of ordinary lay people. However, such a decision should be supported by some additional testing, especially in areas where there is a larger proportion of mother-tongue speakers of Chichewa.

Each of the other three versions in this research project has its own particular strengths and weaknesses. The BL has *familiarity* and *affection* going for it among Protestants, but it remains stylistically unnatural even to those who use it all the time; the BY manifests great *clarity* and *intelligibility*, yet is comparatively lacking in artistic compensation in relation to the biblical text; the hymn version has widespread *popularity*, but is formally tied to a specific, sung melody. Clearly these different translations ought not be set up in competition with one another; rather, people should be shown how to use them all to complement each other within a larger framework of religious communication (evangelization, edification, consolation, etc.).

I conclude that the current policy of the Bible Societies, which aims to produce and promote different types of translation for differing needs, desires, situations, and segments of the general population, is strongly substantiated. This would apply to both the primary characteristics of *quality* (such as the style of rendering, use of supplementary aids for the reader, the manner of page formatting and typography) and also *quantity* (the number of copies printed in relation to the specific constituency concerned and also the size of publication—a small portion versus a full Bible). As to the reformatted BY version, the higher cost of publishing such a space-generous, single-columned text of larger, more legible print size would be a limiting factor. On the other hand, if only portion-sized productions of certain popular pericopes are published (e.g., a selection of familiar psalms), then perhaps the added expense would not be that much when weighed against the increased readability of this design.

One final consideration: Obviously it would require a great deal in terms of *human resources* to produce any sort of a stylistically sensitive or literary functionally equivalent (LiFE) translation. At least one artistically inclined verbal specialist would be needed to compose such a text, someone who can ensure a satisfactory level of exegetical fidelity along with an acceptable TL style, suitably dynamic yet fully appropriate for religious use, even if not for public worship. For the Psalms, especially, an experienced poet would be necessary for success in making the transformation from SL to TL. But that person would also need an adequate amount of biblical background knowledge in order to know how far to go in recreating the text without unduly compromising semantic faithfulness. In addition to the translator(s), other auxiliary staff would have to be trained to review and assess such a version and then offer stylistically oriented constructive criticism. Alternatively, local specialists in the requisite fields could be co-opted for the project. Finally, the intended target group, too, would have to be appropriately educated so that they adequately (if not completely) understand the nature and purpose of the new specialized version, how and why it differs from existing Scripture publications in the TL, and how they can apply such a text for their ultimate spiritual benefit.

10.8.3 The implications for literary translation

I have already discussed what needs to be done in future testing programs and translation projects in order to capitalize on the particular insights revealed by the research reported in this chapter. Now it may be helpful to note areas of special interest and concern having to do with the production and promotion of a specially composed, literary-rhetorical translation of the Bible:

- The particular factor and value of artistry must be isolated to a greater extent—along with its chief stylistic devices (e.g., figurative language, repetition, word-order shifts, intensifiers, phonological devices) to allow a more focused, discriminating evaluation by those being interviewed. This could be done by means of a test that compares only two key texts and their corresponding features at one time (whether complete pericopes, individual passages, or single clauses). For example, a lyric rendering might be compared with corresponding (but reformatted) samples of the popular-language version. Alternatively, more detailed tests of specific features in particular kinds of contexts (co-texts) could be developed. The lyric rendering also needs to be tried out using different genres of biblical discourse such as narrative portions or epistolary segments. Furthermore, it may be necessary to carry out this sort of sophisticated literary assessment more extensively among more knowledgeable respondents such as pastors, teachers, theological students, university students, and more highly educated laypersons.

- More consideration needs to be given to specifying the primary situation of use intended for the artistic version. One of the objectives of the current study was to try to identify some appropriate contexts for the PR's use. One way to do this is to arrange for a special performance setting where testing could be carried out, using different media and formats of text presentation. In central Africa, for example, this could be done by using a *ndakatulo* psalm in an informal worship service of celebration and praise, or a *ndakatulo* psalm could be composed and published as a tract or as a song for a youth choir, or a narrative poetic portion could be presented as a play[343] or broadcast as part of a religious radio drama.[344] In any of these settings, additional audience-involving, tradition-familiar techniques could be utilized to good advantage, such things as background music, periodic points allowing for hand-clapping or "call and response" (either formulaic or spontaneous), interspersed songs and choruses, intervals of drumming, several "character" voices, and a presenter or narrator.
- If the research and testing were better funded, it would be possible to use cassette recordings for transmitting the sample texts and collecting listener responses. Perhaps group sessions could even be

---

[343]The interpersonal drama of Job, for example, would be a possible starting point. A Zambian playwright, Manda Mwila, is currently "bent on bringing the Biblical book of Job onto the stage, in a play he has tagged: 'Job—The Story of Restoration,' " according to the *Sunday Times* of Zambia, April 2, 2000, p. 8.

[344]There is a great potential for novel artistic expression via the medium of radio, since high-powered Christian radio stations have begun broadcasting in Zambia during the past ten years.

video-taped. Mechanically aided transmission would itself need to be assessed, however, in terms of its effectiveness in the socio-cultural settings of southern or central Africa. Would the attainment of greater efficiency or objectivity in test administration be offset by a negative response on the part of respondents to this formal, potentially distracting manner of impersonal communication, the aim of which is to achieve a process of *personal* evaluation? Perhaps some testing via radio broadcast might be carried out in order to learn more generally what the potential and limitations of an electronic medium would be. Radio listeners' feedback can be solicited in the form of letters, telephone calls, or nowadays even by e-mail where the technical facilities are available.

- The overwhelming popularity of the familiar hymn version (HV) has implications for presenting other key Scripture pericopes in hymnic, choral, or some other musically accompanied form, perhaps even entire books, such as the Song of Songs. To investigate this further, a development of Klem's (1982) and Sundersingh's (1999) research (and similar studies) would be called for. Of course, the musical dimension would necessitate another kind of production expertise and additional funding, but the investment in time, effort, and resources would undoubtedly lead to greater contextual relevance in terms of promoting greater, more varied Scripture use, including memorization and public oral expression.[345] The printed format of the HV revealed another important consideration: most readers, second-language speakers in particular, preferred the short meaningful line units. This preference was also expressed in relation to the *ndakatulo* version.

- It became apparent that there is a definite need to discover, train, encourage, and publish the recognized (or even the unrecognized) poets and literary-minded individuals of a given society. Few, if any, artistic Scripture versions will ever be produced if there are no genuine artists available to produce them in the first place. This raises a few problems, however. The financial rewards for gifted Bible translators are relatively small in comparison with what can be earned in the secular market. There is also the issue of freedom of expression. Bible translation tends to constrain artistic creativity: the translator is bound by the essential content of the original text and in many cases also by overly rigid ecclesiastical

---

[345]Sundersingh concludes: "Non-Literates need mnemonic devices to assist their memory. An excellent mnemonic device presented by audio is music. Songs have the capacity to be remembered much longer than even narratives" (1999:194).

expectations or the perceived sacredness of the setting in which the translation will be used. On the other hand, the great potential for increased personal spiritual benefit and stimulation might compensate for these difficulties. One is always impressed by the enthusiastic response to the Scriptures on the part of people who have not lost their ability to appreciate the "heart language" of their mother tongue whereby significant, soul-stirring meaning is best conveyed.

- Our research project served to instill in those tested, and indeed in entire participating congregations, the desire to know more about the activity of Bible translation and the reasons for differences among versions, whether vernacular or English. The possibility of having several distinct types, or styles, of translation available for use in diverse situations and to serve different purposes was strongly supported by a number of respondents. Furthermore, many of the *non*mother-tongue speakers of Chichewa/Chinyanja expressed the desire that such translation and testing be carried out in their own respective languages (all of which belong to the closely related Bantu group). Some people even felt that this kind of formal research should be conducted on a regular basis in local congregations. It would, they felt, encourage more active Bible reading and Bible study, including instruction aimed at enabling a more diligent search for the intended meaning of the original text and a mastery of some of the more difficult portions of Scripture, poetry in particular.

11

Organizing a Literary-Rhetorical Translation Project

In this concluding chapter I will review the core ideas of this book as they relate to the establishment of a translation project. I will assume that the formulators of the project terms of reference (*Brief*) have taken the conse- quential decision to include within its translation purpose (*Skopos*) the aim of producing a literary, functionally equivalent (LiFE) version, whether a complete book of the Bible, such as the Psalms, or an included pericope such as Psalm 23.

Some of the chief obstacles and challenges that face those who are jointly commissioned with the task of carrying out this objective will be summarized here. (Most of them have already been mentioned in the pre- ceding chapters, but not in this particular developmental format.)

11.1 The need for sufficient pre-project planning and research

The critical step of pre-planning as part of establishing an efficient and effec- tive translation project is frequently overlooked in the rush to get things un- derway. In the past, such neglect was perhaps understandable since many organizers may have felt that there were only two major options avail- able—either a literal version or an idiomatic version. The same limited choice applied to important co-variables, such as the medium of communica- tion and the format of text presentation. It was further assumed that they, usually the church leaders, were in the best position to make a choice on be- half of the entire TL community. However, this is not the case nowadays (see sec. 2.8). We now recognize the need to do adequate pre-project research and planning concerning a variety of options in relation to the following three aspects of interlingual message transmission and representation:

• *Textual*—planning with respect to the type of rendering. Will it be more or less dynamic, artistic, rhetorical, and/or novel in terms of the stylistic inventory of appropriate L-R features that may be applied in the TL text?

• *Paratextual*—planning with respect to the supplementary aids that might be employed to guide and enrich a reading of the translation itself, such as sectional headings, introductions, special print formats, a glossary, maps, charts/diagrams, and illustrations.

• *Metatextual*—planning with respect to critical situational circumstances: human and financial resources; potential communication-limiting factors (e.g., ecumenical, financial, temporal, educational, staff-related, existing versions); the chosen channel of message transmission (e.g., print or audio); and of course an accurate assessment of the expressed needs or desires of the primary and secondary audiences. This last point about target-oriented research is crucial, for in one way or another it will affect all of the others.

It is important then to consider what ordinary Bible users wish to see, or hear, in a translation that is meant for them. How can they possibly know whether they would like and be able to use a full literary version or not if they have never been exposed to a good example of one or have never been educated with regard to the reason for its difference from a traditional, more literal translation? Furthermore, they need to be made aware of the other features possible in a "value-added" translation,[346] such as contextualized illustrations, explanatory footnotes, selective cross-references, a simple

---

[346]This term, along with its pertinent application to contemporary Bible translations, comes from a provocative article by Prof. S. Joubert (2002). Joubert's concluding caveat is relevant to those who are planning to produce a LiFE version: "[M]odern translations should address these strange sounds emanating from the original cultural packaging by providing relevant information to assist modern readers in assigning legitimate meanings to the various linguistic signs encapsulated on the pages of the Bible. Without the initial culture shock in encountering a Bible translation we are held prisoners by Western translations of the Bible" (ibid.:41). However, one must take care to distinguish *formal* from *semantic* culture shock. The former would indeed be largely eliminated from a formally domesticated ("naturalized") version; hopefully the latter would not (with regard to issues arising from the historical and sociocultural background, for example, as well as

concordance, and biblical history timeline. in addition to those already mentioned. With respect to medium, it should be asked whether most people would prefer to access the text in written or aural form, in which style or format, and why. These and similar questions can be reliably answered in one way only, that is, by means of a systematic and setting-sensitive program of prior market research in which those for whom the translation is intended are themselves asked and allowed to assess the various available alternatives that are offered by way of illustration.

11.2 Selecting and training the translation team

The most important factor in the preparation of any literary translation is the selection and training of the translation team. This is the key variable that will prevent, limit, or enable ultimate success in this challenging venture. At least one member of the team, which usually comprises three persons, must have the gift of verbal artistry in the TL, that is, as a proficient poet or rhetor in either oral or written vernacular discourse. Without this vital human component, the project will not make much progress no matter how many other resources are available. Ideally, such an individual should have considerable training also in biblical studies so that she or he begins the task with a healthy understanding of and respect for the original text of Scripture.[347] Furthermore, it seems probable that for a genuinely literary, say a poetic, version to succeed, it will have to be initially composed with the genre-based and related artistic and rhetorical essentials already in place—as opposed to these features being subsequently pasted like patchwork into mediocre text by some stylist. The literary foundation has to be firmly laid in the initial draft. Then it can be either corrected exegetically, if need be, or polished up stylistically.

How does one go about finding an individual with the requisite spiritual empathy and artistic talents to do an acceptable job when recomposing a text of Scripture in his or her language? As part of the pre-project investigations described in section 11.1, a search could

---

from the worldview and value system of the biblical text). In any case, translators are obliged in all honesty to explain—perhaps in an introductory preface and/or periodic footnotes—how they have rendered the original text and why, and what has been lost and how. Public educational seminars in various venues and for different constituencies will also undoubtedly be needed, so that active give-and-take discussions of the relevant concerns can take place with the community at large.

[347]It may be extremely difficult to find such a dually gifted individual. The problem with verbal artists who do not know much about the Bible or who have been engaged solely in composing secular literature is that they may feel overly constrained by the requirements of translating Scripture—that is, by the obligation to analyze and functionally represent the meaningful *forms* as well as the *content* of the original sacred text.

simultaneously be made for potential candidates, in fact for the whole team—a capable and committed trio made up of a literary drafter, a biblical exegete, and a specialist in the area of critiquing, revising testing, and doing various research-related tasks. Perhaps an initial trial workshop will have to be conducted with the specific aim of identifying the best-qualified team members from among those who have either applied or been recommended for this special LiFE project. A representative panel of biblical scholars, translation experts, literary critics, and typical members of the target group should make the final selection or recommendation to the project's governing administrative body.

Ideally, the three specialists chosen should have the opportunity of working together for several months before final confirmation, just to make sure that they are not only fully equipped technically for the task, but also compatible and mutually complementing when it comes to working together as a team. During this same period the person who has been chosen to serve as the team leader, or translation coordinator, will have to be evaluated by the project's administrative committee as to his or her ability to serve in this crucial capacity. Many difficult, and at times controversial, decisions will have to be made in the course of their work, and a capable, widely respected manager will have to be found to guide this process as well as the team's day-to-day operations.

Once chosen and confirmed, the team must then be provided with the necessary specialized instruction and training in any areas where they may be deficient. The artist-stylist, for example, would probably benefit from some supplemental education in exegetical analysis, the exegete in literary skills, the researcher in test-sampling techniques—and everyone with regard to modern multimedia and audience-specific communication methods. Even though all this preparation may well take some time, it is indispensable to ensure that the most qualified group of translators is assembled for so rigorous and demanding an assignment as the interlingual, cross-cultural communication of a poetically expressed and rhetorically argued biblical pericope.

A less formal, but no less important course of education also needs to be offered to those who have been selected to serve as reviewers—whether with respect to the text as a whole or only specific aspects of it, such as poetic features, genre evaluation, exegetical accuracy, key theological vocabulary, or extratextual supplements. Reviewers must understand the precise nature of the translation *Brief* and *Skopos* that they have been commissioned with and how they are able to contribute to it. If they cannot appreciate where, how, and why the drafts that they will be examining and listening to differ from a more literal or prosaic rendering, they may see the very features that make a text literary as what they object to the most.

11.3 Compositional-translational procedures

Once the translation team has been assembled, they must first, with the guidance of a translation consultant, agree upon a complete set of daily operational procedures. For example, what strategy can the artist-translator adopt in order to create an acceptable initial draft that is exegetically reliable and also demonstrates the desired stylistic appeal and rhetorical power? Can she or he learn to compose a more vigorous style of vernacular discourse (whatever the genre) without going overboard—that is, without distorting the biblical text and without forcing the literary forms of Scripture into their TL equivalents? Will a special compositional technique need to be devised so as to accent the oral-aural quality in the translation? How can the other team members learn to react to an initial draft in a critical yet sensitive way so that no misunderstanding or hard feelings result?

The procedures need to be jointly considered and established in keeping with the project *Skopos*. Perhaps it has been decided to apply a more limited L-R (LiFE) method, for example only for selected poetic texts of Scripture or making only selective use of the available TL poetic features. How can the team utilize their individual abilities then to cooperatively produce a satisfactory and acceptable result? And how can the inevitable differences of opinion be arbitrated equitably so that a consensus may be achieved in terms of a final approved text? No matter how excellent the individual members of the team, if they lack an adequate step-by-step working plan whereby they can mutually stimulate, correct, complement, and encourage one another, they will not function together well, if at all. If they cannot learn to cooperate fully with one another, they may only frustrate each other's personal efforts and thus hinder or even undo the entire enterprise.

The team, or perhaps its appointed coordinator, needs to work in close conjunction with an experienced translation consultant and an efficient administrative committee representing the target community. With the consultant's guidance, the administrative committee will have to formulate detailed job descriptions and guidelines for each of the team members in accordance with the overall project *Brief*. Then, as new exigencies, obstacles, or resources materialize, their individual working guidelines may need to be revised and elaborated upon, but always on the basis of mutual agreement with regard to the final desired Scripture product.

The specific translation principles and procedures will also have to be clearly communicated to all chief reviewers as well as the leading project supporters and local decision-makers. It is essential that they all fully understand what is going on and have a chance to contribute in some meaningful way to the effort. In addition, the wider community too must be kept well informed. They should know where the work stands at any given moment, what its future course of action is, and how well the project is performing at any stage with regard to the terms of its guiding *Skopos* statement.

11.4 Evaluating and testing the translation

The translation team itself, together with trained reviewers or review teams, are expected to carefully monitor and continually assess the quality (and quantity) of work that is being done. However, at a relatively early stage key representatives of the TL community will also have to be involved, gauging the potential popular reaction to a literary-rhetorical type of Scripture translation, which for many will undoubtedly be quite novel.[348] Does the text meet the primary needs, the expressed desires, and the use-related expectations of a majority of the target audience, as expressed in the project *Skopos* (which they are all hopefully familiar with, at least in summary form)? Does the translation go too far in domesticating the forms of the biblical text? On the other hand, does the translation sufficiently satisfy their criteria and standards of excellence with regard to the written (or oratorical) style and linguistic usage in their language? If not, what alterations can be suggested? It is possible that if these are widespread, some modifications in the team's translation principles, working procedures, and possibly even its personnel may be necessitated.

The need for text-related testing does not end once a version has been published. A program of "product evaluation" must be continued, now in relation to the target population as a whole and to the text's wider use within a range of diverse religious settings. In which ways and how effectively are people making use of the translation that has been prepared for them?[349] What are the major problems that have arisen in terms of understanding and applying the new version? To what extent does this poetically worded and sound-sensitive translation satisfy smaller subgroups of Bible users and meet particular needs and particular uses (e.g., as source

---

[348]Iver Larsen's 2001 article on "acceptability" was published after I completed the initial draft of this chapter. I was pleased to see how closely our respective ideas converge and complement each other with regard to this important issue.

[349]Philip Noss has been carrying out important research in this field of applied translation studies, especially in the area of post-translation "Scripture use" (see Noss 2002).

material for youth choir compositions, radio broadcasting, dramatic performances, popular musical renditions, comic book publications)? Do strong negative public reactions in certain situations and settings suggest any revisions that should be made in the event that a second edition becomes necessary and feasible? Such formal and informal testing needs to be coordinated by some responsible and broadly acceptable agency, perhaps the local Bible Society, and the research results must be properly recorded and saved for future reference.

11.5 Encouraging the TL audience's extensive and intensive involvement

As previously noted, most modern translation theories (from the more foreignizing to the more domesticating) have emphasized the hermeneutical activity and perceptions of the target group for whom a particular version of the Scriptures has been prepared. A program of cooperative, community-based engagement in Bible translation is to be actively encouraged. It should be both extensive (in terms of the numbers of people involved) and intensive (with respect to the degree of actual involvement), whether the focus is a poetic rendition of an entire book, such as the Psalter, or only an individual popular pericope, such as Psalm 23.

The familiar terms *receptors* and *receptor audience* are rather misleading, as is *target audience*, but to a lesser extent. Such terms are far too passive in implication. The ordinary users of the translation, not only the scholars and clergy, need to be engaged in producing the text from beginning (project planning) to end (product evaluation). It is they who are the ultimate "consumers" of the version. That being the case, they must see themselves as joint owners—"stakeholders"—in the communication event being carried out on their behalf. Of course, they cannot do the actual translation work themselves, but they must feel that they do play a meaningful role by directly and indirectly advising the chief project participants: the translators, revisers, testers, and local administrators.

Through their provision of human, material, and financial resources, as well as by their efforts to popularize the project, the text consumers need to shoulder the responsibility of supporting the translation as it is being prepared. They also need to commit themselves to purchasing and using the version once it has been published. This may involve a decision to suspend any negative judgment until they have had a chance to get accustomed to the LiFE rendition in a variety of settings. A great deal of time, expense, and effort goes into producing any Bible translation, especially a literary-rhetorical one; and this can be justified (and the translators' labors at least partially rewarded) only if the new and novel text turns out to contribute in a significant way to the options available to the community for religious as well as literary development. It is up to the people themselves to ensure that this is accomplished—by using the new translation in the manner for which it was intended.

But for the target constituency to be involved in these important ways, it is vital for them to be gradually yet thoroughly instructed by educators from both without and within the community. They need to be made aware of what their particular responsibilities and obligations are. How can they be expected to appreciate or support an innovative sort of Scripture translation if they do not know why, how, by whom, and for whom it has been prepared? This is a matter of great concern, especially in areas where people are already familiar with one or more existing versions that are stylistically very different from the LiFE version being undertaken.

An interactive, community-centered educational program must be implemented as soon as possible, ideally during the initial stages of project planning when the *Skopos* is being discussed and formulated. This effort should be continued for the duration of the translation work so that as many people as possible can contribute feedback to the venture. After publication some basic instruction is still needed in the areas of communication techniques, biblical studies, hermeneutics, translation principles, and literary appreciation in order to prepare people to intelligently access and utilize all the textual and supplementary resources that the new version makes available.[350] This would not be in isolation from or in competition with existing translations, but together with them, in a mutually complementary method of comparative evaluation and text study, coupled with Bible learning and personal application.

Such an energetic program of Scripture engagement will certainly contribute greatly to increasing the relevance of the Word in the users' contemporary life-setting. It will also lay the groundwork for a later systematic critical revision, which should be an explicit aspect of any project *Brief* nowadays. Thus the work of translating any version is not linear, having a definite endpoint; it is rather a dynamic cyclical process involving extensive and intensive research, SL text analysis, TL text production, testing, revision, publication, and then, at a future date, a repetition of these same procedures.

---

[350]As noted in chapter 9, a very successful extensive and intensive audience-educational program has been conducted for the past decade by a number of national Bible Societies in South America (see Omanson 2001). These courses and seminars relate not only to the specific field of Bible translation but also branch off into many related areas of "theological education by extension."

11.6 Recommendations

The following recommendations summarize chapter 11. The special aim of my proposed translation program is to encourage a higher level of target audience involvement in the production of a more idiomatically expressed, rhetorically phrased, artistically toned version of the Scriptures in a local vernacular language. My suggestions concern the interrelated areas of project preparation, selection of translators, popular education, supplementary helps, project organization, community interaction, and project evaluation. These proposals (or appropriate alternatives) need to be considered in the light of the argument of this book, then modified as necessary to meet local needs, and finally adopted during the planning and formulation of a translation *Brief*—those guidelines that set forth the theoretical principles, practical procedures, and pragmatic objectives of the project as a whole.

- *As to project preparation*—The joint, community-based preparation of a comprehensive, but flexible, context-centered *Skopos*, or statement of purpose, must be effected at the very onset of a given translation project (to be periodically reviewed and revised as necessary). First of all, the need or demand for a LiFE rendering should be clearly established by means of a thorough pre-project audience research program. What is its designated target group? In what situations will it be used? Which specific audience needs will it meet? How much initial support does it have? How dynamic or extensive an L-R application is desired: minimal, medial, or maximal with regard to tectonicity, to artistry, to iconicity, and to rhetoricity?
- *As to selection of translators*—Only the most competent and committed to a rigorous work ethic will be equal to the task of Bible translation, an L-R version in particular. This will require proven TL wordsmiths and rhetoricians, proficient in both speech and writing. A great deal of attention will have to be devoted to the process of discovering, motivating, and enlisting team members of this caliber, especially the vernacular artist who is to serve as the principal text drafter. She or he must then be teamed with an academically qualified but also congenial and cooperative exegete who can ensure an adequate measure of fidelity to the original text without stifling the creative initiative of the artist colleague.
- *As to popular education*—It is important to encourage and assist the chosen translators and review specialists to become the best that

they can be, for example, through linguistic and literary studies as well as progressively arranged, practical in-service training sessions or apprenticeship with recognized verbal masters in the community (e.g., an oral storyteller or poet, a popular song composer, or an effective preacher or Bible teacher). In addition, a systematic education of the entire target community is required with regard to the nature and purpose of the project as a whole. Perhaps it will be possible to enlist some TL-speaking scholars and academics (e.g., theological instructors, senior educators, and university lecturers) to assist in this instructional endeavor.[351]

- *As to supplementary helps*—Liberally annotated versions of the Scripture provide needed frames of reference—both contextual (sociocultural and historical) and conceptual (topical, symbolic, worldview-related). They foster a more setting-specific and text-penetrating interpretation of any given passage or pericope. Such locally contextualized supplementary material, from introductory essays to glossary entries, would necessarily include material that pertains to the special nature of the translation itself, for example, references to the prominent structural and stylistic features of either the SL or the TL text. These would be coordinated with other relevant helps for the reader or audience, such as the structural arrangement of a text's larger discourse organization, a thematic outline of a book, a listing of its key terms, or a summary of the rhetorical argument of an epistle.

- *As to project organization*—The establishment of good management principles and the team's working procedures is essential for a successful translation project. This would be an operational structure that gives translators enough time and guidance to do the job along with the necessary encouragement. It must be a goal-oriented and quality-controlled strategy, including the translators' being monitored, administered, and facilitated by a capable project coordinator and a committee composed of key members of the sponsoring target constituency—concerned individuals who understand what

---

[351]There appears to be a great potential for this sort of an interactive program of scholarly assistance to be carried out in many countries of the world, for example, volunteer professors working in the South African university system. The main problem, besides adequate funding, seems to be that many academics are either not aware of the great needs for Bible translation or they do not know how they can help. Perhaps this effort might be facilitated and coordinated through agencies like the Centre for Bible Translation in Africa (University of Stellenbosch) and similar organizations in strategic locations throughout the world.

an L-R translation is all about and are committed to the success of such a version in their language.

- *As to community interaction*—It is necessary to encourage as much local public relations and grass-root support of the translation project as possible in order to stimulate and nourish the idea of joint responsibility and accountability, even if the target audience is relatively narrow (e.g., urban Christian youth). One has to generate a sense of responsible community ownership and promote immediate active usage of the version under preparation so that it will be fully accepted and applied when it is finally published. A novel, stylistically dynamic translation needs to be popularized (made reader/hearer-friendly as well as familiar) well before the time the finished product appears in print or on audiocassettes. This can be done by distributing illustrative and perhaps also instructive samples.

- *As to product evaluation*—An ongoing program of feature-specific text testing has to be promoted from the start. Draft versions must be open to revision in response to audience feedback garnered through both formal and informal methods of assessment from both scholarly and average receptors. This would include encouraging community-based dialogic Scripture study sessions. Suppose the subject for consideration is an Old Testament narrative; the new version could be tried out in the familiar traditional setting of a dramatized oral performance (e.g., by a well-known local griot), then criticism be elicited from the audience. This would be a good way to increase Bible knowledge and at the same time test comprehension. The same would apply to a recital of a LiFE-rendered psalm or prophetic passage in the manner of a royal praise poet.

Our desire is to make it possible for many more people to read and hear the literary artistry and rhetoric of the Christ and his spokesmen (the prophets as well as the apostles) in their mother tongue. Such a new translational option would give them and perhaps heretofore unreached segments of the community the opportunity of becoming as impressed—"amazed" in fact—by the words and deeds of the Master as were his original audiences (see Matt. 7:28–29, Mark 1:22, and Luke 4:32). It is hoped that through this literary means they will be encouraged and in turn motivated to play a more active and responsible role in the ongoing hermeneutical and communicative engagement with the text of Scripture that was initiated and is being maintained for their benefit by this very same Word.

Appendix A
Supplement to Chapter 10

The materials in this appendix are supplementary to chapter 10. There are three sections: A.1, with the samples of Psalm 23[352] referred to in the first paragraph of chapter 10; A.2, the questionnaire used in the testing program; and A.3, a summary of the testing results. The poetic rendering (sec. A.1.8) was the main focus of the testing, the others were presented for comparison to it.

A.1 Sample translations of Psalm 23

A.1.1 Psalm 23 in the Masoretic Text and the RSV

מִזְמוֹר לְדָוִד 1
v. 1 A psalm of David.

יְהוָה רֹעִי לֹא אֶחְסָר׃
The LORD is my shepherd, I shall not want.

בִּנְאוֹת דֶּשֶׁא יַרְבִּיצֵנִי 2
v. 2 He makes me lie down in green pastures;

---

[352]Lefevere observes that one helpful technique for studying a poetic translation "is to compare several translations of the same poem, not in order to make value judgments [though critical evaluation, too, is a valid exercise, if based on explicit criteria of analysis], but to examine the different strategies employed" (cited in Baker, ed. 1998:172). "It also follows that several translations of the same poem will be able to achieve what no one translation can do, that is to highlight different aspects of the same poem, and there is a good case that can be made for multiple translations of the same poem" (ibid.:175)—that is, to gain a more accurate impression of both its artistry and the author-intended message.

עַל־מֵי מְנֻחוֹת יְנַהֲלֵנִי׃
he leads me beside still waters;

3 נַפְשִׁי יְשׁוֹבֵב
v. 3 he restores my soul.

יַנְחֵנִי בְמַעְגְּלֵי־צֶדֶק לְמַעַן שְׁמוֹ׃
He leads me in paths of righteousness for his name's sake.

4 גַּם כִּי־אֵלֵךְ בְּגֵיא צַל מָוֶת
v. 4 Even though I walk through the valley of the shadow of death,

לֹא־אִירָא רָע כִּי־אַתָּה עִמָּדִי
I fear no evil; for thou art with me;

שִׁבְטְךָ וּמִשְׁעַנְתֶּךָ הֵמָּה יְנַחֲמֻנִי׃
thy rod and thy staff, they comfort me.

5 תַּעֲרֹךְ לְפָנַי שֻׁלְחָן נֶגֶד צֹרְרָי
v. 5 Thou preparest a table before me in the presence of my enemies;

דִּשַּׁנְתָּ בַשֶּׁמֶן רֹאשִׁי כּוֹסִי רְוָיָה׃
thou anointest my head with oil, my cup overflows.

6 אַךְ טוֹב וָחֶסֶד יִרְדְּפוּנִי כָּל־יְמֵי חַיָּי
v. 6 Surely goodness and mercy shall follow me all the days of my life;

וְשַׁבְתִּי בְּבֵית־יְהוָה לְאֹרֶךְ יָמִים׃
and I shall dwell in the house of the LORD for ever.

A.1.2 Psalm 23 from the Church of Scotland hymnal[353]

The Lord's my shepherd, I'll not want.
    He makes me down to lie
In pastures green: he leadeth me
    the quiet waters by.
My soul he doth restore again;
    and me to walk doth make.

---

[353]This is a well-known, century-old lyric translation of Psalm 23, originally approved by the Church of Scotland for use in public worship. It is quoted from the reprint edition of *The Psalms in Verse* (Barbour 1995:50-51).

Within the paths of righteousness,
  ev'n for his own name's sake.
Yea, though I walk in death's dark vale,
  yet will I fear none ill:
For thou art with me; and thy rod
  and staff me comfort still.
My table thou hast furnished
  in presence of my foes;
My head thou dost with oil anoint,
  and my cup overflows.
Goodness and mercy all my life
  shall surely follow me:
And in God's house forevermore
  my dwelling-place shall be.

A.1.3 Psalm 23 from The Message *(Peterson 1994:33–34)*

A DAVID PSALM

Yahweh, my shepherd!
  I don't need a thing.
You have bedded me down in lush meadows,
  you find me quiet pools to drink from.
True to your word,
  you let me catch my breath
  and send me in the right direction.

Even when the way goes through
  Death Valley,
I'm not afraid
  when you walk at my side.
Your trusty shepherd's crook
  makes me feel secure.

You serve me a six-course dinner
  right in front of my enemies.
You revive my drooping head;
  my cup brims with blessing.

Your beauty and love chase after me
  every day of my life.
I'm back home in the house of Yahweh
  for the rest of my life.

A.1.4 Psalm 23 in Chichewa Buku Lopatulika (1922), formatted as published

Salimo la Davide	Psalm of David[354]
Yehova ndiye mbusa wanga;	"Jehovah" he is my herdsman; [1]
sindidzasowa.	I will not lack.
Andigonetsa ku busa lamsipu:	He makes me lie down at a pasture of grass: [2]
Anditsogolera ku madzi odikha.	He leads me to still waters.
Atsitsimutsa moyo wanga;	He revives my life; [3]
Anditsogolera m'mabande a cilu-	He leads me in tracks of righteous-
ngamo, cifukwa ca dzina lace.	ness, because of his name.
Inde, ndingakhale ndiyenda m'ci-	Yes, even though I may walk in a val- [4]
gwa ca mthunzi wa imfa,	ley of a shadow of death,
Sindidzaopa coipa; pakuti Inu	I will not fear an evil thing; for You
muli ndi ine:	you are with me:
Cibonga canu ndi ndodo yanu, izi	Your war club and your walking stick, they
zindisangalatsa ine.	they make me happy.
Mundiyalikira gome pamaso pa-	You spread out a square platform before my [5]
nga m'kuona kwa adani anga:	eyes in the seeing of my enemies:
Mwandidzoza mutu wanga ma-	You have poured out on my head
futa; cikho canga cisefuka.	oil; my cup overflows.
Inde ukoma ndi cifundo zidza-	Yes goodness and mercy they will [6]
nditsata masiku onse a moyo	follow me all the days of the life
wanga:	of mine:
Ndipo ndidzakhala m'nyumba ya	And I will stay in the house of
Yehova masiku onse.	"Jehova" all the days.

A.1.5 Psalm 23 in Chichewa Buku Loyera (1998), formatted as published

Salimo la Davide	Psalm of David
Chauta ndiye mbusa wanga,	Chauta he is my herdsman, [1]
sindidzasowa kanthu.	I will not lack anything.
Amandigoneka pa busa	He lays me down at a pasture [2]
lamsipu.	of grass.
Amanditsogolera ku madzi	He leads me to waters
odikha kokapumulirako.	still to go and rest there.
Amatsitsimutsa moyo wanga.	He revives my life. [3]
Amanditsogolera m'njira za	He leads me in ways of
chilungamo	righteousness
malinga ndi ulemerero wa	according to the glory of
dzina lake.	his name.

[354]My literal translation follows the hyphenation of the Chichewa text and includes a representation of the double subject marker, which sounds awkward in English but is emphatic in the vernacular.

Ngakhale ndiyende m'chigwa chamdima wabii, sindidzaopa choipa chilichonse, pakuti Inu Ambuye mumakhala nane. Chibonga chanu ndi ndodo yanu zimanditeteza.	Even though I walk in a valley of darkness of BLACKNESS, I will not fear any thing at all for You Lord you stay with me. Your war club and your walking stick they protect me.	[4]
Inu mumandikonzera chakudya, adani anga akuwona. Mumandilandira bwino podzoza mutu wanga ndi mafuta, mumadzaza chikho changa mpaka kusefukira.	You prepare for me food, while my enemies are looking on. You receive me well by pouring on my head oil, you fill my cup until it overflows.	[5]
Zoonadi, zokoma zanu ndi chikondi chanu zidzakhala ndi ine masiku onse a moyo wanga. Ndidzakhala m'Nyumba mwanu moyo wanga wonse.	In truth, your good things and your love they will stay with me all the days of my life. I will stay in your House my whole life long.	[6]

A.1.6 Psalm 23 in Chichewa Buku Loyera *(1998), reformatted for readability*

Salimo la Davide

Chauta ndiye mbusa wanga,   [1]
  sindidzasowa kanthu.

Amandigoneka pa busa lamsipu.   [2]
Amanditsogolera ku madzi odikha kokapumulirako.

Amatsitsimutsa moyo wanga.   [3]
Amanditsogolera m'njira za chilungamo
  malinga ndi ulemerero wa dzina lake.

Ngakhale ndiyende m'chigwa chamdima wabii,   [4]
  sindidzaopa choipa chilichonse,
  pakuti Inu Ambuye mumakhala nane.
Chibonga chanu ndi ndodo yanu zimanditeteza.

Inu mumandikonzera chakudya, adani anga akuwona.   [5]
Mumandilandira bwino podzoza mutu wanga ndi mafuta,
  mumadzaza chikho changa mpaka kusefukira.

Zoonadi, zokoma zanu ndi chikondi chanu   [6]
  zidzakhala ndi ine masiku onse a moyo wanga.
Ndidzakhala m'Nyumba mwanu moyo wanga wonse.

A.1.7 Psalm 23 in the Chichewa hymn version[355]

Yehova, Mbusa wangadi,	Jehovah, [is] my very own Herdsman,
Ndilibe kusowa;	I lack for nothing;
Andigonetsa bwinoli	He makes me lie down well
Mu msimpu wokoma.	In pleasant green grass.
Ku madzi ake odikha	To his quiet waters
Anditsogolera;	He leads me;
Ndi moyo wanga wofoka	And my weak life
Aulimbikitsa.	He strengthens it.
Anditsogolera m'njira	He leads me in paths
Zakulungamazo;	Those righteous ones;
Chifukwa changa ai, koma	Not for my sake, but
Cha dzina lakelo.	[For the sake] of his very name.
Ndipyola kodi chikwawa	What if I go through a valley
Cha mthunzi wa imfa?	Of the shadow of death?
Ndilibe mantha ngati	I have no fear if
'Nu mundiperekeza.	You accompany me.
Chakudya changa chabwino	My good food
Mwandikonzera pha!	You prepare for me, A LOT!
Pa maso pa adaniwo	Before the eyes of my enemies
Mudyetsa mtimanga.	You feed my heart.
Mwadzoza mutu wanga ndi	You have anointed my head with
Mafuta okoma;	Pleasant oil;
Mwadzaza chikho changadi,	You have filled my own cup,
Inde, chisefuka.	Yes, it overflows.
Zokoma ndi zakuyanja	Good things and friendship
Zidzanditsatako;	They will follow me there;
Ndikhala m'nyumba ya M'lungu	I [will] dwell in the house of God
Ku nthawi zonsezo.	For all times.

A.1.8 Psalm 23 in the ndakatulo poetic rendering

Wanga Mbusa ngwokoma mtima.
  Herdsman of mine he's so good-hearted.
Chauta ndi dzina lake lochukadi.
  Chauta is that most famous name of his.
Mwa iye, ine kusowa kanthu ayi.
  In him, as for me—I lack nothing, not at all.
Gonee! pa zobiriwira andigonetsa.
  DOWN! on fresh greens he makes me lie down.

---

[355]"Yehova Mbusa Wangadi" (*Nyimbo za Mpingo wa Lutheran,* #110).

Malo opumulirako n'kumadzi odikha,
[My] resting place is at quiet waters,
Moyo ine amanditsitsimutsa komweko.
My life he always revives it right there.
M'njira zolungama amanditsogoleramo,
Along straight paths he leads me in them,
Malinga n'dzina lake lomveka—Chauta!
According to his well-known name—Chauta!

M'chigwa cha mdima bii! n'kayendamo,
If in a deep dark valley BLACK! I happen to walk,
Mantha onse balala! poti Chauta alipodi.
All [my] fear GONE! since Chauta is right there.
Inu Abusa, muli pafupi n'zida zotetezera,
O Herdsman, you are close by with weapons for defense,
Ine mtima pansi phee! nthawi zonsezo.
As for my heart, it's completely QUIET! at all times.

Kunena chakudya, ha! ndine mwana-alirenji,
Talk about food, ha! I'm a what-can-the-child-cry-for
Mwandikonzera phwando, adani angoti tong'oo!
You've prepared me a feast, my enemies can just STARE!
Chiko changa cha madalitso chiri nde-nde-nde!
My cup of blessings is full-up BRIM-BRIM-BRIMMING!
Kwanu inu mwandilandiradi ndi manja awiri.
At your home you've welcomed me with two hands.

Indetu, zokoma za chikondi chanu chosasinthika,
Yes indeed, the good things from your unchangeable love,
Zimandilondoladi m'moyo wonse wa pansi pano.
They really follow me during [my] whole life down here.
M'nyumba yanu yoyera, inu Chauta, sindichokamo,
From inside your holy house, Chauta, I don't leave it,
Nchito yanga n'kukutumikirani mpaka muyayaya!
My work is to serve you right up until FOREVER-EVER!

A.2 The questionnaire

In sections A.2.1 and A.2.2 is the original questionnaire that I developed
in mutual consultation with my seminary student assistants. The questions were discussed in class so that they could be readily translated into
Chichewa by each tester for individual or group presentation. They were
later revised based on practical experience during the testing program. (I
have given just the literal back translation of these questions from the
original Chichewa into English.)

A.2.1 Personal background questions (only for those tested as individuals)

Date and Time of Testing _____Place _____

a   What is your name and age (estimate)? (Note sex.)

b.   What is your tribe and where were you born?

c.   Did you go to school? If you went to school, where was this, and for
     how many years did you go? Which language were you taught in at
     school?

d.   How long have you been an active Christian church member? Are
     you baptized—a communicant?

e.   How often do you attend Sunday services (every week, 2–3 times a
     month, once a month, or less)?

f   Do you perform any sort of leadership role in the church? If so, what
     is this?

g.   What is your mother tongue?
     If it is not *Chichewa/Chinyanja,* when did you learn *Chinyanja* and
     how?

h.   How well do you understand *Chinyanja*? Can you read and write this
     language?

i.   How often do you read/study the Bible at home (more than three
     times a week, less, never)?

j.   Do you try to memorize Bible passages? If so, how often and how do
     you do this?

k.   Have you ever studied Psalm 23 before? In which language?

l.   Do you know Psalm 23 well? Do you like it? If so, why do you like it?

m.   Which is your favorite psalm? Favorite book of the Bible? Why do
     you say so?

A.2.2 Practical assessment questions

The following is the basic set of questions, but they can be supplemented or modified as needed. Read the four sample texts one after the other, in a clear, natural way. They are marked as A, B, C, and D. (Text A can be seen in sec. A.1.4, B in A.1.5, C in A.1.7, and D in A.1.8.)[356]

a. Which of the four sample texts—A, B, C, or D—was the most difficult for you to understand?
    Why was this the case—what made this version especially difficult?
    Which other text was difficult to understand?

b. Which *particular verse* of each of these two texts was the most difficult for you to understand?
    Which specific words or phrases caused problems for you?
    Can you suggest any words to make the passage sound clearer or easier to understand at this point?
    Is there any other part of this version that you did not understand properly? If so, which part(s)?

    (To the *tester*: The sample text in question, namely A, B, C, or D, may have to be re-read when specifics are asked for. The tester should also record each place in any of the samples where the respondent did not correctly understand the text, even after a re-reading or two.)

c. Which of the four versions—A, B, C, or D—was the easiest to understand?
    Why do you say so-what is the reason for this version's being easy for you to understand?
    Which version is next easiest to understand?

d. Is there an expression in any of the sample texts that seems to be "a little mistaken" or "inappropriate," for example, too "youthful" to use in a translation of the Bible or to read aloud during a public worship service?

e. Which of the four versions sounds the "sweetest to hear" or "most beautiful?"

---

[356]Text E (A.1.6) is the same as B, except that it has been reformatted for greater readability.

Why do you say this? Which words in particular attracted you to this version?
Give examples of any other expressions in this text that "sounded like a song" to you.
Which version—A, B, C, or D—was the second most beautiful, and why do you think so?

f.   Which version sounds the most "idiomatic" or "genuine" or "idiomatic" or "figurative"?
     Give a specific example of such words from this text.
     Do you like this sort of language? Explain why or why not.

g.   Which version—A, B, C, or D—has the "strongest language" or really "pulled your heart"? Give an example of some words of this type.
     What feeling or attitude does the psalmist seem to demonstrate by the words of the psalm in this version (e.g., sorrow, anger, courage, hope, despair, trust)?

h.   Which of the two sample texts of *Buku Loyera*—B (see sec. A.1.5) or E (see sec. A.1.6)—is "easier" for you to read aloud?
     Can you explain why this text seemed to be easier to read?

     (To the tester: Note any points in the text where the reader makes an obvious mistake. Also indicate whether the person is a good, average, or poor reader.)

i.   Which text, either A, B, C, D, or E, would be easiest for you to memorize, "to enter into your heart"?
     Why do you say this? What causes the words of this version to be easy to learn by heart?
     Which other version do you think would also be easy to learn?

j.   Is there any other comment that you would like to make about any one of these translations?
     Which one did you like best of all, and why do you say so?

     (Note to the tester: The preceding questions, along with any additional ones, may be asked with respect either to *one* of the sample translations or to one translation in comparison with the others being tested. In addition to noting the respondents' answers, testers should also record any noticeable enthusiasm or other emotions expressed during either the text presentation or the interrogation. Not only individuals, but also several groups of people, both large and small, should be tested and their general responses recorded.)

k. Listen again to the words of several verses of sample text C. Do you recognize these words?
    Did you know that you could *sing* these words like a hymn? (Tester: Sing one or two verses of C.)
    Does the fact that you can sing these words change your opinion of this version in any way?
    If so, what do you think about this version now?

l. To test some passages in comparison to the same ones in a different version, first identify which version each of the following passages is taken from—*Buku Lopatulika* (A), *Buku Loyera* (B), or *Ndakatulo* (D). There are three passages in each group: i, ii, iii. Tell which of the three passages in each group you like best and, if possible, why (e.g., "sweet, salty, powerful, attractive, or figurative").

---

1. *M'chigwa cha mdima bii! n'kayendamo,*   (i)
    Mantha onse balala! poti Chauta alipodi

    Inde, ndingakhale ndiyenda m'ci-   (ii)
    gwa ca mthunzi wa imfa,
    Sindidzaopa coipa; pakuti Inu
    muli ndi ine:

    Ngakhale ndiyende m'chigwa   (iii)
    chamdima wabii,
    sindidzaopa choipa chilichonse,
    pakuti Inu Ambuye mumakhala
    nane.

---

2. *Ndipo ndidzakhala m'nyumba ya*   (i)
    Yehova masiku onse.

    M'nyumba yanu yoyera, inu Chauta, sindichokamo,   (ii)
    Nchito yanga n'kukutumikirani mpaka muyaya(ya)!

    Ndidzakhala m'Nyumba mwanu   (iii)
    moyo wanga wonse.

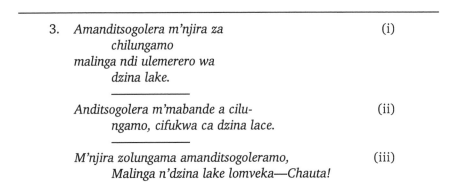

3. *Amanditsogolera m'njira za*   (i)
    chilungamo
    malinga ndi ulemerero wa
    dzina lake.

    Anditsogolera m'mabande a cilu-   (ii)
    ngamo, cifukwa ca dzina lace.

    M'njira zolungama amanditsogoleramo,   (iii)
    Malinga n'dzina lake lomveka—Chauta!

A.3 Statistical summary of results

The results indicated below are a compilation of the information from the
individual testers' record books as reported on the following form. It
should be noted that since not every question was asked of every respondent, the totals given do not match the number of questions. These are the
raw, initial responses. They do not take into account the subsequent discussions that the student-testers had with people to explain the nature
and purpose of the project and the different translations being tested.

SUMMARY TOTALS OF RESEARCH-TESTING   Name:_____

1. How many people did you test—MEN? 59   WOMEN? 31

2. List their numbers according to *mother-tongue* tribe: CHEWA 22,
    NSENGA 10, TUMBUKA 7, TONGA 9, LENJE 9, ILA 1, SOLI 4, SALA
    5, BEMBA 6, NGONI 4, SHONA 2, LUBA 1, NYAKYUSA 2, NDEBELE
    4, KAONDE 2, LUVALE 1, KUNDA 3

3. What was their average age (total number of years divided by the
    number of people)? 35

4. Schooling: Nonliterates? 37   Secondary school graduates? 27

5. Church attendance: How many regular? 70   How many not reg-
    ular attenders? 11

Rating the sample texts of Psalm 23 (A = *Lopatulika*, B = *Loyera*, C = *nyimbo*, D = *ndakatulo*):

		A	B	C	D
6.	Most difficult text to understand:	**63**	8	1	18
7.	Easiest text to understand:	1	**54**	27	8
8.	"Sweetest" (most beautiful) text to hear:	3	17	26	**33**
9.	"Saltiest" (most idiomatic) text:	19	9	1	**46**
10.	Text with the "strongest" language:	**36**	16	4	25
11.	Easiest text to memorize:	3	30	**45**	10
12.	Which text liked "best of all":	7	**33**	25	21
13.	Which preferred for the single passages (Q 1):	7	**22**	X	16

14. Which text is easier to read, B or E (the reformatted version)? B = 15
    E = **38**

15. YOUR PERSONAL COMMENTS (long answer): Has this testing process been of benefit to you? Explain: If yes, how? If no, why? Do you have any other recommendations to make?

A Compendium of Responses to Question 15

"Since I started reading the Bible, I did not know that there are differences in the translations, some easier and others more difficult to understand."

"I have learned how to dig into the text and about the importance of encouraging people to study the Bible in order to make suggestions concerning its translation."

"This testing has taught me how to do interviews and has helped me to know how much our members read and know their Bibles."

"Now I know how and why our translations differ from one another."

"People learned about [Chichewa] poetry and how to use it in [Bible] translation."

"People in Malawi would like to hear the whole book of Psalms as poetry."

"These results would be different [i.e., they would favor the *ndakatulo* version] if such testing were carried out among [mother-tongue] Chichewa speakers."

"This was an opportunity to see how much people want to learn about the Word of God—you could see this in their questions."

"Through this process, we as a [Christian] community can help those who translate the Bible to know where people find difficulties and which [wordings] they appreciate."

Appendix B

An L-R Approach Applied

In section B.1 a number of literary renditions of Psalm 1 are presented, along with some selected commentary, in order to illustrate an L-R (or LiFE) approach to the analysis and translation of Scripture. Some of these renditions are more, others less dynamic than others. They exemplify the variety that is possible when producing this stylistically shaped type of version, for there is not a single "right way" to implement such an approach—it all depends on the specific TL audience and the *Skopos* that has been formulated to serve their Scripture needs. "Just as the same landscape can be painted from a variety of perspectives and with a variety of techniques and tools, so too the same literary text can be portrayed through translation in various ways" (Wilt, trans. 2002c:i).

In section B.2 the focus shifts to a different genre of discourse, namely, Christic rhetoric, where I explore certain aspects of the artistry and persuasiveness of the original biblical text as illustrated by the Sermon on the Mount. In section B.3 the product of literary translation is presented in a specific target language, Chichewa, on a genre-for-genre basis with respect to the Beatitudes and the Lord's Prayer. The Chichewa lyric renderings of these familiar biblical pericopes illustrate how far we might go in endeavoring to produce a "poetic" translation.

B.1 Psalm 1 in the Masoretic Text and nine literary renditions

In section B.1.1 is the original Hebrew text of Psalm 1, which is a tightly-knit poetic composition having both an outer focus and an inner focus. That is, it is didactic and at the same time a profound expression of

sincere personal religious devotion. In B.1.2–B.1.10 a number of artistically composed versions of Psalm 1 are presented and some of their notable poetic features and intentions pointed out. It is assumed that, along
with the various stylistic devices that were utilized to distinguish each
translation from ordinary prose, a serious effort was made to reproduce
the essential functional dynamics of the SL document in religious communicative terms. I will not give a complete comparative evaluation of each
translation—just enough information to provide some relevant textual
background with special reference to the L-R features. A fuller text study
of this nature would be the work of the respective TL committees entrusted with drawing up the initial organizational *Brief* and *Skopos* for
their particular project.

B.1.1 Psalm 1 in Hebrew (Masoretic Text)

Psalm 1, a well-known "wisdom psalm," forms a most fitting introduction
to the Psalter since it firmly grounds the entire collection in the *torah* principles of the covenantal relationship that *YHWH* established to govern all
human and divine interaction in this life.[357]

אַשְׁרֵי הָאִישׁ אֲשֶׁר | 1
לֹא הָלַךְ בַּעֲצַת רְשָׁעִים
וּבְדֶרֶךְ חַטָּאִים לֹא עָמָד
וּבְמוֹשַׁב לֵצִים לֹא יָשָׁב:
כִּי אִם בְּתוֹרַת יְהוָה חֶפְצוֹ   2
וּבְתוֹרָתוֹ יֶהְגֶּה יוֹמָם וָלָיְלָה:
וְהָיָה כְּעֵץ שָׁתוּל עַל־פַּלְגֵי מָיִם   3
אֲשֶׁר פִּרְיוֹ | יִתֵּן בְּעִתּוֹ
וְעָלֵהוּ לֹא־יִבּוֹל
וְכֹל אֲשֶׁר־יַעֲשֶׂה יַצְלִיחַ:

לֹא־כֵן הָרְשָׁעִים   4
כִּי אִם־כַּמֹּץ אֲשֶׁר־תִּדְּפֶנּוּ רוּחַ:
עַל־כֵּן | לֹא־יָקֻמוּ רְשָׁעִים בַּמִּשְׁפָּט   5
וְחַטָּאִים בַּעֲדַת צַדִּיקִים:
כִּי־יוֹדֵעַ יְהוָה דֶּרֶךְ צַדִּיקִים   6
וְדֶרֶךְ רְשָׁעִים תֹּאבֵד:

---

[357]A good case can be made for including the "royal" (Christ-is-LORD) Psalm 2 as part of
this didactic introduction to the Psalter in view of the interlocking lexical inclusion of Pss.
1:1–2:12b ('blessed') and 1:6b–2:12a ('destroyed'). Thus the covenantal charter of the messianic kingdom is the written *torah* of *YHWH*.

The principal theme of Psalm 1 is neatly summarized in antithetical terms at the chiastic close, where the divine agent (יהוה) is finally, hence also climactically, revealed: There are just two "ways" and two "judgments" in this world, one for "the righteous," another for "the wicked" (v. 6). This sharp ethical and spiritual contrast is immediately enunciated in the psalm's first verse (אַשְׁרֵי הָאִישׁ with the opposite figure clearly implied), and it runs like a bold alternating thread throughout the text, with figurative characterizations of the two opposing attitudes and lifestyles set prominently in the middle (vv. 3–4).

The text divides structurally into two unequal halves: A, the righteous in comparison with the wicked (vv. 1–3); and B, the wicked in comparison with the righteous (vv. 4–6). Both portions feature a prominent verbless, almost exclamatory, textual *aperture*: "[Oh, the great] blessedness of the person who..." (1a) versus "Not so the wicked ones, but rather..." (4a). The triads used in the first half of the psalm to describe the faithful (who go undesignated till the very end) give way to paired attributions in the second. The attractive rustic imagery found at the heart of the text stands out in contrast to the conventional legal religious terminology that surrounds it. Although relatively simple in design and poetic style,[358] this psalm artfully, yet also appropriately sets the reverent tone and underlying topic for the book as a whole—namely, the "blessedness" (1a) of "the way of the righteous" (6a) who live "in the Law of the LORD" (2a). Duplicating this soothing spiritual effect in another language and literary/oral tradition presents translators with a great communicative challenge.

B.1.2 Psalm 1 in English from The Psalms In Verse

The translations in The Psalms in Verse (Barbour 1995) were, according to the publisher's introduction, "originally approved by the Church of Scotland to be used in worship over 100 years ago." The text, "based on the King James Version," has been rendered to be "read aloud" as "a testimony to the beauty of God's Holy Word." Thus, it is clearly intended to be a *literary* translation. The archaic KJV language will undoubtedly appeal to a theologically conservative audience, perhaps evoking a religious and devotional setting for worship or a pious meditative atmosphere. Psalm 1 is an example:

---

[358]There are a number of microstylistic and structural features that would require a fuller description in a complete poetic text analysis, for example, the opening alliteration, אַשְׁרֵי הָאִישׁ אֲשֶׁר (1a); the inclusio formed by a reiterated דֶּרֶךְ 'way' (v. 1 and v. 6); or the generally rhythmic flow of the psalm in the first half (note the many waw's) in contrast with the heavily disjunctive and shorter second section.

> *That man hath perfect blessedness*
>   *who walketh not astray*
> *In counsel of ungodly men,*
>   *nor stands in sinners' way,*
> *Nor sitteth in the scorner's chair:*
>   *but placeth his delight*
> *Upon God's law, and meditates*
>   *on his law day and night.*
>
> *He shall be like a tree that grows*
>   *near planted by a river,*
> *Which in his season yields his fruit,*
>   *and his leaf fadeth never:*
> *And all he doth shall prosper well.*
>   *The wicked are not so;*
> *But like are they unto the chaff,*
>   *which wind drives to and fro.*
>
> *In judgment therefore shall not stand*
>   *such as ungodly are;*
> *Nor in th' assembly of the just*
>   *shall wicked men appear.*
> *For why? the way of godly men*
>   *unto the Lord is known:*
> *Whereas the way of wicked men*
>   *shall quite be overthrown.*

In this rendition of Psalm 1 a simple hymnlike, repetitive meter (4/3) is sustained, more or less, throughout (m = minor accent, M = major accent): mM mM mM mM // mM mM mM in every couplet. The imperfect rhyme scheme is also maintained. The rendering stays fairly close in wording to the original text, except for some creative flourishes at the psalm's beginning and ending: "*That man hath* perfect blessedness – who walketh not *astray*..."; "*For why?* the way of godly men – unto the Lord is known...." A major structural flaw may be detected in the very middle of the text, where the prominent break to be found in the original contrastive organization is completely ignored: "And all he doth shall prosper well - the wicked are not so...." In addition to the lack of any formal indication of the key antithesis here, this couplet is closely conjoined visually by the paired typographical format and included within the same stanza unit.

B.1.3 Psalm 1 in English from The Message

Eugene Peterson's version (1994) of Psalm 1 contrasts with the preceding one both in literary style and translational approach. It is not only an issue of dated versus modern language, the whole setting has been transformed into the scenery of today. There is virtually no rhyme and only the occasional rhythmic pattern. Peterson depends, rather, on contemporary imagery to make a forceful impression:

> *How well God must like you—*
> *you don't hang out at Sin Saloon,*
> *you don't slink along Dead-End Road,*
> *you don't go to Smart-Mouth College.*

> *Instead you thrill to Yahweh's Word,*
> *you chew on Scripture day and night.*
> *You're a tree replanted in Eden,*
> *bearing fresh fruit every month,*
> *Never dropping a leaf,*
> *always in blossom.*

> *You're not at all like the wicked,*
> *who are mere windblown dust—*
> *Without defense in court,*
> *unfit company for innocent people.*

> *Yahweh charts the road you take.*
> *The road they take is Skid Row.*

But one may wonder whether Peterson has gone too far in his search for effect, losing the intent of the original in the process, as when he depicts a "Sin Saloon" or "Dead-End Road" or "Smart-Mouth College" in the opening verse. Some exegetical concerns might also be raised, such as the manner in which the Hebrew sense is reflected in 1a ("How well God must like you") or in 6b ("The road *they* take is Skid Row"). On the other hand, we see several felicitous turns of phrase here and there such as "you chew on Scripture day and night" (2b) and "Never dropping a leaf, always in blossom" (3c).

The contrasting styles of Peterson's version and the Scottish version are the result of very different communicative objectives. Perhaps it is best to allow Peterson (1994:6) to speak for himself on his exact motivation and aim in producing his highly contemporary transculturation of the original text:

> In English translation, the Psalms often sound smooth and polished, sonorous with Elizabethan rhythms and diction. As literature, they are beyond compare. But as *prayer*, as the utterances of men and women passionate for God in moments of anger and praise and lament, these translations miss something. *Grammatically* they are accurate. The scholarship undergirding the translations is superb and devout. But as *prayers* they are not quite right. The Psalms in

Hebrew are earthy and rough. They are not genteel. They are not
the prayers of nice people, couched in cultured language. But they
have an immense range of gut-level honesty and passion that provides them with terrific energy.

It would take a college of experts in ancient Hebrew poetry either to
confirm or disprove these last few assertions. In general, I would tend to
agree; however, there is also a certain conventionality and repetitiveness
about the language of the Psalter, in certain psalms at least, that Peterson
does not seem to allow for. To be sure, "honesty," "passion," and "energy"
are definitely present in the original text, but perhaps this is rather more a
reflection of the liturgically familiar than an expression of what is novel
and current. Furthermore, on a stylistic or literary level, one might question the claim—at least with regard to Psalm 1—that this version succeeds in achieving its stated goal of "translating the rhythm and idiom of
the original Hebrew into contemporary English—all the while maintaining the songlike meter and lyrical quality of your favorite translation"
(ibid.). On the other hand, one cannot deny the popularity that Peterson's
The Message has attained among a relatively large target constituency,
mainly younger North American evangelical Protestants.

B.1.4 Psalm 1 in English from Wilt

Like Peterson's version of Psalm 1 in section B.1.3, Timothy Wilt's
(2002c:2) features a contemporary English rhythmic prose style. But
there the similarities end, as seen here:

> *How wonderful it is—*
> *not for those walking where the wicked advise,*
> *not for those standing on the sinner's path,*
> *not for those sitting with cynics, but*
>
> *for those delighting in Yahweh's teachings,*
> *meditating on the Torah day and night!*
>
> *They're like a tree*
> *next to a spring*
> *always thriving*
> *no fading leaves*
>
> *and bearing fruit*
> *at the right time.*
>
> > *Not like the wicked:*
> > *wind-scattered husks.*

> *Not like the wicked, the corrupt,*
> *who cannot stand at judgement time*
> *with those who have lived as they should.*
>
> *Yahweh knows the path of those living as they should.*
>
> *The path of the wicked is being destroyed.*
>
> —For the priesthood

One obvious dissimilarity between Peterson's and Wilt's renderings is that Peterson uses second person for references to the righteous devotee of *YHWH* while Wilt uses third person forms. Wilt also has several nontraditional renderings for individual Hebrew terms and expressions (e.g., "How wonderful it is!" for the initial אַשְׁרֵי and the transliteration "Torah" for תּוֹרָה, which is anticipated by its meaning "teachings"). The point here is "to suggest how primary meanings of the ancient terms could differ from what might be assumed when the Old Testament is read through the lenses of the New Testament or contemporary Christian teaching" (Wilt 2002c:i).

In addition, he introduces two major innovations with respect to the macrostructure. One is the use of the print format and parallel patterning to distinguish utterances that refer to delighters in Yahweh's Torah in contrast to the wicked: no indention indicates the former group versus a large indention for the latter. The other innovation is less noticeable perhaps, but most crucial for those who are reading or hearing the text aloud: After the opening exclamation, the translation is composed—presumably to be also orally articulated—as just six sentences. The first two are longer utterances comprising the first half of the psalm (vv. 1–3), the final four are shorter utterances comprising the second half (vv. 4–6). This structure does reflect the Hebrew text quite closely. Wilt summarizes his literary translation technique as follows:

> I have often restructured [the psalm] texts in the attempt to represent in contemporary English style their genre, thematic accents and coherence of images as well as informational content....I have tried to reflect the Hebrew's use of devices such as wordplay, assonance (repetition of the same sound) and thematically linked ambiguity (a certain word or line can be understood in more than one way, both according with themes of the text), though with less frequency than they occur in the Hebrew texts (ibid.:i).

As examples of this approach, we note how the psalm's crucial medial antithesis is foregrounded by the negative repeated phrase that leads off the second half, "Not like the wicked." Similarly, the conclusion consists of two contrastively short sentences, where the disjunctive (including the visual) style nearly imitates that of the original. This effectively segregates the most personal, all-knowing God, *Yahweh*, from the ultimate fate ("path") of those who disregarded him during their lifetime.

B.1.5 Psalm 1 in English from Boerger

Dr. Brenda Higgie Boerger (2003) provided me with her rendition of Psalm 1, along with the notes and commentary that accompany it, just before she self-published a trial edition of a selection of psalms. She is continuing work on her personal translation of the Psalter and hopes eventually to publish it in its entirety. (The quotations that precede the rendition here were provided in personal communication; those that follow the rendition are from the footnotes of her 2003 book.)

> My goal in this, and all the Psalms, is to capture the inherent meaning of the original compositon, as well as its impact on the readers of that day. To do this, sometimes I deviate considerably from the traditional translations. My stance is that when a literal translation obscures the basic meaning, a different translation should be used.

> We are taught in translation classes to try to find indigenous poetry to translate the poetry of the Bible, but this has not been done for English, so there are no good examples of what this would look like. That is what I am working to accomplish. I am not talking about a poem 'inspired' by the Psalm, but one which represents all its parts and meaning in the receptor language (RL), as well. Therefore, one aim is to convey Hebrew poetry by using verse forms suited to English, and devices such as rhyme, meter, sonics, and imagery, resulting in dynamic scriptures which can be easily memorized or set to music. I strive for a poetry accessible to the general reader....Another goal is to preserve and draw attention to some of the poetic devices of the Hebrew Psalms, in order for English readers to gain an appreciation of them artistically. Despite the fact that many of these devices can be represented in English, and are compatible with English forms, most translations have failed to represent them, or do so in a mundane manner without drawing on their inherent richness. Some English translations value the sparseness and repetition of Hebrew to such a degree that they unnaturally impose it on English, in effect forcing a square peg into a round hole. Instead, the work here aims at using as many of the Hebrew devices as possible, without compromising the natural structures and rhythms of English.

> [In my] search for the poetic environment which best captures the intent or pattern of the Hebrew devices and the mood of the Psalm...I studied Lewis Turco's *The Book of Forms: A Handbook of*

Poetics, Third Edition (2000). It includes not only native English forms, but also foreign language forms which have been borrowed into English. I have found that certain Psalms seem to lend themselves to certain forms, sometimes even naturally falling into the patterns in the form, with little or no adjustment. Where the Hebrew structure doesn't seem to fit any of the specific English forms, I use other English poetic devices (meter, rhyme, heightened language, etc.) so that it is identified as poetry, and I use the layout of the Psalm to make the structure more easily seen by readers.

One of Boerger's (2003) footnotes points out the chiastic pattern of Psalm 1. In it she explains the italics and bolding in her rendition:

> In Psalm 1 we meet our first chiastic pattern, seen in the bolded words "walk," "stand," and "sit" of verse 1, repeated "sit," "stand," and "walk" in verses 5 and 6. The italicized words relate to the theme of walking life's roads: "go," "walk," "course," "road," "path," "trails." In the second part of the pattern, the Hebrew has only 'stand', __, 'way'. I felt it made a tighter composition to repeat them explicitly, in the reverse order. Furthermore, there are rhyming parallels: In the lines with "sit," we find "apart" and "heart." In the lines with "stand," we find "around" and "down."

Psalm 1

WALK WISE
a wisdom psalm
a Heroic Sonnet

1 The wise will show the surest way to *go*:
Don't **walk** your *course* by wicked people's chart,
Don't **stand** around with sinners on the *road*,
Don't **sit** with those who tear our God apart!
2 But you must love the Teachings of the Lord,
And soak its lessons deep into your heart.
So ponder it when waking at first light,
And think about it far into the night.
3 You'll be a tree that's planted by a stream.
Each branch will bear much fruit in its own time.
Your leaves will grow out lush and full and green.
You'll prosper, for that follows God's design.
4 Not so the wicked, not one little bit —
They're just dry husks blown at the wind's command.
5 So with the pure of heart, they cannot **sit**.

For at God's judgment, they'll fall down, not **stand**.
6 While Yahweh guards the *path* the godly **walk**,
The wicked *path* is doomed, *trails* off to naught.

Boerger (2003) labels Psalm 1 as a heroic sonnet, which she defines as follows:

> Heroic sonnets have 18 lines of iambic pentameter verse. An iamb is
> a sequence of two syllables, with the stress on the second. Pentame-
> ter means that there are five stresses in each line, i.e. ten syllables,
> stressed alternately on the even ones. The heroic sonnet is com-
> posed of two heroic octaves plus a heroic couplet. In Psalm 1, the
> first heroic octave is an *ottava rima* (abababcc) and is composed of
> two Sicilian quatrains (dede-fgfg), followed by the heroic couplet
> (hh). The semantics of verses 2 and 3 make implicit information ex-
> plicit to give the requisite 18 lines.

She explains the way she translates 'blessed' at the beginning of Ps. 1:1 as follows:

> I do *not* translate the traditional 'blessed' as either 'blessed' or
> 'happy,' as most English translations do...because this two-syllable
> 'bles-sed' is generally only used in a religious context making it un-
> natural in every day English. Furthermore, most Bible readers
> assume it means "blessed by God." However, Hebrew scholars say
> that 'blessed' means that *a person's circumstances warrant his being
> congratulated.* This focuses on how others perceive the person, not
> on the person's emotional state. The most natural way to convey
> that meaning in English is, "You're lucky!" or "You're fortunate!"
> Even though some people object to these because they say it isn't
> luck, but God, I'm convinced that 'fortunate' is the closest English
> equivalent. Similarly, I object to using 'happy' because we don't
> congratulate people by saying, "You're happy!" The focus is not on
> one's emotional state. Furthermore, the NT beatitudes make no
> sense using happy, as in "*Happy* are those who *mourn* because God
> will comfort them." They're not happy. They're mourning! It is both
> more accurate and more sensible to say, "Fortunate (whether they
> feel it or not) are those who mourn, because God will comfort
> them." I generally use either 'fortunate', 'fulfilled' or 'content',
> though the latter two move the focus from how a person's circum-
> stances are perceived *by others* to how a person perceives them
> *himself.* This latter shift is a compromise, but still preferable to ei-
> ther 'blessed' or 'happy', since one can be content even in the midst
> of mourning. In wisdom psalms I translate this 'wise', since as
> Wendland says, " 'blessed' is frequently used to describe the wise
> person who lives to please God" (2002a:43).

As to the rationale for 'show the surest way to go' in v.1, she says, "The Hebrew emphasizes this statement with a series of sibilants *ashre' haish asher.* I try to duplicate it with 'show the surest way to go' with its rhymed show/go and the sibilants of show/sure." In v. 2, where the Hebrew has *Torah,* she comments, "Hebrew *Torah* is usually translated 'Law' in English. But, there is growing support for 'teachings', which matches more closely the semantic domain of *Torah.*"
Concerning her use of *Yahweh* in v. 6, she says,

> The name of God, the tetragrammaton, YHWH, is translated here as "Yahweh." The tradition for English is to translate it as "LORD" (small caps), giving unnatural sequences like, "The LORD, my Lord." In this translation that sequence is rendered as "Yahweh, my Lord." However, when "Lord" fits the poetic requirements better than "Yahweh," there is the freedom to substitute it. Then *Yahweh* is inserted to preserve its presence in the Psalm, unless it already occurs elsewhere in it. I also [sometimes] translate *Yahweh* as "I AM," as in Psalms 33, 78, 81, 90, 93, 104, 105, and 119.

B.1.6 Psalm 1 in German from Die Gute Nachricht

In the 1982 German translation *Die Gute Nachricht* there appears to have been an attempt to achieve a poetic style of rendering.[359] This is most clearly evident in the figurative expressions to be found in the middle pair of the antithetical verses, 3 and 4, where a rhythmic movement is also developed in the sequence of relatively shorter lines that characterize this section in Hebrew. A similar sort of utterance patterning manifests itself in the opening passage. Verse 2 is composed to stand more obviously as a contrastive parallel to v. 1, a feature that is highlighted by the repeated exclamative aperture *Wie glueclich ist* 'How happy is'. The structural break between the two halves of the psalm is distinctly marked by the emphatic *Ganz anders geht es ihnen* 'It goes quite differently for those...' at the onset of v. 4. The concluding verse of the text is distinguished by a wordplay of thematic significance: *Der Herr* ['the Lord']...*die...hoeren* ['who...listen to']...*den Ungehorsamen* ['the disobedient'].

> 1. Wie glueclich ist,
> wer sich nicht verfueren laesst von denen,
> die Gottes Gebote missachten,
> wer sich nicht nach dem Vorbild
> gewissenloser Menschen richtet

---

[359]I wish to acknowledge the helpful comments of my father, Prof E. H. Wendland, with regard to the German translation. They greatly assisted me in the preparation of this section.

und nicht zusammensitzt mit Leuten,
denen nicht heilig ist,

2. Wie gluecklich ist,
   wer Freude findet an den Weisungen des Herrn,
   wer Tag und Nacht in seinem Gesetz liest
   und darueber nachdenkt.

3. Er gleicht einem Baum,
   der am Wasser steht;
   Jahr fuer Jahr traegt er Frucht,
   Sein Laub bleibt gruen und frisch.
   Ein solcher Mensch hat Erfolg
   bei allem, was er unternimmt.

4. Ganz anders geht es denen,
   die nicht nach Gott fragen:
   Sie sind wie Spreu,
   die der Wind davonblaest.

5. Vor Gottes Gericht koennen sie nicht bestehen,
   und in der Gemeinde des Herrn ist fuer sie kein Platz.

6. Der Herr sorgt fuer die, die auf ihn hoeren;
   aber von den Ungehorsamen bleibt keine Spur.

In the effort to be poetic and meaningful in German, this translation—like any other—loses or conceals several important features of the original text. We note, for example, the closely knit trio of figurative activities referred to in the opening Hebrew tricolon: 'walk...stand...sit'. There is, on the other hand, an overemphasis perhaps upon a strictly legal understanding of the covenantal *torah*, which is rendered first as *die Gottes Gebote* 'God's commandments' in v. 1 (where the Hebrew term does not actually occur), then as *seinem Gesetz* 'his law' in v. 2. Thus the sharp textual contrast between defiant human wisdom (v. 1) and reliable divine wisdom (v. 2), as expressed in the entirety of God's Word (the promises as well as the prescriptions), is thereby blunted. The reiterated key notion of righteousness (צַדִּיקִים) in vv. 5–6 is avoided, probably as an instance of "church language," but the German lexical replacements seem to be rather weak and somewhat off the mark semantically: *der Gemeinde des Herrn* 'the congregation of the Lord' and *den Ungehorsamen* 'the disobedient'. However, a mother-tongue exegete might disagree with these observations.

B.1.7 Psalm 1 in Dutch from the Nieuwe Bijbel Vertaling

The following rendition of Psalm 1 is from the soon-to-be-published Dutch version *Nieuwe Bijbel Vertaling.*[360] Because of the close linguistic correspondence between Dutch and Afrikaans, and also because of the similarity of the Dutch and Afrikaans extralinguistic, socioreligious situations that call for a new translation, it should be of special interest to those who are involved in planning for a possible new Afrikaans version in South Africa.

1 Gelukkig de mens
die niet omgaat met wie kwaad doen,
de weg van zondaars niet betreedt,
bij spotters niet aan tafel zit,

2 maar vreugde vindt in de wet van de HEER,
zich verdiept in zijn wet, dag en nacht.

3 Hij zal zijn als een boom
geplant aan stromend water.
Op tijd draagt hij vrucht,
zijn bladeren verdorren niet.
Al wat hij doet, komt tot bloei.

4 Zo niet de wettelozen!
Zij zijn als kaf
dat verwaait in de wind.

5 Wettelozen houden geen stand waar recht heerst,
noch zondaars in de kring van de rechtvaardigen.

6 De HEER behoedt de weg van de rechtvaardigen,
maar de weg van de kwaden loopt dood.

The key elements of the *Skopos* of the Dutch project are summarized by Kees F. de Blois and Tamara Mewe (2002:218–219) as follows:

> The primary focus...[is] the anticipated use of the translation in church liturgy....It should be a translation that can be read aloud in church (recitable) and be adaptable for chanting purposes. It should have helpful notes and other helps for the reader. It should reflect the literary forms and structures of the source texts, retain as much as possible biblical imagery and metaphor, if functional in contemporary Dutch and expressing the correct intended meaning. The intended liturgical use of the translation implies that marked style

---

[360]Thanks to Dr. Kees de Blois, who provided me with this prefinal version of the new Dutch translation currently in progress under the title *Nieuwe Bijbel Vertaling* and to be published by the Nederlands Bijbelgenootschap.

in the source text at the rhetorical, syntactic and lexical level is reflected somehow in the translation.

In this respect the translational aim of the new Dutch version corresponds to that expressed by Robert Alter in his 1996 English rendition of Genesis (see Alter's preface).[361] In other words, its aim is functional equivalence, "but at a higher, more formal level of language" (de Blois and Mewe 2002:221–222), as illustrated by the reiteration of "biblical 'motiv'-words," refraining from "spelling out contextual implicatures" in the text of the translation and the attempt "to express the 'couleur locale' of the original texts, wherever possible." However, it is not quite clear to me how translators will succeed in "adapting the structure of the [translated] text to the linguistic conventions of the source language" while at the same time allowing "the context and conventions of the target language to prevail" (ibid.). There appears to be a conflict of compositional interest here, although it would require an extended comparative analysis of texts to determine the validity of this concern.

The NBV translators do recognize, according to de Blois and Mewe (2002:224), that "[t]he question of naturalness is considered differently when the translated text is clearly poetic." In that case the TL rendering "can be less redundant than prose," at least in Dutch.[362] A preliminary assessment of how well the team have accomplished their goals may be made on the basis of their prepublication edition of Psalm 1 at the beginning of this section.

The text of the *Nieuwe Bijbel Vertaling* quoted here is actually a revised draft of the text that I first received. Dr. de Blois in personal correspondence provides some interesting comments on this later version in reply

---

[361]The principal difference between the Dutch version's *Skopos* and the one I am proposing for an L-R version (illustrated by the Chitonga and Chichewa examples of secs. B.1.8 and B.1.9) is that my *Skopos* for Bantu versions would seek to transform the salient stylistic forms and rhetorical structures of the biblical texts *holistically* into the most appropriate *functionally equivalent* literary genres and artistic devices available in the TL. In other words, the process of textual re-creation would be carried out not on a feature-for-feature basis, but *globally* at the linguistic level of the larger discourse. Therefore, while much (but by no means all) formal correspondence with respect to the source text would be lost, the essential semantic content would be retained, albeit expressed by idiomatic TL equivalents. Hopefully also the beauty, affective power, and religious relevance of the original text are reproduced in the vernacular by this process of text-domestication—more so than is normally possible by the procedure of formally "exoticizing" or "foreignizing" a translation. (The former term is attributed to James Holmes by de Blois and Mewe 2002:221 and the latter to Lawrence Venuti.) The issue comes down to how best to reflect for the intended audience "the great diversity within the Scriptures in style and genre with its characteristic forms, structures, themes, etc." (ibid.:215). Should it be done more *formally* in terms of the SL or more *functionally* in terms of the TL? My own *Skopos* favors the latter approach.

[362]This statement is substantiated by the fact that a later draft of this text is five words shorter, including a verbless first line: *Gelukkig (is) de mens...*(with *is* dropped out).

to my question why this is felt to be more literary (poetic) in nature than the original.

- Verse 1, line 1: 'Happy the person' instead of 'Happy is the person' is closer to the Hebrew form (no unnecessary explicitation) and functionally more poetic.
- Line 2: *niet omgaan met* replaces *niet in de kring verkeert.* This is closer to the biblical metaphor (*omgaan* for Hebrew הָלַךְ); the line reads better, partly because it is shorter.
- We note an interesting change in translation of 'wicked': the traditional term *goddelozen* is felt by some to have undergone some semantic shift. The younger generation tends to interpret it as people without God, people who don't believe in God, atheists. Curiously, the Hebrew term רְשָׁעִים is now translated in three ways within the same Psalm: in v. 1 as *wie kwaad doen* = 'who commit evil', in vv. 4 and 5 as *wettelozen* = 'lawless ones', and in v. 6 as *kwaden* = 'evil ones'. I suspect this was done for reasons of rhythm and readability.
- Line 3: *de weg betreden* is used rather than *volgen*; the former is slightly more formal/archaic, but aesthetically it sounds better in a psalm.
- Verse 2, line 1, *vreugde* = 'joy', rather than *genoegen* = 'pleasure'.
- Line 2, *zich verdiept in zijn wet* is more suggestive of studying, meditating. The older draft was somewhat unusual exegetically: 'meditate while mumbling'.
- Verse 3, line 1: 'he will be like a tree' rather than 'that person will be like a tree'. Unnecessary explicitation is removed, thus making the line more compact, poetic, and readable. It is still gender-inclusive, since the masculine pronoun points to the 'person' of v. 1.
- Verse 3, line 4: *verdorren* = 'dry up' is more appropriate in connection with leaves than *verwelken* (flowers).
- Verse 5, line 1: the original 'That is why' was dropped at the beginning of this last stanza since it seemed too heavy for the Hebrew עַל־כֵּן. The result is more readable/chantable.
- Line 2: *in de kring van de rechtvaardigen* = 'in the circle of the righteous', instead of the original 'where the righteous are gathered'. The former is more compact and poetic.
- Verse 6, line 1: 'the LORD protects the way of the righteous', rather than 'the LORD knows the way of the righteous'. The earlier draft was too literal and not very intelligible to contemporary speakers.

De Blois concludes that "this second draft of Psalm One reads better in Dutch and is more poetic in terms of rhythm, compactness, and in handling the biblical imagery; in several respects it is also exegetically more accurate" (personal communication).

B.1.8 Psalm 1 in Spanish from Tepox

Alfredo Tepox is the principal translator of the unpublished rendition of Psalm 1 in Spanish that is featured in this section. I wish to thank him for providing it to me. His comments quoted here are taken from his 2001 article on translating biblical poetry into a Spanish functional equivalent version. Though the article is directed specifically to Proverbs 1:1–7, what he says applies equally well to the text of Psalm 1.

Tepox describes his team's effort as a "re-creation" of the Hebrew text: "rather than trying to find a particular equivalent for each term, [we] focused [our] attention on their shared meaning. So—[we] reasoned—as long as the basic meaning was retained, [we] felt free to restructure the word order" (2001:222).

1 Dios bendice	God blesses
a quienes no prestan oído a las	those who pay no attention to
malas compañías,	bad friends,
ni aceptan sus malos consejos,	nor do they accept their bad advice
ni siguen el mal ejemplo	nor do they follow the bad example
de los que se burlan de Dios.	of those who make fun of God.
2 Dios bendice	God blesses
a quienes aman su palabra	those who love His word
y alegres la estudian día y noche.	and happily study it day and night.
3 Son como árboles sembrados	They are like trees that are planted
junto a los arroyos;	by the sides of the brooks;
llegado el momento dan	when the time comes, they give a
mucho fruto	lot of fruit
y no se marchitan sus hojas.	and their leaves do not wither.
¡Todo lo que hacen les sale bien!	Everything they do ends well!
4 Con los malvados no pasa lo mismo;	It is not like that with sinners;
¡son como el polvo que se lleva el	they're like the dust the wind
viento!	carries away!

5 Cuando sean juzgados, nada los salvará; ¡esos pecadores no tendrán parte en la reunión de los buenos!	When the time of their judgment comes, nothing will save them; those sinners won't have any part in the gatherings of good people!
6 En verdad, Dios cuida de los buenos, pero los malvados se encaminan al fracaso.	Actually, God takes care of good people, but the bad people are heading towards failure.

According to Tepox (ibid.), the poetic rhythm and cadence of the Hebrew were reproduced in a contemporary idiom along with a touch of classical Spanish meter, which "allows for lines with one, two, three, or more syllables, as long as the longest line does not exceed sixteen syllables." He recognizes the fact that "since it is basically team poetry, it lacks the flavor a good single poet could give to it." Still, he says, the text manifests a number of attractive poetic and other stylistic features while retaining "the basic components of meaning of [the original] discourse."

The repetition of *Dios bendice* 'God blesses' leads the listener/reader to focus more fully upon the two aspects of goodness that are presented in the two opening verses, namely, the behavioral (v. 1) and the cognitive (v. 2). The climactic line of the first half of the psalm features light alliteration and internal rhyme: *¡Todo lo que hacen les sale bien!* 'Everything they do ends well!' (3e). This is continued in the following line to heighten the antithesis that begins the poem's second half: *Con los malvados no pasa lo mismo* 'It is not like that with sinners' (4a). Additional phonic parallels serve to draw audible attention to the contrast between the continuing fruitfulness of God's people and the ultimate failure of the wicked (in 3c and 6b):

llegado el **mo**men**to** dan **mu**cho *fruto* pero los **m**alvados se encaminan al *fracaso*	'when the time comes, they give a *lot of fruit*' (3c) 'but the bad people are heading towards failure' (6b)

B.1.9 Psalm 1 in the Chitonga ciyabilo poetic genre

This Chitonga[363] poetic piece was composed by the Rev. Salimo Hachibamba, a former Bible translator, who also supplied me with some personal insights regarding its artistic style and structure:

v. 1   Ooyo uukaka kulaya kwababi, mmuntu uulilelekedwe.
       'The one who rejects the advice of the wicked, he's a blessed
       person.'

       Ngoyooyo nzila zyabasizinyonyoono uutazitobeli naaceya.
       'It is that one the way of sinners he does not follow even a little.'

       Aabo basikusampaula Leza, takkali aabo—pe, pe, pe.
       'Those who despise God, he does not sit with—no, no, no.'

v. 2   Uliboobo ulakondwa mumilawo ya Mwami Leza.
       'One like that rejoices in laws of the Lord God.'

       Lyoonse buyo, kusiye buce, nkuyeeya majwi aakwe.
       'All the time, [whether] it's dark [or] it's light, [he] is thinking of
       his words.'

v. 3   Anga ndisamu likomenena munkomwe yamulonga,
       'Like a healthy tree growing on the banks of a river,'

       muciindi ceelede lisakata micelo, bana balyo.
       'in the right time it is loaded with fruits, its children.'

       Kuyuma matu aalyo? Peepe, taasoli naaceya.
       'To dry its leaves? No, not even a little.'

       Ooyo uuli boobo, zyoonse nzyacita zilazwidilila.
       'The one like that, everything he does succeeds.'

v. 4   Atubone basizibi, taawu, tabali boobo pe.
       'Let us see the wicked, no indeed, they are not like that at all.'

---

[363]Chitonga is a southeastern Bantu language spoken by nearly two million people in
Zambia. For further discussion and illustration of the *ciyabilo* genre applied in Bible translation, see Wendland 1994a.

Baide kupepaulwa amuuwo, mbuungu.
'They are blown about with the wind, [like] chaff.'

v. 5   Mulandu mu ciindi calubeta? Leza uyoopa basizibi.
'[What about their] case in the time of judgment? God will give [punishment] to the wicked.'

Kujanika mumbungano yabaluleme? Pee!
'[Could they ever] be found in the congregation of the righteous? No-o!'

Bayoozandulwa, basizinyonyoono, mbobabelele.
'They will be separated, the sinners, all of them.'

v. 6   Bubambwa baluleme! Nkaambo Leza ulikuzi.
'How the righteous are kept [safe]! Because God he knows how[to do it].'

Pele uyoobalobya basizinyonyoono, dooo!
'But he will cause [all] sinners to perish, completely gone!'

The *ciyabilo* is a genre of Tonga lyric poetry that is highly expressive and personal. Traditionally, it was chanted or sung, often to the beat of a drum, on many different sociocultural occasions, usually by a popularly recognized artiste in the community. The typical *ciyabilo* poem features idiomatic, aphoristic (frequently cryptic), and at times abusively critical language. All such derogatory elements must of course be carefully avoided in the more restrained adaptation of this genre to Bible translation, to Psalm 1 in particular. Since the *ciyabilo* is a type of vernacular wisdom literature (or orature), its application in the Psalter would not sound out of place, especially in an audio production. However, some preliminary oral explanation might be needed to clarify for the audience the purpose of this novel translation and why it is appropriate for the Scriptures. People who are familiar only with the old, literal Chitonga version will especially need such an explanation.

The following are the forms and associated functions of the most distinctive features in this lyric rendition of Psalm 1. (A complete description of all its stylistic and structural devices would take us well beyond the scope of this section.)

- *Repetition*—Additional text material of an iterative nature is needed for rhythmic purposes. It hopefully does not increase the total

semantic inventory of the text. It serves to highlight certain elements within the psalm, perhaps more than they would be
foregrounded in the original, for example, '*All the time*, [whether]
it's dark [or] it's light' (v. 2). Some of the following features also exemplify different aspects of the recursive style that contributes to
the overall redundancy in the Tonga translation.

- *Figures and idioms*—Localisms enable the key concepts of the psalm
  to reside comfortably in the Tonga language. They contextualize
  the text verbally and in terms of familiar imagery. An example is 'it
  [a tree] is loaded [i.e., its branches bowed down] with fruits, its
  children' (v. 3). This divinely favored tree is viewed as being
  blessed like a married couple—that is, with many children.
- *Negative emphasis*—The independent negative particle in Chitonga,
  which is usually some form of the particle *pe*, is frequently employed at line endings (less often at beginnings in its longer form,
  Peepe, v. 3b) for the purposes of poetic ballast and/or to stress the
  preceding predication. An example is 'he does not sit with—no, no,
  no' in v. 1.
- *Syntactic movement*—Selected grammatical units may be shifted in
  front of (sometimes after) their usual position in the clause. This
  device is useful for rhythmic purposes or euphony as well as a
  means of focusing the listener's attention on the concepts so dis-
  placed. An example is '*It **is that one** the way of sinners* he does not
  follow * even a little' (in which * marks the spot where the
  front-shifted [italicized] phrase belongs in ordinary Chitonga syntax). This example also illustrates the use of the emphatic demonstrative *ngoyooyo* (its gloss is bold italics), which is common in
  Bantu poetry.
- *Rhetorical questions*—A rhetorical question functions as an attitudinal or emotive qualifier of a given utterance and may also be used
  as an opening structural marker (sometimes contrastive). An example is '[What about their] case in the time of judgment?' in v. 5.
  This question initiates v. 5 and conveys negative overtones concerning the wicked, who are the ones implicitly being referred to.
- *Condensation*—While redundancy is the norm in this genre of
  Chitonga lyric verse, various kinds of shortening, such as ellipsis,
  may appear in order to stress a certain idea or simply for the sake of
  the rhythmic flow of the text as it is being chanted or sung aloud.
  An example is 'God will give [punishment] to the wicked' (v. 5).
  The notion of punishment is clearly implied also in the verb -*pa*
  'give' that is used here.

- *Ideophones*—These distinctive Bantu dramatic predicators create a visual or some other sensory image to generate impact and appeal within any oral text. An example is 'sinners to perish, completely gone!' (*dooo*, v. 6). Ideophones are frequently coupled with other types of exclamatory utterance in the discourse, as in v. 6, 'How the righteous are kept [safe]!'—which is also an example of a condensed (verbless) utterance.
- *Audience engagement*—Many of the previously mentioned stylistic features, coupled with direct speech, operate to overtly or covertly capture the interest and attention of a listening audience. There are some other devices, however, that carry out this function even more obviously. An example is 'Let us see the wicked, no indeed...' (v. 3). Sometimes *atubone* 'let us see', an initial signal of attention, is used to demarcate the onset of a new textual unit, as in the second half of Psalm 1 (v. 4); it sounds as though the poet is actually addressing his hearers.

This Chitonga rendition of Psalm 1 is a text that has been completely poeticized according to vernacular literary conventions, yet without losing very many of the primary stylistic features of the original. Granted, the discourse has been augmented in form as a result of all the lexical bits and pieces that were added to create the necessary colloquial style, rhythm, and line length, but arguably not supplemented with respect to its essential content. As for any critical variation in the intended communicative function or the general emotive tone, I must leave it to mother-tongue listeners to judge.

B.1.10 Psalm 1 in the Chichewa ndakatulo *genre*

Psalm 1 in the Chichewa lyric style has many features in common with the Chitonga rendition—for example, lexical redundancy, idiomatic diction, a rhetorical question, syntactic movements forward and backward, demonstrative highlighting, and frequent exclamatory utterances. Several of these features appear to be accentuated in the Chichewa rendering of Psalm 1. Many more ideophones and exclamatives are dotted throughout the text, as is typical of the *ndakatulo* genre of lyric poetry (see Wendland 1993, chap. 3). An example is *angoti mwaa! basi, watha mwai!* 'they go up MWAA! and away—that's it, their fortune finished!' At times the ideophones occur in related pairs, for example, 'those who do good are *THI!* clasped in the hands of Yahweh, but those who do evil He will cast them *TAYU!* completely away'. The rhythmic dimension of the Chichewa text is also more pronounced; thus the poetic lines, many of which are paired, manifest a more balanced length.

Kudalatu munthu woongoka	How very blessed is the straight person—
nzeru za oipa samverako,	to the wisdom of the wicked he pays no heed,
m'njira ya ochimwa sayendamo,	in the way of sinners he does not walk,
onyoza Chauta sakhala nawo.	with the despisers of Yahweh he has no part.
Koma kukhosi mbee! akamva mau,	But his neck is MBEE! So clear, as he hears the words,
ee, malamulo a Mulungu apo ndipo,	yes, the laws of God, that's where he's at,
usana ndi usiku mtima amaikapo,	day and night his heart is placed there,
kusinkhasinkhatu salekezako.	deep meditation he never abandons.
Ameneyu afanafana ndi mtengo—	This sort of person resembles a tree—
mtengo womera mwa mtsinje wosaphwa.	a tree growing along a drought-resistant stream.
Zipatso zili psa! pokhwima,	Its fruits are PSA! fully ripe at the right time,
onse masamba ali biliwiliwili!	all its leaves are BILIWILIWILI! bright green.
Pakutero ndiko kukhoza iyeyo,	Herein lies the success of that one,
zonse zidzamuyendera bwinodi!	everything will go just great for him!
Nanga oipa nkutero kodi?	Now does the same thing happen for the wicked, do you think?
Ha! mpang'ono pomwedi!	Ha! no, it's not the least bit similar.
Kunena iwo, angonga gaga—	As for them, they are like maize husks—
mungu wouluka ndi mphepo,	like a piece of chaff carried off by the wind,
angoti mwaa! basi, watha mwai!	they go up MWAA! and away— that's it, their fortune finished!
Zimene adzaona nzothetsa nzeru.	What they are going to "see" is quite shocking:
Tsikulo Mulungu mlandu adzawazenga,	On that day an indictment God will serve them with,
ciweruzo cidzawagwera onse pamo— psiti!	judgment will befall them all toge—...burned up!

Pampingo wa okhulupirika adzawachotsatu, sadzakhala nawo pamsonkhano waodala.	From the congregation of the righteous they will be expelled, they will have no part in the assembly of the blessed.
Conco, pali olungama ndi ochimwa:	So, there we have the righteous and sinners:
ocita zabwino ali thi! m'manja mwa Chauta,	those who do good are THI! clasped in the hands of Yahweh,
koma ochita zoipa Iye adzawataya TAYU!	but those who do evil he will cast them TAYU! completely away.
Tere anthu adziwe kuti alipo Mulungutu!	Thus people ought to realize that there is indeed a God!

A few stylistic devices are quite distinctive in this translation. Most noticeable perhaps is a restructuring of the entire text so that it is made up of two equal "stanzas" of fourteen lines each (corresponding to vv. 1–3 and 4–6). The overall discourse organization of the original is thus made to stand out in a more formal way. On the microstructure of the Chichewa version appears another artistic touch that is peculiar to it (and rather difficult to reproduce in English), namely, the use of emphatic postclitics. For example, the very first and last words of the opening stanza illustrate two common ones: *Kudalatu...bwinodi!* 'How very blessed...just great!'

Psalm 1 rendered as a *ndakatulo* lyric poem is as close to a genre-for-genre translation as is possible in Chichewa. Yet many of those who evaluate this text solely on the basis of the English back translation may be inclined to judge it negatively—as pushing the original too far stylistically in the direction of some alien discourse type or a new rhetorical motivation. The Chichewa version might also sound as though it has been overemotivized and is therefore not quite appropriate as an equivalent for the more restrained Hebrew wisdom piece at the start of the Psalter.

Another criticism might stem from what appears to be an addition to the Hebrew text, namely, the last line, 'Thus people ought to realize that there is indeed a God!' Where did that come from? Actually, it stands as a climactic summary of the psalm in general and the final verse (v. 6) in particular. Such a summary is a common feature of the *ndakatulo* genre and would not be deemed out of place in the vernacular; rather, it provides a satisfying close, or "coda," to the piece. A final criticism could be for the loss of the conciseness of the Hebrew caused by so much reiteration of form and content. Does this—or all of these issues—constitute an unwarranted distortion of the biblical text?

Perhaps it does, but on the other hand it is not up to us as outsiders to make the final decision to condemn the Chichewa version on the basis of its stylistic form alone. The ultimate assessment for or against—and in which respects or why—ought to be rendered by the "owners" (*eni-ake*) of the language in keeping with the original *Skopos* statement that was drawn up for this text in its envisaged setting of primary use. Furthermore, any evaluation of the relative *adequacy* (SL focus) and *acceptability* (TL focus) of a given translation in terms of its communicative relevance (coupled with its relative degree of functional equivalence) must be done in the light of a comparison with the entire discourse, not just looking at its individual bits and pieces of structure and style. Once a thorough program of systematic audience testing has been completed (preceded by some explanatory instruction in the vernacular), then those features that are determined by the majority to be inappropriate, misleading, or in error can be eliminated, revised, or corrected as necessary.

B.2 Christic rhetoric: The Sermon on the Mount

As I pointed out in sec. 6.2.1, another good source of artistic-rhetorical practice in the Scriptures is the discourses attributed to Christ. I will explore this subject in somewhat greater detail here in order to further illustrate the importance of taking this stylistic feature into serious consideration during Bible translation, both during the exegetical and also the text-transformational stages.

One author has described Christ's rhetorical techniques in terms of a sports metaphor based on the pitching technique of an American baseball player:

> That made me remember all the times when Jesus himself put stuff on the ball, never delivering a straight fast ball where a curve would be more effective (Matthew 22:18–21; Luke 20:3; John 4:15–16). I'll bet some hot-shot seminarian out there could get a Ph.D. exploring Jesus' use of spin, semantics, and argumentation.... When you see it that way, then, spin is just another word for wisdom. Speaking truth sinlessly does not mean artlessly. (Seu 2001:33)

Similar figures from other sports could of course illustrate the same point.

Consider the expression "You have heard that *it was said*.... But *now I tell you*..." (Matt. 5:21–22), which serves to announce the first development section of the central "body" of the Sermon on the Mount. This is only one example of many that may be understood in a rhetorical sense as well as in their usual theological sense. That is to say, the various admonitions, pleas, encouragements, consolations, warnings, promises, and instructions of Christ, as we have them in the Gospels, are both novel and authoritative in terms of content and intent. This is also true with regard to their stylistic form in service of Christ's diverse persuasive purposes. By *novel*, I do not mean that their style was completely new in every respect. These are innovative texts only when considered as wholes (in terms of form, content, and function)—as complete, audience-contextualized units of communication. Christic rhetoric, as seen in Matthew's Gospel, appears to be a creative amalgam of three principal influences: (1) the Hebrew prophetic tradition; (2) the wisdom school of religious philosophy; and (3) the contemporary Jewish rabbinic method of instruction.[364] Prominent features of each of these three kinds of discourse appear in the foundational speech of Matthew 5–7, examples of which follow (quotations are from the NIV unless noted otherwise):

- Unlimited evangelistic invitation, coupled with unequivocal ethical warning. An example is in 7:13: "Enter through the narrow gate. For wide is the gate and broad is the road that leads to destruction...!"
- Vivid, antithetically expressed didactic maxims concerning human attitudes and behavior. An example is in 7:16b–17: "Do people pick grapes from thorn bushes, or figs from thistles? Likewise every good tree bears good fruit, but a bad tree bears bad fruit."
- Incisive dialogic disputation to highlight contrasting beliefs and characteristics of the kingdom. An example is in 5:21–22: "You have heard that it was said to the people long ago, 'Do not murder...' But I tell you...."

Christic discourse may be identified, analyzed, and assessed from the perspective of either or both of the two main branches of the field of rhetoric, compositional and argumentational. (In actual practice the two are often combined.) In other words, we may examine Christ's speeches as (1) artistic, appealing, attractive verbal constructions (with a focus on *form*)

---

[364]I do not have the space to present a detailed analytical study of Christ's rhetorical style of discourse in comparison to that of the rabbis. (For some rabbinic examples set within a scholarly discussion of their translation, see Neusner 1989.) Suffice it to say that the salient stylistic differences are quite obvious when sample texts are read side by side. It needs to be remembered that the two religious corpuses are really not directly comparable, whether formally or semantically, for their nature and purpose are quite different: In social and religious terms, "Rabbinic literature plainly developed in a way which makes it unlike the Gospels" (B. D. Chilton, cited in Green and McKnight 1992:657). For example, "[T]he very program of the rabbis, of taking up a perennial discussion of purity and promulgating that as Torah caused words or sayings to be ascribed anachronistically to their predecessors" (ibid.). Nevertheless, there are a number of rhetorical techniques that Christ does hold in common with the contemporary Jewish teachers with whom he verbally interacted.

and/or as (2) dynamic, forceful, incisive discourse intended for such purposes as encouragement, indictment, or persuasion (with a focus on
function). Combining these two, we might describe his speeches in more
general rhetorical terms as "effective composition" (employing creative,
convincing, convicting, compelling language) in the service of one or
more of the primary objectives of communication (e.g., informative, expressive, poetic, affective, relational, ritual, and mnemonic).[365] The formal and functional features of this "system of influence" (Wuellner
1991:101) may be manifested on the macro- as well as the microstructure
of a given text or entire corpus. In sections B.2.1–B.2.4 are some examples
from Matthew 5–7 of both.[366]

B.2.1 Architecture: Tectonic textual arrangement in Matthew 5–7

Christ's finely structured hillside catechesis is framed (i.e., by an external, bounding *inclusio*) by references to the physical setting of 5:1–2 and
7:28–29. Its *introduction* comprises eight initial blessings, or beatitudes,
that summarize the essential spiritual and ethical nature of Christ's new
kingdom (5:3–12; note that the eighth, in v. 10, is expanded and thus emphasized by vv. 11–12), followed by the extended reflective similes of salt
and light (5:13–14). The long central portion, the compositional *body*, begins with Christ's programmatic statement on the importance and continued relevance of God's law (5:17–20): "Do not think that I have come to
abolish the Law and the Prophets." This is then clarified and expounded,
as it were, by the six antithetical sections of 5:21–47. These conclude with
the dramatic call for perfection in v. 48 (see the paralleled epiphoric closure at v. 16 and also the Old Testament intertext of Lev. 19:2). The rest of

---

[365]These are similar to the generic types of speech acts that are often cited. However,
speech-act analysis normally moves to a greater level of specificity by means of the notion
of "illocutionary force" such as rebuke, warn, condemn, comfort, encourage, promise, and
bless. A functional analysis of literary discourse may thus be carried out according to various degrees of generality depending on the purpose for which the study is being made. Another example of a broader perspective is that of de Waard and Nida (1986:80), who posit
the following as "the major functions of rhetoric": wholeness, aesthetic appeal, impact, appropriateness, coherence, cohesion, focus, and emphasis. The operation and identification
of these functions depends on the textual and contextual setting, taking into account also
the cognitive dimension of reasoning (i.e., presuppositions, implications, and implicatures)—the primary domain of relevance theory. (As an example see Gutt 1991, chap. 2.)

[366]I present here only a selective rhetorical (form-functional) overview of the Matthew
5–7 pericope. A complete and comprehensive analysis might well follow the format presented in Wuellner's 1991 rhetorical study of Luke 12:1–13:9. Wuellner capably reveals the
compositional dynamics of this text from four integrated perspectives: the rhetorical situation (intentionality), the rhetorical disposition (argumentative sequence), stylistic features
(figures and tropes), and the genre (plus function) of the whole text within the wider discourse structure of Luke's Gospel.

the discourse is basically structured in triads concerning three "acts of righteousness" (6:1 as introduction, 6:2–4, 5–8, [the Lord's Prayer], 16–18); three examples of right choices (6:19–21, 22–23, 24); three lessons of encouragement not to worry (6:25–27, 28–30, 31–34); and three appeals to act with discretion in relation to others (7:1–2 and 12 inclusio; 7:3–5, 6, 7–11). Finally there is a cautionary *epilogue*, which is preceded by an internal macrostructural inclusio at 7:12, "this sums up the Law and the Prophets" (with its parallel in 5:17). This epilogue consists of yet another three contrastive challenges to the Christian life (7:13–14, 15–23, 24–27), the third one acting as a graphic conclusion (end stress) to the discourse as a whole with the exhortation to build wisely on the words of Christ. The Lord's Prayer in 6:9–15 at first appears to be merely a parenthetical comment to explain the instruction of 6:5–8. However, in view of the complete, expertly constructed text, it would seem more likely that it is deliberately made to stand outside the other structural patterns as a way of highlighting both its content and intent (contra Green 2001:292) not only as a model prayer, but more importantly as a crucial portrait of the proper attitude and behavior that should characterize the believer's intimate vertical (6:9–13) and horizontal (6:12b + 14–15) righteous relationships within the kingdom of heaven (cf. 5:6, 10).

The artistic and rhetorical dimension of larger text organization is normally built up on the basis of varied patterns of formal recursion. The reiteration of parallel elements, whether exact (repetition) or corresponding in terms of similarity or contrast (reflection), creates different types of matching constructions either throughout a text or within certain portions of it, generating cohesion and demarcating internal units of discourse. Examples of these constructions include an A–B–A ring construction, chiasmus, inclusio, overlapping terrace, anaphora, and epiphora.[367] By means of such carefully crafted formations a speaker/writer can segment and at the same time unify a discourse by means of varied aesthetic shapes and sizes to create verbal impact and appeal. The conjoined parallels act together to forge distinctive internal relationships and perspectives, thereby highlighting important thematic concepts and pragmatic intentions that can influence the audience to adopt a particular perspective, attitude, or behavior.

---

[367]*Anaphora* is discourse parallelism that marks the respective *beginnings* of different structural units within a text (e.g., "you have heard that it was said" in Matt. 5:21, 27, 31, 33, 38 43). *Epiphora* similarly marks the corresponding *endings* of different units (e.g., "your Father, who sees what is done in secret, will reward you" in Matt. 6:4b, 6b, 18b). Analysts do not always distinguish these two important structural devices in biblical discourse, or they may confuse them with *inclusio*, a more familiar type of structural parallelism (for definitions see the second paragraph of sec. 7.1.6).

We see how stylistic form can enhance rhetorical function in the follow-ing chiastic passage, which is a literal translation of Matt. 5:10–12, Christ's conclusion to the Beatitudes (the parallels are indicated by italics and boldface in the corresponding lettered lines):

A: Blessed are <u>those</u> who have been persecuted **for the sake of** (ἕνεκεν) **righteousness**
B: *because* theirs is the kingdom of *heaven.*
   C: *Blessed* (μακάριοι) are <u>you</u>,
     D: when they shall *reproach* you,
       E: and shall *persecute* [you],
     D': and shall say every evil against you **for the sake of** (ἕνεκεν) **me.**
   C': *Rejoice* and (χαίρετε καὶ) be very glad,
B': *because* your reward is great in *heaven,*
A': for so they *persecuted* the prophets before you.

The stress upon the divine blessings that will come to the Lord's disci-ples (marked by a shift in immediacy from 'those' to 'you', underlined above) despite human persecution is clearly brought out by the tactical arrangement of this text, in which reference to the heavenly reward (B/C) is preceded and followed by reference to earthly reproach (A/D/E). One observes the typical *intensification* of ideas that occurs in the second ("prime") members of each parallel pair. An example is A (enemies perse-cute Christ's followers) => A' (they persecuted even prophets).

But it is also important to take note of the elements (indicated by bold print) that fall more or less *outside* the formal pattern. What is the point and purpose of such suffering from the perspective of believers? It serves both to manifest their righteousness (A) of lifestyle and at the same time to give overt testimony to their faith in Christ ('me' in D'). This privilege comes even in this life for the people of the kingdom of heaven in antici-pation of their eternal, heavenly reward (B/B'). In this respect, they will enter the divine realm in the honorable company of the prophets and will be similarly rewarded, as the progression from A to A' suggests.

The next example, Matt. 7:7–8, illustrates a tightly constructed *linear* pattern consisting of two sets of parallel triads, the second of which re-states and thereby also accents the central appeal and promise that each conveys:

αἰτεῖτε   καὶ δθήσεται ὑμῖν,
ζητεῖτε   καὶ εὑρήσετε,
κρούετε   καὶ ἀνοιγήσεται ὑμῖν·
πᾶς γὰρ ὁ **αἰτῶν**   λαμβάνει

καὶ ὁ ζητῶν   εὑρίσκει
καὶ τῷ **κρούοντι**   ἀνοιγήσεται.

ask   and it will be given to you;
seek   and you will *find*;
knock   and the door will be *opened* to you.
For everyone who **asks**   receives;
he who **seeks**   *finds*;
and to him who **knocks**   the door will be *opened*.

The obvious triadic symmetry and balance here creates a rhythmic flow that moves first in one direction, and then back again in what perhaps constitutes a sonic, as well as an iconic reflection of the certainty of the promise that is thereby highlighted. The concrete, everyday imagery also suggests that this messianic pledge is not reserved just for a future eternity, but is available to ask-seek-knockers in the here and now.[368]

B.2.2 The relevance of the printed format of a text

As was noted in section 2.4.2.5, Pilkington (2000) has extended the discussion of relevance and applied it to a study of stylistic effects in literature. He suggests that the use of figurative language, rhetorical techniques, and various other poetic devices (e.g., meter, alliteration, parallelism, rhyme, strophic structure) encourages a semantic comparison and contrast of the componential and encyclopaedic information that is conceptually attached to the lexical items thus foregrounded. In this way, certain cognitive assumptions and emotive associations are made more prominent, thereby stimulating a mental search for possible relevance. These are the "poetic effects" that form the basis for communicating either "a range of weak implicatures" (i.e., over and above the literal denotation of the text) or "a new concept forming part of the proposition expressed by the utterance" (ibid.:141) that has been stylistically activated. Such features contribute greatly to the impact, appeal, and import that good literature, including many portions of Scripture, generates. They serve "to broaden context, and make both thoughts and feelings

---

[368]Tannehill (1975:45) further explores the possible psychological dimension of this "careful use of repetitive pattern" in the discourses of Christ: It is to generate the "potency for 'resonance'...[which means] that the imaginative power of such material is sufficiently amplified and enriched that it challenges our preconceived perceptions of the world, activates our imaginations through the 'sympathetic vibrations' awakened in the deeper layers of the self, and so opens us to new ways of perceiving, feeling, and acting."

richer, more complex and more precise with regard to actual situations or states of affairs" (ibid.:161).

Certain aspects of this complex interpretative process may be applied to the printed format and typography of literary texts, as illustrated in the selections shown in section B.2.1 (see also Wendland and Louw 1993, chap. 4). The obvious divergence from the usual layout would at these points cause readers to pause in order to determine their significance. For example, in the case of the chiastic formation in the Matt. 5:10–12 passage, a formatted arrangement showing the inverted structure might serve as a visual reflection of the reversal in status that is being referred to.[369] In Matt. 7:7–8, the second passage reproduced above, its balanced parallels may suggest that the individual lines are all part of a complete topical whole.

More subtle indications of style and rhetorical effect can be shown by such typographical features as boldface or italics, possibly to highlight the key terms, reiterated motifs, structural midpoint, or a paradox/surprise at the text's climax (e.g., "rejoice and be very glad!" in Matt. 5:12). Similarly, the shift in mood between Matt. 7:7 and 8 (from appeal to confirmation) might be indicated by the typeface to mark both the parallelism and the modulated tone that pervades the second half of this dual construction. What this contributes to a reader's overall understanding of this pericope would no doubt vary according to the reader's level of print literacy and understanding of the content and purpose of the passage as a whole. But in any case, a sectional introduction or a footnote explaining the significance of the novel typography and format would certainly be an essential extratextual addition.

---

[369]In this case, updated Relevance Theory builds upon the old Russian Formalist poetic principle of "defamiliarization" (*ostraneniye* 'making strange'), in which an effective literary device causes a delay in the automatic conceptual processing of a text (see Pilkington 2000:18). Its meaning, whether local or global, and aesthetic-emotive effect are thereby highlighted, enhancing the communication process. According to Shklovsky (1965:12), "The technique of art is to make objects 'unfamiliar,' to make forms difficult, to increase the difficulty and length of perception because the process of perception is an aesthetic end in itself and must be prolonged.... [T]he author's purpose is to create the vision which results from that deautomatized perception." . This Formalist technique has also been incorporated into the cognitive-based "thematics" approach to literary studies, for example: "[T]hemes must be relatable to human activity that is somehow of a non-routine character, that they are—in terms of a well-known literary theory—foregrounded, and that they are directly involved in human interests and concerns, and that they are thus emotionally charged" (van Peer 2002:255).

B.2.3 Texture: Stylistic devices in rhetorical interaction

Only a summary description and brief illustration of the main stylistic features common to Christic discourse will be presented here. One does not
need to make a very detailed study of the Gospels before concluding that
"Jesus' preaching exemplifies the way in which style, far from adding un-
essential adornment to content, is an essential ingredient to the message it
conveys" (Osborn 1999:232). As was already pointed out, the text of the
Sermon on the Mount is stylistically shaped in order to give it a certain
aesthetic attractiveness and rhetorical forcefulness. This is coupled with a
perceptible augmentation of meaning in the sense of foregrounding, shading, paralleling, contrasting, associating, or intensifying certain elements
so that they serve the interest of the larger theological and ethical themes
being communicated.[370]
The following ten compositional devices or techniques are frequently
manifested as part of the larger rhetorical strategy that Christ employs to
present his persuasive appeal in support of the divinely established principles of ἡ βασιλεία τῶν οὐρανῶν 'the kingdom of heaven':[371]

- *Evocative imagery* most particularly involves use of the "focal instance" and/or metaphor and simile.[372] It can also involve
  metonymy, synecdoche, and personification. In Christic discourse
  graphic imagery serves to evoke the visualization of scenes, intensifying a particular issue, as in Matt. 5:14–16: "You are the light of
  the world. A city on a hill cannot be hidden. Neither do people light

---

[370]Tannehill's treatment of the discourses of Christ is a classic study of the close interrelationship that exists between form, content, and function in a literary text. I fully agree
with his call to "look closely at the form of the synoptic sayings to see how part interacts
with part, modifying and enriching meaning, and how tension between parts twists words
away from their surface meanings and points to something deeper" (1975:16). I have the
further aim of exploring the extent to which such form-bound meaning may be conveyed in
the text of a different language, while retaining a similar significance in terms of meaning,
impact, appeal, and relevance.

[371]It should be pointed out that these features are often combined in their textual realization. Compare the six general (potentially universal) "rhetorical processes" that are posited
by de Waard and Nida (1986:86): (1) repetition, (2) compactness, (3) connectives, (4)
rhythm, (5) shifts in expectancies, both syntactic and semantic, and (6) the exploitation of
similarities and contrasts. Exhortations, the mainstay of rhetorical argumentation, may be
expressed with varying degrees of force or mitigation, ranging from a direct imperative (as
in Matt. 6:5a) to a forceful positive or negative characterization (6:5b). (For an illustration
of this in relation to 1 John, see Wendland 1998c:59–64.)

[372]The "focal instance is a very specific and extreme example [thus related to hyperbole]
which gives it the power of imaginative shock often associated with metaphor" (Tannehill
1975:53). The humorous image of lighting a lamp only to put it under a darkening bushel is
a focal instance.

a lamp and put it under a bushel....in the same way, let your light shine before men...."

- *Contrast, antithesis, and dissociation*[373] are used to embody the overall theme of the hillside discourse. They are effectively reflected on all structural levels of the text to reinforce Christ's theological, ethical argument as a whole and also its various subpoints, as in Matt. 6:16–17: "When you fast, do not look somber as the hypocrites do, for they disfigure their faces to show men that they are fasting.... But when you fast, put oil on your head and wash your face so that it will not be obvious to men that you are fasting...."

- *Hyperbole*, often tinged with *irony* or colored by *caricature*, functions to make a vivid and lasting impression, usually of undesirable human characteristics, as in Matt. 6:5: "...do not be like the hypocrites, for they love to pray standing in the synagogues and on the street corners to be seen by men. I tell you the truth, they have received their reward in full."

- *Ambiguity, enigma, and paradox* are used to raise certain questions or even a measure of doubt within the audience in order to get them to think more deeply about a particular religious or moral issue, or simply to involve them conceptually and emotionally in the argument, as in Matt. 5:37: "Now let your word/speech be 'Yes,' 'Yes,' 'No,' 'No'; but the excess of these is from [the] evil [one]."

- *Rhetorical questions* are used to make an emphatic or emotively or attitudinally marked assertion, not to seek information. As such, they function to persuade, appealing directly to audience affections, as in Matt. 5:46–47: "If you love those who love you, what reward will you get? Are not even the tax collectors doing that? And if you greet only your brothers, what are you doing more than others? Do not even pagans do that?"

- *Condensation and ellipsis*, which are typical of didactic speech, are manipulated for rhythmic (poetic) purposes or to foreground certain crucial contrasts in the text, as in Matt. 6:3–4a: "But your doing alms, let not your left know what your right does, so that your alms might be in secret; and your Father, the one seeing in secret, will repay you."

- *Syntactic movement*, either front- or back-movement out of a normal position in a clause, serves to effect focus or emphasis by creating a

---

[373]Dissociation is a contrastive personal form of argumentation that separates "true reality from its appearance" (Wuellner 1991:109), as we see in Matt. 6:1–4. Another good example is in Matt. 5:17–20, a text which confronts believers with a new (or renewed) vision of reality—namely, the true nature of the kingdom of God.

shift in expectancy, hence novelty, within the discourse, as in Matt. 7:4: "So why do you see the chip, the one in the eye of your brother, but the—in your own eye—beam [front-shift focus] you give no thought to?"

- *Rhythm and sound play* (e.g., alliteration, assonance, paronomasia) interact to embellish the text for a perceptive listening audience, as in Matt. 5:13a–b, where we also note a typical slight shift in the pattern at the end to mark a point of climax where the content is highlighted:

Ὑμεῖς ἐστε τὸ ἅλας τῆς γῆς·	You are the *salt* of the earth;	(9 syllables)
ἐὰν δε τὸ ἅλας μωρανθῇ,	but if the *salt* loses its saltiness,	(9 syllables)
ἐν τίνι ἁλισθήσεται;	how can it be made *salty* again?	(8 syllables)

- *Old Testament citations and allusions*, particularly those that refer to the legal requirements of covenantal living, act as the chief foundation for Jesus' instruction and place him in the line of Jewish prophetic, sapiential, and scribal tradition, as in Matt. 5:43–44 (cf. Lev. 19:18 and Deut. 23:6): "You have heard that it was said, 'Love your neighbor and hate your enemy.' But I tell you: Love your enemies and pray for those who persecute you."
- *Direct speech* within the larger discourse personalizes and dramatizes the account, automatically highlighting particular attitudes, actions, emotions, motives, and thematic motifs, as in Matt. 7:22–23: "Many will say to me on that day, 'Lord, Lord, did we not prophesy in your name...?' Then I will tell them plainly, 'I never knew you....' "

All of these devices operate in varied combinations and proportions throughout Matthew 5–7 to constitute a masterfully arranged instance of religious teaching, as acclaimed also by Christ's contemporaries (Matt. 7:28–29). An excellent illustration of such artfully and incisively composed instruction is in Matt. 6:19–21, which is seen here. It includes a number of these features in rhetorical interaction, for example, a basic rhythm, a bit of rhyme, much soundplay, metaphor, parallel (triadic) contrast, an antithetical aphorism,[374] allusion (possibly to Prov. 23:4–5), and

---

[374]"The 'antithetical aphorism' presents a sharp antithesis in concise form through use of the positive and negative of the same words, or words which are opposites, in the two halves of the saying" (Tannehill 1975:52).

a final shift in syntactic expectancy[375] (i.e., a break in rhythm and content to signal an end stress at 6:21):

Μὴ θησαυρίζετε ὑμῖν	θησαυροὺς	ἐπὶ τῆς γῆς,
ὅπου σὴς	καὶ βρῶσις	ἀφανίζει
καὶ ὅπου κλέπται	διορύσσουσιν	καὶ κλέπτουσιν·
θησαυρίζετε δὲ ὑμῖν	θησαυροὺς	ἐν οὐρανῷ,
ὅπου οὔτε σὴς	οὔτε βρῶσις	ἀφανίζει
καὶ ὅπου κλέπται	οὐ διορύσσουσιν	οὐδὲ κλέπτουσιν·
ὅπου γάρ ἐστιν	ὁ θησαυρός σου,	
ἐκεῖ ἔσται	καὶ ἡ καρδία σου.	

Do not store up for yourselves	*treasures*	on earth,
where moth	and rust	destroy,
and where thieves	break in	and steal.[376]
But store up for yourselves	*treasures*	in heaven,
where moth	and rust	do not destroy,
and where thieves	do not break in	and steal.
For where is	your *treasure*,	
there will be	**also your heart.**	

This passage is yet another example of the "depth rhetoric" that is extensively demonstrated by Christ's words in the Gospels; it is "language which demands decision and action and yet is able to break through the limits of ordinary language, making new action possible by conveying a new vision" (Tannehill 1975:18). This new perspective is not limited to the expressive potential of human discourse but, more importantly, it serves to stimulate effective and insightful communication within the diverse sociocultural settings and interpersonal situations in which language is used. Christic rhetoric is captivating, life-challenging and life-changing speech. It also features occasional humor, down-to-earth realism, and immediate personal relevance.

The Sermon on the Mount includes many memorable lines to motivate its hearers of every age to respond in thought and action to the blessings and the responsibilities of the divine kingdom that the Messiah was in the very process of inaugurating. Such demanding discourse deserves to be formally expressed in such a way that it has a similar effect on local audiences today as well.

---

[375]The final couplet is structurally foregrounded (1) by being placed at the end outside the triadic patterning, (2) by a shift to singular forms (i.e., personalization), and (3) by the unexpected introduction ('there') of 'your heart'.

[376]As Tannehill points out, "The concern for rhythm in vv. 19–20 is shown by the fact that the last verb in each verse is superfluous as far as the meaning goes" (1975:48). I would add that the tight parallelism of these two passages would also be undone if these redundant verbs had been left out.

B.2.4 Argumentation: Strategies of persuasion

As we have seen, the rhetorical characteristics of a particular text are often best revealed in a longer study of the formal development of its explicit or implicit "argument," that is, an exposition of the primary reasoning process that underlies a persuasive composition. While it is not possible here to enter upon a detailed discussion of even a portion of Christ's Discourse on the Mount, I will provide a close "surface reading" of the basic rhetorical-structural development of Matt. 5:17–20, the passage in which the main thesis appears to be set forth. This will illustrate the argumentative technique that characterizes Christic rhetoric as a whole:[377]

A Μὴ νομίσητε
    ὅτι ἦλθον καταλῦσαι τὸν νόμον ἢ τοὺς προφήτας·
    οὐκ ἦλθον καταλῦσαι ἀλλὰ πληρῶσαι.

B ἀμὴν γὰρ λέγω ὑμῖν·
    ἕως ἂν παρέλθῃ ὁ οὐρανὸς καὶ ἡ γῆ,
    ἰῶτα ἓν ἢ μία κεραία
    οὐ μὴ παρέλθῃ
    ἀπὸ τοῦ νόμου,
    ἕως ἂν πάντα γένηται.

B' ὃς ἐὰν οὖν λύσῃ μίαν τῶν ἐντολῶν τούτων τῶν ἐλαχίστων
    καὶ διδάξῃ οὕτως τοὺς ἀνθρώπους,
        ἐλάχιστος κληθήσεται ἐν τῇ βασιλείᾳ τῶν οὐρανῶν
    ὃς δ' ἂν ποιήσῃ
    καὶ διδάξῃ,
        οὗτος μέγας κληθήσεται ἐν τῇ βασιλείᾳ τῶν οὐρανῶν.

---

[377]It is artificial to attempt to describe the Sermon on the Mount as a whole according to the strict stylistic canons of Greco-Roman rhetoric, for example, classifying the text as an instance of the "deliberative" species (see Kennedy 1984, chap. 2; Mack 1990:82), when it seems clear that the other two species are also included (i.e., "judicial," as in 5:21–22 and 27–28, and "epideictic," as in 5:3–12). Similarly, the three modes of artistic proof, *ethos, pathos,* and *logos,* are completely intertwined as Christ, a new rabbi with obvious divine authority, makes varied appeals, warnings, consolations, and commands to a mixed audience of disciples. The *enthymemes of deductive logic become apparent in the periodic occurrences of gar in the text,* but the techniques of inductive reasoning are preeminent in the sequence of similes, metaphors, analogies, examples, intertextual quotations, citations of direct speech, maxims, and brief anecdotes that extend virtually throughout the entire passage. The rhetoric of Christ would appear at one point or another to manifest each of the four primary "motivational genres of discourse": affirmation, reaffirmation, purification, and subversion (Fisher 1970; cf. Wuellner 1991:108, 117).

A' λέγω γὰρ ὑμῖν
    ὅτι ἐὰν μὴ περισσεύσῃ ὑμῶν ἡ **δικαιοσύνη**
    πλεῖον τῶν γραμματέων καὶ Φαρισαίων,
    <u>οὐ</u> μὴ εἰσέλθητε εἰς **τὴν βασιλείαν τῶν οὐρανῶν**.

A   Do not think
    <u>that</u> I have come to abolish the *Law or the Prophets*;
    I have <u>not</u> come to abolish them but to fulfill them.

B   I tell you the truth,
    <u>until</u> heaven and earth disappear,
    not *the smallest letter,* not *the least stroke of a pen,*
    will by any means disappear
    from *the Law*
    <u>until</u> everything is accomplished.

B' <u>Anyone</u> who breaks one of the least of *these commandments*
    and teaches others to do the same
    will be called least in **the kingdom of heaven,**
    but <u>whoever</u> practices
    and teaches [*these commands*]
    will be called great in **the kingdom of heaven.**

A' For [Indeed] I tell you
    <u>that</u> unless your **righteousness** surpasses
    that of the Pharisees and the teachers [of the law],
    you will <u>certainly not</u> enter **the kingdom of heaven.**

The agonistically toned and antithetically patterned arrangement of Matt. 5:17–20 is especially clear in the Greek text. The outer A segments present the correlated theses of Christ's contention concerning his teaching (A) and his disciples' living (A') on the one hand and concerning divine law (A–B) in relation to the heavenly kingdom (A'–B') on the other. Each of the inner B segments serves in characteristic rabbinic midrashic fashion to reinforce, exemplify, or elaborate upon the argument's related thesis by means of a contrastive categorical assertion—thus, B => A and B' => A'.[378]

---

[378]If this perspective on the structure of vv. 17–20 is adopted, the initial postpositioned *oun* 'therefore' of v. 19 functions to link the two halves of the whole section both syntactically and semantically. It thus applies not merely to what is said in v. 19, but to the whole second half of the argument, vv. 19–20 (B'–A'), the ethical portion. Furthermore, the final *gar* of v. 20 is, following Kennedy, better construed not as the marker of an enthymeme (see v. 18), but as a particle of emphasis, 'indeed' (Kennedy 1984:54; *contra* Mack 1990:82). In this case it would be analogous to the usage of Hebrew *kiy* (asseverative).

In v. 17 Jesus begins with a striking assertion about his teaching, hence also about his authority, intended no doubt to prevent popular misunderstandings concerning the true nature of the kingdom of God. It is possibly also a covert denial of an accusation that he was being charged with by religious opponents and rivals—namely, some manner of antinomianism—despite the fact that this was an untenable position, even according to the standards of their own legalistic logic.

Jesus' argument takes the form of a complex set of three intertwined *enthymemes* (abbreviated syllogisms, or logical deductions), which are conveyed for the most part implicitly in the text:

X.   *Major premise:* Unconventional teachers subvert the Scriptures.
     Minor premise: Jesus is an unconventional teacher.
     Conclusion: Jesus is subverting the Scriptures ("the Law and the Prophets").

Y.   *Major premise:* It is impossible for any teacher to subvert the Scriptures ("Law") (not until "all things have been accomplished").[379]
     Minor premise: Jesus is a teacher.
     Conclusion: Jesus cannot subvert the Scriptures.

Z.   *Major premise:* Only someone sent by God can perfectly "fulfill" the Scriptures ("Law").
     Minor premise: Jesus was sent by God.
     Conclusion: Jesus came to perfectly fulfill the Scriptures.

In the case of X, the major premise was a typical, critical exaggeration, the minor premise an unproven suspicion. Nevertheless, the conclusion was valid in the minds of many in the religious establishment. Jesus flatly denies this charge (Y), paraphrasing several well-known passages of Scripture as proof in the form of a figurative hyperbolic oath using the word pairs 'heaven and earth' and 'jot and tittle' in v. 18 (cf. Ps. 119:89; Isa. 40:8; Zech. 1:5–6).[380] In the process he makes an even more controversial claim—that he had come to promote a correct understanding,

---

[379]Christ's ministry initiated the fulfillment of all things as predicted by Old Testament prophecy (cf. Matt. 2:17, 4:14). Christ himself describes the end of the age in graphic detail in the last of his five major discourses in the Gospel of Matthew (24:1–25:46).

[380]Thus, "even if heaven and earth pass away" (which will never happen, unless the Creator allow it), nevertheless, *a fortiori* all the more so, nothing will be abolished/altered/abrogated from God's Law—until "all things" (his complete salvific plan) have been accomplished. Accordingly, all of Christ's teachings focused upon the need to uphold and carry out God's will as expressed in the Scriptures (see Matt. 7:12).

appreciation, and practice of the Scriptures (Z), namely, the "Law" as read and lived in the light of the "Prophets" (5:17–20, 7:12–14, 22:36–40). The pressing implication of Christ's entire evangelistic appeal, his authoritative manner of teaching, and the testimony of his miraculous works was that he was divinely sent to inaugurate the kingdom of God and to interpret the full sense and significance of its demand of perfect righteousness (Matt. 4:23, 5:3–10). Enthymeme Z constitutes the first half of the major theological proposition or thesis of the hillside discourse as a whole, the pragmatic or ethical purpose of which has been clearly stated in v. 16: "that [people] may see your good deeds [in keeping with the Law] and praise your Father in heaven" (cf. v. 20 and also 7:21–24).

The second portion, B'–A', of this rhetorical structure starts off in reverse order from its first half, A–B. The underlying logic of the section is made more perceptible, persuasive, and memorable by the vivid inductive elaboration and exemplification whereby the argument is expressed. Thus v. 19 enunciates—first negatively, then positively—the moral implications and judicial consequences of a person's teaching (confession) and behavior (profession) in relation to God's righteous requirements according to the covenantal obligations of the law (νομου in v. 18 = εντολων τουτων 'these commandments' in v. 19). The hyperbolic, contrastive rhetoric employed here (e.g., ελαχιστων 'least' and μεγας 'great', which indicate *relatively* lesser and greater in importance in the kingdom) is in the rabbinic style and obviously not meant to be taken literally.[381]

Finally, Jesus emphatically and with considerable irony sets the standard higher than the teaching and practice of the local paragons, "the scribes and Pharisees" (20). The Teacher's general "yes…but" affirmation of the covenantal law of the kingdom is subsequently argued with specific details in the rest of the discourse, beginning with a set of six antithetical assertions (5:21–47). These colorful vignettes dramatically reveal by inductive example how the Mosaic legal code needed to be understood and applied in the present context of messianic and eschatological fulfillment (7:21–23), that is, with an inner righteousness that complements and confirms outward religious ritual. This contrast between external appearance and inward reality, between pious practice and one's true heart attitude, between human values and divine requirements, between mere lip service and genuine discipleship,[382] begins with the programmatic Beatitudes

---

[381]For a discussion of some of the rabbinic techniques of argumentation in Matt. 5:17–20, see Keener 1999:175–180. Ellis (1991:130–138) has a more general treatment of this subject.

[382]The Beatitudes stand at the crucial beginning of Christ's great inaugural sermon as "a summary description of the character of the true disciple,…the kind of person the disciple will need to be if he or she is to rise to its demands" (Green 2001:288).

passage and runs like a cohesive thematic thread throughout the rest of the sermon, reaching its emotive climax in the strongly worded prophetic warning (7:15–23) that precedes the artistically fashioned parabolic epilogue (7:24–27).

B.3 Reproducing the rhetoric of Christ in the target language

It is one thing to be able to correctly analyze the stylistic features and text structures along with their associated rhetorical functions in a source language text or corpus. It is more challenging then to *transform* this information so that it conveys the essential message in a given target language and culture. The question is, How does one go about representing the rhetoric of such passages in a functionally *similar* (SL-focus) and contextually *appropriate* (TL-focus) manner in order to achieve an overall interlingual communicative *parity*?

There are two basic steps: First, one must make a complete survey of the rhetorical resources that are available in the oral and written art forms and genres of the TL. Second, one needs to apply these stylistic features translationally in a way that most closely approximates the "functional profile" of the SL document (i.e., the textually marked selection, combination, distribution, and operation of primary functions in the biblical passage at hand). This application to the TL must also be made in accordance with the communication priority determined by the project *Skopos* in view of the intended consumer audience. For example, is the primary emphasis going to be more on representing the forms or representing the meaning of the original message for their benefit? If the latter, a more stylistically domesticated L-R (LiFE) version may be the most relevant. This choice will affect the text's manner of composition as well as the inclusion of extratextual helps (see secs. 5.3 and 9.2.3).

B.3.1 Survey of rhetorical resources in Chichewa

In section B.2.3 some of the main microstylistic features of Christic rhetoric in the Greek New Testament were surveyed. It is interesting to observe that these same artistic forms happen to be significant compositional devices also in Chichewa lyric poetry (*ndakatulo*) and some of its other discourse genres. We find many instances in Chichewa poetic texts of evocative imagery and figurative language, contrast and antithesis, hyperbole and irony, ambiguity and enigma, rhetorical questions, condensation and ellipsis, selective syntactic movements, rhythm and sound play, citation and allusion, and insertions of direct speech.

Moreover, the textual and pragmatic functions of these devices are analogous to what we have observed in the discourse of Christ.
This is not to say that the Greek text may simply be rendered literally in
Chichewa with the same communicative results.[383] On the contrary, such
a procedure quickly gets the translator into serious difficulties, even in
such seemingly straightforward discourse as narrative direct speech.[384]
Attempting to deal with the more complex Christic rhetoric of this sermon
by means of a formal correspondence approach can be communicatively
fatal. The following, for example, is a back-translation of Matt. 7:13–14
from the old Protestant version, *Buku Lopatulika* 'the Sacred Book' (BL),
published ca. 1923:

> Enter at the narrow gateway; because [the] gateway is large, and
> the path departing with it to destruction is broad; and they are
> many who enter at it. For [the] gateway is narrow, and the path
> makes small departing with it to life, in which they who find that
> one [the gateway] are few.[385]

There are not many listeners—or even readers—who are able to derive
any sense at all from this passage in the old Chichewa version. It is
"foreignized" to the point of utter unintelligibility.

A comparative text study is necessary in order to reveal the relative
amounts of the different stylistic features utilized in a representative text.
A secular Chichewa poem would manifest a much higher concentration of
them than would sound natural in a biblical narrative (although more
flexibility would generally be allowed in the affective, figurative discourse of a psalm, the Song of Songs, or a prophetic oracle). Therefore the
Bible translator must carefully discern and select the passages where a dynamic rhetorical feature is required in the vernacular to duplicate the thematic, expressive, and directive ebb and flow of the original text in an
idiomatic and appropriate way. The main aim of the literary (LiFE)

---

[383]This is true for any southeastern Bantu language and any translation that retains most
of the complex sentence constructions along with the abstract/event nouns, passive verbal
constructions, and prepositional phrases (especially *of* phrases) that are found in the original text.

[384]Concentrated theological language and complicated religious argumentation, such as
that of the Epistles, is much more difficult to represent naturally in a Bantu language. Old
Testament poetry is not quite so difficult as the Epistles because of the many genre
near-equivalents available in the TL for use as full or partial translation models. However, a
possible model for New Testament paraenetic literature may be found in the typical vernacular sermons of non-Westernized revivalistic preachers (see Wendland 2000b).

[385]The 1998 popular-language version *Buku Loyera* (BY) renders this as "Enter in at the
narrow gateway. As you know, the gateway that enters in to destruction is large, and its
path is wide open, seeing that the people who pass through that way are many. But the gateway that enters in to life is narrow, and its way is painful [a personification], seeing that the
people who find it are few."

translator is to diligently search for potential functional matches in the TL at points where they are needed and would sound most fitting—ideally as part of a coherent, global, and genre-based strategy of textual re-presentation.

B.3.2 Application: Selected examples from Christ's discourse in Chichewa

I will not go into detail regarding translational application here since style and rhetoric by their very nature must be illustrated and evaluated within and according to the literary standards of the TL. The three examples given below (from the popular-language *Buku Loyera*) are merely suggestive of the communicative potential that is available when representing Christic rhetoric with the translational resources of Chichewa. A comparison with the Greek text (or a literal English version) will reveal at least some of the translators' insight and creativity. How "visible" are their efforts in the text? And how accurate, not only stylistically but also hermeneutically, have the translators been in terms of understanding and re-expressing the original content well?[386]

> *Musamaganiza kuti ndinadzathetsa Malamulo a Mose ndiponso zophunzitsa za aneneri. Inetu sindinadzere kudzawathetsa ai, koma kudzawafikitsa pachimake penipeni.* (Matt. 5:17)
>
> 'Do not keep thinking that I came to put an end to the Laws of Moses as well as the teachings of the prophets. I did not come to put an end to them at all, but rather to cause them to reach their genuine culmination.' (This last expression is a pointed vernacular idiom.)
>
> *Pajatu kumene kuli chuma chako, mtima wakonso kokhala nkomweko.* (Matt. 6:21)
>
> 'As you know, where it is, that wealth of yours, also your heart, its dwelling place is right there.'
> (Note how the epigrammatic quality of the original is reproduced in Chichewa.)
>
> *Chenjera nawoni aneneri onyenga. Amadza kwa inu ali ndi maonekedwe ofatsa ngati nkhosa, koma m'kati mwao ndi mimbulu yolusa* (Matt. 7:15)

---

[386]See Wendland 1998b, chapters 4–5, for a longer discussion of several key biblical expressions and some crucial theological passages in Chichewa and a comparison of the renderings in BL and BY. There is a lot more going on in the vernacular text than I have the space to point out, but the three examples here might at least suggest some of the BY's stylistic idiomaticity and rhetorical incisiveness.

'Just beware of false prophets. They come to you with a harmless appearance like sheep, but on the inside [they] are ferocious wild dogs.' (The last word is the closest local form-functional figurative equivalent to λυκοι.)

In addition to the several striking stylistic similarities pertaining to the manner of rhetorical composition, there are inevitably a number of formal differences in the respective literary inventories and conventions of the SL and TL for genre-comparable texts. Three specific features of Chichewa poetic-persuasive discourse in particular are distinct from Koine Greek (and English as well):

- *Idioms*, both lexical and syntactic. Obviously idioms differ between languages, and a literalist approach completely overlooks the potential of vernacular idioms. An example is in Matt. 5:34 (the idioms are in bold): *Chabwino, koma ine ndikukuuzani kuti muleke **nkulumbira komwe.** Usalumbire kuti, '**Kumwambadi!**' Paja Kumwamba kuli mpando waufumu wa Mulungu.* '**All right**, but as for me I am telling you to stop **any sort of oathing at all.** Don't make an oath saying, "**By heaven!**" As you know, Heaven is the royal seat of God.'
- *Intensifiers*, including various deictic or qualifying particles and enclitics. An example is in 5:24 (the intensifiers are in bold): *Siya chopereka **chakocho** kuguwa **komweko,** ndipo pita, **ka**yambe **wa**yanjana naye mnzakoyo. Pambuyo pake **ndiye** ubwere kudzapereka chopereka chako **chija.*** 'Leave **that** offering **of yours right there** at the altar, and then go, **go** begin by **having become** reconciled with **that** colleague. Afterwards **is when** you may come to **come** offer **that** offering **we've been talking about.**'
- *Ideophones*, which are dramatic, exclamative predicators. An example is in 6:23 (the ideophone is in bold): *Koma ngati kuwala kumene kuli mwa iwe kusanduka mdima, mdima wakewo ndi wochita kuti **goo!*** 'But if the illumination that is in you is transformed into darkness, such darkness is just as if **it's become completely black!**'

In summary, then, we can say that a more dynamic, mediated manner of translating is generally needed to successfully communicate a more literary, that is, stylistically   marked (artfully shaped, rhetorically developed), text in another language and culture.[387] This is necessary not only to promote a fuller understanding and appreciation of the structure and significance of the original text, but also to prevent misunderstanding of the message intent. Problems occur if translators render the SL text too literally (the proverbial path of least resistance) or if they paraphrase it too loosely. Content and intent (including purposeful literary forms) are equally important in any Bible translation.

B.3.3 Two poetic passages rendered poetically in Chichewa

In this section a dynamic LiFE approach is applied to two short, but very familiar pericopes, the Beatitudes and the Lord's Prayer. They have been translated into Chichewa using an oratorical style that is intended to sound as lyrically attractive in the vernacular as in the SL.[388] A poetic rendition of this nature is justified on the basis of a careful analysis of the original text, which, as a number of scholars (e.g., Osborn 1999:225; Tannehill 1975:5; Ryken 1987:118–121) have demonstrated, is of a similar literary character. H. Benedict Green (2001:37) goes so far as to designate these selections as prominent instances of full poetry in Greek. He displays the bifid structure (two-strophe) of the Beatitudes as follows

---

[387]I am positing a continuum of lesser to greater textual "intervention": *manifestation* (interlinear) => *mediation* => *manipulation* (paraphrase). A more mediated version is one in which translators aim to produce a meaningful, linguistically natural, and literarily dynamic (or "turbulent") text in the TL (Hatim and Mason 1997:27–30), yet one in which there is also a concern for preserving a relative parity with regard to communicative functions of the original. However, such intervention must not extend to a manipulated paraphrase of the message, that is, "the process of incorporating into the processing of utterances and texts one's own assumptions, beliefs, etc." (ibid.:220)—or even one's stylistic preferences.

I have here modified Hatim and Mason's discussion (ibid. 146–151) of these evaluative notions, which I find rather confusing. However, we totally agree on the following caveat: "Sign values attaching to particular features in a source language intertextual environment may not necessarily be the same as those perceived by target text readers within their own intertextual environment. It is indeed possible that unintended effects will be relayed by a merely 'manifested', unmediated translation as readers seek to infer meaning from marked uses" (ibid.:161), that is to say, those that are unintentionally generated as the result of a formal correspondence method of translation. An instance of this is seen in BL's rendering of Matt. 5:34: "Do not take an oath at all or pronounce [i.e., even mention the word] Heaven [or, make pronouncement in heaven], because there is the big chair of God." The naïve reader might easily come to the conclusion that the term 'heaven' is taboo or else one is not permitted to speak in the presence of God's throne in heaven.

[388]I composed and back-translated these two poetic texts from Matthew with the assistance of my seminary hermeneutics students, four of whom are mother-tongue Chichewa speakers from Malawi.

(I have included several formatting modifications to highlight the parallel patterns):[389]

I.

Μακάριοι οἱ πτωχοὶ τῷ πνεύματι,   [3]
ὅτι αὐτῶν ἐστιν ἡ βασιλεία τῶν οὐρανῶν.
μακάριοι οἱ πενθοῦντες,   [4]
ὅτι αὐτοὶ παρακληθήσονται.
μακάριοι οἱ πραεῖς,   [5]
ὅτι αὐτοὶ κληρονομήσουσιν τὴν γῆν.
μακάριοι οἱ πεινῶντες καὶ διψῶντες τὴν δικαιοσύνην,   [6]
ὅτι αὐτοὶ χορτασθήσονται.

II.

μακάριοι οἱ ἐλεήμονες,   [7]
ὅτι αὐτοὶ ἐλεηθήσονται.
μακάριοι οἱ καθαροὶ τῇ καρδίᾳ,   [8]
ὅτι αὐτοὶ τὸν θεὸν ὄψονται.
μακάριοι οἱ εἰρηνοποιοί,   [9]
ὅτι αὐτοὶ υἱοὶ θεοῦ κληθήσονται.
μακάριοι οἱ δεδιωγμένοι ἕνεκεν δικαιοσύνης,   [10]
ὅτι αὐτῶν ἐστιν ἡ βασιλεία τῶν οὐρανῶν.

The Lord's Prayer also divides into two primary portions, as shown not only by the content and nature of the petitions but also by the phonological patterning that is evident in each section:

Πάτερ ἡμῶν ὁ ἐν τοῖς οὐρανοῖς,
ἁγιασθήτω τὸ ὄνομά σου·
ἐλθέτω ἡ βασιλεία σου·

---

[389]In addition to the obvious rhythmic repetition and the structural-thematic bounding created by epiphora ('righteousness', vv. 6, 10) and inclusio ('kingdom of heaven', vv. 3, 10), we might note such poetic features as the general balance in lexical weight between the two strophes (thirty-six words each), the prominent thematic shift from a relatively strong internal (I) to a more external (II) manifestation of personal "righteousness," the inner cohesion developed by the semi-rhymed alternation of active and passive verbal forms throughout the text (significantly excluding the first and last beatitudes), periodic stretches of alliteration and assonance, "a complex web of [semantic] relationships between the individual beatitudes" (Green 2001:252, set forth in an impressive, yet also somewhat impressionistic, diagrammatic display on p. 254), and finally, an equally complex web of intertextual parallels and links to the LXX, the Psalter in particular (ibid.:266–267).

γενηθήτω τὸ θέλημά σου,
ὡς ἐν οὐρανῷ καὶ ἐπὶ γῆς·

Τὸν ἄρτον ἡμῶν τὸν ἐπιούσιον
δὸς ἡμῖν σήμερον·
καὶ ἄφες ἡμῖν τὰ ὀφειλήματα ἡμῶν,
ὡς καὶ ἡμεῖς ἀφήκαμεν τοῖς ὀφειλέταις ἡμῶν·
καὶ μὴ εἰσενέγκῃς ἡμᾶς εἰς πειρασμόν,
ἀλλὰ ῥῦσαι ἡμᾶς ἀπὸ τοῦ πονηροῦ.

Matt. 5:3–10, the Beatitudes in Chichewa (Ngodal'anthu)[390]

Ngodalatu anthuwo	Surely how blessed are those people
odzichepetsa mu mtima,	[who are] humble at heart,
popeza Ufumu wakumwamba,	since the Kingdom of heaven,
indedi, aloweratu iwo kale.	yes indeed, they've already entered in.
Ngodalatu anthuwo	Surely how blessed are those people
omvera chisoni m'mtima,	[who] feel sorrow in [their] heart[s],
popeza Mulungu mwini,	since God himself,
inde, adzawasangalatsadi.	yes, he will certainly give them joy.
Ngodalatu anthuwo	Surely how blessed are those people
ofatsa mtima kwambiri,	[who are] most meek at heart,
popeza adzapatsidwa dziko,	since they will be given the land,
indedi, kuti likhale lawolawo.	yes indeed, so it becomes their very own.
Ngodalatu anthuwo	Surely how blessed are those people
omva ludzu la chilungamo,	[who] feel a thirst for righteousness,
popeza Mulungu adzawamwetsa,	since God will give them to drink,
indedi, zofuna zao adzazithetsa.	yes indeed, their wants he'll put to an end.
Ngodalatu anthuwo	Surely how blessed are those people
ochitira anzao chifundo,	[who] treat their fellows mercifully,
popeza Mulungu nawonso	since God for his part too
chake chifundo adzawamvera.	his mercy he'll grant them.
Ngodalatu anthuwo	Surely how blessed are those people
oyera mtima koti mbee!	[who are] pure in heart so BRIGHT!
popeza onse oterewa, zoona,	since all those of this type, truly,
Mulungu mwini adzamuona.	God himself they will see.

---

[390]The initial line of each beatitude may be elided into a single word as here in the Chichewa title.

Ngodalatu anthuwo	Surely how blessed are those people
obweretsa mtendere m'dziko,	[who] bring peace in the land,
popeza kuti Mulungu nayenso	since in fact God he also,
indedi, ana ake eni adza'acha.	yes indeed, his own children he'll call them.
Ngodalatu anthuwo	Surely how blessed are those people
amene amawazunza pansipo	who are persecuted down here below
kamba ka chilungamo chaocho,	on account of that righteousness of theirs,
popeza Ufumu wakumwamba,	since the Kingdom of heaven,
indedi, ndi wao kwamuyayaya!	yes indeed, it's theirs FOREVER!

Matt. 6:9–13, the Lord's Prayer in Chichewa *(Inu 'Tate)*

Inu 'Tate wakumwamba,	O Daddy in heaven,
Dzina lanu lilemekezeke.	may your name be honored.
Wanu Ufumu ukhazikike.	Your Kingdom may it be established.
Kufuna kwanu kuchitike,	May your will be done,
pano pansi ndi kumwambako.	down here and there in heaven.

Choonde tipatseni lero, 'Tate,	Please, give us today, Daddy,
kudya kokwanira moyo wathu.	food sufficient for our life.
Machimo onse mutikhululukire,	Forgive all our sins,
nafe tichite chimodzimodzinso.	and we, let us do the same.
M'zotiyesetsa tisagwemo ayi.	Let us not fall at all into the things that test us.
Kwa Woipa uja, Mdani wathu,	From that Evil One, our Enemy,
mutipulumutse nthawi zonsetu.	deliver us at all times.

Ndithudi, ufumu ndi mphamvu,	To be sure, kingship and power,
ulemunso n'zanu kwamuyaya!	honor too is yours forever![391]

B.3.4 Evaluating a poetic-rhetorical translation

For a full text analysis of the two poetic renditions in sec. B.3.3 they would have to be compared on a line-by-line basis with the original Greek and the two standard Chichewa versions, the older literal *Buku Lopatulika* (BL) and the more recent idiomatic *Buku Loyera* (BY). But perhaps such a detailed contrastive examination is not necessary here. A reading of the English back translations quickly reveals considerable formal differences. The poetic renditions manifest a major stylistic restructuring of the original text, although without a significant loss or distortion of semantic content, no more than in the BL and BY.

---

[391]This concluding doxology, which may be an early textual amplification for liturgical purposes, is included in the Chichewa rendition due to popular demand, despite its absence from the better attested Greek manuscripts.

In addition to the formal differences, the functional disparity is great as well. While both the BL and BY texts can be more or less understood (the former with greater difficulty), there is relatively little that is attractive, forceful, or memorable about them. In contrast, the poetic renditions have a noticeably higher rhetorical impact and appeal, especially when recited aloud in the vernacular. Of course, the BL translation of the Lord's Prayer is beloved, having long been memorized for liturgical and devotional use and thus fulfilling the *ritual* function of communication. But do people really comprehend what they are so reverently saying to the Lord? The words *musatitengere kokatiyesa* 'do not take us along to go and try/test us', for example, are an interpretive challenge, especially for new, unindoctrinated Christians.

In the poetic rendition several major functional implications are highlighted, based on the presence of certain structural features in the original. Note, for example, how the forceful effect of the prominent μακάριοι οἱ 'blessed the' that introduces each beatitude in Matthew 5 is shown by the strophe-initial Chichewa predication *ngodalatu anthuwo* 'surely how blessed—those people!' Also observe how the onset of the climactic passage of the Beatitudes (v. 10), a passage that links the focal thematic expressions 'righteousness' and 'kingdom of heaven', is distinguished in Chichewa by an extra poetic line, rhythm, rhyme, assonance, and a concluding ideophonic expression:

...kamba ka chilungamo chaocho,	...on account of that righteousness of theirs,
popeza Ufumu wakumwamba,	since the Kingdom of heaven
indedi, ndi wao kwamuyayaya!	yes indeed, it's theirs FOREVER!

Certain prominent features also of the Lord's Prayer (Matt. 6:9–13) in Greek are reproduced in the Chichewa poetic rendition. For example, the speaker-directed portion (petitions concerning the pray-er in part two) is clearly demarcated from the immediately preceding addressee-directed, panegyric portion (petitions concerning the Father). This structural-thematic break (v. 11) is shown in Chichewa by an initial particle of appeal and a final reiteration of the vocative of address: *Choonde tipatseni lero, 'Tate,* 'Please, give us today, Daddy'. The emphasis in the Greek conveyed by the initial series of three asyndetic aorist imperatives is shown by an analogous construction in Chichewa, but with the verbs in utterance-final rather than initial position.[392] Another example is the centering effect of the Greek chiasmus, which foregrounds the key term 'kingdom

---

[392]The prominent A–B–A' ring structure formed by these three verbs and their noun subjects (i. e., A/A': passive verbs, neuter nouns; B: active verb, feminine noun) was pointed out by Thom 2001.

[of God]'; this is duplicated in Chichewa by a front-shifted personal pronoun:

Πάτερ ἡμῶν ὁ ἐν τοῖς οὐρανοῖς,
  ἁγιασθήτω τὸ ὄνομά σου·
  ἐλθέτω ἡ βασιλεία σου **Wanu** *Ufumu ukhazikike.*
                        '**Your** Kingdom may it be established.'
  γενηθήτω τὸ θέλημά σου,
ὡς ἐν οὐρανῷ καὶ ἐπὶ γῆς·

This is not to claim that the two poetic renditions are flawless. No translation is. In fact, every translation leaks, losing something, either qualitatively or quantitatively in certain specifiable aspects, whether in terms of form, content, function, or all three. In less flattering terms, "the translator is a traitor" (*traduttore traditore*), whether to a greater or lesser degree.

Even so, it is helpful to evaluate translations according to a more precise scale of assessment (see Wendland 1991:8–10 and also sec. 10.5 of the present work) in regard to their *fidelity* (focusing upon SL meaning), *clarity* (focusing upon TL meaning), *idiomaticity* (focusing upon TL form), and *proximity* (focusing upon SL form). When our poetic-oratorical versions are assessed in terms of communicative loss as weighed against gain, we find a tendency for there to be a noticeable *loss* with respect to verbal consistency, which is useful for word studies and concordance work; certain strategic word placements and structural patterns based on lexical reiteration; the cumulative expressive power and thematic relevance of exact repetition; the familiarizing *mirage* of form, that is, a comforting (for some people), literal near-reflection of the original text. However, these losses also greatly increase the danger of linguistic and literary *alienation*, supporting the notion, as one person put it, that "Christ preaches in Chichewa just like a foreigner—*cha zii!* (i.e., an insipid style)."

On the other hand, we note a significant *gain* with respect to linguistic naturalness, generic appropriateness, verbal impact, memorability, and aesthetic beauty overall—compositional features that more closely match those of the original text in terms of literary excellence and rhetorical power. While Chewa people, for instance, even non-Christians, do realize that Christ lived many years ago in a far-away place and that he spoke a very different language, they also appreciate having his vital message delivered to them in a natural, contemporary manner of speaking. We now have a "Christ who preaches in Chichewa like one of our experts," they say, indeed an attractive, fully *domesticated* discourse. Such textual accommodation automatically increases both the significance and the relevance of what he has to say.

In view of the impossibility of any translation's attaining total communicative equivalence in the TL, perhaps it would be fairer to call a competent translator a "trader" instead of a "traitor," as the familiar proverb has it. The translator who attempts to produce an L-R version must be not only an experienced, qualified, and gifted verbal specialist, but also a skillful trader—able to exchange one feature of the biblical text (selecting from its designated form, content, and intent) for the closest TL equivalent, sometimes gaining, sometimes losing, and sometimes only approximating the original value.

Although no translation is ever complete either semantically or pragmatically, we still need to ask ourselves, How close can we possibly come to the source text of and by which methods? As has been emphasized throughout this book, this question can be answered only on the basis of thorough pre-project research that carefully investigates the needs, desires, capabilities, and resources of the *intended user-group* and also the primary use for which the translation is being made (i.e., its central purpose and envisaged socioreligious and/or ecclesiastical setting). In this way, Bible consumers today—including both patrons and clients of the translated text—are able to interact more fully with the Scriptures as they prepare an edition of the Word that speaks more specifically, meaningfully, and stylistically for them. A literary functionally equivalent (LiFE) version is one way of achieving this challenging goal of interlingual, cross-cultural communication.

Appendix C

Sample Translator-Training Lesson

The sample lesson that follows is intended for use in a Bible translator-training course. It is based on an inductive, interactive method, prepared along the lines of semiprogrammed instruction. The aim is to encourage Zambian translators to think more deeply about the literary-rhetorical features of the biblical text as they analyze it and then render it correspondingly in their mother tongue. This sample lesson, which is based on the Book of Malachi, consists of three parts: The first deals with the *style*, the second with the *structure*, and the third with the *literary-rhetorical translation* of this important prophetic book. The lesson should be used along with other exegetical and translational study aids.

C.1 Malachi's writing style: How Malachi composed his message

In this lesson you will make a survey of the text of the prophet Malachi, paying special attention to his overall *style*, or manner of writing or speaking. During the course of this study, we will be answering questions such as these: What does the text teach us about the way in which Malachi wrote (or spoke)? What were some of the main *literary devices* that he used to help get his ideas across to the people of his time? These features are also important in the writings of many of the other prophets. Can you mention the names of some of these men?

To provide a little background for this lesson, you first need to consider the historical, social, and religious setting in which the prophet Malachi worked—that is, the surrounding situational context for his message.[393] Read the introduction to this book in a standard study Bible such as *The NIV Study Bible* (1985:1423–1424) or the *GNB Study Bible* (pp. 1434–1435). Next read the entire Book of Malachi (only four chapters) in the Bible of your language and, if possible, also in another language. Then review some of the main facts by answering the following questions:

Malachi preached about one hundred years after the Jews were allowed to return from exile in which country? _____
Which nation was ruling most of the world at this time?
_____

Malachi supported the religious reform movements of which two Jewish leaders? _____ and _____

Mention three of the major evils that these servants of God had to condemn in the lives of their fellow countrymen (and women):
   i. _____
   ii. _____
   iii. _____

In order to rebuke and to revive his wayward people, God had sent them two prophets a hundred years before the time of Malachi: Who were these two men? They were:
_____ and _____

What special project did these prophets encourage the people to complete? _____

The project of rebuilding the Temple had been completed, but this remained only an outward sign as far as the lives of the people were concerned. Their hearts had not truly changed, and their actions showed this lack of genuine repentance. They refused to show a reverent response to the LORD's unchanging love to them. So God had to come to them again through the preaching of "my messenger"—which is the meaning of the name *Malachi*. This was a hard message from the Lord, and it required strong language to get the people to listen.

What did you notice about the style of writing as you read through the Book of Malachi? You should have observed, as was pointed out above, that his language is very strong and forceful. Malachi was a powerful preacher; he wanted people to listen to his message and take it to heart.

---

[393]Two books that should be carefully consulted when analyzing and translating the book of Malachi are Clark and Hatton 2002 and Pohlig 1998. They will also help translators answer many of the questions of this lesson. Any points of disagreement with the analysis offered here may be profitably discussed in class.

One really has to read his words *aloud* in order to be able to appreciate his style and its effect.

Malachi's speech is very "rhetorical" in nature—that is, his words are shaped in the form of an argument which is intended to persuade listeners, to affect their feelings, to get them to think seriously about what is being said. Malachi's language should have a definite impact and appeal even today as we listen to it by way of translation.

What is the particular vernacular version that you use? _____

How do Malachi's words sound in your language (YL)? Are they powerful and convincing? Do they sound clear and natural? Explain your answer and give an example from chapter 1:

_____

_____

How would you evaluate the translation in YL? Is it a good one, or mediocre ("lukewarm"), or even poor? Explain what you mean, giving at least one example from the Book of Malachi:

_____

_____

Example: _____

_____

Do you know which language Malachi actually used when he spoke and the language in which his book was written? _____

It is important that his words are expressed as strongly and persuasively today in our language as they are in the original Hebrew in which they were first written. We will be considering this matter of translation more carefully as we study the message of Malachi.

Did Malachi write in prose or poetry? In other words, do his words sound more like Hosea or some other prophet who wrote poetry, or is it more like the historical books of Ezra and Nehemiah (prose) in its manner of expression?

How would you answer this question and why do you say so? _____

_____

You cannot answer this on the basis of how the sentences are printed in your Bible. Full paragraphs do not necessarily indicate prose, and shorter, separate, distinct lines do not necessarily indicate poetry, because the format simply reflects the opinion of today's translators or publishers.

How is the text of Malachi printed in your Bible—as prose or as poetry? Or is there a mixture of both? Give an example of where each type is found in the book: _____

_____

Most Bible scholars think that Malachi's style of writing falls somewhere between pure *prose*, such as we have in Ezra, and prophetic *poetry*, such as we find in Hosea, Joel, or Amos. In any case, Malachi's manner of writing has several prominent characteristics. These *stylistic features* serve to make his language very forceful, even poetic. If we learn to recognize and interpret such artistic and rhetorical devices, we will be able to better understand his message.

There are five STYLISTIC features that we will be giving special attention to since they occur so frequently in this book. The first of these five occurs in the second verse of the first chapter (read 1:2).

Both the SECOND and the third sentences of v. 2 are of what general type? _____

_____

These are NOT questions of the normal kind—that is, they are not "real" questions, asking the addressees to supply some unknown information. Consider the second one: "Was not Esau Jacob's brother?"

Did the LORD not know the answer to this question? Then why did he ask it? _____

_____

Here God wanted to *stress* the fact that Esau was indeed the brother of Jacob. Thus this question is not really asking for some information. Rather, it serves to emphasize a particular point that the speaker is trying to make, whether a forceful *assertion* (positive) or a strong *denial* (negative). We call this type of utterance a *rhetorical question* (abbreviated as RQ).

RQs are commonly used by good speakers in many languages of the world, including the Bantu family here in Africa. Such questions are often specially marked as being rhetorical through the use of a distinct intonation, introductory particles, or a different word order (e.g., by means of a special initial question word like *Kani* "Do you mean to say that" or *Bwanji* "How can you say that" in Chichewa).

How is this question in 1:2b translated in YL? Give a back translation into English:

_____

_____

Is it clear that this is an RQ in your translation? If not, how would you modify, or verbally *mark*, it in YL to indicate that it is *not* a "real" question? Be specific in your explanation.

_____

_____

Now look at the first question of this verse, where the people ask God "How have you loved us?" Here the purpose of the RQ is somewhat different.

Do the people really expect the LORD to give them an explanation of how he showed love to them as a nation in the past? No, in fact what was the point that they were denying by asking this question?

_____

_____

_____

RQs are often accompanied by strong emotions, feelings, opinions, and attitudes on the part of the speaker.

What attitude do the Jews reveal in relation to the LORD by asking him the question of v. 1:2b?_____

_____

As we will see, RQs are very important in the Book of Malachi. Not only do they give emphasis, but they also help to mark the *structure* of the text. That is, they may indicate the beginning of a new point or stage in the prophet's (really the LORD's) argument or legal "case" (*mlandu*) against his disobedient people.

Where does the next RQ appear in chapter 1?_____
Here is where a new _____ begins.

What does the LORD mean to tell the priests by the use of this question in 1:6? What is its implicit (unstated) purpose or communicative function?

_____

Another important feature of Malachi's style of writing, which he used to reinforce his message, is found in 1:8. Here we notice four more _____, a feature which we have just been studying. What is their rhetorical purpose in this passage?

_____

_____

_____

We also observe here that there is a great deal of _____
_____ in Malachi. *Repetition* is the second
important stylistic feature translators need to be aware of. Often such repetition occurs with one of the RQs in the text.

Give another example of this sort of "echoing" repetition in Malachi:

_____

Repetition may be "exact," especially where single words or phrases are
concerned, for example in 2:16 ("I hate"). But more frequently the repetition is "synonymous"; that is, the same or a similar thought is repeated in
different words.

Give an example of synonymous *repetition* from Malachi (as in 1:8):

_____

Often repetition takes the form of *poetic parallelism*, in which one line,
A, says something, and then a second line, B, repeats the essential idea in
different words. Often B adds some emphasis to what was said in A or it is
more specific.

In the spaces below, write two other lines from chapter 1 that are similar in meaning:

A: _____

B: _____

Sometimes the repetition in two related lines is not so easily seen. Often
there may be a definite contrast present. This is called *contrastive parallelism*. We observe this type in the last line of 1:2 and the first line of 1:3.

Write these two parallel lines below and circle the words that contrast
in meaning:

A: _____

B: _____

Sometimes a contrast may cover a number of lines. The whole of 1:12,
for example, contrasts with all of 1:11 (see also 1:4).

At other times, we do not notice the repetition of complete ideas so
much, whether similar or contrastive. Rather, there is an obvious addition, or an association in meaning between lines A and B. Often this association takes the form of some kind of *cause-effect* relationship. This is
called *additive* (or synthetic) *parallelism*. It is illustrated in the first two
clauses of 2:8.

Write these two parallel lines below and observe how B adds an important consequential idea to the meaning of line A:

A: _____

B: _____

Notice how this process continues as the last poetic line of 2:8 sums up the first two lines in the logical relationship of *means-result*. Such verbal repetition in parallel lines demonstrates the rhetorical (argumentative) poetry of Malachi. The LORD is not happy with the spiritual and moral life of his people and therefore has a strong legal case to make against them. He makes this very clear in the forceful language that his prophet uses. It is important to recognize this when trying to understand his message. What point is Malachi trying to emphasize through the use of this or that stylistic feature and what particular feelings does he express by his words?

What emotion does the LORD express along with his utterance of 2:8, and why do you say so?

Another type of repetition in Malachi is more obvious in nature. It frequently involves the use of God's name, 'LORD' (*YHWH*) or the 'LORD Almighty' (*YHWH* of Hosts). Whenever the *personal name* of God is used, it adds some emphasis to whatever is being said. Often this name is found together with the verb 'says'.

How often do you find the expression 'the LORD says' or 'says the LORD (Almighty)' in the first chapter of Malachi? It occurs _____ times.

What fact about the words in Malachi (and all the prophets of God) do these repetitions serve to emphasize (see 1:1)?

Sometimes the repetition of ideas or topics in literary discourse takes the form of a chiasmus, a repetition of lines in reverse order: A—B :: B'—A'. Such a structure is found in 1:2:

A: "I have loved you,"
B: says Yahweh.
B': And you say,
A': "How have you loved us?"

What do you think would be the purpose of this chiastic structure in this verse?

What *reversal* in meaning does this particular form call attention to in the text?

In addition to such contrasts or differences, a chiasmus may also be used to *focus* on important information in the discourse. The point of emphasis usually lies in the *center* of the structure, with additional stress also put at the *end* of the arrangement. An example of this is in 3:1.

Try to fill in the center of the chiastic structure from the clues that are given below. Note that the text cited here is a literal rendering of the original Hebrew:

A: And suddenly he will come to his Temple, the Lord,
    B: whom you are seeking,
        C: namely, _____
    B': whom you are pleased (with).
A': Behold, he comes, says the LORD of Hosts.

Who is being highlighted by the central verbal spotlight of this rhetorical construction? _____

See if you can find another example of this sort of reversed structure in Malachi and explain its particular function in the context concerned.

_____

_____

_____

A third stylistic feature of Malachi's writing is an *exclamation*, a strongly emphatic or especially forceful statement. (In English an exclamation is usually indicated by an exclamation mark.) It is similar to the rhetorical question discussed above, in that it expresses emphasis, but it does not involve the form of a question. In 1:5 the exclamation is embedded in direct speech. *Direct speech* in the prophetic literature is also usually very strong speech in which God or his prophet is talking directly to the reader or hearer.

Find and write down the exclamation found in 1:5:

_____

Why are these words being emphasized? (You need to read the whole section, 1:2–5.)

_____

_____

Find and write down the exclamation found in 1:8:

_____

What is being emphasized? What emotion or attitude accompanies the exclamation?

_____

_____

Exclamatory utterances are often marked by special words, particles, or syntactic constructions that are rather short (sometimes leaving certain words out) or that twist the *word order* (especially in Hebrew). Exclamations appear to be accompanied by very intense emotions and attitudes, whether positive (e.g., praise) or negative (e.g., curse).

Find and write down the exclamation found in 1:13:

_____

What marks this utterance as an exclamation (other than the printed exclamation mark)?

_____

It is necessary for translators to find a way to reproduce the exclamation, including its particular expression of emotion, in a natural way in their language. This must be done by the printed word alone, without the benefit of *intonation* (the tone of one's voice), which is an important aspect of most exclamations.

At times the English version that you are using may not mark a certain utterance as an exclamation, but the context may suggest that it is indeed exclamatory and very emphatic.

Do you see a possible instance of this in 1:10? If so, write what you think the utterance of exclamation is. _____

What *verbal marker*(s) would you use to show that this is an exclamation in YL?

_____

A fourth important stylistic and poetic feature found in Malachi is *figurative language*, that is, words which use images, or pictures, of comparison or association to get the idea across. Figures of speech are forms of indirect language which are not meant to be understood literally. One must look for another meaning that is related in some way to the literal sense.

Identify the figurative language in the first sentence of 1:11:

_____

What important thought does this figure, called a *merismus* (in which two different aspects or elements of a single domain are used to refer to the whole field), serve to emphasize?

_____

Notice that the intended meaning of this figure is given at the beginning of the second clause in 1:11, which includes another common expression that is not to be understood in a literal way.

This second figure of speech is a *metonym*, which substitutes a closely related word for the thing or person that is meant. Notice that this metonym is repeated twice in the last part of v. 11 but with a slight difference in meaning. What are these two meanings?

i. _____

ii. _____

How have these two senses of 'name' been translated into YL? Do people have any difficulty in understanding these references in YL? Explain your answer:

_____

_____

Metaphor is an indirect figurative comparison in which a topic is referred to with a "word picture" or image. In 1:6 there are two instances of metaphor. Write them here:

_____ and _____

These metaphors that ascribe human features or characteristics to God are also called *anthropomorphisms*.

There is another metaphor in 1:7. The word in Hebrew is 'bread'.

How does the NIV render the word 'bread' here? _____

What does the word 'food' or 'bread' refer to here? What is it that is being likened to food?

_____

Can you refer to 'offerings' or 'sacrifices' in your language as 'food'? Explain:

_____

_____

Pick out all the nonliteral language that you can find in 2:11, any word or phrase that is not meant to be understood literally. An example is 'Judah', which refers to the *people* of Judah.

_____

_____

Sometimes nonliteral language may extend over several passages. When it does, it is often combined with the use of graphic *local* imagery, which is very closely related to figurative language, except that it is to be interpreted *literally*, often as part of an example or illustration of some kind. For instance, what are the images that occur (in vv. 13–14) as part of the examples that the LORD gives to prove that the people are "polluting his table" (v. 12)?

_____

_____

Several related figures and images may occur together in a longer passage. Such a combination calls attention to the topic being discussed and emphasizes it by evoking vivid, memorable pictures in the minds of the audience. This enables listeners to better remember the teaching, command, or appeal being presented. A good example of this occurs in 2:1–3. What point or purpose does the imagery emphasize in 2:3?

_____

What is the serious moral problem that the LORD rebukes in 2:3?

_____

_____

The fifth and last stylistic feature in Malachi that we will consider is the most difficult. This device is called *irony*. Here again, the words of the text are not to be understood in a literal sense. Rather, the exact opposite or some contradictory meaning is intended. In most cases the speaker is reproving, correcting, or instructing the listener. When the criticism is meant to be strong in its effect on the listener's personal emotions, attitudes, and self-image, it is termed *sarcasm*.

Consider the expression in 1:8, "Try offering them to your governor!" Yes, this utterance is an exclamation, but it is also an instance of irony. Is the LORD really saying that the Jews should bring crippled animals as a gift to the governor? If not, what does he mean by these words—what does he want them to understand and to feel?

_____

_____

How would you convey this meaning rhetorically in YL? What expressions would you use?

_____

_____

Is it difficult to get this idea across in YL? Explain: _____

_____

Find the example of irony in 1:10. Then explain its intended meaning and the accompanying emotion or attitude:

_____

_____

Expressions involving irony are common in Malachi. The concepts and attitudes that they convey are some of the most difficult to translate into another language because they often depend upon a speaker's *intonation* to show that the words are not to be understood literally.

Is intonation used in YL to mark ironic utterances? Explain how this is done:_____

_____

Is there any other way that you can signal the presence and significance of irony in YL, for example, through the use of a special formula or emotive particle? Explain:

_____

_____

Dramatic (i.e., situational) irony, which is found in the Book of Jonah, is also difficult. It often depends on the discourse structure and plot patterning of the entire text. For example, Jonah, a called prophet of the LORD, tries his best to escape from his assignment! Yet recognizing irony is crucial because a definite and important aspect of meaning is involved; in fact, the meaning is likely to be just the opposite of what the text may appear to say.

Why might this be a special problem for translators of the Bible?

_____

How would you mark the irony of 1:10 in YL?

_____

Do most people reading the Bible in YL understand the irony of 1:8 in a literal way? If so, how would you indicate in YL that an ironic meaning is intended?

_____

_____

What is the dramatic or situational irony that is expressed by the disgusting imagery of 2:3? You may need to consult a commentary for some background information here.

_____

_____

Now do a similar study of the irony, figurative language, and imagery to be found in 2:10–12 and 2:13–16:

_____

_____

_____

_____

In this lesson we have studied five of the important stylistic devices found in the Book of Malachi. List them here with a brief definition of each one:

i. _____

ii. _____

iii. _____

iv. _____

v. _____

Which of these features causes you the most difficulty when translating the Bible in YL? Why?

_____

_____

Are there any other stylistic features that you noticed when reading Malachi which may cause you difficulty when translating the Old Testament?

If you found any, list them below and give an example of each from Malachi:

_____

_____

_____

Why did Malachi use this type of language when preaching his message to the Jews living in and around in Jerusalem? Why did the LORD allow such difficult language to be used in his holy Word?

_____

_____

What was the central message or main theme that Malachi wanted to emphasize through the use of these stylistic features?

_____

_____

This study has shown how the special artistic forms of the biblical text contribute to its total meaning—the meaning that we have to translate as best we can in our language.

How does the presence of these stylistic features influence the way we translate the Scriptures?

_____

_____

_____

In the next portion of our lesson we will see how Malachi has organized his message as a *structure* having several major divisions or sections, each with its own distinct theme and purpose within the text. There is a main theme (namely, how God's people should respond to his unchanging love for them), and under that there are several subthemes. If we can discover these subthemes, or "parts," that fall under the central theme of the message as a whole, they will serve as a map to give us direction as we journey through this important and final book of the Old Testament.

Assignment

Before you go on to the next lesson in section C.2, try to find an example not previously mentioned of each of the five stylistic (L-R) features in Malachi. Write these examples here with their references. Be prepared to identify, explain, and propose a solution for any special translation problems that you find in these examples. Note that where several of these devices occur together, the passage in question normally carries extra emphasis and/or carries some additional point of information. Did you find any instances of this in your investigation? If so, please explain the text and suggest an equivalent rendering in YL that is also forceful and meaningful.

Rhetorical Question: _____

_____

Repetition or *Parallelism:* _____

_____

Direct Speech or *Exclamation:* _____

_____

Figurative Language: _____

_____

Irony or *Sarcasm:* _____

_____

C.2 Structure: How Malachi organized his message

As we examined some of the main features of Malachi's style of writing, we saw that Malachi wrote in a dramatic and forceful way in order to highlight the main points of his message to the Jews of his day. These were people who considered themselves to be very religious, and yet they were living contrary to the will of their covenant God. These people lived according to the outward forms of the Law of God, but their daily behavior denied the true intent and purpose of his commandments.

List the five main features of Malachi's style which help to emphasize his message:

_____

_____

What is the central theme of Malachi's (Yahweh's) message to the people of God?

_____

_____

Why was this message necessary? Why did the people of that time need to hear it?

_____

_____

Do people today need to hear this message? Explain how Bible translation can help make this possible by the way in which the text is rendered in your language.

_____

_____

Our study stresses the need not only for an *accurate* translation, but one that is just as *powerful* and *convincing* as the original in its style of writing. In today's lesson we want to examine Malachi's message in more detail, especially with regard to its *structure*, how the book is organized on the whole. This is not the same thing as its *style, which is its manner of composition.*

To examine the structure we should ask, How is it arranged in terms of its major and minor divisions? What are the main parts and subparts that go along with the central theme (like the parts of a sermon)? Why is the text organized in this way?

The structure, or outline, of a book is a road map. A map helps a person learn the overall route to take on a long journey. This keeps him from getting lost along the way. When we know the outline of a book of the Bible, it is like passing the main places along the way while on a journey. Understanding how a book is organized makes it easier to follow the meaning of its parts, or pericopes. Our study of the Book of Malachi may be arranged into topics according to its overall structure so that each section can act as a meaningful unit on its own. These sections will be related to the larger whole of which they are constituent parts.

What do we mean by the structure of a book? Why is it important to study this?

_____

_____

Why should we examine this structure carefully before we look at the individual parts of the book? How does the larger structure help us to understand the biblical text better?

_____

_____

How can the knowledge of a text's overall structure help in Bible translation? Are translators concerned only about single sentences or paragraphs? Why or why not?

_____

_____

The overall structure of a book is like a _____, which helps us to do what?

_____

Now open up the New International Version Bible (NIV) or the main vernacular Bible that you use and look for the major divisions of Malachi. These are normally indicated in the text by means of *section headings*, that is, titles at the beginning of every major unit. Sometimes a thematic outline of the entire book is given in an introduction, as in *The NIV Study Bible*. The section headings may be regarded as subthemes under the primary central theme of the book as a whole. They are the main elements of the message that the prophet wanted to preach to the people. He wanted them to understand and put these related ideas into practice in their lives as we also should in ours.

Write out the major section headings for Malachi that you find in either the NIV or your Bible. Also give the verse numbers of each section. (A chapter may have more than one section heading.)

Chapter 1 _____

Chapter 2 _____

Chapter 3 _____

Chapter 4

Would any of these NIV headings be difficult to translate in YL? If so, tell which ones and why a literal translation would be difficult or misleading.

What is the intended meaning of the NIV section heading at 2:10—"Judah Unfaithful"?

How could you express this thought more clearly in your language?

It may be useful to compare the NIV's seven headings to those in the Good News Bible (GNB). The GNB's outline, which is reflected in many of the newer vernacular versions of Central Africa, is as follows:

1:1	*[Introduction]*
1:2–5	*The Lord's Love for Israel*
1:6–2:9	*The Lord Reprimands the Priests*
2:10–16	*The People's Unfaithfulness to God*
2:17–3:5	*The Day of Judgment Is Near*
3:6–12	*The Payment of Tithes*
3:13–18	*God's Promise of Mercy*
4:1–6	*The Day of the Lord Is Coming*

Compare these headings from the GNB with those you found in the NIV. Where are the main differences, either in the words of the section headings or the verse number divisions. Write the differences here:

One of the differences occurs at 2:1, where the NIV begins a new section, but the GNB does not. Another difference is at 3:13, where the GNB begins a new section, but the NIV does not.

A structural outline is always shown to be valid by some prominent stylistic features in the text itself, for example, an *inclusio*, a rhetorical question, a larger pattern of repeated words, a special concentration of figurative language and imagery, or any combination of the features that we studied in section C.1. Later we will learn how to examine the biblical text more closely in order to propose and support a credible structural outline.

For now, just study the two places of structural disagreement noted above and see if you can decide which version is correct in its analysis and why. Write your reasons in the space provided below. Note that a new section is often called for where there is some major *break* or *shift* either in form (e.g., a change from prose to poetry, or a change in tense/aspect, or a change of referent) or content (e.g., a change of topic, setting, circumstance, or speaker) or both form and content.

2:1 _____

_____

3:13 _____

_____

The NIV Study Bible (1985) presents the following outline in its introduction to Malachi. It shows how Malachi's major themes are organized and related to one another. (Note: Themes are more precise summaries of content than topics in that themes include a subject and verb, verbal, or qualifier.)

I. Title (1:1)
II. Introduction: God's Covenant Love for Israel Affirmed (1:2–5)
III. Israel's Unfaithfulness Rebuked (1:6–2:16)
    A. The Unfaithfulness of the Priests (1:6–2:9)
        1. They dishonor God in their sacrifices (1:6–14)
        2. They do not faithfully teach the law (2:1–9)
    B. The Unfaithfulness of the People (2:10–16)
IV. The Lord's Coming Announced (2:7–4:6)
    A. The Lord Will Come to Purify the Priests and Judge the People (2:17–3:5)
    B. A Call to Repentance in View of the Lord's Coming (3:6–12)
        1. An exhortation to faithful giving (3:6–12
        2. An exhortation to faithful service (3:13–18)
    C. The Day of the Lord Announced (ch. 4)

Is this thematic outline of the NIV more helpful than a structural outline? Notice that it includes all of the principal divisions but arranges them into several levels. Does this help you better understand how the contents of Malachi are arranged? Explain:

_____

_____

Scholars disagree over such outlines as we can see in the various commentaries on Malachi. Compare the preceding outline with the one found in Clark and Hatton's *Translator's Handbook* (2002:370). Where do the major differences occur? Which outline better represents both the structural and the thematic organization of Malachi?

_____

_____

_____

How can an understanding of the structural and thematic organization of a biblical book help you to translate more accurately? Give one example from Malachi:

_____

_____

_____

A careful study of Malachi's style (which we studied in the last lesson) and structure (this lesson) indicates that his book is written in the form of a *debate* between two parties. (For one possible perspective on the discourse structure of Malachi, see Wendland 1985.) Since this debate involves a formal accusation of one party against the other, it may be termed a *dispute*. It is like what happens in a court of law when someone who has been wronged (the "plaintiff") brings a complaint or charge (a "case") against another person (the "defendant"), who must respond in defense. All this takes place before a judge who will render a decision (a "verdict") according to the law so that justice is done. Is the defendant guilty or innocent? If he is found to be in the wrong, what should the punishment be?

How do you translate the following judicial terms in YL? You may have to do some research before you can answer this question.

"accusation"	_____	"dispute"	_____
"plaintiff"	_____	"case"	_____
"defendant"	_____	"judge"	_____
"verdict"	_____	"guilty"	_____
"innocent"	_____	"law"	_____
"punishment"	_____	"justice"	_____

Study Malachi 1:2 and 1:6. Who are the two parties in the series of cases presented in Malachi?

PLAINTIFF   =   _____

DEFENDANT =   _____

In these verses, God is not just the plaintiff, he is also the supreme

_____.

God renders his judgment in the religious cases against the Jews most clearly in the second half of the book, that is, in chapters 3 and 4. According to which law were these cases being decided? Which law (or laws) had the people violated and where was their judgment found?

_____

The Law of God was the formal agreement, or covenant, that God made with his people. The Law is recorded in the Book of Deuteronomy and elsewhere in the first five books of Moses, known as the Pentateuch.
   Read Deuteronomy 28:1–2. What would happen if the people of Israel obeyed God's Law?

_____

_____

Read Deuteronomy 28:15. What would happen if the people of Israel disobeyed God's Law? _____

_____

Read Deuteronomy 30:1–6. What would the LORD do for his people when they repent?

_____

_____

Read Deuteronomy 29:1. Through whom did God give his Law?

_____

Notice that in this passage the Law is explicitly linked with God's people Israel.
   This important background information illustrates the influence an older biblical text can have upon a later text. Such influence is called *intertextuality*. The Book of Deuteronomy was probably well known to the people Malachi was writing or preaching to. Therefore, when he quoted it, he did not have to explicitly mention the source. Readers and hearers nowadays, however, will frequently not be familiar with this cultural background concerning the history of God's people, where they lived, their way of life, and their worldview.
   How can translators best provide background information to their receptors?

_____

Would it be helpful to include these Deuteronomy references as footnotes in your Bible?

Why or why not? _____

How is the word 'covenant' translated in YL?

Give an example of how this word is used in your everyday life:

_____

_____

What does *berith* 'covenant' refer to? Consult a Hebrew lexicon or Bible dictionary to find out.

_____

Has this key term been well translated in YL? Explain:

_____

Do you have any suggestion for improving how it is translated? Explain:

_____

The important notion of 'covenant' greatly influences our understanding of the whole Old Testament and the New Testament as well. Notice where this concept is introduced in the Book of Malachi.

What is significant about its being placed here? How does it affect the prophet's message as a whole? _____

Read Deuteronomy 29:2 and also Exodus 20:2. What great event do these passages refer to?

_____

God's covenant, which is expressed in the Mosaic Law (or "instructions"), is closely linked to the Good News, the Gospel. We must understand what this covenant is about in order to understand the Gospel—all the things that God graciously did, and continues to do, to deliver his holy and faithful people from evil and preserve their lives.

How is God's gracious working indicated in Malachi 1:2? What key term appears here?

_____

It is important to observe that Yahweh brings seven "cases" against his people. (Seven may be a significant number suggesting completeness.)

These cases forcefully condemn the moral and religious wrongs being committed. They all concern the covenant between Yahweh and his people, which the people have disobeyed in various ways, and they all follow the same general threefold pattern (similar to a catechetical question-and-answer format), even though the specific details may vary.

First, Yahweh makes an *accusation* that either directly or indirectly reproves the people for their lack of faith as reflected in their sinful lives—they are openly violating his clearly stated covenant principles. Second, the people (hypothetically) make a hypocritical reply, an *objection* that impudently questions or complains about what God has just said. Third, Yahweh makes a *response*, replying to their objection by restating his main point, or premise, and supporting it with evidence. This part, which is usually the longest, takes different forms. It may be a further accusation, reproof, warning, exhortation, a promise, or blessing, or any combination of these. The style is quite varied because God wants to get his point across in the most forceful way possible as he urges the people to repent of their wickedness and live righteous lives according to the Law of Moses (see Malachi 4:4).

The key passages of Malachi are listed here to the left. Carefully read each passage, then summarize God's case against his people as expressed in it. (The verse numbers in parentheses refer to the complete case.)

1:2a (1:2–5) _____

1:6–7 (1:6–14) _____

2:1, 8 (2:1–9) _____

2:11, 14 (2:10–16) _____

2:17 (2:17–3:5) _____

3:7–8 (3:6–12) _____

3:13–14 (3:13–18) _____

Notice that chapter 4 is not in the preceding list. What we call chapter 4 was part of chapter 3 in the original Hebrew text. What were the verse numbers of this passage in the original text?

In what ways is 4:1–6 different in terms of form or content from the previous sections found in chapters 1–3?

_____

_____

What is the function or purpose of chapter 4 in relation to Malachi's message as a whole?

_____

_____

Observe that the case presented in 2:1, 8 is somewhat different from the others. In what respects is its structure different from the three-part pattern described above?

_____

_____

Give the verse numbers for the NIV's eight divisions of Malachi:

_____

List two important structural differences that you see when you compare the NIV divisions with that of any other Bible, especially an older version in your language, if there is an older one. Which text division seems to make most sense to you? Give reasons for your opinion:

i. _____

_____

ii. _____

_____

The outline in *The NIV Study Bible* is just one way of analyzing the structure of Malachi. You may find a different method of organization in some other Bible version, handbook, or commentary. In such cases, you must note the differences and then examine the text to see where they occur. In this way you can decide how the discourse is divided into topically related segments. The process of text comparison is crucial for translators to learn and put into practice as they work.

One Hebrew rhetorical device that can sometime help us to make decisions about structure is the inclusio. *Inclusio* is a repetition of significant content at the beginning and ending of a larger unit. The repetition is called inclusio because it "includes" the text in between. In other words, it marks the external boundaries of a distinct section of discourse. We see an example of inclusio in 4:1–3.

What words or ideas are reiterated at the beginning and end of this section?

3:1 _____

3:3 _____

This verbal repetition serves to *highlight* the information found in the center of the paragraph. What thought is emphasized in the center?

_____

_____

See if you can find another example of inclusio as you examine the various discourse units of Malachi. Note the examples of repetition that occur at the beginning and end points of distinct sections (e.g., a paragraph or some larger section):
Beginning (verse ____): _____

_____

Ending (verse ____): _____

_____

Which of the previously listed cases of Yahweh against his people seems to be the most serious? Why (from the perspective of your own society and culture) do you think so?

_____

_____

By these attitudes and behavior the people were acting contrary to their covenant with God. The theme of Malachi as a whole is concerned with this problem. What is this general theme?

_____

_____

How does the structure of Malachi help to emphasize this overall theme and its importance? _____

_____

_____

How is it possible to make *readers* aware of this text structure in your translation? What are some of the devices that you can use to draw their attention to it and clarify its importance to the prophet's message as a whole?

_____

_____

_____

What can you do to make *hearers* aware of the structure? One suggestion is to use transitional expressions to mark the start of a new unit (e.g.,

'Next the LORD Almighty says...' in 1:6). Give some other suggestions that might work for this purpose in YL:

_____

_____

_____

Assignment

In preparation for the next lesson, read, study, and translate Malachi 1:2–5. This is case 1 (or dispute 1). List three important translation problems that you encountered and then tell how you propose solving them in YL.

i. _____

ii. _____

iii. _____

C.3 Translation: A literary-rhetorical version of Malachi 3:6–12

We will now apply some of the things that we have been learning about the style and structure of the Book of Malachi to the preparation of a translation of Malachi 3:6–12. Read through these verses in an English or Hebrew Bible or any other versions at hand. Tell why this is one of the better known portions of Malachi:

_____

_____

In the spaces below, summarize your own analysis of the structural organization, stylistic features, and rhetorical devices that distinguish Malachi 3:6–12.

Structural organization (How is the text arranged into major and minor topics and parts?)

Structural features (What literary devices serve to mark the boundaries of this passage?)

Stylistic features (What literary devices make this text beautiful to listen to?)

Rhetorical features (What literary devices make this text powerful to listen to?)

Now think of how you would best express this passage in your language (YL). First, you must decide what type of translation you wish to prepare in YL. There are basically three types to choose from: literal translation, literary translation, variable translation.

Literal translation is a word-for-word translation. It sticks as close as possible to the original source-language (SL) text. Such a translation is usually very difficult because of its unnaturalness and complexity in the target-language (TL).

Literary translation is a genre-for-genre translation. It utilizes a literary/ oratorical genre that is the closest functional equivalent of the genre found in the SL text, such as a TL praise poem style for a psalm in praise of God. It is difficult to produce because it requires excellent SL exegetes and gifted TL experts.

Variable translation is a middle-of-the-road, "partially literary" translation. It is "as literal as possible, as free as necessary," as the NRSV preface puts it. It is *literal* only when literalness does not produce an unnatural TL text or one that is meaningless or too difficult to understand. It is *literary* to the extent that the translation employs such TL devices as syntactic balance, rhythm, alliteration, parallelism, condensation, effective words and combinations of words, figurative language (e.g., metaphor and simile), and rhetorical features (e.g., rhetorical questions, hyperbole). The chosen features are matched as closely as possible to those of the SL text with respect to both communicative function and value (impact + appeal). Competent translators and translation teams should aim for and be able to achieve this type of a limited LiFE version.

The first of the two texts that follow is a "popular language" translation of Malachi 3:6–12 in Chichewa, formatted as printed in the published version (except that the lines are not justified). In the right column beside it is a literal English back-translation. The second text is a stylistically more dynamic, literary-rhetorical rendition in Chichewa of the same passage, also with an English back-translation. In it a number of artistic and rhetorical features are underlined in order to make it easier to compare the two. After studying the texts, see if you can describe and evaluate what was done in the second one to make it sound more literary or oratorical in Chichewa. Tell whether these same devices would work in YL. If not, what would you suggest as better functionally equivalent forms?

A Popular-Language Version in Chichewa

6 "Ine ndine Chauta, wosasinthika. Nchifukwa chake inu zidzukulu za Yakobe simudaonongeke. 7 Kuyambira masiku a makolo anu mwakhala mu-kuphwanya malamulo anga, simu-dawatsate konse. Ngati mubwerera kwa Ine, Inenso ndidzabwerera kwa inu. Ndikutero Ine Chauta Wampha-mvuzonse. Komabe inu mumati, 'Kodi tingathe kubwerera bwanji?' 8 Ine ndi-kuti, Kodi munthu angathe kubera Mulungu? Komabe inu mumandibera. Inu mumati, 'Kodi timakuberani bwa-nji?' Ine ndikuti, Mumandibera pa zachikumi zanu ndi zopereka zina 9 Ndinu otembereredwa nonsenu, mtu-ndu wanu wonse, chifukwa choti mu-mandibera. 10 Aliyense abwere ndi chichikumi chathunthu ku Nyumba yanga, kuti m'menemo mukhale cha-kudya chambiri. Ndikutero Ine Chauta Wamphamvuzonse. Mundiyese tsono, ndipo muone ngati sinditsekula zipa-ta zakumwamba ndi kukugwetserani madalitso ochuluka. 11 Ndidzaletsa ti-zilombo kuti tisadye mbeu zanu, mipe-sa yanu sidzaleka kubala. Ndikutero Ine Chauta Wamphamvuzonse. 12 Mo-tero anthu a mitundu yonse adzaku-tchulani odala, pakuti dziko lanu lidza-khala lokondweretsa. Ndikutero Ine Chauta Wamphamvuzonse."

6 "I am Chauta, who does not change. For this reason you descendants of Jacob were not destroyed. 7 Beginning from the days of your ancestors you have been smashing my commands, you did not follow them at all. If you return to Me, I too will return to you. I say so Me Chauta almighty. However as for you, you say, 'How are we able to return?' 8 As for me, I say, Is a person able to steal from God? However, as for you, you steal from me. You say, 'How do we steal from you?' I say, You steal from me in your tithes and other offerings. 9 You are cursed all of you, the whole tribe of you, because of this that you steal from me. 10 Let everyone come with the tithe to the House of mine, so that in there might be much food. I say so I Chauta Almighty. Just try me, and see if I don't open up the gates of heaven and cause to fall down blessings a'plenty. 11 I will prevent pests from eating your seeds, your vines will not stop bearing. I say so I Chauta Almighty. 12 There-fore people of all tribes will call you blessed, since your land will be most pleasing. I say so I Chauta Almighty."

A full L-R Version in Chichewa

Note the names for God in this literary rendition: *Chauta* is the Chewa peo-ple's name for the supreme Deity; *Mulungu* is a generic term meaning 'god'; *Mphambe* is a praise name for God that is associated with the powers of creation and the thunder of natural storms.

Ine ndine Chauta, <u>Mulungu</u> wosasinthika<u>ne</u>.   [6]
  I am Chauta, the <u>God</u> who does not change—not <u>me</u>.
Nchifukwa chake inu <u>ana</u> a Yakobe <u>simunathe</u>.
  For this reason you <u>children</u> of Jacob were not <u>finished off</u>.
Kuyambira masiku a makolo anu <u>okanika aja</u>,   [7]
  From the days of your ancestors, <u>those perverse ones</u>,
mukuphwanya malamulo anga, <u>osa</u>watsata konse.
  you are shattering my commands, <u>not</u> follow<u>ing</u> them at all.

<u>Komabe</u> ngati mubwerera kwa ine <u>n'kulapa ndithu</u>,
  However, if you return to me <u>and truly repent</u>,
<u>apo</u> inenso ndidzabwerera kwa inu, <u>osakulangani, ai</u>.
  <u>then</u> I too will return to you, <u>without punishing you, no</u>.
<u>Awa</u> ndi mau anga<u>di</u>, ine Chauta <u>Mulungu Mphambe</u>.
  <u>Those</u> are my <u>very</u> words, I Chauta <u>God-Thunder</u>.
Koma inu mumati, "Kodi tingathe kubwerera bwanji?"
  But as for you, you say, "How are we able to return?"

<u>Apo pali funso</u>: "Munthu angathe kubera Mulungu <u>kodi</u>?"   [8]
  <u>Here's a question</u>: "Can a person steal from God <u>really</u>?"
Kubera mumandibera ndithu, inu simungakane konse.
  To be sure you are always stealing from me, you can't deny it.
Koma <u>mukana pakuti</u>, "<u>Ha</u>! ife timakuberani bwanji?"
  But <u>you deny it saying</u>,
  "<u>Ha</u>! <u>as for us</u>, how do we steal from you?"
"<u>Zoona</u>, mumandibera pa zachikumi ndi zopereka zina."
  "<u>Truly</u>, you steal from me in tithes and other offerings."

<u>Tero</u> muli otembereredwa nonsenu,   [9]
  <u>Thus</u> you are all cursed,
mtundu wonse<u>wu</u> *psiti*!³⁹⁴ <u>Mbala inu</u>!
  <u>this</u> whole tribe <u>together</u>! <u>You</u> <u>thieves</u>!
<u>Choncho</u> abwere <u>onse</u> ku nyumba yanga,   [10]
  <u>So then</u> let <u>them all</u> come <u>to my house</u>,
aliyense abwere ndi chachikumi chakecho.
  everyone let him come with his very own tithe.

Munyumba mwangamu mukhale chakudya moti *tho*!
  In this my house let it be full up! with food,
<u>Awa</u> ndi mau anga<u>di</u>, ine Chauta <u>Mulungu Mphambe</u>.
  <u>Those</u> are my <u>very</u> words, I Chauta <u>God-Thunder</u>.
Mundiyese tsono, <u>muone</u> ngati sinditsegula zipata
  Just try me, <u>see</u> if I don't open up the gates
<u>zakuthambo</u> n'kukugwetserani madalitso <u>ngati mvula</u>.
  of the <u>skies</u> n' cause blessings to fall down <u>like rain</u>.

---

³⁹⁴A Chichewa ideophone (a dramatic predicator) as is *tho*! below.

Ndidzapitikitsa tizilombo kuti tisadye mbeu zanu.   [11]
   I will chase away the pests so they don't eat your seeds.
Ndidzachulukitsa zokolola zonse m'munda mwanu.
   I will increase all the harvested crops in your garden.
Awa ndi mau angadi, ine Chauta Mulungu Mphambe.
   Those are my very words, I Chauta God-Thunder.

Anthu a mitundu yonse adzaona izi ndi kudabwa.   [12]
   People of all nations will see these things and be amazed.
Adzanena kuti ndinu odala a dziko la mwana-alirenji.[395]
   They'll say that you are blessed ones of a bountiful land.
Awa ndi mau angadi, ine Chauta Mulungu Mphambe.
   Those are my very words, I Chauta God-Thunder.

Answer the following questions as you compare the two Chichewa versions of Malachi 3:6–12:

- Which are the most important stylistic features that you detect in the Chichewa L-R version?
- Do you have *similar* devices in YL that could serve as good replacements? Explain.
- Do you have *different* L-R devices in YL that would sound appropriate in this passage? If so, give some examples and tell where you would use them (be specific).
- Do you think that any of the stylistic features found in the Chichewa L-R version distort the meaning of the SL text? If so, which are these and why do you say so?
- Prepare either a full or a limited L-R rendering of this pericope in YL (Malachi 3:6–12) and give an English back-translation below it. Point out three of the special artistic and rhetorical techniques that you have used and tell why you used them where you have.
- Exchange your draft translation for that of a colleague. Prepare a detailed evaluation of his or her version. Suggest any corrections or improvements that seem warranted.

Revise your own translation based on the critique your colleague has given you. Be prepared to present and defend it orally before your colleagues.

---

[395]An idiom meaning 'a land in which a child lacks or cries for nothing'.

Bibliography

Titles marked with an asterisk are recommended as especially suitable for most translators who have had the equivalent of at least a two-year post-secondary course of training in Bible translation. (Note the additional recommendation following the Bibliography.)

Aageson, James. 1993. *Written also for our sake: Paul and the art of biblical interpretation.* Louisville, Ky.: Westminster–John Knox.

Aaron, D. 2001. *Biblical ambiguities: Metaphor, semantics and divine imagery.* Leiden: Brill.

Achtemeier, P. 1990. *Omne verbum sonat:* The New Testament and the oral environment of late Western antiquity. *Journal of Biblical Literature* 109(1):3–27.

Adam, A., ed. 2000. *Handbook of postmodern biblical interpretation.* St. Louis: Chalice.

Alter, Robert. 1981. *The art of biblical narrative.* New York: Basic.*

Alter, Robert. 1985. *The art of biblical poetry.* New York: Basic.*

Alter, Robert. 1987. Introduction to the Old Testament. In Alter and Kermode (eds.), 11–35.

Alter, Robert. 1996. *Genesis: Translation and commentary.* New York: W. W. Norton.

Alter, Robert, and F. Kermode, eds. 1987. *The literary guide to the Bible.* Cambridge, Mass.: Harvard University Press.

Andersen, T. David. 1998. Perceived authenticity: The fourth criterion of good translation. *Notes on Translation* 12(3):1–13.*

Aune, D. 1987. *The New Testament in its literary environment.* Philadelphia: Westminster.

Aune, D. 1991. *Prophecy in early Christianity and the ancient Mediterranean world.* Grand Rapids: Eerdmans.

Austin, J. 1975. *How to do things with words.* Second edition. Cambridge, Mass.: Harvard University Press.

Bailey, J. 1995. Genre analysis. In J. Green (ed.), 197–221.

Bailey, J., and Lyle D. vander Broek. 1992. *Literary forms in the New Testament.* Louisville: Westminster–John Knox.*

Baker, D., and B. Arnold, eds. 1999. *The face of Old Testament studies: A survey of contemporary approaches.* Grand Rapids: Baker.

Baker, M., ed. 1998. *Routledge encyclopedia of translation studies.* London and New York: Routledge.*

Barbour. 1995. *The Psalms in verse.* Uhrichsville, Ohio: Barbour.

Barker, Kenneth L., ed. 1986. *The NIV: The making of a contemporary translation.* Grand Rapids: Zondervan.

Barr, J. 1963. *The Bible in the modern world.* London: SCM.

Barthes, Roland. 1967. *Elements of semiology.* Trans. A. Lavers and C. Smith. Boston: Beacon.

Barton, J. 1984. *Reading the Old Testament: Method in Bible study.* Philadelphia: Westminster.

Barton, J., ed. 1998. *The Cambridge companion to biblical interpretation.* Cambridge and New York: Cambridge University Press.

Bartsch, Carla. 1997. Oral style, written style, and Bible translation. *Notes on Translation* 11(3):41–48.

Bascom, R. 2002. The role of culture in communication. In Wilt (ed.), chapter 3.

Bauer, W., Wm. Arndt, F. Gingrich, and F. Danker. 1979. *A Greek-English lexicon of the New Testament and other Christian literature.* Chicago and London: University of Chicago Press.

Beekman, J., and J. Callow. 1974. *Translating the Word of God.* Grand Rapids: Eerdmans.*

Ben Zvi, E. 2000. Introduction: Writings, speeches, and the prophetic books—setting an agenda. In Ben Zvi and Floyd (eds.), 1–29.

Ben Zvi, E., and M. Floyd, eds. 2000. *Writings and speech in Israelite and ancient Near Eastern prophecy.* Atlanta: Society of Biblical Literature.

Berlin, A. 1985. *The dynamics of biblical parallelism.* Bloomington: Indiana University Press.*

Berlin, A. 1994. *Poetics and interpretation of biblical narrative.* Winona Lake, Ind.: Eisenbrauns.*

Berry, Donald K. 1995. *An introduction to wisdom and poetry of the Old Testament.* Nashville: Broadman and Holman.*

Black, David, and David Dockery, eds. 1991. *New Testament criticism and interpretation.* Grand Rapids: Zondervan.

Bliese, Loren F. 2003. The key word 'name' and patterns with 26 in the structure of Amos. *The Bible Translator* 54(1):121–135.

Boadt, L. E. 1996. Mythological themes and the unity of Ezekiel." In de Regt, de Waard, and Fokkelmann, 211–231.

Boase-Beier, J., and M. Holman, eds. 1999. *The practices of literary translation: Constraints and creativity.* Manchester: St. Jerome.

Bodine, Walter. 2000. The Bible in a world after Babel: On the challenge of Bible translation. *Notes on Translation* 14(4):34–43.

Boerger, Brenda Higgie. 2003. *Poetic oracle English translation of the Psalms.* Trial edition. Private printing.

Bosseaux, Charlotte. 2001. A study of the translator's voice and style in the French translations of Virginia Woolf's *The Waves.* In *CTIS Occasional Papers* 1, M. Olohan (ed.), 55–75.

Breck, J. 1994. *The shape of biblical language: Chiasmus in the Scriptures and beyond.* Crestwood, N.Y.: St. Vladimir's Seminary Press.

Brichto, Herbert. 1992. *Toward a grammar of biblical poetics.* Oxford: Oxford University Press.

Brueggeman, Walter. 1992. *Old Testament theology: Essays on structure, theme, and text.* Minneapolis: Fortress.

Bullinger, E. W. [1899] 1968. *Figures of speech used in the Bible: Explained and illustrated.* Reprint. Grand Rapids: Baker.

Bush, Peter, and Kirsten Malmkjaer, eds. 1998. *Rimbaud's rainbow: Literary translation in higher education.* Philadelphia: John Benjamins.

Caird, G. B. 1980. *The language and imagery of the Bible.* Philadelphia: Westminster.*

Callow, K. 1974. *Discourse considerations in translating the Word of God.* Grand Rapids: Eerdmans.*

Callow, K. 1998. *Man and message: A guide to meaning-based text analysis.* Lanham, Md.: University Press of America.*

Charles, J. 1993. *Literary strategy in the Epistle of Jude.* Scranton: University of Scranton Press.

Chesterman, A. 1997. *Memes of translation: The spread of ideas in translation theory.* Amsterdam and Philadelphia: John Benjamins.

Chesterman, A., and Emma Wagner. 2002. *Can theory help translators? A dialogue between the ivory tower and the wordface.* Manchester: St. Jerome.

Clark, David J. 1999. Review of *Literary structure and rhetorical strategies in the Hebrew Bible* by de Regt, de Waard, and Fokkelman (1996). *UBS Relevant Ramblings,* Series III, October 1999, no pagination. New York: UBS Service Center.

Clark, David J., and Howard A. Hatton. 2002. *A handbook on Haggai, Zechariah, and Malachi.* New York: United Bible Societies.

Clifford, Richard J. 1998. *The wisdom literature.* Nashville: Abingdon.*

Cotterell, P., and M. Turner. 1989. *Linguistics and biblical interpretation.* Downers Grove, Ill.: InterVarsity.*

Davies, G. 1999. *Ezra and Nehemiah.* Berit Olam (Series). Collegeville, Minn.: Liturgical.

Davis, C. 1999. *Oral biblical criticism: The influence of the principles of orality on the literary structure of Paul's Epistle to the Philippians.* Sheffield, England: Sheffield Academic Press.

de Beaugrande, Robert. 1978. *Factors in a theory of poetic translating.* Assen, Netherlands: Van Gorcum.

de Beaugrande, Robert, and W. Dressler. 1981. *Introduction to textlinguistics.* London: Longman.

de Blois, Kees F., and Tamara Mewe. 2002. Functional equivalence and the new Dutch translation project. In Naude and van der Merwe, 214–227.

de Blois, Reinier. 2000. *Towards a new dictionary of Biblical Hebrew based on semantic domains.* Ph.D. dissertation. Vrije Universiteit te Amsterdam.

Deibler, Ellis. 1993. *An index of implicit information in the Gospels.* Dallas: Summer Institute of Linguistics.

Deibler, Ellis. 1999. *An index of implicit information in Acts–Revelation.* Dallas: SIL International.

Delisle, J. 1988. *Translation: An interpretive approach.* Trans. P. Logan and M. Creery. Ottowa: University of Ottowa Press.

de Regt, L. 2003. Signs of redactional development in some Old Testament texts and the translator. Paper read at UBS Triennial Translation Workshop, 16–27 June, Foz do Iguaçu, Brazil.

de Regt, L., J. de Waard, and J. P. Fokkelman, eds. 1996. *Literary structure and rhetorical strategies in the Hebrew Bible.* Assen, Netherlands: Van Gorcum.

de Vries, L. 1999. The notion of genre and the nature of Bible translations. *Notes on Translation* 13(2):26–42.*

de Vries, L. 2001. Bible translations: Forms and functions. *The Bible Translator* 52(3):306–319.*

de Waard, J., and E. A. Nida. 1986. *From one language to another: Functional equivalence in Bible translating.* Nashville: Thomas Nelson.*

Dewey, J. 1980. *Markan public debate: Literary technique, concentric structure, and theology in Mark 2:1–3:6.* Chicago: Scholars Press.

Dooley, R., and S. Levinsohn. 2001. *Analyzing discourse: A manual of basic concepts.* Dallas: SIL International.*

Dorsey, David A. 1999. *The literary structure of the Old Testament: A commentary on Genesis-Malachi.* Grand Rapids: Baker.

Douglas, M. 1993. *In the wilderness: The doctrine of defilement in the Book of Numbers.* Sheffield, England: Sheffield Academic Press.

Douglas, M. 1999. *Leviticus as literature.* Oxford: Oxford University Press.

Duke, R. 1990. *The persuasive appeal of the chronicler: A rhetorical analysis.* Sheffield, England: Almond.

du Plooy, H. 2002. Listening to the wind in the trees: Meaning, interpretation and literary theory. In Naude and van der Merwe (eds.), 266–279.

Duthie, A. 1985. *Bible translations and how to choose between them.* Exeter: Paternoster.

Elliott, J. 1993. *What is social-scientific criticism?* Minneapolis: Fortress.

Elliot, T. S. 1957. *On poetry and poets.* New York: Farrar, Strauss and Cudahy.

Ellis, E. E. 1991. *The Old Testament in early Christianity: Canon and interpretation in the light of modern research.* Grand Rapids: Baker.

Ellis, J. 1989. *Against deconstruction.* Princeton, N.J.: Princeton University Press.

Fawcett, P. 1997. *Translation and language: Linguistic theories explained.* Manchester: St. Jerome.

Fee, G. 1987. *The First Epistle to the Corinthians.* Grand Rapids: Eerdmans.

Fee, G., and D. Stuart. 1993. *How to read the Bible for all its worth.* Second edition. Grand Rapids: Zondervan.*

Finnegan, R. 1970. *Oral literature in Africa.* Oxford: Clarendon.

Finnegan, R. 1977. *Oral poetry: Its nature, significance and social context.* Bloomington: Indiana University Press.

Fisch, H. 1988. *Poetry with a purpose: Biblical poetics and interpretation.* Bloomington: Indiana University Press.

Fisher, W. R. 1970. A motive view of communication. *Quarterly Journal of Speech* 56:131–139.

Floyd, M. H. 2000. "Write the revelation!" (Hab 2:2): Re-imagining the cultural history of prophecy. In Ben Zvi and Floyd (eds.), 103–143.

Follingstad, C. 2001a. *Deictic viewpoint in Biblical Hebrew text.* Dallas: SIL International.

Follingstad, C. 2001b. The problematic particle כִּי—Metarepresentation in Biblical Hebrew in syntagmatic and paradigmatic perspective. Paper presented at Bible Translation 2001, Graduate Institute of Applied Linguistics, Dallas, October 18–20, 2001.

Fox, E. 1995. The five books of Moses: A new translation with introductions, commentary, and notes. New York: Schocken.

Frye, N. 1957. *Anatomy of criticism*. New York: Atheneum.

Gaddis-Rose, Marilyn. 1997. *Translation and literary criticism: Translation as analysis*. Manchester: St. Jerome.

Gerstenberger, E. S. 1988. *Psalms, part 1: With an introduction to cultic poetry*. The Forms of Old Testament Literature, vol. 14. Grand Rapids: Eerdmans.

Gibson, J. 1998. *Language and imagery in the Old Testament*. Peabody: Hendrickson.*

Giese, R. 1995. Literary forms of the Old Testament. In Sandy and Giese (eds.), 5–27.

Gilliard, Frank. 1993. More silent reading in antiquity: *Non omne verbum sonabat. Journal of Biblical Literature* 112(4):689–696).

Gitay, Y. 1991. *Isaiah and his audience: The structure and meaning of Isaiah 1–12*. Assen-Maastricht, Netherlands: Van Gorcum.

Givon, T. 1984. *Syntax: A functional-typological introduction,* vol. 1. Amsterdam and Philadelphia: John Benjamins.

Godfrey, W. Robert. 1999. Music acceptable to God: An argument for greater use of the Psalms. *Modern Reformation* 8(6):34–38.

Green, H. B. 2001. *Matthew, poet of the Beatitudes*. Sheffield, England: Sheffield Academic Press.

Green, J., ed. 1995. *Hearing the New Testament: Strategies for interpretation*. Grand Rapids: Eerdmans.

Green, J., and S. McKnight. 1992. *Dictionary of Jesus and the Gospels*. Downers Grove, Ill.: InterVarsity.

Gross, Carl. 2003. Yes, sir! Yes, sir! Three bags full, sir!: Acceptability as the supreme translation principle in the UBS translation program. Paper read at UBS Triennial Translation Workshop, 16–27 June, 2003, at Foz do Iguaçu, Brazil.

Guthrie, G. 1994. *The structure of Hebrews: A text-linguistic analysis*. Grand Rapids: Baker.

Gutt, Ernst-August. 1991. *Translation and relevance: Cognition and context*. Oxford: Blackwell.

Gutt, Ernst-August. 1992. *Relevance theory: A guide to successful communication in translation*. Dallas: Summer Institute of Linguistics.*

Hargreaves, C. 1993. *A translator's freedom: Modern English Bibles and their language*. Sheffield, England: JSOT.*

Harvey, J. 1998. *Listening to the text: Oral patterning in Paul's letters*. Grand Rapids: Baker.

Hatim, B. 1997. *Communicating across cultures: Translation theory and contrastive text linguistics*. Exeter: University of Exeter Press.

Hatim, B., and I. Mason. 1990. *Discourse and the translator.* London: Longman.

Hatim, B., and I. Mason. 1997. *The translator as communicator.* London: Routledge.*

Heimerdinger, Jean-Marc. 1999. *Topic, focus, and foreground in Ancient Hebrew narratives.* Sheffield, England: Sheffield Academic Press.

Hermans, T. 1996. The translator's voice in translated narrative. *Target* 8(1): 23–48.

Hermans, T. 1999. *Translation in systems: Descriptive and system-oriented approaches explained.* Manchester: St. Jerome.

Holmes, J. 1988. *Translated!: Papers on literary translation and translation studies.* Amsterdam: Rodopi.

House, Juliane. 1977. *A model for translation quality assessment.* Tübingen: Verlag Narr.

House, P. 1988. *Zephaniah: A prophetic drama.* Sheffield, England: Almond.

House, P., ed. 1992. *Beyond form criticism: Essays In Old Testament literary criticism.* Winona Lake, Ind.: Eisenbrauns.

Jakobson, R. 1971. Two aspects of language and two aspects of aphasic disturbances. In *Selected Writings: 2, Word and Language,* 239–259. The Hague: Mouton.

Jakobson, R. 1972. Linguistics and poetics. In *The structuralists from Marx to Levi Strauss,* R. DeGeorge and F. DeGeorge (eds.), 85–122. Garden City, N.J.: Doubleday.

Jakobson, R. 1985. Poetry of grammar and grammar of poetry. In Pomorska and Rudy, 37–46.

Jasper, D. 1998. Literary readings of the Bible. In Barton, chap. 4.

Jin, Di. 2003. Literary translation: Quest for artistic integrity. Manchester: St. Jerome.

Joubert, S. 2002. No culture shock? Addressing the Achilles heel of modern Bible translations. In Naude and van der Merwe (eds.), 30–43.

Jung, Carl. 1953. *Psychological reflections.* Princeton, N.J: Princeton University Press.

Katan, D. 1999. *Translating cultures: An introduction for translators, interpreters and mediators.* Manchester: St. Jerome.*

Keener, C. 1993. *The IVP Bible background commentary: New Testament.* Downers Grove, Ill.: InterVarsity.

Kennedy, G. 1984. *New Testament interpretation through rhetorical criticism.* Chapel Hill: University of North Carolina Press.

Kennedy, G. 1998. *Comparative rhetoric: An historical and cross-cultural introduction.* Oxford: Oxford University Press.

Kennedy, G., trans. and ed. 1991. *Aristotle: On rhetoric—a theory of civic discourse.* Oxford: Oxford University Press.

Kenny, D. 2001. Lexis and creativity in translation: A corpus-based study. Manchester: St. Jerome.

Klem, H. 1982. *Oral communication of the Scripture: Insights from African oral art.* Pasadena, Calif.: William Carey Library.*

Korpel, M.C.A. 2001. *The structure of the book of Ruth.* Pericope Series 2. Assen, The Netherlands: Van Gorcum.

Kugel, J. 1981. *The idea of biblical poetry: Parallelism and its history.* New Haven: Yale University Press.

Kugel, J. 1999. *The great poems of the Bible: A reader's companion with new translations.* New York: Free Press.*

Lambert, J. 1998. Literary translation. In Baker (ed.), 130–133.

Landers, C. E. 2001. *Literary translation: A practical guide.* Clevedon, Buffalo, Toronto, and Sidney: Multilingual Matters.

Lane, William. 1991. *Hebrews 1–8.* Word Biblical Commentary, 47A. Dallas: Word.

Lanham, Richard. 1969. *A handlist of rhetorical terms: A guide for students of English literature.* Berkeley: University of California Press.*

Larsen, I. 2001. The fourth criterion of a good translation. *Notes on Translation* 15(1):40–53.*

Larson, M. 1984. *Meaning-based translation: A guide to cross-language equivalence.* Lanham, Md.: University Press of America. (Second edition, 1998)*

Lausberg, Heinrich. 1998. *Handbook of literary rhetoric: A foundation for literary study.* Leiden: Brill.

Lefevre, Andre. 1981. Beyond the process: Literary translation in literature and literary theory. In *Translation spectrum: Essays in theory and practice,* M. Gaddis-Rose (ed.), 52–59. Albany, N.Y.: SUNY Press.

Levinsohn. S. H. 1987. *Textual connections in Acts.* Atlanta: Scholars Press.

Levinsohn, S. H. 1992. *Discourse features of New Testament Greek: A coursebook.* Dallas: Summer Institute of Linguistics.*

Levinsohn, S. H. 2002. Book review of *Topic, focus, and foreground in Ancient Hebrew narratives,* by J.-M. Heimerdinger. *Journal of Translation and Textlinguistics* 14:126–147.

Levinson, S. 1983. *Pragmatics.* Cambridge: Cambridge University Press.

Levinson, S. 2000. *Presumptive meanings: The theory of generalized conversational implicature.* Cambridge, Mass.: MIT Press.

Lewis, C. S. 1989. *The quotable Lewis,* W. Martindale and J. Root (eds.). Wheaton, Ill.: Tyndale.

Lewis, C. S. 1991. *The inspirational writings of C. S. Lewis.* New York: Inspirational.

Linton, C. 1986. The importance of literary style in Bible translation today. In K. Barker (ed.), 15–31. Grand Rapids: Zondervan.*

Long, B. 1991. *2 Kings.* The Forms of the Old Testament Literature, vol. 10. Grand Rapids: Eerdmans.

Long, V. Phillips. 1994. *The art of biblical history.* Grand Rapids: Zondervan.*

Long, V. Phillips. 1997. Old Testament history: A hermeneutical perspective. In *New international dictionary of Old Testament theology and exegesis,* Willem VanGemeren (ed.), vol. 1, 87–102. Grand Rapids: Zondervan.

Longacre, R. 1989. *Joseph: A story of divine providence. A text theoretical and textlinguistic analysis of Genesis 37 and 39–48.* Winona Lake: Eisenbrauns.

Longacre, R. 1996. *The grammar of discourse.* Second edition. New York: Plenum.

Louw, J. P., and E. A. Nida. 1989. *Greek-English lexicon of the New Testament based on semantic domains.* New York: United Bible Societies.

Lundin, R., C. Walhout, and A. Thiselton. 1999. *The promise of hermeneutics.* Grand Rapids: Eerdmans.

Mack, B. 1990. *Rhetoric and the New Testament.* Minneapolis: Fortress.

Maier, C., ed. 2000. *Evaluation and translation* (special issue of *The Translator* 6[2]). Manchester: St. Jerome.

Maier, J., and V. Tollers, eds. 1979. *The Bible in its literary milieu.* Grand Rapids: Eerdmans.

Malina, B. J. 1993. *The New Testament world: Insights from cultural anthropology.* Revised. Louisville: Westminster–John Knox.*

Malina, B. J., and R. L. Rohrbaugh. 1992. *Social-science commentary on the synoptic Gospels.* Minneapolis: Fortress.

Malina, B. J., and R. L. Rohrbaugh. 1998. *Social-science commentary on the Gospel of John.* Minneapolis: Fortress.

Martin, R. 1989. *Accuracy of translation and the New International Version.* Edinburgh: Banner of Truth Trust.

McCann, J. Clinton, Jr. 1993. *A theological introduction to the Book of Psalms: The Psalms as Torah.* Nashville: Abingdon.

Megrab, R. 1999. Ideological shifts in cross-cultural translation. In Boase-Beier and Holman (eds.), 59–69.

Mitchell, J. P. 1999. *Visually speaking: Radio and the renaissance of preaching.* Louisville, Ky.: Westminster–John Knox.

Mojola, A. 2002. Scripture translation in the era of translation studies. In Wilt (ed.), chapter 2.

Mossop, B. 2001. *Revising and editing for translators.* Manchester: St. Jerome.

Muilenberg, J. 1992. Form criticism and beyond. In P. House (ed.) 49–69.

Munday, J. 2001. *Introducing translation studies: Theories and applications.* London and New York: Routledge.*

Naude, J. 2000. Translation studies and Bible translation. *Acta Theologica* 20(1):1–27.

Naude, J. A., and C. H. J. van der Merwe, eds. 2002. *Contemporary translation studies and Bible translation: A South African perspective. Acta Theologica* Supplementum 2. Bloemfontein: University of the Free State.*

Neeley, Paul. 1996. Basic guidelines for adapting written scriptural texts into song lyrics. *Notes on Translation* 10(2):41–51.

Neusner, J. 1989. *Translating the classics of Judaism: In theory and in practice.* Atlanta: Scholars Press.

Newman, B. M. 2001. *Bible translation: The scene behind the scenes.* New York: American Bible Society.*

Newman, B. M., and P. C. Stine. 1988. *A translator's handbook on the Gospel of Matthew.* New York: United Bible Societies.

Nida, E. A. 1964. *Toward a science of translating.* Leiden: E. J. Brill.

Nida, E. A. 1975. *Exploring semantic structures.* Munich: Wilhelm Fink Verlag.

Nida, E. A. 2000. Creativity in translating. In *I must speak to you plainly: In honor of Robert G. Bratcher,* R. L. Omanson (ed.), 155–166. Carlisle, Cumbria, U.K.: Paternoster.*

Nida, E. A., and J. P. Louw. 1992. *Lexical semantics of the Greek New Testament.* Atlanta: Scholars Press.

Nida, E. A., J. P. Louw, A. Snyman, and J. Cronje. 1983. *Style and discourse: With special reference to the text of the Greek New Testament.* Cape Town: Bible Society of South Africa.

Nida, E. A., and Wm. D. Reyburn. 1981. *Meaning across cultures.* Maryknoll, N.Y.: Orbis.*

Nida, E. A., and C. Taber. 1969. *The theory and practice of translation.* Leiden: Brill.*

Niditsch, S. 1996. *Oral world and written word: Ancient Israelite literature.* Louisville Ky.: Westminster–John Knox.

Niehaus, J. 1993. Obadiah. In *The Minor Prophets,* vol. 2, T. E. McComisky (ed.). Grand Rapids: Baker.

The NIV Study Bible. 1985. Kenneth Barker, general editor. Grand Rapids: Zondervan.

Nogalski, J. and M. Sweeney, eds. 2000. *Reading and hearing the Book of the Twelve.* Atlanta: Society of Biblical Literature.

Nord, C. 1997. *Translating as a purposeful activity: Functionalist approaches explained.* Manchester: St. Jerome.

Norton, D. 2000. *A history of the Bible as literature.* Cambridge: Cambridge University Press.

Noss, P. 1997. Dynamic and functional equivalence in the Gbaya Bible. *Notes on Translation* 11(3):9–24.

Noss, P. 2002. Translators' words and theological readings. *The Bible Translator* 53(3):331–343.

Ogden, G. 2002. Biblical studies and Bible translation. In Wilt (ed.), chapter 5.

Omanson, R., ed. 2001. *Discover the Bible.* Reading, England: United Bible Societies.

Osborn, R. E. 1999. *Folly of God: The rise of Christian preaching.* St. Louis, Mo.: Chalice.

Parunak, H. Van Dyke. 1981. Oral typesetting: Some uses of biblical structure. *Biblica* 62:153–168.

Patrick, D. 1999. *The rhetoric of revelation in the Hebrew Bible.* Minneapolis: Fortress.

Patte, D. 1990a. *The religious dimensions of biblical texts: Greimas's structural semiotics and biblical exegesis.* Atlanta: Scholars Press.

Patte, D. 1990b. *Structural exegesis for New Testament critics.* Minneapolis: Fortress.

Pattemore, S. 2002. Relevance theory, intertextuality and the Book of Revelation. *UBS Bulletin* 194/195:43–60. (*Current Trends in Scripture Translation,* P. A. Noss, ed.).

Pattemore, S. 2003. *Souls under the altar: Relevance theory and the discourse structure of Revelation.* UBS Monograph Series, 9. New York: United Bible Societies.

Petersen, N. 1978. *Literary criticism for New Testament Critics.* Philadelphia: Fortress.

Peterson, E. 1994. *The message: Psalms.* Colorado Springs, Colo.: NavPress.

Pilch, J. 1999. *The cultural dictionary of the Bible.* Collegeville: Liturgical.

Pilch, J., and B. Malina. 1993. *Biblical social values and their meaning: A handbook.* Peabody, Mass.: Hendrickson.*

Pilkington, A. 2000. *Poetic effects.* Amsterdam and Philadelphia: John Benjamins.

Pohlig, James N. 1998. *An exegetical summary of Malachi.* Dallas: Summer Institute of Linguistics.

Pomorska, K., and S. Rudy, eds. 1985. *Roman Jakobson: Verbal art, verbal sign, verbal time*. Minneapolis: University of Minnesota Press.

Porter, S., and R. Hess, eds. 1999. *Translating the Bible: Problems and prospects*. Sheffield, England: Sheffield Academic Press.

Powell, M. 1990. *What is narrative criticism?* Minneapolis: Fortress.

Preminger, A., and T. Brogan, eds. 1993. *The new Princeton encyclopedia of poetry and poetics*. Princeton, N.J.: Princeton University Press.

Reed, J. 1997. *A discourse analysis of Philippians: Method and rhetoric in the debate over literary integrity*. Sheffield, England: Sheffield Academic Press.

Reiss, K. 2000. *Translation criticism—the potentials and limitations*. Trans. E. Rhodes. New York: American Bible Society.*

Robbins, V. 1984. *Jesus the teacher: A socio-rhetorical interpretation of Mark*. Philadelphia: Fortress.

Robbins, V. 1996. *Exploring the texture of texts: A guide to socio-rhetorical interpretation*. Valley Forge, Pa.: Trinity Press International.*

Robinson, D. 1997. *What is translation? Centrifugal theories, critical interventions*. Kent, Ohio: Kent State Press.

Ross, R. 2002. Advances in linguistic theory and their relevance to translation. In Wilt (ed.), chapter 4.

Ryken, L. 1987. *Words of life: A literary introduction to the New Testament*. Grand Rapids: Baker.

Ryken, L. 1992. *Words of delight: A literary introduction to the Bible*. Grand Rapids: Baker.*

Ryken, L. 2002. *The Word of God in English: Criteria for excellence in Bible translation*. Wheaton: Crossway Books.

Ryken, L., ed. 1984. *The New Testament in literary criticism*. New York: Frederick Ungar.

Ryken, L., and T. Longman III, eds. 1993. *A complete literary guide to the Bible*. Grand Rapids: Zondervan.*

Ryken, L.; J. Wilhoit; and T. Longman III, eds. 1998. *Dictionary of biblical imagery*. Downers Grove, Ill.: InterVarsity.*

Sailhammer, J. 1992. *The Pentateuch as narrative: A biblical-theological commentary*. Grand Rapids: Zondervan.

Sandy, D., and R. Giese, Jr., eds. 1995. *Cracking Old Testament codes: A guide to interpreting the literary genres of the Old Testament*. Nashville: Broadman and Holman.*

Sanneh, L. 1989. *Translating the message: The missionary impact on culture*. Maryknoll: Orbis.*

Sasson, J. 1990. *Jonah: A new translation with introduction, commentary, and interpretation*. Anchor Bible. New York: Doubleday.

Schökel, L. A. 1963. Hermeneutics in the light of language and literature. *Catholic Biblical Quarterly* 25:380.

Schökel, L. A. 1988. *A manual of Hebrew poetics*. Rome: Editrice Pontificio Istituto Biblico.*

Schrag, Brian. 1992. Translating song texts as oral compositions. *Notes on Translation* 6(1):44–62.

Scott, D. C., and A. Hetherwick. 1929. *Dictionary of the Nyanja language*. London: Lutterworth Press.

Searle, J. 1969. *Speech acts*. London: Cambridge University Press.

Searle, J. 1979. *Expression and meaning: Studies in the theory of speech acts*. Cambridge: Cambridge University Press.

Seu, Andree. 2001. Original spin. *World*, January 13, 2001.

Sharlemann, R. 1987. Theological text. *Semeia* 40:5–19.

Shklovsky, V. 1965. Art as technique. In *Russian formalist criticism: Four essays*, Lee Lemon and Marion Reis (eds.), 3–24. Lincoln: University of Nebraska Press.

Shuttleworth, M., and M. Cowie. 1997. *Dictionary of translation studies*. Manchester: St. Jerome.

Silberman, L. 1987. Introduction: Reflections on orality, aurality and perhaps more. *Semeia* 39:1–6.

Soards, Marion L. 1994. *The speeches in Acts: Their content, context, and concerns*. Louisville, Ky.: Westminister–John Knox.

Soukhanov, A., ed. 1992. *The American heritage dictionary of the English language*. Third edition. Boston and New York: Houghton Mifflin.

Steen, G. 2002. Metaphor in Bob Dylan's "Hurricane": Genre, language, and style. In *Cognitive stylistics: Language and cognition in text analysis*, E. Semino and J. Culpeper (eds.), 183–207. Amsterdam and Philadelphia: John Benjamins.

Stein, R. 1994. *A basic guide to interpreting the Bible: Playing by the rules*. Grand Rapids: Baker.*

Sterk, J. 2001. Translation and media: How different can we be and still be equivalent? Paper presented at The Conference on Similarity and Translation, New York, May 31–June 1. American Bible Society, New York.

Sternberg, M. 1985. *The poetics of biblical narrative: Ideological literature and the drama of reading*. Bloomington: Indiana University Press.

Stine, Philip C. 1999. Towards developing more effective translation consultants—lessons learned. *Notes on Translation* 13(1):1–8.

Stowers, S. 1986. *Letter writing in Greco-Roman antiquity*. Philadelphia: Westminster.*

Sundersingh, J. 1999. *Toward a media-based translation: Communicating biblical Scriptures to non-literates in rural Tamilnadu, India.* Ph.D. thesis. Fuller Theological Seminary.*

Sweeney, Marvin A. 1996. *Isaiah 1–39: With an introduction to prophetic literature.* The Forms of the Old Testament Literature, vol. 16. Grand Rapids: Eerdmans.

Tannehill, R. C. 1975. *The sword of his mouth.* Semeia Supplements 1. Philadelphia: Fortress.

Tannehill, R. C. 1995. The Gospels and narrative literature. In *The New Interpreter's Bible,* vol. 8, Leander Keck et al. (eds.), 56–70. Nashville: Abingdon.

Tate, W. 1991. *Biblical interpretation: An integrated approach.* Peabody, Mass.: Hendrickson.*

Tepox, A. 2001. The importance of becoming wise: Proverbs 1.1–7. *The Bible Translator* 52(2):216–222.*

Thiselton, A. C. 1999. Communicative action and promise in hermeneutics. In Lundin, Walhout, and Thiselton (eds.), 133–239.

Thom, J. 2001. Literary structure and Bible translation. Paper presented at the annual Congress of the New Testament Society of South Africa, April 18, 2001.

Thomas, K. 1990. Texts oral and choral. Paper presented at UBS ASPRETCON Mini-Workshop, Singapore, July 6–7.

Thuren, L. 1995. *Argument and theology in 1 Peter: The origins of Christian paraenesis.* Sheffield, England: Sheffield Academic Press.

Toury, G. 1995. *Descriptive translation studies and beyond.* Amsterdam: John Benjamins.

Trible, P. 1994. *Rhetorical criticism: Context, method, and the Book of Jonah.* Minneapolis: Fortress.

Tucker, G. M. 1986. Prophetic speech. In *Interpreting the Prophets,* J. L. Mays and P. J. Achtemeier (eds.), 26–40. Philadelphia: Fortress.

Turner, Nigel. 1976. *Style.* Vol. 4 of *A grammar of New Testament Greek,* J. H. Moulton (ed.). Edinburgh: T. & T. Clark.

Valiquette, H. P. 1999. Exodus–Deuteronomy as discourse: Models, distancing, provocation, paraenesis. *JSOT* 85:47–70.

van der Merwe, C. H. J., J. A. Naudé, and J. H. Kroeze. 1999. *A biblical Hebrew reference grammar.* Biblical Languages Series. Sheffield, England: Sheffield Academic Press.

Vanhoozer, K. 1998. *Is there a meaning in this text? The Bible, the reader, and the morality of literary knowledge.* Grand Rapids: Zondervan.

van Peer, W. 2002. Where do literary themes come from? In *Thematics: Interdisciplinary studies,* M. Louwerse and W. van Peer (eds.), 253–263. Amersterdam and Philadelphia: John Benjamins.

Walton, J., V. Matthews, and M. Chavalas. 2000. *The IVP Bible background commentary: Old Testament*. Downers Grove, Ill.: InterVarsity.

Watson, D. 1988. *Invention, arrangement, and style: Rhetorical criticism of Jude and 2 Peter*. Atlanta: Scholars Press.

Watson, D. 1997. The integration of epistolary and rhetorical analysis of Philippians. In *The rhetorical analysis of Scripture: Essays from the 1995 London conference*, S. Porter and T. Olbricht (ed.), 398–426. Sheffield, England: Sheffield Academic Press.

Watson, D., ed. 1991. *Persuasive artistry: Essays in New Testament rhetoric in honor of George A. Kennedy*. Sheffield, England: JSOT.

Watson, W. 1984. *Classical Hebrew poetry: A guide to its techniques*. Sheffield, England: JSOT.

Waugh, L. 1985. The poetic function and the nature of language. In Pomorska and Rudy (eds.), 143–168.

Webster's new world dictionary. 1988. Third college edition, Victoria Neufeldt (ed.). New York: Simon & Schuster.

Wechsler, R. 1998. *Performing without a stage: The art of literary translation*. North Haven, Conn.: Catbird Press.

Wegner, P. 1999. *The journey from texts to translations: The origin and development of the Bible*. Grand Rapids: Baker.

Wendland, E. R. 1979. Stylistic form and communicative function in the Nyanja radio narratives of Julius Chongo. Ph.D. dissertation. University of Wisconsin.

Wendland, E. R. 1981a. Receptor language style and Bible translation: I, A search for "language which grabs the heart." *The Bible Translator* 32(1):107–124.

Wendland, E. R. 1981b. Receptor language style and Bible translation: II, The problem of control in restructuring. *The Bible Translator* 32(3):319–328.

Wendland, E. R. 1982. Receptor language style and Bible translation: III, Training translators about style. *The Bible Translator* 33(1):115–127.

Wendland, E. R. 1984. Biblical Hebrew narrative structure. *Selected Technical Articles Related to Translation* 10:3–36. Dallas: Summer Institute of Linguistics.

Wendland, E. R. 1985. Linear and concentric patterns in Malachi. *The Bible Translator* 36(1):108–121.

Wendland, E. R. 1987a. A communications model for the measurement of fidelity and naturalness in Bible translation. *Occasional Papers in Translation and Textlinguistcs* 2:1–36.

Wendland, E. R. 1987b. *The cultural factor in Bible translation*. New York: United Bible Societies.*

Wendland, E. R. 1988. The "Word of the LORD" and the organization of Amos. *Occasional Papers in Translation and Textlinguistcs* 2(4):1–51.

Wendland, E. R. 1990. 7 X 7 (X 7): A structural and thematic outline of John's Apocalypse." *Occasional Papers in Translation and Textlinguistcs* 4(4):371–387.

Wendland, E. R. 1991. Culture and the form/function dichotomy in the evaluation of translation acceptability. In *Meaningful translation: Its implications for the reader,* J. P. Louw (ed.), 8–40. New York: United Bible Societies.

Wendland, E. R. 1993. *Comparative discourse analysis and the translation of Psalm 22 in Chichewa, a Bantu language of south-central Africa.* Lewiston, N.Y.: Edwin Mellen.

Wendland, E. R. 1994a. Oral-aural dynamics of the Word: With special reference to John 17. *Notes on Translation* 8(1):19–43.

Wendland, E. R. 1994b. A comparative study of 'rhetorical criticism', ancient and modern—With special reference to the larger structure and function of the epistle of Jude. *Neotestamentica* 28(1):193–228.

Wendland, E. R. 1995a. Seeking a path through a forest of symbols: A figurative and structural survey of the Song of Songs. *Journal of Translation and Textlinguistics* 7(2):13–59.

Wendland, E. R. 1995b. *The discourse analysis of Hebrew prophetic literature: Determining the larger textual units of Hosea and Joel.* Lewiston, N.Y.: Mellen Biblical.

Wendland, E. R. 1996a. Finding some lost aspects of meaning in Christ's parables of the lost—and found. *Trinity Journal* 17NS(1):19–65.

Wendland, E.R. 1996b. Obadiah's vision of 'the Day of the Lord': On the importance of rhetoric in the biblical text and in Bible translation. *Journal of Translation and Textlinguistics* 7:54–86.

Wendland, E. R. 1996c. Obadiah's 'day': On the rhetorical implications of textual form and intertextual influence. *Journal of Translation and Textlinguistics* 8:23–49.

Wendland, E. R. 1996d. Text analysis and the genre of Jonah. *JETS* 39(2–3):191–206, 373–395.

Wendland, E. R. 1997. "Blessed is the man who will eat at the feast in the kingdom of God" (Luke 14:15): Internal and external intertextual influence on the interpretation of Christ's parable of the great banquet." *Neotestamentica* 31(1):159–194.

Wendland, E. R. 1998a. What's the 'Good News'?—Check out 'the feet!': Prophetic rhetoric and the salvific centre of Nahum's vision. *Old Testament Studies* 11(1):154–181.

Wendland, E. R. 1998b. *Buku Loyera: An introduction to the new Chichewa Bible translation.* Kachere Monograph 6. Blantrye, Malawi: Christian Literature Association in Malawi.*

Wendland, E. R. 1998c. 'Dear children' versus the 'antichrists': The rhetoric of reassurance in 1 John. *Journal of Translation and Textlinguistics* 11:40–84.

Wendland, E. R. 1999. Scattered bones but a single stick: A rhetorical-stylistic overview of the gospel in Ezekiel 37. *Old Testament Essays* 12(1):149–172.

Wendland, E. R. 2000a. A form-functional, text-comparative method of translation, teaching, and checking. *Notes on Translation* 14(1):7–27.*

Wendland, E. R. 2000b. *Preaching that grabs the heart: A rhetorical-stylistic study of the Chichewa revival sermons of Shadrack Wame.* Kachere Monograph 11. Blantrye, Malawi: Christian Literature Association in Malawi.

Wendland, E. R. 2000c. "Stand fast in the true grace of God!" (5:12)—A text-rhetorical study of the structure and style of 1 Peter. *Journal of Translation and Textlinguistics* 13:25–102.

Wendland, E. R. 2000d. Towards an 'oratorical' Bible translation in a Bantu language: With special reference to Ezekiel's oracle of the 'dry bones' in Chichewa. Paper presented as part of a UBS panel at the International *SBL* Conference in Cape Town, South Africa, July 24–28, 2000.

Wendland, E. R. 2002a. *Analyzing the Psalms: With exercises for Bible students and translators.* Revised edition. Dallas: SIL International.*

Wendland, E. R. 2002b. A literary-rhetorical approach to biblical text analysis and translation. In Wilt (ed.), 179–230.

Wendland, E. R. 2002c. Towards a 'literary' translation of the Scriptures: with special reference to a 'poetic' rendition. In Naude and van der Merwe (eds.), 164–201.

Wendland, E. R., and S. Hachibamba. 2000. A central African perspective on contextualizing the Ephesian potentates, principalities, and powers. *Missiology: An International Review* 28(3):341–363.

Wendland, E. R., and J. P Louw. 1993. Graphic design and Bible reading: Exploratory studies in the typographical representation of the text of Scripture in translation. Cape Town, RSA: Bible Society of South Africa.*

Werth, P. 2000. *Text worlds: Representing conceptual space in discourse:* London: Longman.

Westermann, C. 1967. *Basic forms of prophetic speech.* Philadelphia: Westminster.

Wiesemann, Ursula. n.d. *Discourse analysis.* Electronic copy, privately circulated.

Wiklander, B. 1984. *Prophecy as literature: A text-linguistic and rhetorical approach to Isaiah 2–4.* Stockholm: Liber Tryck.

Williams, D. 1999. *Paul's metaphors: Their context and character.* Peabody, Mass.: Hendrickson.

Wilson, V. 1997. *Divine symmetries: The art of biblical rhetoric.* New York: University Press of America.

Wilt, T. 2002a. Translation and communication. In Wilt (ed.), 27–80.*

Wilt, T., ed. 2002b. *Bible translation: Frames of reference.* Manchester: St. Jerome.*

Wilt, T., trans. 2002c. *Praise, prayer and protest: The David collection (Psalms 1–72)—A liturgy of praise (Psalm 118)—The ABC's of grief (Lamentations).* Private printing. Murfreesburo, Tenn.*

Witherington III, B. 1994. *Jesus the sage: The pilgrimage of wisdom.* Minneapolis: Fortress.

Wonderly, Wm. L. 1968. *Bible translations for popular use.* New York: United Bible Societies.*

Wuellner, Wilhelm. 1991. The rhetorical genre of Jesus' sermon in Luke 12.1–13.9. In *Persuasive artistry: Studies in New Testament rhetoric in honor of George A. Kennedy,* D. F. Watson (ed.), 93–118. Sheffield, England: JSOT.

Young, B. H. 1995. *Jesus the Jewish theologian.* Peabody, Mass.: Hendrickson.

Zogbo, L., and E. R. Wendland. 2000. *Hebrew poetry in the Bible: A guide for understanding and for translating.* New York: United Bible Societies.*

Additional Recommended Reading

Those interested in a literary-rhetorical approach should also take note of the new *Berit Olam* ("The Everlasting Covenant") series of commentaries (Collegeville, Minn.: Liturgical Press–Michael Glazier). This set, which thus far includes studies of Judges, 1 Samuel, 1 Kings, 2 Kings, Ezra and Nehemiah, Ruth and Esther, Leviticus, Numbers, Deuteronomy, and the Twelve Prophets (vols. 1–2), is subtitled *Studies in Hebrew Narrative and Poetry.* According to the published dust jacket, it aims to reflect "the latest developments in the literary analysis of these ancient texts." To be more specific, "The readings of the books of the Hebrew Bible offered here all focus on the final form of the texts, approaching them as literary works, recognizing that the craft of poetry and storytelling that the ancient Hebrew world provided can be found in them and that their truth can be better appreciated [and also more accurately translated, I might add] with a fuller understanding of that art."

Index